DUQUESNE STUDIES

Philological Series

1

John Milton

AN ANNOTATED BIBLIOGRAPHY

1929–1968

DUQUESNE STUDIES
Philological Series

1

JOHN MILTON
AN ANNOTATED
BIBLIOGRAPHY
1929–1968

Compiled By Calvin Huckabay

Revised Edition

Duquesne University Press, Pittsburgh, Pa.
Editions E. Nauwelaerts, Louvain

DUQUESNE STUDIES
PHILOLOGICAL SERIES

Library of Congress Catalog Card Number 73–98551

FOR E. L. MARILLA

PREFACE

This bibliography is an updating and a revision of my earlier work, *John Milton: A Bibliographical Supplement, 1929-1957* (Pittsburgh and Louvain: Duquesne University Press, 1960). It is intended as a supplement to David H. Stevens' *A Reference Guide to Milton from 1800 to the Present Day* (Chicago: University of Chicago Press, 1930) and to Harris F. Fletcher's *Contributions to a Milton Bibliography, 1800-1930* (Urbana: University of Illinois Press, 1931).

My purpose has been to list editions and translations of Milton's works and to note publication of books, articles, and notes concerned with Milton since 1928, the terminal date of Stevens' *Reference Guide*. Most of the items are annotated. Whenever possible, I have examined and verified each item listed. However, in some instances I have found it necessary to rely on the work of others, in the interest of completeness. For example, I have listed the Japanese items compiled by Professor Frank L. Huntley (CL, 13, 1961, 97-113), but I was not able to verify and annotate all the entries because some of them were not available in this country or in the British libraries that I visited. Many of the master's theses that appeared in my 1960 work have been omitted in this edition, and it was not feasible to secure lists of such theses written since 1957. I have attempted to include all doctoral dissertations written since 1928. Some reviews are listed, but the lists of reviews are not intended to be comprehensive in every instance.

I have checked all of the annual lists of Milton studies (since 1928, with the exception of the 1968 lists, which have not yet appeared) and other publications included in the Bibliography section of this work. I have also examined the Milton holdings in the Library of Congress, the Rice University Library, the University of Illinois Library, the Bodleian Library, the Taylorian Library, the Cambridge University Library, the Library of Christ's College, Cambridge, and the British Museum. Numerous individuals have sent offprints to me. A systematic effort has been made to locate items published through October of 1968. Yet I make no claim that this bibliography is complete, because frequently I discover items that I have missed, and they are not always recent items. During the process of editing the entries, the following numbers (but not items) have been eliminated: 78, 124, 277, 349, 380, 1465, 1547, 1582, 1707, 1756, 1931, 1997, and 2251.

The editions of Milton's works are listed chronologically, as are the translations. If there has been a subsequent edition since 1928, the work is listed according to the date of the original edition. Other entries are listed alphabetically, and many entries are cross-listed whenever their scope is sufficient to justify more than a single classification. In listing reviews that appeared in *The Year's Work in English Studies*, I have omitted volume numbers unless the entry was reviewed in a year other than that in which it was published. Italics and quotation marks have been avoided. The general form of the entries is one which seems most suitable for a compilation such as the present one.

In spite of the Milton controversy, and perhaps because of it, the increasing number of Milton items published each year records a considerable interest in Milton as man and artist. A new evaluation of Milton has taken place, and studies published during the past forty years have contributed immeasurably to a better understanding of Milton's life, his age, and his works. The monumental Columbia Edition has appeared since 1928, and four volumes of the Yale Prose Edition have been published. Several good shorter editions have appeared, such as those edited by Professors Merritt Y. Hughes, John Shawcross, and Douglas Bush. A variorum commentary of the poems is in progress, with Professor Hughes as the general editor. The long anticipated biography by Professor William Riley Parker was published at the Clarendon Press this year. Less ambitious undertakings have added new light on Milton, and in recent years there has been considerable interest in the shorter poems, especially in *Lycidas* and *Comus*. At least a dozen anthologies of essays on Milton have been compiled. During the past decade, many works listed by Stevens and long out-of-print have been reissued, as was, for example, David Masson's *Life of Milton*. Finally, I note the widespread celebrations in 1967 of the tercentenary of *Paradise Lost* as evidence of international interest in Milton.

Many individuals have aided me in compiling this bibliography. The reference librarians at all of the libraries where I worked were most cooperative, but I wish especially to thank Mr. Jefferson Caskey of the Houston Baptist College Library, Mr. Richard Perrine of the Rice University Library, Miss Marian Harmon of the University of Illinois Library, and Mr. David Vaisey of the Bodleian Library. Professor John Illo contributed a list of Russian studies, and Professors Maren-Sofie Røstvig and Eric Jacobsen supplied lists of Scandinavian studies. Professors John M. Steadman and C. A. Patrides forwarded lists of their varied publications. Professor Stanley W. Wells of the Shakespeare Institute, University of Birmingham, has sent several entries. Professor John Shawcross has made a number of helpful suggestions and has kindly consented to read the manuscript. In verifying entries and in writing annotations, Miss Judy Bennatte and Mr. Dale Ratheal have been of invaluable assistance. Mrs. Sandra Smith, Mrs. Janice Knox, and Miss Karen Collier typed the manuscript.

My assistants and I have taken many precautions to make this bibliography reasonably free from error. I hope that it will be useful to seasoned Milton scholars and to the Milton scholars of the future. If so, then this labor will not have been in vain.

CALVIN HUCKABAY

Houston, Texas
November, 1968

LIST OF ABBREVIATIONS

AB	American Bookman
AHR	American Historical Review
AI	American Imago
AJP	American Journal of Philology
AL	American Literature
AM	American Mercury
Amer. Rev.	American Review
Ang. Bbl.	Anglia Beiblatt
AN&Q	American Notes and Queries (New Haven, Conn.)
AnM	Annuale Mediaevale (Duquesne U.)
AQ	American Quarterly
AR	Antioch Review
Archiv	Archiv für das Studium der Neuren Sprachen und Literaturen
ArQ	Arizona Quarterly
ASch	American Scholar
ASR	American-Scandinavian Review
AUC	Anales de la Universidad de Chile
AUMLA	Journal of the Australasian Universities Language and Literature Association
AUR	Aberdeen University Review
AWR	The Anglo-Welsh Review (Pembroke Dock, Wales)
BA	Books Abroad
BB	Bulletin of Bibliography
BHM	Bulletin of the History of Medicine
BHS	Bulletin of Hispanic Studies
BJRL	Bulletin of the John Rylands Library
BLR	Bodleian Library Record
BMLA	Bulletin of the Medical Library Association
BMQ	British Museum Quarterly
BNYPL	Bulletin of the New York Public Library
BS	Bibliotheca Sacra
BSTCF	Ball State Teachers College Forum
BSUF	Ball State University Forum
BuR	Bucknell Review

CairoSE	Cairo Studies in English
Camb. Jour.	Cambridge Journal
CanL	Canadian Literature
CE	College English
CHR	Catholic Historical Review
CJ	Classical Journal
CL	Comparative Literature
Class. Bull.	Classical Bulletin
Class. Rev.	Classical Review
CLS	Comparative Literature Studies (U. of Md.)
Com	Commonweal
Com. Rev.	Comparative Review
CP	Classical Philology
CQ	The Cambridge Quarterly
CQR	Church Quarterly Review
CR	The Contemporary Review
Crit	Criterion
CritQ	Critical Quarterly
CritR	The Critical Review (Melbourne; Sydney); also Melbourne Critical Review (MCR)
CSE	Cornell Studies in English
CUF	Columbia University Forum
CW	Catholic World
DA	Dissertation Abstracts
DL	Deutsche Literaturzeitung (Berlin)
DownR	Downside Review
DR	Dalhousie Review
DubR	Dublin Review (London)
DUJ	Durham University Journal
EA	Études Anglaises
E&S	Essays and Studies by Members of the English Association
EHR	English Historical Review
EIC	Essays in Criticism
EIE	English Institute Essays
EIHC	Essex Institute Historical Collections
EJ	English Journal
ELH	ELH; A Journal of English Literary History
ELL	The English Language and Literature (Eng. Lit. Soc. of Korea)
ELN	English Language Notes
ELT	English Literature in Transition (1880-1920)
EM	English Miscellany
ER	English Review
Eras	Erasmus
ES	English Studies

ESA	English Studies in Africa (Johannesburg)
ESELL	Essays and Studies in English Language and Literature (Sendai, Japan)
ESt	Englische Studien
EUQ	Emory University Quarterly
EWR	East-West Review (Doshisha U., Kyoto, Japan)
Expl	Explicator
Flambeau	Le Flambeau: Revue Belge des Questions Politiques et Littéraires
FMod	Filología Moderna (Madrid)
ForumH	Forum (Houston)
FR	Fortnightly Review
FS	Franciscan Studies
GR	Germanic Review
GRM	Germanisch-romanische Monatsschrift, Neue Folge
HispR	Hispanic Review
Hist	History
HJ	Hibbert Journal
HLB	Huntington Library Bulletin
HLQ	Huntington Library Quarterly
HR	Hopkins Review
HTR	Harvard Theological Review
HudR	Hudson Review
ISLL	Illinois Studies in Language and Literature
JA	Jahrbuch für Amerikastudien
JAAC	Journal of Aesthetics and Art Criticism
JBS	Journal of British Studies
JEGP	Journal of English and Germanic Philology
JEH	Journal of Ecclesiastical History
JGE	Journal of General Education
JHI	Journal of the History of Ideas
JMH	Journal of Modern History
JQ	Journalism Quarterly
JR	Journal of Religion
JRUL	Journal of the Rutgers University Library
JWCI	Journal of the Warburg and Courtauld Institute
KR	Kenyon Review
KSJ	Keats-Shelley Journal
L&P	Literature and Psychology
LC	Library Chronicle (U. of Penn.)
LGRP	Literaturblatt für germanische und romanische Philologie
Library	The Library
LJ	Library Journal
LL	Life and Letters
LM	Letterature Moderne

LQHR	London Quarterly and Holborn Review
LSE	Lund Studies in English
MA	Microfilm Abstracts
ManR	Manchester Review
MB	More Books, Bulletin of the Boston Public Library
Merc	(London) Mercury
MFS	Modern Fiction Studies
MGW	Manchester Guardian Weekly
MHRA	Modern Humanities Research Association
MinnR	Minnesota Review
MissQ	Mississippi Quarterly
ML	Music and Letters
MLJ	Modern Language Journal
MLN	Modern Language Notes
MLQ	Modern Language Quarterly
MLR	Modern Language Review
MN	Milton Newsletter
ModA	Modern Age (Chicago)
MP	Modern Philology
MQR	Michigan Quarterly Review
Nat	The Nation (New York)
Nat. and Athen.	The Nation and Athenaeum
N&Q	Notes and Queries
NB	New Books
NC	Nineteenth Century
NCF	Nineteenth Century Fiction
Neophil	Neophilologus (Groningen)
NEQ	New England Quarterly
NER	Nation and English Review
NLB	Newberry Library Bulletin
NM	Neuphilologische Mitteilungen
NMQ	New Mexico Quarterly
NR	New Republic
NS	Die Neueren Sprachen
NSE	Norwegian Studies in English
NSN	New Statesman and Nation
NYHTBR	New York Herald Tribune Book Review
NYTBR	New York Times Book Review
Obs	The Observer
OJES	Osmania Journal of English Studies (Osmania U., Hyderabad)
OR	The Oxford Review
Oxf. Mag.	Oxford Magazine
PAPS	Proceedings of the American Philosophical Society
PBA	Proceedings of the British Academy

PBSA	Papers of the Bibliographical Society of America
PELL	Papers in English Language and Literature
Pers	The Personalist
PhQ	Philosophical Quarterly
PhR	Philosophical Review
PLL	Papers on Language and Literature
PMASAL	Papers of the Mich. Acad. of Science, Arts and Letters
PMLA	PMLA; Publications of the Modern Language Association of America
PQ	Philological Quarterly
PR	Partisan Review
PSE	Princeton Studies in English
PULC	Princeton University Library Chronicle
QFSK	Quellen und Forschungen zur Sprach- und Kulturgeschichte der Germanischen Völker, Neue Folge
QJS	Quarterly Journal of Speech
QQ	Queens Quarterly
QR	Quarterly Review
RA-A	Revue Anglo-Americaine
RC	Revue Critique
RECTR	Restoration and 18th Century Theater Research
REL	Review of English Literature
RenP	Renaissance Papers
RenQuar	Renaissance Quarterly
RES	Review of English Studies
RIP	Rice Institute Pamphlet
RLC	Revue de Littérature Comparée
RLMC	Riv. di Letterature Moderne e Comparate (Firenze)
RLV	Revue des Langues Vivantes (Bruxelles)
RN	Renaissance News
RomN	Romance Notes (U. of N.C.)
RPh	Romance Philology
RR	Romanic Review
RUSE	Rutgers University Studies in English
SAB	South Atlantic Bulletin
SAQ	South Atlantic Quarterly
SatR	Saturday Review (N.Y.), until 1951 published as Saturday Review of Literature (SRL).
Sat. Rev.	Saturday Review (London)
SB	Studies in Bibliography: Papers of the Bibliographical Society of the University of Virginia
SCN	Seventeenth-Century News
Scr	Scrutiny
SEEJ	Slavic and East European Journal
SEER	Slavonic and East European Review

SEL	Studies in English Literature, 1500-1900
SEL (Japan)	Studies in English Literature (Eng. Literary Society of Japan, U. of Tokyo)
SELL	Studies in English Literature and Language (Kyushu U., Fukuoka, Japan)
SFQ	Southern Folklore Quarterly
ShN	Shakespeare Newsletter
ShS	Shakespeare Survey
SN	Studia Neophilologica
SoQ	The Southern Quarterly
SoR	Southern Review
SP	Studies in Philology
Spect	Spectator
SQ	Shakespeare Quarterly
SR	Sewanee Review
SRen	Studies in the Renaissance
SSLL	Stanford Studies in Language and Literature
Sun. Times	(London) Sunday Times
SWR	Southwest Review
TC	Twentieth Century
Th	Thought
TLS	Times Literary Supplement
TQ	Texas Quarterly (U. of Texas)
TRSC	Transactions of the Royal Society of Canada
TSE	Tulane Studies in English
TSL	Tennessee Studies in Literature
TSLL	Texas Studies in Literature and Language
TT	Time and Tide
UCPES	U. of California Pubs., English Studies
UEIES	Uppsala English Institute Essays and Studies
UFMH	U. of Florida Monographs, Humanities Series
UM	University Microfilms
UMSE	U. of Mississippi Studies in English
Universitas	(Wayne State U.)
UTQ	University of Toronto Quarterly
UTSE	University of Texas Studies in English
UWPLL	U. of Wash. Pubs. in Language and Literature
UWR	University of Windsor Review
VQR	Virginia Quarterly Review
VS	Victorian Studies
WHR	Western Humanities Review
WR	Western Review
WWR	Walt Whitman Review
XUS	Xavier University Studies

YCGL	Yearbook of Comparative and General Literature (U. of N.C. Studies in Comp. Lit.)
YR	Yale Review
YSE	Yale Studies in English
YULG	Yale University Library Gazette
YWES	The Year's Work in English Studies
ZAA	Zeitschrift für Anglistik und Amerikanistik (East Berlin)

CONTENTS

BIBLIOGRAPHY

1 AMANO, KEITARO. Milton Bibliography in Japan. Kwansai Univ. Gaku-ho, 1958.

2 ARMS, GEORGE, and JOSEPH M. KUNTZ. Poetry Explication: A Checklist of Interpretation since 1925 of British and American Poems, Past and Present. New York: Swallow, 1950.

3 BALDENSPERGER, FERNAND, and WERNER P. FRIEDERICH. Bibliography of Comparative Literature. New York: Russell and Russell, 1960.
   Contains a bibliography of studies on Milton's influence abroad, pp. 561-2.

4 [BARKER, ARTHUR E.]. A List of Articles on Milton by Arthur E. Barker. SCN, 15, No. 1, 1957, item 16.

5 BATESON, F. W., ed. The Cambridge Bibliography of English Literature. Cambridge: Cambridge Univ. Press; New York: Macmillan, 1941. 4 vols.
   John Milton (1608-1674), by D. H. Stevens, 1, 463-73. Supplement, 1957, pp. 225-37, by W. Arthur Turner, Alberta T. Turner, and W. Edson Richmond.

6 BATESON, F. W. A Guide to English Literature. Garden City: Doubleday, 1965 (Anchor Book). 259pp.
   A Milton reading list, pp. 88-90.

7 BOND, RICHMOND P., and DOUGALD MACMILLAN. Recent Publications: Studies in the Seventeenth and Eighteenth Centuries. SP, 29, 1932, 505-13.

8 BRADSHAW, JOHN. A Concordance to The Poetical Works of John Milton. London: Allen and Unwin, 1965; Hamden, Connecticut: Archon Books, 1965. 412pp.
   First impression, 1894. A reprint of Stevens' No. 24.

9 BUSH, DOUGLAS. English Literature in the Earlier Seventeenth Century, 1600-1660. Oxford History of English Literature, Vol. 5. Oxford: Clarendon Press, 1945. Revised Edition, 1960. viii, 680pp.
   Chronological Tables, pp. 425-59.
   Bibliography, pp. 461-668.
   Milton Bibliography, pp. 615-22.

10 CAMBRIDGE UNIVERSITY. Abstracts of Dissertations Approved for the Ph.D., M.Sc., and M.Litt. Degrees in the Univ. of Cambridge. Cambridge: Cambridge Univ. Press, 1930-31, 1949-50, 1953-54, 1956-57.

11 CAMBRIDGE UNIVERSITY. Titles of Dissertations Approved for the Ph.D., M.Sc., and M.Litt. Degrees in the Univ. of Cambridge. Cambridge: Cambridge Univ. Press, 1957-58—.
   Publications of volumes of summaries discontinued with beginning of this publication.

1

12 Canadian Graduate Theses in the Humanities and Social Sciences. Ottawa: Edmond, Cloutier, 1951.

13 [CANDY, HUGH C. H.]. John Milton. A Catalogue of Works by or Relating to John Milton, Largely Comprising the Library of the Well-Known Milton Scholar, the Late Professor Hugh C. H. Candy. London: Maggs Bros., 1936. 56pp.

14 DAICHES, DAVID. English Literature. The Princeton Studies: Humanistic Scholarship in America. Englewood Cliffs, N.J.: Prentice-Hall, 1964.
Recent Milton scholarship discussed, pp. 32-48.

15 ENGLISH ASSOCIATION. The Year's Work in English Studies, 1920—. Oxford: Oxford Univ. Press, issued annually. Author of Milton sections: L. C. Martin, Arnold Davenport, et al. 1, 1919-20, 81-4; 2, 1920-1, 103-8; 3, 1922, 111-9; 4, 1923, 137-41; 5, 1924, 163-70; 6, 1925, 195-201, 208-9; 7, 1926, 187-92; 8, 1927, 199-205; 9, 1928, 201-4; 10, 1929, 234-8; 11, 1930, 219-30; 12, 1931, 202-3, 206-9; 13, 1932, 205-12, 219-21; 14, 1933, 249-53; 15, 1934, 234-41; 16, 1935, 248-57, 264; 17, 1936, 187-91; 18, 1937, 180-6; 19, 1938, 174-9; 20, 1939, 112-7; 21, 1940, 167-75; 22, 1941, 158-64; 23, 1942, 157-65; 24, 1943, 147-59; 25, 1944, 139-45; 26, 1945, 140-50; 27, 1946, 169-75; 28, 1947, 184-93; 29, 1948, 186, 191-7; 30, 1949, 162-71; 31, 1950, 169, 173-82; 32, 1951, 184-92; 33, 1952, 177-86; 34, 1953, 199-210; 35, 1954, 137-44; 36, 1955, 158-65; 37, 1956, 172-80; 38, 1957, 181-7; 39, 1958, 180-9; 40, 1959, 169-78; 41, 1960, 166-77; 42, 1961, 165-75; 43, 1962, 178-88; 44, 1963, 206-16; 45, 1964, 239-50; 46, 1965, 204-12.

16 English Literature in the Seventeenth Century: Guide to an Exhibition Held in 1957. Oxford: Bodleian Library, 1957. 167pp.
Includes descriptions of ten Milton items exhibited.

17 FISHER, JOHN H. Serial Bibliographies in the Modern Languages and Literatures. PMLA, 66, 1951, 138-56.

18 [FLETCHER, HARRIS F.]. Bibliography of the Writings of Harris F. Fletcher. JEGP, 60, 1961, 847-54. Also in separately published Festschrift issue of JEGP.
Compiled by Isabelle F. Grant.

19 FLETCHER, HARRIS F. Contributions to a Milton Bibliography, 1800-1930, Being a List of Addenda to Stevens's Reference Guide to Milton. University of Illinois Studies in Language and Literature, 16. Urbana: Univ. Of Illinois Press, 1931. Reprinted, New York: Russell and Russell, 1967. 166pp.
Rev: Paul Chauvet, RA-A, 9, 1931, 150-1; S. B. Liljegren, Ang. Bbl., 43, 1932, 369-71; A. Koszul, RC, 65, 1932, 571; Neophil, 17, 1932, 309; D. Saurat, MLN, 48, 1933, 413-4.

20 [FLETCHER, HARRIS F.]. Works on Seventeenth Century Subjects by Harris Francis Fletcher. SCN, 17, No. 1, 1959, item 26.

21 [FRENCH, J. MILTON]. Bibliography of J. Milton French. I. John Milton. II. Other Seventeenth-Century English Literature. Milton Society of America, Annual Dinner Booklet, 1956.
Compiled by William B. Hunter, Jr.

22 GREGORY, RUTH W. American Criticism of Milton, 1800-1938, A Contribution to a Bibliography. Typewritten, Library School, Univ. of Wisconsin, 1938.

23 GROSE, SIDNEY W. Early Editions of Milton's Works in Christ's College Library. Reprinted from Christ's College Magazine, 33, 1921. 8pp.

24 [HANFORD, JAMES HOLLY]. Bibliography of Articles on Milton by James Holly Hanford. SCN, 22, No. 1, 1964, item 10.
   Compiled by David Klein and J. Max Patrick.

25 HANFORD, JAMES HOLLY. A Milton Handbook. Fourth Edition. Revised. New York: Crofts, 1946, 1954.
   Bibliography, pp. 421-47. Other editions of this work are listed under General Criticism.

26 HANFORD, JAMES HOLLY, assisted by CHARLES W. CRUPI. Milton. Goldentree Bibliographies. New York: Appleton-Century-Crofts, 1966, 52pp.
   Intended for graduate and advanced undergraduate students. Contains some helpful annotations and notes.
   Rev: William W. Cobau, SCN, 25, 1967, 35.

27 HENRY E. HUNTINGTON LIBRARY AND ART GALLERY. An Exhibition of William Blake's Watercolor Drawings of Milton's Paradise Lost, May 12-July 31, 1936. San Marino: Huntington Library, 1936. 15pp.

28 HUCKABAY, CALVIN. John Milton: A Bibliographical Supplement, 1929-1957. Duquesne Studies, Philological Series, I. Pittsburgh and Louvain: Duquesne Univ. Press, 1960. Reprinted, New York: AMS Press, 1967. ix, 211pp.
   Rev: Thomas B. Stroup, MissQ, 13, 1960, 143-4; Floyd McAlister, MP, 58, 1961, 281-2; B. A. Wright, RES, 12, 1961, 329; Merritt Y. Hughes, RN, 14, 1961, 121-4; John T. Shawcross, SCN, 19, 1961, 29-34; Lawrence Michel, MLJ, 45, 1961, 51-2; Harris Fletcher, JEGP, 60, 1961, 170-1.

29 HUGHES, MERRITT Y., ed. John Milton. Complete Poems and Major Prose. With Notes and Introductions. New York: Odyssey Press, 1957. xix, 1059pp.
   In the notes, the introductions, and the bibliographies at the end of the introductions, Hughes brings together much of the significant scholarship on Milton since 1930.

30 ------. Paradise Lost. New York: Odyssey Press, 1935.
   Bibliography, pp. liii-lvi.

31 ------. Paradise Lost: A Poem in Twelve Books. A New Edition. New York: Odyssey Press, 1962. lx, 324pp.
   Bibliography of Books Dealing Mainly with Paradise Lost Published since 1934, pp. li-liii; Some Outstanding Editions of Paradise Lost Since 1935, pp. liii-liv; Bibliography of Articles Dealing Mainly with Paradise Lost Since 1957, pp. liv-lx; Unpublished Doctoral Dissertations (Since 1957) Dealing Mainly with Paradise Lost, p. lx.

32 ------. Paradise Regained, the Minor Poems, and Samson Agonistes. New
      York: Odyssey Press, 1937.
        Bibliography, pp. lvi-lxiii.

33 ------. Prose Selections. New York: Odyssey Press, 1947.
        Bibliography, pp. cxxv-cxlvii.

34 ------. The Seventeenth Century in Contemporary Literary Scholarship:
      A Critical Review. Ed. by Lewis Leary (New York: Appleton-Century-
      Crofts, 1958), pp. 67-82.
        Survey of Milton studies, pp. 74-82.

35 HUNTLEY, FRANK L. Milton Studies in Japan. CL, 13, 1961, 97-113.
        A compilation of translations and critical works. Surveys the history of
        Milton studies and concludes that Japanese critics need wider perspectives.

36 Index Translationum. Paris: International Institute of International Co-
      operation, 1932-40. 31 vols.
        Continued in 1948 under the auspices of UNESCO as an annual publication.

37 JENKINS, D. L. Union List of Theses for the Univ. of New Zealand,
      1910-1954. Wellington: New Zealand Library Association, 1956.

38 LIBRARY OF CONGRESS. Catalogue Division. A List of American
      Doctoral Dissertations Printed. Washington: Government Printing
      Office, 1912-40. 27 vols.

39 List of Theses, 1917-1937. SAB, 4, No. 1, 1938, 2-15.
        A list published annually since 1938.

40 LOCKWOOD, LAURA E. Lexicon to the Poetical Works of Milton. New
      York: Burt Franklin, 1966.
        A reprint of Stevens' No. 40, originally published in 1907.

41 McNAMEE, LAWRENCE F. Dissertations in English and American
      Literature: Theses accepted by American, British and German Uni-
      versities, 1865-1964. Foreword by John Hurt Fisher. New York: R. R.
      Bowker Company, 1968. 1124pp.
        Lists author, title, institution, and year of each dissertation. Chapter Eight,
        pp. 293-304, contains a list of 213 dissertations on Milton.

42 Milton Newsletter. 1, 1967—.
        Edited by Roy C. Flannagan and published at Ohio University, this is the
        only periodical devoted exclusively to Milton. Includes notices of recent
        publications, reviews, abstracts of current articles, works in progress, dis-
        sertations, professional meetings, and some original studies.

43 Milton Society of America. Annual Dinner and Meeting. Ed. by William
      B. Hunter, Jr., 1955-61, and by John T. Shawcross, 1962-68.
        A booklet containing business reports, the constitution, the history of the
        society, biographical material on the honored scholar, work-in-progress (all
        from time to time), and membership. The booklet for 1956 contains a
        picture and discussion of the Milton Cottage at Chalfont St. Giles, by Dorothy
        Law, Trustee.

44 MODERN HUMANITIES RESEARCH ASSOCIATION. Annual Bibliography of English Language and Literature. Ed. (1956) by Angus MacDonald and Henry J. Petit, Jr. Cambridge: Bowes and Bowes, Cambridge Univ. Press, 1920—. 1, 1920, 23-4; 2, 1921, 73-4; 3, 1922, 112-4; 4, 1923, 108-10; 5, 1924, 75-7; 6, 1925, 77-9; 7, 1926, 83-5; 8, 1927, 95-7; 9, 1928, 113-4; 10, 1929, 117-8; 11, 1930, 114-6; 12, 1931, 133-6; 13, 1932, 128-31; 14, 1933, 130-3; 15, 1934, 142-5; 16, 1935, 146-8; 17, 1936, 145-8; 18, 1937, 163-6; 19, 1938, 146-8; 20, 1939, 148-51; 21, 1940, 144-7; 22, 1941, 116-9; 23, 1942, 74-6; 24, 1943-4, 147-51; 25, 1945, 77-9; 26, 1946, 61-3; 27, 1947, 122-4; 28, 1948, 127-31; 29, 1949, 138-42; 30, 1950-2, 344-52; 31, 1953-4, 248-53; 32, 1955-6, 294-300; 33, 1957-8, 293-301; 34, 1959, 166-70; 35, 1960, 158-62; 36, 1961, 170-6; 37, 1962, 188-93; 38, 1963, 149-54; 39, 1964, 229-35; 40, 1965, 237-44.

45 MODERN LANGUAGE ASSOCIATION. MLA International Bibliography of Books and Articles on the Modern Languages and Literatures, 1922—. PMLA, 37, 1922, 10-11; 38, 1923, 10-11; 39, 1924, 12-3; 40, 1925, 12; 41, 1926, 13-4; 42, 1927, 28-9; 43, 1928, 27-8; 44, 1929, 33-4; 45, 1930, 37; 46, 1931, 27-8; 47, 1932, 1235-6; 48, 1933, 1326-7; 49, 1934, 1229-30; 50, 1935, 1264-6; 51, 1936, 1237-8; 52, 1937, 1254-6; 53, 1938, 1247-8; 54, 1939, 1240-2; 55, 1940, 1254-6; 56, 1941, 1245-8; 57, 1942, 1251-3; 58, 1943, 1221-3; 59, 1944, 1213-4; 60, 1945, 1223-5; 61, 1946, 1255-7. Until 1946, these bibliographies were published in supplements and are bibliographies of the year indicated. There was no list published in 1947. The following volumes contain the bibliography for the previous year: PMLA, 63, 1948, 51-2; 64, 1949, 31-2; 65, 1950, 54-5; 66, 1951, 63-4; 67, 1952, 34-5; 68, 1953, 119-20; 69, 1954, 103-4; 70, 1955, 138-40; 71, 1956, 141-2; 72, 1957, 210-1; 73, 1958, 166-7; 74, 1959, 133-4; 75, 1960, 210-1; 76, 1961, 168-9; 77, 1962, 185-7; 78, 1963, 148-9; 79, 1964, 163-4; 80, 1965, 126-7; 81, 1966, 140-1; 82, 1967, 147-9; 83, 1968, 131-2. Until 1956, this listing appeared as American Bibliography. Harrison T. Messerole is the current Association Bibliographer.

46 MUMMENDEY, RICHARD. Language and Literature of the Anglo-Saxon Nations as Presented in German Doctoral Dissertations, 1885-1950. Charlottesville: Bibliographical Society of the Univ. of Virginia; Bonn: H. Bouvier, 1954.

47 OCHI, FUMIO. Milton in Japan, 1840-1932. 8pp.
    Mimeograph list in Christ's College Library, Cambridge.

48 OXFORD UNIVERSITY COMMITTEE FOR ADVANCED STUDIES. Abstracts of Dissertations for the Degree of Doctor of Philosophy. Oxford: Clarendon Press, 1925-1940. 12 vols.

49 OXFORD UNIVERSITY COMMITTEE FOR ADVANCED STUDY. Successful Candidates for the Degrees of D. Phil., B. Litt., and B. Sc., with Titles of Their Theses. Oxford Univ. Press, 1940-1962. 18 vols. to 1966.
    Vol. 1 covers 1940-1949; since then, annual lists have been published.

50 [PARKER, WILLIAM RILEY]. Works on Milton by William Riley Parker. SCN, 16, Nos. 3 and 4, 1958, item 185.

51 PATRIDES, C. A., ed. Milton's Epic Poetry: Essays on Paradise Lost and Paradise Regained. A Peregrine Book. Harmondsworth, Middlesex, England: Penguin Books, 1967. 428pp.
An Annotated Reading List, pp. 381-428.

52 PATTERSON, G. M., and others. Index to Theses Accepted for Higher Degrees in the Universities of Great Britain and Ireland. London: Aslib, 1953—.
Fifteen volumes have been published: 1, 1953 for 1950-1; 2, 1955 for 1951-2; 3, 1956 for 1952-3; 4, 1957 for 1953-4; 5, 1957 for 1954-5; 6, 1958 for 1955-6; 7, 1959 for 1956-7; 8, 1960 for 1957-8; 9, 1961 for 1958-9; 10, 1961 for 1959-60; 11, 1962 for 1960-1; 12, 1963 for 1961-2; 13, 1964 for 1962-3; 14, 1966 for 1963-4; 15, 1967 for 1964-5.

53 PINTO, VIVIAN DE SOLA. The English Renaissance: 1510-1688. Introductions to English Literature. Ed. by Bonamy Dobrée. New York: McBride, 1938.
John Milton, a Bibliography, pp. 337-52.

54 POPE, MYRTLE PIHLMAN, ed. A Bibliography of Works by and about John Milton in the Stephen F. Austin State College Library, 1930-1961. Offset typescript. Department of English, Journalism, and Philosophy, Stephen F. Austin State College, Nacogdoches, Texas, November, 1962. [24pp.]
Contains books listed in card catalogue, as well as articles in journals and "hidden" references not listed elsewhere, "such as parts of critical studies in important literary histories and other reference works."

55 Publications of the Modern Language Association: Research in Progress, PMLA, 63, 1948, 199-201; 64, 1949, 141-2; 65, 1950, 160-1; 66, 1951, 187; 67, 1952, 168-9; 69, 1954, 240-2; 71, 1956, 290-1; 73, 1958, 60-1.

56 Recent Studies in the English Renaissance. SEL, 1961—. Arthur Barker, 1, 1961, 147-57; Sears Jayne, 2, 1962, 140-4; Arthur Barker, 3, 1963, 140-50; Walter J. Ong, S.J., 4, 1964, 178-83; Hugh N. MacLean, 5, 1965, 197-203; Ernest Sirluck, 6, 1966, 182-92; Howard Schultz, 7, 1967, 179-89; Kathleen Williams, 8, 1968, 178-85.
Each essay contains a discussion of Milton studies published during the previous year.

57 Recordings of Milton. MN, 1, 1967, 43-4.
Lists all of the readings presently in the Schwann catalog.

58 SEARS, MINNIE E., and MARION SHAW. Essay and General Literature Index, 1900-1933: An Index to About 40,000 Essays and Articles in 2144 Volumes and Collections of Essays and Miscellaneous Works. New York: H. W. Wilson, 1934. 5 vols.
Supplements have been published in 1935, 1941, 1948, 1955, 1960, 1965, 1966, 1967, and 1968. Estelle A. Fidell is the current editor.

59 Seventeenth-Century News. 1, 1942—. Published from 1942 until 1950 as The Seventeenth-Century News Letter.

Edited by J. Max Patrick. Contains lists of current articles, abstracts of articles and papers, and book reviews. It also records the activities of the Milton Society of America.

60 STEVENS, DAVID HARRISON. A Reference Guide to Milton from 1800 to the Present Day. Chicago: Univ. of Chicago Press, 1930. Reprinted, New York: Russell and Russell, 1967. x, 302pp.
Includes items to 1928; well annotated and usually accurate.
Rev. H. J. C. Grierson and A. Melville Clark, YWES, 230; E. N. S. Thompson, PQ, 9, 1930, 317; G. Saintsbury, Bookman, 78, 1930, 161-2; TLS, Apr. 10, 1930, p. 320; N&Q, 158, 1930, 450; E. C. Batho and E. J. Vaughan, MLR, 26, 1931, 203-4; D. Saurat, RES, 7, 1931, 472-4; R[onald] S. C[rane], MP, 28, 1931, 380-1; H. F. Fletcher, MLN, 46, 1931, 539-41; S. B. Liljegren, Ang. Bbl., 43, 1932, 369-71; F. Delattre, Rev. belge de philol. et d'hist., 12, 1933, 309-12.

61 STRATMAN, CARL J. Milton's Samson Agonistes: A Checklist of Criticism. Restoration and 18th Century Theatre Research, 4, 1965, 2-10.
Addenda in SCN, 24, No. 3, 1966, item 16, and by Anthony Low, SCN, 25, No. 1, 1967, item 3.

62 STUDIES IN PHILOLOGY. Recent Literature of the English Renaissance, 1917—. SP, 14, 1917, 225-6; 15, 1918, 216; 16, 1919, 212-3; 17, 1920, 261-2; 18, 1921, 375; 19, 1922, 278-80; 20, 1923, 277-80; 21, 1924, 449-51; 22, 1925, 319-22; 23, 1926, 276-81; 24, 1927, 350-3; 25, 1928, 249-53; 26, 1929, 260-3; 27, 1930, 361-3; 28, 1931, 352-6; 29, 1932, 322-6; 30, 1933, 313-8; 31, 1934, 303-6; 32, 1935, 326-30; 33, 1936, 346-50; 34, 1937, 329-33; 35, 1938, 348-51; 36, 1939, 331-4; 37, 1940, 349-52; 38, 1941, 332-6; 39, 1942, 383-7; 40, 1943, 307-10; 41, 1944, 307-10; 42, 1945, 318-20; 43, 1946, 327-31; 44, 1947, 323-6; 45, 1948, 301-4; 46, 1949, 278-82; 47, 1950, 322-8; 48, 1951, 344-9; 49, 1952, 319-24; 50, 1953, 295-8; 51, 1954, 283-6; 52, 1955, 280-4; 53, 1956, 301-5; 54, 1957, 253-7; 55, 1958, 288-92; 56, 1959, 298-304; 57, 1960, 298-303; 58, 1961, 285-91; 59, 1962, 311-8; 60, 1963, 320-5; 61, 1964, 323-8; 62, 1965, 329-36; 63, 1966, 279-82; 64, 1967, 294-9; 65, 1968, 323-30. Contains items published during the previous year. Dennis Donovan is the current general compiler.

63 TAYLOR, C. R. H. The Milton Collection. The Turnbull Library Record (Wellington, New Zealand), 14, March, 1960, 12-5.
Works collected by Alexander Turnbull.

64 THOMPSON, E. N. S. John Milton: A Topical Bibliography. New Haven: Yale Univ. Press, 1916. xl, 104pp.

65 TROTIER, ARNOLD H., and MARIAN HARMON. Doctoral Dissertations Accepted by American Universities. New York: H. W. Wilson, 1933-55. 22 vols.

66 UNIVERSITY OF DURHAM. Abstracts of Theses for Doctorates. 1931-32 to 1938-39 inclusive.

67 UNIVERSITY OF EDINBURGH. List of Theses Accepted for Doctorates. 1930-31 to 1963-64 inclusive.

68 UNIVERSITY OF ILLINOIS. Collections of First Editions of Milton's Works, University of Illinois Library. An Exhibition, October 1-31,

1953. Introduction and notes prepared by Harris F. Fletcher. Urbana: Univ. of Illinois Press, 1953. 24pp.

69 UNIVERSITY OF LEEDS. Publications and Abstracts of Theses by Members of the University. 1927-28 to 1937-38 inclusive.

70 WATSON, GEORGE, ed. The Concise Cambridge Bibliography of English Literature, 600-1950. Cambridge: Cambridge Univ. Press, 1958. John Milton (1608-1674), pp. 82-3.

71 [WHITING, GEORGE W.] The Miltonic Scholarship of George Wesley Whiting. SCN, 16, No. 1, 1958, item 41.
    A reprint in part of a list of Whiting's published writings, compiled by Ann Gossman (Rice Institute Pamphlet, 44, 1957, vi-viii).

72 [WHITNEY, HENRY AUSTIN, 1826-1889]. The John Milton Collection Formed by Henry Austin Whitney. New York: Alexander Press, [1935]. 21pp.

73 WILLIAMS, WILLIAM P. A Descriptive Catalogue of Seventeenth Century English Religious Literature in the Kansas State Univ. Library (Pamphlet). Manhattan, Kansas: Kansas State Univ. Library, 1966.
    Contains descriptions of copies of Animadversions (1641) and An Apology (1642).

74 [WOODHOUSE, A. S. P.]. Publications of A. S. P. Woodhouse. Essays in English Literature from the Renaissance to the Victorian Age. Presented to A. S. P. Woodhouse, 1964. Ed. by Millar MacLure and F. W. Watt (Toronto: Univ. of Toronto Press, 1964), pp. 334-9.
    Compiled by M. H. M. MacKinnon. Reprinted in part as Seventeenth Century Scholarship of A. S. P. Woodhouse, SCN, 23, Nos. 1 and 2, 1965, item 10.

COLLECTED WORKS: PROSE AND POETRY

75 Milton: Poetry and Prose. With Essays by Johnson, Hazlitt, Macaulay. With an Introduction by A. M. D. Hughes and Notes by Various Scholars. Oxford: Clarendon Press, 1930. xi, 224pp.
First Edition, 1920.

76 The Student's Milton, Being the Complete Poems of John Milton, with the Greater Part of His Prose Works, Now Printed in One Volume, together with New Translations into English of his Italian, Latin, and Greek Poems. Ed. by Frank Allen Patterson. New York: Crofts, 1930. ix, 1090, 41pp. Revised Edition, 1933.
Rev: H. J. C. Grierson and A. Melville Clark, YWES, 225-6; E. C. Batho and E. J. Vaughan, MLR, 26, 1931, 202-3; D. Saurat, RES, 7, 1931, 472-4; H. F. Fletcher, JEGP, 31, 1932, 156-8; R. D. H[avens], MLN, 69, 1934, 558; W. Fischer, Ang. Bbl., 47, 1936, 56-7.

77 The Works of John Milton. Gen. Ed., Frank Allen Patterson. New York: Columbia Univ. Press, 1931-38. 18 vols. in 21.
Vol. 1, Pt. 1: The Shorter English Poems, ed. by Frank Allen Patterson; The Italian Poems, ed. and trans. by Arthur Livingstone; The Latin and Greek Poems, ed. by W. P. Trent in collaboration with Thomas O. Mabbott, with a trans. by Charles Knapp, 1931.
Vol. 1, Pt. 2: Samson Agonistes, ed. by Frank Allen Patterson, 1931. xv, 605pp.
Vol. 2, Pt. 1: Paradise Lost, Books 1-8, ed. by Frank Allen Patterson, 1931.
Vol. 2, Pt. 2: Paradise Lost, Books 9-12, ed. by Frank Allen Patterson, 1931. ix, 547pp.
Vol. 3, Pt. 1: Of Reformation, Of Prelatical Episcopacy, Animadversions . . . against Smectymnuus, The Reason of Church Government, An Apology against a Pamphlet, ed. by Harry Morgan Ayers, 1931.
Vol. 3, Pt. 2: The Doctrine and Discipline of Divorce, ed. by the late Chilton Latham Powell and Frank Allen Patterson, 1931. ix, 585pp.
Vol. 4: The Judgement of Martin Bucer, Tetrachordon, Colasterion, ed. by Chilton Latham Powell; Of Education, Areopagitica, ed. by William Haller, 1931. ix, 368pp.
Vol. 5: The Tenure of Kings and Magistrates, Eikonoklastes, ed. by William Haller, 1932. ix, 352pp.
Vol. 6: A Treatise of Civil Power; Considerations touching the likeliest means to remove Hirelings out of the church; A letter to a Friend Concerning the Ruptures of the Commonwealth; The Present Means, and brief Delineation of a Free Commonwealth . . . In a Letter to General Monk; The Readie and Easie Way to Establish a Free Commonwealth; Brief Notes upon a late Sermon, Titl'd, the Fear of God and the King, &c; Of True Religion, Hæresie, Schism, Toleration; Articles of Peace . . . Observations; A Declaration; or Letters Patents of the

Election of this Present King of Poland; Accedence Commenc't Grammar, ed. by William Haller, 1932. xi, 371pp.

Vol. 7: Joannis Miltoni Angli Pro Populo Anglicano Defensio, ed. by Clinton W. Keyes, with a Trans. by Samuel Lee Wolff, 1932. ix, 587pp.

Vol. 8: Joannis Miltoni Angli Pro Populo Anglicano Defensio Secunda, ed. by Eugene J. Strittmatter, with the Trans. of George Burnett, London, 1809, Revised by Moses Hadas, 1933. vii, 266pp.

Vol. 9: Joannis Miltoni Angli Pro Se Defensio contra Alexandrum Morum Ecclesiasten, ed. by Eugene J. Strittmatter, with the Trans. of George Burnett, London, 1809, Revised by Moses Hadas, 1933. vii, 308pp.

Vol. 10: The History of Britain; A Brief History of Moscovia, ed. by George Philip Krapp, 1932. ix, 387pp.

Vol. 11: Artis Logicae Plenior Institutio, ed. and trans. by Allan H. Gilbert, 1935. xv, 538pp.

Vol. 12: The Familiar Letters of John Milton, ed. by Donald Lemen Clark with the Trans. of David Masson; The Prolusions of John Milton, ed. by Donald Lemen Clark with a Trans. of Bromley Smith; An Early Prolusion by John Milton and Miscellaneous Correspondence in Foreign Tongues, ed. and trans. by Thomas Ollive Mabbott and Nelson Glenn McCrea; English Correspondence by John Milton, Collected and Ed. by Thomas Ollive Mabbott; Correspondence of Milton and Mylius, Collected, Ed., and Trans. by Thomas Ollive Mabbott and Nelson Glenn McCrea, 1936. xi, 415pp.

Vol. 13: The State Papers of John Milton, Collected and Ed. by Thomas Ollive Mabbott and J. Milton French, including (1) Literae Pseudo-Senatus Anglicani, 1676, with the Translation of Edward Phillips, 1694, and (2) Additional Material, with Translations by Several Hands: Letters from the Skinner Manuscript, State Papers from Various Sources, English State Papers by John Milton now first printed from the Columbia Manuscript, Major State Documents Translated by Milton, 1937. xv, 646pp.

Vol. 14: De Doctrina Christiana, Bk. 1, Chs. 1-6, ed. with the Trans. of Charles R. Sumner, D. D., by James Holly Hanford and Waldo Hilary Dunn, 1933. vii, 403pp.

Vol. 15: De Doctrina Christiana, Bk. 1, Chs. 7-20, 1933. viii, 409pp.

Vol. 16: De Doctrina Christiana, Bk. 1, Chs. 21-33, 1934. viii, 381pp.

Vol. 17: De Doctrina Christiana, Bk. 2, 1934. viii, 587pp.

Vol. 18: The Uncollected Writings of John Milton, ed. by Thomas Ollive Mabbott and J. Milton French with Trans. by Nelson Glenn McCrea and Others, including (1) Proposalls; (2) Latin Documents by Milton in the Scriptum Parliamenti, 1652; (3) Additional State Papers; (4) Milton's Commonplace Book, ed. by James Holly Hanford, with a Trans. by Nelson Glenn McCrea; (5) Additions to the Commonplace Book; (6) Outlines for Tragedies; (7) Character of the Long Parliament; (8) Toland's Additions to the History of Britain, contributed by Harris Fletcher; (9) Essays from the Columbia Manuscript; (10) Additional Correspondence; (11) Fugitive, Lost, and Projected Works; (12) Book Inscriptions; (13) Introduction to Raleigh's Cabinet Council;

(14) Marginalia. Appendices: (1) New Discovered Texts of Hobson Poems, Contributed by William R. Parker; (2) Poems Ascribed to Milton; (3) Apothegmata and Records of Conversations; (4) Legal Documents; (5) Joannis Philippi Angli Responsio; (6) Supposed Collaborations; (7) Index to Pro Populo; (8) Index to History of Britain; (9) Apocryphal Prose Works; (10) Conversations with Mylius; (11) Marginalia on Malvezzi; 1938. xv, 656pp.

> Rev: G. R. Elliott, AB, Sept., 1931, pp. 74-6; H. W. Garrod, Nat., 132, 1931, 681-2, 135, 1932, 175-6, and 143, 1936, 498-9; TLS, Sept. 3, 1931, p. 987, June 23, 1932, p. 461, Jan. 26, 1933, p. 54, July 4, 1935, p. 435, Mar. 20, 1937, p. 226, Apr. 23, 1938, p. 283, and Jan. 7, 1939, p. 8; A. M. Witherspoon, SRL, Aug. 8, 1931, pp. 33-5, and Dec. 24, 1938, p. 19; A. Tate, NR, 68, 1931, 266-8; D. Saurat, RES, 8, 1932, 340-3, 10, 1934, 229-31, 14, 1938, 349-52, and 16, 1940, 221; F. S. Boas, YWES, 13, 1932, 219, and 16, 1935, 264; H. Darbishire, RES, 9, 1933, 61-2, 319; H. J. C. Grierson, RES, 9, 1933, 316-9; B. A. Wright, MLR, 29, 1934, 452-8, 31, 1936, 79-83, 32, 1937, 96, 33, 1938, 432, and 35, 1940, 88-9; H. F. Fletcher, JEGP, 33, 1934, 132-44, 300-5, and 38, 1939, 147-52, 292-300; L. C. Martin, YWES, 18, 1937, 181-2, and 19, 1938, 174-5; Maurice Kelley, MLN, 51, 1936, 463-6; W. C. Abbott, AHR, 44, 1938, 101-4; N&Q, 175, 1938, 394-6, and 176, 1939, 35.

79 PATTERSON, FRANK A., and FRENCH R. FOGLE. An Index to the Columbia Edition of the Works of John Milton. New York: Columbia Univ. Press; London: Milford, 1940. 2 vols. xxviii, 1073, and xi, 214pp. Vol. 1: A-K; Vol. 2: L-Z.

> Rev: L. C. Martin, YWES, 175; TLS, Nov. 16, 1940, p. 583; D. F. Smith, NMQ, 10, 1940, 187-9; H. F. Fletcher, JEGP, 40, 1941, 146-8; R. T. F., Pers., 22, 1941, 309; A. W. Witherspoon, SRL, No. 14, 1941, p. 11; A. S. P. Woodhouse, UTQ, 10, 1941, 504-5; W. C. Abbott, AHR, 46, 1941, 978-9; W. R. Parker, MLN, 57, 1942, 405-6.

80 John Milton: Selections from His Works and Tributes to His Genius. Arranged by Isaac Foot and Presented to Him by Nancy Astor. Newtown, Montgomeryshire: Privately printed by The Welsh Outlook Press, 1935.

> Contains poetry and prose; tributes from a host of admirers, pp. 103-46.

81 Complete Poetry and Selected Prose of John Milton. With English Metrical Translations of the Latin, Greek, and Italian Poems. Ed. by E. H. Visiak, with a Foreword by Sir Arnold Wilson. London: Nonesuch Press; New York: Random House, 1938. xxvii, 860pp. Reprinted by Nonesuch, 1948.

> Rev: L. C. Martin, YWES, 180-1; K. John, NSN, N.S., 15, 1938, 698-700; John Hayward, Spect., Apr. 15, 1938, p. 680; CR, 154, 1938, 128; N&Q, 175, 1938, 233-4; D. Saurat, FR, 164, 1938, 367-8; RES, 16, 1940, 219-20.

82 A Shorter Milton. Selected and Edited by F. J. Tickner. Nelson Classics. London: Nelson and Sons, 1938. vi, 263pp.

> Contains many of minor poems, selections from Paradise Lost and Paradise Regained, Samson Agonistes, and selections from the prose works.

83 Complete Poetry and Selected Prose of John Milton. New York: Modern Library, 1942. vi, 756pp.

84 Milton. Selected Poetry and Prose. Ed. by C. R. Bull. Melbourne: Melbourne Univ. Press, 1948, 1950, 1956. x, 148pp.

85 The Portable Milton. Ed. by Douglas Bush, with an Introduction. New York: Viking Press, 1949. 693pp. Reprinted, 1962, 1968 (with updated bibliography).

86 John Milton. Ed. by Maynard Mack. Vol. 2 of English Masterpieces. Englewood Cliffs, N.J.: Prentice-Hall, 1950. Second Edition, 1961. 346pp.
    Introduction, pp. 1-28. Contains twelve of the minor poems, Areopagitica, and selections from Paradise Lost and Samson Agonistes.

87 Complete Poetry and Selected Prose of John Milton. Introduction by Cleanth Brooks. New York: Modern Library, 1950. xxiv, 756pp.

88 Paradise Lost and Selected Poetry and Prose. Ed. by Northrop Frye. New York: Holt, Rinehart and Winston, 1951. xxxviii, 601pp.

89 John Milton. Complete Poems and Major Prose. Ed. by Merritt Y. Hughes, with Notes and Introductions. New York: Odyssey Press, 1957. xix, 1059pp. Reprinted, 1962.
    Rev: Agnes M. C. Latham, YWES, 181; SCN, 15, 1957, 29; Irene Samuel, RN, 11, 1958, 138-41; EA, 11, 1958, 351-2; F. T. Prince, MLR, 56, 1961, 299-300.

90 The Compact Milton. Selections from the Poems and Areopagitica. Ed. with an Introduction by H. S. Taylor. New York: Barron's Educational Series, 1966. 305pp.

COLLECTED POEMS

91 Poems of John Milton. With an Introduction by Sir Henry Newbolt. London: Nelson and Sons, 1929. xiv, 530pp.
Reissued, 1930 (?).

92 The Complete Poems of John Milton. Printed together with New Translations into English of his Italian, Latin, and Greek Poems. Ed. by Frank Allen Patterson. New York: Crofts, 1930. ix, 439pp. Revised Edition, 1933.
Contains the poetry published in The Student's Milton.

93 The Poems of John Milton. Ed. with an Introduction by Frank Allen Patterson. Modern Readers' Series. New York: Macmillan, 1930. ix, 439pp.

94 The English Poems of John Milton, from the Edition of the Late H. C. Beeching, D. D. London: Oxford Univ. Press, 1932. vii, 488pp.
Several editions "from Beeching" are listed in Stevens.

95 The Poetical Works of John Milton, edited after the original texts by H. C. Beeching. London: Oxford Univ. Press, Humphrey Milford, 1932, 1935. xiii, 554pp.

96 John Milton. Poems. Ed. and arranged with a Preface by H. J. C. Grierson. New York: Coward-McCann, 1933. 2 vols.
Apparently a reprint of Grierson's 1925 edition, Stevens' No. 261.

97 The Poetical Works of John Milton. Introduction by W. H. D. Rouse. Everyman's Library. New York: Dutton; London: Dent, 1933. xvi, 554pp.
See Stevens' No. 254, first published ca. 1909.

98 The Poetical Works of John Milton. Ed. after the original texts by the Reverend H. C. Beeching, M. A., including William Cowper's Translation of the Latin and Italian Poems, with an Introduction by Charles Grosvenor Osgood. New York: Oxford Univ. Press, 1935. xxxi, 599pp.

99 The Complete Poems of John Milton with Complete Notes by Thomas Newton, D. D., Bishop of Bristol. Illustrated by Gustave Doré and Others. New York: Union Library Assn., Crown Publishers, 1936. ix, 665pp.

100 The Poems of John Milton, with an Introduction and Notes by James Holly Hanford. Nelson's English Series. New York: T. Nelson, 1936. lxxxviii, 582pp. Second Edition, 1953.

101 Selected Poems of John Milton. With Introduction and Notes by James Holly Hanford. New York: Thomas Nelson, 1936. lxxxviii, 138pp.

102 The Poetical Works of John Milton. Ed. after the original texts of H. C. Beeching. New edition with translations of the Italian, Latin and Greek

Poems from the Columbia University edition, and a Reader's Guide by W. W. Skeat. London: Oxford Univ. Press, 1938, 1946. xiii, 679pp.
Rev: N&Q, 175, 1938, 341-2; P. Meissner, DL, 60, 1939, 916-18.

103 The English Poems of John Milton. With an Introduction by Charles Williams, and a Reader's Guide to Milton Compiled by Walter Skeat. World's Classics Series. Oxford: Oxford Univ. Press; London: Milford, 1940, xxii, 545pp; London: Oxford Univ. Press, 1958. xx, 543pp.
Rev: D. C. Macgregor, RES, 17, 1940, 479-81; TLS, May 11, 1940, p. 235, July 26, 1940, p. 359, and Aug. 9, 1940, p. 385; Margaret Willy, English, 4, 1942, 108.

104 The Complete Poetical Works of John Milton. A New Text, ed. with an introduction and notes by Harris Francis Fletcher. New Cambridge Edition. Boston: Houghton Mifflin, 1941. xiii, 574pp.
A revision of William V. Moody's Cambridge Edition. The Life and Times of John Milton, 1608-1674, pp. 1-39.
Rev: E. N. S. T[hompson], PQ, 20, 1941, 188-92; A. S. P. Woodhouse, JEGP, 41, 1942, 99-102; W. R. Parker, MLN, 57, 1942, 686.

105 John Milton's Complete Poetical Works, Reproduced in Photographic Facsimile. Ed. by Harris Francis Fletcher. Urbana: University of Illinois Press, 1943-8. 4 vols.
Vol. 1: Poems &c. upon Several Occasions, 1673. Poems, both English and Latin, 1645. With Fugitive Printings, Manuscript Copies, and Their Collations, 1943. vi, 465pp.
Vol. 2: The First Edition of Paradise Lost, with the Plans and Lists of Epic Subjects from the Trinity College Manuscript, the Manuscript of Book I, with Translations and Collations, 1945. vi, 634pp.
Vol. 3: The Second Edition of Paradise Lost, 1948. iv, 455pp.
Vol. 4: The 1671 Edition of Paradise Regained and Samson Agonistes, 1948. iv, 316pp.
Rev: TLS, July 8, 1944, p. 335, and Aug. 17, 1946, p. 390; W. W. Greg, MLR, 39, 144, 409-17; J. Milton French, JEGP, 43, 1944, 474-8, 45, 1946, 458-64, and 48, 1949, 413-20; E. N. S. Thompson, PQ, 23, 1944, 185-6, and 25, 1946, 287-8; L. C. Martin, YWES, 26, 1945, 140-1, and 29, 1948, 191-2; Maurice Kelley, MLN, 60, 1945, 188-92, 63, 1948, 208-9, and 66, 1951, 103-6; B. A. Wright, Library, 4th Ser., 25, 1945, 87-94; Helen Darbishire, RES, 23, 1947, 170-3, and ibid., N.S., 2, 1951, 386-9; A. H. Gilbert, SAQ, 46, 1947, 289-90; W. R. Parker, PBSA, 41, 1947, 33-52, and 43, 1949, 361-4.

106 The Portable Milton: Paradise Lost, Paradise Regained, Samson Agonistes, and Comus, Other Selections. Ed. by Douglas Bush. Viking Paperbound Portables. New York: The Viking Press, 1949, 1962. 693pp.

107 AUDEN, W. H., and N. H. PEARSON, eds. Poets of the English Language. Vol. 3: Milton to Goldsmith. New York: Viking Press, 1950.
Includes the usual short lyrics, parts of Paradise Lost, and all of Samson Agonistes, accompanied by brief introductory comments.
Rev: Bonamy Dobrée, Spect., Sept. 5, 1952, p. 304.

108 The Poetical Works of John Milton. Ed. by Helen Darbishire. Oxford: Clarendon Press, 1952-5. 2 vols. Vol. 1: Paradise Lost, 1952. xxv, 326pp. Vol. 2: Paradise Regained, Samson Agonistes, Poems upon Severall

Occasions Both English and Latin, 1955. xx, 376pp. Reprinted, 1962, 1967.

Sets forth the case for a reformed text, 1, ix-xviii. Includes textual notes and commentaries.

Rev: Arnold Davenport, YWES, 33, 1952, 182, and 36, 1955, 161; TLS, Dec. 26, 1952, p. 854; Louis Bonnerot, EA, 5, 1952, 253; B. A. Wright, MLR, 47, 1952, 577-9, and RES, 8, 1957, 78-94; Richard Murphy, Spect, Mar. 20, 1953, pp. 352, 354; George Watson, CR, 184, 1953, 61-2; H. J. C. Grierson, MLR, 48, 1953, 335-6; C. V. Wedgwood, TT, Sept. 3, 1955, pp. 1142-3; reply by E. C. Kitson, ibid., Sept. 10, 1955, p. 1169; R. O. Evans, SCN, 14, No. 1-2, 1956, 5-6.

109 The Complete English Poems of Milton. Ed. by John Gawsworth. London: Macdonald, 1953. xxxv, 513pp.

110 John Milton. Poems. Selected with an Introduction by L. D. Lerner. London: Penguin Books, 1953. 316pp.

Rev: TLS, Aug. 21, 1953, p. 537.

111 HARRISON, G. B., gen. ed. Major British Writers. New York: Harcourt, Brace, 1954, 1959. 2 vols.

Douglas Bush, ed., Milton section. General introduction, 1, 401-13.

112 A Selection of Poems by John Milton. With an Introduction by Howard Sergeant. London: Grey Walls Press, 1954. 64pp.

113 John Milton. Poems. Ed. by B. A. Wright. Everyman's Library. London: Dent; New York: Dutton, 1956. xlii, 479pp.

Reformed text with introductory discussion of principles.

Rev: J. B. Broadbent, MLR, 52, 1957, 626-7; Kenneth Muir, London Mag., 4, No. 8, 1957, 8, 70, 73, 75, 77; J. B. Leishman, RES, 9, 1958, 82-5; J. B. Broadbent, ES, 39, 1958, 265-9; F. W. Bateson, TLS, July 4, 1958, p. 377.

114 John Milton. Milton's Dramatic Poems. Ed. by Geoffrey and Margaret Bullough. London: Univ. of London, Athlone Press, 1958; Fairlawn, New Jersey: Essential Books, 1958. 224pp. Fifth Impression, 1967.

Rev: J. B. Broadbent, ES, 39, 1958, 265-9; TLS, May 9, 1958, p. 259; SCN, 16, 1958, 35; F. T. Prince, MLR, 54, 1959, 419.

115 The Poetical Works of John Milton. Ed. by Helen Darbishire. With Translations of the Italian, Latin, and Greek Poems from the Columbia Univ. Edition. Oxford Standard Authors. Revised Edition. London and New York: Oxford Univ. Press, 1958. xii, 628pp.

Rev: E. E. Duncan-Jones, MLR, 53, 1958, 243-4; SCN, 16, 1958, 35; J. B. Broadbent, ES, 39, 1958, 265-9; TLS, June 20, 1958, p. 346, and comments by F. W. Bateson, July 4, 1958, p. 377, and B. A. Wright, Aug. 1, 1958, p. 435, and J. C. Maxwell, Aug. 15, 1958, p. 459, and Peter Alexander, Aug. 22, 1958, p. 471; H. F. Fletcher, JEGP, 58, 1959, 296-7; Maria Wickert, Anglia, 78, 1960, 103-4; K. M. Lea, RES, 11, 1960, 84-5.

116 BALD, R. C. Seventeenth-Century English Poetry. The Harper English Literature Series, under the editorship of the late Karl J. Holzknecht. New York: Harper and Brothers, 1959. ix, 591pp.

Contains many of the minor poems and selections from Paradise Lost and Paradise Regained.

117 John Milton. The Poems of John Milton. Ed. by Helen Darbishire. London: Oxford Univ. Press, 1961. x, 679pp.
   Reprints original editions of 1645, 1671, 1673, and 1674.
   Rev: John T. Shawcross, SCN, 20, 1962, 7; Edgar Mertner, Anglia, 82, 1964, 247-59.

118 John Milton. Paradise Lost and Other Poems. Ed. by Edward LeComte. Mentor Books. New York: New American Library, 1961, 1964. 414pp.
   Includes Samson Agonistes and Lycidas.
   Rev: John T. Shawcross, SCN, 20, 1962, 30-1.

119 The Poetical Works of John Milton. Globe Edition. With Introductions by David Masson. London: Macmillan and Co., 1961; New York: St. Martin's Press, 1961. xi, 625pp.
   A reprint of Stevens' No. 209, first published in 1877 and reprinted numerous times.

120 John Milton. Paradise Lost. Paradise Regained. Samson Agonistes. With a new Introduction by Harold Bloom. New York: Collier Books, 1962. 350pp.

121 John Milton. Poems and Selected Prose. Ed. and with an Introduction by Marjorie Hope Nicolson. New York: Bantam Books, 1962. vi, 597pp.

122 The Complete English Poetry of John Milton (Excluding His Translations of Psalms 80-88). Arranged in Chronological Order with an Introduction, Notes, Variants, and Literal Translations of the Foreign Language Poems by John T. Shawcross. The Stuart Editions. New York: New York Univ. Press, 1963. Issued also in The Anchor Seventeenth Century Series, Garden City: Anchor Books, Doubleday, 1963. xv, 574pp.
   This edition contains thirteen illustrations from Jacob Tonson's 1688 edition of Paradise Lost. Selected bibliography, pp. 567-70.
   Rev: K. William Fried, SCN, 21, 1963, 14.

123 John Milton. The Complete English Poems of John Milton. Ed. by John Jump. New York: Washington Square Press, 1964. 465pp.

125 Milton. Ed. by William G. Madsen. New York: Laurel Editions, Dell Publishing Co., 1964, 190pp.
   Introduction, pp. 7-32. Contains some of minor poems, excerpts from nine books of Paradise Lost, and most of Samson Agonistes.

126 John Milton. The Complete Poetical Works of John Milton. Ed. by Douglas Bush. Cambridge Edition. Boston: Houghton Mifflin, 1965. xxxiii, 570pp.
   Rev: Barbara Lewalski, SCN, 23, 1965, 53-4.

127 John Milton. Complete English Poems. Ed. with an Introduction by John Gawsworth [Including Gustave Doré's illustrations to Paradise Lost]. Boston: Ginn, 1966. xxxv, 513pp.

128 John Milton. Poetical Works. Ed. by Douglas Bush. Oxford Standard Authors. London: Oxford Univ. Press, 1966. xxxi, 570pp.
   Rev: TLS, Sept. 1, 1966, p. 779; J. C. Maxwell, N&Q, N.S., 13, 1966, 397-9; Martin Mueller, Archiv, 204, 1968, 458-9.

129 The Argo Book of Recorded Verse. 3: Milton. Ed. by George H. W. Rylands. London: Oxford Univ. Press in Association with the British Council, 1968. x, 292pp.

> Nine records and accompanying texts are available. Contains several of the shorter poems; selections from Paradise Lost, Paradise Regained, and Samson Agonistes; and all of Comus.

PARADISE LOST

130   John Milton. Paradise Lost, Book I. Ed. by G. E. Hollingworth and A. F. Watt. Lycidas. Ed. by S. E. Goggin. London: Univ. Tutorial Press, 1930, 1938. xix, 58pp.

131   John Milton. Paradise Lost, Book I. Ed. by H. C. Beeching. Oxford: Clarendon Press; London: Milford, 1931. 131pp.
   First Edition, 1887. Bound with E. K. Chambers' edition of Book 2 (see below).

132   John Milton. Paradise Lost, Book II. Ed. by E. K. Chambers. Oxford: Clarendon Press; London: Milford, 1931. 112pp.
   First Edition, 1893. Bound with Beeching's edition of Book 1.

133   John Milton. Paradise Lost, Books I, II. Ed. by G. E. Hollingworth and A. F. Watt. London: W. B. Clive, Univ. Tutorial Press, 1931. 106pp.

134   John Milton's Paradise Lost. Arranged and ed. by G. M. Davis. London: Bell's English Language and Literature Series, 1931. vii, 139pp.

135   The Manuscript of Paradise Lost. Book I. Ed. by Helen Darbishire. Oxford: Oxford Univ. Press, 1931. xlvii, 38, 74pp.
   Contents: Introduction, collotype facsimile of the text of the first edition of Book 1, with a transcript of the manuscript on opposite pages, and notes. The editor emphasizes the importance of the manuscript as an indication of Milton's methods of preparing his copy.
   Rev: G. B. Harrison and L. C. Martin, YWES, 202-3; TLS, Dec. 3, 1931, p. 977; G. R. Elliott, AB, 74, 1931, 457-9; MGW, 25, 1931, 295; S. B. Liljegren, Ang. Bbl., 43, 1932, 378-9; B. A. Wright, MLR, 27, 1932, 334-8; R. F. Russell, Merc, 25, 1932, 502; Paul Chauvet, RA-A, 9, 1932, 549-50; A. W. Pollard, Library, N.S., 13, 1932, 219-21; MB, 7, 1932, 395-6; W. F. P. Stockley, TLS, Feb. 18, 1932, p. 112; R. W. Chapman, TLS, Sept. 29, 1932, p. 691; H. J. C. Grierson, RES, 9, 1933, 229-34; M[ario] P[raz], La Cultura, 12, 1934, 726.

136   Paradise Lost. A Poem in Twelve Books. The Author John Milton. London: Cresset Press, 1931. xii, 442pp.
   Printed at the Shakespeare Head Press, Oxford. "This text of Paradise Lost has been set in type from a copy of the second edition, revised and augmented by the author, printed at London by S. Simmons in 1674. The plates and illustrations were designed and engraved on wood by D. Galanis." Limited edition of 195 copies; printed on Batchelor's hand-made paper; ten copies printed on Roman Vellum.
   Rev: TLS, Dec. 24, 1931, pp. 1033-4.

137   John Milton. Paradise Lost, Books I and II. Ed. by George C. Irwin. With an Introduction by Guy Boas. London: Macmillan, 1934, 1938, 1952. v, 165pp.

138   John Milton. Paradise Lost. Ed. by A. W. Verity. Cambridge: Cambridge Univ. Press, 1934. 2 vols.
   A reprint of Stevens' No. 755, published in 1910.

139 Milton's Paradise Lost, Book I. Ed. by Constance Mary Le Plastrier and
J. P. Guinane, with an Introduction and Notes. Sydney: Shakespeare
Head Press, 1934.

140 Paradise Lost. Books I and II, by John Milton and Essay on Milton by
Lord Macaulay. Ed. by H. A. Treble. Laurel and Gold Series. London
& Glasgow: Collin's Clear-Type Press, 1934, 1935. 224pp.

141 John Milton. Paradise Lost. Ed. by Merritt Y. Hughes. New York:
Odyssey Press, 1935. lvi, 422pp.
Penetrating introduction. Selected bibliography, liii-lvi. Basis of the text is
the 1674 edition of the poem.
Rev: B. A. Wright, MLR, 33, 1938, 432-4; W. R. Parker, MLN, 54, 1939, 75.

142 John Milton. Paradise Lost. Ed. by Merritt Y. Hughes. Garden City:
Doubleday, 1935. lvi, 422pp.

143 John Milton. Paradise Lost. Book IV. Ed. by S. E. Goggin. London:
Univ. Tutorial Press, 1936, 1948, 1949. 73pp.
Reissues of Book 4 from the 1907 edition of Books 4 and 5 (Stevens' No.
1087).

144 John Milton. Paradise Lost. Book VI. Ed. by A. J. F. Collins . . . and
S. E. Goggin. London: Univ. Tutorial Press, 1936. 68pp.
A reissue of Book 6 from the 1910 edition of Books 5 and 6 (Stevens'
No. 1092).

145 John Milton. Paradise Lost. Books IX and X. . . . Ed. by Cyril Aldred.
Scholar's Library. London: Macmillan and Co., 1936. xxxvii, 125pp.

146 John Milton. Paradise Lost. Ed. with Notes by James Holly Hanford. New
York: T. Nelson, 1936. 205pp.

147 Paradise Lost and Paradise Regained, by John Milton, with an Introduction by William Rose Benét and Illustrations by Carlotta Petrina. San
Francisco: J. H. Nash for Members of the Limited Editions Club, 1936.
xiii, 441pp.
Rev: C. P. Rollins, SRL, Jan. 16, 1937, p. 21.

148 John Milton. Paradise Lost. Books I and II. Ed. by Alfred E. Ikin. 2 pt.
Brodie's Chosen English Texts. London: James Brodie, 1937.

149 John Milton. Paradise Lost. Books IX and X. Ed. by A. W. Verity. Pitt
Press Series. Cambridge: Cambridge Univ. Press, 1937. lxxii, 166pp.
A reprint of a volume of a series, first published 1891-96. See Stevens' No. 235.

150 John Milton. Paradise Lost. The Text of the First Edition Prepared for
Press by J. Isaacs. Waltham Saint Lawrence, England: Golden Cockerel
Press, 1937. 378pp.
Two hundred numbered copies.
Rev: TLS, June 26, 1937, p. 484; H. O. Wolfe, Obs., Aug. 8, 1937.

151 John Milton. Paradise Lost, Book I. Ed. by H. C. Beeching. On the
Elements of Milton's blank verse in Paradise Lost [by R. S. Bridges].
Oxford: Clarendon Press, 1938. 153pp.
Another of the several reprints "from Beeching."

152 John Milton. Paradise Lost. Book II. Ed. by E. K. Chambers. Oxford: Clarendon Press Series, 1938. 118pp.
  This edition reprinted separately, not with the Beeching edition, as it was in 1931.

153 John Milton. Paradise Lost, Books I and II. Ed. by David Shillan and Orion S. Playfair. With a portrait by N. A. D. Wallis. London: Longmans, 1938, 1958. vii, 216pp.
  Contains lengthy introduction and selected criticism from Addison to Tillyard.

154 John Milton. Paradise Lost. Books I-IV. Ed. with Introduction and Notes by M. Macmillan. London: Macmillan, 1938-1952. 4 vols.
  Stevens lists M. Macmillan as the editor of the first three books of Paradise Lost, 1888, 1896 (Nos. 1042, 1054).

155 John Milton's Paradise Lost, Books I and II. Ed. with Introduction and Notes by G. H. Cowling. London: Methuen, 1939. xviii, 64pp.
  Contains an appendix on Milton's cosmology.

156 John Milton. Paradise Lost. Books III and IV. Ed. by A. W. Verity. Pitt Press Series. Cambridge: Cambridge Univ. Press, 1940. lxxii, 141pp.
  A reprint of one volume of the 1891-96 series. See Stevens' Nos. 235 and 255.

157 John Milton. Paradise Lost: Illustrations by William Blake. Prefaces by Philip Hofer and John T. Winterich. New York: Heritage Press, 1940. xx, 311pp.
  Blake's illustrations reproduced in color.

158 John Milton. Paradise Lost and Other Poems. Ed. with an Introduction by Maurice Kelley. New York: Walter J. Black, 1943. xx, 386pp.
  Rev: E. L. Tinker, NYTBR, July 25, 1943, p. 25.

159 Milton's Paradise Lost. First Book. Ed. by Roger J. McHugh. Dublin: Browne and Nolan, 1945. 80pp.

160 John Milton. Paradise Lost. Chicago: H. Regnery for The Great Books Foundation, 1949. 314pp.

161 John Milton. Paradise Lost. Books I and II. Ed. by A. W. Verity. Pitt Press Series. Cambridge: Cambridge Univ. Press, 1952. lxxiv, 172pp.
  First edition, 1893. Reprinted 21 times.

162 John Milton. Paradise Lost, Books I and II. Ed. by R. R. Pedley. London: Chatto and Windus, 1956. 173pp.
  "This edition reproduces as exactly as possible the second edition of the poem published in 1674."

163 John Milton. Paradise Lost: Books I and II. Ed. by E. M. W. Tillyard, and with notes by Phyllis B. Tillyard. London: Harrop, 1956. 210pp.

164 John Milton. Paradise Lost. Dolphin Books. Garden City: Doubleday, 1960. 280pp.

165 John Milton. Paradise Lost, Books IX and X. Ed. with an Introduction and Notes by E. M. W. Tillyard. London: Harrop, 1960. 172pp.

166 John Milton. Paradise Lost, Books I and II. Ed. by T. Crehan. London: Univ. of London Press, 1961. 160pp.

167 John Milton. Paradise Lost: A Poem in Twelve Books. A New Edition. Ed. by Merritt Y. Hughes. New York: Odyssey Press, 1962. lx, 324pp.
   Introduction, pp. xv-l. Text is reproduced from the editor's 1957 Milton: Complete Poems and Major Prose. Extensive notes embody much of the recent scholarship. Extensive bibliography. Includes Edward Phillips' Life of Milton, pp. 309-324.
   Rev: John T. Shawcross, SCN, 20, Autumn, 1962, 30.

168 John Milton. Paradise Lost: Books I and II. Ed. by F. T. Prince. London: Oxford Univ. Press, 1962. 205pp.
   Contains a lengthy introduction and commentaries (70 pages) on the two books. Appendices: Paradise Lost and Epic Structure; The Universe, the Cosmos and the Angels; The Verse; Milton's Critics; The Chronology of Milton's Life.

169 Paradise Lost, Book II, by John Milton. With Introduction, Notes and Exercises by Patrick J. Kennedy. Dublin: M. H. Gill and Son, 1963 (?). 122pp.
   Edited for students who are preparing for certificate examinations of the Department of Education.

170 John Milton. Paradise Lost, Books I and II. Ed. with Introduction and Commentary by B. Rajan. New York: Asia Publishing House, 1964; Bombay: Popular Press, 1964. xliv, 115pp.
   Introduction, pp. ix-xli. Extensive commentary.

171 John Milton. Paradise Lost. Books IX and X. Ed. by A. W. Verity. Pitt Press Series. Cambridge: Cambridge Univ. Press, 1964. lxxii, 166pp.
   First edition, 1896. Reprinted 8 times.

172 From Paradise Lost: Selections from John Milton's Poem. Ed. by H. S. Taylor. London: Heinemann, 1965. 209pp.
   Designed for young students. Contains selections from all books, except Book 7.

173 John Milton. Paradise Lost. Books I and II. Ed. by J. C. Suffolk. London: Univ. Tutorial Press, 1965. 108pp.
   Designed to assist students in advanced examinations.

174 Milton's Paradise Lost. Ed. by B. P. Misra. Book I. Kitab Ghar, Givalior 1, Madhya Pradesh, India, 1965. 168pp.

175 John Milton. Paradise Lost and Paradise Regained. Ed. by Christopher Ricks. The Signet Classic Poetry Series. New York and Toronto: The New American Library; London: The New English Library, 1968. xliv, 45-400pp.
   In the Introduction the editor discusses some of the modern objections to Paradise Lost. Partially modernized text based on the 1667 edition. Contains a selected bibliography.

176   John Milton. Paradise Lost: 1667. A Scolar Press Facsimile. Menston,
      England: The Scolar Press Limited, 1968.
         Reproduced from a copy in possession of the Scolar Press, except for ap-
         proximately seventy-five pages reproduced from copies in the British Mu-
         seum. The appendix includes the variant title pages of 1667, 1668, and
         1669, "along with the new preliminary matter which Simmons added in
         1668, perhaps to spur the lagging sales."

PARADISE REGAINED

177 Paradise Regain'd. A Poem in Four Books. The Author John Milton. London: The Cresset Press, 1931. 88pp.

    Printed at the Shakespeare Head Press, Oxford. "This text of Paradise Regain'd has been set in type from a copy of the first edition, printed at London by John Milton for John Starkey in 1671." Illustrated by D. Galanis. A limited edition of 195 copies. Printed on Batchelor's handmade paper; ten copies printed on Roman vellum.
    Rev: TLS, Dec. 24, 1931, pp. 1033-4.

178 John Milton. Paradise Regained. London: Partridge, 1932. x, 187pp.

179 John Milton. Paradise Regained. Newly Edited with an Introduction and Commentary by E. H. Blakeney. London: Scholartis Press and E. Partridge, 1932. ix, 187pp.

180 Paradise Lost and Paradise Regained, by John Milton, with an Introduction by William Rose Benét and Illustrations by Carlotta Petrina. San Francisco: J. H. Nash for Members of the Limited Editions Club, 1936. xiii, 441pp.

181 John Milton. Paradise Regained, the Minor Poems and Samson Agonistes. Complete and Arranged Chronologically. Ed. by Merritt Y. Hughes. New York: Odyssey Press; Garden City: Doubleday, 1937. lxiii, 633pp.

    A selected bibliography, pp. lvi-lxiii. Good introductions.

182 John Milton. Paradise Regained. Samson Agonistes. 1671. A Scolar Press Facsimile. Menston, England: The Scolar Press Limited, 1968.

    "Reproduced (original size) from a copy in possession of The Scolar Press, except for the pages listed below [in the prefatory note], reproduced by permission of the Trustees of the British Museum...." A selection of the best pages from four copies.

183 John Milton. Paradise Lost and Paradise Regained. Ed. by Christopher Ricks. The Signet Classic Poetry Series. New York and Toronto: The New American Library; London: The New English Library, 1968. xliv, 45-400pp.

    "The text of Paradise Regained is based on the first edition, 1671." Partially modernized.

SAMSON AGONISTES

184 samson agonistes a dramatic poem the author john milton. florence: stamperia del santuccio, 1930/31. 76pp.
Printed in semi-uncial characters without capitals.

185 John Milton. Samson Agonistes. Printed under the direction of Victor Hammer. Florence: Stamperia del Santuccio, 1931.
Rev: TLS, Mar. 17, 1932, p. 186; SRL, 7, 1932, 451.

186 John Milton. Samson Agonistes and English Sonnets. Introduction and Notes by A. M. Percival. Sonnets, ed. by W. Bell. New York: Macmillan, 1931. xlviii, 219pp.
A reprint of Stevens' No. 1141, published in 1890.

187 John Milton. Samson Agonistes: A Dramatic Poem. With wood engravings by Robert A. Maynard. Harrow Weald: Raven Press, 1931. xi, 63pp.
An edition limited to 275 copies.
Rev: B. H. Newdigate, Merc, 25, 1931, 200-1; Frank Kendon, FR, N.S., 131, 1932, 113-6.

188 Milton's Samson Agonistes, with Introduction, Notes, Glossary and Indexes by A. W. Verity. Cambridge: Cambridge Univ. Press, 1932. lxvi, 171pp.
A reprint of Stevens' No. 1142, published in 1892.

189 John Milton. Samson Agonistes. Ed. by A. J. Wyatt and A. J. F. Collins. The Sonnets. Ed. by A. R. Weeks. London: Univ. Tutorial Press, 1932. viii, 160pp.

190 John Milton. Samson Agonistes. A Dramatic Poem. The Author John Milton. Florence: Stamperia del Santuccio, 1933.
Rev: Bibliofilia, 35, 1933, 105-6.

191 John Milton. Samson Agonistes. With Introduction and Notes by A. M. Percival. London: Macmillan, 1933, 1951, 1958. xlvii, 202pp.
First Edition, 1890, Stevens' No. 1141.

192 John Milton. Samson Agonistes. Ed. with Introduction and Notes by John Churton Collins. Oxford: Clarendon Press, 1935. 94pp.
A reprint of Stevens' No. 1139, published in 1883.

193 John Milton. Paradise Regained, the Minor Poems and Samson Agonistes. Complete and Arranged Chronologically. Ed. by Merritt Y. Hughes. New York: Odyssey Press; Garden City; Doubleday, 1937. lxiii, 633pp.
A selected bibliography, pp. lvi-lxiii. Good introductions.

194 John Milton. Samson Agonistes. Ed. by Sir Edmund K. Chambers. London and Glasgow: Blackie and Son, 1938? 146pp.

195 John Milton. Samson Agonistes. Ed. by J. E. Bradshaw. Brodie's Chosen English Texts. London: James Brodie, 1949. 93pp. Bath: James Brodie, 1963. 103pp.

196 John Milton. Samson Agonistes, and Shorter Poems. Ed. by Arthur E. Barker. Crofts Classics. New York: Appleton-Century-Crofts, 1950. xii, 114pp.

197 John Milton. Samson Agonistes. Ed. by F. T. Prince, with an Introduction, Notes, and Appendices. London and New York: Oxford Univ. Press, 1957, 1960. 144pp.

198 John Milton. Samson Agonistes: the Poem and Materials for Analysis. Selected and edited by Ralph E. Hone. San Francisco: Chandler Publications, 1966. 284pp.
    Rev: Ralph W. Condee, SCN, 25, 1967, 28-9.

199 John Milton. Samson Agonistes and the Shorter Poems. Ed. by Isabel Gamble MacCaffrey. Signet Classics. New York: New American Library, 1966. xxxvii, 216pp.
    Introduction, pp. vii-xxxvii.
    Rev: Ralph W. Condee, SCN, 25, 1967, 28-9.

200 John Milton. Paradise Regained. Samson Agonistes. 1671. A Scolar Press Facsimile. Menston, England: The Scolar Press Limited, 1968.
    "Reproduced (original size) from a copy in possession of The Scolar Press, except for the pages listed below [in the prefatory note], reproduced by permission of the Trustees of the British Museum...." A selection of the best pages from four copies.

201 John Milton. Samson Agonistes. Ed. with Introduction and Notes by Michael Davis. English Classics, New Series. London: Macmillan, 1968. xliv, 163pp.

MINOR POEMS AND SELECTED MINOR POEMS

202 COFFIN, ROBERT P. TRISTRAM, and ALEXANDER M. WITHER-
SPOON, eds. Seventeenth-Century Prose and Poetry. New York: Har-
court Brace, 1929, 1946. Second Edition, ed. by Witherspoon and Frank
J. Warnke. New York: Harcourt, Brace and World, 1957, 1963. xxvi,
1094pp.
Contains approximately 25 of the shorter poems, including the Songs from
Comus, pp. 881-99.

203 Early Poems of John Milton. Selected and ed. by Mercy A. Brann.
Illustrations by Isabel Bacheler. New York: Holt, 1929. xi, 235pp.

204 John Milton. The Nativity Ode, Lycidas, Sonnets, etc. Ed. by William
Bell. London: Macmillan, 1929. xx, 230pp.
A reprint of Stevens' No. 283, published in 1889. Often reprinted.

205 Lycidas, by John Milton; with four original etchings by Philip Evergood.
New York: H. L. Binsse, 1929.

206 The Sonnets of Mr. John Milton, both English and Italian. Maastricht:
Halycon Press, 1929. 28pp.
Printed with the italic type cut by Christoffel Van Dyck (1601-70).

207 Shorter Poems of John Milton. Selected and edited by Harold T. Eaton.
Chicago & New York: Lyons and Carnahan, 1929. 136pp.

208 John Milton. Arcades. Shaftesbury: The High House Press, 1930. 8pp.
Edition limited to 100 copies and printed on handmade paper.

209 The Latin Poems of John Milton. Ed. by Walter MacKellar. Cornell Stud.
in Eng., 15, New Haven: Yale Univ. Press for Cornell Univ.; London:
Milford, 1930. xli, 382pp.
Introd. pp. 1-67. Includes English prose translations.
Rev: H. J. C. Grierson and A. Melville Clark, YWES, 228; E. N. S. Thomp-
son, PQ, 9, 1930, 320; L. Bradner, MP, 28, 1930, 116-7; C. S. Northrup,
Cornell Alumni News, 32, 1930, 392; D. Saurat, RES, 6, 1930, 473; TLS, Apr.
24, 1930, p. 533; E. C. Batho and E. J. Vaughan, MLR, 26, 1931, 203; J. H.
Hanford, MLN, 46, 1931, 534-6; S. Gaselee, Class. Rev., 45, 1931, 155-6, and
N&Q, 163, 1932, 249; H. F. Fletcher, JEGP, 31, 1932, 158-9; C. W. Brodribb,
N&Q, 162, 1932, 188; T. O. Mabbott, N&Q, 162, 1932, 263-4, and 163, 1932,
170; V.R., N&Q, 163, 1933, 209, 371; F. Delattre, Rev. belge de philol. et
d'hist., 12, 1933, 315.

210 John Milton. On the Morning of Christ's Nativity. Flansham, Bognor
Regis, Sussex: Pear Tree Press, 1930. 19pp.
A hand-printed edition of 100 copies.

211 Minor Poems by John Milton. Ed. by S. E. Allen. Reviews by H. Y.
Moffett. Illustrations by W. M. Berger. New York: Macmillan, 1930.
xliii, 140pp.

A revision of Stevens' No. 339, published in 1912. Also contains Macaulay's Essay on Milton and Arnold's Address on Milton.

212 John Milton. Samson Agonistes and English Sonnets. Introduction and Notes by A. M. Percival. Sonnets, ed. by W. Bell. New York: Macmillan, 1931. xlviii, 219pp.
A reprint of Stevens' No. 1141, published in 1890.

213 Comus, A Masque by John Milton. Abridged and Arranged for School Performance by Lucy Chater. London: Allen and Unwin, 1931. 32pp.
First published, 1911 (Stevens' No. 449).

214 Milton's Minor Poems . . . Ed. by W. J. Halliday. Selected English Classics. London: Ginn & Co., 1931. xxxvii, 131pp.

215 Milton's Ode On the Morning of Christ's Nativity, L'Allegro, Il Penseroso, and Lycidas. Ed. by A. W. Verity. Pitt Press Series. Cambridge: Cambridge Univ. Press, 1931. li, 172pp.
First Verity edition, 1891 (Stevens' No. 285). Reprinted at least ten times by 1931.

216 John Milton. Comus. Illustrated by Blair Hughes-Stanton. Newton, Wales: Gregynog Press, 1931; London: Gregynog Press, 1932.
Limited Edition of 250 copies.
Rev: R.E.R., NSN, N.S., 3, 1932, xii, xiv; B. H. Newdigate, Merc, 25, 1932, 294.

217 The Hymn on the Morning of Christ's Nativity, by John Milton. Birmingham: Birmingham School of Printing, 1932. 12pp.
Type set and cast by students at the British school.

218 John Milton. L'Allegro. Glen Head, Long Island: Ashlar Press, 1932. 15pp.
Four hundred copies. Woodcut on title page by Rudolph Ruzicka.

219 John Milton. Il Penseroso. Glen Head, Long Island: Ashlar Press, 1932. 16pp.
Woodcut on the title page by Rudolph Ruzicka.

220 John Milton. Milton's Minor Poems. Ed. with Notes by Oliver Elton. Oxford: Clarendon Press, 1932. 101, 16, 16, 24, 6, 26pp.
Edited with separated pagination but bound in one volume are Comus, L'Allegro, Il Penseroso, and Arcades. Nineteen of the sonnets are edited by W. Worrall.

221 Milton's Minor Poems, with Descriptive Poetry of the Eighteenth, Nineteenth, and Twentieth Centuries. Ed. by Kenneth W. Wright. New York: Noble, 1932. x, 168pp. Reprinted, 1934, 1935.
Descriptive poems by George Crabbe, William Wordsworth, Rupert Brooke, and Edna St. Vincent Millay.

222 John Milton. Samson Agonistes. Ed. by A. J. Wyatt and A. J. F. Collins. The Sonnets. Ed. by A. R. Weeks. London: Univ. Tutorial Press, 1932. viii, 160pp.

223 Four Poems by John Milton: L'Allegro, Il Penseroso, Arcades, Lycidas. With Wood-Engravings by Blair Hughes-Stanton. Newtown, Montgomeryshire, Wales: Gregynog Press, 1933. 33pp.
   Edition limited to 250 copies; Beeching text; hand-set in Gill Perpetua Type by John Hugh Jones and Idwal Jones. Leather binding.

224 John Milton. On the Morning of Christ's Nativity. Madison, N.J.: Golden Hind Press, 1933. 16pp.
   A limited edition of 100 copies.

225 The Cambridge Manuscript of John Milton. Lycidas and Some of the Other Poems Reproduced from the Collotype Facsimile. With a Bibliographical Note by Frank A. Patterson. New York: Columbia Univ. Press for the Facsimile Text Society; London: Milford, 1933.
   "An offset reproduction of the collotype of W. Aldis Wright, who in 1899 printed the manuscript."
   Rev: A. H. Gilbert, SAQ, 33, 1934, 111-2; H. F. Fletcher, JEGP, 13, 1934, 338.

226 John Milton. Epitaphium Damonis. Printed from the First Edition [1645]. With a new translation by W. W. Skeat. In memory of Israel Gollancz. New York: Macmillan; Cambridge: Cambridge Univ. Press, 1933. 21pp.
   Rev: A. Brandl, Archiv, 164, 1933, 134; TLS, July 13, 1933, p. 482; N&Q, 165, 1933, 143-4; J. H. Hanford, MLN, 51, 1936, 53-4; E. Bensly, RES, 12, 1936, 92-3.

227 Milton's Sonnets, with Introduction, Notes, Glossary and Indexes by A. W. Verity. Cambridge: Cambridge Univ. Press, 1933. xxxii, 78pp.
   A reprint of Stevens' No. 630, published in 1895.

228 Early Poems of John Milton. Selected and Ed. by Mercy A. Brann. Illustrated by Isabel Bacheler. New York: Holt, 1934. xi, 235pp.

229 Four Poems by John Milton: L'Allegro, Il Penseroso, Arcades, Lycidas. With wood-engravings by Blair Hughes-Stanton. London: Gregynog Press, 1934. 33pp.

230 John Milton. Minor Poems. New York: Columbia Univ. Press for the Facsimile Text Society, 1934. 120pp. Reprinted, 1935.
   A facsimile of the 1645 volume.

231 Milton's L'Allegro, Il Penseroso, Comus, and Lycidas. Ed. by Martin W. Sampson. New York: Holt, 1934. xxxii, 96pp.

232 John Milton. Lament for Damon and Other Latin Poems. Rendered into English by Walter Skeat, with an Introduction by E. H. Visiak. Oxford: Oxford Univ. Press, 1935.
   Rev: H. I. Bell, Class. Rev., 50, 1936, 204-5; Arnold Wilson, NC, 119, 1936, 495-506; E.L., RA-A, 13, 1936, 516; TLS, Jan. 11, 1936, p. 26; N&Q, 170, 1936, 17; W. R. Parker, MLN, 52, 1937, 388.

233 John Milton. The Hymn on the Morning of Christ's Nativity. Worcester: Edenezer Baylis and Son, 1935. 12pp.

234 Milton's Minor Poems. Ed. by Tom Peete Cross. Illustrations by Marguerite Benjamin. Boston: Ginn, 1936. viii, 129pp.

235 John Milton. Paradise Regained, the Minor Poems and Samson Agonistes. Complete and Arranged Chronologically. Ed. by Merritt Y. Hughes. New York: Odyssey Press; Garden City; Doubleday, 1937. lxiii, 633pp.
A selected bibliography, pp. lvi-lxiii. Good introductions.

236 John Milton. On the Morning of Christ's Nativity. With a Wood Engraving by Alison McKenzie. Newtown, Wales: Gregynog, 1937.

237 The Mask of Comus. The Poem Originally Called A Mask Presented at Ludlow Castle, 1634, &c., ed. by E. H. Visiak. The Airs of Five Songs Reprinted from the Composer's Autograph Manuscript, ed. by Hubert J. Foss, with a Foreword by the Earl of Ellesmere. Ornamented by M. R. H. Farrar. London: Nonesuch Press, 1937. xxiv, 44pp.
Rev: TLS, Jan. 15, 1938, p. 40; B. H. Newdigate, Merc, 37, 1938, 455; E. M. W. Tillyard, NC, 124, 1938, 479-81; MGW, Jan. 28, 1938, p. 75.

238 Shorter Poems of John Milton. Ed. by B. A. Wright. The Scholars Library. London: Macmillan; New York: St. Martin's Press, 1938. Reprinted, 1944, 1948, 1950, 1952, 1957, 1959, 1961. xliv, 209pp.
Contains a lengthy introduction; many of the well-known poems, including L'Allegro, Il Penseroso, Arcades, Comus, and Lycidas; notes, and an appendix on Milton's cosmology.

239 John Milton. Comus and Selected Poems [i.e., those in Palgrave's Golden Treasury, Book II]. Ed. by A. S. Collins. London: Univ. Tutorial Press, 1938, 1953. xxiv, 116pp.
For students preparing for the school certificate examination of the Northern Universities Joint Matriculation Board.

240 John Milton. Comus. Ed. with Notes by Oliver Elton. Clarendon Press Series. Oxford: Clarendon Press, 1938. 101pp.
First Elton edition, 1891 (Stevens' No. 433).

241 John Milton. Lycidas. With Introduction and Notes by W. Bell. London: Macmillan, 1938. 48pp.
First Bell edition, 1898.

242 Milton's English Sonnets. Ed. with Notes by W. Bell. London: Macmillan, 1938. 11, 36pp.
Sections from Bell's 1889 edition of Lycidas and the sonnets (Stevens' No. 283).

243 Comus, by John Milton. With Introduction and Notes by W. Bell. London: Macmillan, 1939, 1950. xx, 117pp.
First Bell edition, 1890 (Stevens' No. 431).

244 Justa Edovardo King. Reproduced from the Original Edition, 1638, with an Introduction by Ernest C. Mossner. New York: Columbia Univ. Press for the Facsimile Text Society, 1939. 61pp.
Reproduces the first edition of Lycidas.

245 John Milton. Comus. Ed. by J. M. Evans. Brodie's Chosen English Texts. London: James Brodie, 1939. 79pp.

246 John Milton Poems. Mount Vernon, New York: Peter Pauper Press, 1940. 91pp.
> Contains L'Allegro, Il Penseroso, Comus, Lycidas, and many of the other minor poems.

247 John Milton. Comus. With Introduction and Notes by W. Kersley Holmes. Blackie's Smaller English Classics. London and Glasgow: Blackie, 1943. vi, 42pp.

248 Lycidas. By John Milton. Lines Composed a Few Miles above Tintern Abbey and Ode on the Intimations of Immortality. By William Wordsworth. With Introduction, Notes and Exercises by Patrick J. Kennedy. Dublin: M. H. Gill & Son, 1944. 135pp.

249 John Milton. L'Allegro and Il Penseroso. Illustrated by Bernard Meninsky. London: Wingate, 1947. 28pp.

250 John Milton. Lycidas and Comus. With Introduction and Notes by W. Bell. London: Macmillan, 1947. xx, 117pp.
> First edition, 1899.

251 John Milton. Poems. L'Allegro, Il Penseroso, Comus, Lycidas, and the Complete Minor Poems. Mount Vernon, New York: The Peter Pauper Press, 1947. 91pp.

252 Lament for Damon. The Epitaphium Damonis of Milton. Trans. by Helen Waddell. UTQ, 16, 1947, 341-8.

253 Milton: Minor Poems and Sonnets. With Introduction and Notes by J. M. Evans. Brodie's Chosen English Texts. London: James Brodie, 1947. 64pp.

254 VAN SINDEREN, ADRIAN. Blake, the Mystic Genius. Syracuse: Syracuse Univ. Press, 1949. 119pp.
> Blake's text of L'Allegro and Il Penseroso and illustrations in color, pp. 45-112. Notes on the Poems, pp. 113-5.

255 Poems of Mr. John Milton: the 1645 Edition with Essays in Analysis. Ed. by Cleanth Brooks and John E. Hardy. New York: Harcourt, Brace, and Co., 1951; London: Dennis Dobson, 1957. Reprinted, New York: Gordian Press, 1968. xxi, 353pp.
> Part 1: The Poems, pp. 3-94; Part 2: Essays in Analysis, pp. 95-270; several appendices.
> Rev: J. H. Hanford, YR, 41, 1951-2, 634-6; Arnold Davenport, YWES, 33, 1952, 179-80; Ben R. Redman, SRL, June 21, 1952, p. 41; Kester Svendsen, SR, 60, 1952, 548-54; T. B. Stroup, SCN, 10, 1952, 48; Max Selinger, BA, 27, 1953, 193; QR, 295, 1957, 483; TLS, July 12, 1957, p. 428; Frank Kermode, RES, 9, 1958, 319-20.

256 John Milton. Comus. Adapted by John Dalton. With Music by Thomas A. Arne. London: Stainer and Bell, for the Royal Musical Association, 1951. xxpp., score (161pp.) .

257 FEASEY, LYNETTE, ed. And so to the Playhouse. London: George G. Harrap, 1951. 192pp.

Contains an edition of Comus, pp. 19-54; a note on the production of the play, pp. 55-9.

258 Comus and Some Shorter Poems of Milton. Ed. by E. M. W. and Phyllis B. Tillyard. London: Harrap, 1952. 223pp.

259 English Pastoral Poetry from the Beginnings to Marvell. Ed. by Frank Kermode. London: Harrap, 1952.
Includes L'Allegro, two songs from Arcades, passages from Comus, and Lycidas.

260 On the Morning of Christ's Nativity. John Milton, compos'd 1629. Lexington, Kentucky: Carolyn Reading, 1952. No pagination.
Introduction by Thomas B. Stroup. A limited edition of fifty copies; set in Victor Hammer's American Uncial type.

261 Milton: Comus. Ed. by A. S. Collins. Third Edition. London: Univ. Tutorial Press, 1953. xxii, 61pp.
Introduction and Notes are drawn from the edition of S. E. Goggin and A. F. Watt.

262 A Selection of Poems by John Milton With an Introduction by Howard Sergeant. Crown Classics. London: Grey Walls Press, 1954. 64pp.

263 The Shorter Poems of John Milton. Ed. by B. A. Wright. London: St. Martin's Press, 1954.

264 John Milton. L'Allegro (and) Il Penseroso, with the Paintings by William Blake together with a Note upon the Poems by W. P. Trent (and) a Note upon the Paintings by Chauncey Brewster Tinker. New York: Heritage Press, 1954; New York: Limited Editions Club, 1954. 43pp.

265 The Masque of Comus. The Poem by John Milton, with a Preface by Mark Van Doren. The Airs by Henry Lawes, with a Preface by Hubert Foss. Cambridge: Cambridge Univ. Press for members of the Limited Editions Club, 1954; New York: Heritage Press, 1955. 57pp.

266 John Milton. L'Allegro, Il Penseroso and Lycidas. Complete Paraphrases by N. Stockwell and Professor E. E. Denny. Farnham, Surrey: Normal Press, 1961. 12pp.

267 Milton's Lycidas: The Tradition and the Poem. Ed. by C. A. Patrides. Foreword by M. H. Abrams. New York: Holt, Rinehart and Winston, 1961. xx, 246pp.
Contains text, plus extensive critical apparatus. See this entry under Minor Poems: Criticism for complete annotation.
Rev: Harry G. Merrill, SCN, 19, 1961, 8.

268 BATEMAN, T. SOMERSET. Milton's Sonnets: A Complete Paraphrase. Farnham and East Dulwich: Normal Tutorial Series, 1962. 10pp.
First printed, 1904 (Stevens' No. 646).

269 John Milton. Early Poems (On the Morning of Christ's Nativity, L'Allegro and Il Penseroso, Lycidas). Con Introduzione e Note di Ferruccio Ferrari. Torino: G. B. Paravia, 1963. xix, 52pp.
Contains an introduction (pp. vii-xviii) and notes.

270 John Milton. Minor Poems. Ed. by Ann Phillips. London: Univ. Tutorial Press, 1966. 175pp.
>   Includes Comus, Nativity Ode, At a Solemn Music, L'Allegro, Il Penseroso, Lycidas, and the English sonnets. General Introduction, pp. 1-18. Introduction to Comus, pp. 19-27. Notes, pp. 101-73.

271 John Milton. Samson Agonistes and the Shorter Poems. Ed. by Isabel E. Gamble MacCaffrey. Signet Classics. New York: New American Library, 1966. xxxvii, 216pp.
>   Introduction, pp. vii-xxxvii.

272 Milton's Sonnets. Ed. by E. A. J. Honigmann. London: Macmillan; New York: St. Martin's, 1966. x, 210pp.
>   Includes both Italian and English sonnets. General Introduction, pp. 29-82; Collation and Commentary, pp. 83-204.
>   Rev: C. B. Cox, Spect, Nov. 4, 1966, p. 590; QR, Jan., 1967, pp. 121-2; John Buxton, RES, 19, 1968, 73-5; W. J. Barnes, QQ, 75, 1968, 161-6.

273 The Sonnets of Milton. With Introduction and Notes by J. S. Smart. With a preface by B. A. Wright. Oxford: Clarendon Press, 1966. 177pp.
>   First edition, 1921 (Stevens' No. 651). Introduction, pp. 1-39. Extensive notes.
>   Rev: C. B. Cox, Spect, Nov. 4, 1966, p. 590; Charles L. Davies, SCN, 15, 1967, 66-7.

274 Milton's Lycidas: Edited to Serve as an Introduction to Criticism. Ed. by Scott Elledge. New York and London: Harper and Row, 1966. xxii, 330pp.
>   A volume designed to counter the Brooks and Warren approach to literary criticism and to demonstrate what T. S. Eliot means in his essay, Tradition and the Individual Talent. Contents: The 1638 text of Lycidas, with textual variations; five classical pastoral elegies; selections from two classical consolations; nine Renaissance pastorals; selections on the theory of the monody; five contemporary elegies; selections from Justa Edovardo King; Milton's accounts of his early training; England in 1637; selected commentaries on Lycidas from Joseph Warton to W. H. Auden; a bibliography of pastoral poetry; and a bibliography of books and articles about Lycidas.
>   Rev: Francis E. Moran, SCN, 25, 1967, 28.

275 John Milton. Comus and Other Poems. Ed. by F. T. Prince. Oxford: Oxford Univ. Press, 1968. 197pp.
>   Rev: TLS, Sept. 12, 1968, p. 1003.

COLLECTED PROSE WORKS AND
INDIVIDUAL SELECTIONS

276 Milton on Education. The Tractate of Education with Supplementary
   Extracts from Other Writings from Milton. Ed. by Oliver Morley
   Ainsworth. New Haven: Yale Univ. Press, 1928.
   Rev: E. N. S. Thompson, PQ, 8, 1929, 95; Denis Saurat, RES, 5, 1929, 480;
   Marjorie Nicolson, MLN, 45, 1930, 197-9; H. F. Fletcher, JEGP, 29, 1930,
   464-5.

278 John Milton. Areopagitica and Other Prose Writings. Ed. with an Introduction by William Haller. New York: Macmillan, 1929. xvii, 170pp.
   First published in 1927, Stevens' No. 1269. Contents: Areopagitica, autobiographical passages from the prose works, Of Education, The Ready and
   Easy Way.

279 A Brief History of Moscovia and of Other less-known Countries lying
   eastward of Russia as far as Cathay. Gathered from the Writings of
   Several Eye-witnesses by John Milton. To which are added other
   Curious Documents. Ed. by Prince D. S. Mirsky. London: Blackamore
   Press, 1929. 120pp.
   Rev: TLS, Dec. 5, 1929, p. 1024; ER, 50, 1930, 523-4.

280 Milton's Prose. Selected and Edited with an Introduction by Malcolm W.
   Wallace. The World's Classics. London: Oxford Univ. Press, 1931.
   476pp.
   First published in 1925 (Stevens' No. 1266). Reprinted, 1937, 1942, 1947,
   1949, 1959.

281 John Milton. Private Correspondence and Academic Exercises. Translated
   from the Latin by Phyllis B. Tillyard. With an Introduction and Commentary by E. M. W. Tillyard. Cambridge: Cambridge Univ. Press,
   1932. xxxix, 143pp.
   A translation of the original 1674 text of Milton's Prolusiones oratoriae
   and familiar letters.
   Rev: Spect, 148, 1932, 460; QR, 258, 1932, 391; N&Q, 162, 1932, 162; C.
   Saltmarshe, AB, 81, 1932, 319; A. Fremantle, Merc, 26, 1932, 274-5; H. Read,
   Crit, 11, 1932, 746-7; A. Brandl, DL, 53, 1932, 835-7; B. A. Wright, MLR, 28,
   1933, 259-62; C. G. Osgood, MLN, 48, 1933, 473-6; Paul Chauvet, RA-A, 10,
   1933, 238; NC, 119, 1936, 495-506.

282 John Milton's Areopagitica. Ed. with an Introduction and Notes by John
   W. Hales. Oxford: Clarendon Press, 1932. xlv, 160pp. Reprinted, 1939.
   First edition, 1866 (Stevens' No. 1230). Reprinted several times.

283 John Milton. Areopagitica. New York: Columbia Univ. Press for the
   Facsimile Text Society, 1934, 1935.
   Reproduced from the edition of 1644.

284 John Milton. Areopagitica. With a Commentary by Sir Richard C. Jebb

and with supplementary material. Pitts Press Series. Cambridge: Cambridge Univ. Press, 1940, xi, 130pp.
A reissue of the edition of 1918, Stevens' No. 1263.

285 John Milton. Areopagitica, A Speech for the Liberty of Unlicensed Printing. With an Introduction and Notes by H. B. Cotterill. Macmillan's English Classics. London: Macmillan, 1941, 1952. xi, 118pp.
A reprint of Stevens' No. 1250, published in 1904.

286 Areopagitica by John Milton. Christchurch: Caxton Press, 1941. 55pp.
A limited edition of 150 copies.

287 HAUG, RALPH A. An Annotated Edition of John Milton's The Reason of Church-Government Urg'd against Prelaty. Doctoral diss., Ohio State Univ., 1944. Abs., Ohio State Univ. Abstracts of Dissertations, No. 45, 1943-4, pp. 129-37.

288 John Milton. Areopagitica. Maidstone: Typography Department of the Maidstone School of Art and Crafts, 1944. 59pp.
"In commemoration of the Tercentenary of the Publication of the Areopagitica by John Milton, November, 1644." Monotype text set by teachers and cast by students in the Maidstone School.

289 John Milton. Prose Selections. Ed. by Merritt Y. Hughes. New York: Odyssey Press, 1947. cxci, 454pp.
Introduction contains biographical accounts by Aubrey, Edward Phillips, and the anonymous biographer. Selected bibliography, pp. cxxv-cxlvii.

290 John Milton. Areopagitica. Chicago: H. Regnery for the Great Books Foundation, 1949. 65pp.

291 JOCHUMS, MILFORD C., ed. John Milton's An Apology against a Pamphlet. . . . Doctoral diss., Univ. of Illinois, 1949. 583pp. Illinois Studies in Language and Literature, 35. Urbana: Univ. of Illinois Press, 1950. vi, 255pp.
Rev: Davis P. Harding, JEGP, 50, 1951, 549-51; A. E. Barker, MLR, 47, 1952, 394-5; D. M. Wolfe, MLN, 68, 1953, 271-2; Ernest Sirluck, MP, 50, 1953, 201-5; B. A. Wright, RES, 5, 1954, 85-6.

292 STAHL, HERBERT M. An Annotated Edition of The Reason of Church Government urg'd againt prelaty and Lord Brooke's A discourse opening the nature of that episcopacie which is exercised in England. Doctoral diss., Univ. of Washington, 1950.

293 John Milton. Areopagitica and Of Education, with Autobiographical Passages from Other Prose Works. Ed. by G. H. Sabine. Crofts Classics. New York: Crofts, 1951. xii, 110pp.

294 BLACKFORD, PAUL W. A Translation and Edition of Joannis Miltoni Angli pro Populo anglicano Defensio contra Claudii Anonymi, alias Salmasii, Defensionam Regiam. Doctoral diss., Northwestern Univ., 1951. Abs., Summaries of Doctoral Dissertations, Northwestern Univ., 18, 1951, 10-14.

295 SMITH, CALVIN C. An Edition of Milton's Prolusiones Oratoriae. Master's thesis, Duke Univ., 1952.

296 Complete Prose Works of John Milton. Don M. Wolfe, gen. ed. New Haven: Yale Univ. Press, 1953. To be published in 8 vols.

"The purpose of the Complete Prose Works of John Milton is to present annotated texts of Milton's prose in the ascertainable order of its composition, bringing to bear in notes, prefaces, and volume introductions the accumulated scholarship of the past century."

Vol. 1, 1624-1642: Introduction, by Don M. Wolfe (vol. ed.); Prolusions (1628-1632), trans. and prefaces by Phyllis B. Tillyard with notes and prefaces by Kathryn A. McEuen; Private Correspondence (1627-1641), trans., notes, and prefaces by W. Arthur Turner and Alberta T. Turner; Commonplace Book (1630?-1655?), trans., preface, and notes by Ruth Mohl; Of Reformation, preface and notes by Don M. Wolfe and William Alfred; Of Prelatical Episcopacy, preface and notes by J. Max Patrick; Animadversions, preface by Rudolf Kirk with notes by Rudolf Kirk, assisted by William P. Baker; Reason of Church Government, preface and notes by Ralph A. Haug; An Apology against a Pamphlet, preface and notes by Frederick L. Taft. Appendices: (A) Legal Index, trans. by Ruth Mohl with preface and notes by Maurice Kelley; (B) A Postscript, preface and notes by Don M. Wolfe; (C) The London Petition (Dec. 11, 1640); (D) Constitutions and Canons Ecclesiastical (1640); (E) The Oath Ex-Officio, by Don M. Wolfe; (F) The Legion of Smec, by Frederick L. Taft and Ashur Baizer; (G) The Bishops, by Leo F. Solt, Ashur Baizer, Franklin R. Baruch, and J. Hillis Miller, Jr.; (H) Theme on Early Rising, trans., preface, and notes by Maurice Kelley and Donald Mackenzie; (I) Textual Guide; 1953. xvi, 1073pp.

Vol. 2, 1643-1648: Introduction, by Ernest Sirluck (vol. ed.); Doctrine and Discipline of Divorce (August 1, 1643), preface and notes by Lowell W. Coolidge; Of Education (June, 1644), preface and notes by Donald C. Dorian; The Judgement of Martin Bucer (July 15, 1644), preface and notes by Arnold Williams; Areopagitica (November, 1644), preface and notes by Ernest Sirluck; Tetrachordon (March 4, 1645), preface and notes by Arnold Williams; Colasterion (March 4, 1645), preface and notes by Lowell W. Coolidge; Private Correspondence (1647-1648), trans., notes and preface by W. Arthur Turner and Alberta T. Turner; Textual Notes; Doctrine and Discipline of Divorce: Spelling and Punctuation Changes in 1644. Appendices: (A) The Star Chamber Decree of 1637 with notes by Ernest Sirluck; (B) The Licensing Order of 1643, with notes by Ernest Sirluck; (C) Little Non-Such: A Satire on Milton's Divorce Argument? by Ernest Sirluck; Milton as Translator: Notes on Milton's Method of Translation in The Judgement of Martin Bucer, by Arnold Williams.

Vol. 3, 1648-1649: Introduction, by Merritt Hughes (vol. ed.); Part One: Religious and Civil Strife; Part Two: Milton's Anatomy of Kingship; Part Three: Articles of Peace. The Tenure of Kings and Magistrates; Observations upon the Articles of Peace; Eikonoklastes. Preface and Notes to all three of above works by Merritt Hughes. Appendices: (A) Textual Notes to The Tenure; (B) Textual Notes to Eikonoklastes. 652pp.

Vol. 4, 1650-1655: Introduction, by Don M. Wolfe (vol. ed.); Part One: A Defence of the People of England; preface and notes by William J. Grace; trans. by Donald Mackenzie. A Second Defence of the English People; preface and notes by Donald A. Roberts; trans. by Helen North; 1966. 686pp. Part Two: Pro Se Defensio; preface and notes by Kester Svendsen; trans. by Paul W. Blackford; Milton's Private Correspondence (1651-1655), trans., prefaces, and notes by W. Arthur and Alberta T. Turner. Appendices: (A) The Phillips' Response, preface and notes by Robert W. Ayers; trans. by James I. Armstrong; (B) Salmasius: Opponent of Milton, by Kathryn A. McEuen; (C) Selections from Defensio Regia; trans. by Kathryn A. McEuen: (D) Selections from Du Moulin, Regii Sanguinis Clamor; preface and trans. by Paul W. Blackford; (E) Selections from More's Fides Publica and Supplementum, preface and trans. by Paul W. Blackford; (F) Variants in the London edition of Milton's Defensio, by Robert W. Ayers; (G) Authorized Editions of Milton's Defensio, Defensio Secunda, and Pro Se Defensio, by Robert W. Ayers; (H) Corrections to the Columbia Text of Milton's Pro Populo Anglicano Defensio, by Robert W. Ayers; 1966. 687-1166pp.
Volumes in preparation:

Vol. 5: French Fogle (vol. ed) ; History of Britain, ed. by French Fogle; State Papers, ed. by J. Max Patrick and trans. by Paul W. Blackford.

Vol. 6: Robert W. Ayers and Austin Woolrych (vol. eds.) ; A Treatise of Civil Power, ed. by William J. Grace; Considerations Touching the Likeliest Means, ed. by William J. Grace; Letter to a Friend, ed. by Robert W. Ayers; Readie & Easie Way, ed. by Robert W. Ayers; Brief Notes on a Late Sermon, Proposalls of Certaine Expedients, and Outlines for Tragedies, ed. by James Holly Hanford.

Rev: D. C. Allen, MLN, 69, 1954, 116-20; TLS, July 30, 1954, p. 484; reply to Allen and TLS reviewer by Arthur Turner, ibid., Sept. 24, 1954, p. 609; Walter Taplin, Spect, June 4, 1954, pp. 690-3; J. Max Patrick and others, SCN, 12, 1954, 1-4, 14-5; J. George, Aberdeen Univ. Rev., 36, 1955, 55-8; F. T. Prince, RES, 6, 1955, 316-8; Barbara Kiefer [Lewalski], Church Hist., 25, 1956, 88-90; I. A. Shapiro, MLR, 51, 1956, 244-6; SCN, 17, 1959, 30; Arthur Axelrad, SCN, 17, 1959, 30-1; J. Max Patrick, JMH, 32, 1960, 279-80; G. B. Evans, JEGP, 59, 1960, 497-505; William Haller, Church Hist., 29, 1960, 364-5; Ralph Laurence, English, 13, 1960, 68-9; QQ, 67, 1960, 138; J. I. Cope, RN, 13, 1960, 250-2; SCN, 18, No. 1, 1960, item 7; SCN, 18, No. 2-3, 1960, item 13; TLS, Apr. 29, 1960, p. 274; Kenneth Muir, MLR, 56, 1961, 406-7; K. M. Lea, RES, 12, 1961, 204-7; TLS, Apr. 12, 1963, p. 250; William Haller, ELN, 1, 1963, 146-51; Joseph Frank, SCN, 21, 1963, 34-6; Samuel Mintz, RN, 16, 1963, 346-8; Walter J. Ong, S.J., SEL, 4, 1964, 178-9; Kenneth Muir, MLR, 59, 1964, 109; Alastair Fowler, N&Q, N.S., 11, 1964, 113-4; John M. Steadman, JEGP, 63, 1964, 516-21; K. M. Lea, RES, 15, 1964, 321-3; John R. Mulder, SCN, 24, 1966, 57-8; J. B. Broadbent, ES, 38, 1957, 275-8, and 48, 1967, 243-6; John M. Steadman, RenQuar, 20, 1967, 395-400.

297 AYERS, ROBERT W. A Translation and Critical Edition of the John Phillips-John Milton Johannis Philippi Angli Responsio. Doctoral diss., Rutgers Univ., 1955. Abs., DA, 15, 1955, 2531.

298 John Milton. Areopagitica and Other Prose Works. Introduction by Kathleen M. Burton. Everyman's Library. New York: Dutton: Dent, 1955. xii, 306pp.
Rev: O. Lutaud, EA, 9, 1956, 162.

299 John Milton. Areopagitica. Ed. by F. B. Pinion. Brodie's Chosen English Texts. London: Brodie, 1956. 96pp.

300 John Milton. Areopagitica. Paris: Aubier, 1956. 241pp.
Rev: M. Y. Hughes, EA, 10, 1957, 155-6.

301 MOODY, LESTER DEANE, ed. John Milton's Pamphlets on Divorce. Doctoral diss., Univ. of Washington, 1956. Abs., DA, 17, 1957, 855-6.
Fully annotated.

302 COFFIN, ROBERT P. TRISTRAM, and ALEXANDER M. WITHER-SPOON, eds. Seventeenth-Century Prose and Poetry. New York: Harcourt Brace, 1929, 1946. Second Edition, ed. by Witherspoon and Frank J. Warnke. New York: Harcourt, Brace and World, 1957, 1963. xxvi, 1094pp.
Contains: Of Education, pp. 388-94; Areopagitica, pp. 395-417.

303 SHAABER, M. A., ed. Seventeenth-Century English Prose. The Harper English Literature Series, under the editorship of the late Karl J. Holzknecht. New York: Harper and Brothers, 1957. xii, 480pp.
Contains Areopagitica, pp. 231-60.

304 John Milton. Selections from The Reason of Church Government, An Apology for Smectymnuus, and Of Education; Preface to Paradise Lost; Preface to Samson Agonistes. In Critical Essays of the Seventeenth Century. Ed. by J. E. Spingarn (Bloomington: Indiana Univ. Press, 1957), Vol. 1.
A reprint of Stevens' No. 1254, first published in 1908.

305 Milton's Prose Writings. Everyman's Library. Introduction by Kathleen M. Burton. Revised Edition. London: Dent, 1958; New York: Dutton, 1958. xi, 367pp.
Contains Of Reformation, An Apology for Smectymnuus, Of Civil Power, On Christian Doctrine (selections), Of True Religion, Areopagitica, The Tenure of Kings and Magistrates (selections), Eikonoklastes (selections), The Ready and Easy Way, and other prose works.
Rev: O. Lutand, EA, 12, 1959, 353.

306 Milton's Eikonoklastes: An Annotated Edition. Ed. by Sonia Miller. Doctoral diss., Univ. of Illinois, 1958. Abs., DA, 19, 1959, 2602-3.

307 John Milton. Areopagitica and Of Education. Ed. with Introduction and Notes by Michael Davis. New York: St. Martin's Press, 1963. 132pp.

308 Liberty of Printing, by John Milton. London: Coptic Press, 1964. 13pp.
Selections from Areopagitica.

309 HORWOOD, ALFRED J., ed. A Commonplace Book of John Milton. New York: Johnson Reprints; London: Camden Society, 1965.
A reprint of the 1876 edition (Stevens' No. 1232).

310   John Milton. Areopagitica. English Reprints. Ed. by Edward Arber (New York: AMS Press, 1966), 1, 1-80.
Stevens' No. 1224, published in 1868.

311   FERRY, ANNE D., ed. Religious Prose of Seventeenth-Century England. The Borzoi Anthology of Seventeenth-Century English Literature. New York: Alfred A. Knopf, 1967. 258pp.
Includes selections from Of Reformation, Animadversions, The Reason of Church Government, and An Apology.

312   The Prose of John Milton. Selected and Edited from the Original Texts with Introductions, Notes, Translations, and Accounts of All His Major Prose Writings. General Introduction by J. Max Patrick, Editor. The Stuart Editions. New York: New York Univ. Press, 1967. Issued also in The Anchor Seventeenth-Century Series. Garden City: Doubleday and Co., 1967. xxxv, 675pp.

Individual selections edited by Everett H. Emerson, Arthur M. Axelrad, Thomas R. Hartmann, William B. Hunter, Jr., Barbara Keifer Lewalski, John R. Mulder, John T. Shawcross, and J. Max Patrick.
Rev: Joseph Frank, SCN, 26, 1968, 31.

313   John Milton. Prose Works, 1641-1650. Scolar Press Facsimiles. Menston, England: The Scolar Press Limited, 1967-68. 3 vols.
Vol. 1: Contains Of Reformation, Of Prelatical Episcopacy, The Reason of Church Government, Animadversions, and An Apology Against a Pamphlet. "The tracts have been reproduced from the presentation volume of eleven prose pamphlets which Milton gave to the Bodleian Library in 1645 or 1646 at the request of his friend John Rous, Bodley's Librarian." Includes Milton's presentation inscription.
Vol. 2: Contains the remaining six tracts in the presentation volume, mentioned above: The Doctrine and Discipline of Divorce, The Judgement of Martin Bucer, Colasterion, Tetrachordon, Areopagitica, and Of Education. The text of the Doctrine and Discipline is the revised, second edition of 1644.
Vol. 3: Contains Eikonoklastes and The Tenure of Kings and Magistrates. Reproduced "from the copies of the revised, second edition of 1650 preserved together in a volume in the Bodleian Library."

TRANSLATIONS

Paradise Lost

314 John Milton: Shitsurakuen. Trans. by Kinji Yasutake. Kobe: Sainichian, 1929. 188pp.
A Japanese translation. Also includes Paradise Regained and Samson Agonistes.

315 John Milton. Paradise Lost, Book I. Trans. by Kinji Yasutake, 1929.

316 John Milton. Shitsurakuen. Trans. by Tenrai Shigeno. Tokyo: Shinco Sha, 1929. 12, 516pp.
A Japanese translation.

317 John Milton. El Paráiso perdido. Edición illustrada. Barcelona: Ediciones Iberia, 1932. 119pp.

318 John Milton. Paradise Lost, Book I. Trans. by Tetsuzo Okada. In Eishibun-no-Henei (A Glimpse of English Verse), 1932.
Japanese.

319 John Milton. Kadotettu paratiisi. Runoelma. Suomentanut Yrjö Jylhä. Toinen painos. Helsinki: Werner Söderström, 1933. Reprinted, 1952. xvi, 362pp.
The first complete metrical translation into Finnish.

320 John Milton. Il Paradiso Perduto. Trad. di Alessandro Muccioli. Florence: La Nuova Italia, 1933. 459pp.

321 John Milton. Il Paradiso Perduto. Tradotto de Lazzaro Papi con Illustrazioni di Gustavo Doré. Milano: Casa Editrice Sonzogno, 1938. xii, 282pp. Reprinted, 1943.

322 John Milton: Il Paradiso Perduto. Trad. di Giuseppe Nicolussi. Naples: Studio di propaganda, 1938.

323 John Milton. Rakuen Shoshitsu. Trans. by Takeshi Fujii. Tokyo: Iwanami Shoten, 1938-1941, 1950. 3 vols. Illus.

324 John Milton. El Paráiso perdido. Santiago de Chile: Ediciones Ercilla, 1940. 310pp.

325 John Milton. El Paráiso Perdido. Traduccion del Inglés por Dionisio Sanjuan con un Estudio Biográfico por F.R. de Chateaubriand. Notas de Addison, Saint Maur y Otros y 13 Ilus. Madrid: M. Aguilar, 1946. 647pp.

326 John Milton. Shitsurakuen. Trans. by Tenrai Shigeno. Tokyo: Oizumi Shoten, 1948. 2 vols.
A Japanese translation.

327 John Milton. Das Verlorene Paradies. Trans. by B. Pick. Cologne: Kolner Universitätsverlag, 1948. 139pp.

328 John Milton. Il Paradiso Perduto. Trad. di D. Petoello. Turin: Un. Tip. Ed. Torinese, 1950. 547pp.

329 John Milton. El paradis perdut. Traducció de Joseph M. Boix i Selva. Barcelona: Aiguaforto de Ramon de Capmany, 1950. 2 vols.
Translation by a Catalan poet.

330 John Milton. Paradis Perdu. Tome I, Livres I à VI. Tome II, Livres VII à XII. Introd., Trad., et Notes de Pierre Messiaen. Paris: Aubier, 1951, 1955, resp. 295, 320pp.
Rev: Jacques Blondel, EA, 5, 1952, 158-60.

331 John Milton. El paradis perdut. Traducción i Notes per J. M. Boix i Selva. Barcelona: Editorial Alpha, 1953. 459pp.
Rev: M. Dole, Arbor, 31, 1955, 150-2.

332 John Milton. El Paraiso Perdido. Trad. per Pablo Laredo. Barcelona: Editorial Alpha, 1955. 224pp.

333 John Milton. O Paráíso Perdido. Trans. by Antônio José de Lima Leitão. São Paulo: Logos, 1956. 2 vols.

334 John Milton. Poterjannyj Raj. Vozvraščennyl Raj. Trans. by Vahtang Celidze. Tbilisi: Gosijdat Gruz, 1956.
A Russian translation of Paradise Lost and Paradise Regained.

335 John Milton. Paradise Lost, Books I-VI. Peking, 1958. 309pp.
A Chinese translation, listed in the catalogue at Christ's College, Cambridge, but unavailable for examination.

336 John Milton. Paraisa e Humbur (poemë). Trans. by Alqi Kristo. Tiranë: N. Sh. Botimeve Naim Frasheri, 1960.
An Albanian translation.

337 John Milton. Ztraceny Ráj. Trans. by Josef Jungmann. Praha: Snklhu, 1960.
A Czech translation.

338 John Milton. Det Förlorade Paradiset. Trans. by Frans G. Bengtsson. Stockholm: Natur och kultur, 1961. 354pp.

339 John Milton. Silragwon. Trans. by Jeong-sig Yu. Seoul: Dongyangsa, 1961. 178pp.
A Korean translation.

340 John Milton. O Paráíso Perdido. Trans. by Torrigri Guimarães. São Paulo: Ed. Brasil, 1962. 195pp.

341 BUYLLA, JOSE BENITO A. La traducción de Jovellanos del libro primero del Paraíso Perdido, de Milton. FMod, IV, No. 10, 1963, 1-47.
Includes annotated translation of Book 1.

342 John Milton. Silragwon. Bogragwon. Trans. by Jeong Yu. Seoul: Eulyumunhwasa, 1963.
Korean translation of Paradise Lost and Paradise Regined.

343   John Milton. Silragwon. Tusa Samson. Trans. by Chang-bae Lee. Seoul:
      Jeong-eumsa, 1963. 537pp.
        Korean translation of Paradise Lost and Samson Agonistes.

344   John Milton. Paraisa e Humbur. Trans. by Alqi Kristo. Prištinë: Rilindja,
      1964.
        An Albanian translation.

345   El Paraiso Perdido. Por Juan Milton. Traducción de Juan Mateos.
      México: Editorial Diana, S.A., 1964. 376pp. Cartoné.

346   Johann Miltons episches Gedichte von dem Verlohrnen Paradiese.
      Faksimiledruck der Bodmerschen Übersetzung von 1742. Mit einem
      Nachwort von Wolfgang Bender. Stuttgart: Metzler, 1965. 33, 621pp.
        Part of the series, Deutsche Neudrucke, a facsimile edition of the translation
        by Johann Jakob Bodmer.

347   John Milton. El Paráiso Perdido. Trans. by A. Espiña. Madrid: Medi-
      terraneo, 1965.

348   John Milton. Paraíso Perdido. Trad. por Antonio José Lima Leitão.
      Brazil, n.d.

350   John Milton. El Parásio Perdido. Trans. by Dionisio Sanjuan. Madrid:
      Espasa-Calpe, 1966. 234pp.

SHORTER POEMS

351 John Milton. Comus. Trans. by Tenrai Shigeno. Japan, 1929.

352 John Milton. Den Stærke Samson. Paa Dansk ved uffe Birkedol. Kjöbenhaun: H. C. Bakkes Boghandel, 1930. 78pp.
A Danish translation of Samson Agonistes.

353 John Milton. Lycidas. Trans., notes, and introd. by Amina Mastrostefano. Ascoli Piceno: E. Tassi, 1930. 65pp.

354 Les Sonnets anglais et italiens de Milton. Traduits en sonnets français et commentes par E. Saillens. Paris: Fischbacher, 1930. 79pp.
Rev: Paul Chauvet, RA-A, 9, 1932, 336.

355 John Milton. Samson Agonistes. Trans. by Tenrai Shigeno. Japan, 1934.

356 John Milton. Paradise Regained. Trans. by K. Azegami. Japan, 1936.
Huntley: Accompanied by generous notes. "A complete and definitive translation."

357 Milton: l'Allegro, il Penseroso et Samson Agonistes. Tr. avec une introd. par Floris Delattre. Paris: Aubier, 1937. xcii, 151pp. Reprinted, 1945.
Rev: Paul Dottin, ESt., 72, 1937, 107; Emile Legouis, EA, 1, 1937, 252-3; W. Fischer, Ang. Bbl., 49, 1938, 264.

358 John Milton. Lycidas. Trans. by Torao Taketomo. Japan, 1939.

359 John Milton. Tōgisha Samuson. Tokyo: Iwanami Shoten, 1941. 117pp.
A Japanese translation of Samson Agonistes.

360 Milton. Liriche e drammi. Trans. and ed. by Alberto Castelli. Milan: Montuoro, 1941. 228pp.
Includes several sonnets, Samson Agonistes, Lycidas, L'Allegro, and Il Penseroso.

361 John Milton. Lament for Damon. Trans. by Helen Waddell. Privately printed, 1943. 12pp.
"In memory of George Frederick Waddell Martin, killed March 7, 1942, and of his brothers-in-arms who died young.'

362 John Milton. Sansone Agonista. A Cura di Marco Lombardi. Milan: Bompiani, 1943. 186pp. Reprinted, 1945.
Also includes translations of Comus and the Italian sonnets. Appendix: I versi italiani di Milton.

363 Milton. L'Allegro-Il Penseroso. A cura di Lauro Roberti-Fletcher. Florence: Fussi, 1946. 51pp.

364 Milton. Simson der Kämpfer. Trans. by H. Ulrich and ed. by R. Schneider. Freiburg, 1947.

365 John Milton. Ode alla Nativita, ad un concerto sacro, Allegro, Penseroso,

Arcadi, Como, Licida. Versione col testo a fronte, introduzione e note a cura di Carlo Izzo. Florence: G. C. Sansoni, 1948. xli, 272pp.

366 John Milton. Sansone agonista, Sonetti. Versione col testo a fronte, introduzione e note a cura di Carlo Izzo. Florence: G. C. Sansoni, 1948. xxxiv, 250pp.

367 John Milton. Samson Agonistes. Translated by Christian E. Kreipe. Introduction and Notes by Karl Denner. Kentucky Microcards, Series A, No. 25, 1949.
     Apparently the translation published at Halle in 1926 (see Stevens' No. 1183), with the Introduction and Notes prepared for this series.

368 John Milton. Sansón Agonistes. (La escena del Sansón y Dalila.) Versión de José Garciá Nieto y Charles David Ley. Madrid, 1949.

369 John Milton. Shimson Ha-Givvor. Trans. by Reuven Avinoam. Tel-Aviv: Massada, 1950.

370 John Milton. Le Paradis reconquis, Étude critique. Traduction et notes par Jacques Blondel. Paris: Aubier, 1955. 270pp.
     Rev: Merritt Y. Hughes, MLN, 71, 1956, 602-3.

371 John Milton. Sámson. Trans. by Tihamer Dybas. Budapest: Uj Magyar Kiado, 1955. 111pp. Illus.
     The first translation into Hungarian.

372 John Milton. Ode sur la Nativité. Trans. by Claude Summer. Addis Ababa, Ethiopia: Univ. College Press, 1956. 25pp.

373 John Milton. I Sonetti. Traduzione metrica di Bruno Fattori (con testo a fronte). Milano: Ceschina, 1958. 87pp.

374 John Milton. Simson der Kämpfer (Samson Agonistes) Deutsch-Englisch. Aus dem Englischen übersetzt von Hermann Ulrich. Einleitung V. Anselm Schlösser. Berlin: Aufbau-Verlag, 1958. 163pp.
     Rev: Tibor Lutter, ZAA, 7, 1959, 419-21.

375 John Milton. Kamengeki Comus. Trans. by Shigeo Saino. Tokyo: Nan'un-dô, 1960.

376 John Milton. Pahan Sita. Trans. by Gamani Pathberiza. Colombo, Ceylon: M. D. Gunasena and Co., 1960.
     L'Allegro and Il Penseroso.

377 John Milton. Versek. Trans. by Géza Képes, Agnes Nemes Nagy et al. Budapest: Europa, 1960.
     The Minor Poems.

378 D'HAEN, CHRISTINE. John Milton: Lycidas. Tirade (Amsterdam), 7, 1963, 673-83.
     On the pastoral background of Lycidas. Translation of the poem into Dutch, pp. 679-83.

379   Le Comus de John Milton: masque neptunien. Par Jacques Blondel. Paris:
      Presses Universitares de France, 1964. 142pp.
          Lengthy introduction and commentary. French translation, pp. 95-121.
          Rev: M. T. Jones-Davies, EA, 19, 1966, 186-7; D. C. Allen, JEGP, 65,
          1966, 339-40; Joachim Stephan, ZAA, 15, 1967, 193-6; Clifford Leech, MLR,
          62, 1967, 702-3.

381   John Milton. Samson-Borec. Trans. by Ě. Kvitaišvili and Z. Kiknadze.
      Tbilisi, Russia: Nakaduli, 1966.
          A Georgian translation of Samson Agonistes.
          See also item Nos. 334, 342, and 343.

AREOPAGITICA AND OTHER PROSE

382 A Translation of Milton's Areopagitica. By Humphrey Lunch. Gaitsford Prize for Greek Prose. Oxford: Blackwell, 1932. 8pp.

383 John Milton. Areopagitica. Traduzione e prefacione di S. Breglia. Bari: Laterza, 1933. xxxii, 134pp.
Rev: TLS, Feb. 2, 1933, p. 76; Nuova Riv. Storica, 17, 1933, 579-80.

384 John Milton. Om Trykkafrihed. Areopagitica. Trans. by A. C. Krebs. Copenhagen: Berlingske Forlag, 1936.

385 John Milton. Areopagitica, traducción y prólogo de José Carner. Mexico City: Fondo de cultura economica, 1941. 104pp.
"Primera edicion espanola, 1941."

386 John Milton. Areopagitica. Rede für die Pressfreiheit und gegen die Zenser. Basel: E. Ganzmann, 1944. iv, 95pp.

387 John Milton. Areopagitica. Rede für die Pressfreiheit und gegen die Zensur. Paris: Aubier, 1945.

388 Genron-to-Jiyū (Speech and Freedom). Trans. by Kenji Ishida, Shungo Yoshida, and Seichi Ueno. Tokyo: Shingetsusha, 1948. 148pp.
Milton's only prose work translated into Japanese before 1961.

389 John Milton. Genron-to-Jiyū. Trans. by Seichi Ueno, Kenji Ishida, and Singo Yoshida. Tokyo: Iwonomi World Classics, n.d.
Areopagitica. Reprint of above item.

390 John Milton. Shuppan No Jiyû. Trans. by Mitsuo Umezkai et al. Tokyo: Kawade shobô, 1955. 382pp. Illus.
Areopagitica. Also contains selections from Locke and Hume and an introduction.

391 Milton: Areopagitica pour la Liberté d'Imprimer sans Autorisation ni Censure. Ed. and trans. with notes by O. Lutaud. Collection Bilingue des Classiques Etrangers. Paris: Aubier, 1956. 240pp.
English text and French translation on opposite pages.
Rev: Merritt Y. Hughes, EA, 10, 1957, 155-6; SCN, 15, 1957, item 8; S. B. Liljegren, ZAA, 5, 1957, 211-2.

392 John Milton. Rikon no Susume. Trans. by Tetsusaburo Nishiyama. Tokyo: Ruri-shoten, 1961.
The Doctrine and Discipline of Divorce.

393 John Milton. Areopagitica. Trans. by Šašibhushan Dasgupta. Calcutta: Jignasa (for Sahitya Akademi, New Delhi), 1963. 135pp.
A Bengali translation.

394 John Milton. Areopagitica. Trans. by Balakrishna Rao. New Delhi: Sahitya Akademi, 1965. 75pp.
A Hindi translation.

GENERAL CRITICISM

395 ADAMS, ALBERT C. A Study of the Ethics of John Milton. Doctoral diss., Univ. of Missouri, 1961. Abs., DA, 22, 1961, 3184.

396 ADAMS, ROBERT MARTIN. Empson and Bentley: Something About Milton Too. PR, 21, 1954, 178-89.
Concerning Empson's remarks in Some Versions of Pastoral.

397 ------. Ikon: John Milton and the Modern Critics. Ithaca: Cornell Univ. Press, 1955; London: Cumberlege, 1956; Ithaca: Cornell Paperbacks, 1966. xvii, 231pp.
Intends to clear away some modern misconceptions of Milton. Chapters include Reading Comus, The Devil and Doctor Jung, The Text of Paradise Lost, Empson and Bentley: Scherzo, Milton's Reading, Milton's Verse: Efforts at a Judgment, and Milton and Magnanimity. Chapters 1, 3, and 4, noted elsewhere, are reprints, in altered form, of previous articles.
Rev: Arnold Davenport, YWES, 159; R. O. Evans, SCN, 13, 1955, 41-2; Marvin Mudrick, HudR, 9, 1956, 126-33; C. M. Coffin, QQ, 63, 1956, 138-44; TLS, June 15, 1956, p. 362; Kester Svendsen, BA, 30, 1956, 331; F. T. Prince, RES, 8, 1957, 457-8; Frank Kermode, EIC, 7, 1957, 196-207; Edgar Mertner, Anglia, 76, 1958, 327-9; Everett H. Emerson, ES, 42, 1961, 381-3.

398 ADAMSON, J. H. Milton and the Creation. JEGP, 61, 1962, 756-78.
An examination of the ex Deo theory of creation, how it arose, who its proponents were, and why Milton accepted it.

399 ------. Milton's Arianism. HTR, 53, 1960, 269-76.
Gives supporting evidence for William B. Hunter's thesis (HTR, 52, 1959, 9-35) and offers one qualification.

400 ADDINGTON, MARION H. Milton: Some Parallels. N&Q, 164, 1933, 132-3.
The influence of Sylvester and Shakespeare.

401 AGAR, HERBERT. Milton and Plato. Doctoral diss., Princeton Univ., 1928. Princeton: Princeton Univ. Press, 1928; Oxford: Oxford Univ. Press, 1931. Reprinted, Gloucester, Mass.: Peter Smith, 1965. 76pp.
Rev: F. S. Boas, YWES, 12, 1931, 206.

402 ALDRIDGE, ALFRED O. Milton's and Pope's Conception of God and Man. BS, 96, 1939, 444-58.
"... Milton's approach to the problem of justifying God to man is theological, while Pope's is ethical."

403 ALLAIN, MATHÉ. The Humanist's Dilemma: Milton, God, and Reason. CE, 27, 1966, 379-84.
Milton was faced with the dilemma of a religion based on absolute biblical authority and his belief in the free will of rational beings; "the dilemma splits Paradise Lost, is explored in Paradise Regained, and finds its full resolution in Samson Agonistes."

404 ALLEN, DON CAMERON. The Harmonious Vision: Studies in Milton's
     Poetry. Baltimore: Johns Hopkins Press, 1954. xx, 125pp.
       "Milton, true son of Eve, expended the full powers of his life towards the
       recapture of the harmonious vision." Chapters include The Search for the
       Prophetic Strain; L'Allegro and Il Penseroso, The Higher Compromise: On
       the Morning of Christ's Nativity and A Mask, The Translation of a Myth:
       The Epicedia and Lycidas, The Idea as Pattern: Despair and Samson
       Agonistes, Description as Cosmos: The Visual Image in Paradise Lost, Reali-
       zation and Climax: Paradise Regained.
       Rev: Arnold Davenport, YWES, 137-8; Barbara Lupini, English, 10, 1954,
       105-6; R. Florence Brinkley, SAQ, 53, 1954, 598; Merritt Y. Hughes, MP,
       52, 1954, 211-4; E. L. Marilla, MLQ, 16, 1955, 54-6; SCN, 13, 1955, 10;
       Douglas Bush, MLN, 70, 1955, 58-60; Denis Saurat, EA, 8, 1955, 344-5;
       L. C. Martin, MLR, 50, 1955, 240-1; J. B. Broadbent, ES, 37, 1956, 276-7;
       J. C. Maxwell, RES, 7, 1956, 106-7.

405 ------. Some Theories of the Growth and Origin of Language in Milton's
     Age. PQ, 28, 1949, 5-16.
       Discusses "the activities and the methods of contemporary philologists in
       Milton's age . . . ," especially those concerning the origin of language and
       causes for language change.

406 ALLEN, RALPH K. Milton's Creative Unitarianism. Doctoral diss., Univ.
     of Washington, 1953. Abs., DA, 13, 1953, 791. 329pp.

407 ANAND, MULK RAJ. The Example of Milton. Freedom of Expression.
     Ed. by Herman Ould (London: Hutchinson, 1945), pp. 142-51.
       On Milton, liberty, and the Indian Revolution.

408 ANDERSON, WARREN D. Notes on the Simile in Homer and His
     Successors: II. Milton. CJ, 53, 1957, 127-33.
       ". . . Milton, like Homer, bases the validity of many of his similes on a
       hypothesis of identity." Milton was able to lend "reality to the unreal by
       means of comparisons drawn as nearly as possible from the same realm."

409 ANIKST, A. Milton. History of English Literature (Moscow, 1945), 1,
     175-200.

410 ------. A Poet of the English Revolution. Soviet Culture, Dec. 9, 1958.
       On the 350th anniversary of Milton's birth.

411 ANSELOT, NOËL. Un nouvel aspect de Milton. Le Flambeau, 34, 1951,
     277-82.
       "Dans la production littéraire anglaise, un nom marque un temps: John
       Milton."

412 ARTHOS, JOHN. Dante, Michelangelo, and Milton. London: Routledge
     and Kegan Paul, 1963; New York: Humanities Press, 1964. xii, 124pp.
       "Dante, Michelangelo, and Milton . . . , like Longinus . . . rested in the con-
       viction that poetry depended on truth. . . . What their theories have to do
       with their achievements and how far these bear Longinus out is the subject
       of this study." Milton discussed, pp. 90-120.
       Rev: TLS, Nov. 14, 1963, p. 928; J. B. Beer, MLR, 60, 1965, 594-8; John
       Buxton, RES, 16, 1965, 198-9; Rosemary Woolf, CritQ, 7, 1965, 290-1.

413 ATKINS, JOHN W. The Last Phase: Jonson and Milton. English

Literary Criticism: The Renascence (London: Methuen, 1947; 2nd Edition, New York: Barnes and Noble, 1952) , pp. 312-42.
 Considers Milton's remarks on rhetoric, the nature and function of poetry, the poet, rhyme, blank verse, and Greek tragedy.
 Rev: D. C. A[llen], MLN, 63, 1948, 508; E. H. W. Meyerstein, English, 7, 1948, 138-9; F. G. Mackarill, LL, 57, 1948, 268-72; G. D. Willcock, RES, 25, 1949, 70-1; M. T. Herrick, JEGP, 48, 1949, 286-9; H. S. Wilson, UTQ, 18, 1949, 402-5.

414 BAILEY, JOHN. Milton. Home Univ. Library. Revised Edition. New York: Henry Holt; London: Williams and Norgate, 1930, 1932. 256pp.
 Reprint of Stevens' No. 2417, first published in 1915.
 "An introduction to the scope of Milton's art that has merit. The major poems are dealt with in brief but definite analysis" (Stevens' annotation) .

415 BAILEY, MARGARET LEWIS. Milton and Jakob Boehme: A Study of German Mysticism in Seventeenth-Century England. New York: Haskell House, 1964. vii, 200pp.
 A reprint of Stevens' No. 2410. Considers Boehme and England in general and discusses the similarity between Milton and Boehme.

416 BAKER, CHARLES E. Milton's Italian Relations. Doctoral diss., Cornell Univ., 1933. Abs., Ithaca: Cornell Univ. Press, 1933.

417 BAKER, HERSCHEL. The Race of Time: Three Lectures on Renaissance Historiography. The Alexander Lectures, 1965. Toronto: Univ. of Toronto Press, 1967.
 Records Milton's changing attitude toward the Arthurian legend.

418 ------. The Wars of Truth: Studies in the Decay of Humanism in the Earlier Seventeenth Century. London: Staples Press, 1952. Cambridge: Harvard Univ. Press, 1952. xi, 390pp.
 Milton discussed, passim, as the last great exemplar of Renaissance humanism in England.
 Rev: TLS, Mar. 6, 1953, p. 157.

419 ------. Where Liberty Lies: Freedom of Conscience in Milton's Day and in Ours. SWR, 41, 1956, 1-13.
 On liberty and freedom as dominant themes in Milton's work.

420 BARKER, ARTHUR E. Seven Types of Milton Criticism. UTQ, 25, 1956, 494-506.
 A review of recent criticism.

421 ------, ed. Milton: Modern Essays in Criticism. A Galaxy Book. New York: Oxford Univ. Press, 1965. vii, 483pp.
 An anthology of thirty-three selections on Milton, all previously published. Each essay is listed in this bibliography under its appropriate classification.
 Rev: Agnes M. C. Latham, YWES, 204.

422 ------. Structural and Doctrinal Pattern in Milton's Later Poems. Essays in English Literature from the Renaissance to the Victorian Age Presented to A. S. P. Woodhouse (Toronto: Univ. of Toronto Press, 1964) , pp. 169-94.
 Milton's idea of Christian liberty "serves as a focus for Milton's developing

preoccupations and might provide a further means of clarifying the cruxes of his later poems."

423 BARNES, W. J. Some Recent Studies in Milton. QQ, 75, 1968, 161-6.
Discusses Joseph Summers' Lyric and Dramatic Milton, John Steadman's Milton and the Renaissance Hero, and E. A. J. Honigmann's edition of the sonnets.

424 BARTHOLOMEW, RUTH. Some Sources of Milton's Doctrine of Free Will. Doctoral diss., Western Reserve Univ., 1945.

425 BASTIAN, MARGARETHE. Das Problem der Versuchung bei Milton. Doctoral diss., Marburg, 1930. Marburg: Franz Fischer, 1930. 78pp.

426 BATESON, F. W. Milton. NSN, Aug. 19, 1950, p. 181.
Animadversions on Rex Warner's review (NSN, Aug. 12, 1950, p. 181) of his English Poetry, A Critical Introduction. Defends his comments on Milton.

427 BATTENHOUSE, HENRY M. Milton. Poets of Christian Thought: Evaluations from Dante to T. S. Eliot (New York: Ronald Press, 1947), pp. 44-62.
A sentimental interpretation.

428 BAUGH, ALBERT C., ed. A Literary History of England. New York: Appleton-Century-Crofts, 1948. Second Edition, 1967.
Contains three chapters on Milton, written by Tucker Brooke: Milton, The Last Elizabethan, pp. 673-80; Milton's Latin Poems and Prose Works, pp. 681-8; Milton in the Restoration, pp. 689-98. In the second edition, the Milton bibliography is updated by M. A. Shaaber.
Rev: Delancey Ferguson, NYHTBR, May 2, 1948, p. 11; Charles Duffy, NYTBR, May 23, 1948, p. 25; TLS, Mar. 26, 1949, p. 202; J. J. Parry, JEGP, 48, 1949, 147-9; René Wellek, MP, 47, 1949, 39-45.

429 BAUMGARTNER, PAUL R. Milton and Patience. SP, 60, 1963, 203-13.
Paradise Lost, Paradise Regained and Samson Agonistes "manifest a new and real conviction in the Christian virtue of patience and in its corollaries, dependence on and submission to, the will of God."

430 BAYLEY, JOHN. . . . The Ways of Man to Man. Spect, July 30, 1965, pp. 154-5.
Comments on the revised edition of William Empson's Milton's God.

431 BECK, RICHARD J. Milton and the Spirit of his Age. ES, 42, 1961, 288-300.
Deals with three aspects of seventeenth-century thought to which Milton contributed.

432 BEER, JOHN. Milton, Lost and Regained. PBA, 50, 1965, 143-68. Reprinted in pamphlet form, London: Oxford Univ. Press, 1965. 26pp.
An appreciative survey of Milton's poetry. Feels that Milton is an elusive figure whose "work lies in a penumbra immediately behind the birthright of the modern world."

433 BELLOC, HILAIRE. On Milton. Selected Essays. Introduction by J. B. Morton (London: Methuen, 1948, 1950), pp. 63-8.
An essay originally published in Belloc's On Anything (1910). Appreciative.

434   BENJAMIN, EDWIN B. Fame, Poetry, and the Order of History in the
      Literature of the English Renaissance. SRen, 6, 1959, 64-84.
          Briefly traces Milton's attitudes toward fame in History of Britain, Lycidas,
          Paradise Lost, Paradise Regained, and other works.

435   BENTLEY, J. A. Undergraduate Disparagement of Milton. DR, 26, 1945-
      46, 421-32.
          Deplores the then current neglect of Milton.

436   BERKELEY, DAVID S. A Milton Guide. Offset typescript. Stillwater,
      Oklahoma, 1965. v, 460pp.
          Contains pertinent questions and answers on works ranging from On the
          Morning of Christ's Nativity to Samson Agonistes, including the prose. "The
          value of this work as the compiler sees it is to cause the student to come to
          grips in as full and as varied a way as possible with Milton's art and
          thought.... The compiler believes that a penetrating, just, and comprehen-
          sive synthesis will be made easier by a perusal of these pages."

437   BETHELL, S. L. The Cultural Revolution of the Seventeenth Century.
      London: Denis Dobson, 1951. 161pp.
          Passim.

438   ------. Essays on Literary Criticism and the English Tradition. London:
      Denis Dobson, 1948.
          Classifies poetry as the Shakespeare-Donne type and the Spenser-Milton-
          Tennyson type.

439   BITTING, MARY E. Contempt of the World in the Poetry of John
      Milton: A Study in Milton's Changing Personal and Artistic Emphases.
      Master's thesis, Univ. of North Carolina, 1937.

440   BLAKE, WILLIAM. Seconds livres prophetiques, contenant Milton. Trad.
      de l'anglais avec une introduction par Pierre Berger. Paris: Rieder,
      1930. 256pp.
          Rev: TLS, June 1, 1933, p. 376.

441   BLAU, SHERIDAN D. Milton's Salvational Aesthetic. JR, 46, 1966,
      282-95.
          Suggests that Milton transformed Elizabethan critical theories in order to
          develop a new concept of poetry, which would "serve the specific purposes
          of a Puritan theocracy."

442   BLISSETT, WILLIAM F. The Historical Imagination in the English
      Renaissance, Studied in Spenser and Milton. Doctoral diss., Univ. of
      Toronto, 1950. Abs., Univ. of Toronto . . . Final Oral Examinations
      for the Degree of Doctor of Philosophy, Session 1949-50.

443   BOLLIER, E. P. T. S. Eliot and John Milton: A Problem in Criticism.
      TSE, 8, 1958, 165-92.
          Surveys Eliot's critical principles and theories which are relevant to under-
          standing his views on Milton and traces the development of these views
          from 1919 to 1947.

444   BRAND, C. P. Torquato Tasso: A Study of the Poet and of His Contribu-
      tion to English Literature. Cambridge: Cambridge Univ. Press, 1965.
      xi, 344pp.
          Considers Tasso's influence on Milton.

445 BRILL, MARY C. Milton and Ovid. Doctoral diss., Cornell Univ., 1935. Abs., Cornell Univ. Abstracts of Dissertations. Ithaca: Cornell Univ. Press, 1935. 6pp.

446 BRINKLEY, ROBERTA F. Milton and the Arthurian Story. Arthurian Legend in the Seventeenth Century. Johns Hopkins Monographs in Literary History, 3 (Baltimore: Johns Hopkins Press, 1932), pp. 126-41. Reprinted, London: Cass, 1967.
  A consideration of Milton's concept of and respect for the Arthurian legend and of probable and possible reasons for his not continuing his idea of an epic about Arthur.
  Rev: TLS, July 21, 1932, pp. 521-2; A. G. van Kranendonk, ES, 15, 1933, 69-71; J. J. Parry, MLN, 48, 1933, 267-8; C. B. Millican, RES, 10, 1934, 101-2; H. Marcus, Ang. Bbl., 45, 1934, 50-2.

447 BROADBENT, J. B. Links Between Poetry and Prose in Milton. ES, 37, 1956, 49-62.
  In his poetry, Milton often repeats ideas that he has stated in the prose. "A knowledge of the repetitions will occasionally help us to elucidate a passage in the poems by reference to the prose...."

448 BROADUS, EDMUND K. John Milton and the Puritans. The Story of English Literature (Revised Edition, New York: Macmillan, 1931), pp. 196-228.
  Rev: TLS, Apr. 28, 1932, p. 314; G. H. C., QQ, 39, 1932, 572-4.

449 BRODRIBB, C. W. Milton and Buchanan. N&Q, 158, 1930, 185.
  Similarities between Buchanan's Latin poems and the poetry of Milton.

450 ------. Milton and Two Latin Poets. N&Q, 159, 1930, 129.
  On Milton's indebtedness to Manlius and Statius.

451 ------. Milton's Bellman. N&Q, 182, 1942, 273.
  Dekker's Bell-man (1608) "bears very closely on Milton's words."

452 BROOKS, CLEANTH. Milton and Critical Re-Estimates. PMLA, 66, 1951, 1045-54.
  A paper read before the Milton group of MLA, Dec. 28, 1950. Suggests, i.a., the need for further study of myth and metaphor and symbolic structure, commending modern critics' concern in these areas.

453 ------. Milton and the New Criticism. SR, 59, 1951, 1-22.
  Milton not radically different from Donne in his use of metaphor.

454 BROWN, CALVIN S. Music and Literature. A Comparison of the Arts. Athens: Univ. of Georgia Press, 1948. xi, 287pp.
  Considers the influence of music on Milton's poetry.

455 BROWN, STUART G. A Note on Poetry and Prophecy. SR, 49, 1941, 107-15.
  Wordsworth (1937).
  Remarks on Grierson's concept of prophetic poetry in his Milton and

456 BRUNNER, HILDEGARD. Miltons persönliche Beziehungen zur Aristokratie und seine aristokratische Geisteshaltung. Doctoral diss., Bonn, 1933. Published as Miltons persönliche und ideelle Welt in ihrer

Beziehung zum Aristokratismus. Bonner studien zur englische Philologie, 19. Bonn: Hanstein, 1933. 50pp.
    Rev: W. Milch, Die Literatur, 36, 1933, 52; Lit. Zentralblatt, 84, 1933, 694; A. Brandl, Archiv, 164, 1933, 135; Paul Chauvet, RA-A, 11, 1934, 256-7; G.-K. Bauer, GRM, 22, 1934, 249-50; H. F. F[letcher], JEGP, 33, 1934, 338; J. H. Hanford, MLN, 51, 1936, 53-4; W. Schmidt, Literaturblatt, 57, 1936, 34-5.

457   BRYANT, JOSEPH A., JR. The Evolution of Milton's Conception of History. Doctoral diss., Yale Univ., 1948.

458   ------. Milton's Views on Universal and Civil Decay. SAMLA Studies in Milton. Ed. by J. Max Patrick (Gainesville: Univ. of Florida Press, 1954), pp. 1-19.
    Asserts that "it was Milton's political theory, not his cosmology, that caused him occasionally to reflect soberly and perhaps fearfully on such objects as degeneration, decay, and the fate of the age."

459   ------. A Note on Milton's Use of Machiavelli's Discorsi. MP, 47, 1950, 217-21.
    Milton did not know Machiavelli's important critical writings until late in his career.

460   BURGESS, ANTHONY. The Milton Revolution. Spect, April 28, 1967, pp. 487-8.
    A review article on Patrick Murray's Milton: The Modern Phase and E. M. W. Tillyard's revised Milton. Appreciative.

461   BURKE, KENNETH. Responses to Pressure. Poetry, 51, 1937-8, 37-42.
    Review article on Grierson's Wordsworth and Milton (1937).

462   BURNS, NORMAN THOMAS. The Tradition of Christian Mortalism in England: 1530-1660. Doctoral diss., Univ. of Michigan, 1967. Abs., DA, 28, 1968, 5045-A. 192pp.
    "The purpose of this study is to elucidate the intellectual milieu in which young Thomas Browne, Milton, Hobbes, and Richard Overton, author of the notorious Mans Mortallitie (1643), came to believe that the soul is dead until it is resurrected with the body on the Last Day."

463   BUSH, DOUGLAS. Arthur Woodhouse: Scholar, Critic, Humanist. Essays in English Literature from the Renaissance to the Victorian Age Presented to A. S. P. Woodhouse, 1964. Ed. by Millar MacLure and F. W. Watt (Toronto: Univ. of Toronto Press, 1964), pp. 320-33. Reprinted in Bush's Engaged and Disengaged (Cambridge: Harvard Univ. Press, 1966), pp. 79-96.
    Contains an appreciative analysis of Woodhouse's studies in Milton.

464   ------. Classical Influences in Renaissance Literature. Martin Classical Lectures, Oberlin College, 13. Cambridge: Harvard Univ. Press, 1952. 60pp.
    Passim.
    Rev: Rudolf Gottfried, MLN, 68, 1953, 505-6; Northrop Frye, RN, 6, 1953, 47-8; Hardin Craig, JEGP, 52, 1953, 255-6.

465   ------. The Critical Significance of Biographical Evidence: John Milton.

EIE, 1946 (New York: Columbia Univ. Press, 1947), pp. 5-19.
Biographical evidence is often abused in the case of Milton, but often it is useful in re-creating circumstances of composition and in throwing light on the text.

466 ------. English Literature in the Earlier Seventeenth Century, 1600-1660. Oxford History of English Literature, 5. Oxford: Clarendon Press, 1945. Revised Edition, 1960. viii, 680pp.
Chapter XII, Milton, pp. 377-420. "He [Milton] is seen, in the first place, as the last great exponent of Christian humanism in its historical continuity.... In the second place, recent criticism has brought fresh perceptiveness to the study of Milton's poetic art and heritage and has done much to reanimate and enrich the traditional conception of the great classical artist among modern poets...."
Chronological Tables, pp. 425-59.
Bibliography, pp. 461-8.
Milton Bibliography, pp. 615-22.
Rev: L. C. Martin, YWES, 132-4; Geoffrey Tillotson, English, 6, 1946, 28-30; DUJ, N.S., 7, 1946, 66-7; J. H. P. P., Library, 5th Ser., 1, 1946, 79-81; C. J. Sisson, MLR, 41, 1946, 432-3; H. B. Charlton, MGW, 54, 1946, 49; H. J. C. Grierson, Spect, Jan. 18, 1946, p. 68; J. F. Macdonald, Canadian Forum, 26, 1946, 187; L. C. Martin, RES, 23, 1947, 167-9; M. E. Prior, MP, 45, 1947, 139-42; H. F. Fletcher, JEGP, 46, 1947, 315-7; Arthur Barker, UTQ, 16, 1947, 206-10; R. Kirk, MLQ, 9, 1948, 108-9; M. Y. Hughes, MLN, 63, 1948, 190-4; Arthur Barker, JEGP, 62, 1963, 617-28; SCN, 20, 1963, 50-1.

467 ------. English Poetry. The Main Currents from Chaucer to the Present. New York: Oxford Univ. Press, 1952. 222pp.
Milton discussed, pp. 68-79.

468 ------. The Isolation of the Renaissance Hero. Reason and Imagination: Studies in the History of Ideas, 1600-1800. Ed. by J. A. Mazzeo (New York: Columbia Univ. Press, 1962; London: Routledge and Kegan Paul, 1962), pp. 57-69.
Considers, i.a., Adam, Samson, and the Son of Paradise Regained.

469 ------. Milton. Mythology and the Renaissance Tradition in English Poetry (Minneapolis: Univ. of Minnesota Press; London: Oxford Univ. Press, 1932), pp. 248-86. Reprinted, Library of Literary History and Criticism, No. 3, New York: Pageant Book Co., 1957; New York: W. W. Norton, 1963.
Studies influences exerted by Ovid et al. Views Milton's handling of mythology as the culmination of the Renaissance tradition.

470 ------. Milton. The Renaissance and English Humanism (Toronto: Univ. of Toronto Press, 1939; reprinted, 1941, 1956), pp. 101-34.
Sees Milton as the last great exponent of Christian humanism in its historical continuity.
Rev: W. G. Rice, UTQ, 9, 1940, 238-42; A. Walker, RES, 16, 1940, 337-8; R. V. Cram, Classical Weekly, 33, 1940, 212-3; TLS, Jan. 18, 1941, p. 32; B. E. C. Davis, MLR, 36, 1941, 256-8.

471 ------. Notes on Milton's Classical Mythology. SP, 28, 1931, 259-72.

472 ------. Science and English Poetry, a Historical Sketch, 1590-1950. The
Patten Lectures, Indiana Univ., 1949. New York: Oxford Univ. Press,
1950.
Milton discussed in a chapter entitled The New Science and Seventeenth
Century Poets, pp. 27-50.
Rev: Geoffrey Bullough, YWES, 12-3.

473 ------. Science and Literature in the Seventeenth Century. Seventeenth
Century Science and the Arts. Ed. by Hedley H. Rhys (Princeton:
Princeton Univ. Press, 1961), pp. 29-62. Reprinted in Engaged and Disengaged (Cambridge: Harvard Univ. Press, 1966), pp. 180-206.
The bibliography that accompanies the original publication is omitted in the
reprint. Milton's attitude toward science noted, passim. Concludes that "the
writers of poetry and prose whom we chiefly read and reread are the great
race who lived before or outside the Enlightenment."

474 ------. Virgil and Milton. CJ, 47, 1952, 178-82, 203-4.
A paper read before the New England Classical Association in 1950. Concerned with Vergilian influence in a general way, including Milton's blending
of pagan with Christian themes.

475 BUTLER, P. R. Rivers of Milton and Spenser. QR, 291, 1953, 373-84.
"Let rivers, then, and streams be our business, as two great poets mention
them...."

476 BUXTON, CHARLES R. Prophets of Heaven and Hell. Virgil, Dante,
Milton, Goethe. An Introductory Essay. Cambridge: Cambridge Univ.
Press, 1945. Reprinted, New York: Haskell House, 1966. xv, 115pp.
Discusses, i.a., the poems as works of art, the historical value of the poems,
the moral and intellectual effect of the poems, and the poems as documents
expressing the basic ideas of Western civilization.
Rev: TLS, Aug. 25, 1945, p. 406; DUJ, 7, 1945, 31-2; N&Q, 189, 1945, 131-2;
V. de S. Pinto, English, 5, 1945, 207-10; A. D. Lindsay, MGW, Oct. 5, 1945,
p. 178; B. Ifor Evans, CR, 159, 1946, 60-1; B. A. Wright, MLR, 41, 1946, 76-7;
J. S. Collis, FR, 945, 1946, 146-7; L. C. Martin, RES, 22, 1946, 243-4.

477 CAMPBELL, LILY B. The Christan Muse. HLB, No. 8, 1935, pp. 29-70.
Milton represents the culmination of a movement which opposed the "pagan-
izing and secularizing of literature throughout the Renaissance."

478 CARVER, P. L. The Sources of Macaulay's Essay on Milton. RES, 6,
1930, 49-62.
A study of the essay as the final stage in a process of thought and of unconscious borrowings as a result of Macaulay's retentive memory.

479 CAWLEY, ROBERT R. Milton and the Literature of Travel. PSE, 32,
Princeton: Princeton Univ. Press, 1951. 158pp.
"An attempt to show how Milton used the travel literature in his poetry,
which among the travel books were his favorites, how he adapted their
materials to his poetic purposes, and how his lines were enriched by the
abundant and colorful details provided by those books."
Rev: J. H. Hanford, YR, 41, 1951-2, 634-6; Allan Gilbert, SAQ, 51, 1952,
465-6; H. F. Fletcher, JEGP, 51, 1952, 294; A. I. Carlisle, RES, 4, 1953,
288-9; Jacques Blondel, EA, 6, 1953, 359-60.

480 CHAFFURIN, LOUIS. Milton. Les Langues modernes, 36, 1938, 441-7.

481 CHAMBERS, R. W. Poets and Their Critics: Langland and Milton. Warton Lecture on English Poetry. Proceedings of the British Academy, 27, London: Milford, 1942. 48pp.
Rev: TLS, Aug. 22, 1942, p. 419; William R. Parker, MLN, 59, 1944, 205-6.

482 CHESTERTON, GILBERT K. Milton and Merry England. The Man Who Was Chesterton. Comp. and ed. by R. T. Bond (New York: Dodd, 1937), 631-46.
Reprint of Stevens' No. 2482, published in 1921-2. Discusses Milton's grand style.

483 ------. Taste for Milton. Handful of Authors (New York: Sheed and Ward, 1953), 75-7.
A reprint of an 1908 essay, apparently unnoticed by Stevens or Fletcher.

484 CHEW, AUDREY. Joseph Hall and John Milton. ELH, 17, 1950, 274-95. Published also in pamphlet form.
Similarities and differences in ideas.

485 CHRISTENSEN, PARLEY A. On Liberty in Our Time. Milton and Mill. WHR, 6, 1952, 110-8.

486 CLARK, EVERT M. Milton and the Warfare of Peace. SAQ, 45, 1946, 195-208.
Milton long ago realized that the ultimate guarantees of world peace are neither political nor military but moral.

487 ------. Milton and Wither. SP, 56, 1959, 626-46.
A study of Wither's influence upon Milton.

488 ------. Milton's English Poetical Vocabulary. SP, 53, 1956, 220-38.
On the size and origins of Milton's vocabulary.

489 CLARK, G. N. The Seventeenth Century. Oxford: Oxford Univ. Press, 1929. 384pp.
Passim.

490 CLARK, IRA G., III. The Son of God in Milton's Works. Doctoral diss., Northwestern Univ., 1966. Abs., DA, 27, 2525A-6A.

491 COHEN, WILLIAM H. Romantic Criticism of Milton. Master's thesis, Univ. of Florida, 1954.

492 COLERIDGE, SAMUEL T. Coleridge on the Seventeenth Century. Ed. by Roberta F. Brinkley. Introduction by Louis I. Bredvold. Durham: Duke Univ. Press, 1955.
Reproduces Coleridge's lectures, comments, and marginalia on Milton, passim, but there are two main chapters: Milton/Prose, pp. 471-3; Milton/Poetry, pp. 541-611.
Rev: J. M. Raines, BA, 30, 1956, 89; Lucyle Werkmeister, Pers, 37, 1956, 314-5; Roland M. Frye, SAB, 22, 1956, 14-5; George Whalley, UTQ, 25, 1956, 259-62; G. B. Evans, JEGP, 55, 1956, 337-8.

493 ------. Shakespeare and Milton: Seven Lectures. Scholarly Reprints. New York: Burt Franklin, 1968. 295pp.
Apparently a reprint of John Payne Collier's 1856 edition, Stevens' No. 2008.

494 COLIN CLOUT. Milton's "Two Men I Honour. . . ." N&Q, 185, 1943, 45.
> Reproduces a letter to Benedetto Buonmattei dated Sept. 10, 1638, expressive of Milton's interest in the purity of the mother tongue.

495 CONIBEAR, MABEL RUTH. Milton's Attitude Toward the Bible as Reflected in His Poetry and Prose Works, and in His Letters. Master's thesis, Alberta Univ., 1932. 260pp.

496 CONKLIN, GEORGE N. Biblical Criticism and Heresy in Milton. Doctoral diss., Columbia Univ., 1949. New York: King's Crown Press, 1949.
> Holds that Milton's doctrinal heterodoxies derive largely from his method of Biblical criticism.
> Rev: H. F. Fletcher, JEGP, 49, 1950, 254-5; W. S. Hudson, Rev. of Religion, 15, 1950, 60-2; T. S. K. Scott-Craig, MLN, 65, 1950, 567-8; C. Smyth, CQR, 150, 1950, 266-8; E. L. Allen, RES, 2, 1951, 281-2; Nathaniel H. Henry, PQ, 30, 1951, 223-4.

497 COOPER, BRIAN G. Milton's Spirituality. The Aryan Path, 38, 1967, 296-300.

498 COOPER, LANE. Abyssinian Paradise in Coleridge and Milton. Late Harvest (Ithaca: Cornell Univ. Press, 1952), pp. 59-64.
> Milton's and Coleridge's use of Purchas' Pilgrimage (1617). Reprint of Stevens' No. 2268, published in 1906.

499 CORMICAN, L. A. Milton's Religious Verse. Pelican Guide to English Literature, Vol. 3: From Donne to Marvell, ed. by Boris Ford (Harmondsworth, Middlesex: Penguin Books, 1956, 1960), pp. 173-92.

500 CRAIG, HARDIN, ed. A History of English Literature. New York: Oxford Univ. Press, 1950.
> Milton discussed, pp. 322-39.

501 CROSLAND, GEORGE N. Milton and the Ironic Temper. Doctoral diss., Univ. of California (Los Angeles), 1961.

502 CRINÒ, ANNA MARIA. Le Opere di Milton a Firenze nel Seicento. Italia, 28, 1951, 108-10.

503 CURRY, WALTER C. Milton's Ontology, Cosmogony, and Physics. Lexington: Univ. of Kentucky Press, 1957. 226pp.
> Chapters: Milton's Dual Concept of God as Related to Creation; Milton's Chaos and Old Night; The Consistence and Qualities of Chaos; The Genesis of Milton's World; The Lordship of Milton's Sun; Some Travels of Satan and the Road to Hell; Milton's Scale of Nature. Appendix: Milton's Light Exhaling from Darkness: A Study in Symbols. The Lordship of Milton's Sun and the appendix are here printed for the first time; the other chapters are revisions of earlier articles.
> Rev: William B. Hunter, Jr., SCN, 15, 1957, 29; Kester Svendsen, BA, 32, 1958, 80-1; Harry F. Robins, JEGP, 57, 1958, 135-6; Burton O. Kurth, Pers, 39, 1958, 317-8; Maria Wickert, Anglia, 78, 1960, 104-6; Bernhard Fabian, NS, 1963, pp. 140-1.

504 CUTLER, BRUCE. The Facts of Human Defeat. Poetry, 93, 1959, 404-8.
Review article on Milton studies by Elio Chinol, W. C. Curry, Rose Macaulay,
and Arnold Stein.

505 DAICHES, DAVID. A Critical History of English Literature. London:
Secker and Warbury, 1960; New York: Ronald Press Co., 1960. 2 vols.
Milton, 1, 390-457, and passim. Contains a good summary of Milton's
creative output. Sees Milton as the last English poet to "use as his poetic
heritage everything that Western civilization . . . had so far achieved."
Rev: William Walsh, NSN, Oct. 8, 1960, pp. 533-4; Willard Thorp,
NYHTBR, Nov. 27, 1960, p. 32; Raymond Williams, MGW, Sept. 29, 1960,
p. 10.

506 ------. Religion, Poetry, and the Dilemma of the Modern Writer. Literary
Essays (Edinburgh: Oliver and Boyd, 1956) , pp. 206-25.
Shows how Milton answered the question of the justice of God and relates
Milton's dilemma to the modern dilemma.

507 DANE, NATHAN. Milton's Callimachus. MLN, 56, 1941, 278-9.
Milton used a 1514 text.

508 DANIELLS, ROY. Baroque Form in English Literature. UTQ, 14, 1945,
393-408.
Milton, pp. 406-8. The recognition of a baroque period might be the means
of establishing the unity of seventeenth-century literature.

509 ------. Milton, Mannerism and Baroque. Toronto: Univ. of Toronto
Press, 1963. 229pp.

A search for analogies between Milton's art and the other arts. ". . . I have
attempted a clarification of the Mannerist traits in Milton's earlier work and
the Baroque elements in his great poetic trilogy." Chapters: Introduction;
Mannerism; Comus and Lycidas; Baroque; Paradise Lost: Unity, Power,
and Will; Paradise Lost: Space and Time; Paradise Lost: Personages and
Plot; Paradise Lost: Paradox and Ambiguity; Milton and Spenser; Puritanism and Baroque; Paradise Lost and Roman Baroque; Paradise Regained;
Samson Agonistes.
Rev: J. B. Beer, MLR, 60, 1965, 594-8.

510 DAS GUPTA, R. K. Milton on Shakespeare. ShS, 14, 1961, 98-101.
Concludes that Shakespeare "was not a force in Milton's literary life and
that he realized that the older poet represented a moral universe and an
order of poetry which were different from his own."

511 ------. Milton's Theory of Poetry. Doctoral diss., Exeter College, Oxford,
1957.

512 D[AVENPORT], A[RNOLD]. Possible Echoes from Sidney's Arcadia in
Shakespeare, Milton, and Others. N&Q, 194, 1949, 554-5.
Cites Paradise Lost, 2, 126-8, Samson Agonistes, 1-2, and Lycidas, 6.

513 DE SELINCOURT, ERNEST, ed. Milton. English Poets and the National
Ideal (Oxford: Clarendon Press, 1940) , pp. 34-60.
Milton and liberty. A reprint of a 1915 essay.

514 DE SOET, F. D. Puritan and Royalist Literature in the Seventeenth Cen-

tury. Doctoral diss., Amsterdam, 1932. Amsterdam: Gedrukt, 1932.
163pp.
> Milton discussed, pp. 10-56. Concerned with Milton's political and religious
> views.

515 DEUTSCH, ALFRED, O. S. B. Milton After Vatican Council II. American Benedictine Review, 18, 1967, 236-44.
> A discussion of Catholic scholarship on Milton. Feels that attitudes of scholars
> such as H. Belloc have become outdated and that "Milton might gain some
> of the prestige among Catholic men of letters that he has long held in the
> non-Roman world."

516 Devil's Advocate. TLS, June 24, 1960, p.401.
> Remarks on Empson's studies.

517 DICKSON, DAVID W. D. Milton's Use of Light. Doctoral diss., Harvard Univ., 1949.

518 DIEKHOFF, JOHN S. Critical Activity of the Poetic Mind: John Milton. PMLA, 55, 1940, 748-72.
> On Milton's method of composition. Points up the consciousness of the
> poet's artistry.

519 ------. The General Education of a Poet: John Milton. JGE, 14, 1962, 10-21.
> On Milton's ideal of the educated man and its relevance to his career in
> poetry.

520 DOBRÉE, BONAMY. Milton and Dryden: A Comparison and Contrast in Poetic Ideas and in Poetic Method. ELH, 3, 1936, 83-100.
> Printed also in the Johns Hopkins Alumni Magazine, 25, 1937, 125-44.

521 DOBSON, E. J. Milton's Pronunciation. Language and Style in Milton: A Symposium in Honor of the Tercentenary of Paradise Lost. Ed. by Ronald David Emma and John T. Shawcross (New York: Frederick Ungar, 1967), pp. 154-92.
> Uses the works of John Wallis and Richard Hodges as principal sources.
> "In general Milton's pronunciation would seem to have been very much
> what one would expect of an educated Londoner of his time."

522 DRAWVER, PAULINE SUE. Milton's Knowledge and Use of Aristotle. Doctoral diss., Univ. of Illinois, 1964. Abs., DA, 25, 1965, 4684-5.

523 DUBBEL, S. EARL. Leisure at Horton. SAQ, 36, 1937, 163-70.
> On the benefits of a retirement such as Milton's.

524 DURRETT, R. W. Do the Epic Poets Reveal Themselves to Us by Their Failures? CJ, 25, 1930, 500-6.
> Milton failed to some extent, but "the good in him far outweighs the bad."

525 DWORSKY, BESA R. Milton and the Rabbinical Bible. TLS, Apr. 25, 1935, p. 272.
> Reply by Theodor Gaster, TLS, May 9, 1935, p. 301.

526 EASTLAND, ELIZABETH W. Milton's Ethics. Doctoral diss., Vanderbilt Univ., 1941. Abs., Bulletin of Vanderbilt Univ., 41, No. 10, 1941, 17-9. Published in summary form. Nashville: Vanderbilt Univ. Press, 1946.

527 EASTMAN, FRED. John Milton. Men of Power: Sixty Minute Biographies (Nashville: Cokesbury Press, 1938), 2, 137-84.

528 EGLE, A. Milton und Italien. Doctoral diss., Freiburg im Breisgau, 1940. 147pp.

529 EISIG, K. T. Moral Criteria in Renaissance Literary Criticism, with Special Reference to Milton. Master's thesis, Univ. of London, 1952.

530 ELIOT, T. S. Milton. Annual Lecture on a Master Mind. Henriette Hertz Trust of the British Academy. Oxford: Oxford Univ. Press, 1947. 19pp. Reprinted in SR, 56, 1948, 185-209; in On Poetry and Poets (London: Faber, 1957), pp. 165-83; in the Modern Critical Spectrum, ed. by Gerald J. and Nancy M. Goldberg (Englewood Cliffs, N.J.: Prentice-Hall, 1962), pp. 175-86.
   Still does not like Milton the man but retracts somewhat from his 1936 position that Milton's influence has been bad.
   Rev: L. C. Martin, YWES, 185-6; TLS, Dec. 13, 1947, p. 65; Desmond McCarthy, Sun. Times, Nov. 9, 1947, p. 3; B. A. Wright, MLR, 43, 1948, 530-2; W. Weintraub, Kultura, 4, 1948, 129-31.

531 ------. A Note on the Verse of John Milton. E&S, 21, 1936, 32-40. Reprinted in On Poetry and Poets (London: Faber, 1957), pp. 156-64; in The Modern Critical Spectrum, ed. by Gerald J. and Nancy M. Goldberg (Englewood Cliffs, N.J.: Prentice-Hall, 1962), pp. 169-74; and in Milton: A Collection of Critical Essays, ed. by Louis L. Martz (Englewood Cliffs, N.J.: Prentice-Hall, 1966), pp. 12-18.
   Milton's rhetoric is "not necessarily bad in itself" but "is likely to be bad in its influence; and it may be considered bad in relation to the historical life of a language as a whole."
   Rev: L. C. Martin, YWES, 187-8.

532 ------. What is a Classic? London: Faber, 1945. 32pp.
   An address delivered before the Vergil Society on Oct. 16, 1944. Argues that Milton's style is not a classic style because "it is a style of a language still in formation, the style of a writer whose masters were not English, but Latin and to a less degree Greek."

533 ------. Milton: Two Studies. London: Faber, 1968.
   Includes the 1936 essay and the 1947 lecture.

534 ELLIOTT, G. R. Milton and Miss Moore. SRL, 6, 1929, 30.
   Disparages Miss Moore's romantic notions of Milton made in her criticism of his review of Spurgeon's Keats's Shakespeare (SRL, 5, 1929, 1105).

535 ------. Milton and the Present State of Poetry. The Cycle of Modern Poetry (Princeton: Princeton Univ. Press; London: Milford, 1929), pp. 135-94
   Milton should be our guide in the development of modern poetry.
   Rev: TLS, June 20, 1929, p. 491; Norman Foerster, AL, 1, 1929, 331-4, and AB, 70, 1929, 214-5; H. H. Clark, SRL, Aug. 17, 1929, p. 52; Irving Babbitt, Forum, 82, Oct., 1929, xviii, xx, xxii, xxiv.

536 ------. Revival of the Poet of Hope. AB, 72, 1930, 341-9.
   Milton is the greatest poet of human hope in English and perhaps in all secular literature.

537 ELLEDGE, SCOTT, ed. Eighteenth-Century Critical Essays. Ithaca, New York: Cornell Univ. Press, 1961. 2 vols.
Contains several essays and excerpts of essays on Milton by writers such as Addison, Dennis, Johnson, and J. Warton.

538 EMERSON, EVERETT H. English Puritanism from John Hooper to John Milton. Durham: Duke Univ. Press, 1968. xii, 313pp.
Contains an introductory essay, English Puritanism, 1550-1641, and includes selections of works of twenty Puritan writers. Includes comments on Milton's Puritanism, pp. 279-87, and a portion of Of Reformation, pp. 287-93.

539 EMPSON, WILLIAM. Milton and Bentley. Some Versions of Pastoral (London: Chatto and Windus, 1935; Harmondsworth: Penguin Books, 1966), pp. 149-94. Reprinted in Milton: A Collection of Critical Essays. Ed. by Louis L. Martz (Englewood Cliffs, N.J.: Prentice-Hall, 1966), pp. 19-39.
Uses Bentley's criticism of Paradise Lost as a springboard for his own remarks on the poetry.
Rev: TLS, Nov. 30, 1935, p. 798; reply by Empson, ibid., Dec. 7, 1935, p. 838; D. Hawkins, Spect, Nov. 15, 1935, p. 828.

540 ENELOW, HYMAN GERSON. Milton: His Memory and Message. Selected Works, with a Memoir by F. A. Levy (Kingsport, Tennessee: privately printed, 1935), 2, 221-9.

541 FERRAU, ANTONIO. Milton rivoluzionarie. Rassegna italiana, 34, 1933, 716-22.

542 FIDO, MARTIN. Milton on Love. OR, No. 3, 1966, 47-66.
Holds that Milton portrays love in a profound and mature way and that "Milton exhibits in his poetry sexual responses which have a triumphant normality...."

543 FINK, ZERA S. Immortal Government: The Free Commonwealth. The Classical Republicans (Evanston: Northwestern Univ. Press, 1945), pp. 90-122. Reprinted, 1962.
An account of Milton's efforts to achieve a mixed state in England.

544 ------. Milton and the Theory of Climatic Influence. MLQ, 2, 1941, 67-80.
A study of the theory as it appears in Milton's works with the conclusion "that the ultimate effect on Milton's poetical ambition was to emphasize and make him more dependent upon the idea of divine inspiration which he had inherited from the Renaissance...."

545 ------. Milton's Retirement to Horton and Renaissance Literary Theory. ES, 22, 1940, 137-8.

546 ------. The Theory of the Mixed State and the Development of Milton's Political Thought. PMLA, 57, 1942, 705-36.
Emphasizes Milton's belief in the superiority of the mixed state.

547 FIORE, AMADEUS P., O. F. M. Th'Upright Heart and Pure: Essays on John Milton Commemorating the Tercentenary of the Publication of Paradise Lost. Pittsburgh and Louvain: Duquesne Univ. Press, 1967.
Contains a Preface by Fiore, and essays by M. Y. Hughes, W. B. Hunter, Jr.,

M. Kelley, E. Le Comte, B. Rajan, J. T. Shawcross, W. Shumaker, J. M. Steadman, K. Svendsen, R. West, and B. A. Wright, each of which is listed under its appropriate classification.
Rev: Thomas R. Hartmann, SCN, 26, 1968, 33-4.

548 ------. The Influence of Augustine on Milton's Work. Doctoral diss., Univ. of London, 1961.

549 FISCH, HAROLD. Jerusalem and Albion: The Hebraic Factor in Seventeenth-Century Literature. New York: Schocken, 1964. ix, 301pp.
Part Three: Milton, pp. 117-72. Describes Milton's Hebraic use of the Covenant-idea in the prose works and in the major poems.

550 FISHER, PETER F. Milton's Theodicy. JHI, 17, 1956, 28-53.
Feels that Milton solves the problem of evil on the level of prophetic faith, not on the level of argument.

551 FISHER-SHORT, W. John Milton and the Problems of Literary Criticism —an Examination of Some Twentieth-Century Critics of Milton. Master's thesis, Manchester Univ., 1952.

552 FIXLER, MICHAEL. Apocalypticism and the Millennium in the Work of John Milton. Doctoral diss., Univ. of Chicago, 1961. Published as Milton and the Kingdoms of God. Evanston: Northwestern Univ. Press, 1964. 293pp.
Report on dissertation, SCN, 21, 1963, item 20. Traces Milton's shifting conception of the Kingdom of God from the period of his early poems through the completion of Paradise Regained.
Rev: Agnes M. C. Latham, YWES, 240; Christopher Ricks, NSN, Oct. 9, 1964, p. 542; TLS, Nov. 5, 1964, p. 996; Virginia R. Mollenkott, SCN, 23, 1965, 27; Howard Sargeant, English, 15, 1965, 191-2; Howard Schultz, MP, 63, 1966, 357; Barbara Lewalski, Church Hist., 35, 1966, 244-5; John Buxton, RES, 17, 1966, 202-3; John M. Steadman, MLR, 63, 1968, 940-2.

553 FLETCHER, HARRIS F. Milton (Index Poeticus) —The Theatrum Poetarum by Edward Phillips. JEGP, 55, 1956, 35-40.
"As I now see the Theatrum, it stands out as a work almost completely produced by Milton, though not of course in the form in which it was printed."

554 [FLETCHER, HARRIS F.] Milton Studies in Honor of Harris Francis Fletcher. JEGP, 60, 1961, 609-854 (all of No. 4, October). Reprinted, Urbana: Univ. of Illinois Press, 1961.
Contains articles by D. C. Allen, Douglas Bush, J. Milton French, Allan H. Gilbert, Davis P. Harding, Merritt Y. Hughes, Maurice Kelley and Samuel D. Atkins, William R. Parker, H. F. Robins, Paul R. Sellin, Charles H. Shattuck, Ernest Sirluck, John M. Steadman, Kester Svendsen, E. M. W. Tillyard, and Don M. Wolfe. Each article is listed in its appropriate section.
Rev: B. A. Wright, RES, 14, 1963, 297-301.

555 ------. Milton's Copy of Gesner's Heraclides, 1544. JEGP, 47, 1948, 182-7.
On Milton's markings and marginalia.

556 ------. Milton's Homer. JEGP, 38, 1939, 229-32.
The 1560 edition by Eustathius.

557 ------. Milton's Rabbinical Readings. Urbana: Univ. of Illinois Press,
     1930. Reprinted, Hamden, Conn.: Shoe String Press, 1967; New York:
     Gordian Press, 1968. 344pp.
        Chapters: Milton's References to the Rabbis in His Prose Works, The Rab-
        binical Materials Milton Cited or Used, Rabbinical Commentaries on Crea-
        tion, The Creation of the Visible Universe in Paradise Lost, The Creation
        of the Earth and Its Forms of Life in Paradise Lost, Some Loyal Angels, and
        Some Rebel Angels.
        Rev: H. J. C. Grierson and A. M. Clark, YWES, 226-7; TLS, Jan. 1, 1931,
        p. 14; J. A. Montgomery, JEGP, 30, 1931, 291-3; E. C. Baldwin, MLN, 66,
        1931, 536-7; S. B. Liljegren, Ang. Bbl., 43, 1932, 373-7; Paul Chauvet, RA-A,
        9, 1932, 240-1; G. W. Whiting, N&Q, 162, 1932, 344-7, and RES, 8, 1932,
        450-3; Zu Miltons rabbinischen Studien, Ang. Bbl., 44, 1933, 154-9.

558 ------. Milton's Semitic Studies and Some Manifestations of Them in his
     Poetry. New York: Gordian Press, 1966. x, 155pp.
        A reprint of Stevens' No. 2571, first published in 1926. "Reaches firmly into
        new evidence that Saurat had touched, while obviously giving only an open-
        ing into the most fruitful present field of Milton research outside of England
        records. The author affirms that Milton's concept of the Holy Spirit is in
        the Jewish Shekinah and other rabbinical matter; that his ideas can be
        demonstrated as derived from Semitic origins" (Stevens' annotation).

559 FLUCHÈRE, HENRI. John Milton, Poète Vivant? EA, 20, 1967, 408-15.
        An examination of the critical writings of T. S. Eliot, F. R. Leavis, and
        others, in relation to John Milton.

560 FOERSTER, DONALD M. Homer, Milton, and the American Revolt
     Against Epic Poetry: 1812-1860. SP, 53, 1956, 75-100.
        Discusses the Romantic attack on the epic as that attack was launched in
        America and provides further illumination on "some of the basic trends in
        American critical thinking prior to the Civil War."

561 FORREST, JAMES FRENCH. The Evil Thought in the Blameless Mind:
     A Study in the History of a Moral Idea, Its Literary Representation, and
     Its Particular Relationship to the Works of John Milton. Doctoral
     diss., Cornell Univ., 1960. Abs., DA, 21, 1961, 3449.

562 FOSTER, JOAN M. The Influence of Spenser on Milton. Master's thesis,
     King's College, Univ. of London, 1945.

563 FOSTER, WILLIAM. Milton and India. TLS, Apr. 6, 1933, p. 248.
        Milton knew how to pronounce Indian names properly.

564 FRANK, JOSEPH. John Milton's Movement toward Deism. JBS, 1, 1961,
     38-51.
        Holds that in much of Milton's later work, including Paradise Lost, he has
        moved toward a deistic philosophy. Reply by William Haller, ibid., pp. 52-7.
        Rev: SCN, 20, 1962, 31-2.

565 ------. The Unharmonious Vision: Milton as a Baroque Artist. CLS, 3,
     1966, 95-108.
        Holds that "Milton's poetry generally becomes more Baroque as his theology
        becomes less assured, that, in fact, the reciprocal movement is like a teeter-
        totter: as the see of his aesthetic confidence rises, the saw of his religious
        conviction sinks."

566 FRASER, RUSSELL. On Milton's Poetry. YR, 56, 1966, 172-96.
"Milton is the poet of esthetic scientism. His achievement is to attempt the reformation of poetry, that its language may be made to convey the truth with absolute totality and precision."

567 FREEDMAN, MORRIS. A Note on Milton and Dryden as Satirists. N&Q, N.S., 1, 1954, 26-7.
Points out neglected resemblances.

568 ------. Milton and Dryden. Doctoral diss., Columbia Univ., 1953. Abs., DA, 14, 1954, 109. Ann Arbor: UM, 1954. 203pp.

569 FREITAG, WOLFGANG. Milton und seine Zeitgenossen in ihrem Verhaltnis zur Musik. Doctoral diss., Freiburg, 1949. 218pp.

570 FRENCH, J. MILTON. Chips from Milton's Workshop. ELH, 10, 1943, 230-42.
Changes made by Milton in his workbook reveal his method of writing poetry.

571 ------. John Milton's Songs of Experience. SCN, 15, 1957, 6-7.
A speech delivered before the Milton Society at its annual dinner on Dec. 28, 1956. Insists that Milton's life experiences contributed to the texture of Paradise Lost, Paradise Regained, and Samson Agonistes.

572 ------. Milton's Annotated Copy of Gildas. Harvard Studies and Notes in Phil. and Lit., 20, 1938, 75-80.

573 ------. Some Notes on Milton. N&Q, 188, 1945, 52-5.
Discusses the following points: Milton's alleged misconduct in Italy, editions of Salmasius' Responsio, Salmasius' reward for writing his Responsio, the burning of Milton's Defensio abroad, Milton's connection with John Phillips' Responsio of 1652, Milton Taunted with Blindness, and the effect of Milton's Defensio on More.

574 FRENCH, ROBERTS W. St. Giles, Cripplegate. MN, 2, 1968, 48, 53.
Reports on the progress of the reconstruction of St. Giles, Cripplegate, including plans for the future improvement of the area.

575 FRIEDERICH, WERNER P. Dante's Fame Abroad, 1350-1850. Rome: Edizioni di Storia e Letteratura, 1950. 582pp.
Considers similarities between Dante and Milton and surveys the scholarship on Dante's influence on Milton, pp. 201-10.

576 FRYE, ROLAND M. Milton and the Modern Man. QR, 288, 1950, 373-9.
Suggests that we turn to Milton for strength and guidance.

577 ------. The Teachings of Classical Puritanism on Conjugal Love. Studies in the Renaissance (Ren. Soc. of America) , 2, 1955, 148-59.
Explores one area of misconception and uncertainty about Puritanism, namely the teachings of classical Puritanism on physical love in marriage.

578 GABRIELI, VITTORIO. Milton agonista. Cultura, 5, 1967, 316-34.

579 GÄCKLE, OSKAR. Die unsichtbare Welt in Miltons Denken und ihre Wirkung auf seinen Freiheitsbegriff. Doctoral diss., Heidelberg, 1944. 208pp.

580   GAINES, ERVIN J. Merchant and Poet: a Study of Seventeenth Century
         Influences. Doctoral diss., Columbia Univ., 1953. Abs., DA, 14, 1954, 110.
         Considers Milton's anti-Utopian ideas.

581   GASTER, THEODOR. Milton and the Rabbinical Bible. TLS, May 9,
         1935, p. 301.

582   GERRIETTS, JOHN S. A Study of the Imaginal Qualities of Poetry,
         Based on Descriptive Passages of Milton and Coleridge. Doctoral diss.,
         Loyola Univ. (Chicago), 1954.

583   GIBBS, PAUL T. Milton's Use of the Law of Nature. Doctoral diss., Univ.
         of Washington, 1938. Abs., Univ. of Washington Abstracts of Theses,
         3, 1938, 319-21.

584   GILBERT, ALLAN H. Milton's Defense of Bawdry. SAMLA Studies in
         Milton. Ed. by J. Max Patrick (Gainesville: Univ. of Florida Press,
         1953), pp. 54-71.
         Draws passages from many of Milton's works to illustrate the poet's attitude
         toward obscenity.

585   ------. Some Critical Opinions on Milton. SP, 33, 1936, 523-33.
         Discusses recent Milton scholarship.

586   GOLDBERG, GERALD J. AND NANCY M., eds. The Modern Critical
         Spectrum. Englewood Cliffs, N.J.: Prentice-Hall, 1962. xiv, 344pp.
         Contains three articles on Milton by T. S. Eliot and A. S. P. Woodhouse, all
         of which are listed in appropriate sections.

587   GOODE, JAMES. Milton and Longinus. TLS, Aug. 21, 1930, p. 668.
         Cites passages from the Prolusions to indicate Milton's knowledge of
         Longinus.

588   GOTO, KAZUO. L. P. Smith: Milton and his Modern Critics, and the
         Tendency of Recent Criticism. Kobe Univ. Modern Age, 6, 1954.

589   ------. Milton and the Future of English Poetry. Kobe Univ. Modern
         Age, 10-12, 1955.

590   ------. Milton Today. Kobe Univ. Kenkyu, 5, 1954.

591   GRABILL, PAUL EZIDIUS. Milton's Text, Study, and Use of Chaucer.
         Master's thesis, Univ. of Illinois, 1951.

592   GRACE, WILLIAM. Ideas in Milton. Notre Dame and London: Univ.
         of Notre Dame Press, 1968. viii, 295pp.
         Aims "to delineate the main complexes of ideas to be looked for in the
         reading of Milton, as an aid, especially for the undergraduate student,
         toward reclarifying and rethinking the question that Milton, as an artist,
         perennially raises."
         Rev: MN, 2, 1968, 67-8.

593   GRAVES, ROBERT. The Ghost of Milton. The Common Asphodel: Col-
         lected Essays on Poetry, 1922-1949 (London: Hamish Hamilton, 1949),
         pp. 315-25.
         "I have included 'The Ghost of Milton' as a minority report justifying my

dismay at the recent revival of Milton-worship. To me, Milton has always been a monster and a renegade. . . ."

594 GRAY, F. CAMPBELL. Milton's Counterpoint: Classicism and Romanticism in the Poetry of John Milton. SR, 43, 1935, 134-45.
Points out that in Milton's verse there is a love of beauty but that there is a love of form and order which is prerequisite to it. "But the romanticist, the individualist, crops out continually in the thought contained within these forms."

595 GREAVES, MARGARET. The Blazon of Honour: A Study in Renaissance Magnanimity. London: Methuen, 1964; New York: Barnes & Noble, 1964. 140pp.
Chapter 6, pp. 94-111, is a discussion of magnanimity in Milton's work, especially in Paradise Lost.

596 GREBANIER, BERNARD. A Simplified Approach to Milton. Great Neck, New York: Barron's Educational Series, Inc., 1964. 57pp.
Contains summaries and analyses of the major poems, selected minor poems, and Areopagitica. A student guide.

597 GREENE, D. J. Sooth in Keats, Milton, Shakespeare, and Dr. Johnson. MLN, 65, 1950, 514-17.
See also A. C. Luttrell, N&Q, 196, 1951, 405-7, and Greene again in N&Q, 197, 1952, 204-5. On the meaning of sooth.

598 GREGG, ANN LIVINGSTON. Milton's Attitude Toward Medieval England. Master's thesis, The American Univ., 1963. Abs., Master's abstracts, 3, No. 1, 1965, 17.

599 GRIERSON, SIR HERBERT J. C. Criticism and Creation: Essays and Addresses. London: Chatto and Windus, 1949.
Contains two articles on Milton: The Metaphysics of Donne and Milton, pp. 35-48; Milton and Political Liberty, pp. 71-94.
Rev: TLS, Feb. 17, 1950, p. 106; Janet Smith, NSN, Feb. 18, 1950, pp. 196, 198; M. H. M. MacKinnon, Canadian Forum, 30, 1950, 214.

600 ------. John Milton: l'homme et le poéte. RA-A, 6, 1929, 19-36, 97-114.

601 ------. John Milton: The Man and the Poet. Cross Currents in English Literature of the Seventeenth Century, or, the World, the Flesh, and the Spirit, Their Action and Relations. Being the Messenger Lectures on the Evolution of Civilization, Cornell University, 1926-27 (London: Chatto and Windus, 1929), pp. 232-73. Reprinted, Baltimore: Peregrine Books, 1966. 320pp.
See also passim.
Rev: TLS, Jan. 16, 1930, p. 41; George Saintsbury, Bookman, 77, 1930, 330; Mario Praz, ES, 12, 1930, 117-9; Marjorie Nicolson, MLN, 46, 1931, 205-6; D. A. Roberts, SRL, 8, 1931, 218.

602 ------. Milton and Liberty. MLR, 39, 1944, 97-107.
On Milton's Arianism and his concept of civil and religious liberty.

603 ------. Milton and Wordsworth: Poets and Prophets. A Study of Their Reactions to Political Events. Cambridge: Cambridge Univ. Press;

New York: Macmillan, 1937. x, 185pp. Reprinted, 1950, 1956, 1960, 1963.

Traces Milton's view of prophetic poetry and of his own prophetic mission from youth to the publication of Samson Agonistes. Chapter 7: Wordsworth and the French Revolution, a Contrast with Milton.

Rev: TLS, Mar. 6, 1937, p. 167; N&Q, 172, 1937, 252; E[dwin] G. G[reen-law], CR, 151, 1937, 154-7; J. Kooistra, ES, 19, 1937, 122-5; B. de Selincourt, Obs, Mar. 7, 1937; E. Muir, Merc, 35, 1937, 83-4; E. Sackville-West, NSN, June 5, 1937, p. 936; Mario Praz, Crit, 17, 1937, 154-7; E[dwin] G. G[reen-law], CW, 145, 1937, 752-3; P. Hutchinson, NYTBR, June 20, 1937, p. 6; I[rvin] E[dwin], Jour. of Philosophy, 34, 1937, 639-40; C. A. Hawley, Unity, 120, 1937, 100; Mark Van Doren, Nat., 145, 1937, 22-3; K. Burke, Poetry, 51, Oct., 1937, 37-42; QR, 268, 1937, 368; N. C. Smith, English, 1, 1937, 435; J. Veldkamp, Neophil, 23, 1937, 63-5; Emile Legouis, EA, 1, 1937, 330-1; E. C. Batho, MLR, 33, 1938, 70-1; Denis Saurat, RES, 14, 1938, 225-8; reply by Grierson, ibid., 458-60; F. R. Leavis, Scr, 7, 1938, 104-14; H. F. B.-S., Oxf. Mag., Mar. 10, 1938, pp. 526-7; E. M. W. Tillyard, MLN, 53, 1938, 381-3; W[illiam] H[aller], ELH, 5, 1938, 24; George Williamson, MP, 36, 1938, 77-9; W. Mann, Ang. Bbl., 50, 1939, 206-9; S. G. Brown, SR, 49, 1941, 107-15.

604 GRIERSON, SIR HERBERT J. C., and J. C. SMITH. Milton. A Critical History of English Poetry (London: Chatto and Windus, 1944; New York: Oxford Univ. Press, 1946), pp. 172-86.

Rev: Gwyn Jones, LL, 43, 1944, 170, 172, 174; TLS, Dec. 2, 1944, pp. 582-3; Raymond Mortimer, NSN, Nov. 11, 1944, pp. 324-5; Sheila Shannon, Spect, Nov. 24, 1944, pp. 484, 486; B. I. Evans, MGW, Feb. 23, 1945, p. 107; Herman Peschmann, English, 5, 1945, 192; Babette Deutsch, NYHTBR, Dec. 1, 1946, p. 46; Leonard Bacon, SRL, Dec. 7, 1946, p. 70; F. A. Pottle, YR, 36, 1947, 731-4; D. C. A[llen], MLN, 62, 1947, 360; Earl Daniels, CE, 8, 1947, 443-4.

605 GUIDI, AUGUSTO. La Figure di Cristo nel poema di Milton. Humanitas, 1, 1946, 403-6.

From the Nativity Ode to Samson Agonistes.

606 ------. John Milton. Brescia: Morcelleana, 1940. 195pp.

Topics: Poesie giovanili, Il Paradiso Perduto, Le ultime opere.

607 GULLETTE, GEORGE A. Methodology in Milton's Source Studies. Doctoral diss., Univ. of Michigan, 1945. Abs., DA, 6, No. 2, 1945, 53-5. 279pp.

608 ------. Some Inadequacies of Method in the Study of Milton's Sources. Papers of the Michigan Academy, 32, 1948 for 1946, 447-56.

Reply by Arnold Williams, ibid., p. 707.

609 HALL, VERNON, JR. Milton. A Short History of Literary Criticism (New York: New York Univ. Press, 1963), pp. 52-5.

On Milton's theory of poetry.

610 HALLECK, REUBEN P. John Milton. The Story of English Literature. Revised Edition (New York: American Book Co., 1937), pp. 238-52.

611 HALLER, WILLIAM. The Future of Milton Studies. SCN, 15, 1957, 4-6.

A speech delivered before the Milton Society at its annual dinner on Dec. 28, 1956.

612 ------. Hail Wedded Love. ELH, 13, 1946, 79-97. Reprinted in Milton: Modern Judgements, ed. by Alan Rudrum (London: MacMillan, 1968), pp. 296-312.
The background of Milton's ideas concerning marriage and divorce.

613 ------. Milton and the Protestant Ethic. JBS, No. 1, 1961, 52-7.
A reply to Joseph Frank's assertion of Milton's deism, ibid., pp. 38-51.

614 ------. Poet of the Devil's Party, and God's. SRL, 32, Nov. 19, 1949, p. 22.
Review article of Hanford's John Milton, Englishman (1949).

615 ------. What Needs My Shakespeare? SQ, 3, 1952, 3-16.
From a speech given at the Folger Library in celebration of Shakespeare's birthday, April 23, 1951. The author notes a close affinity between the basic themes of Milton and Shakespeare.

616 HAMPSTEN, RICHARD FRANKLIN. Studies in Milton's Blank Verse. Doctoral diss., Univ. of Washington, 1963. Abs., DA, 25, 1964, 1210.

617 HANFORD, JAMES HOLLY. John Milton, Poet and Humanist: Essays by James Holly Hanford. Foreword by John S. Diekhoff. Cleveland: Western Reserve Univ. Press, 1966. 286pp.
A collection of eight essays, each previously published and each noted in this bibliography under its appropriate classification.

618 ------. Milton and the Art of War. John Milton, Poet and Humanist (Cleveland: Western Reserve Univ. Press, 1966), pp. 185-223.
A reprint of Stevens' No. 1331, published in 1921. "Milton read widely in military literature, both ancient and modern. A careful analysis of his use of military material in his writings. It is unlikely that he served in the army" (Stevens' annotation).

619 ------. Milton and the Return to Humanism. John Milton, Poet and Humanist (Cleveland: Western Reserve Univ. Press, 1966), pp. 161-84.
A reprint of Stevens' No. 2444, published in 1919. An important study in the history of Milton criticism. Interprets Milton as a Christian humanist and man of the Renaissance, rather than as a Puritan.

620 ------. A Milton Handbook. New York: Appleton-Century-Crofts, 1926. x, 304pp. Revised Edition, 1933. Third Edition, 1939. Fourth Edition, 1946. Reprinted, 1954.
Chapters: Materials for Milton's Biography, The Prose Works, The Minor Poems, Paradise Lost, Paradise Regained and Samson Agonistes, Milton's Style and Versification, Milton's Fame and Influence. Appendices: Milton and the Universities, Milton's "Biographia Literaria," The Milton Portraits, Milton's Private Library, Milton and His Printers, Milton in Italy. There is a bibliography, pp. 421-48, Fourth Edition.
Rev: L. C. Martin, YWES, 14, 1933, 169; Commonweal, 17, 1933, 588; W. Fischer, Ang. Bbl., 46, 1935, 243-4; William R. Parker, MLN, 56, 1941, 392-3; L. C. Martin, YWES, 27, 1946, 169.

621 ------. Milton in Current Criticism. EJ, 28, 1939, 342-8.
Discusses the criticism of T. S. Eliot, H. J. C. Grierson, E. M. W. Tillyard, W. Haller.

622 ------. The Temptation Motive in Milton. John Milton, Poet and Humanist (Cleveland: Western Reserve Univ. Press, 1966), pp. 244-63.

A reprint of Stevens' No. 2436, published in 1918. "A careful study of the development of Milton's moral principles. The keen sense of enjoyment evident in his early poems gave way to the Puritan concept that life is a moral conflict" (Stevens' annotation).

623 ------. That Shepherd Who First Taught the Chosen Seed: A Note on Milton's Mosaic Inspiration. UTQ, 8, 1939, 403-19.
On Milton's belief in his divine inspiration.

624 HARASHIMA, YOSHINORI. Milton as a Music Lover. Oberon, 14, 1936.

625 ------. Milton's Taste and Doctrine of Music. SEL (Japan), 18, 1938, 531-43.
Milton and music, and Milton's views on the celestial harmony.

626 HARBESON, GERALDINE M. Nature in the Poetry of Milton and Spenser. Master's thesis, Florida State College for Women, 1944.

627 HARDELAND, GERTRUD. Miltons Anschauungen von Staat, Kirche, Toleranz. Doctoral diss., Göttingen, 1934. Studien zur englischen Philologie, 81. Halle: Niemeyer, 1934. 175pp.
Rev: H. Scherpbier, ES, 16, 1934, 224-6; W. F. Schirmer, Dt. Litzt, 55, 1934, 2180-2; A. B[randl], Archiv, 166, 1934, 139; H. F. Fletcher, JEGP, 34, 1935, 120-1; H. O. Wilde, Ang. Bbl., 46, 1935, 240; L. C. Martin, YWES, 238-9; Denis Saurat, MLN, 51, 1936, 263-4; W. Schmidt, LGRP, 57, 1936, 35-6; A. Koszul, RC, 69, 1936, 211-2.

628 HARDING, DAVIS P. Milton and Ovid: A Study of the Influence of Ovid and his Renaissance Editors and Commentators on Milton's Poetry. Doctoral diss., Univ. of Illinois, 1943. Published as Milton and the Renaissance Ovid. Univ. of Illinois Studies in Language and Literature, 30, No. 4. Urbana: Univ. of Illinois Press, 1946. 105pp.
Throws new light on Milton's debt to Ovid by examining the editions which Milton might have used. Explains Milton's successive changes in his attitude toward Ovid.
Rev: L. C. Martin, YWES, 169-70; Michael Krouse, MLN, 62, 1947, 135-8; Douglas Bush, CP, 62, 1947, 132-3; A. M. Clark, CR, 61, 1948, 128-9; A. N. Jeffares, ES, 27, 1948, 182-5; M. Y. Hughes, MLQ, 10, 1949, 113-5.

629 HARDISON, O. B., JR. The Enduring Monument: A Study of the Idea of Praise in Renaissance Literary Theory and Practice. Chapel Hill: Univ. of North Carolina Press, 1962. xvi, 240pp.
Considers Milton an exponent of the theory of praise. On the genre of Paradise Lost, pp. 88-92. Also, passim.

630 HARDY, J. E. Critical Pretense. SR, 62, 1954, 509-19.
A review article of Arnold Stein's Answerable Style (1953). "...we begin to get, in this book, a Milton criticism to match the new Milton influence."

631 HARKNESS, G. Eschatology in the Great Poets. Religion in Life, 22, 1952, 85-99.
Milton's views discussed, pp. 94-6.

632 HARRINGTON, DAVID V. John Milton, Education, and the Modern Church College. Cresset, 29, 1966.

Feels that all of Milton's works have some bearing on education. Deals especially with Raphael's and Michael's instruction in Paradise Lost.

633 HARRIS, VICTOR. All Coherence Gone. Chicago: Univ. of Chicago Press, 1949.
Concerned with the controversy on the decay of nature. Milton's views discussed, pp. 160-3.

634 HARRISON, T. P. They Tell of Birds: Chaucer, Spenser, Milton, Drayton. Austin: Univ. of Texas Press, 1956. xviii, 159pp.
Milton, pp. 85-108. Concludes that "for Milton the bird world was largely useful in providing symbols of despicable human beings."

635 HAUG, RALPH A. Milton and Archbishop Ussher. N&Q, 185, 1943, 66-7.
Evidence shows that Ussher was unaware of the tracts Milton wrote against him. Replies by E. H. Visiak, p. 146, and T. O. M[abbott], pp. 293-4.

636 HAVILAND, THOMAS P. John Milton—Religious Liberal. Christian Register, 118, 1939, 261-3.

637 HAYS, H. R. The Dangerous Sex: The Myth of Feminine Evil. New York: G. P. Putnam's Sons, 1964.
Discusses Milton and female sexuality, pp. 170ff.

638 HAZLITT, WILLIAM. On Shakespeare and Milton. The Proper Study: Essays on Western Classics. Ed. by Quentin Anderson and Joseph A. Mazzeo (New York: St. Martin's Press, 1962), pp. 383-96.
Hazlitt's article listed in Stevens, No. 1876, first published in 1818-19.

639 HEINRICH, HELLMUT. John Miltons kirchenpolitik, puritanische ideen zum problem staat und kirche. Berlin: Junker and Dünnhaupt, 1942. 132pp.

640 HENRY, NATHANIEL H. Milton and Hobbes: Mortalism and the Intermediate State. SP, 48, 1951, 234-49.
Milton's mortalism in the Socinian tradition.

641 ------. Milton's Puritanism: A Study of the Theological Implications of his Thought. Doctoral diss., Univ. of North Carolina, 1942. Abs., Univ. of North Carolina Record, Research in Progress, No. 383, 1942, pp. 74-5.

642 HESSE, ERNST. John Miltons mystisch-theistisches Weltbild. Mit ein anh.: Miltons Gedanken über Jugenderziehung. Doctoral diss., Leipzig, 1934. Dresden: Gittel, 1934. 64pp.
Summarizes the sources and the nature of Milton's ideas.
Rev: Lit. Zentrablatt, 85, 1934, 1135.

643 HESSELBERG, ARTHUR K. A Comparative Study of the Theories of Ludovicus Molina, S. J., and John Milton. Doctoral diss., Catholic Univ., 1952. Abs., Catholic Univ. Studies in Politics, Government, and International Law, Abstract Series, 2. Washington: Catholic Univ. Press, 1952. 26pp.

644 HIBBITTS, JOHN B. Milton's Heresy. Master's thesis, Dalhousie Univ., 1946. 204pp.

645 HIGHET, GILBERT. The Classical Tradition. Greek and Roman Influences on Western Literature. New York: Oxford Univ. Press; Oxford: Clarendon Press, 1949. xxxviii, 763pp. Reprinted, 1957.
Almost all of Milton's works discussed, passim, in the light of the classical background.
Rev: H. W. Garrod, Spect, Sept. 30, 1949, pp. 424, 426; G. F. Whicher, NYHTBR, Dec. 18, 1949, p. 7; TLS, Jan. 6, 1950, p. 12; F. M. Cambellack, CL, 2, 1950, 376-9; C. A. Robinson, Jr., SRL, Mar. 4, 1950, p. 21.

646 HILL, CHRISTOPHER. The Politics of John Milton. Listener, 70, September 12, 1963, 383-5.
An appreciative essay. Notes that Milton continued to deal with political problems in the poetry written after the Restoration.

647 HINDLEY, DOUGLAS. Milton and Christian Humanism. Doctoral diss., Stanford Univ., 1950. Abs., Abstracts of Dissertations, Stanford Univ., 25, 1950, 130-3.

648 HIRSCH, FRANZ. Die Rolle der klassischen Mythologie in der geistigen Entwicklung Miltons. Doctoral diss., Wien, 1944. 107pp.

649 HOOPES, ROBERT. Right Reason in the English Renaissance. Cambridge: Harvard Univ. Press; Oxford: Oxford Univ. Press, 1962. viii, 248pp.
Chapter 10: Milton "Prime Wisdom," pp. 186-200. "Milton stands as the last great literary voice of the concept of right reason, indeed of rational and ethical Christianity itself. . . ."

650 HOVEY, R. BENNETT. Milton's Attitude Toward Science. Isis, 35, 1944, 32.

651 HOWARTH, HERBERT. Eliot and Milton: The American Aspect. UTQ, 30, 1961, 150-62.
On T. S. Eliot's attitudes toward Milton.

652 HOWARTH, R. G. Milton and Camoens. Southerly (Sidney, Australia), 11, 1950, 57-8.
Believes that Milton could have read Camoens in the original.

653 HUGHES, MERRITT Y. Lydian Airs. Ten Perspectives on Milton (New Haven and London: Yale Univ. Press, 1965), pp. 1-11.
On Milton and music.

654 ------. A Meditation on Literary Blasphemy. JAAC, 14, 1955, 106-15.
Attacks on Shakespeare and Milton.

655 ------. Milton and the Sense of Glory. PQ, 28, 1949, 107-24. Reprinted in Ten Perspectives on Milton (New Haven and London: Yale Univ. Press, 1965), pp. 12-34.
On the ethical, theological, political, and sectarian implications of Milton's sense of glory.

656 ------. The Seventeenth Century in Contemporary Literary Scholarship: A Critical Review. Ed. by Lewis Leary (New York: Appleton-Century-Crofts, 1958), pp. 67-82.
Survey of Milton studies, pp. 74-82.

Rev: D. S. Murphy, QQ, 73, 1966, 295-6; TLS, Mar. 31, 1966, 264; F. T. Prince, RES, 18, 1967, 332-4; Wayne Shumaker, ELN, 4, 1967, 214-6.

657 ------. Ten Perspectives on Milton. With a Foreword by Douglas Bush. New Haven and London: Yale Univ. Press, 1965. xv, 291pp.
The Foreword is an appreciative essay on Professor Hughes. Nine of the ten essays are reprints, and each is listed in this bibliography under its appropriate classification.
Rev: F. T. Prince, RES, 18, 1967, 332-4; N. W. Bawcutt, N&Q, 212, 1967, 114-6; Robert F. Clayton, Library Journal, 90, 2555-6.

658 HUNT, E. L. Reading for Honors and Common Sense. School and Society, 42, 1935, 726-32.
Milton's writings on education from the standpoint of practical citizenship.

659 HUNTER, WILLIAM B., JR. Milton and Thrice Great Hermes. JEGP, 45, 1946, 327-36.
On Milton's indebtedness to the Hermetic writings for ideas about the soul and the cosmos.

660 ------. A Milton Evening. Milton Society of America, 1954.
Tributes to Douglas Bush and C. S. Lewis, and brief quotations from their work; biographical statements.

661 ------. Milton on the Incarnation: Some More Heresies. JHI, 21, 1960, 349-69.
"It is my purpose here to explore Milton's conception of the union of God and man which we call the Incarnation, to indicate something of the philosophical and religious background of this conception, and to show how the underlying theories permeate other areas of his thought."

662 ------. Milton on the Nature of Man; a Study in Late Renaissance Psychology. Doctoral diss., Vanderbilt Univ., 1946. Abs., Bulletin of Vanderbilt Univ., 47, No. 11, 1947, 13-4. Summary, Nashville: Joint Univ. Libraries, 1946. 33pp.

663 ------. Milton's Power of Matter. JHI, 13, 1952, 551-62.
Illustrates the meaning of the term, Power of Matter, and suggests its implications regarding Milton's conception of the soul.

664 ------. New Words in Milton's English Poems. Essays in Honor of W. C. Curry (Nashville: Vanderbilt Univ. Press, 1954), pp. 241-59.
Contrary to accepted opinion, Milton "has enriched our vocabulary in a number of ways."

665 HUNTLEY, JOHN FARINGDON. The Educational, Theological, and Literary Principles of Milton's Poetic Art. Doctoral diss., Univ. of Chicago, 1961.

666 IGLESIAS, ANTONIO. An Open Letter to Milton—Formidable Pamphleteer. SRL, Aug. 23, 1952, pp. 20-1, 33-4.
Relates Milton's efforts to achieve liberty to the recent struggle of liberals against the "professed defenders of personal freedom."

667 IZZO, CARLO. Storia della Letteratura Inglese dalle Origini alla Restaurazione. Milano: Nuova Accademia Editrice, 1961. 622pp.
Chapter 7: John Milton, pp. 517-61.

668 JARRETT-KERR, MARTIN. Milton, Poet and Paraphrast. EIC, 10, 1960, 373-89.
"...I wish to suggest that Milton, that supreme craftsman, injured himself, from Paradise Lost onwards, first by working too hard, and second by revering too much."

669 JEFFREY, LLOYD N. Virgil and Milton. Class. Outlook, 31, 1954, 69-70.

670 JONAS, LEAH. John Milton. Divine Science: The Aesthetic of Some Representative Seventeenth-Century English Poets. Columbia Univ. Studies in English and Comparative Literature, 151 (New York: Columbia Univ. Press, 1940), pp. 166-200.
On Milton and his theory of poetry and how he disciplined himself to become a great poet.

671 KATO, SADA. Milton and Temptation. Nanzan Univ. Academia, 21, 1958.

672 KATO, TAKEO. Milton's Unitarian Religious Thought. Osaka Univ. Sozo, 1951.

673 KEENE, THELMA B. Biographers and Critics on Milton's Opinions of Woman. Master's thesis, Duke Univ., 1940.

674 KELLEY, MAURICE. "J" and "I" in Milton's Script. MLR, 44, 1949, 545-7.
On the principle of banishing "J" or the consonantal "I" from the text of the Latin poems.

675 ------. Milton and Miracles. MLN, 53, 1938, 170-2.
Holds that Milton accepts miracles.

676 ------. Milton's Arianism Again Considered. HTR, 54, 1961, 195-205.
Argues against denials of Milton's Arianism.

677 KELLEY, MAURICE, and SAMUEL D. ATKINS. Milton's Annotations of Aratus. PMLA, 70, 1955, 1090-1106.
An index to Milton's intellectual development.

678 KELLY, F. JOSEPH. Milton and Dante: A Few Points of Contrast. CW, 132, 1930, 170-3.

679 KENRICK, EDWARD F. The Origin and Development of Milton's Thought on the Trinity: First Period, 1608-1625. Doctoral Diss., Fordham Univ., 1951. Abs., Fordham Univ. Diss., 18, 1952, 60-3.

680 KERMODE, FRANK, ed. The Living Milton: Essays by Various Hands. London: Routledge and Kegan Paul, 1960, paperback, 1963; New York: Macmillan, 1961. 180pp.
Contains essays by John Wain, J. B. Broadbent, G. S. Fraser, David Daiches, Donald Davie, Frank Kermode, W. W. Robson, F. W. Bateson, Michael Hamburger, and Berard Bergonzi, each of which is listed in its appropriate section.
Rev: William Empson, MGW, Sept. 22, 1960, p. 10; Agnes M. C. Latham, YWES, 40, 1960, 167-8; G. D. Klingopulus, Spect, No. 6907, 1960, 740-1; TLS, Dec. 30, 1960, p. 848; Kathleen Nott, Obs, Nov. 20, 1960, p. 29;

Christopher Ricks, TC, 169, 1961, 314-5; B. R. McElderry, Jr., Pers, 43, 1962, 273; F. T. Prince, RES, 13, 1962, 78-9.

681 KING, ROY. Psyche's Tasks—Milton's Sense of Self. Studies in Six Seventeenth Century Writers (Athens: Ohio Univ. Press, 1966), pp. 193-218.
Suggests that modern interpretations of the Cupid-Psyche myth parallel important motifs in Milton's poetry and are suggestive of the way he organized his world.

682 KIRKLAND, E. C. A Collection and Explanation of the Folklore in Milton's English Poems. Doctoral diss., Northwestern Univ., 1934. Abs., Northwestern Univ., Summaries of Ph.D. Dissertations, 2, 1934, 5-11.

683 KNIGHT, G. WILSON. Chariot of Wrath: the Message of John Milton to Democracy at War. London: Faber and Faber, 1942. 194pp.
Relates passages in the major poems and in Milton's other works to the struggle of the democratic nations against totalitarianism.
Rev: L. C. Martin, YWES, 163-4; N&Q, 182, 1942, 336; TLS, May 30, 1942, p. 271; B. S., MGW, July 31, 1942, p. 65; S. Addleshaw, CQR, 134, 1942, 121-3; E. E. Kellett, NSN, Aug. 29, 1942, p. 146; Geoffrey Tillotson, English, 4, 1943, 130-1; F. O. Mathiessen, NR, 108, 1943, 674-5.

684 ------. The Frozen Labyrinth: An Essay on Milton. The Burning Oracle: Studies in the Poetry of Action (London: Milford; Oxford: Oxford Univ. Press, 1939), pp. 59-113.
Rev: TLS, Sept. 2, 1939, pp. 514, 516; H. I'A Fausett, MGW, Sept. 8, 1939, p. 194; A. C., SRL, Sept. 16, 1939, p. 20; G. G. Sedgwick, UTQ, 9, 1940, 246-8; Wilfrid Gibson, English, 3, 1940, 35-6; B. E. C. Davis, MLR, 35, 1940, 268-9; K. Tillotson, RES, 17, 1941, 245-6; G. H. C., QQ, 48, 1941, 88-90.

685 ------. Milton. The Golden Labyrinth: A Study of British Drama (London: Phoenix House, 1962), pp. 124-9.
Comus, Paradise Lost, Paradise Regained, and Samson Agonistes considered in the light of the church-state controversy of the seventeenth century.

686 KOEHLER, GEORGE STANLEY. Milton and the Roman Elegists. Doctoral diss., Princeton Univ., 1942. Ann Arbor: UM, 1952. 208pp.

687 Idea and Image. TLS, Sept. 5, 1958, p. 497.
Editorial approval of Rosemond Tuve's remarks on Milton's images and themes (The Listener, Aug. 28, 1958). Reply by F. R. Leavis, TLS, Sept. 19, 1958, p. 529; and a lengthy answer to it, TLS, Sept. 26, p. 545; also letter by William Empson, TLS, Oct. 3, p. 561. Leavis states that the academic world has never faced the case against Milton. Empson agrees with Leavis and offers animadversions on Milton's God.

688 KRANIDAS, THOMAS. Milton and the Rhetoric of Zeal. TSLL, 6, 1965, 423-32.
Examines the relationship of Puritan "rhetoric of zeal" to "Anglican via media and its claims for moderation."

689 ------. Milton's Concept of Decorum. Doctoral diss., Univ. of Washington, 1962. Abs., AD, 23, 1963, 4360. Published as The Fierce Equation: A Study of Milton's Decorum. The Hague: Mouton, 1965. 165pp.
The first chapter deals with the background of decorum. The second is an

attempt to deduce Milton's concept of decorum from his prose writings, and the third is a study of decorum in Paradise Lost.

Rev: Edgar Mertner, Anglia, July, 1968, 225-9; W. H. Ussery, SCN, 25, 1967, 1-2; Anne Davidson Ferry, MLQ, 28, 1967, 494-6.

690 KURTH, BURTON O. Milton and the English Traditions of Biblical Heroic Narrative. Doctoral diss., Univ. of California (Berkeley), 1955.
See also item No. 1495.

691 LANGDON, IDA. Milton's Theory of Poetry and Fine Art: An Essay with a Collection of Illustrative Passages from His Works. New York: Russell and Russell, 1965. x, 342pp.

A reprint of Stevens' No. 2536, published in 1924. "A well-arranged gathering of passages to illustrate the author's conclusions regarding the varied interests of Milton in the records of critical theory as well as in current experiences of his day" (Stevens' annotation).

692 LARSON, MARTIN A. Milton and Puritanism—Clarified. PQ, 9, 1930, 308-11.

Milton stood alone, a heretic. Reply by E. N. S. Thompson, pp. 311-2.

693 LAWRENCE, W. B. Milton and the Aeroplane. N&Q, 196, 1951, 282.

Query, "Is there anywhere in Milton, akin to that of the poet Gray, a prophesy of the coming of the aeroplane?" Reply by Howard Parsons, N&Q, 196, 1951, 372, who cites Paradise Lost, 6, 771, and concludes that Milton "conceived the coming of the aeroplane."

694 LAWRY, JON S. The Shadow of Heaven: Matter and Stance in Milton's Poetry. Ithaca: Cornell Univ. Press, 1968. xv, 416pp.

An interpretation of much of Milton's poetry. "Matter" of the title refers to Milton's subjects, while "stance" refers to the "devices of participation within the subject by author and audience." Lawry shows that most of the matter appears in the early poetry and reappears in "the larger field of the later works," with some alterations in subject and form.

Rev: MN, 2, 1968, 66-7.

695 LEAVIS, F. R. The Common Pursuit. London: Chatto and Windus, 1952. Reprinted, Baltimore: Peregrine Books, 1963.

Contains two reprints of articles on Milton: Mr. Eliot and Milton, pp. 9-32; In Defense of Milton, pp. 33-43. The first article, occasioned by Eliot's 1947 recantation, originally appeared in SR, 57, 1949, 1-30, and contains a re-statement of the author's case against Milton's style. The second article first appeared in Scr, 7, 1938, 104-14.

696 ------. Milton's Verse. Scr, 2, 1933, 123-36. Reprinted in Revaluation: Tradition and Development in English Poetry (London: Chatto and Windus, 1936), pp. 42-67; and in Milton's Epic Poetry: Essays on Paradise Lost and Paradise Regained, ed. by C. A. Patrides (Harmondsworth: Penguin Books, 1967), pp. 15-32.

"Milton's dislodgement, in the past decade, after his two centuries of predominance, was effected with remarkably little fuss."

697 Leavis Works Not on Pyre. The Times, June 14, 1962, p. 7f.

Cambridge students defer to F. R. Leavis' retirement but proceed to burn T. S. Eliot's poems.

698 LE COMTE, EDWARD S. Milton as Satirist and Wit. Th'Upright

Heart and Pure. Ed. by Amadeus P. Fiore, O. F. M. (Pittsburgh and Louvain: Duquesne Univ. Press, 1967), pp. 45-59.
Gives numerous examples of Milton's satire and wit and points out the need for a more thorough study of the subject.

699 ------. A Milton Dictionary. London: Peter Owen, 1961; New York: Philosophical Library, 1961. 358pp.
Contains three classes of entries: hard words in Milton's verse and prose, allusions, characters, friends, opponents, vocabulary; a descriptive entry for each of Milton's works; and entries concerning his father and mother, his wives, his nephews, his biographers and editors, and his leading critics. References are located by line number for the poems and by page number of the Columbia Edition.
Rev: Agnes M. C. Latham, YWES, 166; J. Max Patrick, SCN, 19, 1961, 34; Hamilton T. Tyler, JAAC, 21, 1962, 331-2; Isabel G. MacCaffrey, RN, 15, 1962, 46-7.

700 ------. Yet Once More: Verbal and Psychological Pattern in Milton. New York: Liberal Arts Press, 1954. ix, 192pp.
A study of Milton's borrowing from himself.
Rev: E. W. Robbins, MLN, 70, 1955, 141-3; Robert M. Adams, MP, 52, 1955, 207-11; Kester Svendsen, BA, 30, 1956, 222-3; TLS, Jan. 20, 1956, p. 38; reply by Le Comte, ibid., Mar. 9, 1956, p. 149.

701 LEGOUIS, EMILE. Milton. A History of English Literature. By Emile Legouis and Louis Cazamian. Trans. by W. D. MacInnes (London: Macmillan, 1927), pp. 589-612. Revised editions, 1933, 1957.
Rev: TLS, Aug. 3, 1933, p. 526; B. de Selincourt, Obs, July 23, 1933; L. Abercrombie, Spect, 151, 1933, 130.

702 ------. Milton. A Short History of English Literature. Trans. by V. F. Boyson and J. Coulson (Oxford: Clarendon Press, 1934), pp. 165-70.

703 LEGOUIS, PIERRE. Les Amours de Dieu chez Collins et Milton. RA-A, 8, 1930, 136-8.

704 LEVER, KATHERINE. Milton and Homer, the Monarch of the Mount. BuR, 12, No. 2, 1964, 57-64.
Says that Milton cannot be considered superior to Homer since Milton "has not ever engaged Homer on his own ground."

705 LEVINSON, RONALD B. Milton and Plato. MLN, 46, 1931, 85-91.
Provides some footnotes and marginalia to Agar's Milton and Plato.

706 LEWIS, C. S. The Discarded Image. An Introduction to Medieval and Renaissance Literature. Cambridge: Cambridge Univ. Press, 1964. 232pp.
An account of the Medieval Model. Relates Milton, passim

707 ------. Variation in Shakespeare and Others. Rehabilitations and Other Essays (Toronto: Macmillan, 1936), pp. 159-80.
Discusses the differences between Shakespeare's and Milton's uses of variation.

708 LIEVSAY, JOHN LEON. Milton Among the Nightingales. RenP, 1958-60, pp. 36-45.
Feels that Milton came to consider the nightingale as a bird peculiarly his own and as symbolic of his own poetic voice.

709 LILJEGREN, S. B. Fourteen Studies in Milton. New York: Haskell
      House, 1967. xlii, 160pp.
        A reprint of Stevens' No. 2437, published in 1919 as Studies in Milton. Con-
        tains a lengthy introduction, three disparaging chapters on Milton's Italian
        journey, and eleven chapters on Milton and the Pamela prayer. "Calls
        Milton a Renaissance type—egotistic, unscrupulous, Stoic (like Raleigh and
        Marlowe). Attempts to demonstrate that Milton could not have visited
        Galileo; that he and the printer Dugard interpolated the Pamela prayer from
        Arcadia in Eikonbasilike. Obviously wrong in saying English criticism has
        been governed by Puritan tradition in judging Milton" (Stevens' annota-
        tion).

710 ------. Some Notes on Milton Criticism. UEIES, 16, 1956, xx-xxv.
        Animadversions on R. W. Chambers, L. B. Wright, and other Miltonists.

711 ------. Supplementary Note on H. F. Fletcher, Milton's Rabbinical Read-
      ings, Ang. Bbl., 45, 1934, 20-3.
        Questions some of Fletcher's major conclusions.

712 LOANE, GEORGE G. Milton and Chapman. N&Q, 175, 1938, 456-7.
        Cites correspondences which "establish a possibility or even a probability of
        Milton's knowledge of Chapman."

713 LOOTEN, C. C. J. Milton quelques aspects de son génie. Paris: Desclée
      de Brouwer, 1938. 247pp.
        Animadversions on Tillyard's, Saurat's, and Belloc's interpretations of Milton.
        Discusses Milton the pamphleteer, Milton the republican and regicide,
        Milton the historian, Milton and the idea of the poet, Milton and music,
        Paradise Lost, and the theology of Milton.

714 ------. Milton et l'idée du Poète. RA-A, 9, 1931, 1-15.

715 ------. Milton et la musique. RA-A, 8, 1931, 393-408.
        Discusses Milton's relations with musicians, the importance he attaches to
        music in his scheme of education, and the influence of the art on his verse.

716 LOVE, CHRISTOPHER C. The Scriptural Latin Plays of the Renaissance
      and Milton's Cambridge Manuscript. Doctoral diss., Univ. of Toronto,
      1950. Abs., Univ. of Toronto . . . Final Oral Examinations for the
      Degree of Doctor of Philosophy, Session 1949-50.

717 LUMIANSKY, ROBERT M. Milton's English Again. MLN, 55, 1940,
      591-4.
        Argues against the belief in the alien character of Milton's vocabulary.

718 LUTTER, TIBOR. John Milton, az Angol Polgári Forradalom Költoje
      (John Milton, Poet of the English Bourgeois Revolution). Budapest:
      Akadémiai Kiadó, 1956. 223pp.
        Summary in English by the author, p. 222. In "this first comprehensive
        Hungarian study" Lutter is especially interested in showing how the English
        Revolution is reflected in Milton's poetry and prose.

719 MacCALLUM, HUGH REID. Milton and Figurative Interpretation of
      the Bible. UTQ, 31, 1962, 397-415.
        "Milton gained much from the ancient figurative traditions which had been
        inherited and modified by writers of the Renaissance."

720 ------. Milton and the Study of Scripture. Doctoral diss., Univ. of Toronto, 1960.

721 MACKAIL, J. W. The Springs of Helicon: A Study in the Progress of English Poetry from Chaucer to Milton. Lincoln: Univ. of Nebraska Press, 1962. xxvi, 207pp.
A reprint of Stevens' No. 2345, first published in 1909. Milton discussed, pp. 135-204.

722 MACKELLAR, WALTER. Milton and Pindar. TLS, Dec. 3, 1931, p. 982.
A reply to L. R. Farnell, TLS, Oct. 1, 1931, p. 754. Cites evidence of Milton's acquaintance with Pindar.

723 MACKENZIE, PHYLLIS. Milton's Visual Imagination: an Answer to T. S. Eliot. UTQ, 16, 1946, 17-29.
Shows how Eliot has unjustly and incorrectly compared Milton and Shakespeare.

724 MACKINNON, MALCOLM H. M. Milton's Theory and Practice of the Epic, Examined in Relation to Italian Renaissance Literary Criticism. Doctoral diss., Univ. of Toronto, 1948.

725 MACKLEM, MICHAEL. Love, Nature, and Grace in Milton. QQ, 56, 1949, 534-47.
"My suggestion is that for Milton, as for Spenser, this duality of humanism and Puritanism, reason and revelation, nature and grace, is resolved by the Neo-Platonic doctrine of love."

726 MADSEN, WILLIAM G. The Idea of Nature in Milton's Poetry. Doctoral diss., Yale Univ., 1952. Published in Three Studies in the Renaissance: Sidney, Jonson, and Milton (New Haven: Yale Univ. Press, 1958), pp. 181-283.
Topics: Nature in Comus; Nature in Paradise Lost; Nature, Man and God; Nature and Grace; The Poetic Vision.

727 ------. From Shadowy Types to Truth: Studies in Milton's Symbolism. New Haven and London: Yale Univ. Press, 1968. 208pp.
"The thesis of this book is that Milton's symbolic theory and practice can best be understood in the context of theories of biblical interpretation that were current in his day, and, in particular, that the doctrine of typology throws more light on the symbolic structure of the major poems as well as on Milton's philosophical and religious presuppositions than do the currently fashionable theories about metaphoric or mythic structure and Neo-platonic allegoria." Parts of this study have been previously published and are listed in this bibliography under their appropriate classifications. Includes, i.a., chapters on Lycidas, Paradise Lost, Paradise Regained, and Samson Agonistes.
Rev: TLS, July 25, 1968, p. 795; MN, 2, 1968, 32.

728 MAJOR, JOHN M. Milton's View of Rhetoric. SP, 64, 1967, 685-711.
A detailed analysis. "Milton acquired a thorough knowledge of rhetoric at St. Paul's and Cambridge (and probably Horton); admired and used to great advantage in his own writings the valid rhetoric of the ancients, while rejecting with scorn the inferior art taught in the schools of his day; under the influence of certain philosophers, authors, and cultural movements, and

no doubt for aesthetic and personal reasons as well, acquired gradually a distaste, amounting at times to an outright hostility, for rhetoric itself as false and deceptive."

729 MANUEL, M. The Seventeenth-Century Critics and Biographers of Milton. Doctoral diss., Univ. of Wisconsin, 1956. Abs., DA, 16, 1956, 2166-7. Published in Trivandrum, India, 1962.

730 MARILLA, ESMOND L. Milton and Bacon: a Paradox. ES, 36, 1955, 106-11. Reprinted in Milton and Modern Man: Selected Essays (University, Alabama: Univ. of Alabama Press, 1968), pp. 118-24.
   Milton agrees that fruitless speculation is undesirable and approves Bacon's concern for scientific advancement as a means for man's material improvement; he differs from Bacon by regarding such mastery as an instrument of man's purpose in life.

731 ------. Milton and Modern Man: Selected Essays. Preface by Douglas Bush. University, Alabama: Univ. of Alabama Press, 1968. 149pp.
   A collection of Marilla's studies with some revisions on Paradise Lost, Paradise Regained, Samson Agonistes, and Lycidas. Also includes his essay on Milton and Bacon, above, and a general introduction. In this bibliography, each essay is entered separately under its appropriate classification.
   Rev: MN, 2, 1968, 65-6.

732 MARTZ, LOUIS L., ed. Milton: A Collection of Critical Essays. Twentieth Century Views. Englewood Cliffs, N.J.: Prentice-Hall, Inc., 1966. vii, 212pp.
   Contains twelve previously published essays by T. S. Eliot, W. Empson, C. S. Lewis, B. Rajan, F. T. Prince, A. J. A. Waldock, G. Hartman, D. Bush, W. B. C. Watkins, A. Stein, E. M. W. Tillyard, and J. H. Summers. Each is noted in its appropriate section in this bibliography.
   Rev: John L. Lievsay, SAQ, 66, 1967, 260-3.

733 MAYOUX, JEAN-JACQUES. Aspects de l'Imagination de Milton. EA, 20, 1967, 378-98.
   A study of the metaphysical and intellectual aspects of the imagery of Milton. The author stresses the cultural and mythical sources of Milton's style. Attention is given to Paradise Lost, Samson Agonistes, and Comus.

734 MAZZEO, JOSEPH A., ed. Reason and Imagination: Studies in the History of Ideas, 1600-1800. New York: Columbia Univ. Press; London: Routledge and Kegan Paul, 1962. viii, 321pp.
   Studies in Honor of Marjorie Hope Nicolson. Contains essays relating to Milton by D. Bush, A. O. Lovejoy, A. D. Ferry, W. Haller, M. A. N. Radzinowicz, and G. A. Finney, all of which are listed in their appropriate sections.
   Rev: John Steadman, RN, 15, 1962, 343-6.

735 McCOLLEY, GRANT. Milton's Technique of Source Adaptation. SP, 35, 1938, 61-110.
   Milton sometimes utilizes ideas in his sources in their original order and sometimes in reverse order.

736 ------. The Seventeenth-Century Doctrine of the Plurality of Worlds. Annals of Science, 1, 1936, 385-430.

737 ------. The Theory of a Plurality of Worlds as a Factor in Milton's Attitude Toward the Copernican Hypothesis. MLN, 47, 1932, 319-25.
Feels that Milton considered it expedient to indicate suspended judgment on both the theory and the hypothesis.

738 McDAVID, RAVEN I., JR. Milton as a Political Thinker. Doctoral diss., Duke Univ., 1935.

739 McDILL, JOSEPH M. Milton and the Pattern of Calvinism. Doctoral diss., Vanderbilt Univ., 1939. Nashville: The Author, 1942. xxiii, 432pp.

740 McLACHLAN, H. The Religious Opinions of Milton, Locke, and Newton. Manchester: Manchester Univ. Press, 1941. vii, 221pp.
Examines the views of each writer and the history of the theological movement to which he belongs.
Rev: TLS, July 19, 1941, p. 344; Lee Atkinson, LQHR, Oct., 1941, pp. 491-2; E. H. W. Meyerstein, English, 4, 1942, 23-4; F. M. Higham, Hist, N.S., 27, 1942, 87-8.

741 McNAMEE, MAURICE B., S. J. Honor and the Epic Hero: A Study of the Shifting Concept of Magnanimity in Philosophy and Epic Poetry. New York: Holt, Rinehart, 1960.
Chapter 9: Magnanimity in Milton, pp. 160-78. "It is the purpose of this chapter to show that Milton's concept of honor and glory is in many ways a conscious abrogation of the notion as it was described by Aristotle in his discussion of magnanimity."

742 MEGROZ, RODOLPHE L. Milton Agonistes. Thirty-One Bedside Essays (Hadleigh, Essex: Tower Bridge Publications, 1951), pp. 99-102.
Comments on E. H. Visiak's studies. Agrees that Milton has been unjustly maligned and neglected.

743 MERTNER, EDGAR. Die Bedeutung der kosmischen Konzeption in Miltons Dichtung. Anglia, 69, 1950, 105-34.

744 MILLER, MILTON. Milton's Imagination and the Idyllic Solution. WR, 13, 1948, 35-43.
Appreciative. "... for Milton's idyll is the idyll of the good and the triumph of man's will over evil in the figure of a redeeming Christ."

745 Milton Bombarded. TLS, Nov. 9, 1940, p. 567; Nov. 16, 1940, p. 579.
Refers to L. P. Smith's Milton and His Modern Critics (1940). Holds that the present detraction may be due to the decline of classical learning.

746 Milton Memorial Lectures, 1908. Read before the Royal Society of Literature. Ed. with an Introduction by Percy W. Ames. New York: Haskell House, 1964. xiii, 222pp.
A reprint of Stevens' No. 2330, first published in 1909. "Lectures by G. C. Williamson, W. H. Hadlow, E. H. Coleridge, W. E. A. Axon, E. H. Pember, E. B. Saintsbury, H. G. Rosedale, E. Dowden, Sir Edward Brabrook. Contents noted, Archiv, cxxii (1909), 451" (Stevens' annotation).

747 Milton Society of America. Minutes of Annual Meeting, Philadelphia, 1960. SCN, 18, 1960, 47-8.

748   Milton Society of America. Report on the MLA Meeting, 1961. SCN,
      20, 1962, 17-8.
         Includes exerpts from the address of Harris F. Fletcher, honored in Chicago
         by the Milton Society for his outstanding scholarship.

749   Milton Society of America. The 1962 Milton Society Meeting. SCN, 21,
      1963, item 19.
         Contains a summary of an address on Milton in Italy, delivered by James
         H. Hanford.

750   Milton Society of America. The 1965 Milton Society Meeting. SCN, 24,
      No. 3, 1966, item 17.

751   Milton Society of America. Notice of 1966 meeting in Chicago. MN, 1,
      1967, 3.

752   Milton Society of America. MN, 2, 1968, 6-7.
         Report on the 1967 meeting in Chicago, with Walter C. Curry as the honored
         scholar. Contains comment on William R. Parker's address, in which he
         discussed his problems in writing Milton: A Biography.

753   A Milton Tercentenary. TLS, Sept. 22, 1945, p. 451.
         Remembers distinguishing and singular facts about the 1645 poems.

754   Milton without the Epic. TLS, Sept. 2, 1955, 501-2.
         Milton's poetic career is a progress from one great form to another; Samson
         Agonistes is not an ebb tide.

755   MILWARD, PETER, S. J. Christian Themes in English Literature. In-
      troduction by Masao Hirai. Tokyo: Kenkyusha, 1967. xvi, 296pp.
         Milton's work cited, passim.

756   MIMS, EDWIN. John Milton, Dissenter and Heretic. The Christ of the
      Poets (New York: Abingdon-Cokesbury Press, 1948), pp. 100-18.

757   ------. Milton and the Modern World. Golden Book, April, 1931, pp. 87-9.
         On the relevance of Milton's ideas today.

758   MIYANISHI, MITSUO. Milton as an Artist. Kyoto Univ. Eibungaku
      Hyoron, 1, 1954.

759   ------. Milton's Evolutionary Ideas. Albion (Japan), 4, 1936.

760   ------. A Study of Milton. Kyoto: Apollonsha, 1961. 340pp.

761   The MLA Convention and the Milton Society. SCN, 17, No. 2, 1959,
      item 66.
         Report on the 1958 meeting.

762   MLA Conference on Milton. MN, 2, 1968, 5-6.
         Report on the 1967 meeting in Chicago, with comments on papers read by
         Louis Martz, Stanley Fish, and B. Rajan.

763   MOLLENKOTT, VIRGINIA R. The Bible, the Classics, and Milton.
      Christianity Today, 9, Jan. 1, 1965, 331-3.
         "The marriage of Hebraism and Hellenism at their finest was a reality in
         the mind of John Milton."

764 ------. Milton and the Apocrypha. Doctoral diss., New York Univ., 1964. Abs., DA, 27, 1966, 212A-213A.

765 MÖLLER, ALFRED. Zu Miltons rabbinischen Studien. Ang. Bbl., 44, 1933, 154-9.
Comments prompted by Liljegren's attack on Fletcher's studies.

766 MONTGOMERY, SARA DRAKE. John Milton—Alexander Pope, A Study in Contrast. Master's thesis. Univ. of Georgia, 1938.

767 MORAND, PAUL PHELPS. De Comus à Satan: L'oeuvre poetique de John Milton expliquée par sa vie. Paris: Didier, 1939. 262pp.

   Rev: E. N. S. T[hompson], PQ, 19, 1940, 223; E. M. W. Tillyard, MLN, 55, 1940, 635-6.

768 MORRIS, JOHN N. Empson's Milton. SR, 70, 1962, 673-7.
A review article on Milton's God, by William Empson. The book is "as much an anti-Christian polemic as it is a piece of literary criticism."

769 MOSER, WILLARD C. The Meaning of Soul and Spirit in Milton's Works. Doctoral diss., Tulane Univ., 1968. 190pp.

770 MOUNTS, CHARLES E. "Sooth" in De La Mare, Keats, and Milton. MLN, 62, 1947, 271-2.
To Milton the word means "truth," while to Keats and De La Mare it means "smooth."

771 MUELLER, MARTIN. Sixteenth-Century Italian Criticism and Milton's Theory of Catharsis. SEL, 6, 1966, 139-50.
Sees a close resemblance between Milton's theory and theories current in Italy in the sixteenth century.

772 MULLEN, CECIL. Milton's Poetry, Viewed in the Light of Catholic Doctrine. Master's thesis, Ottawa Univ., 1935. 112pp.

773 MURDOCH, WALTER. On Two Poets. 72 Essays (Sydney: Angus and Robertson, 1947), pp. 317-21.
Contrasts the temperaments of Shakespeare and Milton.

774 MURRAY, JOHN FRANKLIN, S. J. Milton's Conception of Original Justice and of Original Sin. Doctoral diss., Univ. of New Mexico, 1957. Abs., DA, 18, 1958, 583.

775 MURRY, JOHN MIDDLETON. Heaven—and Earth. London: Cape, 1938. 383pp.
Contains three chapters on Milton: Milton: I Am That Satan, pp. 147-57; Milton: Lear Without Cordelia, pp. 158-67; Milton: Tendering the Whole, pp. 168-83. On Milton's "curious version of Christian morality." Quite unsympathetic.

776 ------. Heroes of Thought (New York: Julian Messner, 1938), pp. 142-77.
Argues that Milton has no charity.

777 MYHR, IVAR L. [MRS. E. H. DUNCAN]. The Evolution and Practice of Milton's Epic Theory. Doctoral diss., Vanderbilt Univ., 1940. Abs.,

Bulletin of Vanderbilt Univ., 40, No. 10, 1940, 14-5. Published in summary form. Nashville: Joint Univ. Libraries, 1942. 53pp.

778   NAKAGIRI, NOBUYA. Milton and Chastity. Meiji Gakuin Ronso (Japan), 34, 1954.

779   ------. An Outline of Studies in Spenser, Donne, and Milton. Meiji Gakuin Ronso (Japan), 29, 1952.

780   ------. Phoebus Apollo and the Music of the Spheres. Meiji Gakuin Ronso (Japan), 29, 1953.

781   ------. Present-day Milton Studies with Special Reference to T. S. Eliot. Meiji Gakuin Ronso (Japan), 21, 1951.

782   ------. Recent Milton Critics (incomplete). Meiji Gakuin Ronso (Japan), 34, 1954.

783   NAZARI, EMILIO. Problemi Miltoniani. Palermo: A. Priulla, 1951. 250pp.
Chapter topics: Milton's trip to Italy and his religious uncertainties, classical and Italian elements in Paradise Lost, and some considerations on the life and personality of Milton.

784   NEILSON, WILLIAM A. On Milton's Conception of Poetry. Studies in the History of Culture: The Disciplines of the Humanities (Menasha, Washington: George Banta, 1942), pp. 156-60.

785   NICOLSON, MARJORIE HOPE. The Breaking of the Circle: Studies in the Effect of the New Science upon Seventeenth Century Poetry. The Norman Wait Harris Lectures Delivered at Northwestern Univ., July, 1949. Evanston: Northwestern Univ. Press, 1950. Revised Edition. New York: Columbia Univ. Press, 1960.
Milton discussed passim and pp. 160-6. "In the astronomy of Paradise Lost Milton, whether he realized it or not, broke the Circle of Perfection."
Rev: Samuel Mintz, Isis, 43, 1952, 98-100; Joan Bennett, RES, 3, 1952, 178-80; William Blackburn, SAQ, 51, 1952, 469-70; H. J. C. Grierson, MLR, 47, 1952, 390-2.

786   ------. John Milton: A Reader's Guide to His Poetry. New York: Farrar, Straus, 1963; London: Thames and Hudson, 1964. xv, 385pp.
"In preparing this volume I have had in mind particularly three groups of readers: the general reader, who may have read no Milton, or at most, the Minor Poems and possibly the first two books of Paradise Lost; the undergraduate, often reading Milton for the first time; the English teacher who is not a 'Milton specialist,' but who must teach Milton in a 'survey course' or in a course in Renaissance literature from Spenser to Milton."
Rev: J. Max Patrick, SCN, 21, No. 4, 1963, 69-70; N. J. C. Andreasen, CE, 26, 1964, 244; John M. Steadman, Archiv, 204, 1968, 460-1.

787   ------. The Microscope and English Imagination. Smith College Studies in Modern Language, 16, 4. Northampton, Massachusetts: Banta, 1935. 92pp.
A background study.
Rev: L. I. Bredvold, PQ, 15, 1936, 167-8; W. J. Schmidt, Ang. Bbl, 47, 1936, 250; F. R. Johnson, MLN, 52, 1937, 229-31.

788 ------. Milton and the Bible. The Bible and Its Literary Associations. Ed. by Margaret B. Crook (New York: Abingdon Press, 1937), pp. 278-308.
Discusses the effect of the Bible upon Milton, Biblical themes and allusions in his poetry, and the transformation of his sources.

789 ------. Mountain Gloom and Mountain Glory: The Development of the Aesthetics of the Infinite. Ithaca: Cornell Univ. Press, 1959; New York: W. W. Norton, 1963. 403pp.
Milton, passim.

790 ------. Voyages to the Moon. New York: Macmillan, 1948, 1960.
Milton, passim. A background study.

791 NOTT, KATHLEEN. Old Puritan Writ Large. The Emperor's Clothes (Bloomington: Indiana Univ. Press, 1954), pp. 159-93. Reprinted, 1958.
Agrees with the New Critics that "Milton the poet was the portentous and comet-like cause which accounted for much of the devastation in poetic language."

792 NOYES, ALFRED. A French View of Milton. The Opalescent Parrot (London: Sheed and Ward, 1929), pp. 55-70.
Censures Taine and Saurat for their criticism of Milton.

793 O'BRIEN, GORDON W. The Avatars of Dignity: A Study in the Imagery of Humanism. Doctoral diss., Ohio State Univ., 1951. Abs., DA, 18, 1958, 1789-91.
Shows how Milton employs certain images and themes to set forth his conception of the dignity of man.

794 ------. Renaissance Poetics and the Problem of Power. Chicago: Institute of Elizabethan Studies, 1956. xxvi, 127pp.
Milton given a prominent place, for "... he was the last of these for whom the Renaissance concept of the dignity of man and of the aims of human knowledge went far toward creating the form and theme of his discourse."

795 OCHI, EIJI. The So-Called Struggle between Good and Evil in Milton. Hiroshima Univ. Bungakubu Reports, 1954.

796 OCHI, FUMIO. Milton Ronko (Essays and Studies in Milton). n.d. vi, 350pp.
In Japanese.

797 ------. Milton's View of Rome. SEL (Japan), 21, 1942.

798 ------. A Study of Milton. Kyoto: Doshisha Univ. Press, 1953. 345pp.
Chapters: The Organic Relationship between Milton's Latin and English Poems, Three Persons Who Influenced Milton—Diodati, Young, and His Father, The Italian Trip, Milton's Debt to Greece, Italy, and England, The Technique of the Epic Catalogue, and others.

799 O'CONNOR, JOHN J. A Note on the Meaning of the Word Novel in the Seventeenth Century. N&Q, 198, 1953, 477-8.
Milton's De Doctrina Christiana not the first work in which the word appeared signifying "a fictitious prose narrative or tale of considerable length."

800 O'DONNELL, SISTER JOHN MARY. Introducing Milton to Culturally Handicapped Students. EJ, 56, 1967, 561, 565.

Describes her experiences with a group at Notre Dame High School, Maylan, Pennsylvania.

801 OGDEN, H. S. V. The Principles of Variety and Contrast in Seventeenth Century Aesthetics, and Milton's Poetry. JHI, 10, 1949, 159-82.
Shows, i.a., how the principles affected Milton's poetry and some of the graphic art of the seventeenth century.

802 ORAS, ANTS. Notes on Some Miltonic Usages: Their Background and Later Development. Acta et Commentationes Universitatis Tartuensis, Dorpatensis, B. 43, 3. Tartu: Kruger, 1938. 133pp.
Rev: W. Héraucourt, Ang. Bbl., 50, 1939, 198-200; P. Meissner, DL, 60, 1939, 919-20; H. Scherpbier, Neophil, 24, 1939, 312.

803 ------. Spenser and Milton: Some Parallels and Contrasts in the Handling of Sound. Sound and Poetry, EIE, 1956 (New York: Columbia Univ. Press, 1957), pp. 109-33.
Feels that Spenser's approach is pre-Neo-Aristotelian, while Milton's reflects an absorption of Renaissance principles and points beyond them.

804 ORSINI, NAPOLEONE. La lingua poetica inglese: Note storiche. Anglica, 1, 1946, 139-48, 193-203, 241-52.
Includes remarks on Milton and Shakespeare.

805 ------. Studii sul Rinascimento italiano in Inghilterra. Con alcuni testi inglese inediti. 5, Milton's Machiavelli Studies. Florence: Sansoni, 1937. 141pp.
Rev: A. Zanco, Rivista italiana del dramma (Rome), Jan. 15, 1938.

806 OSBORNE, LAWRENCE J. Changes in Milton's Theology from The Nativity Ode through Of True Religion. Doctoral diss., Stanford Univ., 1952. Abs., Abstracts of Diss., Stanford Univ., 27, 1953, 232-3.

807 OSGOOD, CHARLES G. The Classical Mythology of Milton's English Poems. New York: Stechert-Hafner, 1964, 198pp.; New York: Gordian Press, 1964, lxxxv, 111pp.; New York: Haskell House, 1964.
Reprints of Stevens' No. 2225, first published in 1900.

808 ------. Milton. Poetry as a Means of Grace: Studies in Dante, Spenser, Milton and Johnson (Princeton: Princeton Univ. Press; London: Milford, 1941), pp. 80-105. Reprinted, Stapleton, New York: Gordian Press, 1965.
General remarks addressed to theological students.
Rev: Douglas Bush, MLN, 58, 1943, 222.

809 ------. Milton. The Voice of England: A History of English Literature (New York: Harper and Bros., 1935; Second Edition, 1952), pp. 237-51.

810 ------. Virgil and the English Mind. The Tradition of Virgil (Princeton: Princeton Univ. Press, 1930), pp. 23-40.
Especially concerned with Vergil's influence on Milton.

811 PARKS, GEORGE B. The Decline and Fall of the English Renaissance Admiration of Italy. HLQ, 31, 1968, 341-57.
Brief mention of Milton's references to Italy.

812   PARSONS, EDWARD S. Milton's Seasonal Inspiration. MLN, 49, 1934, 46.
      Cites a parallel from Cowper, who says that he writes best during the winter.

813   PARSONS, HOWARD. Milton and the Aeroplane. N&Q, 196, 1951, 372.
      A reply to W. B. Lawrence's query (N&Q, 196, 1951, 282). States that Paradise Lost 6, 771, is evidence that Milton "conceived the coming of the aeroplane."

814   PATRICK, J. MAX. An Editorial Tribute to Watson Kirkconnell. SCN, 26, 1968, 1-2.
      An appreciative account of Kirkconnell's achievements, including his editions of Milton's analogues.

815   PATRICK, J. MAX, ed. SAMLA Studies in Milton. Essays on John Milton and His Works by Members of the South Atlantic Modern Language Association. Foreword by James H. Hanford. Gainesville: Univ. of Florida Press, 1953. xiii, 197pp.
      A collection of essays by J. A. Bryant, Jr., R. H. West, A. H. Gilbert, R. H. Bowers, Alvin Thaler, T. B. Stroup, L. P. Boone, and Ants Oras. Each essay is listed in this bibliography under its appropriate classification.
      Rev: Arnold Davenport, YWES, 199-200; R. Wood, MLN, 70, 1955, 448-50; Colin Williamson, SN, 27, 1955, 269-71; Edgar Mertner, Anglia, 76, 1958, 322-5; J. B. Broadbent, ES, 41, 1960, 348.

816   PATRIDES, C. A. Milton and Arianism. JHI, 25, 1964, 423-9.
      "... I feel obliged to insist that the application of the term 'Arian' to Milton distorts his views and confounds the important differences between 'subordinationism' and the Arian mythology."

817   ------. Milton and the Christian Faith: a Study of His Orthodoxy. Doctoral diss., Wadham College, Oxford, 1957.

818   ------. Milton and the Christian Tradition. Oxford: Clarendon Press, 1966. xvi, 302pp.
      "The centre of the present study is Milton's conception and presentation of the principal themes of the Christian faith." Chapters: The Doctrine of the Godhead, The Doctrine of Creation, The Nature of Nature, The Fall of Angels and Man, The Restoration of Man, The Christian Idea of Love, The Concept of Grace, The Christian View of History, The Eschata of History.
      Rev: C. B. Cox, Spect, Nov. 4, 1966, p. 590; John Drewett, CQR, Oct.-Dec., 1967, p. 535; J. B. Hibbitts, DR, 47, 1967, 101-2; TLS, Apr. 27, 1967, p. 353; John R. Mulder, SCN, 25, 1967, 1; John T. Shawcross, RenQuar, 20, 1967, 515-7; L. R. N. Ashley, Bibliothèque d'Humanisme et Renaissance, 29, 1967, 495-7; H. W. Donner, ES, 49, 1968, 164-6.

819   ------. Paradise Lost and the Language of Theology. Language and Style in Milton: A Symposium in Honor of the Tercentenary of Paradise Lost. Ed. by Ronald David Emma and John T. Shawcross (New York: Frederick Ungar, 1967), pp. 102-19.
      Questions the conclusions of Maurice Kelley (This Great Argument) and others who feel that De Doctrina Christiana represents Milton's mature thought. "Milton performing in the cool sphere of theology, largely met with disaster in De Doctrina."

820 ------. The Phoenix and the Ladder: The Rise and Decline of the Christian View of History. UCPES, 29. Berkeley and Los Angeles: Univ. of California Press, 1964. 101pp.
    Milton's views of history discussed, pp. 58-68. Sees Paradise Lost as the termination of an era in the history of thought.

821 ------. Psychopannychism in Renaissance Europe. SP, 60, 1963, 227-9.
    "...mortalism, and particularly psychopannychism, was far more widely disseminated than we have been led to believe."

822 ------. Renaissance and Modern Thought on the Last Things: A Study in Changing Conceptions. HTR, 51, 1958, 169-85.
    Draws illustrations from Milton and several others.

823 ------. The Renaissance View of Time: A Bibliographical Note. N&Q, N.S., 10, 1963, 408-10.
    "Milton was one of the few great writers of the Renaissance to depart from the traditional view of time."

824 ------. The Scale of Nature and Renaissance Treatises on Nobility. SN, 36, 1964, 63-8.
    A background study.

825 PETER, JOHN. Reflections on the Milton Controversy. Scr, 19, 1952, 2-15.
    On Leavis and his adversaries.

826 PITMAN, M. R. The Description of Landscape in Poetry from Spenser to Milton. B. Litt. thesis, Lady Margaret Hall, Oxford, 1964.

827 POLE, DAVID. Milton and Critical Method. BJA, 3, 1963, 245-58.
    Compares the conclusions and the critical approaches in The Muse's Method, An Introduction to Paradise Lost, by Joseph H. Summers, The Metaphoric Structure of Paradise Lost, by Jackson I. Cope, Poetry and the Fountain of Light, by H. R. Swardson.

828 POUND, EZRA. Literary Essays. Ed. by T. S. Eliot. New York: New Directions, 1954. Reprinted, 1960.
    Contains scattered disparaging references to Milton.

829 POWYS, JOHN C. Milton. The Enjoyment of Literature (New York: Simon and Schuster, 1938), pp. 238-75.
    General laudatory remarks.

830 PRAZ, MARIO. John Milton. Storia della Letteratura Inglese (Florence: Sansoni, 1937), pp. 155-65.

831 ------. Rapporti tra la letteratura italiana e la letteratura inglese. Letteratura Comparate (Milan: Marzorati, 1948), pp. 145-96.
    Considers Milton's relations with Italy in general, pp. 67-9.

832 PRIEST, HAROLD M. Tasso in English Literature, 1575-1675. Doctoral diss., Northwestern Univ., 1933. Abs., Summaries of Dissertations, Northwestern Univ., 1, 1933, 5-9.
    Considers Milton as the second great English poet to be influenced profoundly.

833 PRINCE, F. T. The Influence of Tasso and Della Casa on Milton's Diction. RES, 25, 1949, 222-36.
Sees a positive influence.

834 ------. The Italian Element in Milton's Verse. Oxford: Clarendon Press, 1954, 1962. xv, 183pp.
"My endeavor has been to show that this Italian influence on Milton's verse is deeper than it had been thought to be, especially as it affects the epic poetry."
Rev: Arnold Davenport, YWES, 138; TLS, Mar. 5, 1954, p. 152; CE, 16, 1954, 75; Sergio Baldi, Riv. di, Let. Mod., 5, 1954, 308-10; K. M. Lea, RES, 6, 1955, 203-4; Denis Saurat, EA, 8, 1955, 344-5; Wilhelmina Gordon, QQ, 63, 1956, 312-3.

835 ------. Lost and Regained. FMLS, 3, 1967, 310-4.
Categorizes Milton critics into two camps, (1) the prophets, and (2) the "doctors of the law, scribes, or priests." Concludes that both types of critics are needed.

836 PRITCHARD, JOHN P. The Fathers of the Church in the Works of John Milton. CJ, 33, 1937, 79-87.
"Milton's patristic knowledge is more than simply matter got up for specific polemical purposes; it is part and parcel of his being."

837 PUHALO, DUŠAN. Milton i mi. Živi jezici, 2, 1960, 29-38.

838 PURCELL, JAMES M. Milton y los siete tipos de ambigüedad. Estudios (Duquesne Univ.), 1, 1953, 23-9.

839 PURNELL, ROSENTENE BENNETT. John Milton and the Doctrine of Sympathy: Deontology and Ambiance. Doctoral diss., Univ. of Oklahoma, 1967. Abs., DA, 28, 1967, 1056-A.
"This study aims to demonstrate that much of Milton's perception and expression of the unity of existence lies in his sublime and personal response to the doctrine of sympathy as it was used in the secular and religious contexts of the available tradition."

840 QUILLER-COUCH, SIR ARTHUR T. Milton. Cambridge Lectures (London: Dent, 1943), pp. 207-58.
A reprint of an item in Stevens' No. 2496, published in 1922.

841 RADER, KATHERINE. The Soliloquy in Milton's English Poems. Doctoral diss., Univ. of Oklahoma, 1952.

842 RAJAN, BALACHANDRA. The Constant Core. EWR, 3, 1967, 113-25.
On the wholeness and the continuity of Milton's poetry. "With Milton, the overall pattern is therefore best described in terms of that seventeenth century symbol of perfection, the circle."

843 ------. Simple, Sensuous, and Passionate. RES, 21, 1945, 289-301. Reprinted in Milton: Modern Essays in Criticism. A Galaxy Book. Ed. by Arthur E. Barker (New York: Oxford Univ. Press, 1965), pp. 3-20.
Milton's aesthetic credo.

844 RALEIGH, SIR WALTER A. Milton. New York: Benjamin Blom, 1967. xx, 286pp.

A reprint of Stevens' No. 2226, first published in 1900. Often quoted for Raleigh's assertion that Paradise Lost "is an eternal monument to dead ideas." "Among the best appreciations of Milton's poetry" (Stevens' annotation).

845 RALLI, AUGUSTUS. Milton. Poetry and Faith (London: John Lane, 1951), pp. 131-43.
Appreciative.
Rev: TLS, Apr. 27, 1951, p. 640.

846 RANSOM, JOHN CROWE. Mr. Empson's Muddles. Southern Rev., 4, 1938, 322-39.
Comments on Empson's Milton and Bentley (1935).

847 RASCOE, BURTON. Milton the Conscience. Titans of Literature: From Homer to the Present (New York: Putnam, 1932), pp. 276-96.
Repeats all the old charges against Milton.
Rev: A. Colton, SRL, 9, 1932, 252, 357-60.

848 RAY, DON E. Milton and the Elizabethan Tradition of Christian Learning. Doctoral diss., Rice Univ., 1957.

849 READ, HARLAN E. A Great Poet Whose Contributions to Freedom Were Written in Prose. Fighters for Freedom: The Story of Liberty Throughout the Ages (New York: McBride, 1946), pp. 164-7.
Laudatory.

850 READ, HERBERT. The Poet and His Muse. BJA, 4, 1964, 99-108.
In surveying this relationship, discusses "Milton as representative of the relation of the Renaissance poet to his Muse...."

851 RECK, JOSEF. Das Prinzip der Freiheit bei Milton. Erlangen: Dörres, 1931. 55pp.

852 REESING, JOHN. Milton's Philosophical View of Nature. Doctoral diss., Harvard Univ., 1954.

853 ------. Milton's Poetic Art: A Mask, Lycidas, and Paradise Lost. Cambridge: Harvard Univ. Press, 1968. x, 208pp.
A collection of eight previously unpublished essays, each of which is listed under its appropriate classification in this bibliography. "In brief, the fundamental assumption behind all these essays is the familiar view of Milton as a classical-humanist-Christian poet of the English Renaissance."

854 ------. Postscript. Milton's Poetic Art: A Mask, Lycidas, and Paradise Lost (Cambridge: Harvard Univ. Press, 1968), pp. 123-35.
A concluding essay in which the author brings together "generalizations about Milton's thought and art that have gradually clarified themselves with the writing of these essays." Discusses, i.a., the theme of divine rescue in Milton and Milton's observance of decorum and obedience to genre.

855 REEVES, JAMES. A Short History of English Poetry, 1340-1940. London: Heinemann, 1961. xvi, 228pp.
Milton, pp. 98-105.

856 REWIS, HELEN S. The Conflict between Humanism and Puritanism: Milton and His Predecessors. Master's thesis, Emory Univ., 1937.

857 RICHARDS, I. A. The Places and the Figures. KR, 11, 1949, 17-30.
Critical comment on D. L. Clarke's John Milton at St. Paul's School (1948).

858 RICHTER, WALTER. Der Hiatus im englischen Klassizismus (Milton,
Dryden, Pope). Freiburg i Br. Schrambert: Gatzer und Hahn, 1934.
139pp.

859 RICKS, CHRISTOPHER. In Defense of Milton. New York Review,
June 9, 1966, pp. 27-8.
Review article of recent studies by D. Bush, N. Frye, and B. Lewalski.
Discusses the Milton controversy.

860 ------. The Ways of God. NSN, 70, August 27, 1965, 292-3.
A review-article on William Empson's reissued Milton's God. Feels that
Empson's critics have not conceded enough.

861 RILEY, EDGAR H. Milton's Tribute to Virgil. SP, 26, 1929, 155-65.
Brings together Milton's scattered references to Vergil.

862 RILEY, SISTER MARY GERALDINE, R. S. M. Infinite Variety in Milton: A Study of John Milton's Concept of Woman as Shown in His
Works. Doctoral diss., Rutgers Univ., 1962. Abs., DA, 23, 1962, 2119.

863 ROBERTS, DONALD R. The Music of Milton. PQ, 26, 1947, 328-44.
Relates Milton's verse to the music of his era.

864 ROBERTS, E. A. Essays on Milton, with Selections from His Works.
King's Treasuries of Literature. London: Dent, 1930.

865 ROBINS, HARRY F. If This Be Heresy: A Study of Milton and Origen.
ISLL, 51. Urbana: Univ. of Illinois Press, 1963. 196pp.
"A primary purpose of this study is to demonstrate that Milton as a theologian is deeply indebted to early Christian thought, of which Origen is, in
some ways, the best representative." Contents: Ante-Nicene Christianity,
Origen and Heresy; An Outline of Milton's Theology: Its Heresies; Origen
and Milton; Milton's Muse.
Rev: Agnes M. C. Latham, YWES, 209; J. Max Patrick, SCN, 21, No. 4, 1963,
58; Walter J. Ong, S. J., SEL, 4, 1964, 181-2; Cooper R. Mackin, BA, 39,
1965, 215; J. B. Beer, MLR, 60, 1965, 434-6; A. B. Chambers, MP, 63, 1965,
61-6; C. A. Patrides, JEGP, 64, 1965, 586-9; John Carey, RES, 16, 1965,
427-9; Maurice Kelley, SCN, 23, No. 1-2, 1965, 3; B. M. G. Reardon, N&Q,
N.S., 13, 1966, 396-7; Maren-Sofie Røstvig, ES, 48, 1967, 347-8.

866 ROBSON, W. W. More Empson than Milton. OR, No. 1, 1966, 19-28.
A review article on W. Empson's Milton's God. Concludes that Empson
has "done good service to Milton and to poetry."

867 ROGERS, KATHERINE M. The Troublesome Helpmate: A History of
Misogyny in Literature. Seattle: Univ. of Washington Press, 1966.
Milton's views toward women discussed, pp. 151-9 and passim. "John Milton,
the greatest of the Puritans, clearly illustrates the nature and limits of their
misogyny."

868 ROSCELLI, WILLIAM JOHN. The Metaphysical Milton (1625-1631).
TSLL, 8, Winter, 1967, 463-84.
Supports his contention that Milton has a direct connection with the

metaphysical poets but feels that Milton owes no debt to a specific metaphysical poet.

869 ------. Milton and the Body Politic. Doctoral diss., Ohio State Univ., 1960. Abs., DA, 21, 1960, 877-8.

870 ROSS, MALCOLM M. Milton and the Protestant Aesthetic. Poetry and Dogma: the Transfiguration of Eucharistic Symbols in Seventeenth-century English Poetry (New Brunswick: Rutgers Univ. Press, 1954), pp. 183-204.
    The Christian symbols in Milton's poetry are externalized, but they cease to be ritualistic in the Protestant context of Milton's thought.

871 ------. Milton and Sir John Stradling. HLQ, 14, 1951, 129-46.
    Suggests several parallels between Stradling's Divine Poems (1625) and Milton's poems.

872 ------. Milton's Royalism: A Study of the Conflict of Symbol and Idea in the Poems. Doctoral diss., Cornell Univ., 1941. Published as Cornell Studies in English, 34. Ithaca: Cornell Univ. Press, 1943. xiii, 150pp.
    On the royalist symbolism in the anti-royalist context of Milton's poetry. Deals with the contradiction between the symbol and the idea in Paradise Lost and its resolution in his last poems. Chapters: The Elizabethan Background, The Problem of the Early Poems and the Early Plans, Paradise Lost, The Last Poems, Conclusion.
    Rev: Maurice Kelley, MLN, 59, 1944, 578-9; H. F. Fletcher, JEGP, 43, 1944, 253-4; TLS, May 27, 1944, p. 263; Arthur Barker, Canadian Forum, 24, 1944, 189; B. A. Wright, RES, 21, 1945, 66-8; William R. Parker, MLQ, 6, 1945, 106-7; Kirby Neill, CHR, 31, 1945, 241-2; Louise Brown, JMH, 17, 1945, 89.

873 RUDRUM, ALAN, ed. Milton: Modern Judgements. London: Macmillan, 1968. 320pp.
    A collection of essays, all previously published, by J. H. Summers, Arthur Barker, J. B. Leishman, Wayne Shumaker, Stanley Eugene Fish, Arnold Williams, Murray W. Bundy, Cleanth Brooks, Rosalie L. Colie, Lawrence A. Sasek, William G. Madsen, M. M. Mahood, J. B. Broadbent, and William Haller. In this bibliography each essay is listed under its appropriate classification.
    Rev: TLS, July 25, 1968, p. 795.

874 RUNTZ-REES, C. Flower Garlands of Poets: Milton, Shakespeare, Spenser, Marot, and Sannazarro. Mélanges offerts à M. Abel LeFranc, 1936, pp. 75-90.

875 SÁEZ, RICHARD. The Redemptive Circle: Illusion and The Beneficence of Evil in Tasso, Milton, and Calderon. Doctoral diss., Yale Univ., 1967. Abs., DA, 28, 1968, 4608-A-9-A.

876 ST. CLAIR, FOSTER Y. The Myth of the Golden Age from Spenser to Milton. Doctoral diss., Harvard Univ. 1931. Abs., Summaries of Theses, Harvard Univ. 1931, pp. 242-4.

877 SAINTSBURY, GEORGE. Milton. The Cambridge History of English Literature (Cambridge: Cambridge Univ. Press; New York: Macmillan, 1933), 7, 108-61.
    A reprint of Stevens' No. 2379, published in 1911.

878 SAITO, TAKESHI. Milton's Christian Thought. Tokyo Shingaku Dia-gaku, Shingaku, No. 5, 1953.

879 SALTMARSHE, C. John Milton, Letter Writer. Bookman (London), 81, 1932, 319-20.

880 SAMARIN, R. The Creative Road of John Milton. Moscow: State Library, n.d. 124pp.
   Doctoral diss., The Gorky Institute of World Literature of the Academy of Sciences of the USSR.

881 ------. Milton and Russian Culture. Soviet Literature, No. 1, 1959, 168-73.

882 ------. On John Milton's Theory. Reports and Accounts of the Faculty of Philology of the Moscow State Univ., 5, 1948, 47-51.
   Concerning Milton's theory of the epic.

883 SAMBROOK, A. J. Milton's Creation Heresy Paralleled. ES, 46, 1965, 330-1.
   Milton's views on Creation were shared by his "most famous ... royalist literary adversary, the editor and part author of Eikon Basilike—John Gauden (1605-1662)."

884 SAMPSON, GEORGE. Milton. The Concise Cambridge History of English Literature (Cambridge: Cambridge Univ. Press, 1941), pp. 357-70.
   Rev: L. B. Wright, MLQ, 3, 1942, 493; Edith J. Morley, RES, 18, 1942, 375-8.

885 SAMUEL, IRENE. Dante and Milton: The Commedia and Paradise Lost. Ithaca: Cornell Univ. Press, 1966. x, 299pp.
   Concerned mainly with the Commedia in Paradise Lost, but the appendices list Milton's references to Dante before Paradise Lost and contain excerpts from studies on the relationship of the two poets.
   Rev: James H. Sims, BA, 42, 1968, 129.

886 ------. Milton's References to Plato and Socrates. SP, 41, 1944, 50-64.
   Early poems contain references to the philosophers, while the later poems incorporate Platonic theories.

887 ------. Platonism in the Poetry of John Milton. Doctoral diss., Cornell Univ., 1940. Abs., Cornell Univ. Abstracts of Theses, 1940, pp. 44-7. Published as Plato and Milton. Cornell Studies in English, 35. Ithaca: Cornell Univ. Press, 1947. xii, 182pp. Reprinted, 1965.
   Rev: TLS, June 14, 1947, p. 299; J. M. French, MLN, 63, 1948, 280-2; C. R. T., QQ, 55, 1948, 109; L. C. Martin, YWES, 185-6; Lionel Stephenson, Pers, 30, 1949, 207-8.

888 SAUNDERS, J. W. Milton, Diomede, and Amaryllis. ELH, 22, 1955, 254-86.
   On Milton's relationship to his audience.

889 SAURAT, DENIS. Milton et le materialisme chrètien en Angleterre. Paris: Rieder, 1928. 243pp.
   Stevens' No. 2609.
   Rev: Paul Chauvet, RA-A, 6, 1929, 172-4; C. B., Rev. historique, 54, 1929, 407-8; André Leroy, Rev. d'histoire de la philosophie, 2, 1929, 427-9; René Pruvost, Rev. de synthese historique, N. S., 21, 1929, 125; R. S. Crane, MP, 27, 1930, 361-4; B. Fehr, Ang. Bbl., 42, 1931, 161-9.

890 ------. Milton: Man and Thinker. Second Edition. London: Dent, 1944,
1946; Hamden, Conn.: Archon Books, 1964; London: Bailey Brothers,
1964. xiv, 291pp.
   Originally published in 1925, Stevens No. 2565. Aim is to determine the
   human and lasting element in Milton's thought. Part One: The Man; Part
   Two: The System; Part Three: The Great Poems; Part Four: The History
   of Miltonic Ideas (discussions of Hebraic and Christian sources, the Fathers,
   the Zohar and the Kabbalah, Fludd, and the Mortalists). Lengthy annotation
   in Stevens.
   Rev: B. Fehr, Ang. Bbl., 42, 1931, 161-9; TLS, Sept. 16, 1944, p. 451; Joan
   Bennett, NSN, Sept. 2, 1944, pp. 156-7; Charles Williams, Spect, Aug. 18,
   1944, p. 154; E. M. Forster, La France libre, Oct. 16, 1944, pp. 449-50;
   A. S. P. Woodhouse, UTQ, 15, 1946, 200-5.

891 SAYERS, DOROTHY. Dante and Milton. Further Papers on Dante (New
York: Harper, 1957), pp. 148-82.
   A comparative study rather than one of influence. "Milton was a Dante
   deprived of Beatrice . . . in the whole range of her significance."
   Rev: TLS, Dec. 13, 1957, p. 758.

892 SCHIRMER, WALTER F. Die epische Dichtung und John Milton. Ge-
schichte der englischen Literatur von den Anfängen bis zur Gegenwart
(Halle: Niemeyer, 1937), pp. 322-41.
   Rev: H. S. V. Jones, JEGP, 36, 1937, 617-8; H. Lüdeke, ES, 20, 1938, 219-23;
   M. Wildi, DL, 59, 1939, 702-8; W. E. Süskind, Die Literatur, 40, 1939, 758;
   F. Brie, ESt., 72, 1939, 283-6; H. G. Fiedler, English, 2, 1939, 247-9; W.
   Fischer, Ang. Bbl., 51, 1940, 49-54; S. B. Liljegren, SN, 13, 1940, 154-8.

893 SCHMIDT, ERIKA. Miltons Weltschau. Doctoral diss., Berlin-Frei, 1956.
324pp.

894 SCHNEIDER, R. Milton zwischen Politik und Geschichte. Die Literatur,
38, 1936, 314-8.

895 SCHORK, W. Die Dramenpläne Miltons. Freiburg i. Quakenbrück: Trute,
1934. 92pp.
   Rev: H. O. Wilde, Ang. Bbl., 46, 1935, 239; J. H. Hanford, JEGP, 36, 1937,
   584-6; A. B., Archiv, 167, 1935, 141.

896 SCHULTZ, HOWARD. Milton and Forbidden Knowledge. MLA Revolving Fund Series, 17. New York: Modern Language Assn. of America,
1955. vii, 309pp.
   A comprehensive study of the subject of forbidden knowledge in Christian
   tradition and in the Renaissance. Gives special attention to Milton.
   Rev: Arnold Davenport, YWES, 159-60; Donald Howard, SCN, 13, 1955,
   43-4; D. C. Allen, MP, 54, 1956, 138-9; H. F. Fletcher, JEGP, 55, 1956,
   322-3; J. I. Cope, MLN, 71, 1956, 529-32; H. L. Short, HJ, 55, 1956, 405-6;
   Frank Kermode, EIC, 7, 1957, 196-207; B. O. Kurth, Pers, 37, 1957, 102-
   3; Barbara K. Lewalski, Rev. of Religion, 22, 1957, 198-202; Ernest Sirluck,
   Church Hist., 26, 1957, 189-92; Kenneth Muir, RES, 8, 1957, 443-4.

897 ------. Obscurantism in Milton and the Humanistic Tradition. Doctoral
diss., Harvard Univ., 1940. Abs., Harvard Univ., Summaries of Theses,
1940, pp. 356-60.

898   SCOTT, WILLIAM O. Ramism and Milton's Concept of Poetic Fancy.
      PQ, 42, 1963, 183-9.

      On Milton's approach to logic and its implications for his poetic theory
      and practice.

899   SEEBACHER, JACQUES. Comment Peut-on Être Milton? Le Paradis
      Perdu: 1667-1967. Ed. by Jacques Blondel (Paris: Minard Lettres
      Modernes, 1967), pp. 241-50.
      To be a Milton a Miltonic blindness is necessary. Personal myth and history
      are hidden in the heart of the work if it is to be Miltonic.

900   SELLIN, PAUL R. The Poetic Theory of Daniel Heinsius and English
      Criticism of the Seventeenth Century: Jonson, Milton, and Dryden.
      Doctoral diss., Univ. of Chicago, 1963. Leyden: published for the Sir
      Thomas Browne Institute at the University Press, 1964.

901   ------. Sources of Milton's Catharsis: A Reconsideration. JEGP, 60, 1961,
      712-30.
      A re-examination of the influence of Antonio Minturno and Giambattista
      Guarini on Milton and a suggestion of another source—Daniel Heinsius'
      De tragoedise constitutione.

902   SENIOR, JOHN. Milton and Eliot. Nat, 161, 1945, 186-7.
      A review of Douglas Bush's Paradise Lost in Our Time (1945). Calls the
      book an "intelligent, healthy counter-criticism to the current praise for the
      modern metaphysical school of poetry."

903   SEWELL, ELIZABETH. The Orphic Voice: Poetry and Natural History.
      New Haven: Yale Univ. Press, 1960. x, 463pp.
      Considers the Orpheus myth in writers from Shakespeare to Rilke. Com-
      ments on the progress of Orpheus through Milton's works, passim.

904   SHAWCROSS, JOHN T. A Metaphoric Approach to Reading Milton.
      BSUF, 8, Summer, 1967, 17-22.
      "An awareness of the meanings which a word accrued for Milton leads to
      new, deeper, more meaningful interpretations, to levels of imagery which
      unite a poem in an additional way, and to further meanings for other
      related words."

905   ------. Milton's Debt to Shakespeare: An Analysis of the Alleged Parallels.
      MA thesis, New York Univ., 1950. 365pp.

906   ------. Milton's Spelling: Its Biographical and Critical Implications. Doc-
      toral diss., New York Univ., 1958. Abs., DA, 22, 1961, 567-8.
      Description of plan and some of conclusions reached, SCN, 19, 1961, item 65,

907   ------. One Aspect of Milton's Spelling: Idle Final E. PMLA, 78, 1963,
      501-10.
      A discussion of spelling in Milton's works as it relates to printer's errors and
      to the identification of the dates of manuscripts. Gives evidence, based on a
      full examination of Milton's orthography, "concerning Milton's use or
      omission of idle final 'e'."

908   ------. Orthography and the Text of Paradise Lost. Language and Style
      in Milton: A Symposium in Honor of the Tercentenary of Paradise Lost.

Ed. by Ronald David Emma and John T. Shawcross (New York: Frederick Ungar, 1967), pp. 120-53.

"My aim has been to call in doubt hypotheses of the correctness of the text in terms of Milton's 'desires' or practices, to indicate the confusion of textual transmission and correction that must have occurred, and to suggest that the second edition has only some authority, not full authority, over the first edition."

909 ------. What We Can Learn from Milton's Spelling. HLQ, 26, 1963, 351-61.

Suggests "how the study of Milton's orthography corrects certain assumptions and how it tells us important things about his life and his works."

910 SIEBERT, THEODOR. Untersuchungen über Milton Kunst vom psychologischen Standpunkt aus. Anglia, N.F., 42, 1930, 67-82.

911 ------. Wahrheit und Wahrhaftigkeit bei Milton. ESt, 64, 1929, 53-64.

912 SIEGEL, BEN. Elements of the Old Testament in Early Seventeenth Century English Poetry. Doctoral diss., Univ. of Southern California, 1957. Abs., Abstracts of Diss., Univ. of Southern California, 1957, pp. 97-9.

Mentions that Milton combined Puritan reverence for Scripture with the seventeenth-century intellectual's refusal to be bound to the law.

913 SIEGEL, PAUL N. Milton and the Humanist Attitude toward Women. JHI, 11, 1950, 42-53.

Shows that in depicting marriage Milton drew from humanists like Castiglione and from Puritan domestic conduct book writers like Mrs. Hutchinson.

914 SIRE, JAMES WALTER. Miltonic Criticism and the Problem of the Reader's Belief. Doctoral diss., Univ. of Missouri, 1964. Abs., DA, 25, 1965, 4129.

915 SIRLUCK, ERNEST. Milton and the Law of Nature. Doctoral diss., Univ. of Toronto, 1949.

916 ------. Milton's Political Thought: A Survey Preliminary to the Investigation of the Classical Influence. Master's thesis, Univ. of Toronto, 1941. 226pp.

917 SMITH, LOGAN PEARSALL. Milton and His Modern Critics. London: Oxford Univ. Press, 1940. Reprinted, Boston: Little, Brown, 1941. 88pp.

Shows how "certain modern critics have daringly attempted to scale the heavens and dislodge him [Milton] from his consecrated throne."

Rev: L. C. Martin, YWES, 171-2; N&Q, 189, 1940, 360; John Hayward, Spect, Nov. 8, 1940, pp. 482-4; Peter Quennell, NSN, N.S., Nov. 16, 1940, pp. 496-9; E. Johnson, NR, 104, 1941, 800-1; A. M. Witherspoon, SRL, July 12, 1941, p. 8; D. A. Roberts, NYTBR, May 25, 1941, p. 5; B. A. Wright, MLR, 36, 1941, 407; William R. Parker, RES, 17, 1941, 346-7; W. Gibson, English, 4, 1941, 189-90; Orlo Williams, Natl. Rev., 116, 1941, 236-41; F. A. Voight, NC, 130, 1941, 211-21; Theodore Maynard, CW, 153, 1941, 760-1.

918 SPAETH, SIGMUND G. Milton's Knowledge of Music: Its Source and Significance in His Works. Foreword by Warner G. Rice. Ann Arbor Paperbacks. Ann Arbor: Univ. of Michigan Press, 1963, 1964.

A reprint of Stevens' No. 2407, first published in 1913. A thorough exposition of music in Milton's day and of Milton's knowledge and use of music.

Rev: NYTBR, Apr. 26, 1964, p. 46.

919 SPENCER, T. J. B. John Milton: the Great Rival. Listener, 70, July 25, 1963, 123-4.
On Milton's "sense of rivalry with the poets of the past."

920 ------. Longinus in English Criticism: Influences before Milton. RES, N.S., 8, 1957, 137-43.
"In view of the English interest in Longinus in the immediately preceding years and the lively appreciativeness of Frances Junius ... the solitary mention in the tractate Of Education can hardly be regarded as of much interest or significance."

921 ------. Milton, the First English Philhellene. MLR, 47, 1952, 553-4.
Assembles various passages to show that Milton hoped the Greeks could overthrow the Turks.

922 SPEVACK-HUSMANN, HELGA. The Mighty Pan: Miltons mythologische Vergleiche. Doctoral diss., Münster, 1959. Published in the series, Neue Beitrage zur englischen Philologie, 1. Münster: Aschendorff, 1963. 150pp.
A study of Milton's use of myths, especially in Paradise Lost.
Rev: Ernest Schanzer, MLR, 59, 1964, 108; Horst Oppel, NS, 1964, 149-50; Joachim Stephan, ZAA, 13, 1965, 197-201; Charles Witke, MP, 63, 1965, 162-3; J. Blondel, EA, 18, 1965, 182; Inga-Stina Ewbank, RES, 16, 1965, 72-3.

923 STARKMAN, M. K. The Militant Miltonist; or the Retreat from Humanism. ELH, 26, 1959, 209-28.
Focuses on "the critical temper in England and America of the war and postwar period, roughly the last fifteen years, as Milton criticism clarifies it."

924 STARNES, DeWITT T. The Hesperian Gardens in Milton. UTSE, 31, 1952, 42-51.
A consideration of Stephanus and Natalis Comes as sources of Milton's identification of the garden with the Elysian Field and the Isles of the Blest.

925 ------. John Milton and Renaissance Dictionaries. UTSE, 1943, pp. 50-65.
Suggests that Milton was indebted to some or all of the dictionaries.

926 ------. Proper Names in Milton: New Annotations. A Tribute to G. C. Taylor (Chapel Hill: Univ. of North Carolina Press, 1952), pp. 38-61.
Argues "that the reference books, especially the lexicons and dictionaries known to Milton and his contemporaries, are often the best guides to the author's meaning."

927 ------ and ERNEST W. TALBERT. Milton and the Dictionaries. Classical Myth and Legend in Renaissance Dictionaries: A Study of Renaissance Dictionaries in Their Relation to the Classical Learning of Contemporary English Writers (Chapel Hill: Univ. of North Carolina Press, 1955), pp. 226-39.
Milton probably used the Thesaurus of Robert Stephanus and the Dictionarium of Charles Stephanus.
Rev: D. C. Allen, MLN, 71, 1956, 598; R. A. Fraser, SAQ, 55, 1956, 511-2; W. J. Ong, S. J., Class. Bull., 32, 1956, 70; Archer Taylor, RN, 9, 1956, 108-10; Douglas Bush, MP, 54, 1957, 200-2; Michel Poirier, EA, 10, 1957, 247-8; C. R. Thompson, SQ, 8, 1957, 233-5; R. R. Bolgar, RES, 9, 1958, 63-5.

928 STEADMAN, JOHN M. Chaste Muse and Casta Juventus: Milton, Minturno, and Scaliger on Inspiration and the Poet's Character. Italica, 40,
1963, 28-34.
> An examination of the antithesis between heavenly inspiration and the effects
> of love and wine against the background of Renaissance poetic theory and
> mythography.

929 ------. Ethos and Dianoia: Character and Rhetoric in Paradise Lost.
Language and Style in Milton: A Symposium in Honor of the Tercentenary of Paradise Lost. Ed. by Ronald David Emma and John T. Shawcross (New York: Frederick Ungar, 1967), pp. 193-232.
> Examines ethos and dianoia, character and thought, in light of the Aristo-
> telian classifications, and shows how Milton applies rhetorical and logical
> principles in Paradise Lost, especially in the longer speeches.

930 ------. Milton's Epic Characters: Image and Idol. Chapel Hill: Univ. of
North Carolina Press, 1968. xiii, 343pp.
> "This volume explores the intellectual background of Paradise Lost and
> Paradise Regained, with particular emphasis on problems of characterization.
> Though its end is literary criticism, its method is primarily that of the history
> of ideas." Most of the chapters have been published previously but have
> been revised for this study. Each chapter is entered separately under its
> appropriate classification in this bibliography. Appendices: Renaissance Def-
> initions of the Hero, pp. 319-24; Heroes and Daemons, pp. 324-6; Mazzoni
> on the Nature of the Hero, pp. 327-30.

931 ------. Milton and Mazzoni: The Genre of the Divina Commedia. HLQ,
23, 1960, 107-22.
> "That Milton subscribed to Mazzoni's conception of Dante's poem as a
> 'comedy' seems practically certain."

932 ------. Milton and the Renaissance Hero. Oxford: Clarendon Press, 1967.
xiii, 209pp.
> A consideration of (1) Milton's "treatment of the heroic formulae commonly
> accepted as ethical and literary norms, (2) his distinction between their valid
> and invalid modes, and (3) his revaluation of the epic tradition in terms of
> this dichotomy." Discusses, i.a., the critiques of fortitude, sapience, leadership,
> amor, and magnanimity.
> Rev: James H. Sims, SCN, 26, 1968, 2-3; VQR, 44, 1968, lxi; W. J. Barnes,
> QQ, 75, 1968, 161-6.

933 STEIN, ARNOLD. Milton and Metaphysical Art: an Exploration. ELH,
16, 1949, 120-34.

934 STILLMAN, DONALD G. Milton as Proof Reader. MLN, 54, 1939, 353-4.
> Concludes that "Milton's carefully revised manuscript was closer to his
> wishes than the first edition."

935 STOLL, ELMER E. Criticisms Criticized: Spenser and Milton. JEGP, 41,
1942, 451-77.
> A review of recent criticism. Latter portion reprinted in From Shakespeare
> to Joyce, pp. 413-21.

936 ------. From Shakespeare to Joyce: Authors and Critics, Literature and
Life. New York: Doubleday, 1944. x, 442pp.

Contains three articles on Milton, which are noted in their appropriate sections.

937 ------. Milton Classical and Romantic. PQ, 23, 1944, 222-47.
"...Milton seems too well balanced and disciplined, too sober and responsible, for a Romantic."

938 ------. Milton, Puritan of the Seventeenth Century. Poets and Playwrights (Minneapolis: Univ. of Minnesota Press, 1930), pp. 241-95. Reprinted, London: Russell and Russell, 1965; Minneapolis: Univ. of Minnesota Paperback, 1967. London: Oxford Univ. Press, 1967.
An appreciative account of Milton and how he reveals himself in his works.

939 ------. Milton a Romantic. RES, 8, 1932, 425-36.
On the interests of the Romantic poets and romantic elements in Milton's poetry, especially Paradise Lost.

940 STOLLMAN, SAMUEL S. Milton and Judaism. Doctoral diss., Wayne State Univ., 1964. Abs., DA, 25, 1965, 5264.

941 STRACHEY, LYTTON. Milton. Spectatorial Essays (London: Chatto and Windus, 1964), pp. 104-8.
A reprint of a 1908 essay. Emphasizes the artistic side of Milton's works, not the theological.

942 STROUP, THOMAS B. Implications of the Theory of Climatic Influence in Milton. MLQ, 4, 1943, 185-9.
Believes that the theory influenced Milton's interpretation of the universe and had a bearing on his attitude toward his own work.

943 ------. Religious Rite and Ceremony in Milton's Poetry. Lexington: Univ. of Kentucky Press, 1968. ix, 83pp.
Suggests that the words of ritual and liturgy, learned during Milton's youth, "often echo in his verses as cues to their occasions and suggest to wary readers the motifs of their forms deep within the poem." Chapters: The Minor Poems, Paradise Lost, Paradise Regained, Samson Agonistes.
Rev: Anthony Low, SCN, 26, 1968, 3-4; H. E. Bowen, SAB, 33, 1968, 20-1; MN, 2, 1968, 10.

944 SUMMERS, JOSEPH H., ed. The Lyric and Dramatic Milton. Selected Papers from the English Institute. With a Foreword. New York and London: Columbia Univ. Press, 1965. xii, 190pp.
Contains papers read at the English Institute in 1963 and 1964 by L. L. Martz, C. L. Barber, I. G. MacCaffrey, W. G. Madsen, E. Weismiller, and J. H. Summers. Three papers are on the Minor Poems, and three are on Samson Agonistes. In this bibliography each paper is listed under its individual author.
Rev: Agnes M. C. Latham, YWES, 207-8, 211; J. Max Patrick, SCN, 24, 1966, 21-2; J. C. Maxwell, N&Q, N. S., 13, 1966, 397-9; Jackson I. Cope, RN, 19, 1966, 164-6; W. J. Barnes, QQ, 75, 1968, 161-6; Edgar Mertner, Anglia, 86, July, 1968, 225-9.

945 ------. Milton and the Cult of Conformity. YR, 46, 1957, 511-27. Reprinted in Milton: Modern Judgements, ed. by Alan Rudrum (London: MacMillan, 1968), pp. 29-43.
Appreciative analysis of Milton's position in the twentieth century. "How-

ever much we may disagree with or disbelieve in specific items in Milton's cosmos, the major poems provide as exciting and challenging literary experiences as we are likely to discover in an age which has been justly labeled both 'the age of anxiety' and 'the age of conformity.' "

946   SVENDSEN, KESTER. Cosmological Lore in Milton. ELH, 9, 1942, 198-223.
        Gives "an examination of the cosmological phenomena of the sublunar vault as Milton refers to them in his prose as well as in his poetry. A collateral purpose ... [is] ... a demonstration of the usefulness to the study of Milton of such popular encyclopedias of science as Bartholomew's De Proprietatibus Rerum (1535), Caxton's Mirrour of the World (1481), La Primaudaye's The French Academie (1618), and John Swan's Speculum Mundi (1643)."

947   ------. Milton and the Encyclopedias of Science. SP, 39, 1942, 303-27.
        Offers three generalizations: "first, the vernacular encyclopedias of science popular in the Middle Ages and the Renaissance constitute a most significant portion of the background against which Milton's works should be studied; second, the bulk of Milton's science is ... the traditional heritage of the seventeenth century from the Middle Ages ... and third, the widespread dissemination in and by these encyclopedias of scientific ideas and terms also in Milton makes definite source ascription as to particulars of science distinctly hazardous."

948   ------. Milton and Science. Cambridge: Harvard Univ. Press, 1956. viii, 304pp.
        "What is proposed here, then, is a comprehensive study of natural science in Milton, based on the medieval and Renaissance encyclopedias of science in the vernacular but extending to popular learning in any form and occasionally including documents in new science as these are relevant."
        Rev: Arnold Davenport, YWES, 173-4; Stephen Merton, SCN, 15, 1957, 3-4; W. B. Hunter, Jr., MLN, 72, 1957, 620-2; F. R. Johnson, RN, 10, 1957, 201; W. R. Gilman, QJS, 43, 1957, 90-1; Wilhelmina Gordon, QQ, 64, 1957, 621-2; E. M. Clark, BA, 31, 1957, 198-9; Douglas Bush, Isis, 48, 1957, 494-5; M. G. Parks, DR, 37, 1957, 302-8; V. de S. Pinto, N&Q, N. S., 4, 1957, 273-4; R. H. Syfret, RES, 9, 1958, 322-4; J. Bronowski, MLR, 53, 1958, 106-7; Allan Gilbert, SAQ, 57, 1958, 513-6; D. H. M. Woollam, Camb. Rev., 78, 1958, 420, 423.

949   ------. Milton's Use of Natural Science, with Special Reference to Certain Encyclopedias of Science in English. Doctoral diss., Univ. of North Carolina, 1940. Abs., Univ. of North Carolina Record, No. 359, 1943, pp. 85-7.

950   SWEDENBERG, H. T., Jr. The Theory of the Epic in England, 1650-1800. Univ. of California Publications in Eng., 15. Berkeley: Univ. of California Press, 1944. 396pp.
        Milton discussed, passim, but the study contains no detailed analysis of the poet's epic theory.

951   SYPHER, WYLIE. The Metaphysicals and the Baroque. PR, 11, 1944, 3-17.
        Examines Donne, Milton, and various others in light of Eliot's criticism of artificial language. Concludes that Milton is the greatest of the Baroque poets.

952   TATE, ALLEN. Notes on Milton. NR, 68, 1931, 266-8.
        A review article of Patterson's edition of the works plus critical remarks on

Milton. "It is high time that the modern poets, who feel strongly other seventeenth-century influences, came to a better view of Milton's significance and style."

953 TAYLOR, DICK, JR. Grace as a Means of Poetry: Milton's Pattern for Salvation. TSE, 4, 1954, 57-90.
Milton believed that salvation came only by God's grace but that man had to prove himself eligible by trial and temptation. This provides an organizing pattern for the major poems.

954 TAYLOR, GEORGE C. Milton's English. N&Q, 178, 1940, 56-7.
Milton's vocabulary does not favor Latin rather than native English words.

955 ------. Milton's Use of Du Bartas. Cambridge: Harvard Univ. Press; London: Milford, 1934. 129pp.

956 ------. Some Patristic Conventions Common to Shakespeare and Milton. SP, 28, 1931, 652-6.
Points out that Shakespeare and Milton held many opinions in common and holds that source hunters forget the commonplaceness of many of the ideas of the age.

957 TAYLOR, IVAN E. John Milton's Views on the Teaching of Foreign Languages. MLJ, 33, 1949, 528-36.

958 [KELLY] TERESA, SISTER MARGARET. A Paradise Remembered. Thought, 22, 1947, 483-94.
Considers the influence of Dante and Italy on Milton.

959 THALER, ALWIN. Shakespeare and Milton Once More. SAMLA Studies in Milton. Ed. by J. Max Patrick (Gainesville: Univ. of Florida Press, 1953), pp. 80-99.
Supplements his earlier studies in tracing reminiscences of Shakespeare's works in Milton.

960 ------. Shakespearean Recollection in Milton: A Summing Up. Shakespeare and Our World (Knoxville: Univ. of Tennessee Press, 1966), pp. 139-227.
Study is intended to prove that "the form and substance of Milton's work was significantly influenced by his Shakespearean memories...." Cites parallels from thirty-five of Shakespeare's plays and the nondramatic poems. Shows an abundance of parallels in Paradise Lost, Paradise Regained, and Samson Agonistes.

961 ------. Shakespeare's Silences. Cambridge: Harvard Univ. Press, 1929.
Contains two articles on Milton: The Shakespearean Element in Milton, pp. 139-208; Milton in the Theatre, pp. 209-56. Both are reprints of Stevens' Nos. 2566 and 487, resp. The first is supplemented by Thaler in his Shakespeare and Milton Once More (SAMLA Studies in Milton, pp. 80-99).

962 THOMPSON, ELBERT N. S. Essays on Milton. New York: Russell and Russell, 1967. 217pp.
A reprint of Stevens' No. 2416, published in 1914. "An interesting collection of studies with original contributions. Contains: Milton, The Last of the Elizabethans; Milton's Temperament and Ideals; The True Bearing of Milton's Prose; Epic Structure of Paradise Lost; The Sources of Paradise Lost; The Theme of Paradise Lost; Milton's Art" (Stevens' annotation).

963 THOMPSON, HARLEY S. Cicero's Influence on Milton. Doctoral diss.,
     Yale Univ. 1947.

964 THOMPSON, J. A. K. The Classical Background of English Literature.
     London: Allen and Unwin, 1948.
     Milton discussed, pp. 192-8.

965 THOMPSON, L. S. European Books. American Book Collector, 18, 1967,
     28.
     Reviews various European reference works, including Eugenio Garin's
     Geschichte und Dokumente der abendländischen Pädagogik (Rowhalt, 1966)
     which contain commentary on the writings of Milton and others.

966 THORPE, JAMES, ed. Milton Criticism: Selections from Four Centuries.
     New York: Rinehart, 1950. Reprinted, London: Routledge and Kegan
     Paul, 1956, 1962, 1965; New York: Octagon Books, 1966. 376pp.
     Part One contains essays and excerpts from critics ranging from Addison
     to C. S. Lewis and T. S. Eliot; in Part Two Thorpe presents excerpts and
     brief comments from critics from Marvell to Arnold.
     Rev: Arnold Davenport, YWES, 175-6; CE, 11, 1950, 471; T. B. Stroup, SCN,
     8, No. 1, 1950, 2; TLS, Sept. 28, 1951, p. 613; G. S. Fraser, NSN, Oct. 27, 1951,
     pp. 468-9.

967 THWAITES, MICHAEL. Milton Blind. London: Blackwell, 1938. 8pp.
     The year's Newdigate poem. On Milton's ability to inspire modern man
     to trust God.

968 TILLYARD, E. M. W. John Milton (1608-74). Chamber's Encyclopaedia
     (New Edition, London: George Newnes, 1955), 9, 416-9.

969 ------. The Literary Kinds and Milton. Stil- und Formprobleme in der
     Literatur, 5, 1960, 95-103. Reprinted in Essays, Literary and Educa-
     tional by E. M. W. Tillyard (London: Chatto and Windus, 1962), pp.
     71-9.
     The traditional genres were centers of convention for Milton, and they left
     him a freedom which he needed in order to write his own poem.

970 ------. The Metaphysicals and Milton. London: Chatto and Windus, 1956.
     Reprinted, 1960, 1965. 87pp.
     Proposes to examine the alleged opposition of the metaphysicals to Milton.
     Rev: TLS, Dec. 27, 1956, p. 10; NSN, Nov. 3, 1956, pp. 565-6; Christopher
     Hill, Spect, Nov. 23, 1956, pp. 751-2; Kenneth Muir, London Mag., 4, No. 8,
     1957, pp. 8, 70ff; M. Poirier, EA, 10, 1957, 257-8; J. Max Patrick, SCN, 15,
     1957, 29; Helen Gardner, Oxf. Mag., 76, 1957-8, 240; A. J. Smith, RES, 9,
     1958, 205-7.

971 ------. Milton and the Classics. Essays by Diverse Hands: Being the
     Transactions of the Royal Society of Literature of the United King-
     dom, N.S., 26, 1953, 59-72.
     Milton indebted but not to the extent indicated by many of the source
     hunters.

972 ------. Milton. London: Chatto and Windus; New York: Dial Press, 1930.
     viii, 396pp. Reprinted, London: Chatto and Windus, 1931; New York:
     Barnes and Noble, 1963. Revised Edition, with a Preface by Phyllis B.

Tillyard. London: Chatto and Windus, 1966; New York: Collier-Macmillan, 1967; Harmondsworth: Penguin Books, 1968. viii, 340pp.

Contains sections on the early poems, the period of the prose, Milton's beliefs, and the later poems. Appendices, i.a., on Thomas Young, the dating of the sonnets, and Spenser's influence on Milton. The revised edition is substantially the same work as the 1930 edition.
Rev: H. J. C. Grierson and A. Melville Clark, YWES, 219-22; TLS, May 22, 1930, p. 431; H. Read, Crit, 10, 1930, 192-5; Marjorie Nicolson, MP, 28, 1930, 239-41; G. R. Potter, Univ. of California Chron., 32, 1930, 504-7; George Saintsbury, Bookman, 78, 1930, 161-2; O. Burdett, Merc, 22, 1930, 466-7; K. M. L., Oxf. Mag., Oct. 16, 1930, p. 34; Spect, May 3, 1930, p. 475; O. Burdett, Sat. Rev., 169, 1930, 591; T. E. Welby, WER, 1, 1930, 235-6; E. N. S. Thompson, PQ, 10, 1931, 223-4; H. F. Fletcher, JEGP, 30, 1931, 592-4; W. P. Mustard, AJP, 52, 1931, 92-3; Edwin Greenlaw, MLN, 46, 1931, 527-8; Paul Chauvet, RA-A, 8, 1931, 256-7; J. J. Reilly, CW, 134, 1931, 244-5; F. Delattre, Rev. belge. de Philol. et d'hist., 12, 1933, 309-12; QR, Apr., 1967, p. 233.

973 ------. Milton. London: Longmans for the British Council, 1952. 54pp.
Brief comments on many of the works.

974 ------. The Miltonic Setting: Past and Present. Cambridge: Cambridge Univ. Press; New York: Macmillan, 1938; London: Chatto and Windus, 1938, 1946, 1949, 1957, 1961. xii, 208pp.
Several chapters are reprints. Chapters L'Allegro and Il Penseroso, Milton and Keats, Milton and Primitive Feeling, Milton and Prophetic Poetry, Milton and Protestantism, Milton's Visual Imagination, Milton's Style, Milton and the English Epic Tradition, the Growth of Milton's Epic Plans.
Rev: L. C. Martin, YWES, 175-6; QR, 271, 1938, 182; Denis Saurat, FR, 144, 1938, 367-8, and RES, 14, 1938, 473-4; T. O. Mabbott, Com, 28, 1938, 190; A. M. Witherspoon, SRL, June 18, 1938, p. 16; G. W. Whiting, MP, 36, 1938, 215-7; D. A. Roberts, Nat, 147, 1938, 272; TLS, Mar. 12, 1938, p. 169; F. R. Leavis, Scr, 7, 1938, 104-14; Merc, May, 1938, p. 82; Charles Williams, Crit, 17, 1938, 738-40; N&Q, 174, 1938, 252; B. A. Wright, MLR, 35, 1939, 236-8; A. Brandl, DL, 59, 1939, 1496-9; William R. Parker, MLN, 55, 1940, 215-8; R. Stamm, ESt, 75, 1942, 250-2; TLS, June 26, 1947, p. 380; H. B. C., MGW, June 20, 1947, p. 10.

975 ------. Poetry Direct and Oblique. London: Chatto and Windus, 1934. 286pp.
Milton's works cited in a number of instances to illustrate the differences between direct and implied meaning in poetry.
Rev: TLS, Apr. 26, 1934, p. 298; M. Roberts, Spect, 153, 1934, 23; F. Kendon, FR, 142, 1934, 123-4.

976 ------. Studies in Milton. London: Chatto and Windus, 1951. 176pp. Reprinted, 1955, 1960, 1964.
A number of chapters are reprints. Chapters: Arnold on Milton; the Crisis of Paradise Lost; Satan; Satan, Gabriel, and the Plowman; Adam and Eve in Paradise; Milton's Humour; The Action of Comus; The Christ of Paradise Regained and the Renaissance Heroic Tradition; Private Correspondence and Academic Exercises; Theology and Emotion in Milton. Appendices: Milton and Statius; Milton and Philostratus.
Rev: L. C. Martin, YWES, 116-7; M. C. Bradbrook, NSN, Aug. 4, 1951, pp. 133-4; F. S. Boas, FR, 1016, 1951, 564-5; Hugh I'A Fausset, MGW, July 19,

1951, p. 12; TLS, July 27, 1951, p. 464; Bonamy Dobrée, Spect, Aug. 3, 1951, pp. 166-8; M. G., Twentieth Century, 150, 1951, 171-2.

977 TOUSLEY, MARION. Milton as Mythmaker. Master's thesis, Louisiana State University, 1939.

978 TRINTERUD, L. J. William Haller, Historian of Puritanism. Journal of British Studies, 5, 1966, 33-55.
A summary and evaluation of Haller's many studies on Puritanism. Gives some attention to Haller's interpretation of Milton.

979 [TSUJI], HIROKO KUSAKABE. Syntax and Rhetoric in Milton's Poems. Annual Reports of Studies (Doshisha Women's College), 17, December, 1966, 270-92.

980 TUNG, MASON. The Search for Perfection in John Milton. Doctoral diss., Stanford Univ., 1962. Abs., DA, 23, 1962, 2142-3.

981 TURNER, AMY L. The Visual Arts in Milton's Poetry. Doctoral diss., Rice Univ. 1955.

982 TUVE, ROSEMOND. Baroque and Mannerist Milton? JEGP, 60, 1961, 817-33.
Questions the usefulness of categorizing the poems of great writers, with special reference to Milton.

983 TUVESON, ERNEST L. Millennium and Utopia: A Study in the Background of the Idea of Progress. Berkeley: Univ. of California Press, 1949.
On the rise of the idea that a millennium was being brought about by God. Milton, passim.
Rev: G. N. Conklin, RN, 3, 1950, 47-8; G. R. Stephenson, NYTBR, Mar. 5, 1950, p. 18.

984 UEKI, TOSHŪCHI. An Examination of Milton's Use of Myth and Legend. Hyozo Prefectural Normal School (Japan), Education Research Institute Reports, 1948.

985 ------. Milton's View of Women. Kobe University Educational Research Reports (Japan), 3, 1951.

986 ULLANAESS, S. P. N. John Milton. Kirke og Kultur, 63, 1958, 228-34.
On Milton's high and universal status.

987 VALENTE, LEONE. Milton. La poesia inglese ad il suo contributo alla conoscenza dello spirito (Firenze: Valecchi, 1947), pp. 97-130.

988 VECHTMAN-VETH, A. C. E. A Guide to English Studies: Suggestions for the Study of Milton and Dryden. ES, 11, 1929, 137-40.

989 VIA, JOHN A. Studies in the Imagery of Milton's Poetry and Prose to 1642. Doctoral diss., Univ. of Illinois, 1967. Abs., DA, 29, 1968, 580-A. 426pp.

990 VILLANI, FELICE. Criteri e tendenze della piu recente critica Miltoniana. Letterature Moderne, 5, Dec., 1954, 637-46.
On the recent criticism of E. M. W. Tillyard, C. S. Lewis, C. Williams, B. Rajan, and others.

991 ------. Modelli italiani de Milton. Giornale Italiano de Filologia, 8, 1955, 52-7.

Mainly appreciative remarks on the work of F. T. Prince concerning the Italian influence on Milton.

992 VISIAK, E. H. The Animus Against Milton. Derby, England: The Grasshopper Press, 1945. 9pp.

Notices several aspects of anti-Miltonic criticism.

Rev: N&Q, 188, 1945, 176.

993 ------. Milton Agonistes: A Metaphysical Criticism. New York: Haskell House, 1966.

A reprint of Stevens' No. 2521, published in 1923. "A psychological study, not literary in purpose and not fully tempered by a knowledge of Milton's mind; attempts to show his interest in Satan due to war with self" (Stevens' annotation).

994 ------. Notes on Milton. N&Q, 174, 1940, 184-6, 276-8, 311-4, 453-4.

Topics discussed, resp., are Milton's development towards Quakerism, Samson Agonistes, Milton's egotism, and Milton's personality.

995 ------. Notes on Milton. N&Q, 180, 1941, 133-4, 313, 316.

The subjects include Milton's genius and Milton's idea of chastity, resp.

996 ------. Notes on Milton. N&Q, 183, 1942, 250.

On familiarized phrases and their sources.

997 ------. The Portent of Milton: Some Aspects of His Genius. London: W. Laurie, 1958.

Most of the chapters are revised reprints of earlier publications, but the title essay, The Portent of Milton—The Power, pp. 15-46, is here published for the first time. Other chapters: Victorian Veneration, Milton in His Own Times, Creative Genius, Invested Power, Sublimity and Humanism, Comus, Milton's Marriages, Milton on Divorce, Milton's Prose, Milton's Digression, Milton's Magic Shadow.

Rev: Derek Stanford, TT, Apr. 1958, p. 500; TLS, Mar. 21, 1958, pp. 158-9; SCN, 16, 1958, 23-4; Jackson I. Cope, SAQ, 58, 1959, 482-3.

998 VIVANTE, LEONE. John Milton, 1608-1674. English Poetry and Its Contribution to the Knowledge of a Creative Principle (London: Faber, 1950), pp. 61-75.

On Milton and light.

999 VOGT, KARL F. Milton als Publizist. Eine Untersuchung über die puritanische Auffassung von der Sendung Englands in 17. Jahrhundert. Doctoral diss., Tübingen. Würzburg: R. Mayr, 1933. 100pp.

Rev: A. B[randl], Archiv, 166, 1934, 139-40; H. O. Wilde, Ang. Bbl., 46, 1935, 241.

1000 VOIGT, F. A. Milton Thou Shouldst be Living. . . . NC, 130, 1941, 211-21.

A review of recent books.

1001 VOLTAIRE, FRANÇOIS. Essay on Milton. Ed. by Desmond Flower. Cambridge: Cambridge Univ. Press, 1954. xiv, 29pp. Also privately printed, Cambridge, 1954.

1002   WAIN, JOHN. Strength and Isolation: Pessimistic Notes of a Miltonolater. The Living Milton (London: Routledge and Kegan Paul, 1960), pp. 1-11.
    Appreciative. On the urgency of studying Milton.

1003   WARNER, REX. John Milton. London: Max Parrish, 1949. 112pp.
    A general discussion of Milton's life and art.
    Rev: TLS, Apr. 28, 1950, p. 255; letter by E. M. W. Tillyard, ibid., May 5, 1950, p. 277; NSN, Mar. 11, 1950, p. 284; P. Russell, NER, 135, 1950, 72-4; Howard Doughty, Nat, 170, 1950, 429-30.

1004   WARREN, KATHRYN L. Milton's Concept of the Creation and Nature of Man: An Inquiry into Their Origins. Master's thesis, Univ. of South Carolina, 1951.

1005   WATKINS, J. W. N. Milton's Vision of a Reformed England. Listener, 61, 1959, 168-9, 172.
    Holds that Milton's insistence on external reform stemmed from his erroneous belief that moral truths are self-evident.

1006   WATKINS, WALTER B. C. An Anatomy of Milton's Verse. Baton Rouge: Louisiana State Univ. Press, 1955. Reprinted, Hamden, Connecticut: Shoe String Press, 1965. x, 151pp.
    Chapters: Sensation, Creation, Temptations. In Sensation, Watkins discusses the sensory elements in the poetry; in Creation and in Temptation, he traces those themes in poems ranging from Comus to Samson Agonistes.
    Rev: Arnold Davenport, YWES, 176-7; Marvin Mudrick, HudR, 9, 1956, 126-33; Charles M. Coffin, QQ, 63, 1956, 138-44; TLS, Jan. 20, 1956, p. 38; D. C. Allen, MLN, 71, 1956, 532-3; R. W. Condee, CE, 18, 1956, 176; Kester Svendsen, BA, 30, 1956, 331; Everett H. Emerson, SCN, 15, 1957, 28; K. M. Lea, RES, 7, 1957, 309-10.

1007   WATSON, E. A. F. The Animal World in the Poetry and Drama of the Sixteenth and Seventeenth Centuries, with Special Reference to Spenser, Shakespeare, and Milton. B. Litt. thesis, Lady Margaret Hall, Oxford, 1964.

1008   WATSON, GEORGE. Ramus, Miss Tuve, and the New Petromachia. MP, 55, 1958, 259-62.
    Rejects R. Tuve's linking of the metaphysical style with Ramism (in her Elizabethan and Metaphysical Imagery, 1947) because the only poets who are plausibly Ramists—Sidney, Jonson, and Milton—are not metaphysical.

1009   WEDDELL, FITZ-JOHN. References to Nature in the English Poems of John Milton. Master's thesis, Columbia Univ., 1932. 100pp.

1010   WEDGWOOD, C. V. John Milton. Seventeenth Century English Literature. Home Univ. Library (Oxford: Oxford Univ. Press, 1950; reprinted as A Galaxy Book, New York: Oxford Univ. Press, 1961), pp. 108-19.
    Rev: TLS, Oct. 6, 1950, p. 626; H. R. Charlton, MGW, Nov. 2, 1950, p. 11; R. G. Cox, Scr, 18, 1951, 56-9.

1011   WEIDHORN, MANFRED. Dreams in Seventeenth-Century English Literature. Doctoral diss., Columbia Univ., 1963. Abs., DA, 26, 1965, 1638.

"The last chapter gathers Milton's few remarks on the dream and his uses of it in lyric, masque, vision, sonnet, and epic."

1012 WESEMAN, FRIEDRICH. Milton and das Naturrecht. Versuch eines Beitrages zur Geschichte der Menschenrechte. Doctoral diss., Hamburg, 1949. 151pp.

1013 WEST, ROBERT. Milton as Philosophical Poet. Th'Upright Heart and Pure. Ed. by Amadeus P. Fiore, O. F. M. (Pittsburgh and Louvain: Duquesne Univ. Press, 1967), pp. 131-41.
An appreciative essay. "The poet's way is not the philosopher's way, but perhaps his engagement with the issues does entitle Milton to the adjective 'philosophical'."

1014 WHITELEY, M. Verse and Its Feet. RES, N.S., 9, 1958, 268-78.
Reply by F. T. Prince, ibid., pp. 278-9. On Prince's comments in The Italian Element in Milton's Verse.

1015 WHITING, GEORGE W. The Father to the Son. MLN, 65, 1950, 191-3.
Milton follows the Greek Fathers and St. Ambrose in believing that in creating man the Son was the external efficiency of God.

1016 ------. Milton and Cockeram's Dictionaire. N&Q, 193, 1948, 555-8.
This work (1623) is useful in determining the meaning of Milton's words.

1017 ------. Milton and This Pendant World. Austin: Univ. of Texas Press, 1958. xviii, 364pp. Reprinted, New York: Octagon, 1967.
"The purpose of this study of Milton's poetry and the religious tradition is to interpret Milton in an age increasingly skeptical, in a culture dominated by the assumptions of the natural and historical sciences and by the illusions of progress and enlightenment." Chapters: Comus, Jonson, and the Critics; Lycidas, the Corrupt Clergy, and the Reformation; The Mysterious Stairs, the Glassy Sea and the Golden Compasses; Paradise Lost, Protestantism, and the Retreat from Christianity; The Pattern of Time and Eternity; Samson Agonistes and the Geneva Bible; The Paradise Within; Bibliography, Index.
Rev: Agnes M. C. Latham, YWES, 181; Wilhelmina Gordon, QQ, 65, 1958, 712-3; SCN, 17, 1959, item 65; Albert H. Carter, RN, 12, 1959, 117-9; Burton O. Kurth, Pers, 41, 1960, 402-3; A. S. P. Woodhouse, MP, 57, 1960, 272-4; Carl S. Meyer, Concordia Theol. Monthly, 31, 1960, 392-3; Fitzroy Pyle, RES, 11, 1960, 329-31; Karl Brunner, Eras, 14, 1961, 297-8.

1018 ------. Milton and the Return from Avilion. N&Q, N.S., 7, 1960, 442-3.
On Milton and the Matter of Britain.

1019 ------. Milton in The Classical Tradition. N&Q, 197, 1952, 556-60.
I.e., the book by Gilbert Highet.

1020 ------. Milton's Literary Milieu. Chapel Hill: Univ. of North Carolina Press; London: Oxford Univ. Press, 1939. Reprinted, London: Russell and Russell, 1964. xii, 401pp.
"The definite purpose of this volume is to compare ideas in Milton's poetry and prose with those in contemporary writing, hexaemeral, historical, cartographical, psychological, theological, poetical, and controversial."
Rev: B. A. Wright, MLR, 35, 1940, 393-4; E. N. S. T[hompson], PQ, 19, 1940, 414-5; Douglas Bush, JEGP, 39, 1940, 418-20; A. R. Benham, MLQ, 1, 1940, 558-9; A. M. Witherspoon, SRL, Jan. 20, 1940, p. 7; A. S. P. Woodhouse, UTQ, 10, 1941, 502-4; P. L. Carver, RES, 20, 1944, 163-6.

1021 ------. Milton's Rules for -ed. MLN, 49, 1934, 166-8.
      Disagrees with H. Darbishire on Milton's spelling practices.

1022 ------. Notes on Milton's Rabbinical Readings. N&Q, 162, 1932, 344-6.
      On the study by Harris F. Fletcher.

1023 ------. Pareus, the Stuarts, Laud, and Milton. SP, 50, 1953, 215-29.
      On Milton and Pareus' doctrine of royal responsibility.

1024 WILDE, HANS-OSKAR. Miltons geistesgeschichtliche Bedeutung. Heidel-
      berg: Winter, 1933. 144pp.
      Rev: Lit. Zentralblatt, 84, 1933, 790; J. H. Hanford, MLN, 51, 1936, 53-4.

1025 ------. Miltons personliche und ideele Welt in ihrer Beziehung zum
      Aristokratismus. Bonn: Hanstein, 1933. 50pp.

1026 WILDING, MICHAEL. Milton's Critics: Another Ten Years. MCR, No.
      7, 1964, pp. 126-35.
      "The essential case, in fact, against Milton hasn't in any real way been
      answered."

1027 WILKENFELD, ROGER B. Theoretics or Polemics? Milton Criticism
      and the Dramatic Axiom. PMLA, 82, 1967, 505-15.
      Analyzes historical criticism of Milton's dramatic quality. Argues that "the
      term [dramatic] has been drained of meaning if not of imaginative energy,"
      and should be re-examined by critics and readers.

1028 WILLEY, BASIL. Eustace Mandeville Wetenhall Tillyard, 1889-1962.
      Proceedings of the British Academy, 49, 1963, 387-405. Issued also as a
      pamphlet, London: Oxford Univ. Press, 1965.

1029 ------. The Seventeenth Century Background: Studies in the Thought of
      the Age in Relation to Poetry and Religion. London: Chatto and
      Windus, 1934. viii, 315pp.
      Milton discussed, pp. 69-76 (on Scriptural interpretation), pp. 219-63 (the
      heroic poem in a scientific age), and passim. There have been several re-
      prints of this study, including paperback editions (e.g. Penguin, 1962).
      Rev: TLS, Apr. 19, 1934, p. 269; H. J. C. Grierson, Scr, 3, 1934, 294; Walter
      Graham, JEGP, 42, 1943, 468-9; Arthur Barker, PRv, 52, 1943, 413-4; D. C.
      Allen, MLN, 59, 1944, 437-8.

1030 WILLIAMS, ARNOLD. Conservative Critics of Milton. SR, 49, 1941,
      90-106.
      On the criticism of T. S. Eliot, H. J. C. Grierson, and E. M. W. Tillyard.

1031 ------. Methods and Achievements in the Use of Milton's Sources: a
      Defense. Papers of the Michigan Academy, 32, 1948 for 1946, 471-80.
      A reply to Gullette, ibid., pp. 447-56.

1032 WILLIAMS, CHARLES. John Milton. The Image of the City and Other
      Essays. Selected by Anne Ridler (London: Oxford Univ. Press, 1958),
      pp. 26-36.
      A reprint of Williams' Introduction in his edition of The English Poems of
      John Milton (1940).

1033 ------. Milton. The English Poetic Mind (Oxford: Clarendon Press,
      1932), pp. 110-52. Reprinted, London: Russell and Russell, 1963.

Interprets Milton's poetry as a battle between gods and false gods.
Rev: TLS, June 16, 1932, p. 443; B. E. C. Davis, MLR, 28, 1933, 112-3; K.
Arns, ESt, 68, 1933, 119-20.

1034 ------. The New Milton. Merc, 36, 1937, 225-61. Reprinted in The Image
of the City and Other Essays. Selected by Anne Ridler (London: Oxford
Univ. Press, 1958), pp. 19-25.
Favors a kindlier interpretation.

1035 WILLIAMSON, GEORGE. Milton and the Mortalist Heresy. SP, 32, 1935,
553-79.
Emphasizes the importance of Browne's Religio Medici (1642) in inspiring
the mortalist controversy, rather than Overton's Mans Mortallitie (1643).

1036 ------. Milton and Others. Chicago: Univ. of Chicago Press, 1965; London:
Faber and Faber, 1965. 227pp.
Contains essays, some reprints, on Milton, Dryden, Marvell, Donne, Vaughan,
and Browne. In this bibliography, the essays on Milton are listed under their
appropriate classification.
Rev: Agnes M. C. Latham, YWES, 204, 207, 211, 212; TLS, Oct. 28, 1965,
p. 960; C. F. Williamson, RES, N. S., 17, 1966, 435-6; Geoffrey Bullough,
English, 16, 1966, 19-20; John L. Lievsay, SAQ, 66, 1967, 260-3; N. W.
Bawcutt, N&Q, N.S., 14, 1967, 114-6.

1037 ------. Milton the Anti-Romantic. MP, 60, 1962, 13-21. Reprinted in Mil-
ton and Others (Chicago: Univ. of Chicago Press; London: Faber and
Faber, 1965), pp. 11-25.
Considers Milton's allusions to romances of chivalry in his chief poetic works.

1038 ------. Seventeenth-Century Contexts. London: Faber and Faber, 1960.
Contains reprints of several essays, i.a., Milton and the Mortalist Heresy
and The Obsequies for Edward King.
Rev: TLS, Aug. 26, 1960, p. 547; G. M., NSN, Sept. 17, 1960, p. 400.

1039 WILSON, ARNOLD. New Light on Milton. NC, 119, 1936, 495-506.
On the contributions of Belloc, Skeat, Visiak and P. B. and E. M. W. Tillyard. Censures Belloc for his attitude toward Milton the man.

1040 WILSON, HENRY. Milton's Reaction to His Blindness. Medical History,
4, 1960, 186-95.
Men "should draw comfort from the resilience of a haughty poet who was
not defeated by his blindness but suppressed his human disappointment
from his prose, only to sublimate it in his poetry."

1041 WOLFE, DON M., ed. Leveller Manifestoes of the Puritan Revolution.
Foreword by Charles A. Beard. New York and London: Nelson, 1944.
xvi, 440pp.
Rev: H. N. Brailsford, NSN, Aug. 26, 1944, pp. 140-1; E. N. S. Thompson,
PQ, 23, 1944, 287; William Haller, MLN, 60, 1945, 135-6; H. J. C. Grierson,
MLR, 40, 1945, 138-40; J. R. Roberts, MLQ, 6, 1945, 105-6; A. S. P. Wood-
house, UTQ, 15, 1945, 99-100; Godfrey Davies, Pol. Sci. Quar., 60, 1945,
155-6.

1042 ------. Limits of Miltonic Toleration. JEGP, 60, 1961, 834-46.
"The limits of Milton's toleration ... are clearly defined in his undeviating
hostility toward freedom of Catholic conscience; and his failure to speak for

the Jews can only be interpreted, in the light of contemporary agitation, as a reluctance to permit them freedom of worship."

1043 ------. Milton and Hobbes: A Contrast in Social Temper. SP, 41, 1944, 410-26.
"Among seventeenth-century thinkers, no two critics offer more diverse or contradictory interpretations of root social issues than John Milton and Thomas Hobbes." Their "ideological contrasts throw into sharp focus Milton's philosophical position in the stirring public affairs that absorbed the middle years of his life."

1044 ------. Milton and the Theory of Democracy. Doctoral diss., Univ. of Pittsburgh, 1930. Abs., Univ. of Pittsburgh, Abstracts of Theses, 6, 1930, 206-12.

1045 ------, ed. A Milton Evening. Milton Society of America, 1948.
Tributes to J. H. Hanford and brief quotations from his work; biographical statements.

1046 ------, ed. A Milton Evening. Milton Society of America, 1951.
Tributes to R. D. Havens and H. J. C. Grierson and brief quotations from their work; biographical statements.

1047 ------, ed. Milton Evening. Milton Society of America, 1953. Published as a supplement to SCN, 11, Winter, 1953, ed. by J. Max Patrick.
Tributes to Helen Darbishire and D. L. Clark and brief quotations from their work; biographical statements. Articles: D. L. Clark, John Milton and the fitted stile or lofty, mean, or lowly, pp. 5-9; a letter from Sir H. J. C. Grierson, p. 9, for his selection as honored scholar two years before; and Helen Darbishire, The Chronology of Milton's Handwriting, p. 11.

1048 ------. Milton, Lilburne, and the People. MP, 31, 1934, 253-72.
"The purpose of this study is to clarify Milton's various attitudes toward his countrymen and their capacity for self-government by contrasting them with the beliefs of his contemporary, John Lilburne."

1049 ------. Milton under Glass. TLS, May 18, 1956, p. 304.
A defense of recent Milton scholarship.

1050 ------. Milton's Conception of the Ruler. SP, 33, 1936, 253-72.
"Inherited from Plato and Aristotle, modified by Christian doctrine, the conception of a leader holding his position by virtue of his superior integrity alone dwelt in Milton's mind persistently from youth to old age."

1051 WOLFF, CYNTHIA GRIFFIN. Literary Reflections of the Puritan Character. JHI, 29, 1968, 13-32.
The author examines the Puritan character from psychological, religious and sociological points of view. Brief reference to Milton.

1052 WOODHOUSE, A. S. P. The Approach to Milton: a Note on Practical Criticism. TRSC, 38, 1944, 201-13.
Censures the New Critics and defends the "conservative or solid" type of criticism.

1053 ------. Background for Milton. UTQ, 10, 1941, 504-5.
A review of recent Milton studies.

1054 ------. The Historical Criticism of Milton. PMLA, 66, 1951, 1033-44. Reprinted in The Modern Critical Spectrum. Ed. by Gerald J. and Nancy M. Goldberg (Englewood Cliffs, N.J.: Prentice-Hall, 1962), pp. 233-43.
A paper read before the Milton group of MLA on Dec. 28, 1950.

1055 ------. Milton and His Age. UTQ, 5, 1935, 130-9.
Comments on studies by Hanford, Sewell, Willey, Saurat, Powicke, and Cassirer.

1056 ------. Milton the Poet. Sedgewick Memorial Lecture, University of British Columbia. Toronto: J. M. Dent, 1955. 30pp.
Attacks Eliot, Brooks, Empson, and Bodkin and considers six distinctive marks of Milton the poet.
Rev: SCN, 14, 1956, 1.

1057 ------. Milton, Puritanism, and Liberty. UTQ, 4, 1935, 483-513.
On the contribution of Puritanism to Milton's concept of Christian liberty. Compares Milton and Roger Williams.

1058 ------. Notes on Milton's Early Development. UTQ, 13, 1943, 66-101.
On the dates and interrelations of the early poems and prolusions.

1059 ------. Notes on Milton's Views on the Creation: the Initial Phase. PQ, 28, 1949, 211-36.
On Milton's relation to the orthodox doctrine and on his break with it on the question of creation ex nihilo.

1060 ------. The Poet and His Faith: Religion and Poetry in England from Spenser to Eliot and Auden. Chicago and London: Univ. of Chicago Press, 1965. xii, 304pp.
Chapter 4, Milton, pp. 90-122. Discusses Milton's poetry from the Cambridge period through Samson Agonistes. Sees the poems as a coalescence of a religious and an aesthetic experience.
Rev: R. G. Cox, N&Q, N. S., 14, 1967, 79-80; R. W. Battenhouse, SAQ, 66, 1967, 126-7.

1061 ------. Some Reflections on How to Read Milton. SCN, 16, No. 1, 1958, item 54.
Address at annual Milton Society dinner, 1957.

1062 WRENN, C. C. The Language of Milton. Studies in English Language and Literature Presented to Karl Brunner on the Occasion of His Seventieth Birthday. Ed. by S. Korniger. Weiner Beiträge zur Englischen Philologie, 65 (Wein-Stuggart: Wilhelm Braumuller, 1957), pp. 252-67.
Appreciative.

1063 WRIGHT, B. A. Shade for Tree in Milton's Poetry. N&Q, N.S., 5, 1958, 205-8.
Insists that Milton extensively used shade as a metonymy for tree.

1064 WRIGHT, F. A., and T. A. SINCLAIR. A History of Later Latin Literature from the Middle of the Fourth to the End of the Seventeenth Century. London: Routledge, 1931. vii, 417pp.
Milton's Latin works discussed, pp. 396-7. Holds that Latin literature ends with Milton's death in 1674.

1065   WYLD, H. C. The significance of -'n and -en in Milton's Spelling. ESt,
       70, 1935, 138-48.
         Examines and enlarges upon H. Darbishire's discussion in her introduction
         to The Manuscript of Milton's Paradise Lost, Book I (1931).

1066   Young Critical Eyes Turn on Great Poets. The Times, Sept. 22, 1960,
       p. 15d.
         Calls Kermode's The Living Milton a commando raid defying F. R. Leavis
         and others.

1067   ZAGARIA, R. Serafino da Salandra, Inspiratore di Milton. Bari: Resta,
       1950. 86pp.

1068   ZAGORIN, PEREZ. John Milton. A History of Political Thought in the
       English Revolution (London: Routledge, 1954), pp. 106-20.
         "The vast amount of writing that has appeared ... serves, I think, to obscure
         the fact that as a political theorist and systematic thinker, he was not of the
         first order."

1069   ZANCO, AURELIO. Le concezione della donna in Milton. LM, 4, 1953,
       636-52.
         On Milton's treatment of women.

1070   ZWICKY, LAURIE B. Milton's Use of Time: Image and Principle.
       Doctoral diss., Univ. of Oklahoma, 1959. Abs., DA, 20, 1959, 1030.

PARADISE LOST

1071 ADAMS, JOHN R. The Theism of Paradise Lost. Pers, 22, 1941, 174-80.

1072 ADAMS, ROBERT M. Literature and Psychology: A Question of Significant Form. L&P, 5, 1955, 67-72.
Takes Paradise Lost as an example in which the artist's concern embodied not only form and theme, but audience reaction to his impression-creating attempt. "In other words, the literary form is not invariably the most significant form."

1073 ------. The Text of Paradise Lost: Emphatic and Unemphatic Spellings. MP, 52, 1954, 84-91.

1074 ADAMSON, J. H. The Christ Themes in Paradise Lost. Doctoral diss., Harvard Univ., 1956.

1075 ------. Kepler and Milton. MLN, 74, 1959, 683-5.
An interpretation of Paradise Lost, 8, 122-5, in the light of Kepler's theory of the sun's attractive virtue.

1076 ------. The War in Heaven: Milton's Version of the Merkabah. JEGP, 57, 1958, 690-703.
Suggests that "... Milton's account of the War in Heaven is a Christian adaptation of the Merkabah theme...."

1077 ADDISON, JOSEPH. Criticism on Milton's Paradise Lost. English Reprints. Ed. by Edward Arber (New York: AMS Press, 1966), 2, 1-152.
Stevens' No. 12, published in 1868.

1078 ------. Criticism on Paradise Lost. Edited with Introduction by Albert S. Cook. New York: Phaeton Press Series, 1968. 224pp.
A reprint of the 1924 edition.

1079 ------. Paradise Lost as an Epic. The Practice of Criticism. Ed. by Sheldon P. Zitner and others (Chicago: Scott, Foresman and Co., 1966), pp. 1-14.
A reprint of three of Addison's Spectator essays (1712).

1080 ALLEN, DON CAMERON. The Legend of Noah: Renaissance Rationalism in Art, Science, and Letters. Illinois Studies in Language and Literature, 33, Nos. 3-4. Urbana: Univ. of Illinois Press, 1949. 221pp. Reprinted, 1963.
Paradise Lost, passim.
Rev: Arnold Williams, JEGP, 49, 1950, 581-3.

1081 ------. Milton and the Creation of Birds. MLN, 63, 1948, 263-4.
Milton's letting the "egg come before the chicken" a common seventeenth-century idea.

1082 ------. Milton and the Descent to Light. JEGP, 60, 1961, 614-30. Reprinted in Milton: Modern Essays in Criticism. Ed. by Arthur Barker (New York: Oxford Univ. Press, 1965), pp. 177-95.

In the vertical movement of Paradise Lost, Milton "joins himself to the procession, heathen and Christian, of those who acted in the great allegory of faith, who descended to ascend, who entered the darkness to see the light."

1083 ------. Milton and the Love of Angels. MLN, 76, 1961, 489-90.
On Raphael's description of the union of spirits (Paradise Lost, 8, 620-9) and the concept of the ideal union of lovers.

1084 ------. Milton and the Name of Eve. MLN, 74, 1959, 681-3.
On Paradise Lost, 10, 867-72. "Clement of Alexandria in his Protrepticus says that the Hebrew name Eve when aspirated is identical with the feminine of serpent."

1085 ------. Milton and Rabbi Eliezer. MLN, 63, 1948, 262-3.
Parallels between Paradise Lost and Eliezer's Pirkê.

1086 ------. Milton and the Sons of God. MLN, 61, 1946, 73-9.
On Paradise Lost, 11, 573-87.

1087 ------. Milton's Amarant. MLN, 72, 1957, 256-8.
On Milton's transplanting the flower to heaven.

1088 ------. Milton's Busiris. MLN, 65, 1950, 115-6.
On Paradise Lost, 1, 306-9.

1089 ------. Milton's Eve and the Evening Angels. MLN, 75, 1960, 108-9.
On parallels between Paradise Lost, 4, 449-76, and 8, 250ff., and the traditional distinction between the angels of light and those of darkness.

1090 ------. Milton's Winged Serpents. MLN, 59, 1944, 537-8.
Paradise Lost, 7, 482-4, refers to winged serpents, not dragons.

1091 ------. Paradise Lost, I, 254-255. MLN, 71, 1956, 324-6.

1092 ------. The Scala Religionis in Paradise Lost. MLN, 71, 1956, 404-5.
On Paradise Lost, 8, 253ff.

1093 ------. Two Notes on Paradise Lost. MLN, 68, 1953, 360-1.
On Paradise Lost, 3, 510-11, and 10, 327-29.

1094 ALLISON, ALEXANDER W. A Heterodox Note on Milton's Orthodoxy. PMASAL, 48, 1963, 621-8.
Paradise Lost is only as coherent an embodiment as possible of a system of doctrine itself containing obscurities and unresolved contradictions.

1095 AMES, ELIZABETH MORRIS. The Garden Poetry Tradition in Seventeenth-Century England. Master's Thesis, The American Univ., 1964. 131pp. Abs., Master's Abstracts, 2, No. 3, 1964, 12.
Discusses Milton's Garden of Eden passages in Paradise Lost.

1096 ARYANPUR, MANOOCHER. Paradise Lost and the Odyssey. TSLL, 9, 1967, 151-66.
"Homer's influence on Paradise Lost is rarely concentrated in particular passages; it is diffused throughout whole scenes."

1097 ASHLEY, JACK DILLARD. Cosmic Symbolism in Paradise Lost. Doctoral diss., Vanderbilt, 1960. Abs., DA, 21, 1961, 2701.

1098 AUTRY, RANDALL F. Milton's Beelzebub. Master's thesis, Duke University, 1945.

1099 BAKER, BRUCE P., II. Ironic Contrast in Milton's Paradise of Fools. N&Q, N.S., 13, 1966, 378.
The Paradise of Fools contrasts with the Paradise of Eden.

1100 BAKER, DONALD C. Mammon and Mulciber: An Old Chestnut. N&Q, N.S., 4, 1957, 112-3.
Insists that Mammon and Mulciber are two distinct figures.

1101 ------. On Satan's Hair. N&Q, N.S., 4, 1957, 69-70.
The evil connotations of Paradise Lost, 2, 706-11.

1102 BALDWIN, EDWARD C. Milton and Phineas Fletcher. JEGP, 33, 1934, 543-6.
Milton's indebtedness in Paradise Lost, 10, 504-21.

1103 ------. Some Extra-Biblical Semitic Influences upon Milton's Story of the Fall of Man. JEGP, 28, 1929, 366-401.
"We may confidently affirm that he was acquainted with the products of Jewish learning, and that in the extra-canonical Jewish books may be found precedents for his elaborations of the Genesis story. In view of this fact, the notion formerly held that Milton indulged his inventive faculty in supplementing 'the letter of revelation' must be considerably modified."

1104 BALDWIN, T. W., ALLAN H. GILBERT, and THOMAS O. MABBOTT. A Double Janus. PMLA, 56, 1941, 583-5.
In support of Gilbert, PMLA, 54, 1939, 1026-30.

1105 The Ballet Paradise Lost. MN, 1, 1967, 30-1.
On the first performance of the work by Roland Petit, on Feb. 23, 1967, at the Royal Opera House, Covent Garden.

1106 BANKS, THEODORE H. The Meaning of Gods in Paradise Lost. MLN, 54, 1939, 450-4.
Lists three senses which need to be distinguished.

1107 BARKER, ARTHUR E. . . . And on his Crest Sat Horror: Eighteenth Century Interpretations of Milton's Sublimity and His Satan. UTQ, 11, 1942, 421-36.

1108 ------. Structural Pattern in Paradise Lost. PQ, 28, 1949, 16-30. Reprinted in Milton: Modern Essays in Criticism. A Galaxy Book (New York: Oxford Univ. Press, 1965), pp. 142-55.
Feels that in shifting the number of books from ten to twelve for the 1674 edition, Milton made his poem more epic than tragic, with the center coming between Books 6 and 7, "with evil on the one hand frustrated, and on the other creation and recreation."

1109 BARNETT, PAMELA R. Theodore Haak, F. R. S. (1605-1690): The First German Translator of Paradise Lost. Anglica Germanica: British Studies in Germanic Languages and Literatures, III. The Hague: Mouton and Co., 1962. 274pp.
Two chapters of special interest: Fourteen—The subsequent history of the manuscript Verlustigtes Paradeis and Berge's printed version, pp. 160-7.

Fifteen—A Critical discussion of Das Verlustigte Paradeis, pp. 168-86. Appendix 3: Das Verlustigte Paradeis, pp. 189-260.
Rev: Jackson I. Cope, Isis, 55, 1964, 241; K. G. Knight, MLR, 60, 1965, 142.

1110 BEKKER, HUGO. The Religio-Philosophical Orientations of Vondel's Lucifer, Milton's Paradise Lost, and Grotius' Adamus Exul. Neophil., 44, 1960, 234-44.
"That the difference between Vondel's Lucifer and Milton's Satan is . . . determined by the difference between the Catholic versus the Protestant commitment becomes evident when we consider the Lucifer motif as . . . handled by . . . Hugo Grotius."

1111 BELL, MILLICENT. The Fallacy of the Fall in Paradise Lost. PMLA, 68, 1953, 863-83.
Adam and Eve are never purely good but fallen and capable of redemption from the start.

1112 BENHAM, ALLEN R. Things Unattempted Yet in Prose or Rime. MLQ, 14, 1953, 341-7.
"The things hitherto unattempted in the theme of the fall and restoration of man is to put the old story into a pattern derived from the ancient Greek and Latin epics."

1113 BENNETT, JOSEPHINE W. Milton's Use of the Vision of Er. MP, 36, 1939, 351-8.
Milton uses the passage from Plato in Paradise Lost.

1114 BERCOVITCH, SACVAN. Three Perspectives on Reality in Paradise Lost. UWR, 1, 1965, 239-56.
The angelic, the demonic, and the human, each unfolding on its own level.

1115 BERGEL, LIENHARD. Milton's Paradise Lost, I, 284-95. Expl, 10, 1951, item 3.

1116 BERKELEY, DAVID S. "Precieuse" Gallantry and the Seduction of Eve. N&Q, 196, 1951, 337-9.

1117 BERGER, HARRY, JR. Archaism, Vision, and Revision: Studies in Virgil, Plato, and Milton. Centennial Review, 11, 1967, 24-52.
Demonstrates that Haeckel's theorem that "cultural history is recapitulated in the development of the individual work" holds true for Paradise Lost as well as it does for the Republic and the Aeneid. "Like Plato and Virgil, Milton sees the critical moment of action and freedom occurring now, in the unique revision or re-creation of experience by the poetic will of man, and not then, in the archaic or archetypal and fabled time of ancient gods and heroes."

1118 BERRY, BOYD McCULLOCH. The Doctrine of the Remnant, 1550-1660. A Study in the History of English Puritanism and Paradise Lost. Doctoral diss., Univ. of Michigan, 1966. Abs., DA, 27, 1967, 2144-A.-45A.
Discusses Milton's treatment of Noah in Book 11 within the context of the Puritan tradition of the remnant.

1119 BERTSCHINGER, M. Man's Part in the Fall of Woman. ES, 31, 1950, 49-64.
Evaluates Milton's treatment of the Fall in the light of contemporary criticism, showing that "Eve's fall constitutes . . . a sequence of events."

1120 BEUM, ROBERT. So Much Gravity and Ease. Language and Style in
Milton: A Symposium in Honor of the Tercentenary of Paradise Lost.
Ed. by Ronald David Emma and John T. Shawcross (New York:
Frederick Ungar, 1967), pp. 333-68.
> Surveys previous studies of Milton's versification and counters some of the
> conclusions of F. T. Prince. Feels that "Milton was an Englishman before
> he was an eclectic humanist."

1121 BIRRELL, T. A. The Figure of Satan in Milton and Blake. Satan. Ed. by
Bruno de Jésus-Marie (London: Sheed and Ward, 1951), pp. 379-93.
> Attempts to show how Milton "keeps the figure of Satan under control—
> what happens to the Satan symbol."

1122 BLACK, MINDELE CHANA. Studies in the Epic Language of Paradise
Lost. Doctoral diss., Radcliffe College, 1956.

1123 BLACKER, IRWIN R. Did Milton Visit Hell? SCN, 9, 1951, 54.
> "The geysers of the Lardarello area near Florence may have suggested
> Milton's infernal topography."

1124 BLANCHARD, ELIZABETH SHEILA. Structural Patterns in Paradise
Lost: Milton's Symmetry and Balance. Doctoral diss., The Univ. of
Rochester, 1966. Abs., DA, 27, 1966, 1332-A.

1125 BLISSET, WILLIAM. Caesar and Satan. JHI, 18, 1957, 221-32.
> On the likenesses between the various figures of Caesar and those of Satan,
> especially Milton's.

1126 BLONDEL, JACQUES. Le Merveilleux dans le Paradis Miltonien. EA,
20, 1967, 348-56.
> A study of the supernatural quality of the fourth book of Paradise Lost.
> Emphasis is placed on the concrete nature of Eden and the possible significance
> of this terrestial paradise.

1127 ------. Milton poète de la Bible dans le Paradis Perdu. 1: Situation et
sources de l'épopée biblique. 2: Thématique biblique. Archives des
lettres modernes, Nos. 21-2, 1959. 87pp.
> Considers the English background of Paradise Lost and discusses sources of
> the epic. Contains chapters on Milton's characters, before and after the Fall.

1128 ------. Milton's Eden. English Studies Today, Fourth Series (Roma:
Edizioni di Storia e Letteratura, 1966), pp. 255-65.
> The vision of Eden is no perfunctory episode but provides an anticipation
> of the paradise within.

1129 ------, ed. Le Paradis Perdu, 1667-1967. Paris: Minard Lettres Modernes,
1967. 279pp.
> A collection of Tercentenary essays by Jacques Blondel, Pierre Brunel,
> Robert Couffignal, Helen Gardner, Jean Gillet, René Lejosne, Max Milner,
> Mario Praz, Paul Rozenberg, Jacques Siebacher, Raymond Tschumi. Each
> essay is listed in this bibliography under its individual author in its appropriate
> section.
> Rev: Pierre Legouis, EA, 20, 1967, 435-7.

1130 BODKIN, MAUD. Archetypal Patterns in Poetry: Psychological Studies
of the Imagination. London: Oxford Univ. Press, 1934. 340pp. Reprinted, 1963.

An application of Jung's hypothesis regarding the psychological significance of poetry. Comments, i.a., on the Paradise-Hades pattern in Paradise Lost, on Plato's Phaedo myth and Paradise Lost, on the image of woman in Paradise Lost, and on Satan as devil and hero.
Rev: TLS, Jan. 10, 1935, p. 18; LL, 11, 1935, 491-3; S. H. Hooke, Folk-Lore, 46, 1935, 176-9; E. L. Walton, NYTBR, Feb. 3, 1935, p. 16; G. D. Willcock, MLR, 31, 1936, 91-2.

1131 ------. Literature and the Individual Reader. L&P, 10, 1960, 39-44.
On Paradise Lost. Disagrees with Lewis and Eliot. "...those inconsistencies, unions of opposites, noted by the poet's critics, have their function."

1132 BOGGS, EARL R. Selected Precepts of Freedom to Choose in Paradise Lost. Peabody Journal of Education, 30, 1953, 276-84.

1133 BØGHOLM, N. Milton and Paradise Lost. Copenhagen: Levin and Munksgaard; London: Williams and Norgate, 1932. 132pp.
Discusses the human interest, the theology and philosophy, the style and language, and other poetical treatments of Genesis.
Rev: L. C. Martin, YWES, 209; TLS, Sept. 29, 1932, p. 694; S. B. Liljegren, Ang. Bbl., 43, 1932, 379-80; K. M. L., Oxf. Mag., June 8, 1934, p. 773.

1134 BOHANAN, VALERIE FOLTS. Some Views of Time and History in Milton's Paradise Lost. Doctoral diss., Emory Univ., 1967. Abs., DA, 28, 1968, 5006-A-7-A. 254pp.

1135 BOLTWOOD, ROBERT M. Turnus and Satan as Epic Villains. CJ, 47, 1952, 183-6.
"...just as Milton uses Satan to explain the presence of sin and evil in the world, so Virgil uses Turnus as heroic opposition to Aeneas' design on Italy. In both instances the characters, one primarily villainous and the other primarily heroic, are employed as means to an end greater in each case than themselves."

1136 BOND, DONALD F. Milton's Paradise Lost, V, 100-113. Expl, 3, 1945, item 54.

1137 BONHAM, SISTER M. HILDA, I. H. M. Milton's Ways with God: A Survey of the Criticism on the Representation of the Deity in Paradise Lost (1929-1963). Doctoral diss., Univ. of Michigan, 1964. Abs., DA, 25, 1965, 7240.

1138 BOONE, LALIA P. The Language of Book VI, Paradise Lost. SAMLA Studies in Milton. Ed. by J. Max Patrick (Gainesville: Univ. of Florida Press, 1953), pp. 114-27.
Determines how much of the language of Book 6 is native and how much is archaic. Illustrates a practical methodology for linguistic analysis.

1139 BOSWELL, JACKSON C. Milton and Prevenient Grace. SEL, 7, 1967, 83-94.
Holds that a reading of Paradise Lost, supported by references to Paradise Regained and the prose works, "demonstrated clearly that Milton did believe in prevenient grace even when he was arguing most strongly for predestination."

1140 BOWRA, C. M. Milton and the Destiny of Man. From Virgil to Milton (London: Macmillan, 1945), pp. 194-247. Reprinted, 1961, 1962.
On Paradise Lost as an epic form.
Rev: L. C. Martin, YWES, 143-4; TLS, Apr. 28, 1945, p. 198; Gwyn Jones, LL, 46, 1945, 128-32; V. de S. Pinto, Eng, 5, 1945, 207-10; Bonamy Dobrée, Spect, May 25, 1945, p. 480; Rose Macaulay, NSN, May 26, 1945, p. 340; A. J. Grant, CR, 168, 1945, 318-9; H. L. T., QQ, 52, 1945, 377-8; A. S. P. Woodhouse, UTQ, 15, 1946, 200-5; Leonard Bacon, SRL, Feb. 16, 1946, 44-5; B. A. Wright, RES, 22, 1946, 330-1; A. Norman Jeffares, ES, 27, 1946, 121-3.

1141 BOYETTE, PURVIS E. Milton and the Sacred Fire: Sex Symbolism in Paradise Lost. Doctoral diss., Vanderbilt Univ., 1966. Abs., DA, 27, 1967, 3420-A.

1142 ------. Milton's Eve and the Neoplatonic Graces. Renaissance Quarterly, 20, 1967, 341-4.
"The themes of Love and Fertility are . . . linked through Milton's allusions to the Graces and to the Zephyr-Flora configuration, which together function as an exposition of a Neoplatonic metaphysic of Love."

1143 ------. Something More About the Erotic Motive in Paradise Lost. TSE, 15, 1967, 19-30.
". . . my purpose in this paper is to extend the limits of the published criticism by examining in depth the metaphysical implications of sexual love in Paradise Lost and to indicate some of the philosophical and literary sanctions for Milton's treatment of sex."

1144 BRIGGS, K. M. The Anatomy of Puck: An Examination of Fairy Beliefs among Shakespeare's Contemporaries and Successors. New York: Hillary House, 1959.
Contains a discussion of the spiritual creatures in Paradise Lost.

1145 BROADBENT, J. B. Milton's Heaven. Milton's Epic Poetry: Essays on Paradise Lost and Paradise Regained. Ed. by C. A. Patrides (Harmondsworth: Penguin Books, 1967), pp. 133-56.
A reprint, with minor changes, of Chapter 4 of Some Graver Subject: An Essay on Paradise Lost (1960).

1146 ------. Milton's Hell. ELH, 21, 1954, 161-92.
On the geography and literary background.

1147 ------. Milton's Paradise. MP, 51, 1954, 160-76.
"So I propose to offer some evidence to support my theory that the place in the poem has a background of facts in the world and because the geographical element is inseparable from the literary, to show how Milton used the facts to solve a peculiar artistic problem and to compare his Paradise in other respects with various poetic descriptions of similar places."

1148 ------. The Rhetoric of Paradise Lost. Doctoral diss., St. Catharine's College, Oxford, 1956.

1149 ------. Some Graver Subject: an Essay on Paradise Lost. London: Chatto and Windus, 1960. Reprinted with an additional preface, London: Schocken Books, 1967. 303pp.
Chapters: Introduction, Hell, Pandemonium and Chaos, Heaven, The World,

Paradise, Antecedentia, The War in Heaven, Creation, The Fall, Exile, Conclusion.
Rev: Luke Parsons, CR, No. 1134, 1960, 402-3; TLS, July 8, 1960, p. 434; William Empson, Listener, 64, 1960, 196; Frank Kermode, Spect, July 22, 1960, p. 140; John Steadman, MLQ, 22, 1961, 403-5; Laurence Lerner, EIC, 11, 1961, 104-10; Walter Mackellar, Criticism, 4, 1962, 374-6; Howard Schultz, MP, 60, 1962, 136-8; O. B. Hardison, Jr., Th, 37, 1962, 455-6.

1150   BRODRIBB, C. W. Milton and Valerius Flaccus. N&Q, 175, 1938, 399.
       The opening of Paradise Lost seems to correspond with that of Valerius Flaccus' Argonautica.

1151   ------. Paradise Lost: A Book a Year? N&Q, 163, 1932, 417-8.
       Suggests that the epic was written between 1655 and 1665, with Milton working from the autumn to the spring of each year.

1152   ------. Paradise Lost: I. 756: Capital v. Capitol. N&Q, 179, 1940, 370-1.
       Favors capitol.

1153   BROOKE-ROSE, CHRISTINE. Metaphor in Paradise Lost: A Grammatical Analysis. Language and Style in Milton: A Symposium in Honor of the Tercentenary of Paradise Lost. Ed. by Ronald David Emma and John T. Shawcross (New York: Frederick Ungar, 1967), pp. 252-303.
       Classifies "Milton's metaphors by form rather than by their content" and "shows their suitability to purposes that have been misunderstood by critics [such as Waldock] working with criteria formulated almost entirely with reference to novels" (editors' Preface).

1154   BROOKS, CLEANTH. Eve's Awakening. Essays in Honor of W. C. Curry (Nashville: Vanderbilt Univ. Press, 1954), pp. 281-98. Reprinted in Milton: Modern Judgements, ed. by Alan Rudrum (London: Macmillan, 1968), pp. 173-88.
       By using certain dominant images in his account of the creation of Adam and Eve, Milton implies the nature of the fall.

1155   BROWN, J. R. Some Notes on the Native Elements in the Diction of Paradise Lost. N&Q, 196, 1951, 424-8.
       On Milton's probable indebtedness to earlier English writers, especially Spenser.

1156   BRUFFE, KENNETH A. Satan and the Sublime: The Meaning of the Romantic Hero. Doctoral diss., Northwestern Univ., 1964. Abs., DA, 26, 1965, 2203-4.
       Holds that during the late eighteenth and early nineteenth centuries "Satan, because he was seen to be 'sublime,' tended to become more and more a correlative for the 'new way of thinking,' a tendency which culminated in the evolution of a 'Satanic Principle' which manifested itself most prominently in the character of the Byronic hero."

1157   BRYAN, ROBERT A. Adam's Tragic Vision in Paradise Lost. SP, 62, 1965, 197-214.
       On Paradise Lost, 11, 385-411. "Despite their exotic associations, the names in these lines present a view of the 'progress'—the translatio peccati—of sin, death, and destruction."

1158 BRYCE, GEORGE P. The Biblical Allusions in Milton's Paradise Lost. Master's thesis, McMaster University, 1940. 161pp.
Finds 913 references from the Old Testament and 490 from the New Testament.

1159 BUCKALEW, MARY. The Heavenly Dialogues: Milton and the Tradition. Doctoral diss., Texas Christian Univ., 1967.

1160 BUCKWALTER, KATHRYN M. Criticism of Paradise Lost Since 1890. Master's thesis, Duke Univ., 1942.

1161 BULLOUGH, GEOFFREY. Milton and Cats. Essays in English Literature from the Renaissance to the Victorian Age (Toronto: Univ. of Toronto Press, 1964), pp. 103-24.
Feels that there may be a relationship between Milton's treatment of Adam and Eve in Paradise Lost, Books 4 and 8, and that in a poem by the Dutch poet-statesman, Jacob Cats (1577-1660).

1162 BUNDY, MURRAY W. Eve's Dream and the Temptation in Paradise Lost. Research Studies of the State College of Washington, 10, 1942, 273-91.
Interprets the dream as an essential part of the narrative and ties Adam's discourse on dreams closely into the structure of the tragedy.

1163 ------. Milton's Exalted Man. Essays in American and English Literature Presented to Bruce Robert McElderry, Jr. Ed. by Max F. Schulz (Athens: Ohio Univ. Press, 1967), pp. 197-220.
Milton emphasizes virtues, rather than vices, in presenting Christ's encounter with Satan and his final victory over Satan.

1164 ------. Milton's Prelapsarian Adam. Research Studies of the State College of Washington, 13, 1945, 163-84. Reprinted in Milton: Modern Judgements, ed. by Alan Rudrum (London: MacMillan, 1968), pp. 151-72.

1165 BURDEN, DENNIS H. The Logical Epic: A Study of the Argument of Paradise Lost. London: Routledge and Kegan Paul; Cambridge: Harvard Univ. Press, 1967. ix, 206pp.
"This book is a study of the logic of the theme of Paradise Lost.... It argues that Milton, making Paradise Lost the right Christian poem, was very aware of how it could be made into the wrong unchristian poem, and that this awareness made for extensive and dynamic application." Chapters: The Logic of God's Providence, The Presentation of God in Paradise Lost, The Garden, The Satanic Poem, Hapless Eve, The Contention about Knowledge, The Provocative Fruit, The Fall of Adam, The Aftermath. Rev: TLS, Aug. 17, 1967, p. 745; Stella P. Revard, JEGP, 67, July, 1968; YR, 57, June, 1968, 589.

1166 BURKE, HERBERT C. The Poles of Pride and Humility in the Paradise Lost of John Milton. Doctoral diss., Stanford Univ., 1954. 250pp. Abs., DA, 14, 1954, 1707.

1167 BUSH, DOUGLAS. Characters and Drama. Milton: A Collection of Critical Essays. Ed. by Louis L. Martz (Englewood Cliffs, N.J.: Prentice-Hall, 1966), pp. 109-20.
A chapter reprinted from Paradise Lost in Our Time (1945).

1168 ------. Ironic and Ambiguous Allusion in Paradise Lost. JEGP, 60, 1961, 631-40.
> Shows that irony and ambiguity are not exclusively modern devices and that ironic allusion is an important element in Paradise Lost.

1169 ------. Paradise Lost in Our Time. Some Comments. Ithaca: Cornell Univ. Press; London: Milford, 1945; Glouchester, Mass.: Peter Smith, 1957. iv, 117pp.
> Delivered as the Messenger Lectures, Cornell Univ., November, 1944. A refutation of the conception that Paradise Lost is a monument to dead ideas. Chapters: The Modern Reaction Against Milton, Religious and Ethical Principles, Characters and Drama, and The Poetical Texture.
> Rev: L. C. Martin, YWES, 145-6; E. N. S. Thompson, PQ, 24, 1945, 192; C. R. T., QQ, 52, 1945, 378-9; John Senior, Nat, Aug. 25, 1945, pp. 186-7; L. E. A. Byrns, Th, 26, 1946, 553-4; George Cookson, Eng, 6, 1946, 140; B. A. Wright, MLR, 41, 1946, 74-6; J. Milton French, JEGP, 45, 1946, 110-4; Z. S. Fink, MLN, 61, 1946, 199-200; A. S. P. Woodhouse, UTQ, 15, 1946, 200-5; TLS, Aug. 17, 1946, p. 390; L. C. Knights, MGW, 55, 1946, 150; Joan Bennett, NSN, Oct. 5, 1946, p. 250; B. M., DR, 26, 1946, 251-2; A. Norman Jeffares, ES, 27, 1946, 182-5; Kathleen Tillotson, RES, 23, 1947, 173-4; Desmond McCarthy, Sun. Times, Nov. 2, 1947, p. 3.

1170 ------. Paradise Lost in Our Time: Religious and Ethical Principles. Milton: Modern Essays in Criticism. A Galaxy Book. Ed. by Arthur E. Barker (New York: Oxford Univ. Press, 1965), pp. 156-76.
> Reprint of a chapter of Bush's 1945 volume.

1171 ------. Paradise Lost: The Poetical Texture. Milton's Epic Poetry: Essays on Paradise Lost and Paradise Regained. Ed. by C. A. Patrides (Harmondsworth: Penguin Books, 1967), pp. 33-54.
> A reprint of Chapter 4 of Paradise Lost in Our Time (1945), revised in part by Bush.

1172 ------. Recent Criticism of Paradise Lost. PQ, 28, 1949, 31-43.

1173 BUTLER, A. Z. The Pathetic Fallacy in Paradise Lost. Essays in Honor of W. C. Curry (Nashville: Vanderbilt Univ. Press, 1954), pp. 269-79.
> Uses Paradise Lost as the prime example of the necessity for using the pathetic fallacy.

1174 BUXTON, CHARLES R. Milton's Paradise Lost. A Politician Plays Truant. Essays on English Literature (London: Christophers, 1929), pp. 60-82.

1175 BUXTON, JOHN. A Note on Paradise Lost, X, 71-79. RES, 15, 1964, 52-3.
> Them (1. 79) refers to these thy transgressors (1. 72); illustrate (1. 78) "means 'to make illustre' in the sense proposed by Tasso."

1176 BYARD, MARGARET. The Idea of Harmony and Paradise Lost. Doctoral diss., Columbia Univ., 1962. Abs., DA, 23, 1962, 2113.
> Report on this dissertation, SCN, 21, 1963, item 21.

1177 CAIRNS, E. E. The Theology of Paradise Lost. BS, 105, 1948, 478-91; 106, 1949, 106-18.
> Considers De Doctrina Christiana as a gloss on Paradise Lost.

1178 CAIRNS, HUNTINGTON, ALLEN TATE, and MARK VAN DOREN. Milton: Paradise Lost. Invitation to Learning (New York: New Home Library, 1942), pp. 307-21.
A symposium. Transcript of a direct recording broadcast by the Columbia Broadcasting System.

1179 CAMERON, A. BARRY. Report on the Tercentenary Celebration of Paradise Lost. SCN, 26, 1968, 17.
At the Univ. of Western Ontario. Contains brief notices of papers read by Roy Daniells, Northrop Frye, Arthur Barker, Hugh MacCallum, and B. Rajan.

1180 CARLISLE, A. I. A Study of the Trinity College MS., Pages 35-41, and Certain Authors Represented in Milton's Commonplace Book, in Their Relationship to Paradise Lost and Paradise Regained. B. Litt. thesis, St. Hugh's, Oxford, 1952.

1181 CARNALL, GEOFFREY. Milton's Paradise Lost, III, 481-483. N&Q, 197, 1952, 315-6.
Suggests that the clue to the meaning may be found in the Sphaera (1639) of Johannes de Sacrobosco, pp. 11-3.

1182 CARVER, P. L. The Angels in Paradise Lost. RES, 16, 1940, 415-31.
Considers Milton's problems in presenting angels as characters and suggests who the primary influences were.

1183 CHAMBERS, A. B. Chaos in Paradise Lost. JHI, 24, 1963, 55-84.
"Chaos is as true an exemplar as hell of that state which everywhere prevails when the laws of providence are set aside, when the ways of God to man are opposed and overturned."

1184 ------. Milton's Proteus and Satan's Visit to the Sun. JEGP, 62, 1963, 280-7.
On Paradise Lost, 3, 599-605. Milton uses Proteus to "illuminate Satan's visit to the sun"; from this point in Paradise Lost Satan spirals downward into night.

1185 ------. The Mind Is Its Own Place: Paradise Lost, I. 253-255. RN, 16, 1963, 98-101.
Sees Satan's speech as a curious mixture of truth and error.

1186 ------. More Sources for Milton. MP, 63, 1965, 61-6.
Review article on James H. Sims' The Bible in Milton's Epics and Harry F. Robins' If This Be Heresy.

1187 ------. Sin and Sign in Paradise Lost. HLQ, 26, 1963, 381-2.
On the naming of Sin (Paradise Lost, 2, 758-61) and the meaning of "portentous."

1188 ------. Three Notes on Eve's Dream in Paradise Lost. PQ, 46, 1967, 186-93.
Discusses the implications of Satan's appearance as a toad to the external observer, of his appearance as an angel within Eve's mind, and of his inspiring the dream through Eve's ear.

1189 ------. Wisdom at One Entrance Quite Shut Out: Paradise Lost, III, 1-55. PQ, 42, 1963, 114-9. Reprinted in Milton: Modern Essays in Criticism.

A Galaxy Book. Ed. by Arthur E. Barker (New York: Oxford Univ. Press, 1965), pp. 218-25.
> On Milton's blindness, "the purpose of mortal vision, and the symbolism of the eyes of the soul."

1190 CHAMPION, LARRY S. The Conclusion of Paradise Lost: A Reconsideration. CE, 27, 1966, 384, 389-94.
> Feels that the Nimrod passage in Book 12 has central architectonic importance because "it becomes an earthly parallel to the spatial rebellion of evil, the construction of Pandemonium, the operation of the basic irony, and the controlling pattern of the felix culpa." It prepares the way for the "final statement of man's liberty in theological terms."

1191 CHATMAN, SEYMOUR. Milton's Participial Style. PMLA, 83, 1968, 1386-99.
> "The history of the rise of the participial style has yet to be written. One of its greater moments surely is Paradise Lost. The disposition to convert verbs into noun-modifying participles, particularly past participles, imparts a highly characteristic flavor to Milton's style. To understand the effect fully we need (I) to review the grammar of the participles and particularly those details of chief significance to Milton's practice; (II) to survey the history of their use in English poetry, comparing Milton's practice with those of his predecessors and successors; and, finally (III), to weigh the esthetic and semantic values which they contribute to the texture of Milton's poetry."

1192 CHILDERS, CHARLES L. Milton's Doctrine of God, Studied in the Light of Historical Christianity. Doctoral diss., Vanderbilt Univ., 1959. Abs., DA, 20, 1959, 1781-2.

1193 CHINOL, ELIO. La caduta dal Paradiso terrestre. Per un' interpretazione del libro IX del Paradiso Perduto di Milton. EM, 6, 1955, 9-30.
> The Fall from Earthly Paradise. An analysis of Book 9 of Paradise Lost. Questions the view that 9, 780-4, is the central passage in the epic and stresses the significance of the fall of Satan.

1194 ------. Il dramma divino e il dramma umano nel Paradiso perduta. Bellavista (Napoli): Arti grofiche, 1958. 163pp.
> A study of the divine drama and the human drama of Paradise Lost. Contains a chapter on contemporary criticisms of Paradise Lost.
> Rev: Bruce Cutler, Poetry, Mar., 1959, pp. 404-5.

1195 CIARDI, JOHN. A Poem Talks to Itself: One Thing Calls Another into Being. SatR, Jan. 24, 1959, pp. 12-3.
> On Paradise Lost, 9, 494-503. This passage "is an example of poetry elevated to sublimity by the rich and powerful development of its diction into music-like themes."

1196 CIRILLO, ALBERT R. Noon-Midnight and the Temporal Structure of Paradise Lost. ELH, 29, 1962, 372-95. Reprinted in condensed form in Milton's Epic Poetry: Essays on Paradise Lost and Paradise Regained. Ed. by C. A. Patrides (Harmondsworth: Penguin Books, 1967), pp. 215-32.
> ". . . the effect is that of a double time scheme whereby events that are being expressed in temporal terms . . . are simultaneously occurring in the eternal present which is the central setting of the poem."

1197   CLAIR, JOHN. A Note on Milton's Arianism. Essays and Studies in Language and Literature. Ed. by Herbert H. Petit (Pittsburgh: Duquesne Univ. Press; Louvain: Editions E. Nauwelaerts, 1964), pp. 44-8.
>   Traces the progress of the Son in Paradise Lost from his "begetting" to his "final" equality with the Godhead and concludes that although Milton expresses some Arian views, the term Arian is too rigid to apply to him.

1198   CLARK, EVERT M. Milton's Abyssinian Paradise. UTSE, 29, 1950, 129-50.
>   On Paradise Lost, 4. Milton indebted to Samuel Purchas and Peter Heylyn.

1199   CLARK, IRA G., III. The Son of God in Milton's Works. Doctoral diss., Northwestern Univ., 1966. Abs., DA, 27, 2525A-6A.

1200   CLEMENTS, REX. The Angels in Paradise Lost. QR, 264, 1935, 384-93.
>   ". . . Milton's angels are like himself—individual personalities of godlike strength. They do not fit easily into any scheme or classification."

1201   COFFIN, CHARLES MONROE. Creation and the Self in Paradise Lost. Ed. by C. A. Patrides. ELH, 29, 1962, 1-18. Reprinted with Prefatory Note by John Crowe Ransom in Kenyon Alumni Bull., 20, No. 4, 1962, 11-7.
>   ". . . the general pattern of the Human-Divine relationship is drawn for us in terms of association, disassociation, and preparation for reassociation."

1202   ------. Study Questions on Milton's Paradise Lost. New York: Crofts, 1938. vi, 2pp.

1203   COLIE, ROSALIE L. Paradoxia Epidemica: The Renaissance Tradition of Paradox. Princeton: Princeton Univ. Press, 1966. xx, 553pp.
>   Chapter Five, Affirmations in the Negative Theology: Eternity, pp. 169-89, is a consideration of Paradise Lost. ". . . Milton presents these particular paradoxes so that their oppositions are at once fused and yet made clear."
>   Rev: Sister Miriam Joseph, ELN, 5, 1967, 142-7.

1204   ------. Time and Eternity: Paradox and Structure in Paradise Lost. JWCI, 23, 1960, 127-38. Reprinted in Milton: Modern Judgements, ed. by Alan Rudrum (London: MacMillan, 1968), pp. 189-204.
>   Milton's "efforts to reconcile poetically the paradoxes involved in the concepts eternity and time, of foreknowledge and free will, affected the structure and technique of his poem."

1205   CONDEE, RALPH W. The Formalized Openings of Milton's Epic Poems. JEGP, 50, 1951, 502-8.
>   Analysis indicative of Milton's attempt to imitate both Homer and Virgil.

1206   ------. Milton's Theories Concerning Epic Poetry: Their Sources and Their Influence on Paradise Lost. Doctoral diss., Univ. of Illinois, 1949. Abs., Urbana: Univ. of Illinois Press, 1949.

1207   CONRATH, JOHN BERNARD. The Orthodoxy of Paradise Lost. Doctoral diss., State Univ. of Iowa, 1946. Abs., Univ. of Iowa, Doctoral Dissertations: Abstracts and References, 6, 1953, 369-71.

1208 COOLIDGE, JOHN S. Great Things and Small: The Virgilian Progression. CL, 1965, 1-23.
      ". . . Milton's use of the traditional phrase [to compare great things with small] draws this central element in Virgil's work into the even more comprehensive design of Milton's own Christian humanism."

1209 COPE, JACKSON I. The Metaphoric Structure of Paradise Lost. Baltimore: The John Hopkins Press, 1962. 182pp.
      Contents: Poets and Critics: The Metaphoric School; Ramistic Implications; Time and Space as Miltonic Symbol; Scenic Structure in Paradise Lost; The Creating Voice. ". . . examines the structural components of Paradise Lost, light, darkness, and vertical movement, and finds that they imitate metaphorically the over-all theme of the epic."
      Rev: H. F. Fletcher, QJS, 48, 1962, 321-2; Barbara Lewalski, MP, 61, 1963, 122-6; Roland M. Frye, JEGP, 62, 1963, 390-4; Kenneth Muir, CritQ, 5, 1963, 96; Geoffrey Bullough, English, 14, 1963, 153-4; Richard L. Drain, ES, 44, 1963, 286-8; Dean Morgan Schmitter, RN, 16, 1963, 145-7; J. A. Bryant, Jr., SAQ, 62, 1963, 121-2; TLS, Feb. 15, 1963, pp. 101-2; Thomas R. Hartmann, SCN, 21, 1963, 17; R. L. Colie, PQ, 43, 1964, 425-8; Edgar Mertner, Anglia, 82, 1964, 247-59; John Buxton, RES, 15, 1964, 319-21; N. Neri, BHR, 27, 1965, 350-1.

1210 ------. Milton's Muse in Paradise Lost. MP, 55, 1957, 6-10.
      Spiritual illumination as opposed to physical blindness.

1211 ------. Satan's Disguises: Paradise Lost and Paradise Regained. MLN, 73, 1958, 9-11.
      "The disguises of Satan form a link between the epics."

1212 ------. Time and Space as Miltonic Symbol. ELH, 26, 1959, 497-513.
      Considers spatial dimension in Paradise Lost and Paradise Regained "as the aesthetic shape of the myth through which Milton created meaning for the boundless spaces viewed by Galileo. . ."

1213 CORCORAN, SISTER MARY IRMA. Milton's Paradise with Reference to the Hexameral Background. Doctoral diss., Catholic Univ., 1945. Washington: Catholic Univ. of America Press, 1945, 1967 (paperback reprint). xvi, 149pp.
      Rev: L. C. Martin, YWES, 141-2; Arnold Williams, MLN, 61, 1946, 352-3; Grant McColley, JEGP, 45, 1946, 464-6; Harris Fletcher, MLQ, 7, 1946, 359-61; Sister M. Teresa, Th, 23, 1948, 340-1; Arthur Barker, MLR, 44, 1949, 110-1.

1214 COWLING, GEORGE. Milton's Paradise Lost. Shelley and Other Essays (Melbourne: Melbourne Univ. Press; London: Oxford Univ. Press, 1936), pp. 131-56.
      Emphasizes the grand style of the epic in a manner similar to the late Victorians.

1215 CRAWFORD, JOHN W. Another Biblical Allusion in Paradise Lost. SCN, 15, 1967, 66.
      Moloch's speech (2, 65-70) alludes to 2 Philippians 2:4 and Leviticus 10:1-2, in his use of the words "Tartarean" and "strange fire."

1216 CROSSETT, JOHN. Milton and Pindar. N&Q, N.S., 9, 1962, 217-8.

On Paradise Lost 3, 365-9, and parallels in Olympian 2, 83-5, Olympian 13, 93-5, and Pythian 1, 1-4.

1217   CRUNDELL, H. W. The Power to Reason: A Milton Paradox. N&Q, 185, 1943, 113.
Reply to K. Svendsen, N&Q, 184, 1943, 368-70.

1218   CURRY, WALTER C. The Consistence and Qualities of Milton's Chaos. Vanderbilt Studies in the Humanities, 1, 1951, 56-70.

1219   ------. The Genesis of Milton's World. Anglia, 70, 1951, 129-49.
Outlines the order of progress from chaos to cosmos.

1220   ------. Milton's Chaos and Old Night. JEGP, 46, 1947, 38-52.
Defends "the hypothesis that the conception of the divinity of both Chaos and Night was in accordance with the doctrines of Neoplatonic theology in its interpretation of Orphic and Pythagorean cosmogony."

1221   ------. Milton's Dual Concept of God as Related to Creation. SP, 47, 1950, 190-210.
Proposes to "disengage Milton's philosophy of the Divine nature from theological controversy and to show how consistently his dual concept of Deity in relation to the world is developed in the Christian Doctrine and embodied in Paradise Lost."

1222   ------. Milton's Scale of Nature. SSLL. Ed. by Hardin Craig. Stanford: Stanford Univ. Press, 1941, pp. 173-92.
In Paradise Lost. Shows that "Milton's doctrine concerning the scale of nature represents a distinguished syncretism of elements derived from a variety of philosophical traditions."

1223   ------. Some Travels of Milton's Satan and the Road to Hell. PQ, 29, 1950, 225-35.
Especially concerned with the wandering and adventures of Satan. Discusses concepts of infinity, time and space, visual perspectives, directions, and distances in Paradise Lost.

1224   CUTTS, JOHN P. The Miserific Vision: A Study of Some of the Basic Structural Imagery of Paradise Lost. EM, 14, 1963, 57-72.
"Much of the imagery and close symmetry of Paradise Lost is based on a parody of traditional concepts of God, the Trinity and Heaven." "The beatific vision is parodied by what I shall call . . . the miserific vision."

1225   DAHLBERG, CHARLES. Paradise Lost V, 603, and Milton's Psalm II. MLN, 67, 1952, 23-4.
Interprets "begot" as "invested with kingship."

1226   DAICHES, DAVID. The Opening of Paradise Lost. The Living Milton (London: Routledge and Kegan Paul, 1960), pp. 55-69.
An analysis of the first twenty-six lines of Paradise Lost.

1227   DANIEL, NAT V., JR. The Theology of Paradise Lost, III, 183-184, Re-examined. RenP, 1963 (Durham, N.C.: Southeastern Renaissance Conference), pp. 21-9.
Suggests that the Bible is the best gloss on the epic and that "where the Bible is ambiguous, Paradise Lost is more than likely to be equally and similarly ambiguous."

1228 DANIELLS, ROY. Humour in Paradise Lost. DR, 33, 1953, 159-66.

1229 ------. Milton, Mannerism and Baroque. Toronto: Univ. of Toronto
Press, 1963. 229pp.
A search for analogies between Milton's art and the other arts. "...I have
attempted a clarification of the Mannerist traits in Milton's earlier work and
the Baroque elements in his great poetic trilogy." Chapters: Introduction;
Mannerism; Comus and Lycidas; Baroque; Paradise Lost: Unity, Power, and
Will; Paradise Lost: Space and Time; Paradise Lost: Personages and Plot;
Paradise Lost: Paradox and Ambiguity; Milton and Spenser; Puritanism and
Baroque; Paradise Lost and Roman Baroque; Paradise Regained; Samson
Agonistes.
Rev: Agnes M. C. Latham, YWES, 208-9; H. R. MacCallum, Canadian Forum,
43, 1963, 186; J. Max Patrick, SCN, 21, 1963, 36; Walter J. Ong, S. J., SEL,
4, 1964, 179-80; B. Rajan, CanL, No. 21, 1964, 55-8; Sidney Warhaft, QQ, 71,
1964, 137-8; Millar MacLure, UTQ, 33, 1964, 420-2; J. B. Beer, MLR, 60,
1965, 594-8.

1230 DANIELS, EDGAR F. Milton's Doubtful Conflict and the Seventeenth-
Century Tradition. N&Q, N.S., 8, 1961, 430-2.
"The doubtful conflict of Paradise Lost re-enforces the central purpose of the
poem: to justify God's ways to man (and Satan) by illustrating the decree
of free will."

1231 ------. Milton's Fallen Angels—Self-Corrupted or Seduced? N&Q, N.S.,
7, 1960, 447-50.
Presents theological and literary traditions to support both points of view.

1232 ------. The Seventeenth-Century Conception of Satan with Relation to
the Satan of Paradise Lost. Doctoral diss., Stanford Univ., 1952. Abs.,
Abstracts of Dissertations, Stanford Univ., 27, 1953, 217-9.

1233 ------. Thomas Adams and Darkness Visible (Paradise Lost, I, 62-3).
N&Q, N.S., 6, 1959, 369-70.
Asserts that Milton reflects Thomas Adams' A Commentary or, Exposition
upon the Divine Second Epistle Generall, Written by the Blessed Apostle
St. Peter (1633), p. 505., which "indicates the origin of the doctrinal
paradox."

1234 DARBISHIRE, HELEN. Milton's Paradise Lost. Oxford: Oxford Univ.
Press, 1951. 51pp.
Delivered as the James Bryce Memorial Lecture at Somerville College.
Discusses the criticism of Bentley and Johnson.

1235 DAVIDSON, GUSTAV. A Dictionary of Angels, Including the Fallen
Angels. New York: The Free Press; London: Collier-Macmillan, 1967.
xxxii, 387pp.
Contains frequent references to Milton's handling of angels in Paradise Lost.

1236 DAVIE, DONALD. Syntax and Music in Paradise Lost. The Living
Milton (London: Routledge and Kegan Paul, 1960), pp. 70-84.
Argues that the structure of Paradise Lost is architectural, not musical.

1237 DAY, DOUGLAS. Adam and Eve in Paradise Lost, IV. TSLL, 3, 1961,
369-81.

". . . Adam and Eve's simple, charming idyll in Boox IV" dramatically fore-shadows the Fall of Man.

1238 DAY-LEWIS, CECIL. The Grand Manner. Nottingham: John Clough, 1952. 26pp.
Comments, i.a., on the opening lines of Paradise Lost, 3.

1239 DELASANTA, RODNEY KENNETH. The Epic Voice. Doctoral diss., Brown Univ., 1962. Abs., DA, 23, 1963, 2524.
In the Arcadia, the Faerie Queene, and Paradise Lost.

1240 DE MAISÈRES, MAURY THIBAUT. Les Poèmes Inspirées du Début de la Genèse â l'Epoque de la Renaissance. Louvain, 1931.

1241 DEMARAY, HANNAH DISINGER. Disorderly Order in the Garden Literature of Browne, Marvell, and Milton. Doctoral diss., Univ. of Southern California, 1968. Abs., DA, 29, 1968, 256-A-7-A. 142pp.

1242 DEMARAY, JOHN G. The Thrones of Satan and God: Backgrounds to Divine Opposition in Paradise Lost. HLQ, 31, 1967, 21-33.
Finds many parallels between Comus and Paradise Lost, especially with reference to the "opposed chairs of the noble peer and the evil Comus placed at the opposite ends of the performing space" and the "opposed thrones of God and Satan placed so far apart in the poet's epic."

1243 DENNIS, LEAH. The Puzzle of Paradise Lost. Univ. of California Chronicle, 34, 1932, 195-200.
Milton the artist and moralist vs. Satan.

1244 DE PILATO, S. Un Inspiratore italiano del Paradiso Perduto di Milton: P. Serafino della Salandra. Potenza: Marchesiello, 1934. 26pp.

1245 DEUTSCH, ALFRED H. Some Scholastic Elements in Paradise Lost. Doctoral diss., Univ. of Illinois, 1945.

1246 DI CESARE, MARIO A. Advent'rous Song: The Texture of Milton's Epic. Language and Style in Milton: A Symposium in Honor of the Tercentenary of Paradise Lost. Ed. by Ronald David Emma and John T. Shawcross (New York: Frederick Ungar, 1967), pp. 1-29.
". . . I will discuss certain motifs of the poem by close examination of some of the words Milton uses, some Latinate elements in his diction and syntax, some images and metaphors, allusions and patterns. . . . But my major concern is to approach them [the motifs] by way of the stylistic elements that contribute to the texture of Paradise Lost as an epic whole."

1247 ------. Vida's Christiad and Vergilian Epic. New York: Columbia Univ. Press, 1964. x, 372pp.
Argues, passim, for Vida's influence on Milton.

1248 DICKSON, DAVID W. D. Milton's Son of God: A Study in Imagery and Orthodoxy. PMASAL, 36, 1952, 275-81.

1249 DIEKHOFF, JOHN S. Eve, the Devil, and Areopagitica. MLQ, 5, 1944, 429-34.
Milton is not being inconsistent in letting Eve paraphrase Areopagitica (PL, 9, 322-41).

1250 ------. The Function of the Prologues in Paradise Lost. PMLA, 57, 1942, 697-704.
Each of the four prologues has a narrative and a rhetorical function, and each marks a stage in the argument and furnishes ethical proof.

1251 ------. Milton's Paradise Lost: A Commentary on the Argument. New York: Columbia Univ. Press; London: Oxford Univ. Press, 1946. Reprinted, New York: The Humanities Press, 1958. 161pp.
Chapters: Milton's Theory of Poetry, Two Rhetorical Aids to Proof, The Evil of Satan, Man's Guilt, God's Justice, God's Providence and Mercy, The Way of Virtue.
Rev: L. C. Martin, YWES, 171-2; F. R. Fogle, Rev. of Religion, 12, 1947, 66-71; A. S. P. Woodhouse, UTQ, 16, 1947, 433-5; TLS, Mar. 29, 1947, p. 140; E. M. W. Tillyard, RES, 23, 1947, 363-4; Allan H. Gilbert, SAQ, 46, 1947, 289-90; E. M. Pope, MLN, 63, 1948, 444-5.

1252 ------. The Trinity Manuscript and the Dictation of Paradise Lost. PQ, 28, 1949, 44-52.
On Milton's habits of composition and correction.

1253 DOLAN, PAUL J. Milton and Eliot: A Common Source. N&Q, N.S., 13, 1966, 379-80.
Both Milton (in Paradise Lost, 1, 242) and T. S. Eliot (in epigraph to his Marina) utilize a line from Seneca's Hercules Furens (1. 1138).

1254 DORRIS, GEORGE E. Paolo Rolli and the First Italian Translation of Paradise Lost. Italica, 42, 1965, 213-25.
An appreciative essay on Rolli's translation (1729, 1735) with comments on other translations. See also Dorris' doctoral dissertation, Paolo Rolli and the Italian Circle in London: 1715-1744, Northwestern Univ., 1962.

1255 DOUGLAS, NORMAN. On Paradise Lost. LL, 58, 1948, 86-118.
Translates "a paper by a certain Zicari tracing the origin of Milton's Paradise Lost to a sacred tragedy entitled Adam Caduto...which was written by a Calabrian monk named Salandra."

1256 DOUGLASS, JAMES W. Milton's Dance of Life. Downside Review, 80, 1962, 243-9.
In Paradise Lost, Milton "insists rather on seeing the freedom of each action in terms of the hierarchical staircase of being."

1257 DUGGAN, SISTER MARY KATHLEEN, G.N.S.H. Irony in Milton's Paradise Lost: Its Modes and Its Thematic Implications. Doctoral diss., St. Louis Univ., 1964. Abs., DA, 25, 1965, 4685.

1258 DUNCAN, EDGAR H. The Natural History of Metals and Minerals in the Universe of Milton's Paradise Lost. Osiris, 11, 1954, 386-421.
Stresses Robert Fludd's concepts.

1259 ------. Satan-Lucifer: Lightning and Thunderbolt. PQ, 30, 1951, 441-3.
Parallel between Paradise Lost, 2, 927-38, and Comenius' explanation of thunderbolts.

1260 DUNCAN, JOSEPH E. Milton's Four-in-One Hell. HLQ, 20, 1957, 127-36.
Feels that Milton unites four different conceptions of hell so that it becomes "a potent symbol in which the sinner, the cause of sin, and the punishment for sin merge significantly."

1261 DUNCAN-JONES, E. E. Musical Hinges: Milton and Saint-Amant. N&Q, N.S., 11, 1964, 337.
Notes a parallel to the "Harmonious sound" of the gates of Heaven (Paradise Lost, 7, 206) in Saint-Amant's Moyse Sauné.

1262 DURR, ROBERT A. Dramatic Pattern in Paradise Lost. JAAC, 13, 1955, 520-6.
"Attention seldom focuses exclusively upon the episode at hand, but complimentary and contrasting episodes juxtapose themselves in our minds...."

1263 DUSTDOOR, P. E. Legends of Lucifer in Early English and in Milton. Anglia, 54, 1930, 213-68.
". . . an exposition of the multifarious legends of Lucifer prevalent in Early English and . . . a comparative study of the Early English versions of the Angelic revolt on the one hand and Milton's version of it is Paradise Lost on the other."

1264 EHRSTINE, JOHN. The Faces of an Ironic God. Universitas, 3, 1965, 51-63.
An examination of God's speeches in Paradise Lost, with the conclusion that they successfully reflect the ironic nature of existence.

1265 EISENSTEIN, SERGEI. The Film Sense. Trans. by Jay Leyda. Toronto: Longmans, 1943, 1957.
A director's view of Paradise Lost, pp. 52-7.

1266 ELTON, WILLIAM. Paradise Lost and the Digby Mary Magdalene. MLQ, 9, 1948, 412-4.
A passage from the play anticipates the infernal council and temptation scenes in Paradise Lost.

1267 EMERSON, EVERETT H. Milton's War in Heaven: Some Problems. MLN, 69, 1954, 399-402.
The fact that the Son is called upon to end the war reflects Milton's idea that good cannot overcome evil completely without God's help.

1268 ------. The New Criticism of Paradise Lost. SAQ, 54, 1955, 501-7.

1269 EMPSON, WILLIAM. Adam and Eve. Listener, 64, 1960, 64-5.
Interprets various events of the fall, including Eve's dream, Raphael's visit, Eve's temptation and fall, Adam's fall, the quarrel, and Adam's hatred.

1270 ------. Emotion in Words Again. KR, 10, 1948, 579-601. Reprinted as All in Paradise Lost in The Structure of Complex Words (London: Chatto and Windus, 1951), pp. 101-4.
"All," which occurs 612 times in Paradise Lost, appears in nearly every scene of emotional pressure.

1271 ------. Eve. Milton's Epic Poetry: Essays on Paradise Lost and Paradise Regained. Ed. by C. A. Patrides (Harmondsworth: Penguin Books, 1967), pp. 157-78.
A reprint of Chapter 4 of Empson's Milton's God (1961), with some paragraphs omitted.

1272 ------. Heaven's Awful Monarch. Listener, 64, 1960, 111-2, 114.
Despite strong cases for the falls of Satan, Eve, and Adam (Listener, 64.

1960, 11-3, 64-5), affirms Milton's justification of God through analysis of events in Heaven.

1273 ------. The Loss of Paradise. The Northern Miscellany of Literary Criticism (Hull: Hull Printers, Ltd., 1953), pp. 17-8.

"The root of the startling power of Milton is that he could accept and express this downright horrible conception of God and yet keep somehow alive, underneath it, all the breadth and generosity, the welcome of all noble pleasure, which had been prominent just before it in the development of European history."

1274 ------. Milton's God. London: Chatto and Windus, 1961; Norfolk, Connecticut: New Directions, 1961. 280pp. Revised Edition, London: Chatto and Windus, 1965.

Feels that the traditional God of Christianity is very wicked. "He [Milton] is struggling to make his God appear less wicked. . . and does succeed in making him noticeably less wicked than the traditional Christian one; though, after all his efforts, owing to his loyalty to the sacred text..., his modern critics still feel. . . that there is something badly wrong about it all." Chapters: Critics, Satan, Heaven, Eve, Adam, Delilah, and Christianity.

Rev: Agnes M. C. Latham, YWES, 170-1; Frank Kermode, MGW, Sept. 21, 1961, p. 11; A. Alvarez, NSN, Sept. 29, 1961, pp. 442-3; Rex Warner, London Mag., Oct., 1961, pp. 81, 83, 85; R. L. Brett, CritQ, 3, 1961, 285-7; William Empson, ibid., p. 368; David Daiches, Spect, No. 6953, 1961, 434-5; J. B. Broadbent, TT, 42, 1961, 1572; TLS, Sept. 29, 1961, p. 646; Empson, ibid., Oct. 6, 1961, p. 663; YR, N. S., 51, June, 1961, p. 14; Helen Gardner, Listener, 66, 1961, 521-2; Barbara Everett, MLR, 57, 1962, 415-7; Kenneth Burke, Nat, June 16, 1962, pp. 540-1; Douglas Bush, NYTBR, Mar. 11, 1962, pp. 4-5; John N. Morris, SR, 70, 1962, 673-7; William Riley Parker, VQR, 38, 1962, 332-5; QR, Jan., No. 633, 1962, pp. 121-2; Thelma Herring, AUMLA, 19, 1963, 141-4; [Summary of series of letters in TLS], SCN, 20, 1963, 57-8, "skirmishes between Empson and practically everybody"; John M. Steadman, Archiv, 200, 1963, 299-301; Margaret M. Byard, SCN, 21, No. 4, 1963, 60. Of Revised Edition: Agnes M. C. Latham, YWES, 46, 1965, 205; Philip Hobsbaum, Listener, 74, 1965, 388-9; John Bayley, Spect, July 30, 1965, pp. 154-5; Christopher Ricks, NSN, Aug. 27, 1965, pp. 292-3.

1275 ------. Milton's God. TLS, Oct. 6, 1961, p. 663.

Dislikes the TLS review of his book, Milton's God.

1276 ------. Satan Argues His Case. Listener, 64, 1960, 11-3.

Attempts reconstruction of Satan's early history from indications in the dialogues of Paradise Lost. Traces Satan's high motives and his development before the Fall.

1277 ------. The Satan of Milton. HudR, 13, 1960, 33-59.

On Satan's case in Paradise Lost. Tries to follow Milton's "whole account of the tragedy of Satan."

1278 ETHEL, GARLAND. Hell's Marching Music. MLQ, 18, 1957, 295-302.

Paradise Lost, 1, 549-65.

Suggests that Plutarch's Lycurgus be added to the source possibilities for

1279 EVANS, J. M. Traditional Elements in Some English Treatments of the Fall of Man. Doctoral diss., Merton College, Oxford, 1963. 330pp. Pub-

lished as Paradise Lost and the Genesis Tradition. Oxford: Clarendon
Press, 1968. xiv, 314pp.
    "My major concern, then, will be with the evolution of the Fall story, of
    which the parallels singled out by some of the scholars I have mentioned
    are often the natural result, rather than with the precise connexions between
    the parallels themselves." Contents (abbreviated): Introduction: The Study
    of a Tradition, The Exegetical Tradition, The Literary Tradition, Paradise
    Lost and the Tradition. Extensive bibliography.
    Rev: TLS, Sept. 12, 1968, p. 1003.

1280 EVANS, ROBERT O. Milton's Use of "E're" in Paradise Lost. N&Q, N.S.,
     1, 1954, 337-9.
     Uses Milton's spellings of "ere" and "e're" as the basis of a discussion con-
     cerning Darbishire's editorial principles.

1281 ------. Paradise Lost 1, 580-587: An Additional Comment. NM, 62,
     1961, 196-205.
     On Milton's reasons for naming Charlemagne instead of Roland in the
     passage.

1282 ------. Proofreading of Paradise Lost. N&Q, N.S., 2, 1955, 383-4.
     Discusses Darbishire's and R. M. Adams' opposing views on "improving" the
     text of the epic.

1283 FARRELL, THOMAS, JR. The Classical Biblical Epic in England.
     Doctoral diss., Univ. of Iowa, 1950.
     Traces the acceptance of the classical biblical epic as a literary form from
     the Anglo-Saxon period to the seventeenth century.

1284 FARRISON, W. EDWARD. The Classical Allusions in Paradise Lost,
     Books I and II. EJ, 22, 1933, 650-3.

1285 FENDERSON, LEWIS H. The Onomato-Musical Element in Paradise
     Lost. CLAJ, 9, 1966, 255-64.
     Shows how Milton uses vowels and consonants to create a poetic language
     "that is endless in its variety of shades and gradations."

1286 FERRY, ANNE DAVIDSON. The Authority of the Narrative Voice in
     Paradise Lost. In Defense of Reading. Ed. by Reuben A. Brower and
     Richard Poirier (New York: Dutton, 1952), pp. 76-93.
     Emphasizes the role of Milton as narrator in Paradise Lost. "The role of
     the narrator as interpreter to the fallen reader of the unfallen world. . . de-
     termines the distinctives style of Paradise Lost."

1287 ------. The Bird, the Blind Bard, and the Fortunate Fall. Reason and
     the Imagination. Studies in the History of Ideas, 1600-1800. Ed. by J. A.
     Mazzeo (New York: Columbia Univ. Press; London: Routledge and
     Kegan Paul, 1962), pp. 183-200.
     On the closing lines of Paradise Lost (12, 645-9). "Our feelings are controlled
     here by the tone of the narrative voice, the mingling of attitudes which has
     characterized that tone from the opening of the epic."

1288 [FERRY], ANNE DAVIDSON. Innocence Regained: Seventeenth-Century
     Reinterpretations of the Fall of Man. Doctoral diss., Columbia Univ.,
     1956. Abs., DA, 17, 1957, 847-8.

1289 ------. Milton and the Miltonic Dryden. Cambridge: Harvard Univ.
      Press, 1968. 238pp.
      Part One: Paradise Lost and Absalom and Achitophel, pp. 21-121. "... un-
      covers an intricate pattern of connections between the two poems, and reveals
      how Dryden depicted human corruption by exploring the dangers of fallen
      language, in all its abuses and confusions."

1290 ------. Milton's Epic Voice: The Narrator in Paradise Lost. Cambridge:
      Harvard Univ. Press, 1963. xv, 187pp.
      "He [Milton] makes use repeatedly of elaborate devices to keep us continually
      aware of the role of the narrator as interpreter to us of the poem's meaning."
      Chapters: Tone—The Bird and the Blind Bard, Point of View and Comment,
      Simile and Catalogue, Sacred Metaphor, Allegory and Parody, and Vision as
      Structure.
      Rev: Agnes M. C. Latham, YWES, 211-2; Helen Gardner, Listener, 70, 1963
      575; Patrick Cruttwell, MGW, Aug. 29, 1963, p. 11; Kenneth Muir, CritQ,
      5, 1963, 275-6; Paul Fussell, Jr., SRL, Sept. 7, 1963, p. 35; TLS, Sept. 20,
      1963, p. 706; Edward S. Le Comte, RN, 17, 1964, 133-5; Geoffrey Bullough,
      English, 15, 1964, 24-5; Scott Elledge, SAQ, 63, 1964, 590-1; J. B. Beer. MLR,
      60, 1965, 594-8; John Buxton, RES, 16, 1965, 198-9; Martin S. Blaze, SCN, 23,
      1965, 1-2; John G. Demaray, Pers, 46, 1965, No. 3.

1291 FIELDS, ALBERT W. Milton and Self-knowledge. PMLA, 83, 1968, 392-9.
      Examines Milton's concept of self-knowledge as seen in Paradise Lost,
      Paradise Regained, and Samson Agonistes, and compares Milton's view
      with other Classical and Christian ideas of self-knowledge.

1292 FIORE, AMADEUS, P., O.F.M. The Paradox of the Angelic Fall in
      Paradise Lost. Duquesne Review, 46, Spring, 1966, 15-26.
      "The irony of Satan's situation is part of the Christian paradox that the
      corruption of the best becomes the worst and from the worst God brings
      forth the best, and this functions significantly for the central irony of the
      whole epic."

1293 ------. The Problem of 17th-Century Soteriology in Reference to Milton.
      FS, 15, 1955, 48-59, 257-82.
      Considers the redemptive element in De Doctrina Christiana, Paradise
      Lost, and Paradise Regained in relation to the Renaissance milieu.

1294 ------. Satan Is a Problem. The Problem of Milton's "Satanic Fallacy"
      in Contemporary Criticism. FS, 17, 1957, 173-87.
      Uses La Driere's theory of voice and address to show that Satan is a
      "damned fool" throughout the epic.

1295 FISCH, HAROLD. Hebraic Style and Motifs in Paradise Lost. Language
      and Style in Milton: A Symposium in Honor of the Tercentenary of
      Paradise Lost. Ed. by Ronald David Emma and John T. Shawcross
      (New York: Frederick Ungar, 1967), pp. 30-64.
      "... I would prefer to begin with a broad account of the way in which the
      'Rabbinic Bible' presented those key biblical passages on which the main
      story of Paradise Lost is based, and then see whether this presentation seems
      in any way relevant to Milton's telling of the story."

1296 FISH, STANLEY. Further Thoughts on Milton's Christian Reader. CritQ,
      7, 1965, 279-84.
      An examination of the mechanics by which the reader discovers his limitations.

1297 ------. The Harassed Reader in Paradise Lost. CritQ, 7, 1965, 162-82.
Holds that the poem's center of reference is its reader and that Milton makes the reader fall as Adam did, with the same awareness.

1298 ------. Milton's God: Two Defences and a Qualification. Southern Review (Australia), 2 1966, 116-36.
A discussion of Paradise Lost, 3, 56-134, consisting of a formal defense and a rhetorical defense, with the qualification that God has a captive audience after line 92.

1299 ------. 'Not so much a teaching as an intangling': Milton's Method in Paradise Lost. Milton: Modern Judgements, ed. by Alan Rudrum (London: Macmillan, 1968), pp. 104-35.
A reprint of the first chapter of Surprised by Sin: the Reader in Paradise Lost, below.

1300 ------. Standing Only: Christian Heroism in Paradise Lost. CritQ, 9, 1967, 162-78.
Satan is an example of the epic hero, but he is the antithesis of the Christian hero, "and a large part of the poem is devoted to distinguishing between the two and showing the superiority of the latter."

1301 ------. Surprised by Sin: the Reader in Paradise Lost. London: Macmillan; New York: St. Martin's, 1967. xi, 344pp.
"My subject is Milton's reader, and my thesis, simply, that the uniqueness of the poem's theme—man's first obedience and the fruit thereof—results in the reader's being simultaneously a participant in the action and critic of his own performance."
Rev: TLS, Aug. 17, 1967, p. 745.

1302 FLANNAGAN, ROY C. Milton's Eve. Doctoral diss., Univ. of Virginia, 1966. Abs., DA, 28, 1967, 627-A.

1303 ------. Vallombrosa and Valdarno. MN, 2, 1968, 47-8.
Discusses Milton's use of Vallambrosa and Valdarno. Describes Vallambrosa, suggesting reasons why Milton might have gone there, and offers some possible locations of Valdarno.

1304 FLETCHER, HARRIS F. Milton and Ben Gerson. JEGP, 29, 1930, 41-52.
On Paradise Lost, 7.

1305 ------. Milton's Demogorgon—Prolusion I and Paradise Lost, II, 960-5. JEGP, 57, 1958, 684-9.
"Milton's two usages. . .almost certainly came directly from a printed edition of Boccaccio's De genealogiis deorum, perhaps that of 1532."

1306 FORD, JANE F. Satan as an Exemplar of Evil in Paradise Lost. Doctoral diss., Univ. of Pittsburgh, 1934. Abs., Univ. of Pittsburgh Bulletin, 10, 1934, 546-7.

1307 FORD, P. JEFFREY. Paradise Lost and the Five-Act Epic. Doctoral diss., Columbia Univ., 1966. Abs., DA, 28, 1967, 2207-A.
". . . essentially a study of the two editions of Paradise Lost."

1308 FORREST, JAMES FRENCH. The Evil Thought in the Blameless Mind: A Study in the History of a Moral Idea, Its Literary Representation, and

Its Particular Relationship to the Works of John Milton. Doctoral diss., Cornell Univ., 1960. Abs., DA, 21, 1961, 3449.

1309 FOX, ROBERT C. The Allegory of Sin and Death in Paradise Lost. MLQ, 24, 1963, 354-64.
". . . my thesis is that Sin and Death represent the respective sin of lust and gluttony in addition to their nominal concepts."

1310 ------. The Character of Mammon in Paradise Lost. RES, N.S., 13, 1962, 30-39.
". . . Mammon is primarily a symbol of the vice commonly termed avarice or covetousness. . . ."

1311 ------. The Character of Moloch in Paradise Lost. NS, 1962, pp. 389-95.
Moloch is to some extent an embodiment of Aristotle's concept of rashness, but he may also be partially patterned after Dante's Amata.

1312 ------. Milton's Paradise Lost, II, 226-228. Expl, 18, 1959, item 4.
On the meaning of "ignoble ease."

1313 ------. Milton's Sin: Addenda. PQ, 42, 1963, 120-21.
Additional analogues to Steadman's list in PQ, 29, 1960, 93-103.

1314 ------. Satan's Triad of Vices. TSLL, 2, 1960, 261-80.
Reduces Satan's motive for any action to "one of three basic vices: pride, envy, or revenge."

1315 ------. The Seven Deadly Sins in Paradise Lost. Doctoral diss., Columbia Univ., 1957. 225pp. Abs., DA, 17, 1957, 1328.

1316 FRASER, JOHN. Paradise Lost, Book IX: A Minority Opinion. MCR, No. 7, 1964, pp. 22-33.
A reading of 400 lines of Book IX shows that "a full surrender is incompatible with a full concentration of one's faculties and that there are failures of mind in a number of those lines that are positively disturbing."

1317 FREEDMAN, MORRIS. Dryden's Reported Reaction to Paradise Lost. N&Q, N.S., 5, 1958, 14-6.
Insists that Dryden always preferred rhyme to blank verse, despite some statements to the contrary.

1318 ------. John Milton, Nathanael Carpenter, and Satan. N&Q, N.S., 4, 1957, 293-5.
Notes similarities between Paradise Lost and Carpenter's Achitophel (1627).

1319 ------. Satan and Shaftesbury. PMLA, 74, 1959, 544-7.
"The close dependence of Absalom and Achitophel on Paradise Lost suggests how aptly Milton's material lent itself to contemporary political commentary and, simultaneously, how densely political it was in itself."

1320 FRENCH, ROBERTS WALKER. Verbal Irony in Paradise Lost. Doctoral diss., Brown Univ., 1965. Abs., DA, 26, 1965, 354-5.

1321 FRISSELL, HARRY L. Milton's Art of Logic and Ramist Logic in the Major Poems. Doctoral diss., Vanderbilt Univ., 1951. Abs., Bulletin of Vanderbilt Univ., 51, 1951, 22-3. Ann Arbor: UM, 1952. 250pp.

1322 FRYE, NORTHROP. The Return of Eden: Five Essays on Milton's Epics. Toronto: Univ. of Toronto Press, 1965; London: Routledge and Kegan Paul, 1965.

> The first four essays, designed as an introduction to Paradise Lost, were originally delivered at Huron College in 1963. The fifth in its original form appeared in MP (53, 1956, 227-38) as The Typology of Paradise Regained. Titles: The Story of All Things, The Breaking of the Music, Children of God and Nature, The Garden Within, and Revolt in the Desert.
> Rev: Barbara Lewalski, CE, 27, 1966, 643-4; W. G., Criticism, 7, 1966, 389-94; Alice Hamilton, DR, 46, 1966, 411-3; W. J. Barnes, QQ, 73, 1966, 455-7; J. Max Patrick, SCN, 24, 1966, 2-3; Patrick Cruttwell, HudR, 19, 1966, 498-502; C. A. Patrides, RES, 18, 1967, 330-2; J. B. Broadbent, ELN, 4, 1967, 216-8; John Lievsay, SAQ, 66, 1967, 260-3; Joseph H. Summers, JEGP, 46, 1967, 146-9.

1323 FRYE, ROLAND MUSHAT. God, Man, and Satan: Patterns of Christian Thought and Life in Paradise Lost, Pilgrim's Progress, and the Great Theologians. Princeton: Princeton Univ. Press, 1960. 184pp.

> Uses a metaphorical interpretation to make Paradise Lost and Pilgrim's Progress meaningful to twentieth-century man, pp. 21-91.
> Rev: Agnes M. C. Latham, YWES, 170; Howard Schultz, RN, 13, 1960, 334-6; EUQ, 16, 1960, 190-1; Ernest Sirluck, MP, 59, 1961, 68-9; Merritt Y. Hughes, MLN, 76, 1961, 650-3; T.S.K. Scott-Craig, Religion in Life, 30, 1961, 144-6; J. A. Bryant, Jr., SAQ, 60, 1961, 347-8; Glen Cavalierd, Theology, 64, 1961, 393; J. Franklin Murray, Th., 36, 1961, 133-4; L. R. Dawson, Christian Century, 28, Mar. 1, 1961, p. 269; Barbara Everett, MLR, 57, 1962, 415-7; Stanley R. Hopper, Theology Today, 19, 1962, 131-3.

1324 GAGE, CLARA S. The Sources of Milton's Concepts of Angels and the Angelic World. Doctoral diss., Cornell Univ., 1936. Abs., Ithaca: Cornell Univ. Press, 1936. 6pp.

1325 GARDNER, EDWARD H. Paradise Lost, I, 549-555. MLN, 62, 1947, 360.

1326 GARDNER, HELEN. A Reading of Paradise Lost. Oxford: Oxford University Press, 1965, 1967 (paperback). x, 131pp.

> Except for appendices, delivered as the Alexander Lectures, Univ. of Toronto, 1962. Contents: Paradise Lost Today, The Universe of Paradise Lost, The Cosmic Theme, The Human Theme. Appendix A: Milton's Satan and the Theme of Damnation in Elizabethan Tragedy; Appendix B: Milton's First Illustrator (John Baptist Medina).
> Rev: Agnes M. C. Latham, YWES, 208-9; A. C. Partridge, ESA, 9, 1966, 213-5; TLS, Mar. 31, 1966, p.264; Patrick Cruttwell, HudR, 19, 1966, 498-502; J. C. Maxwell, N&Q, N. S., 13, 1966, 397-9; Merritt Y. Hughes, JEGP, 46, 1967, 262-6; William A. Armstrong, English, 16, 1967, 148-9; William Empson, NSN, Dec. 24, 1965, pp. 1004; J. B. Beer, MLR, 63, 1968, 186-8.

1327 ------. L'Univers du Paradis Perdu. Le Paradis Perdu: 1667-1967. Ed. by Jacques Blondel (Paris: Minard Lettres Modernes, 1967), pp. 13-36.

> A translation by Michèle Bellot-Antony of a chapter from Gardner's A Reading of Paradise Lost.

1328 ------. Milton's Satan and the Theme of Damnation in Elizabethan Tragedy. ES, N.S., 1, 1948, 46-66. Reprinted in Milton: Modern Essays in Criticism, A Galaxy Book, ed. by Arthur E. Barker (New York: Oxford

Univ. Press, 1965), 205-17; and in slightly revised form in A Reading
of Paradise Lost (1965, 1967), above.

"It is on the tragic stage that we find the idea of damnation in English
literature before Paradise Lost—in Marlowe's Faustus, in Shakespeare's
Macbeth, and in Beatrice-Joanna of Middleton and Rowley."

1329   GARVIN, KATHARINE. Snakes in the Grass (with Particular Attention
to Satan, Lamia, Christabel). REL, 2, No. 2, 1961, 11-27.

A brief survey of serpent literature as reflected in Milton, Keats, and
Coleridge.

1330   GHIRADELLA, ROBERT V. Types of Irony in Paradise Lost. Doctoral
diss., New York Univ., 1964. Abs., DA, 25, 1964, 1891-2.

1331   GIAMATTI, A. BARTLETT. The Earthly Paradise and the Renaissance
Epic. Doctoral diss., Yale Univ., 1964. Princeton: Princeton Univ. Press,
1966. 374pp.

Considers writers from Dante to Milton. Chapter Six, Milton, pp. 295-
355. Milton's garden is a reflection of Adam and Eve and includes the
potential for change, which is part of their nature. "The earthly paradise in
Paradise Lost. . . blends all the previous images of the beautiful place
into one."

1332   ------. Milton and Fairfax's Tasso. RLC, 40, 1966, 613-5.

Suggests, i. a., that Paradise Lost, 4, 135-6, and 9, 495-503, echo Fairfax's translation, rather than Tasso's Italian text.

1333   GILBERT, ALLAN H. Critics of Mr. C. S. Lewis on Milton's Satan. SAQ,
47, 1948, 216-25.

Defends Lewis in opposing the idea that Satan is heroic or noble.

1334   ------. A Double Janus (Paradise Lost XI, 129). PMLA, 54, 1939, 1027-30.

Replies by T. W. Baldwin, PMLA, 56, 1941, 583-4; by A. H. Gilbert, PMLA,
584; by T. O. Mabbott, PMLA, 584-5.

1335   ------. Form and Matter in Paradise Lost, Book III. JEGP, 60, 1961,
651-63.

Discusses Milton as a theologian and Milton's use of divinities as epic
characters.

1336   ------. On the Composition of Paradise Lost. A Study of the Ordering
and Insertion of Material. Chapel Hill: Univ. of North Carolina Press,
1947. viii, 185pp. Reprinted, New York: Octagon Books, 1966.

A study of the evolution of Paradise Lost from its inception to its final form.
Chapters: Long Choosing, The Outline of Paradise Lost, The Passages In-
fluenced by the Tragedies, The Middle Epic Shift of the War in Heaven,
The Middle Epic Shift of Creation, Late Epic Material.
Rev: Ernest Sirluck, MP, 45, 1948, 273-5; G. G., Pers, 29, 1948, 311-2; M. B.
Seigler, SAB, 13, 1948, 3, 315-6; H. F. Fletcher, JEGP, 57, 1948, 202-3;
M. Y. Hughes, Ital, 25, 1948, 259-61; J. S. Diekhoff, MLN, 64, 1949, 129-30;
S. B. Liljegren, SN, 21, 1949, 79-80; Kester Svendsen, MLQ, 10, 1949, 534;
A. N. Jeffares, ES, 31, 1950, 185-6; B. A. Wright, RES, N. S., 1, 1950, 268-70;
V. de S. Pinto, Eras, 3, 1950, 161-3.

1337   ------. A Parallel between Milton and Boiardo. Ital, 20, 1943, 132-4.

"In adapting passages from the Orlando Innamorato for the war in heaven,

Milton retains something of the comedy of the boasters suddenly vanquished and forced to flee in terror 'bellowing.' "

1338 ------. The Qualities of the Renaissance Epic. SAQ, 53, 1954, 372-8.
A paper read before the Renaissance group of the MLA, 1952. Pays particular attention to the significance of Orlando Furioso. Paradise Lost, passim.

1339 ------. The Theological Basis of Satan's Rebellion and the Function of Abdiel in Paradise Lost. MP, 40, 1942, 19-42.
Finds the basis in Psalms 2 and Hebrews 1.

1340 GILLESPIE, HELEN. The Story of Adam and Eve from Caedmon to Milton. Master's thesis, Duke Univ., 1937.

1341 GILLIAM, J. F. Scylla and Sin. PQ, 29, 1950, 345-7.
On Paradise Lost, 2, 650-1.

1342 GIOVANNINI, MARGARET. Milton's Paradise Lost, IV, 131-193. Expl, 12, 1953, item 1.

1343 GLAESENER, H. Le Voyage de Milton en Italie. Prélude au Paradis perdu. RLC, 13, 1936, 294-329.

1344 GOHN, ERNEST S. The Christian Ethic of Paradise Lost and Samson Agonistes. SN, 34, 1962, 243-68.
"The purpose of this paper is to show that throughout his work, and particularly in Paradise Lost and Samson Agonistes, Milton never lost sight of the didactic aim outlined in his early treatise [Reason of Church Government].... This paper also purports to demonstrate that the doctrinal ends of Milton's poems become clearer when viewed against a background of Renaissance ethical theory."

1345 GORDON, D. J. Two Milton Notes. RES, 18, 1942, 318-9.
1. Precious Bane: a Recollection of Boethius in Paradise Lost? (1, 692).
2. The Golden Chersoness. (Paradise Regained, 4, 74).

1346 GOSSMAN, ANN. Man Plac't in a Paradise: A Comparative Study of Milton, St. Ambrose, and Hugh St. Victor. Master's thesis, Rice Institute, 1954.

1347 ------. Milton, Prudentius, and the Brood of Sin. N&Q, N.S., 4, 1957, 439-40.
Suggests Prudentius' Hamartagenia as one of the sources for Milton's treatment of Sin at Hell's gates.

1348 ------. Milton's Paradise Lost, II, 1013. Expl, 19, 1961, item 51.
On Milton's use of the "Pyramid of fire."

1349 ------. Two Milton Notes; 1: Milton, Plutarch, and Darkness Visible; 2: The Iron Rod and Golden Sceptre in Paradise Lost. N&Q, N.S., 8, 1961, 182-3.
1. Milton's darkness visible may echo Plutarch's Concerning Nature (fifteenth question).
2. Nathanael Culverwell, "who cites Plutarch. . . in defence of Right Reason" furnishes "an interesting analogue for Milton's golden sceptre and iron rod in Paradise Lost, II, 327-8, and V, 886-7."

1350   ------. The Use of the Tree of Life in Paradise Lost. JEGP, 65, 1966, 680-87.

> "The Tree of Life. . . is important as a focus of certain ironic tensions that are carefully developed throughout Paradise Lost" and as "an illustration of Milton's application of the Renaissance belief in Right Reason as a guide to choice of values and to the right use of all created things."

1351   GRACE, WILLIAM J. Notes on Robert Burton and John Milton. SP, 52, 1955, 578-91.

> I.a., Burton and the Limbo of Vanity and the catalogue of fallen angels.

1352   ------. Orthodoxy and Aesthetic Method in Paradise Lost and the Divine Comedy. CL, 1, 1949, 173-87.

1353   GRAHAM, W. Paradise Lost, Books IV and IX (John Milton). Notes on English Literature Series. Oxford: Basil Blackwell, 1966. 79pp.

> Introductions designed for students; suitable critical approaches indicated.

1354   GRANSDEN, K. W. Paradise Lost and the Aeneid. EIC, 17, 1967, 281-303.

> Gives examples of the method Milton uses to "convert the style and mannerisms of the Aeneid into his English epic."

1355   GRANT, ISABELLE FITCH. The Publication of Paradise Lost from 1667 to 1800, with a Handlist of Editions. Master's thesis, Univ. of Illinois, 1937.

1356   GRAY, JAMES ARTHUR. The Form and Function of Rhythm in the Versification of Paradise Lost. Doctoral diss., Univ. of Washington, 1967. Abs., DA, 28, 1967, 1785-A.

1357   GREEN, CLARENCE C. The Paradox of the Fall in Paradise Lost. MLN, 53, 1938, 557-71.

> "The form that the paradox takes in Paradise Lost is of particular interest, for it reveals how complex were the traditional and philosophical influences that went into the shaping of Milton's mind."

1358   GREENE, DONALD. The Sin of Pride: A Sketch for a Literary Exploration. NMQ, 34, Spring, 1964, 8-30.

> Sees Samson Agonistes as an example of self-psychoanalysis in literature and cites Satan and Eve as examples of neurotic psychology.

1359   GREENE, THOMAS. Milton. The Descent from Heaven: A Study in Epic Continuity (New Haven: Yale Univ. Press, 1963), pp. 363-418.

> Interprets the convention of Raphael's descent to Adam in Book Five of Paradise Lost in its historical and literary perspective and shows how the descent harmonizes with the rest of the poem.

1360   GREENFIELD, STANLEY B. Milton's Paradise Lost, XII, 629-632. Expl, 19, 1961, item 57.

> On the Ev'ning Mist and the Labourer's heel.

1361   GROSE, CHRISTOPHER WALDO. Some Uses of Sensuous Immediacy in Paradise Lost. HLQ, 31, 1968, 211-22.

> Demonstrates that Milton actually links sensuous immediacy with rhetoric, that sensuous immediacy in fact is an organic part of Milton's rhetorical argument. Places particular emphasis on Book 1.

1362 ------. The Rhetoric of the Miltonic Simile. Doctoral diss., Washington
Univ., 1966. Abs., DA, 27, 1966, 1785-A.
"The purpose of this dissertation is first to consider Milton's theory of
simile, available in the early Logic, and within Paradise Lost itself, and
secondly, to read closely the heroic similes of Milton's first epic with this
theory in mind."

1363 GROSS, BARRY. Free Love and Free Will in Paradise Lost. SEL, 7,
1967, 95-106.
Adam and Eve have "to give up love of self in order to discover their
proper roles in relation to each other and to God."

1364 GRÜN, RICHARD H. Das Menschenbild John Miltons in Paradise Lost:
Eine Interpretation seines Epos im Lichte des Begriffes Disobedience.
Frankfurter Arbeiten aus dem Gebiete des Anglistik und der Amerika-
Studien, Heft 2. Heidelberg: Winter, 1956. 100pp.
Rev: K. H. Darenberg, NS, 1956, pp. 502-3; T. Riese, Archiv, 195, 1958,
59; SCN, 16, 1958, 34-5; Edgar Mertner, Anglia, 76, 1959, 326-7.

1365 GUERLAC, HENRY. The Poets' Nitre. Isis, 45, 1954, 243-55.
Milton's references to nitre and nitrous foam are in accord with popular
Renaissance ideas concerning the cause of thunderstorms and earthquakes.

1366 GUIDI, AUGUSTO. John Milton. Brescia: Morcelleana, 1940. 195pp.
Contains a section on Paradise Lost.

1367 GURTEEN, S. H. V. The Epic of the Fall of Man: A Comparative Study
of Caedmon, Dante and Milton. New York: Haskell House, 1964. xi,
449pp.
A reprint of Stevens No. 2718, first published in 1896.

1368 GUTHKE, KARL S. Goethe, Milton und der humoristische Gott: Eine
Studie zur poetischen Weltordnung im Faust. Goethe, 22, 1960, 104-11.
Quotes Paradise Lost, 5, 721-32; 5, 735-7; 8, 75-84; 8, 399-406; passages which
are indicative of God's humor.

1369 HAGENBÜCHLE, ROLAND. Sündenfall und Wahlfreiheit in Miltons
Paradise Lost. Schweizer Anglistische Arbeiten, 5. Bern: Francke
Verlag, 1967. vii, 144pp.
Chapters: Der Südenfall im puritanischen Zeitalter Miltons, Der literarische
Hintergrund, Der Sündenfall in Paradise Lost, Theodizee-Gedanke und an-
thropozentrisches Weltbild, Die neue Würde des Menschen.

1370 HÄGIN, PETER. The Epic Hero and the Decline of Heroic Poetry: A
Study of the Neoclassical English Epic with special reference to Milton's
Paradise Lost. The Cooper Monographs. Bern: Francke, 1964. 181pp.
Focuses attention on the history of the epic hero. Chapter 5: The Hero of
Paradise Lost, pp. 146-69.
Rev: Agnes M. C. Latham, YWES, 243-4.

1371 HAIR, P. E. H. Milton and Sierra Leone. N&Q, N.S., 13, 1966, 23-4.
On Paradise Lost 10, 703.

1372 HALKETT, JOHN GEORGE. Milton and the Idea of Matrimony: A
Study of Milton's Divorce Tracts and Paradise Lost. Doctoral diss.,
Northwestern Univ., 1964. Abs., DA, 25, 1964, 3570.

1373 HALL, AMY V. Milton and The City of God. Doctoral diss., Univ. of
      Washington, 1941. Abs., Univ. of Washington, Abstracts of Theses, 6,
      1942, 267-8.

1374 HALLER, WILLIAM. The Tragedy of God's Englishman. Reason and
      the Imagination: Studies in the History of Ideas, 1600-1800. Ed. by J. A.
      Mazzeo (New York: Columbia Univ. Press; London: Routledge and
      Kegan Paul, 1962), pp. 201-11.
      On the political events in England after 1640 and their bearing on
      Milton's choosing of an epic subject.

1375 HAMILTON, G. ROSTREVOR. Hero or Fool? A Study of Milton's
      Satan. London: Allen and Unwin, 1944. 41pp.
      Rev: TLS, Nov. 4, 1944, p. 540; A. S. P. Woodhouse, UTQ, 15, 1946, 200-5.

1376 HAMMERLE, KARL. To Save Appearances (Par. L VIII 82), ein
      Problem der Scholastik. Anglia, 62, 1938, 368-72.
      On the philosophical background of Milton's concept of the universe.

1377 HAMMOND, MASON. Concilia Deorum from Homer through Milton.
      SP, 30, 1933, 1-16.

1378 HANFORD, JAMES HOLLY. The Dramatic Element in Paradise Lost.
      John Milton, Poet and Humanist (Cleveland: Western Reserve Univ.
      Press, 1966), pp. 224-43.
      A reprint of Stevens' No. 956, published in 1917. "Influence of Elizabethan
      drama on Milton; his preference for classical drama; psychological and
      dramatic aspects of Paradise Lost; use of elements of Elizabethan tragedy;
      growth of plan" (Stevens' annotation).

1379 ------. Paradise Lost Annotated by Thomas Edwards. PULC, 23, 1962,
      123-4.
      Recognizes Edwards' extensive notes to Paradise Lost, probably prepared
      for publication and now existing "as marginalia in a fine copy of the 'Thir-
      teenth Edition,' published by Jacob Tonson in 1729. . . ."

1380 HANKINS, JOHN E. Milton and Olaus Magnus. Studies in Honor of
      T. W. Baldwin. Ed. by Don C. Allen (Urbana: Univ. of Illinois Press,
      1958), pp. 205-10.
      Cites several parallels which "suggest that Olaus' Epitome (1558) had a
      considerable influence in providing the descriptive materials for Milton's
      account of Hell and in stimulating his poetic imagination."

1381 ------. The Pains of the Afterworld: Fire, Wind, and Ice in Milton and
      Shakespeare. PMLA, 71, 1956, 482-95.
      On Shakespeare's and Milton's use of the medieval pains of punishment.

1382 HARDING, DAVIS P. The Club of Hercules: Studies in the Classical
      Background of Paradise Lost. Illinois Studies in Language and Litera-
      ture, 50; Urbana: Univ. of Illinois Press, 1962. 134pp.
      "In the following pages I have merely attempted to suggest, not rigidly to
      define, some of the ways in which Milton has turned that literature [Latin
      and Greek] to account at every level of the poem's meaning—the plot, struc-
      ture, characterization, and pre-eminently style."
      Rev: Irene Samuel, Classical World, 56, Feb. 19, 1963, p. 144; John M.

Raines, ELN, 1, 1963, 68-70; Stephen Merton, SCN, 21, 1963, 16-7; TLS, Feb. 15, 1963, pp. 101-2; Arnold Stein, RN, 16, 1963, 348-50; Charles Garton, N&Q, N. S., 11, 1964, 353-4; John Buxton, RES, 15, 1964, 319-21.

1383 - - - - - -. Milton's Bee-Simile. JEGP, 60, 1961, 664-9.
The simile of the bees in Paradise Lost, 1, 767-76, is reminiscent of one in Vergil's Fourth Georgic.

1384 HARDISON, O. B., JR. The Enduring Monument: A Study of the Idea of Praise in Renaissance Literary Theory and Practice. Chapel Hill: Univ. of North Carolina Press, 1962. xvi, 240pp.
Considers Milton an exponent of the theory of praise. On the genre of Paradise Lost, pp. 88-92. Also, passim.

1385 HARDY, JOHN P. Dr. Johnson as a Critic of the English Poets Including Shakespeare. Doctoral diss., Magdalen College, Oxford, 1965.
Chapter 7: Johnson's Criticism of Paradise Lost.

1386 - - - - - -. Johnson and Raphael's Counsel to Adam. Johnson, Boswell and Their Circle. Essays Presented to Lawrence Fitzroy Powell in Honour of His Eighty-Fourth Birthday (Oxford: Clarendon Press, 1965), pp. 122-36.
Johnson's praise of Raphael's counsel to Adam concerning scientific inquiry is "to be viewed in the context of his Christian interpretation of Socratic humanism."

1387 HARGREAVES, H. A. Report on the Tercentenary Celebration of Paradise Lost. SCN, 26, 1968, 17-8.
At the Univ. of Alberta. Contains brief summaries of papers read by John C. Bryce, Charles Davis, J. Max Patrick, Ernest Sirluck, and John M. Steadman. Also notes the performance of Psychedelic Satan, a dramatic reading from Paradise Lost.

1388 HARPER, GEORGE M. The World's First Love Story. Literary Appreciations (New York: Bobbs-Merrill, 1937), pp. 70-88.
Discusses the Adam-Eve story in Paradise Lost. Calls Milton the "most seductive painter of female delights," etc.

1389 HARRINGTON, DAVID V. A Defense of the Felix Culpa in Paradise Lost. Cresset, 28, 1965, 12-4.
Points out that Milton's aim is to justify God's ways to man, not to decide whether the fall was fortunate or not.

1390 HART, JEFFREY. Paradise Lost and Order: I Know Each Lane and Every Valley Green. CE, 25, 1964, 576-82.
"There is evidence in the poem itself that associates Eden before the Fall with the England of Elizabeth, and the Fall itself with the break-up of that harmonious vision of man, society, and cosmos which had been the legacy of sixteenth-century humanists...."

1391 HARTMAN, GEOFFREY. Milton's Counterplot. ELH, 25, 1958, 1-12.
Reprinted in Milton: Modern Essays in Criticism, A Galaxy Book, ed. by Arthur E. Barker (New York: Oxford Univ. Press, 1965), pp. 386-97; and in Milton: A Collection of Critical Essays, ed. by Louis L. Martz (Englewood Cliffs, N.J.: Prentice-Hall, 1966), pp. 100-8.

142   *An Annotated Bibliography*

On Paradise Lost. ". . . God's omnipotent knowledge that the creation will outlive death and sin. . . may be characterized as the counterplot."

1392 HARTWELL, KATHLEEN. Lactantius and Milton. Cambridge: Harvard Univ. Press, 1929. xv, 220pp.
Amasses considerable evidence of Lactantius' influence in the works of Milton. Rev: TLS, Oct. 3, 1929, p. 770; D. H. Stevens, CP, 24, 1929, 414-5; C. W. Brodribb, TLS, Oct. 10, 1929, p. 794; Denis Saurat, RES, 6, 1930, 473-5; R. S. Crane, MP, 27, 1930, 361-4; H. F. Fletcher, JEGP, 29, 1930, 465-6; S. B. Liljegren, DL, 51, 1930, 1232-3; G. Kitchin, MLR, 25, 1930, 215-6; F. Delattre, Rev. belge de Philol. et d'hist., 12, 1933, 309-12.

1393 HAVENS, P. S. Dryden's Tagged Version of Paradise Lost. Parrott Presentation Volume (Princeton: Princeton Univ. Press, 1935), pp. 383-97.

1394 HAVILAND, THOMAS P. Milton for the Young. LC, 3, 1935, 46-8.
A humorous description of a recent library acquisition, The Story of Paradise Lost for Children, by Eliza W. Bradburn, the daughter of Wesley's friend, Samuel Bradburn.

1395 HAYS, H. R. The Dangerous Sex: The Myth of Feminine Evil. New York: G. P. Putnam's Sons, 1964.
Discusses Milton and female sexuality, pp. 170 ff.

1396 HEMBY, JAMES B. A Study of Irony in Paradise Lost. Doctoral diss., Texas Christian Univ., 1965.

1397 HERBERT, CAROLYN. Comic Elements in the Scenes of Hell of Paradise Lost. Renaissance Papers, 1956 (Columbia: Univ. of South Carolina Press, 1956), pp. 92-101.
". . . much of the scenes in Hell revolves laughingly around the characters representing pride. . . ."

1398 HERBST, EDWARD L. Classical Mythology in Paradise Lost. CP, 29, 1934, 147-8.
Observes that "Milton excluded references to classical mythology from the speeches of his characters, and uses them only when he speaks in his own person."

1399 HERBSTER, S. I. Paradise Lost: A Study for the Modern Preacher. Lutheran Church Quarterly, 4, 1931, 377-89.

1400 HERMAN, WILLIAM R. Heroism and Paradise Lost. CE, 21, 1959, 13-7.
Examines the main characters in the light of two contrasting concepts of the hero—the Hellenic and the Biblical.

1401 HERTZ, NEIL H. Wordsworth and the Tears of Adam. SIR, 7, Autumn, 1967, 15-33.
Concerned in general with the problem of encounter of poet with poet. Sees a connection between Milton's story of the Flood in Paradise Lost, 11, and Wordsworth's poetry, especially The Ruined Cottage.

1402 HIBERNICUS. Milton: Two Verbal Parallels: Autumn Leaves. N&Q, 184, 1943, 85.
The leaves simile and Chapman's translation of Homer and Heywood's Brazen Age.

1403 ------. Mulciber's A Summer Day (Paradise Lost, 1, 744). N&Q, 180, 1941, 27.

1404 HILDEBRAND, G. D. The Power of Chastity in Paradise Lost. N&Q, 197, 1952, 246.
On Paradise Lost, 9, 309-12, 373-4, and 455-66.

1405 HILL, D. M. Johnson as Moderator. N&Q, N.S., 3, 1956, 517-22.
Regards Johnson's method in assessing Paradise Lost (Life of Milton) as that of a moderator.

1406 ------. Satan on the Burning Lake. N&Q, N.S., 3, 1956, 157-9.
Since the whale is the symbol of Satan in the bestiaries, Milton's long simile in Book 1 is not a digression.

1407 HOBSBAUM, PHILIP. The Criticism of Milton's Epic Similes. SN, 36, 1964, 220-31.
Comments on studies by E. M. W. Tillyard, J. B. Broadbent, D. Daiches, K. Muir, and others.

1408 ------. The Milton Controversy: A Documentation. The Use of English, 14, 1963, 180-6.
A review of Milton criticism since 1900, with the conclusion that "to attempt to interpret the whole work [Paradise Lost] seems to be a venture doomed to failure, at least so far as any general acceptance of the interpretation is concerned."

1409 HOLLOWAY, JOHN. Paradise Lost and the Quest for Reality. FMLS, 3, 1967, 1-14.
Points out the "strong link which exists between Milton and Francis Bacon," and the links between Milton and Shakespeare. Calls Milton "the first of our great moderns."

1410 HOOKER, WALLACE K. Time, Value, and Moral Process in Milton's Paradise Lost. Doctoral diss., Texas Christian Univ., 1966.

1411 HORRELL, JOSEPH. Milton, Limbo, and Suicide. RES, 18, 1942, 413-27.
On the meaning of the Limbo passage in Paradise Lost 3, and Adam and Eve's discussion of suicide in Paradise Lost, 11.

1412 HOWARD, DONALD R. Milton's Satan and the Augustinian Tradition. Renaissance Papers, 1954 (Columbia: University of South Carolina Press, 1954), pp. 11-23.
An exposition of Augustine's doctrine of evil, with its emphasis on nothingness, with the assertion that "Milton's portrayal of Satan reflects his acquaintance with this well known theological concept."

1413 HOWARD, LEON. The Invention of Milton's Great Argument: A Study of the Logic of God's Ways to Men. HLQ, 9, 1946, 149-73.
An analysis of Milton's logic and its relationship to the meaning of Paradise Lost.

1414 HOWELL, A. C. Anibal Galindo's Spanish Translation of Milton's Paradise Lost. RLC, 36, 1962, 438-43.
Prose translation, published in Ghent in 1868. Reviews Galindo's comments on Paradise Lost and notes that the translator, a Colombian, found in the poem inspiration for the struggle of Latin-American nations to attain liberty.

1415 - - - - - -. Milton's Paradise Lost, Book I, Line 506. AN&Q, 3, 1965, 85.
      Cites unnoted echo of longum est dicere in Cicero's speech In Gaium Verrem
      Actionis Secundae (1. 156).

1416 HUCKABAY, CALVIN. Satan and the Narrative Structure of Paradise
      Lost: Some Observations. SN, 33, 1961, 96-102.
      Even though Satan dominates most of the action in Books 1 and 2 and parts
      of the narrative of Books 3 and 4, Milton never lets the reader lose sight
      of man as the central figure.

1417 - - - - - -. The Satanist Controversy of the Nineteenth Century. Studies in
      English Renaissance Literature. Ed. by Waldo F. McNeir (Baton Rouge:
      Louisiana State Univ. Press, 1962), pp. 197-210.
      Traces the development of the controversy over Satan's position in Paradise
      Lost from its inception with William Blake (1790) to its fruition with
      Sir Walter Raleigh (1900).

1418 HUGHES, MERRITT Y. Devils to Adore for Deities. Studies in Honor of
      Dewitt T. Starnes. Ed. by Thomas P. Harrison and others (Austin:
      Univ. of Texas Press, 1967), pp. 241-58.
      On Milton's treatment in Paradise Lost, 1, of the demons who are to be
      adored as deities. Considers the background of Milton's approach and feels
      that the fallen angels are to be considered as individuals, not as patterned
      examples of the Seven Deadly Sins.

1419 - - - - - -. The Filiations of Milton's Celestial Dialogue. Ten Perspectives on
      Milton (New Haven and London: Yale Univ. Press, 1965), pp. 104-35.
      On Paradise Lost, 3, 80-343.

1420 - - - - - -. Merit in Paradise Lost. HLQ, 31, 1967, 3-20.
      "Our particular interest is the poet's solution of his hard problem: how to
      establish the merits of the Messiah who Raphael tells Adam was with no
      explanation presented to the angels on God's 'holy Hill.' "

1421 - - - - - -. Milton and the Symbol of Light. SEL, 4, 1964, 1-33. Reprinted in
      Ten Perspectives on Milton (New Haven and London: Yale Univ.
      Press, 1965), pp. 63-103.
      A study of the role of light in Paradise Lost. Contains a survey of other
      studies of Milton's light.

1422 - - - - - -. Milton's Celestial Battle and the Theogonies. Studies in Honor
      of T. W. Baldwin. Ed. by Don C. Allen (Urbana: Univ. of Illinois
      Press, 1958), pp. 237-53. Reprinted in Ten Perspectives on Milton (New
      Haven and London: Yale Univ. Press, 1965), pp. 196-219.
      "The thesis of the present study is that Milton definitely conceived his
      celestial battle as representing events which were none the less actual for
      surmounting the reach of human sense, and that he found evidence for their
      occurrence and models for their likening to corporal forms in the classical
      accounts of the Titans and giants on the gods of Olympus, of which the
      best is Hesiod's Theogony."

1423 - - - - - -. Milton's Limbo of Vanity. Th'Upright Heart and Pure. Ed. by
      Amadeus P. Fiore, O.F.M. (Pittsburgh and Louvain: Duquesne Univ.
      Press, 1967), pp. 7-24.
      Defends the passage in Paradise Lost, 3, 440-97, and finds its source in Plato
      and the Neoplatonists and to some extent in the Italian poets.

1424 ------. Myself Am Hell. MP, 54, 1956, 80-94. Reprinted in Ten Perspectives on Milton (New Haven and London: Yale Univ. Press, 1965), pp. 136-64.
Explains the symbolism of Paradise Lost, 4, 73-79.

1425 ------. Satan and the Myth of the Tyrant. Essays in English Literature from the Renaissance to the Victorian Age Presented to A. S. P. Woodhouse (Toronto: Univ. of Toronto Press, 1964), pp. 125-48. Reprinted in Ten Perspectives on Milton (New Haven and London: Yale Univ. Press, 1965), pp. 165-95.
Discusses Milton's Satan as ectype and archetype, observes various attempts to identify him with historical and literary figures, and surveys psychiatric analyses of him.

1426 ------. Satan Now Dragon Grown (Paradise Lost, X, 529). EA, 20, 1967, 356-69.
On the transformation scene in Book 10 and Milton's final treatment of Satan. "Fallen angels as well as fallen men might be symbolized by the celebrated metamorphoses of the ancient poets, and of all fallen creatures Satan was most eligible for transformation into the serpent."

1427 HULME, HILDA M. On the Language of Paradise Lost: Its Elizabethan and Early Seventeenth-Century Background. Language and Style in Milton: A Symposium in Honor of the Tercentenary of Paradise Lost. Ed. by Ronald David Emma and John T. Shawcross (New York: Frederick Ungar, 1967), pp. 65-101.
Considers, i.a., the influence of Shakespeare, Spenser, Giles and Phineas Fletcher, and Du Bartas and tries "to establish what Milton . . . remembered and re-used from those writings of his Elizabethan predecessors which he had read before his blindness or which he was having read to him again while he was at work on his later poems."

1428 HUNT, WINIFRED. On Even Ground: A Note on the Extramundane Location of Hell in Paradise Lost. MLQ, 23, 1962, 17-9.
The location of Milton's hell "provides imagery vital for conveying Milton's attitude toward both Satan and man's world in Paradise Lost."

1429 HUNTER, WILLIAM B., JR. Eve's Demonic Dream. ELH, 13, 1946, 255-65.
"My purpose is to show that the poet conceived of this dream in terms of contemporary dream and demon lore."

1430 ------. The Heresies of Satan. Th'Upright Heart and Pure. Ed. by Amadeus P. Fiore, O.F.M. (Pittsburgh and Louvain: Duquesne Univ. Press, 1967), pp. 25-34.
Argues that Milton is "consciously picturing Satan as a heretic of the dynamic monarchian persuasion. . . ."

1431 ------. Holy Light in Paradise Lost. RIP, 46, 1960, 1-14.
Outlines some of the neoplatonic and patristic traditions behind the opening of Book 3 and attempts to show that Milton addresses "the Son of God as Holy Light."

1432 ------. The Meaning of Holy Light in Paradise Lost III. MLN, 74, 1959, 589-92.

"I wish to urge that the collocation of the two images light-sun and stream-fountain reveals that Milton had in mind the identification of this Holy Light with the Son of God."

1433 ------. Milton's Arianism Reconsidered HTR, 52, 1959, 9-35.
"... the various 'Arian' passages in the Christian Doctrine and Paradise Lost fall into place as revelations of a tradition which antedates even the Council of Nicaea. It seems that we may assert positively that Milton was not an Arian."

1434 ------. Milton's Urania. SEL, 4, 1964, 35-42.
Further contention that in the invocations in Books 1, 7, and 9 of Paradise Lost, Milton is addressing the Son of God.

1435 ------. Prophetic Dreams and Visions in Paradise Lost. MLQ, 9, 1948, 277-85.
Shows the background of divine revelation in rabbinical and Neo-Platonic theory.

1436 ------. Satan as Comet: Paradise Lost, II, 708-11. ELN, 5, 1967, 17-21.
Argues against the postulate that Milton's comet was actually a comet which he viewed at age ten, in 1618. Theorizes instead that Satan is made similar to a supernova. "But one should claim no great profundity in Milton's knowledge of science."

1437 ------. Two Milton Notes. MLR, 44, 1949, 89-91.
On Paradise Lost, 8, 94-7, and 12, 632-4, 642-4.

1438 HUNTLEY, FRANK L. A Justification of Milton's Paradise of Fools (P.L. III, 431-499). ELH, 21, 1954, 107-13.
Relates the passage to the rest of the poem.

1439 ------. Milton, Mendoza, and the Chinese Land-Ship. MLN, 69, 1954, 404-7.
On Paradise Lost, 3, 431-42. Mendoza credited with the account of the land ship.

1440 HUNTLEY, JOHN F. Aristotle's Physics as a Gloss on Paradise Lost, VIII.152. PQ, 44, 1965, 129-32.
"... Aristotle's Physics helps the reader to interpret the physical, moral, and spiritual implications of Paradise Lost VIII. 152 and permits him to see that here Milton draws still another element into the complex pattern of reciprocity and antagonism which animates so much of the poem."

1441 ------. The Ecology and Anatomy of Criticism: Milton's Sonnet 19 and the Bee Simile in Paradise Lost, I. 768-76. JAAC, 24, 1966, 383-91.
Discusses "the use of historical fact in the work of literary interpretation," with references to Sonnet 19, and "proposes a non-Homeric, non-Virgilian, rather 'Miltonic' interpretation of the bee simile...."

1442 HUTCHERSON, DUDLEY R. Milton's Adam as Lover. UMSE, 2, 1961, 1-11.
Feels that the source of Adam's competence as lover lies in Milton's own marital experiences.

1443 ------. Milton's Eve and Other Eves. UMSE, 1, 1960, 12-31.
A consideration of Milton's Eve and her predecessors in Genesis, Caedmon, Du Bartas, and elsewhere.

1444 ------. Milton's Epithets for Eve. Univ. of Virginia Studies, N. S., 4, 1951, 253-60.
>In the James Southall Wilson Festschrift.

1445 HUTSON, ARTHUR E., and PATRICIA McCOY, eds. Epics of the Western World. New York: Lippincott, 1954. 512pp.
>Contains an introduction to Paradise Lost, pp. 449-57, and a summary, pp. 458-97.

1446 HYMAN, LAWRENCE W. Paradise Lost: The Argument and the Rhythmic Pattern. MinnR, 5, 1965, 223-8.
>Suggests that the heart of the poem lies in its contradictory elements, its cyclical pattern. Paradise Lost "is great, not because it answers a problem, nor because it explains the meaning of life, but because it creates through its own rhythm a pattern which we recognize as inherent in our lives."

1447 ------. Poetry and Dogma in Paradise Lost. CE, 29, 1968, 529-35.
>In the basic incompatibility of Milton's moral or theological dogma and the seeming reality of life lies the tragedy of the poem—"the source of its dramatic intensity." The modern reader should argue not whether the characters *should* have acted as they did but rather *why* they had to act in the face of this fundamental conflict.

1448 ------. The Publication of Paradise Lost. Journal of Historical Studies, 1, 1967, 50-64.
>On the circumstances surrounding the publication of Paradise Lost and its reception, including the reactions of Dryden and Marvell.

1449 ILLO, JOHN. Animal Sources for Milton's Sin and Death. N&Q, N.S., 7, 1960, 425-6.
>On Sylvester's Bartas: His Devine Weekes and Workes (1611) as a possible influence on Milton's Sin and Death.

1450 ------. Milton, Dowland, and Eve's Love for Adam. SCN, 19, 1961, item 67.
>Cites parallels between John Dowland's "Now cease, my wandering lies" and Eve's speech in Paradise Lost, 9, 961-89.

1451 IWAHASHI, TAKEO. Poetic Metaphysics of Paradise Lost. Japan: Christian Thought Series, 1933.
>The first part discusses time and space, astronomy, and anthropology of Paradise Lost; the second notes various critical opinions and contains Iwahashi's evaluation of the poem; the third part deals with theological topics.

1452 J., W. H. Paradise Lost: "Lose" or "Loose." N&Q, 174, 1938, 438.
>Concerning Belial's speech in Paradise Lost, 2.

1453 JAHANGER, RUSTAM PESTANJI MODI. Vondel and Milton. Bombay: K. and J. Cooper, 1942. 326pp.
>Includes a verse translation of Vondel's Lucifer.
>Rev: Helen Darbishire, RES, 19, 1943, 330.

1454 JAMISON, SISTER M. THECLA. The Twentieth-Century Critics of Milton and the Problem of Satan in Paradise Lost. Doctoral diss., Catholic Univ., 1952. On microcards, Catholic Univ.

1455 JOHNSON, FRANCIS RARICK. Astronomical Thought in Renaissance England: A Study of the English Scientific Writings from 1500 to 1645. Baltimore: Johns Hopkins Press, 1937. xiii, 357pp.
The astronomy of Paradise Lost, pp. 282-87.

1456 JONES, BUFORD. A Thoreauvian Word Play and Paradise Lost. Emerson Society Quarterly, 47, 1967, 65-6.
Compares and contrasts man's state in Paradise Lost and in Walden.

1457 JONES, FRED L. Paradise Lost, I, 549-62. MLN, 49, 1934, 44-5.
The description of the march of the fallen angels is from Plutarch's Life of Lycurgus.

1458 JONES, PUTNAM F. Satan and the Narrative Structure of Paradise Lost. If by your art ((Pittsburgh: Univ. of Pittsburgh Press, 1948), pp. 15-26.
The debate over Satan's role has its basis in the narrative structure of the poem.

1459 JONES, ROGER IOAN STEPHENS. The Epic Simile in Paradise Lost. B. Litt. thesis, Jesus College, Oxford, 1967. 160pp.

1460 JONSSON, INGE. William Empson, John Milton och Var Herre. Samlaren, 84, 1963, 95-119.
Critical of Empson's Milton's God. Feels that Empson pays insufficient attention to scholarly research and to Milton's text.

1461 JOSEPH, SISTER MIRIAM, C.S.C. Orthodoxy in Paradise Lost. Laval Théologique et Philosophique, 8, 1952, 243-84.
"... it seems fair to conclude that an intelligent Catholic reader can enjoy in Paradise Lost the expression of dogmatic, moral, and philosophical truths impregnated with a power to poetry, the power not merely to teach but to delight and move."
Rev: SCN, 13, 1955, 11-2.

1462 JUMP, J. D. John Milton and the Arabian Wind. N&Q, 196, 1951, 270-2.
On Paradise Lost, 4, 153-66.

1463 KASTOR, FRANK S. In His Own Shape: The Stature of Satan in Paradise Lost. ELN, 5, 1968, 264-9.
Notes Milton's vagueness in picturing Satan and points out that Milton describes the external Satan by stature, which combines shape and size and is conveyed through metaphor and simile. Satan's stature is largest in heaven (planetary), smaller in hell (mountainous), and smallest on earth (man-sized).

1464 ------. Lucifer, Satan, and the Devil: A Genesis of Apparent Inconsistencies in Paradise Lost. Doctoral diss., Univ. of California, Berkeley, 1963. Abs., DA, 24, 1964, 5386-7.

1466 KEHLER, DOROTHEA. Paradise Lost, X 860-862. MN, 2, 1968, 45.
Suggests that "Milton drew upon a single source—the memorable refrain from Spenser's Epithalamium...."

1467 KEITH, A. L. Personification in Milton's Paradise Lost. EJ, 17, 1929, 399-409.
Observes that "Milton personifies abstract ideas much more freely than

concrete objects. Abstractions are more difficult to comprehend unless endowed with personality. Certainly they are thus given an emotional appeal. This emotional quality pervades the entire poem and is due to nothing so much as to the personification."

1468 KELLETT, E. E. Macbeth and Satan. LQHR, July, 1939, pp. 289-99.
On Milton's early interest in Macbeth as a subject for a poem and resemblances between Shakespeare's character and Satan.

1469 ------. The Puns in Milton. LQHR, 159, 1934, 469-76.

1470 KELLEY, MAURICE W. Milton's Arianism Again Considered. HTR, 54, 1961, 195-205.
Argues against denials of Milton's Arianism by William Hunter (HTR, 52, 1959, 9-35) and Roland M. Frye (God, Man, and Satan, 1960), pp. 75-6.

1471 ------. Milton's De Doctrina Christiana as a Gloss upon Paradise Lost. Doctoral diss., Princeton Univ., 1934. Published as This Great Argument: a Study of Milton's De doctrina christiana as a Gloss upon Paradise Lost. Princeton Studies in English, 22. Princeton: Princeton Univ. Press: Oxford: Oxford Univ. Press, 1941. Reprinted, Gloucester, Mass.: Peter Smith, 1962. xiv, 269pp.
Rev: T. B. Stroup, MLQ, 3, 1941, 327-30; A. Williams, MP, 40, 1941, 103-4; T. Maynard, CW, 155, 1941, 506-7; J. S. Diekhoff, SR, 50, 1941, 266-7; G. L. Kane, CHR, 28, 1941, 143-4; B. M., DR, 22, 1941, 249; Douglas Bush, MLN, 58, 1943, 220-2; N. H. Henry, PQ, 22, 1943, 92-3; G. C. Taylor, Shakespeare Assn. Bull., 18, 1943, 92-5; A. S. P. Woodhouse, PRv, 52, 1943, 206-8; H. J. C. Grierson, MLR, 39, 1944, 97-107.

1472 ------. Milton's Use of Begot in Paradise Lost, V, 603. SP, 38, 1941, 252-65.

1473 ------. Paradise Lost, VII, 8-12, and the Zohar. MLR, 29, 1934, 322-4.

1474 ------. The Theological Dogma of Paradise Lost, III, 173-202. PMLA, 52, 1937, 75-9. Reprinted in Milton: Modern Essays in Criticism. A Galaxy Book. Ed. by Arthur E. Barker (New York: Oxford Univ. Press, 1965), 226-32.
The passage is in accord with the Arminian views in De Doctrina Christiana.

1475 KELLOGG, ALFRED L. Some Patristic Sources for Milton's Gehenna. N&Q, 195, 1950, 10-3.
Jerome and Bede.

1476 KELLY, SISTER MARGARET TERESA. The Influence of Dante's Paradise upon Milton. Doctoral diss., Cornell Univ., 1938. Abs., Cornell Univ. Abstracts of Theses, 1938, pp. 33-5.

1477 KENRICK, EDWARD F. Paradise Lost and the Index of Prohibited Books. SP, 53, 1956, 485-500.
A translation placed on the Index, 1734.

1478 KERMODE, FRANK. Adam Unparadised. The Living Milton (London: Routledge and K. Paul, 1960), pp. 85-123.

A defense of Paradise Lost against Waldock, Graves, and others. "In fact, modern reader as I am, I find Paradise Lost wonderfully satisfying...

because Milton's poem seems to me enduringly to represent, or better to embody, life in a great symbolic attitude."

1479   KIM, SUN SOOK. Ethics in Milton's Paradise Lost. ELL (Korea), No. 5, 1958 (?), pp. 1-27.

1480   KIRKCONNELL, WATSON. A Slice of Canada: Memoirs. Toronto: Univ. of Toronto Press for Acadia Univ., 1967. 393pp.
An autobiography, including the author's account (pp. 222-32) of his work in editing The Celestial Cycle, noted below.

1481   ------. The Celestial Cycle: the Theme of Paradise Lost in World Literature, with Translations of the Major Analogues. Toronto: Univ. of Toronto Press, 1952. Reprinted, New York: Gordian Press, 1968. xxvii, 701pp.
Part 1: Analogues, in whole or in part.
Part 2: Descriptive catalogue of analogues.
Rev: Arnold Davenport, YWES, 184-5; D. C. A[llen], MLN, 68, 1953, 281; E. M. W. Tillyard, RES, 4, 1953, 405; James R. Naiden, CL, 5, 1953, 375-7; C. L. B., DR, 33, 1953-4, 37; A. E. Barker, UTQ, 23, 1954, 195-8; Malcolm Ross, QQ, 60, 1953-4, 440; Edgar Mertner, Anglia, 72, 1954-5, 489-92; J. Blondel, EA, 8, 1960, 74-5.

1482   ------. Some Latin Analogues of Milton, with a Chronological Checklist. TRSC, 3rd. Series, 40, 1946, 173-89.
Presents the "appended chronological lists of analogues of Milton's Paradise Lost, in all languages and from all periods." The list contains 225 analogues.

1483   KIVETTE, RUTH MONTGOMERY. Milton on the Trinity. Doctoral diss., Columbia Univ., 1960. Abs., DA, 21, 1960, 189-90.

1484   KLAMMER, ENNO. The Fallacy of the Felix Culpa in Milton's Paradise Lost. Cresset, 23, No. 8, 1960, 13-4.
Examines six passages in Paradise Lost and concludes that the theory of the fortunate fall becomes a fallacy which Milton refutes.

1485   KNIGHT, DOUGLAS. The Dramatic Center of Paradise Lost. SAQ, 63, 1964, 44-59.
Milton's poetic order "finds that point where poet and reader can step from their private individual exploration of the world into their common human exploration of it."

1486   KNIGHTLEY, WILLIAM J. The Perfidy of the Devils' Council. UMSE, 5, 1964, 9-14.
"This nearness of Satan's work to the work of Christ, particularly since it anticipates events totally unknown to Satan, is the measure of his brilliance as well as his perfidy."

1487   KNOTT, JOHN R., JR. The Pastoral Day in Paradise Lost. MLQ, 29, 1968, 168-82.
Shows that Milton uses the pastoral convention of the three primary times of the day (dawn, noon, and evening) to emphasize the bliss of Adam and Eve before the Fall. The closing lines of the poem "owe their extraordinary power to the fact that the rhythm of nature is not restored."

1488   ------. The Visit of Raphael: Paradise Lost, Book V. PQ, 47, 1968, 36-42.

Focuses attention on the dinner which is shared by Adam and Raphael. Feels that it enhances the humility and also the majesty of Adam and Eve.

1489   KORETZ, GENE. Milton's Paradise Lost, IX, 910. Expl, 12, 1954, item 53. On the meaning of "these wilde Woods forlorn."

1490   KRANIDAS, THOMAS. Adam and Eve in the Garden: A Study of Paradise Lost, Book V. SEL, 4, 1964, 71-83.
Sees an integration of the human and the comic existing within Milton's concept of decorum.

1491   ------. Milton's Concept of Decorum. Doctoral diss., Univ. of Washington, 1962. Abs., DA, 23, 1963, 4360. Published as The Fierce Equation: A Study of Milton's Decorum. The Hague: Mouton, 1965. 165pp.
The first chapter deals with the background of decorum. The second is an attempt to deduce Milton's concept of decorum from his prose writings, and the third is a study of decorum in Paradise Lost.
Rev: Agnes M. C. Latham, YWES, 46, 1965, 206; W. H. Ussery, SCN, 25, 1967, 1-2; A. D. Ferry, MLQ, 28, 1967, 494-6.

1492   ------. Satan's First Disguise. ELN, 2, 1964, 13-5.
Examines Satan's "theatrical glitter" (Paradise Lost, 3, 634-644) and relates it "to some other aspects of Milton's thought."

1493   KROUSE, F. MICHAEL. Milton's Paradise Lost, IV, 349. Expl, 7, 1949, item 44.

1494   KUROTA, KENJIRO. The Early Reception of Paradise Lost. Ehime Univ. Helicon (Japan), 3, 1953.

1495   KURTH, BURTON O. Milton and Christian Heroism: Biblical Epic Themes and Forms in Seventeenth Century England. UCPES, 20. Berkeley: Univ. of California Press, 1959. 152pp. Reprinted, Hamden, Connecticut: Shoe String Press, 1966.
Shows that "the concept of a Christian epic based on Biblical subject matter was widespread enough in the first half of the seventeenth century to be called one of the characteristic ideas, or ideals of the age" and that "Milton was as much the culmination of an English tradition of sacred heroic poetry as the more general Renaissance and Continental aspirations to write the Christian epic."
Rev: Agnes Latham, YWES, 40, 1959, 174; Frank Kermode, MLR, 4, 1960, 591-2; Merritt Y. Hughes, MLN, 76, 1961, 551-6; French Fogle, Personalist, 42, 1961, 409-11; Nell P. Eurich, SCN, 19, 1961, 28-9; William Riley Parker, JEGP, 65, 1962, 180-1; J. Blondel, EA, 18, 1965, 182-3.

1496   LANDY, MARCIA. Tercentenary Celebration of Paradise Lost. SCN, 26, 1968, 31-3.
At the Univ. of Pittsburgh. Contains summaries of the following papers: Thomas Kranidas, Visions and Revision in Paradise Lost; Joseph Summers, Milton and the Celebration of Creation; Louis L. Martz, Tragic Transformation in Samson Agonistes; Arnold Stein, The Metamorphoses of Satan; O. B. Hardison, Written Records and Truths of Spirit in Paradise Lost; Mario Di Cesare, Paradise Lost and Epic Tradition; John Steadman, Milton's Rhetoric: Satan and the Unjust Discourse; Michael Fixler, Myth and Mystery in Paradise Lost; Jackson Cope, Paradise Regained: Inner Ritual; and Northrop Frye, The Revelation of Eve.

1497   LANGENFELT, GÖSTA. The OE. Paradise Lost. Anglia, 55, 1931, 250-65.

1498   LANGTON, EDWARD. Satan, a Portrait. A Study of the Character of
       Satan through All the Ages. London: Sheffington, 1946; New York:
       Macmillan, 1947.
          A background study.

1499   LASCELLES, MARY. The Rider on the Winged Horse. Elizabethan and
       Jacobean Studies Presented to Frank Percy Wilson in Honour of His
       Seventieth Birthday (Oxford: Clarendon Press, 1959), pp. 173-98.
          A consideration of Milton's use of Pegasean Wing in Paradise Lost, 7, 4, in
          terms of the poet's vocation.

1500   LAUTER, PAUL. Milton's Siloa's Brook. N&Q, N.S., 5, 1958, 204-5.
          On the relevance of John 9: 1-11, 30-39 to the beginning of Paradise Lost.

1501   LAWRY, JON S. Euphrasy and Rue: Books XI and XII, Paradise Lost.
       BSUF, 8, Summer, 1967, 3-10.
          Shows that "Books XI and XII balance the regenerative conditions and
          assurances of Paradise."

1502   ------. Reading Paradise Lost: The Grand Masterpiece to Observe. CE,
       25, 1964, 582-6.
          Offers a scheme for a class reading of Paradise Lost in "three parts of four
          books each...."

1503   ------. The Shadow of Heaven: Matter and Stance in Milton's Poetry.
       Ithaca: Cornell Univ. Press, 1968. xv, 416pp.
          See Chapter 4: Most Reason is That Reason Overcome: Choice in Paradise
          Lost, pp. 121-288.

1504   LE COMTE, EDWARD S. Milton's Infernal Council and Mantuan.
       PMLA, 69, 1954, 979-83.
          Supplies addenda to Kirkconnell's list of analogues.

1505   LEE, HERBERT G. The Justification Theme in Milton's Work with
       Special Reference to Paradise Lost. Master's thesis, Univ. of North
       Carolina, 1947.

1506   LEGOUIS, PIERRE. Dryden Plus Miltonien Que Milton? EA, 20, 1967,
       370-7.
          A detailed study of Dryden's adaptation of Paradise Lost in The State of
          Innocence.

1507   LEJOSNE, ROGER. Satan Républicain. Le Paradis Perdu: 1667-1967.
       Ed. by Jacques Blondel (Paris: Minard Lettres Modernes, 1967), pp.
       87-103.
          Discusses the political characteristics in Paradise Lost and holds that the
          poem is a kind of political pamphlet in disguise.

1508   LEVER, J. W. Paradise Lost and Anglo-Saxon Tradition. RES, 23, 1947,
       97-106.
          Argues for the influence of the Caedmonian Genesis.

1509   LEVIN, HARRY. Paradises, Heavenly and Earthly. HLQ, 29, 1966,
       305-24.

A Founder's Day address, delivered on Feb. 28, 1966. Discusses the Paradises of Dante, Milton, and others.

1510 LEVY, BABETTE. Milton's Paradise Lost (and other works): A Critical Analysis in Depth. Bar Notes Literature Study and Examination Guides. New York: Barrister Publishing Co., Inc., 1966. With charts by Joan Butterworth Grady. 124pp.
A student outline.

1511 LEWALSKI, BARBARA KIEFER. Paradise Lost Introduced and Structured in Space. MP, 61, 1963, 122-6.
A review article on The Muse's Method: An Introduction to Paradise Lost, by Joseph Summers and The Metaphoric Structure of Paradise Lost, by Jackson I. Cope. Notes similarities of objectives and convictions and divergences in method and approach.

1512 ------. Structure and the Symbolism of Vision in Michael's Prophecy, Paradise Lost, Books XI-XII. PQ, 42, 1963, 25-35.
"The evidence...suggests that the prophecy is a highly complex aesthetic structure, organized so as to project the great themes of the poem on the epic screen of all human history, and at the same time...to promote Adam's own development as a dramatic character."

1513 LEWIS, C. S. A Preface to Paradise Lost. Being the Ballard Methews Lectures Delivered at University College, North Wales, 1941, Revised and Enlarged. London: Oxford Univ. Press, 1942. 139pp. Reprinted, 1942, 1943, 1944, 1946, 1951, 1954, 1956, 1959. Issued as an Oxford Paperback, 1960. 152pp.
Contents: Epic Poetry, Is Criticism Possible?, Primary Epic, The Technique of Primary Epic, The Subject of Primary Epic, Virgil and the Subject of Secondary Epic, The Style of Secondary Epic, Defence of This Style, The Doctrine of the Unchanging Human Heart, Milton and St. Augustine, Hierarchy, The Theology of Paradise Lost, Satan, Satan's Followers, The Mistake about Milton's Angels, Adam and Eve, Unfallen Sexuality, The Fall, Conclusion, Appendix: Notes on Certain Passages.
Rev: TLS, Nov. 28, 1942, p. 528, and Dec. 5, 1942, p. 595; N&Q, 183, 1942, 359-60; L. C. Martin, YWES, 160-1; Jackson Knight, Spect, Nov. 13, 1942, p. 460; Denis Saurat, NSN, Nov. 14, 1942, pp. 325-6; L. C. Knights, Scr, 11, 1942, 146-8; H. J. C. Grierson, MLR, 38, 1943, 143-8; E. H. W. Meyerstein, English, 4, 1943, 129-30; E. W. Wagenknecht, NYTBR, May 23, 1943, p. 10: DUJ, 4, 1943, 71-2; W. R. Parker, MLN, 59, 1944, 205-6; Irene Samuel, PRv, 53, 1944, 580-90; B. A. Wright RES, 20, 1944, 78-84; E. E. Stoll, RES, 20, 1944, 108-24.

1514 ------. Satan, Milton: Modern Essays in Criticism. A Galaxy Book, ed. by Arthur E. Barker (New York: Oxford Univ. Press, 1965), pp. 196-204.
A reprint of the chapter on Satan in Lewis' Preface to Paradise Lost.

1515 ------. The Style of Secondary Epic. Milton: A Collection of Critical Essays. Ed. by Louis L. Martz (Englewood Cliffs, N.J.: Prentice-Hall, 1966), pp. 40-55.
A chapter reprinted from Lewis' A Preface to Paradise Lost.

1516 LEWIS, RICHARD B. Milton's Use of Logic and Rhetoric in Paradise Lost to Develop the Character of Satan. Doctoral diss., Stanford Univ., 1949. Abs., Abstracts of Dissertations, Stanford Univ., 24, 1950, 155-8.

1517 LIEB, MICHAEL J. The Dialectics of Creation: Patterns of Birth and Regeneration in Paradise Lost. Doctoral diss., Rutgers Univ., 1967. Abs., DA, 28, 1968, 4135-A. 351pp.

1518 L[OANE], G[EORGE] G. Paradise Lost: Lose or Loose. N&Q, 176, 1939, 89.
Milton habitually uses "loose" for what we write "lose."

1519 LOANE, GEORGE G. A Phrase in Paradise Lost (Book IV, 11, 408-10). N&Q, 180, 1941, 387.
Replies by E. H. V., N&Q, 181, 1941, 27; by Loane, p. 68; by E. H. V., pp. 95-6.

1520 ------. Ridges of War. N&Q, 175, 1938, 313.
On Paradise Lost, 6, 233. Suggests that "ridges" refers to spaces between masses of troops.

1521 ------. A Simile of Milton. N&Q, 175, 1938, 434-5.
On Paradise Lost, 4, 159-66.

1522 LODGE, ANN. Satan's Symbolic Syndrome. A Psychological Interpretation of Milton's Satan. PsyR, 43, 1956, 411-22.
Suggests that "...Milton's Satan represents what in clinical psychology would be considered a classical case of paranoia, displaying in highly abstracted and symbolic form, all the essential characteristic symptoms."

1523 LONG, ANNE BOWERS. The Relations Between Classical and Biblical Allusions in Milton's Later Poems. Doctoral diss., Univ. of Illinois, 1967. Abs., DA, 28, 1968, 5022-A. 382pp.

1524 LOOTEN, M. C. Milton et les amours de dieu. RA-A, 8, 1931, 345-6.
Attacks Legouis on Paradise Lost, 7, 8-12.

1525 LOREDANO, GIOVANNO FRANCESCO. The Life of Adam (1640). A Facsimile Reproduction of the English Translation of 1659 with an Introduction by Roy C. Flannagan with John Arthos. Gainesville, Fla.: Scholars' Facsimiles and Reprints, 1967. xxi, 86pp.
Flannagan and Arthos consider Loredano's work as an analogue and as a possible source of Paradise Lost.
Rev: Douglas Higgins, SCN, 26, 1968, 3.

1526 LOVEJOY, ARTHUR O. Milton and the Paradox of the Fortunate Fall. ELH, 4, 1937, 161-79. Reprinted in Essays in the History of Ideas (Baltimore: Johns Hopkins Press, 1948), pp. 277-95; and in Milton's Epic Poetry: Essays on Paradise Lost and Paradise Regained, ed. by C. A. Patrides (Harmondsworth: Penguin Books, 1967), pp. 55-73.
A study of the background of Adam's speech in Paradise Lost, 12, 466-78.

1527 ------. Milton's Dialogue on Astronomy. Reason and the Imagination: Studies in the History of Ideas, 1600-1800. Ed. by J. A. Mazzeo (New York: Columbia Univ. Press; London: Routledge and Kegan Paul, 1962), pp. 129-42.
On Adam and Raphael's discussion in Books 7 and 8 of Paradise Lost. Concludes that Milton's attitude is extremely pragmatic and anti-intellectual and therefore ironic.

1528 LOW, ANTHONY. The Parting in the Garden in Paradise Lost. PQ, 47, 1968, 30-5,
   In Book 9. Feels that Adam errs in permitting Eve to part from him and that Adam "abdicates his proper responsibilities," with the "important consequence of making him more nearly responsible for the fall."

1529 LUCAS, F. L. Literature and Psychology. Ann Arbor Paperbacks. Ann Arbor: Univ. of Michigan Press, 1957, 1962.
   On Milton's conscious and unconscious attitude toward Satan, pp. 111-8.

1530 ------. Satan's Witness. TLS, Nov. 18, 1960, p. 741.
   On the meaning of witness'd in Paradise Lost, 1, 57.

1531 LUMIANSKY, ROBERT M., and HERSCHEL BAKER, eds. Critical Approaches to Six Major English Works: Beowulf through Paradise Lost. Philadelphia: Univ. of Pennsylvania Press, 1968. 256pp.
   Irene Samuel is the author of the essay on Paradise Lost, pp. 209-53. ". . . includes a survey of the critical approaches to the work which have been advocated during the last several decades."

1532 LUMPKIN, BEN W. Fate in Paradise Lost. SP, 44, 1947, 56-68.
   Contrary to the utterances of Satan, Milton, God, and the forces of God use the word to mean a divine decree or the will of God.

1533 LUTTER, TIBOR. Miltons Verlorenes Paradies: ein Interpretationsversuch. ZAA, 5, 1957, 378-403.
   Considers Milton's choice of theme and relates the epic to the Puritan Revolution.

1534 MABBOTT, THOMAS O. Milton and Nonnos. N&Q, 197, 1952, 117-8.
   Paradise Lost, 4, 340ff., echoes a passage in the Dionysiaca.

1535 MacCAFFREY, ISABEL E. GAMBLE. Paradise Lost as Myth. Doctoral diss., Radcliff College, 1954. Cambridge: Harvard Univ. Press, 1959. 229pp.
   Contents: Introduction, The Meaning of Myth, Milton's Myth, Structural Patterns in Paradise Lost, The Language of Paradise Lost, Into Our First World: Milton's Imagery, Satan's Voyage, Conclusion, Select Bibliography, Index.
   Rev: Agnes M. C. Latham, YWES, 40, 1959, 174; Frank Kermode, MLR, 55, 1960, 591-2; Allan Pritchard, DR, 40, 1960, 107-9; QQ, 67, 1960, 491-2; B. A. Wright, RES, 11, 1960, 11; SCN, 18, No. 1, 1960, item 2; Milledge B. Seigler, Expl, 19, No. 5, 1961, review 3; Laurence Lerner, EIC, 11, 1961, 108-10.

1536 ------. The Meditative Paradigm. ELH, 32, 1965, 388-407.
   A review article on Louis L. Martz's The Paradise Within: Studies in Vaughan, Traherne, and Milton (1964). "The sixty-page essay devoted to Paradise Lost in this book offers a new analysis of the poem's structure based on the meditative paradigm." Deals also with Paradise Regained.

1537 MacCALLUM, H. R. Milton and Sacred History: Books XI and XII of Paradise Lost. Essays in English Literature from the Renaissance to the Victorian Age Presented to A. S. P. Woodhouse (Toronto: Univ. of Toronto Press, 1964), pp. 149-68.

Working within the context of Christian belief about history, Milton selects and arranges his material to make doctrine coalesce with aesthetic pattern.

1538 MACKELLER, WALTER. Milton and Grotius. TLS, Dec. 15, 1932, p. 963.
Argues that in Paradise Lost, 11, 661-71, Milton is referring to Hugo Grotius.

1539 MACKIN, COOPER R. Aural Imagery as Miltonic Metaphor: The Temptation Scenes of Paradise Lost and Paradise Regained. Explorations of Literature. Ed. by Rima Drell Reck (Baton Rouge: Louisiana State Univ. Press, 1966), pp. 32-42.
Suggests that the aural imagery in Book 9 "is a metaphor for the ultimate meaning of Satan's temptation and that it serves the same function in the temptation scenes in Paradise Regained."

1540 MACKINNON, MALCOLM, H. M. Milton's Theory and Practice of the Epic, Examined in Relation to Italian Renaissance Literary Criticism. Doctoral diss., Univ. of Toronto, 1948.

1541 MADSEN, WILLIAM G. Earth the Shadow of Heaven: Typological Symbolism in Paradise Lost. PMLA, 75, 1960, 519-26. Reprinted in Milton: Modern Essays in Criticism. A Galaxy Book. Ed. by Arthur E. Barker (New York: Oxford Univ. Press, 1965), pp. 246-63.
Contends that in Paradise Lost, 5, 571-6, "Milton is using 'shadow' not in its Platonic or Neoplatonic sense but in its familiar Christian sense of foreshadowing or adumbration; and that the symbolism of Paradise Lost is typological rather than Platonic."

1542 ------. The Fortunate Fall in Paradise Lost. MLN, 74, 1959, 103-5.
"Adam's Fall opens up for man an entirely new dimension of experience: if it was possible for man before the Fall to participate with the angels... after the Fall he may participate with the Godhead itself."

1543 ------. The Idea of Nature in Milton's Poetry. Three Studies in the Renaissance: Sidney, Jonson, Milton. Yale Studies in English, 138. Ed. by Benjamin C. Nangle (New Haven: Yale Univ. Press, 1958), pp. 181-283.
Topics: Nature in Comus; Nature in Paradise Lost; Nature, Man and God; Nature and Grace; The Poetic Vision.
Rev: SCN, 16, 1958, 23; M. Wickert, Anglia, 78, 1960, 104-6; Agnes M. C. Latham, YWES, 181-2.

1544 MAGON, LEOPOLD. Die drei ersten deutschen Versuche einer Übersetzung von Miltons Paradise Lost. Gedenkschrift für Ferdinand Josef Schneider (Weimar, 1956), pp. 39-82.
On German translations of Paradise Lost.

1545 MAHOOD, MOLLY MAUREEN. Poetry and Humanism. New Haven: Yale Univ. Press; London: Jonathan Cape, 1950. Reprinted, Port Washington, N. Y.: Kennikat Press, 1967. 335pp.
Contains two articles of interest: Milton: the Baroque Artist, pp. 169-206, in which Mahood holds that Paradise Lost is expressive of the humanism of the metaphysical poets rather than that of the earlier Renaissance; and Milton's Heroes, pp. 207-51, in which Samson and Satan are presented as contrasting figures.

1546 MALONE, KEMP. Grundtvig on Paradise Lost. Renaissance Studies in Honor of Hardin Craig (Stanford: Stanford Univ. Press, 1941), pp. 320-3.
The article also appears in PQ, 20, 1941, 512-5.

1548 MANLEY, FRANCIS [FRANK]. Paradise Parched. MLN, 74, 1959, 7-9.
On Paradise Lost, 12, 632-6.

1549 MANLEY, FRANK. Milton and the Beasts of the Field. MLN, 76, 1961, 398-403.
Observes that in the account of land animals (Paradise Lost, 7, 449-98) Milton includes those whose manner of existence raised discussion among biblical commentators such as Benedictus Pererius: the crossbreed, the amphibians, the insects.

1550 ------. Moloch on Demonic Motion. MLN, 76, 1961, 110-6.
On Paradise Lost, 2, 70-81.

1551 MANNING, CLARENCE A. A Russian Translation of Paradise Lost. SEER, 13, 1935, 173-6.
Reproduces and comments on the introduction to a 1780 translation.

1552 MARILLA, ESMOND L. The Central Problem of Paradise Lost: The Fall of Man. Essays and Studies in English Language and Literature, 15. Uppsala: A. -B. Lundequistska Bokhandeln; Copenhagen: Ejnar Munksgaard; Cambridge: Harvard Univ. Press, 1953. 36pp. Reprinted in Milton and Modern Man: Selected Essays (University, Alabama: Univ. of Alabama Press, 1968), pp. 27-55.
"My purpose here is to bring the details of the scene [the fall of Adam and Eve] under careful focus and to argue for my view that the episode is a painstaking and carefully unified dramatization of issues which, in Milton's opinion, are always active in shaping the course of human history."
Rev: Arnold Davenport YWES, 206; Pierre Legouis, EA, 7, 1954, 119; J. Milton French, SN, 26, 1954, 201-2.

1553 ------. Milton on Conjugal Love among the Heavenly Angels. MLN, 68, 1953, 485-6. Reprinted in Milton and Modern Man: Selected Essays (University, Alabama: Univ. of Alabama Press, 1968), pp. 103-5.
On Raphael's comment in Paradise Lost, 8.

1554 ------. Milton on Vain Wisdom and False Philosophie. SN, 25, 1953, 1-5. Reprinted in Milton and Modern Man: Selected Essays (University, Alabama: Univ. of Alabama Press, 1968), pp. 98-102.
On Paradise Lost, 2, 557-68.

1555 ------. Milton's Pandemonium. NS, 4, 1960, 167-74. Reprinted in Milton and Modern Man: Selected Essays (University, Alabama: Univ. of Alabama Press, 1968), pp. 87-97.
"The purpose of the present study is to bring under close examination the action embraced in these books [1 and 2] and to argue that Pandemonium, the climax of that action in Book II, represents a carefully devised integral element in the artistic framework of the poem."

1556 ------. Milton's Paradise of Fools. ES, 42, 1961, 159-64. Reprinted in Milton and Modern Man: Selected Essays (University, Alabama: Univ. of Alabama Press, 1968), pp. 106-13.

On the passage in Paradise Lost, 3, 416-98, and its relationship to Milton's theme and purpose.

1557 ------. A Reading of Two Episodes in Paradise Lost. EA, 12, 1959, 135-41. Reprinted in Milton and Modern Man: Selected Essays (University, Alabama: Univ. of Alabama Press, 1968), pp. 78-86.
The organic importance of the war in Heaven (Book 6) and Satan's altercation with the guardian angels (Book 4) is the emphasis which they place on the battle between good and evil, a battle which good will win and which prefigures the ultimate establishment of Christ's kingdom on earth.

1558 MARSHALL, WILLIAM H. Paradise Lost: Felix Culpa and the Problem of Structure. MLN, 76, 1961, 15-20. Reprinted in Milton: Modern Essays in Criticism. A Galaxy Book. Ed. by Arthur E. Barker (New York: Oxford Univ. Press, 1965), pp. 336-41.
On the Paradox of the Fortunate Fall. "... the confusion caused by the meaning and structural function of the theme of felix culpa in the poem carries at least implications of a kind of failure on Milton's part."

1559 MARTZ, LOUIS L. Paradise Lost: The Journey of the Mind. The Paradise Within: Studies in Vaughan, Traherne, and Milton (New Haven and London: Yale Univ. Press, 1964, 1966), pp. 105-67. xix, 217pp.
Uses the Augustinian principle of "the indwelling teacher" as the central approach in exploring the style, organization, and meaning of Paradise Lost.
Rev: H. C. White, YR, 54, 1964, 440; Isabel G. MacCaffrey, ELH, 32, 1965, 388-407; John M. Wallace, JEGP, 64, 1965, 732-8; Joan Bennett, MP, 63, 1965, 160-2; QR, No. 644, 1965, 236; John M. Steadman, RN, 18, 1965, 164-7; Gale H. Carrithers, Jr. SAQ, 64, 1965, 418; James H. McCabe, Th, 40, 1965, 294-5; John R. Mulder, SCN, 23, No. 1-2, 1965, 3-4; TLS, June 3, 1965, p. 456; John Carey, N&Q, N. S., 13, 1966, 35-6; L. C. Martin, RES, 17, 1966, 90-1; J. L. Murphy, ELN, 3, 1966, 223-5.

1560 MAXWELL, I. R. Waldock and Milton. Southerly (Sidney, Australia), 12, 1951, 14-6.
Criticizes Waldock's Paradise Lost and Its Critics (1947).

1561 MAXWELL, J. C. "Gods" in Paradise Lost. N&Q, 193, 1948, 234-6, 242.

1562 ------. Paradise Lost, XI, 829-38. MLR, 45, 1950, 515-6.
Echoes Spenser's Faerie Queene, 2, 12, and Homer's alleged Hymn to Apollo (11. 74-8).

1563 ------. The Sensible of Pain: Paradise Lost, 2, 278. RES, 5, 1954, 268.
Interprets the phrase as "that element in our pain which is apprehended by the senses."

1564 MAZIÈRES, THIBAUT DE. Les poèmes inspirés du début de la Genèse à l'époque de la Renaissance. Louvain, 1931.
Considers Paradise Lost.

1565 McADAMS, JAMES R., ed. Abstracts of Papers Read at the 1967 MLA Meetings. SCN, 26, 1968, 18-9.
Contains, i.a., abstracts of B. Rajan's Paradise Lost: The Providence of Style, of Irene Samuel's Paradise Lost among the Commentators, 1942-1967, and of Louis L. Martz's A Poem Written in Ten Books.

1566 ------. Milton's Epic Synthesis: A Study of the Association of Paradise Lost and Paradise Regained. Doctoral diss., New York Univ., 1966.

1567 McCARTHY, THOMAS J. Some Theological Aspects of Paradise Lost. Master's thesis, Univ. of Western Ontario, 1933. 130pp.
"Milton's works mirror the eclecticism of the age and indicate the prevailing trend of religious thought."

1568 McCOLLEY, GRANT. The Astronomy of Paradise Lost. SP, 34, 1937, 209-47.
Analyzes "the principal distinguishing characteristics and prestige of the most influential astronomical conceptions of the period, including in this analysis some discussion of the comments and reactions of Milton."

1569 ------. The Book of Enoch and Paradise Lost. HTR, 31, 1938, 21-39.
Milton knew more of I Enoch than is commonly acknowledged.

1570 ------. The Epic Catalogue of Paradise Lost. ELH, 4, 1937, 180-91.
Suggests that the important precedent for the catalogue of Lucifer's peers in Book 1 of Paradise Lost "was not Homer and the Iliad, but Alexander Ross and the Pansebeia; or, A View of all Religions in the World" (London, 1653).

1571 ------. Macbeth and Paradise Lost. SAB, 13, 1938, 146-50.
Milton's indebtedness.

1572 ------. Milton and Moses Bar-Cepha. SP, 38, 1941, 246-51.
Parallels.

1573 ------. Milton's Ariel. N&Q, 177, 1939, 45.
Basil and Procopius were Milton's authorities for his making Ariel a follower of Satan.

1574 ------. Milton's Battle in Heaven and Rupert of Saint Heribert. Spect, 16, 1941, 230-5.
Parallels suggest that Milton had read the twelfth-century theologian.

1575 ------. Milton's Dialogue on Astronomy: The Principal Immediate Sources. PMLA, 52, 1937, 728-62.
On Paradise Lost, 8. Suggests Bishop John Wilkins and Alexander Ross.

1576 ------. Milton's Golden Compasses. N&Q, 176, 1939, 97-8.
On Milton's following convention in using the metaphor in Paradise Lost, 7, 224-33.

1577 ------. Paradise Lost. HTR, 32, 1939, 181-235.
"...I suggest that Paradise Lost was designed as a non-sectarian epic and more or less deliberately modelled as well as based upon conservative religious literature...."

1578 ------. Paradise Lost: An Account of Its Growth and Major Origins, with a Discussion of Milton's Use of Sources and Literary Patterns. Chicago: Packard and Co., 1940. Reprinted, New York: Russell and Russell, 1963. 362pp.
Relates Milton's epic to the literature from which it sprang.
Rev: L. C. Martin, YWES, 169-70; Garland Greever, Pers, 22, 1941, 308; M. Kelley and T. S. K. Scott-Craig, MLN, 27, 1942, 295-6; S. A. Nock, SR, 49, 1942, 561-5.

1579 ------. The Theory of the Diurnal Rotation of the Earth. Isis, 26, 1937, 392-402.

1580 McKENZIE, LEROY R. Some Aspects of Milton's Concept of Order as Revealed through Key Terms, Patterns, and Images in Paradise Lost. Doctoral diss., Univ. of Ottawa, 1962.

1581 McKERAHAN, ANNABELLE L. Paradise Lost: A Sublimation of the Philosophical Concepts Found in Milton's Prose. Doctoral diss., Univ. of Pittsburgh, 1936. Abs., Univ. of Pittsburgh, Abstracts of Theses, 20, 1936, 168-74.

1583 McMANUS, HUGH FRANCIS. Milton's Son of God as Celestial Man. Doctoral diss., Columbia Univ., 1967. Abs., DA, 28, 1968, 5023-A-4-A. 115pp.

1584 MEIER, HANS HEINRICH. Xanaduvian Residues. ES, 48, 1967, 145-55.
      Compares several elements in Coleridge's Kubla Khan with Paradise Lost and feels that the key to understanding Kubla Khan is the "notion of an exotic earthly paradise corresponding with Milton's paradise in Paradise Lost and with Spenser's Garden of Adonis in the Faerie Queene...."

1585 MENZIES, W. Milton: The Last Poems. E&S, 24, 1938, 80-113.
      On the poems as an expression of the poet's inner feelings at the time of composition.

1586 MEYERSTEIN, E. H. W. Ramiel (Paradise Lost, VI, 372), N&Q, 189, 1945, 255.
      Asks, "Where did Milton get the name?"

1587 MILLER, DOROTHY DURKEE. Eve. JEGP, 61, 1962, 542-7.
      Comments on Eve's position in the hierarchy, before and after the Fall.

1588 MILLER, MILTON. Paradise Lost: the Double Standard. UTQ, 20, 1951, 183-99.
      The fallen angels exemplify the heroic standard of virtue, while Christ exemplifies the super-heroic standard of self-sacrifice.

1589 MILLS, RALPH DELANO. The Logic of Milton's Narrative of the Fall: A Reconsideration. Doctoral diss., Ohio State Univ., 1966. Abs., DA, 27, 1967, 2506-A.

1590 MILNER, MAX. Le Satan de Milton et L'Épopée Romantique Française. Le Paradis Perdu: 1667-1967. Ed. by Jacques Blondel (Paris: Minard Lettres Modernes, 1967), pp. 219-40.
      Discusses to what extent Milton's Satan has aided or hampered the development of the epic in France after 1820.

1591 MINER, EARL. Felix Culpa in the Redemptive Order of Paradise Lost. PQ, 47, 1968, 43-54.
      Points out that "there is a carefully calculated redemptive order in Paradise Lost inclusive of all God's angelic and human creatures." The fall should be "regarded as fortunate but only for few and in no wise a contradiction of anything earlier in the poem."

1592 MIYANISHI, MITSUO. Charles Williams and the Structure of Paradise Lost. Kyoto Univ. Eibungaku Hyoron, 4, 1957.

1593 ------. The Problem of Evil in Paradise Lost. Albion (Japan), 5, 1934.

1594 MOAG, JOSEPH STEWART. Traditional Patterns of Dialogue and Debate in Milton's Poetry. Doctoral diss., Northwestern Univ., 1964. Abs., DA, 25, 1965, 6598-9.

1595 MOHL, RUTH. Studies in Spenser, Milton and the Theory of Monarchy. New York: Columbia Univ. Press, 1949. Reprinted, New York: Ungar, 1962.
Two essays of interest: The Theme of Paradise Lost, pp. 66-93; and Milton and the Idea of Perfection, pp. 94-132. In the first essay, Mohl argues that Milton's purpose was to present the theme of the making of the greater man—not simply the greater man Christ but the human being everywhere. In the second, the author places Milton on the side of the Christian humanists, "whose conception of perfection implies life and growth."
Rev: E. Sirluck, MP, 48, 60-4; Mindele Black, QQ, 57, 1950, 580-2; E. S. Gohn, MLN, 65, 1950, 562-4.

1596 MOLLENKOTT, VIRGINIA R. The Cycle of Sins in Paradise Lost, Book XI. MLQ, 27, 1966, 33-40.
"The first three visions form elaborations of the sins of Satan, Eve, and Adam, respectively; the fourth vision further elaborates the first; and the fifth elaborates the second."

1597 ------. A Note on Milton's Materialistic Angelology. SCN, 22, No. 1, 1964, item 9.
"...Milton entertained the possibility that maybe—just maybe—Heaven would be more like earth than men generally imagine."

1599 MOONEY, HARAY J. [Tercentenary Conference at the Univ. of Pittsburgh]. MN, 2, 1968, 29-30.
Comments on papers read by Thomas Kranidas, Joseph Summers, Louis Martz, Arnold Stein, O. B. Hardison, Jr., Mario DiCesare, John Steadman, Michael Fixler, Jackson Cope, and Northrop Frye.

1600 MORITZ-SIEBECK, BERTA. Der Limbus-Passus in Miltons Paradise Lost (III, 440-97). Anglia, 79, 1962, 153-76.
In defense of the passage. Discusses Milton's reasons for the inclusion of the passage and analyzes its parts.

1601 ------. Untersuchungen zu Miltons Paradise Lost: Interpretation der beiden Schlussbucher. QFSK, 12. Berlin: Walter de Gruyter, 1963. vii, 274pp.
Shows that the last two books of Paradise Lost are thematically and architectonically the triumphant conclusion to the poem.
Rev: Inga-Stina Ewbank, RES, 16, 1965, 225; Joachim Stephan, ZAA, 13, 1965, 193-7; Herbert Grabes, Archiv, 202, 1965, 293-4.

1602 MORRIS, HARRY. Some Uses of Angel Iconography in English Literature. CL, 10, 1958, 36-44.
Gives examples from Bartolomaeus Anglicus, Spenser, Heywood, and Milton.

1603 MORRIS, JOHN N. Milton and the Imagination of Time. SAQ, 67, 649-58.
"Paradise Lost, in short, takes place in the present moment. The drama

enacted in its lines is the typological first term of a relationship in which each reader's encounter with the poem is intended to be the second."

1604 ------. Paradise Lost Now. ASch, 33, 1963, 65-83.
"I should like to suggest that Milton's moral notions, viewed in all their complication, have in them something interesting and immediately valuable to us."

1605 MORRISION, NAN DANSBY. Principles of Structure in Paradise Lost. Doctoral diss., Univ. of South Carolina, 1967. Abs., DA, 28, 1968, 4606-A-7-A. 326pp.

1606 MORSE, J. MITCHELL. La Pucelle and Paradise Lost. CL, 9, 1957, 238-42.
Chapelain's poem as a possible source.

1607 MUELLER, MARTIN E. The Tragic Epic: Paradise Lost and the Iliad. Doctoral diss., Indiana Univ., 1966. Abs., DA, 27, 1967, 2506-A.

1608 MUIR, LYNETTE R. A Detail in Milton's Description of Sin. N&Q, N.S., 3, 1956, 100-1.
The hounds in Sin's womb may derive from Malory's Questing Beast.

1609 MULDROW, GEORGE McMURRY. The Beginnings of Adam's Repentance. PQ, 46, 1967, 194-206.
Analyzes the repentant Adam, "the sinful man who because of God's mercy can take the necessary steps in his regeneration and who, as he takes those steps, becomes fully the hero of the epic."

1610 ------. The Theme of Man's Restoration in Milton's Later Poetry. Doctoral diss., Stanford Univ., 1960. Abs., DA, 21, 1960, 1193.

1611 MÜLLER, URSULA. Miltons Satan. Die Gestalt Lucifers in der Dichtung vom Barock bis zur Romantik (Berlin: Emil Ebering, 1940), pp. 40-50.

1612 M[UNSTERBERG], M. Precursors of Paradise Lost. MB, 19, 1944, 24.
Andreini's L'Adamo and Vondel's Lucifer.

1613 MURRAY, JOHN FRANKLIN, S. J. Milton's Conception of Original Justice and of Original Sin. Doctoral diss., Univ. of New Mexico, 1957. Abs., DA, 18, 1958, 583.

1614 MURRAY, PATRICK. Milton: The Modern Phase, A Study of Twentieth Century Criticism. London: Longmans, 1967, ix, 163pp.
"A survey of the work of twentieth-century scholars." Deals exclusively with criticism of Paradise Lost.
Rev: TLS, Aug. 17, 1967, p. 745; Anthony Burgess, Spect, No. 7244, April 28, 1967, 487-8; MN, 1, 1967, 31.

1615 ------. Paradise Lost: A Christian Poem in a Post-Christian Age. Studies, 60, No. 219, Autumn, 1966, 277-84.
Suggests that "critics and champions of Milton alike have seriously exaggerated the extent to which his greatest work is out of touch with modern taste."

1616 MUSGROVE, S. Is the Devil an Ass? RES, 21, 1945, 302-15.
"The Satan of the first two books, even if magnificent . . . is still intellectually rotten and is still evil incarnate."

1617 MUTSCHMANN, HEINRICH. Further Studies Concerning the Origin of Paradise Lost (The Matter of the Armada). Dorpat, Estonia: Mattiessen, 1934. 55pp.

> Milton's first epic plans were to glorify Britain in an epic and to celebrate the defeat of the Armada. Echoes of such planning remain in Paradise Lost, especially in Book 6, which contains numerous parallels to contemporary accounts.
> Rev: L. C. Martin, YWES, 235-6; TLS, Sept. 13, 1934, p. 616; H. O. Wilde, Ang. Bbl., 46, 1935, 238-9; Denis Saurat, MLN, 51, 1936, 263-4; E. H. Visiak, NC, 119, 1936, 506-12.

1618 ------. Milton's Projected Epic on the Rise and Future Greatness of the Britannic Nation together with a Reprint of the Anonymous Pamphlet, Great Britain's Ruin Plotted by the Seven Sorts of Men, 1641. Dorpat, Estonia: J. G. Krüger, 1936.

> Rev: TLS, Aug. 1, 1936, p. 633; S. Addleshaw, CQR, 124, 1937, 330-3; E. M. W. Tillyard, MLN, 53, 1938, 381-3; reply to Tillyard by Mutschmann, ibid., 54, 1939, 398.

1619 [MYERS], CATHERINE RODGERS. John Milton: Paradise Lost. Barnes and Noble Book Notes, 819. New York: Barnes and Noble, 1966. 93pp.

1620 NAZARI, EMILIO. Problemi Miltoniani. Palermo: A. Priulla, 1951. 250pp.

> Considers, i.a., the classical and Italian elements in Paradise Lost, pp. 44-217.

1621 NELSON, LAWRENCE E. Streamlining Satan. Our Roving Bible (New York: Abington-Cokesbury, 1945), pp. 93-9.

1622 NEUMANN, HARRY. Milton's Adam and Dostoyevsky's Grand Inquisition on the Problem of Freedom Before God. Pers, 48, July, 1967, 317-27.

> "While Milton was confident that loss of Eden would, in time, teach man to cherish his freedom, the Inquisition, if not Dostoyevsky, insisted that man's congenital servility prevents the transformation of his tragic fall into the first act of a divine comedy."

1623 NEWMEYER, EDNA. The Poet's Province: Wordsworth's Manuscript Notes in Paradise Lost. Doctoral diss., The City Univ. of New York, 1966. Abs., DA, 27, 1966, 1343A-1344A.

1624 NICHOLS, MARGARET ANN. The Garden Tradition and Dramatic Experience in Marvell and Milton. Doctoral diss., Univ. of Illinois, 1966. Abs., DA, 27, 1967, 2156-A.

> Examines "Milton's representation of the experience of Adam and Eve in the Garden of Eden in the context of Milton's modification of the elementary patristic notions, his conception of the Creation and God's art as it manifests itself in His planting of Paradise, and the relation between the pre- and post-lapsarian human and natural conditions."

1625 NICOLSON, MARJORIE HOPE. The Breaking of the Circle: Studies in the Effect of the New Science upon Seventeenth Century Poetry. Evanston: Northwestern Univ. Press, 1950; Revised Edition, New York: Columbia Univ. Press, 1960.

> Discusses the astronomy of Paradise Lost, pp. 160-6 (1950 edition).

1626   ------. Milton and the Telescope. ELH, 2, 1935, 1-32.
"Milton's imagination . . . was stimulated less by books about the new astronomy than by the actual sense experience of celestial observation." This
experience "made Paradise Lost the first modern cosmic poem, in which a
drama is played against a background of interstellar space."

1627   ------. Milton's Hell and the Phlegraean Fields. UTQ, 7, 1938, 500-13.
Suggests that Milton may have remembered his visit to the Phlegraean Fields
in southern Italy.

1628   ------. The Discovery of Space. Medieval and Renaissance Studies: Pro-
ceedings of the Southeastern Institute of Medieval and Renaissance
Studies, Summer, 1965. Ed. by O. B. Hardison, Jr. (Chapel Hill: Univ.
of North Carolina Press, 1966), pp. 40-59.
Deals, i.a., with Milton's treatment of space in Paradise Lost. "Milton's
world-scheme was Ptolemaic, but his universe was the indefinite universe of
Galileo and of Bruno."
Rev: E. J. Devereux, RenQ, 21, 1968, 89-91.

1629   ------. The Telescope and Imagination. MP, 32, 1935, 233-60.
A background study. "Indeed, we may, without mere rhetoric or exaggera-
tion, see in that majestic picture in Paradise Lost a symbolic scene of the
seventeenth-century attitude toward the new awareness of space which the
telescope caused."

1630   NORFORD, DON PARRY. Trial by Contrary: A Study of Milton's Later
Poems. Doctoral diss., Columbia Univ., 1966. Abs., DA, 28, 1967, 2218-A.

1631   Note on Paradise Lost, II, 1052-3. N&Q, N.S., 5, 1958, 222.
Finds a possible reflection of Dante's Paradiso, 28, 19-21.

1632   OCHI, FUMIO. Milton's Satirical Spirit and the Paradise of Fools. SEL
(Japan), 7, 1956.

1633   OGDEN, H. S. V. The Crisis of Paradise Lost Reconsidered. PQ, 36, 1957,
1-19. Reprinted in Milton: Modern Essays in Criticism. A Galaxy Book.
Ed. by Arthur E. Barker (New York: Oxford Univ. Press, 1965), pp.
308-27.
Argues against Tillyard and Bell that Adam and Eve, though not perfect
before the Fall, are by no means already fallen, "that the Fall is the central
theological event in the poem, and that it is likewise the climax of the
narrative."

1634   ORAS, ANTS. Darkness Visible: Notes on Milton's Descriptive Proce-
dures in Paradise Lost. All These to Teach: Essays in Honor of C. A.
Robertson. Ed. by Robert A. Bryan and others (Gainesville: Univ. of
Florida Press, 1965), pp. 130-43.
On Milton and Poussin, Claude Lorrain and Rembrandt.

1635   ------. Echoing Verse Endings in Paradise Lost. South Atlantic Studies
for Sturgis E. Leavitt (Washington: Scarecrow Press, 1953), pp. 175-90.

1636   ------. Goddess Humane (Paradise Lost IX, 732). MLR, 49, 1954, 51-3.
Prefers the reading "human" to "humane."

1637   ------. Milton's Blank Verse and the Chronology of His Major Poems.

SAMLA Studies in Milton. Ed. by J. Max Patrick (Gainesville: Univ. of Florida Press, 1953), pp. 128-97.
Accepts the traditional chronology.

1638 ORCHARD, THOMAS N. The Astronomy of Milton's Paradise Lost. New York: Haskell House, 1967. viii, 288pp.
A reprint of Stevens' No. 939, first issued in 1896 and revised in 1913. "Well illustrated. Presents an account of astronomical theory up to Milton's time. Considerable revision and abridgement in the second edition" (Stevens' annotation).

1639 PAKENHAM, THOMAS. On the Site of the Earthly Paradise. TLS, Feb. 15, 1957, p. 104.
Replies by E. Ullendorff and W. G. L. Randles, Mar. 8, 1957, p. 151. On Milton's indebtedness to Purchas and to Urreta, a Spanish Dominican, for his account of the true and of the false Paradise.

1640 PAOLUCCI, ANNE. Dante's Satan and Milton's Byronic Hero. Italica, 41, 1964, 139-49.
"Milton's Satan, if properly understood, does not detract from Dante's poetic representation, but, rather, intensifies it."

1641 PARISH, JOHN E. Milton and an Anthropomorphic God. SP, 56, 1959, 619-25.
Shows that Milton wrote Paradise Lost, 3, 80-172, and 8, 352-451, with stories in mind from Genesis 18, Exodus 32, and Numbers 14.

1642 ------. Milton and God's Curse on the Serpent. JEGP, 58, 1959, 241-7.
On the progressive revelation to Adam of the full meaning of the curse, climaxed by Adam's speech (12, 469-73) on God's goodness and mercy.

1643 ------. Milton and the Rape of Proserpina. ES, 48, 1967, 332-5.
Calls attention to the "subtle use Milton makes in Paradise Lost of Ovid's story of the rape of Proserpina."

1644 ------. Milton's Paradise Lost, VI, 362-368. Expl, 24, 1965, item 15.
Raphael refers to himself in the third person and preserves the motif of the mysterious guest. In the passage Milton also invents a parallel to an incident in the Book of Tobit.

1645 ------. Pre-Miltonic Representations of Adam as a Christian. RIP, 40, No. 3, 1953, 1-24.
Reviews "the attitude which Christians in the first centuries of the Church and during the Middle Ages had toward Adam himself and toward the question whether or not he knew anything of the Redeemer who was to be born" and then examines "the way Milton had Adam reflect on the enigmatic words of his Judge and gradually come to realize their full significance."

1646 ------. Standing Prostrate: The Paradox in Paradise Lost, X, 1099, and XI, 1. EM, 15, 1964, 89-101.
The apparent inconsistency of Adam and Eve's falling prostrate and standing repentant at the same time is intentional ambiguity on Milton's part.

1647 PARSONS, COLEMAN O. The Classical and Humanist Context of Paradise Lost, II, 496-505. JHI, 29, 1968, 33-52.
On the background of Milton's passage against war. Feels that Milton adopts

and sharpens "Erasmus' paradox of diabolical concord in the spreading of discord. . . ."

1648 PATRICK, J. MAX. The Influence of Thomas Ellwood upon Milton's Epics. Essays in History and Literature. Presented by Fellows of the Newberry Library to Stanley Pargellis. Ed. by Heinz Bluhm (Chicago: The Newberry Library, 1965), pp. 119-32.
> Holds that Miltonists have underestimated Ellwood in intelligence and judgment and suggests that the didacticism and simplicity of Paradise Regained was a result of the Quaker's reaction to Paradise Lost.

1649 ------. Milton and Thomas Ellwood—A Reconsideration. MN, 2, 1968, 2-4.
> Questions some of the conclusions of Elizabeth McLaughlin in MN, 1, 1967, 17-28, including those dealing with the state papers and Ellwood's reaction to Paradise Lost. Reply by Mrs. McLaughlin, ibid., pp. 4-5.

1650 PATRICK, JOHN M. Milton, Phineas Fletcher, Spenser, and Ovid—Sin at Hell's Gates. N&Q, N.S., 3, 1956, 384-6.

1651 ------. Milton's Conception of Sin as Developed in Paradise Lost. Utah State Univ. Monograph Series, Vol. 7, No. 5. Logan: Utah State Univ. Press, 1960. 72pp.
> ". . . I shall attempt, then, to discover what Milton actually had to say about the fact of Adam's sin, in what the sin seems to have consisted, and in how Adam came to commit it—and something as to the effect Milton observes that this sin had upon Adam himself and upon his posterity."
> Rev: J. M. Steadman, PQ, 40, 1961, 159-60; C. F. Williamson, SN, 33, 1961, 210-2; Frank Kermode, MLR, 56, 1961, 470.

1652 ------. More on the Dorian Mood in Paradise Lost. N&Q, N.S., 4, 1957, 196-7.
> Suggests that in 1, 549-61, Milton may have in mind a passage from Ammianus Marcellinus' Res Gestae.

1653 PATRIDES, C. A. Adam's Happy Fault and XVIIth-Century Apologetics. FS, 23, 1963, 238-43.
> Adam's speech (12, 469-78) considered in the light of the seventeenth–century background.

1654 ------. The Bloody and Cruell Turke: The Background of a Renaissance Commonplace. SRen, 10, 1963, 126-35.
> The acceptance of the Turkish terror reflects a belief in the "sufferance of God," as does Paradise Lost, 4, 1006-1009.

1655 ------. The Godhead in Paradise Lost: Dogma or Drama. JEGP, 64, 1965, 29-34.
> ". . . I hope to demonstrate that in Paradise Lost the unity of the godhead is not impaired; for the most part, indeed, Milton does not seem to distinguish between the Father and the Son."

1656 ------. I Nove Ordini degli Angeli: Storia di una Idea. Sophia: Rassegna critica di Filosofia e Storia della Filosofia, 33, 1965, 341-8.
> Discusses various schemes of angelic rank and notes Milton's Protestant avoidance of a rigid classification.

1657 ------. John Milton: The Poet Who Gave Us Paradise. The Observer (Colour Supplement), August 13, 1967, pp. 3-9.

> Accompanied by several illustrations of the expulsion scene. Holds that the visual arts of Italy influenced Milton's conception of Paradise and points out that in turn we owe our conception mostly to Milton.

1658 ------. Milton and His Contemporaries on the Chains of Satan. MLN, 73, 1958, 257-60.

> Shows that the restraint of Satan by God was a belief widely held in Milton's day.

1659 ------. Milton and the Protestant Theory of the Atonement. PMLA, 74, 1959, 7-13.

> Shows that although Milton's God is legalistic and although some will continue to call him a dictator, it should be remembered that Milton reflects views held by his contemporaries and by many of his Protestant predecessors.

1660 ------, ed. Milton's Epic Poetry: Essays on Paradise Lost and Paradise Regained. A Peregrine Book. Harmondsworth, Middlesex, England: Penguin Books, 1967. 428pp.

> A collection of essays, all previously published. Contributors on Paradise Lost are F. R. Leavis, D. Bush, A. O. Lovejoy, A. J. A. Waldock, A. Stein, K. Widmer, J. B. Broadbent, W. Empson, J. H. Summers, A. R Cirillo, F. T. Prince, C. Ricks, and B. Rajan. In this bibliography, each essay is listed according to its author.

1661 ------. Paradise Lost and Language of Theology. Language and Style in Milton: A Symposium in Honor of the Tercentenary of Paradise Lost. Ed. by Ronald David Emma and John T. Shawcross (New York: Frederick Ungar, 1967), pp. 102-19.

> "...points out that the theology of Paradise Lost and the language that expresses it, and not the theology and language of the unfinished De Doctrina Christiana, properly represent the mature Milton's beliefs" (editors' Preface).

1662 ------. Paradise Lost and the Mortalist Heresy. N&Q, N.S., 4, 1957, 250-1.

> Suggests a reconsideration of the belief that the mortalism of De Doctrina Christiana is reflected in the epic, since Adam (10, 808-13) is hardly in a position to argue about death.

1663 ------. Paradise Lost and the Theory of Accommodation. TSLL, 5, 1963, 58-63.

> The theory applies to the Deity and serves "as the basis of the 'extended metaphor' of the war in Heaven."

1664 ------. The Phoenix and the Ladder: The Rise and Decline of the Christian View of History. USPES, 29. Berkeley and Los Angeles: Univ. of California Press, 1964. 101pp.

> Milton's views of history discussed, pp. 58-68. Sees Paradise Lost as the termination of an era in the history of thought.

1665 ------. The Protevangelium in Renaissance Theology and Paradise Lost. SEL, 3, 1963, 19-30.

> Cites support from tradition and from Protestant apologists for Milton's identification of the "seed" with Christ in Paradise Lost, 10, 179-90.

1666 ------. Renaissance and Modern Views on Hell. HTR, 57, 1964, 217-36.
      Discusses Milton's conception of Hell "as a condition and as a place."

1667 ------. Renaissance Ideas on Man's Upright Form. JHI, 19, 1958, 256-8.
      Notes Milton's use of the concept in Paradise Lost, 4, 288-89, and 7, 506-10.

1668 ------. Renaissance Interpretations of Jacob's Ladder. Theologische
      Zeitschrift, 18, 1962, 411-8.
      Contemporary interpretations of Jacob's Ladder and Milton's handling of the
      stairs in Paradise Lost, 3, 502-15.

1669 ------. Renaissance Thought on the Celestial Hierarchy: The Decline of a
      Tradition. JHI, 20, 1959, 155-66.
      Toward the end of a long tradition, Milton declined to use a dogmatic
      classification of the angels.

1670 ------. Renaissance Views on the Unconfused Orders Angellick. JHI,
      23, 1962, 265-7.
      Protestant writers "avoided strict classification of angels, preferring to speak
      vaguely of the 'unconfused orders Angellick' or to state cautiously that they
      have 'sundry names.' "

1671 ------. The Salvation of Satan. JHI, 28, 1967, 467-78.
      A discussion of theories on the possible salvation of Satan, with the suggestion
      that in Paradise Lost "the dramatic context demanded that Satan's redemption
      should at least be entertained as a possibility." Hence Satan's speech in
      4, 93-104.

1672 ------. The Tree of Knowledge in the Christian Tradition. SN, 34, 1962,
      239-42.
      Several references to Milton. Concerned with the raison d'être and the name
      of the Tree of Knowledge.

1673 PEARCE, DONALD R. The Style of Milton's Epic. YR, N.S., 52, 1963,
      427-44. Reprinted in Milton: Modern Essays in Criticism. A Galaxy
      Book. Ed. by Arthur E. Barker (New York: Oxford Univ. Press, 1965),
      pp. 368-85.
      Claims "that the 'remote grandeur' of Milton's language in Paradise Lost
      originates in the formalities of classic prose. . . ."

1674 PECHEUX, MOTHER MARY CHRISTOPHER, O.S.U. Abraham,
      Adam, and the Theme of Exile in Paradise Lost. PMLA, 80, 1965,
      365-71.
      "It is the purpose of this article to explore further the Abraham-Adam
      parallel in the last two books, showing in particular the relationship between
      Abraham's departure from Ur and Adam's from Paradise."

1675 ------. The Concept of the Second Eve in Paradise Lost. PMLA, 75,
      1960, 359-66.
      On the background of the epithet second Eve referring to Mary in Paradise
      Lost, 5, 385-387, and 10, 183, and how Milton exploited the connotations.

1676 ------. The Conclusion of Book VI of Paradise Lost. SEL, 3, 1963, 109-17.
      Suggests that the rout of the rebel angels foreshadows Christ's casting the
      devils into swine.

1677 ------. O Foul Descent!: Satan and the Serpent Form. SP, 62, 1965, 188-96.

On Satan's reluctance to assume a serpent form as a "direct contrast to the willingness of the Son to assume corporeal form."

1678 ------. The Second Adam and the Church in Paradise Lost. ELH, 34, 1967, 173-87.
Parallels the basic elements of (1) the Unholy Trinity, (2) the Holy Trinity, (3) the Creation of Eve—all with the concept of the church, "the bride of Christ, issuing from the side of Christ on the cross, as Eve had come from Adam."

1679 PELLETIER, ROBERT R. The Revolt of Islam and Paradise Lost. KSJ, 14, 1965, 7-13.
Suggests "a general similarity in important words and combinations of words, phrasing, sentiment, and imagery."

1680 ------. Satan and Prometheus in Captivity. N&Q, N.S., 7, 1960, 107-8.
Presents some verbal similarities in descriptions of Satan and Shelley's Prometheus as captives.

1681 ------. Unnoticed Parallel Between Ahasuerus and Satan. KSJ, 11, 1962, 12-4.
Notes verbal similarities in Queen Mab and Paradise Lost. Concludes that the grandeur of Shelley's Ahasuerus (Queen Mab) derives from Milton's Satan.

1682 PEQUIGNEY, FARRE JOSEPH. Paradise Lost, Epic of Inwardness. Doctoral diss., Harvard Univ., 1959.

1683 PETER, JOHN DESMOND. A Critique of Paradise Lost. New York: Columbia Univ. Press, 1960; London: Longmans, 1960, 1961, 1962. 172pp.
"...I have tried to trace the epic's successes and failures quite impartially, and ... the attempt has done nothing to abate my regard for those successes which it can fairly claim." This study, however, is a disparagement of Milton's poem.
Rev: Agnes M. C. Latham, YWES, 41, 1960, 171; William Empson, Listener, 64, 1960, 750, 753; TLS, Nov. 11, 1960, p. 726; F. L. Lucas, TLS, Nov. 18, 1960, p. 741; Frank Kermode, MLR, 56, 1961, 407-8; Isabel G. MacCaffrey, MLN, 76, 1961, 647-50; Laurence Lerner, EIC, 11, 1961, 104-10; Kester Svendsen, RN, 14, 1961, 200-3; Joseph H. Summers, JEGP, 61, 1962, 181-4; J. Franklin Murray, Th, 37, 1962, 139-40; W. W. Robson, RES, 13, 1962, 198-200.

1684 PHILLIPS, NORMA. Milton's Limbo of Vanity and Dante's Vestibule. ELN, 3, 1966, 177-82.
On reflections of Dante's vestibule of hell (Inferno, 3, 16-69) in Milton's Limbo of Vanity or Paradise of Fools (Paradise Lost, 3, 440-97).

1685 PILATO, S. DE. Un inspiratore del Paradiso Perduto: P. Serafino della Salandra. Potenza: Marchesiello, 1934. 26pp.
Rev: G. N. Giordano-Orsini, Leonardo, 6, 1935, 19-20.

1686 PINEAS, RAINER. Dekker's The Whore of Babylon and Milton's Paradise Lost. ELN, 2, 1965, 257-60.
Notes "similarities between parts of Books 1 and 2 of Milton's poem and the opening of Dekker's anti-Catholic play...."

1687 POLE, DAVID. Milton and Critical Method. British Journal of Aesthetics, 3, 1963, 245-58.
Comments on Joseph H. Summers' The Muse's Method, Jackson I. Cope's The Metaphoric Structure of Paradise Lost, and H. R. Swardson's Poetry and the Fountain of Light. Critical of Summers and Cope but more appreciative of Swardson's work. A disparagement of recent interpretations of Paradise Lost.

1688 POLSGROVE, ALMUS BALLOW. Eve of Paradise Lost. MA thesis, Mississippi State Univ., 1964. 101pp. Abs., Mississippi State Univ. Abstracts of Theses, 1963-4 (1965), p. 52.

1689 POWELL, F. TOWNSHEND. Francis Atterbury. TLS, Mar. 3, 1932, p. 155
On Atterbury's copy of Paradise Lost.

1690 PRAZ, MARIO. Le Metamorfosi di Satan. La Carne, La Morte e il Diavolo nella Letterature Romantica (Milan and Rome: Soc. Editrice, 1930), pp. 49-90. Reprinted in The Romantic Agony, trans. by Angus Davidson (London: Oxford Univ. Press, 1933), pp. 51-92.

1691 P[RAZ], M[ARIO]. Milton e l'ortografia. La Cultura, 12, 1934, 726-7.
A review of H. Darbishire's The Manuscript of Paradise Lost (1931).

1692 PRESCOTT, ANNE LAKE. The Reception of Du Bartas in England. SRen, 15, 1968, 144-73.
Concerned mainly with the Elizabethan reception, but feels that Du Bartas' decline in popularity was brought about "not by Dryden's scorn but by Milton's emulation. Until Paradise Lost there had been no poem which both closely duplicated the Septmaines in aim and far excelled them in quality."

1693 PRINCE, F. T. Milton e Tasso. RLMC, 13, 1960, 53-60.
On Jerusalem Delivered and Paradise Lost.

1694 ------. On the Last Two Books of Paradise Lost. E&S, 11, 1958, 38-52. Reprinted in Milton's Epic Poetry: Essays on Paradise Lost and Paradise Regained. Ed. by C. A. Patrides (Harmondsworth: Penguin Books, 1967), pp. 233-48.
Considers the significance and effect of the books.

1695 PRITCHARD, HUGH C. A Study of Repetition as an Architectonic Device in Paradise Lost. Master's thesis, Univ. of North Carolina, 1942.

1696 PUJALS, ESTABAN. Estructura y concepto de El Paraíso perdido de Milton. Atlántida, 5, 1967, 209-19.
Examines the genesis, internal structure, and theme of Paradise Lost. Suggests that critics have not sufficiently considered the sacramental presence of human love.

1697 PURCELL, J. M. Rime in Paradise Lost, MLN, 59, 1944, 171-2.
Corrects Diekhoff's list of couplets (PMLA, 41, 1934, 539-43) and the numerical list of rhyme schemes.

1698 PURSELL, WILLENE VAN LOENEN. Love's Place in the Orderly System of Marriage in Paradise Lost. Love and Marriage in Three English

Authors: Chaucer, Milton and Eliot (Stanford Honors Essays in Humanities, 7, Stanford, California, 1963), pp. 16-33. 58pp.
Relates the Adam-Eve relationship to the Renaissance concept of order.

1699 PUTZEL, ROSAMUND. A Re-examination of the Place of the Holy Spirit in Paradise Lost. Master's thesis, Univ. of North Carolina, 1951.

1700 QUARE. Paradise Lost in Latin. N&Q, 174, 1938, 442-3.
Notes the existence of a complete Latin hexameter translation by William Dobson.

1701 QVARNSTRÖM, GUNNAR. Dikten och den Nya Vetenskapen. Det Astronautiska Motivet. Acta Reg. Societatis Humaniorum Litterarum Lundensis, No. 40. Lund: C.W.R. Gleerup, 1961. xii, 304pp.
A study of the cosmic voyage, with indications of the new science of numerical composition, Two chapters devoted to Paradise Lost. Summary in English, pp. 275-90.

1702 ------. The Enchanted Palace: Some Structural Aspects of Paradise Lost. Stockholm: Almqvist and Wiksell, 1967. 189pp.
An analysis based upon the author's point of view of numbers. Argues that the poem has a balanced Christocentric structure and that the temporal scheme consists of 33 days, 11 of which comprise the actions of Satan. Examines the length and position of the epic speeches and the division of Paradise Lost into structural units. Chapters: Epic Chronology, The Christocentric Structure, The Structure of Epic Speeches, The Epic Modulation of Time, and Interpretations.

1703 R., V. Milton: A Familiar Quotation. N&Q, 165, 1933, 65.
Paradise Lost, 2, 146.

1704 RADER, KATHERINE. The Soliloquy in Milton's English Poems. Doctoral diss., Univ. of Oklahoma, 1952.

1705 RADZINOWICZ, MARY ANN NEVINS. Eve and Dalila: Renovation and the Hardening of the Heart. Reason and the Imagination: Studies in the History of Ideas, 1600-1800. Ed. by J. A. Mazzeo (New York: Columbia Univ. Press; London: Routledge and Kegan Paul, 1962), pp. 155-81.
Holds that Eve and Dalila are dramatizations of the struggle to achieve true freedom and virtue after a fall. In Eve, Milton depicts renovation; in Dalia, the process of the hardening of the heart.

1706 RAILO, EINO. Kadotetun Paratiisin maailmankuva (The Weltbild of Paradise Lost). Valvoja-Aika (Helsingfors), 1932.

1708 RAJAN, BALACHANDRA. The Language of Paradise Lost. Milton: A Collection of Critical Essays. Ed. by Louis L. Martz (Englewood Cliffs, N.J.: Prentice-Hall, 1966), pp. 56-60.
Reprinted from Rajan's edition of Books 1 and 2 of Paradise Lost (1964).

1709 ------. Paradise Lost: The Critic and the Historian. UWR, 1, 1965, 42-50.
Feels that both the historian and the critic are needed to understand the complex and creative balance that is achieved between the poem and its heritage.

1710 ------. Paradise Lost: The Hill of History. HLQ, 31, 1967, 43-63.

An analysis of Books 11 and 12, with comments on Milton's view of history, which "is not without affinities to the thinking of today."

1711 ------. Paradise Lost and the Seventeenth Century Reader. Doctoral diss., Cambridge Univ., 1946. London: Chatto and Windus, 1947, 1966; Toronto: Oxford Univ. Press, 1962; New York: Barnes and Noble, 1966; Ann Arbor: Univ. of Michigan Press (Paperback), 1967. 171pp.
Relates the epic to seventeenth-century thought and presents a critical analysis of its structure.
Rev: L. C. Martin, YWES, 189-90; TLS, Oct. 18, 1947, 539; Joan Bennett, NSN, Nov. 8, 1947, pp. 375-6; F. E. Hutchinson, Spect, Oct. 31, 1947, pp. 567-8; B. A. Wright, RES, 25, 1949, 75-83; A. S. P. Woodhouse, UTQ, 18, 1949, 202-5; A. N. Jeffares, ES, 30, 1949, 92-3.

1712 ------. The Style of Paradise Lost. Milton's Epic Poetry: Essays on Paradise Lost and Paradise Regained. Ed. by C. A. Patrides (Harmondsworth: Penguin Books, 1967), pp. 276-97.
A reprint, with minor changes, of pp. xix-xxxviii of Rajan's 1964 edition of Books 1 and 2 of Paradise Lost.

1713 RANSOM, JOHN CROWE. God Without Thunder. New York: Harcourt Brace, 1930. x, 334pp.
Discusses the Promethean elements of Satan, pp. 127-33.

1714 ------. The Idea of a Literary Anthropologist and What He Might Say of the Paradise Lost of Milton. KR, 21, 1959, 121-40.
Discusses Milton's historical predicament in treating the ancient narrative recorded in Genesis.

1715 READ, HERBERT. Milton. A Coat of Many Colors (London: Routledge, 1945), pp. 132-3.
On the virtues of Paradise Lost.

1716 REESING, JOHN. An Essay for the Tercentenary of Paradise Lost. Milton's Poetic Art: A Mask, Lycidas, and Paradise Lost (Cambridge: Harvard Univ. Press, 1968), pp. 71-86.
On the revised structure of the 1674 edition of Paradise Lost. Suggests "that one of his objects in changing to a twelve-book arrangement was to make even the mathematical dimensions of the poem reflect its explicit—and physical—division into two parts. By this simple strategy he was able, without losing any of the resonances between Book V and the new Book XI, to alert his readers that they should listen especially for resonances between the new Book XII and Book VI."

1717 ------. A Poem about Loss. Milton's Poetic Art: A Mask, Lycidas, and Paradise Lost (Cambridge: Harvard Univ. Press, 1968), pp. 53-68.
On the last three books of Paradise Lost. Deals with the "transformation in the meaning of three key words: 'loss,' 'death,' and 'wrath'" and shows how this transformation affects the consciousness of Adam and Eve and the reader.

1718 ------. Miltonic Sensibility in Paradise Lost. Milton's Poetic Art: A Mask, Lycidas, and Paradise Lost (Cambridge: Harvard Univ. Press, 1968), pp. 107-119.
"In this essay I shall try to identify the action of Milton's sensibility in Paradise Lost, a wonderfully alert and supple responsiveness which, in hold-

ing together all the varied materials of the poem, contributes importantly to the achievement of the distinctive quality we all feel."

1719 ------. The Rhythm of Paradise Lost: Books XI and XII. Milton's Poetic Art: A Mask, Lycidas, and Paradise Lost (Cambridge: Harvard Univ. Press, 1968), pp. 89-104.
An analysis of the tempo and sound effects achieved in the last two books of Paradise Lost. Feels that in the final lines of the poem "Milton achieves a sense of order restored, in the soul, in the family, in the race."

1720 REGAN, DORIS B. Paradise Lost: An Enduring Monument. Reading and Collecting, 1, Oct., 1937, 11-2.

1721 REVARD, STELLA PURCE. The Dramatic Function of the Son in Paradise Lost: A Comment on Milton's Trinitarianism. JEGP, 66, 1967, 45-58.
Regrets that much scholarly reaction of late has been "an attempt to reconcile Milton's theological doctrines with orthodox trinitarianism." Holds that it would be a mistake to call Milton's views in De Doctrina Christiana anti-trinitarian, "for basically they are not so."

1722 ------. Milton's Critique of Heroic Warfare in Paradise Lost V and VI. SEL, 7, 1967, 119-39.
"The account of the war in Heaven ... unfolds the archetypal pattern in which evil, the corrupting disease of the universe, begins and flourishes."

1723 ------. Milton's Eve and the Evah of Sir William Alexander's Doomes-day. PLL, 3, 1967, 181-6.
Disagrees that the closest "literary ancestor" to Eve is "the golden Aphrodite of Homer," and compares Eve with a figure she considers a better parallel, Alexander's Evah.

1724 ------. The War in Heaven: A Study of the Tradition in Paradise Lost. Doctoral diss., Yale Univ., 1966. Abs., DA, 27, 1967, 3434-A.

1725 REYNOLDS, JOHN S. The Similes in Book I of Paradise Lost Compared with Those in Book I of The Faerie Queene. Master's thesis, Univ. of North Carolina, 1940.

1726 RICE, WARNER G. Fate in Paradise Lost. PMASAL, 31, 1947 for 1945, 299-306.

1727 RICHARDSON, JANETTE. Virgil and Milton Once Again. CL, 14, 1962, 321-31.
Syntactical echoes of the Aeneid in Paradise Lost "suggest that Milton was deliberately attempting to write Virgilian English."

1728 RIGTER, G. H. Milton's Treatment of Satan in Paradise Lost. Neophil, 42, 1958, 309-22.
Satan and the Fall of Man reveal a conflict in Milton between reason and emotion: "this conflict ... is the psychological basis of the whole of Paradise Lost."

1729 ROBERTSON, D. S. The Odyssey and Paradise Lost. TLS, May 4, 1940, pp. 219, 221.

1730 ROBINS, HARRY F. The Cosmology of Paradise Lost: A Reconsideration. Doctoral diss., Indiana Univ. 1951.

1731 ------. The Crystalline Sphere and the Waters Above in Paradise Lost. PMLA, 69, 1954, 903-14.
    Holds that Milton places the crystalline sphere in its usual place and that he derives the waters above from theological sources and does not identify them with the crystalline sphere.

1732 ------. Milton's Golden Chain, MLN, 69, 1954, 76.

1733 ------. Satan's Journey: Direction in Paradise Lost. JEGP, 60, 1961, 699-711.
    Corrections of and additions to Curry's observations in his Milton's Ontology, Cosmogony, and Physics.

1734 ------. That Unnecessary Shell of Milton's World. Studies in Honor of T. W. Baldwin. Ed. by Don C. Allen (Urbana: Univ. of Illinois Press, 1958) , pp. 211-9.
    "In this paper I shall present my reasons for regarding the outside shell as an unnecessary and unjustified addition to the astronomy of Paradise Lost." Does not believe the physics of Paradise Lost deserving of solemn scientific inquiry.

1735 ROSE, PATRICIA A. Essentials of Epic Poetry: A Comparative Study of the Iliad, the Chanson de Roland, and Paradise Lost. Master's thesis, Florida State Univ., 1955.

1736 ROSENBERG, DONALD MAURICE. Milton and the Laughter of God. Doctoral diss., Wayne State Univ., 1966. Abs., DA, 27, 1966, 1039A.

1737 ROSS, MALCOLM M. Poetry, Belief, and Paradise Lost. DR, 28, 1948, 177-88. Reprinted in Poetry and Dogma (New Brunswick: Rutgers Univ. Press, 1954) , pp. 205-27.
    Holds that a correct understanding of the poem is possible not by a suspension of disbelief but in spite of disbelief. "Beyond this, the range of appreciation must depend upon the kind and degree of belief."

1738 RØSTVIG, MAREN-SOFIE. Renaissance Numerology: Acrostics or Criticism? EIC, 16, 1966, 6-21.
    Defends the theory of numerical composition in general and of Milton's use of it in the composition of Paradise Lost.

1739 ROZENBERG, PAUL. Don, Amour et Sujétion dans le Paradis Perdu. Le Paradis Perdu: 1667-1967. Ed. by Jacques Blondel (Paris: Minard Lettres Modernes, 1967) , pp. 105-40.
    Discusses the relationship of God's gift of love and submission in Paradise Lost.

1740 RUDRUM, ALAN. A Critical Commentary on Milton's Paradise Lost. Macmillan Critical Commentaries. London: Macmillan, 1966. v, 101pp.
    Contains discussions on Satan and his followers, Adam and Eve, Milton's similes, and Milton's verse; questions for discussion; and a selected bibliography.

1741 RUDWIN, MAXIMILIAN. The Devil in Legend and Literature. Chicago: Open Court, 1931. 354pp.
A background study.

1742 ------. Open Court, 43, 1929.
The volume contains several articles relevant to Paradise Lost: The Legend of Lucifer, pp. 193-208; The Number and Names of the Devils, pp. 282-93; The Form of the Fiend, pp. 321-40; The Organization of Pandemonium, pp. 463-73; Journeys to Hell, pp. 566-70; Diabolus Simia Dei, pp. 602-11; The Synagogue of Satan, pp. 728-48.

1743 RUPP, ERNEST FORDON. Six Makers of English Religion, 1500-1700. New York: Harper, 1957. 125pp.
Chapter Four: John Milton and Paradise Lost, pp. 74-91, "Yet there is much to ponder, much to meditate, much to learn, from a serious and attentive Christian reading of Paradise Lost."
Rev: George S. Gunn, Scottish Jour. of Theology, 11, 1958, 215-6.

1744 RUSCHE, HARRY. Biblical Allusion and Imagery in a Passage of Paradise Lost. ES, 49, 1968, 332-4.
On the wolf-sheep imagery of Paradise Lost, 4, 183-93. "Milton selects his images of destruction and deceit to presage the new role of Satan: the animal, the thief, who destroys the peace of the sheepcote, the perfection of Paradise."

1745 RYKEN, LELAND. Milton and the Apocalyptic. HLQ, 31, 1968, 223-38.
Seeks to identify and illustrate the poetic theories and philosophic outlook with which Milton approached the problem of portraying the "apocalyptic in humanly comprehensible terms." Feels that Milton was strongly influenced by the Medieval and Renaissance theory of accommodation and that Milton shows some influence of Platonism.

1746 S., W. W. The Forbidden Fruit, N&Q, 183, 1942, 226-7.
A query concerning the idea that the fruit was an apple. Replies by Hibernicus and George Percival-Kaye, p. 323; by Sayar, p. 383.

1747 SAFER, ELAINE. The Use of Cross Reference to Develop Polarities in Paradise Lost and Paradise Regained. Doctoral diss., Western Reserve Univ., 1966. Abs., DA, 28, 1967, 2221-A.

1748 ST. GEORGE, PRISCILLA P. Psychomachia in Books V and VI of Paradise Lost. MLQ, 27, 1966, 185-96.
The War in Heaven contrasts two states of being and hints at the psychomachia of the Christian soul in Homeric terms.

1749 SAMUEL, IRENE. Dante and Milton: The Commedia and Paradise Lost. Ithaca: Cornell Univ. Press, 1966. x, 299pp.
The purpose is "to collect the evidence about Milton's interest in Dante and see what he may have learned from the Commedia that bears upon his writing of Paradise Lost." Appendices list Milton's references to Dante before Paradise Lost and contain excerpts from studies on the relationship of the two poets.
Rev: M. Babin, CL, 18, 1966, 269-72; TLS, Oct. 12, 1967, p. 972; M. A. Radzinowicz, RenQuar, 20, 1967, 517-9; James H. McCabe, Th, 42, 1967, 291-2.

1750 ------. The Dialogue in Heaven: A Reconsideration of Paradise Lost, III,

1-417. PMLA, 72, 1957, 601-11. Reprinted in Milton: Modern Essays in Criticism. A Galaxy Book. Ed. by Arthur E. Barker (New York: Oxford Univ. Press, 1965), pp. 233-45.
On the centrality of the episode to the entire action of the poem.

1751 ------. Milton on Learning and Wisdom. PMLA, 64, 1949, 708-23.
In Paradise Lost and Paradise Regained Milton expands, not retracts, what he has said earlier about studies.

1752 ------. Paradise Lost and the Survey Course. CE, 11, 1950, 195-8.
Suggests Book 9, rather than Books 1 and 2, as "most nearly representative of the whole" work.

1753 ------. The Proems of the Commedia and Paradise Lost: Higher Argument Remains. BuR, 12, No. 3, 1964, 31-46. Reprinted with revisions in Dante and Milton (Ithaca: Cornell Univ. Press, 1966), pp. 47-66.
". . . major themes of the four prologues in Paradise Lost have precedents in Dante."

1754 ------. Purgatorio and the Dream of Eve. JEGP, 63, 1964, 441-9. Reprinted in Dante and Milton (Ithaca: Cornell Univ. Press, 1966), pp. 3-13.
A comparison of Eve's dream in Book 5 of Paradise Lost and Dante's first dream on Mount Purgatory. In spite of differences, "something of the purgatorial associations of dreams in Dante impresses itself on Milton's handling of the sequence."

1755 ------. Satan and the Diminisht Stars. MP, 59, 1962, 239-47. Reprinted in Dante and Milton (Ithaca: Cornell Univ. Press, 1966), pp. 14-28.
On Milton's sun-and-star images in Paradise Lost as reminiscent of Dante's comparable system of symbols.

1757 ------. The Valley of Serpents: Inferno XXIV-XXV and Paradise Lost X. 504-577. PMLA, 78, 1963, 449-51. Reprinted in Dante and Milton (Ithaca: Cornell Univ. Press, 1966), pp. 105-16.
A comparison of the "transformation-scenes, of the thieves in Inferno and the fallen angels in Paradise Lost into serpents."

1758 SAMUELS, CHARLES THOMAS. The Tragic Vision of Paradise Lost. Univ. of Kansas City Rev., 27, 1960, 65-78.
Shows that the tragic vision is not dominant because Milton writes the epic "from the point of view of God, and from the point of view of God tragedy is farce."

1759 SASEK, LAWRENCE A. The Drama of Paradise Lost, Books XI and XII. Studies in English Renaissance Literature. Ed. by Waldo F. McNeir (Baton Rouge: Louisiana State Univ. Press, 1962), pp. 181-96. Reprinted in Modern Essays in Criticism. A Galaxy Book, ed. by Arthur E. Barker (New York: Oxford Univ. Press, 1965), pp. 342-56, and in Milton: Modern Judgements, ed. by Alan Rudrum (London: MacMillan, 1968), pp. 205-18.
An exposition of the last two books of Paradise Lost, seen as a dramatic presentation in which the character of Adam is molded into an example of Christian fortitude.

1760 ------. Milton's Paradise Lost, II, 226-228. Expl, 16, 1958, item 30.
Defines Milton's notion of true peace.

1761 ------. Satan and the Epic Hero: Classical and Christian Tradition. Doctoral diss., Harvard University, 1953.

1762 SAURAT, DENIS. Gods of the People. London: John Westhouse, 1947. 190pp.
Concerned with the evolution of ideas by "unknown people." Draws examples from the thought of Spenser and Milton and others.

1763 SAURO, SISTER JOAN STANISLAUS. Teaching Paradise Lost. EJ, 56, 1967, 757-8, 765.
Advocates various approaches of teaching Paradise Lost and "rendering the ways of Milton palpable to the contemporary student."

1764 SCHAAR, CLAES. Vida, Ramsay, and Milton's Bees. ES, 46, 1965, 417-8.
[Cf. Paradise Lost, 1, 768-775] "As regards the 'Council in Hell' motif, Neo-Latin poets had in fact established the bee simile as an ingredient before Milton introduced it into the first book of Paradise Lost."

1765 SCHANZER, ERNEST. Milton's Fall of Mulciber and Troia Britannica. N&Q, N.S., 4, 1957, 379-80.
Suggests Heywood's work (1609) as a source for Paradise Lost, 1, 740-6.

1766 ------. Milton's Hell Revisited. UTQ, 24, 1955, 136-45.
Feels that the actual fall from Heaven is merely a geographical adjustment to spiritual events already accomplished. Sees many parallels, in reality burlesques, between God and Heaven and Satan and Hell.

1767 SCHEUERLE, WILLIAM. Satan the Cormorant. Thoth, 3, 1962, 18-23.
Examines some similes (Paradise Lost, 4) depicting "Satan's steady degeneration to the wolf-thief-cormorant figure" (Paradise Lost, 4, 183-96) as he approaches man.

1768 SCHIRMER, W. F. Das Problem des religiösen Epos im 17. Jahrhundert in England. Deutsche Vierteljahrschrift, 14, 1936, 60-74.
Sees Paradise Lost as a fusion of the warring elements, the new religious feeling and the emergent scientific philosophy.

1769 SCHLINGHOFF, MARGOT. Miltons Bildersprache im Paradise Lost. NS, 8, 1959, 263-71.
A study of the imagery in Paradise Lost.

1770 SCHÜCKING, LEVIN L. Die Spiegelung der puritanischen Ehe in Miltons Verlorenem Paradies. Die Familie im Puritanismus (Leipzig and Berlin: Verlog und Druck von B. G. Teubner, 1929), pp. 70-83. Reprinted, Bern and Munich: Francke Verl, 1964.

1771 SCHULTZ, HOWARD. Satan's Serenade. PQ, 27, 1948, 17-26.
On the dream episode in the Garden.

1772 ------. Warlike Flutes: Gellius, Castiglione, Montaigne, and Milton. MLN, 64, 1949, 96-8.
On the flutes of Paradise Lost, 1, 550-4.

1773 SCOTT-CRAIG, T. S. K. Milton's Paradise Lost, V, 108-111. Expl, 3, 1945, item 37.

1774 ------. Milton's Paradise Lost, V, 108-109. Expl, 24, 1965, item 24.
The retiring power is fancy rather than reason.

1775 ------. Miltonic Tragedy and Christian Vision. The Tragic Vision and the Christian Faith. Ed. by Nathan A. Scott, Jr. (New York: Association Press, 1957), pp. 99-122.
Argues against Johnson, and holds that in Paradise Lost and Paradise Regained "we have almost ideal examples of tragic vision illuminated by biblical faith, and of biblical faith transforming the tragic vision of life."

1776 SCUDDER, HAROLD H. Satan's Artillery. N&Q, 195, 1950, 334-47.
On Paradise Lost, 6, 568-78.

1777 SEAMAN, JOHN EUGENE. The Chivalric Cast of Milton's Epic Hero. ES, 49, 1968, 97-107.
In Paradise Lost and Paradise Regained. Discusses Christ in relation to the Homeric tradition. Sees Christ as the only victorious figure in Paradise Lost, "a regally Homeric figure in a context of heroic challenge...."

1778 ------. The Epic Art of Paradise Lost: A Study of Milton's Use of Epic Conventions. Doctoral diss., Stanford Univ., 1962. Abs., DA, 23, 1962, 2120-1.

1779 ------. Homeric Parody at the Gates of Milton's Hell. MLR, 62, April, 1967, 212-3.
Sees an ironic parallel between the meeting of Satan and Sin and Death and the encounter between Glaukos and Diomedes in the Iliad, 7, 119-236.

1780 SEDELOW, SALLY YEATES. The Narrative Method of Paradise Lost. Doctoral diss., Bryn Mawr College, 1960. Abs., DA, 21, 1960, 1556-7.

1781 SELDIN, M. Review Notes and Study Guide to Paradise Lost and Other Works of Milton. New York: Monarch Press, 1963, 1964, 1966. 154pp.
A student outline.

1782 SENSABAUGH, GEORGE F. Milton on Learning. SP, 43, 1946, 258-72.
On Raphael's discourse to Adam.

1783 SERONSY, CECIL C. Samuel Daniel and Milton. N&Q, 197, 1952, 135-6.
Possible borrowings in Paradise Lost and Paradise Regained.

1784 SEWELL, ARTHUR. Milton's Christian Doctrine and Its Relation to Paradise Lost. B. Litt. thesis, Queen's College, Oxford, 1933. iv, 142pp.
See No. 3036 for information concerning publication of this study.

1785 ------, and DENIS SAURAT. Two Notes on Milton. I. Did Milton Change His Views after Paradise Lost? II. The Interpretation of Paradise Lost, Book VII, 11. 168ff. RES, 15, 1939, 73-80.
The authors have opposing views on both issues. Sewell reiterates his view in RES, 15, 1939, 335.

1786 SEWELL, ELIZABETH. The Human Metaphor. South Bend: Univ. of Notre Dame Press, 1964. 212pp.

Considers, i.a., Paradise Lost, Paradise Regained, and Samson Agonistes in Chapter 4, Individual Life as Myth: The Figure of Suffering and Effort, pp. 114-55.

1787 SHARROCK, ROGER. Godwin on Milton's Satan. N&Q, N.S., 9, 1962, 463-5.
"William Godwin in his Political Justice issued what may well be the first manifesto of the Satanist school."

1788 SHAWCROSS, JOHN T. The Balanced Structure of Paradise Lost. SP, 62, 1965, 696-718.
Examines the organization and reorganization of Paradise Lost and considers its "thesis, style, and genre in light of its structure."

1789 ------. The Chronology of Milton's Major Poems. PMLA, 76, 1961, 345-58.
Suggests that Paradise Regained "seems to lie near but somewhat later than Samson Agonistes and, except for late work, before Paradise Lost as it now stands."

1790 ------. The Metaphor of Inspiration in Paradise Lost. Th'Upright Heart and Pure. Ed. by Amadeus P. Fiore, O.F.M. (Pittsburgh and Louvain: Duquesne Univ. Press, 1967), pp. 75-85.
"As I read Paradise Lost, therefore, I am struck by the metaphor of inspiration with its sexual overtones: the poem itself is the creation of God and the poet; it simulates an act of generation through psychological motif, subject matter, strategically placed proems, and rhythm; it deals with creation which is bodily, conceptual, and physical; and it suggests constant generation through impregnation of its readers with its message."

1791 ------. Orthography and the Text of Paradise Lost. Language and Style in Milton: A Symposium in Honor of the Tercentenary of Paradise Lost. Ed. by Ronald David Emma and John T. Shawcross (New York: Frederick Ungar, 1967), pp. 120-53.
"My aim has been to call in doubt hypotheses of the correctness of the text in terms of Milton's 'desires' or practices, to indicate the confusion of textual transmission and correction that must have occurred, and to suggest that the second edition has only some authority, not full authority, over the first edition."

1792 ------. Paradise Lost. Philadelphia: Educational Research Associates, 1966.
A study guide with extensive commentaries.

1793 ------. The Son in His Ascendance: A Reading of Paradise Lost. MLQ, 27, 1966, 288-401.
Sees both climaxes in Paradise Lost (in Books 3 and 9) as part of a greater pyramidic structure, with its center in Book 6. "God's mercy and the Son's ascendance within the poem—actual or implied—remove any real suspense or plotting in heroic terms."

1794 SHERRY, BEVERLY THELMA CHADWICK. Style and Action in Paradise Lost. Doctoral diss., Bryn Mawr, 1966. Abs., DA, 27, 1967, 3470-A.

1795 SHIGENO, TENRAI. A Study of Milton's Paradise Lost. Tokyo: Kenkyūsha, 1932.
> The first lengthy Japanese study of Paradise Lost.

1796 SHUMAKER, WAYNE. The Fallacy of the Fall in Paradise Lost. PMLA, 70, 1955, 1185-7.
> Disagrees with Bell, PMLA, 68, 1953, 863-83. Reply by Bell, pp. 1187-97, a rejoinder by Shumaker, pp. 1197-1202, and a surrejoinder by Bell, p. 1203.

1797 ------. Paradise Lost: The Mythological Dimension. BuR, 10, 1961, 75-86. Abs., SCN, 19, 1961, item 17 (Paper read in English 6 section of MLA, 1960). Reprinted in Unpremeditated Verse, Chapter One, pp. 3-25 (1967, see below).
> Inquires "whether the poem's extraordinary power ... does not derive partly from its capacity, as myth, to stimulate the deepest and most primitive layers of human consciousness."

1798 ------. Paradise Lost and the Italian Epic Tradition. Th'Upright Heart and Pure. Ed. by Amadeus P. Fiore, O.F.M. (Pittsburgh and Louvain: Duquesne Univ. Press, 1967), pp. 87-100.
> Points out that Milton rejects the complicated plot, the use of magic, and the valor, honor, and romantic love of Boiardo, Ariosto, and Tasso, and that Milton thus creates an epic which "has attained, even for scientifically oriented minds, a relevance which forbids us to discuss it as merely charming."

1799 ------. Unpremeditated Verse: Feeling and Perception in Paradise Lost. Princeton: Princeton Univ. Press, 1967. x, 230pp.
> The first part focuses on the embodiment of feeling; the second part, on perception. Chapters: Paradise Lost as Myth; The Narrative Plan; Three Examples of Affective Tonality; Animism; The Epic World as Sentient; Synecdoche and Metonymy; Visual Perception; Auditory Perception; Somatic Perception; Affect and Percept on the Mount of Speculation.
> Rev: YR, 57, June, 1968, 589.

1800 SIEBERT, THEODOR. Egozentrisches in Miltons Schreibweise, mit besonderer Berucksichtigung des Satan in Paradise Lost. Anglia, 43, 1931, 57-83.

1801 SIEGEL, PAUL. A Paradise within Thee in Milton, Byron, and Shelley. MLN, 56, 1941, 615-7.
> Considers Paradise Lost, Cain, and The Revolt of Islam.

1802 SIMON, IRÈNE. The Thesis of Paradise Lost. RLV, 29, 1963, 83-6.
> Summarizes main points in G. A. Wilkes' study, The Thesis of Paradise Lost. Agrees with his major contention.

1803 SIMS, JAMES H. Paradise Lost: Arian Document or Christian Poem? EA, 20, 1967, 337-47.
> Surveys the controversy on Milton's alleged Arianism and argues that "Paradise Lost is a Christian poem, accepted by and acceptable to orthodox Christian readers, and not an Arian document."

1804 ------. The Use of the Bible in Milton's Epic Poems. Doctoral diss., Univ. of Florida, 1959. Published as The Bible in Milton's Epics. Gainesville: Univ. of Florida Press, 1962. 283pp.

"Altogether, 1364 individual citations to Scripture have been recorded by Milton's editors from Hume to Hughes. Yet none of the editors, commentators, or scholars have attempted to bring together and systematize Milton's use of the Bible in his major poems; this is the task I have undertaken here, and I have, in the process, added 816 Biblical citations to particular lines of the two epics."
Rev: Virginia R. Mollenknott, SCN, 21, 1963, 34; J. A. Bryant, Jr., SAQ, 62, 1963, 607-9; Charles Garton, N&Q, N. S., 11, 1964, 353-4; Edgar Mertner, Anglia, 82, 1964, 247, 59; J. B. Beer, MLR, 60, 1965, 434-6.

1805   SIRLUCK, ERNEST. Paradise Lost: A Deliberate Epic. Churchill College, Cambridge, Overseas Fellowship Lecture No. 1. Cambridge: W. Heffer and Sons, 1967. 30pp.
A paper read on May 17, 1966, at Churchill College. Considers the nature of epic poetry in light of Paradise Lost, analyzing the organizing principle of the poem, and the influence of the dramatic form upon that work. Explains what is meant by justifying the ways of God to man.
Rev: TLS, Feb. 8, 1968, p. 134.

1806   SLAUGHTER, E. E. Milton's Demogorgon. PQ, 10, 1931, 310-2.
On Paradise Lost, 2, 963-5. Locrine a possible source.

1807   SMITH, CALVIN C. Milton's Satan and the Elizabethan Stage Villain. Doctoral diss., Duke Univ., 1957.

1808   SMITH, HALLETT. No Middle Flight. HLQ, 15, 1952, 159-72.
"... Milton was able to speak out ... not only because he believed the argument, but also because he had found an area of belief which encompassed at once serious doctrine and poetic fiction."

1809   SMITH, PAUL R. A Comparison of Paradise Lost and Mundorum Explicatio. Master's thesis, Univ. of Georgia, 1951.

1810   SMITH, REBECCA W. The Source of Milton's Pandemonium. MP, 29, 1931, 187-98.
His recollection of St. Peter's Cathedral.

1811   SPADALA, ENRICO. Tre i principi dei diavoli: Lucifer di Dante. Plutone di Tasso, Satana di J. Milton. Ragusa: Puglisi, 1937. 116pp.

1812   SPAETH, J. DUNCAN. Epic Conventions in Paradise Lost. Elizabethan Studies . . . in Honor of George F. Reynolds. Univ. of Colorado Studies, Ser. B., Studies in the Humanities, 2 (Boulder: Univ. of Colorado Press, 1945), pp. 201-10.

1813   SPEVACK-HUSMANN, HELGA. The Mighty Pan: Miltons mythologische Vergleiche. Neue Beiträge zur englischen Philologie, 1. Münster: Aschendorff, 1963. 105pp.
A 1959 Münster dissertation. Deals especially with Milton's use of myths in Paradise Lost. See this item under General Criticism for reviews.

1814   Stage Version of Paradise Lost. The Times, Feb. 12, 1960, p. 9d.
On an adaptation by James Roose Evans at the Vanbrugh Theatre.

1815   STANLEY, E. G. Ripeness is All. N&Q, N.S., 14, 1967, 228-9.
Michael's speech to Adam (Paradise Lost, 11, 535-8) uses "the Ciceronian idea of ripeness for death."

1816   STAPLETON, LAURENCE. Perspectives of Time in Paradise Lost. PQ, 45, 1966, 734-48.
  "The past as well as the present dimension of time belongs to the perspective of Paradise Lost. But although the past has a very far reach for Milton—because of his heterodox theories—the subjective feeling of the past is not important in his narrative as it is, for example, in Virgil. . . ."

1817   STARNES, D. T. Gehenna and Tophet. N&Q, 192, 1947, 369-70.
  Addenda to Whiting, N&Q, 192, 1947, 225-30.

1818   - - - - - -. Tityos and Satan. N&Q, 197, 1952, 379-80.
  In some particulars, Milton may have been thinking of the story of Tityos in his description of Satan's size in Paradise Lost, 1, 194-8, 209-10.

1819   STAVROU, C. N. Milton's Satan: One Word More. Univ. of Kansas City Rev., 25, 1958, 157-60.
  Interprets Satan as a complex character—a foil to God, the embodiment of evil, and the prototype of Adam and hence of man.

1820   STEADMAN, JOHN M. Achilles and Renaissance Epic. Moral Criticism and Literary Tradition. Lebende Antike, Symposion für Rodalf Sühnel. Ed. by Horst Meller and Hans-Joachim Zimmermann (Berlin, 1967), pp. 139-54.
  Discusses Alamanni, Tasso, and other Renaissance precursors of Milton.

1821   - - - - - -. Adam and the Prophesied Redeemer (Paradise Lost, XII, 359-623). SP, 56, 1959, 214-25. Reprinted in revised form in Milton's Epic Characters: Image and Idol (Chapel Hill: Univ. of North Carolina Press, 1968), pp. 72-81.
  Milton's fusion of conventional elements in the final books of Paradise Lost "represents, on the whole, an original contribution to a fairly common theme—Adam's foreknowledge of Christ his redeemer."

1822   - - - - - -. Allegory and Verisimilitude in Paradise Lost: The Problem of the Impossible Credible. PMLA, 78, 1963, 36-9.
  In his allegorical representations Milton follows the critical thought of the Italian Renaissance, whereas his disparaging neoclassical critics "bore the hallmark of seventeenth-century France."

1823   - - - - - -. Archangel to Devil: The Background of Satan's Metamorphosis. MLQ, 21, 1960, 321-35. Reprinted in revised form in Milton's Epic Characters: Image and Idol (Chapel Hill: Univ. of North Carolina Press, 1968), pp. 281-97.
  On the transformation scene in Book 10 of Paradise Lost. Shows how Milton utilized the tradition but altered its timing in the sequence of events.

1824   - - - - - -. The Bee-Simile in Homer and Milton. N&Q, N.S., 3, 1956, 101-2.
  On Paradise Lost, 1, 768-76.

1825   - - - - - -. Bitter Ashes: Protestant Exegesis and the Serpent's Doom. SP, 59, 1962, 201-10. Reprinted in revised form in Milton's Epic Characters: Image and Idol (Chapel Hill: Univ. of North Carolina Press, 1968), pp. 298-315.
  On Milton's debt to Christian exegetical tradition in Book 10 of Paradise Lost.

1826 ------. Busiris, the Exodus, and Renaissance Chronography. Revue belge de philologie et d'histoire, 39, 1961, 794-803.
On Paradise Lost. "In the light of Renaissance chronography, the conventional criticism of Milton's historical allusion [to Busiris, in Paradise Lost, 1, 307] seems, on the whole, invalid."

1827 ------. The Classical Hero: Satan and Gentile Virtue. Milton's Epic Characters: Image and Idol (Chapel Hill: Univ. of North Carolina Press, 1968), pp. 209-23.
"For Milton the inherent contradictions in Renaissance ideas of heroic virtue and the merit of pagan worthies proved a poetic asset. They gave him a traditional basis both for his heroic idol and for the standards by which he exposed its fallacy. They lent versimilitude and probability both to his portrait of the Satanic hero and to the iconoclastic scene in which he shattered it."

1828 ------. Dante's Commedia and Milton's Paradise Lost: A Consideration of the Significance of Genre for Source Studies and Comparative Literature. Doctoral diss., Princeton Univ., 1954. Abs., DA, 15, 1955, 593-4.

1829 ------. Demetrius, Tasso, and Stylistic Variation in Paradise Lost. ES, 47, 1966, 329-41.
Holds that stylistic variation in Paradise Lost is consistent with both the tone of the poem and the quality and action of the characters within the poem and points out that Milton's use of stylistic variation parallels that of his contemporaries.

1830 ------. The Devil and Pharaoh's Chivalry. MLN, 75, 1960, 197-201.
On the three comparisons in Milton's extended simile in Paradise Lost "describing the hopeless state of Satan's fallen legions."

1831 ------. Ethos and Dianoia: Character and Rhetoric in Paradise Lost. Language and Style in Milton: A Symposium in Honor of the Tercentenary of Paradise Lost. Ed. by Ronald David Emma and John T. Shawcross (New York: Frederick Ungar, 1967), pp. 193-232.
Examines ethos and dianoia, character and thought, in light of the Aristotelian classification, and shows how Milton applies rhetorical and logical principles in Paradise Lost, especially in the longer speeches.

1832 ------. Eve's Dream and the Conventions of Witchcraft. JHI, 26, 1965, 567-74.
Suggests Milton's probable skepticism regarding the existence of witches.

1833 ------. Felicity and End in Renaissance Epic and Ethics. JHI, 23, 1962, 117-32. Reprinted in revised form in Milton's Epic Characters: Image and Idol (Chapel Hill: Univ. of North Carolina Press, 1968), pp. 105-22.
Sees the idea of beatitude as the cornerstone of Milton's argument and fable in Paradise Lost and Paradise Regained.

1834 ------. From the Safe Shore: Milton and Tremellius. Neophil, 44, 1960, 218-9.
The Junius-Tremellius Bible approved the reading of Paradise Lost, 1, 310.

1835 ------. The God of Paradise Lost and the Divina Commedia. Archiv, 195, 1959, 273-89.

"Both approaches to the concept of God" were "specific responses to different literary requirements, and they reflected a deliberate emphasis on different aspects of deity."

1836 ------. Grosseteste on the Genealogy of Sin and Death. N&Q, N.S., 6, 1959, 367-8.
> Grosseteste's sermon on Luke 12:13 as an analogue of the genealogy in Paradise Lost and of Milton's concept of the darkness of hell-fire.

1837 ------. Heroic Virtue and the Divine Image in Paradise Lost. JWCI, 22, 1959, 88-105. Reprinted in revised form in Milton's Epic Characters: Image and Idol (Chapel Hill: Univ. of North Carolina Press, 1968), pp. 23-43.
> Milton portrays in Messiah the divine archetype of heroic virtue; in Satan he shows the counterfeit of genuine heroism; in Adam "he delineates the original perfection of the divine image in man, its obscuration by sin, and its partial recovery through repentance and faith."

1838 ------. Image and Idol: Satan and the Element of Illusion in Paradise Lost. JEGP, 59, 1960, 640-54. Reprinted in revised form in Milton's Epic Characters: Image and Idol (Chapel Hill: Univ. of North Carolina Press, 1968), pp. 227-40.
> The divine testimony of the Father, Son and angels constitutes right reason, while the proud imaginations of Satan create a deliberate picture of illusion and of Satan's fallacies.

1839 ------. Islamic Tradition and That Divelish Engin. Hist. Ideas News Letter, 4, 1958, 39-41.
> Medieval Moslem commentators furnish a parallel to the Renaissance idea that the devil invented the cannon.

1840 ------. John Collop and the Flames without Light (Paradise Lost, I, 62-3). N&Q, N.S., 2, 1955, 382-3.

1841 ------. Leviathan and Renaissanse Etymology. JHI, 28, 1967, 575-6.
> Primarily concerned with Hobbes. Notes that Leviathan had been glossed as a symbol of the Devil by St. Gregory and that Milton could exploit this interpretation "for the commonplace it was, in Paradise Lost."

1842 ------. Magnific Titles: Satan's Rhetoric and the Argument of Nobility. MLR, 61, 1966, 561-71. Reprinted in revised form in Milton's Epic Characters: Image and Idol (Chapel Hill: Univ. of North Carolina Press, 1968), pp. 263-77.
> Satan makes false use of rhetoric, in his appeal to nobility when he addresses his followers by their titles. This contrasts with Christ who makes no claim to adulatory titles and honors which his tempter offers him.

1843 ------. Mammon and Heav'ns Pavement (Paradise Lost, I, 682). N&Q, N.S., 7, 1960, 220.
> "In Mammon's attitude to Heav'ns Pavement Milton gives us the negative image—a picture in reverse—of the Senecan ideal."

1844 ------. Man's First Disobedience: The Causal Structure of the Fall. JHI, 21, 1960, 180-97. Reprinted in revised form in Milton's Epic Characters: Image and Idol (Chapel Hill: Univ. of North Carolina Press, 1968), pp. 139-59.

"...the causal structure of the fall in Paradise Lost serves essentially to exonerate God and to place the principal blame for man's sin and misery on man himself."

1845 ------. Meaning and Name: Some Renaissance Interpretations of Urania. NM, 64, 1963, 209-32.
On the various interpretations of Urania and of the Muses and their relationship to divine poetry, especially Paradise Lost.

1846 ------. Men of Renown: Heroic Virtue and the Giants of Genesis 6:4 (Paradise Lost, XI, 638-99). PQ, 40, 1961, 580-6. Reprinted in revised form in Milton's Epic Characters: Image and Idol (Chapel Hill: Univ. of North Carolina Press, 1968), pp. 177-93.
The concept of heroic virtue inherent in Genesis 6:4 is "an idea of cardinal importance in Milton's heroic poetry."

1847 ------. Milton and the Argumentum Paris: Biblical Exegesis and Rhetoric. Archiv, 202, 1966, 347-60. Reprinted in revised form in Milton's Epic Characters: Image and Idol (Chapel Hill: Univ. of North Carolina Press, 1968), pp. 160-73.
"...re-examine[s] the Biblical sources of Satan's insistence on equality with God and his rhetorical exploitation of the 'argument of the equal' (the argumentum paris) in justifying his rebellion and exhorting his companions to revolt."

1848 ------. Milton and Patristic Tradition: The Quality of Hell-Fire. Anglia, 76, 1958, 116-28.
"Milton expresses essentially the same conception of Hellfire as Gregory, Aquinas, Rolle, and Chaucer before him."

1849 ------. Milton and St. Basil: The Genesis of Sin and Death. MLN, 73, 1958, 83-4.
Suggests that St. Basil's Sixth Homily on the Hexaemeron may have been an influence upon Milton.

1850 ------. Milton and Wolleb Again (Paradise Lost, I, 54-56, 777). HTR, 53, 1960, 155-6.
On the influence of Wolleb's Compendium Theologiae Christianae on Paradise Lost.

1851 ------. Milton, Fulgentius, and Edward Browne: A Note on the Tantalus Myth. N&Q, N.S., 13, 1966, 391-2.
The deceptive apples of Fulgentius's Mythologican parallel Paradise Lost, 10, 547ff.

1852 ------. A Milton-Ariosto Parallel: Satan and Rodomonte (Paradise Lost, 4, 181). ZRP, 77, 1961, 514-6.
Satan's leap over the wall of Paradise is paralleled by Rodomonte's method of entering a citadel in Orlando Furioso, Canto 14. This strengthens the link between Paradise Lost and the tradition of epic and romance and points up ethical similarities.

1853 ------. A Milton-Claudian Parallel. N&Q, N.S., 3, 1956, 202.
Compares the opening of the infernal portals, Paradise Lost, 2, 881ff., and a passage in Claudian's Consulatu Stilichonis.

1854 ------. Milton, Virgil, and St. Jerome (Paradise Lost, III, 160-170). N&Q,
      N.S., 6, 1959, 368-9.
      On Valeria Falconia Proba and St. Jerome as possible sources for Milton's
      Christian echo of the Aeneid, 664-5.

1855 ------. Milton and the Renaissance Hero. Oxford: Clarendon Press, 1967.
      xiii, 209pp.
      A consideration of (1) Milton's "treatment of the heroic formulae commonly
      accepted as ethical and literary norms, (2) his distinction between their
      valid and invalid modes, and (3) his revaluation of the epic tradition in
      terms of this dichotomy." Discusses, i.a., the critiques of fortitude, sapience,
      leadership, amor, and magnanimity.
      Rev: TLS, Feb. 8, 1968, p. 134; John Buxton, RES, 19, 1968, 319-20.

1856 ------. Milton's Giant Angels: An Additional Parallel. MLN, 75, 1960,
      551-3.
      On Paradise Lost, 7, 605.

1857 ------. Milton's Walls of Glass (Psalm 136). Archiv, 198, 1961, 34-7.
      On Milton's "metrical paraphrase of Psalm 136:15" and Paradise Lost, 7,
      293, and 12, 197. ". . . the comparison of the Red Sea to 'Two Wals of Glasse'
      flanking the route of the Hebrews originated neither with Milton nor with
      Du Bartas, but with patristic commentators on Exodus 14 and 15 and on
      Psalm 136."

1858 ------. Mimesis and Idea: Paradise Lost and the Seventeenth-Century
      World-View. EUQ, 20, 1964, 67-80. Reprinted in revised form in Mil-
      ton's Epic Characters: Image and Idol (Chapel Hill: Univ. of North
      Carolina Press, 1968), pp. 3-20.
      Regards Paradise Lost as "both 'an imitation of action'—man's fall and
      expulsion from Eden—and an imitation of a system of ideas, the moral and
      physical universe of seventeenth-century Puritanism."

1859 ------. Milton's Epic Characters: Image and Idol. Chapel Hill: Univ. of
      North Carolina Press, 1968. xiii, 343pp.
      This item is annotated under General Criticism.

1860 ------. Miracle and the Epic Marvellous in Paradise Lost. Archiv, 198,
      1961, 289-303.
      On Milton's conscious attempts "to arouse wonder—the 'propria operations'
      of the heroic poem." Examines "1) Milton's own references to the wonder
      aroused by divine or diabolical agency in the course of the poem and 2) the
      traditional theological distinction between God's 'miracles' and Satan's
      'wonders.' "

1861 ------. Moses Prologizes: Milton and Ezekiel's Exagoge. N&Q, N.S., 11,
      1964, 336-7.
      "It is possible, therefore, to regard Milton's preference for the Greek verb
      in his outline of Paradise Lost as a conscious or unconscious debt to the
      Ezekielis Eductio."

1862 ------. Nature's Prime (Paradise Lost, V, 294-5) and William Byrd. N&Q,
      N.S., 5, 1958, 472-3.
      Milton's line echoes a similar phrase in Byrd's madrigals No. 8 and No. 28,
      First Sett of Italian Madrigalls (1590).

1863 ------. Pandaemonium and Deliberative Oratory. Neophil, 48, 1964, 159-76. Reprinted in revised form in Milton's Epic Characters: Image and Idol (Chapel Hill: Univ. of North Carolina Press, 1968), pp. 241-62.
The "infernal councillors" "are rhetoricians rather than dialecticians. Their arguments fall within the province of deliberative oratory."

1864 ------. Paradise Lost, 1667-1967. HLQ, 31, 1967, 1.
The editor's introduction to the Milton Tercentenary Issue (November), which includes articles by Merritt Y. Hughes, John G. Demaray, Maurice Kelly, B. Rajan, James Thorpe, and Edward Weismiller. In this bibliography each of these tercentenary articles is listed according to section and author. The issue also contains several Blake illustrations and three portraits of Milton from the Huntington Collections.

1865 ------. Paradise Lost and the Tragic Illustrious. Anglia, 78, 1960, 302-16.
Though critics have argued that Paradise Lost is more tragic than heroic, Milton "apparently made no clear-cut distinction between epic and tragedy."

1866 ------. Peripeteia in Milton's Epic Fable. Anglia, 81, 1963, 429-52.
In the major poems Milton makes use of the Aristotelian concept of peripeteia to emphasize the moral process of God's law.

1867 ------. The Quantum Mutatus Theme and the Fall. AN&Q, 2, 1964, 83.
On echoes of Aeneid, 2, 274-75, in Burton's The Anatomy of Melancholy, Valmarana's Daemonomachia, Milton's Paradise Lost, 1, 84-85, and William Hog's translation of Paradise Lost.

1868 ------. Recognition in the Fable of Paradise Lost. SN, 31, 1959, 159-73.
An analysis of four scenes of discovery: Satan's first meeting with Sin and Death; Satan's detection by the guardian angels: Man's knowledge of good and evil by eating the fruit; Adam's recognition of Christ as redeemer.

1869 ------. Satan's Metamorphoses and the Heroic Convention of the Ignoble Disguise. MLR, 52, 1957, 81-5. Reprinted in revised form in Milton's Epic Characters: Image and Idol (Chapel Hill: Univ. of North Carolina Press, 1968), pp. 194-208.
Believes that Satan's voluntary disguises possess a recognizable affinity with the heroic tradition.

1870 ------. Sin, Echidna and the Viper's Brood. MLR, 56, 1961, 62-6. Translated and reprinted by Casa Editrice Astrolahio, Rome, as Peccato, Echidna e la Nidiata della Vipera. Intelligenza, No. 1, 1962, 55-8.
"Though Milton borrowed from Spenser the idea of investing the mythical serpent-woman with characteristics of the female viper, he derived the major outlines of his figure not from the Faerie Queene, but directly from Hesiod's Theogony and conventional viper lore."

1871 ------. Sin and the Serpent of Genesis 3: Paradise Lost, II, 650-53. MP, 54, 1956, 217-20.

1872 ------. Spirit and Muse: A Reconsideration of Milton's Urania (Paradise Lost I, 1-26). Archiv, 200, 1963, 353-7.
"There is ... considerable justification for regarding the first twenty-six lines of Paradise Lost as two distinct invocations to two different powers—the first, a personification of the gift of sacred utterance or 'Celestial Song'; the second, God himself."

1873 ------. The Suffering Servant and Milton's Heroic Norm. HTR, 54, 1961,
      29-43. Reprinted in revised form in Milton's Epic Characters: Image and
      Idol (Chapel Hill: Univ. of North Carolina Press, 1968), pp. 58-71.
         In Paradise Regained "Milton modelled his exemplary hero not on any
         ideal extrinsic to the Biblical Messiah, but on the character of the historic
         Christ as revealed in the Scriptures and interpreted by Protestant theolo-
         gians."

1874 ------. Tantalus and the Dead Sea Apples (Paradise Lost, X, 547-73).
      JEGP, 64, 1965, 35-40.
         In fusing the legend of the Dead Sea apples and the Tantalus myth, Milton
         achieves a parody of the temptation of man. This heightens the punishment
         and everlasting humiliations of Satan.

1875 ------. Tradition and Innovation in Milton's Sin: The Problem of
      Literary Indebtedness. PQ, 39, 1960, 93-103.
         "... by investing his figure with the form of the conventional woman-serpent
         as well as attributes reminiscent of particular parallels, Milton enhanced
         the propriety, verisimilitude, and probability of his otherwise incredible
         monster."

1876 ------. The Tragic Glass: Milton, Minturno and the Condition Humaine.
      Th'Upright Heart and Pure. Ed. by Amadeus P. Fiore, O.F.M. (Pitts-
      burgh and Louvain: Duquesne Univ. Press, 1967), pp. 101-15.
         Concerned with the human condition in Paradise Lost and Samson Agonistes.
         Notes similarities and differences between Minturno's and Milton's use of
         the mirror metaphor in tragedy and concludes, "In universalizing Samson's
         predicament into a 'mirror of our fickle state,' Milton bears eloquent witness
         to the gravity and universality of the tragic vision."

1877 ------. Urania, Wisdom and Scriptural Exegesis (Paradise Lost, VII, 1-12).
      Neophil, 47, 1963, 61-73.
         Re-examines the background and significance of the close relationship be-
         tween Urania and Wisdom.

1878 STEIN, ARNOLD. Answerable Style. Milton's Epic Poetry: Essays on
      Paradise Lost and Paradise Regained. Ed. by C. A. Patrides (Harmonds-
      worth: Penguin Books, 1967), pp. 92-120.
         A reprint of pp. 119-62 of Stein's Answerable Style: Essays on Paradise
         Lost (1953).

1879 ------. Answerable Style: Essays on Paradise Lost. Minneapolis: Univ. of
      Minnesota Press, 1953. ix, 166pp. Reprinted, Seattle and London: Univ.
      of Washington Press, 1967.
         Chapters: Satan, The War in Heaven, A Note on Hell, The Garden, The
         Fall, Answerable Style.
         Rev: Cleanth Brooks, KR, 15, 1953, 638-47; J. H. Hanford, SCN, 11, 1953,
         29; TLS, May 7, 1954, p. 298; C. S. Holmes, SR, 62, 1954, 509-19; Kester
         Svendsen, BA, 28, 1954, 223; MGW, Feb. 4, 1954, p. 10; John E. Hardy, SR,
         62, 1954, 509-19; Wayne Shumaker, MLN, 69, 1954, 516-8; E. Duncan-Jones,
         MLR, 50, 1955, 106-7.

1880 ------. Milton's War in Heaven—An Extended Metaphor. ELH, 18, 1951,
      201-20. Reprinted in Answerable Style (Minneapolis: Univ. of Minn.
      Press, 1953; Seattle: Univ. of Washington Press, 1967), pp. 17-37. Re-

printed also in Milton: Modern Essays in Criticism. A Galaxy Book. Ed. by Arthur E. Barker (New York: Oxford Univ. Press, 1965), 264-83.

1881 ------. The Paradise Within and the Paradise Without. MLQ, 26, 1965, 586-600.
Review article on L. L. Martz's The Paradise Within.

1882 ------. Satan: The Dramatic Role of Evil. PMLA, 65, 1950, 221-31. Reprinted in Answerable Style (Minneapolis: Univ. of Minnesota Press, 1953; Seattle: Univ. of Washington Press, 1967), pp. 3-16.

1883 STEWART, FLORENCE M. Paradise Lost, Bk. I, 636: Different. N&Q, 166, 1934, 79.
Milton uses "different" in its old sense of "deferent."

1884 STOCKLEY, W. F. P. Paradise Lost, 1, 301. TLS, Feb. 18, 1932, p. 112.

1885 STOLL, ELMER E. Belial as an Example. MLN, 48, 1933, 419-27.
Of literature as imagination rather than life.

1886 ------. From the Superhuman to the Human in Paradise Lost. UTQ, 3, 1933, 3-16. Reprinted in From Shakespeare to Joyce (New York: Doubleday, 1944; New York: Frederick Ungar, 1965), pp. 422-35.

1887 ------. Give the Devil His Due: a Reply to Mr. Lewis. RES, 20, 1944, 108-24.
Attacks Lewis' interpretation of Satan in his Preface to Paradise Lost.

1888 ------. A Postscript to Give the Devil His Due. PQ, 28, 1949, 167-84.
Further reasons for Milton's attributing to Satan qualities such as courage, fortitude, and perseverance.

1889 ------. Was Paradise Well Lost? Poets and Playwrights (Minneapolis: Univ. of Minnesota Press, 1930), pp. 203-9. Reprinted, London: Russell and Russell, 1965.

1890 STRAUMANN, HEINRICH. Miltons Epos von den Abtrünnigen. Stufen einer Sinndeutung-Zurich: Institut Orell Füssli, 1960. 16pp.
A lecture delivered on April 29, 1960, at the University of Zürich.

1891 STRODE, LENA VIRGINIA. A Study of Descriptive Techniques in Narrative Poetry from Chaucer to Milton. Doctoral diss., Univ. of Denver, 1961. Abs., DA, 23, 1962. 228pp.
Examines Books 1-4 of Paradise Lost.

1892 STROUP, THOMAS B. Parallel Entrances and Exits in Paradise Lost. TSL, 6, 1961, 71-5.
Discusses similarities and/or contrasts between appearances of the major characters at the beginning and the end of the poem.

1893 ------. Religious Rite and Ceremony in Milton's Poetry. Lexington: Univ. of Kentucky Press, 1968. ix, 83pp.
Contains a chapter on Paradise Lost, pp. 15-47.

1894 SUMMERS, JOSEPH H. The Final Vision. Milton: A Collection of

Critical Essays. Ed. by Louis L. Martz (Englewood Cliffs, New Jersey: Prentice-Hall, 1966), 183-206.
A reprint of a chapter from Summers' The Muse's Method: An Introduction to Paradise Lost.

1895   ------. Grateful Vicissitude in Paradise Lost. PMLA, 69, 1954, 251-64. Reprinted in The Muse's Method (Cambridge: Harvard Univ. Press, 1962), pp. 71-86.
Feels that we cannot properly read the poem unless we can share imaginatively Milton's conception of grateful vicissitude, eternal movement and change, which continues so long as God's creatures continue to exist.

1896   ------. The Muse's Method: An Introduction to Paradise Lost. Cambridge: Harvard Univ. Press, London: Chatto & Windus, 1962. x, 227pp.
"We should ... approach Paradise Lost with a trace of diffidence and with a healthy capacity to doubt our preconception and our first judgment." Chapters: The Beginning; Satan, Sin, and Death; Grateful Vicissitude; The Two Great Sexes; The Pattern at the Center; The Ways of the Fall; The Voice of the Redeemer; The Final Vision.
Rev: Agnes M. C. Latham, YWES, 183; Thomas R. Hartmann, SCN, 20, 1962, 29-30; Barbara Lewalski, MP, 61, 1963, 122-6; Harry F. Robins, JEGP, 62, 1963, 807-8; Kenneth Muir, CritQ, 5, 1963, 96; TLS, Feb. 15, 1963, p. 101; Arnold Stein, RN, 16, 1963, 348-50; F. N. Lees, N&Q, N.S., 11, 1964, 114-6; John Buxton, RES, 15, 1964, 319-21; Edgar Mertner, Anglia, 82, 1964, 247-59.

1897   ------. Paradise Lost: The Pattern at the Centre. Milton's Epic Poetry: Essays on Paradise Lost and Paradise Regained. Ed. by C. A. Patrides (Harmondsworth: Penguin Books, 1967), pp. 179-214.
A reprint of Chapter 5 of The Muse's Method: An Introduction to Paradise Lost.

1898   ------. The Two Great Sexes in Paradise Lost. SEL, 2, 1962, 1-26. Reprinted in The Muse's Method (Cambridge: Harvard Univ. Press, 1962), pp. 87-111.
A chapter from Summers' The Muse's Method. Feels that the theme of the "two great sexes" is central to Paradise Lost and shows how Milton employs sexual metaphor throughout the poem.

1899   ------. The Voice of the Redeemer in Paradise Lost. PMLA, 70, 1955, 1082-9. Reprinted in The Muse's Method (Cambridge: Harvard Univ. Press, 1962), pp. 176-85.
Milton uses Eve's speech in Book 10 in which she offers herself as a redeemer, however inadequate she is to fill that role, as a mirror of the redemptive actions of the Son.

1900   SUNDELL, ROGER HENRY. Internal Commentary in the Major Poems of John Milton. Doctoral diss., Washington Univ., 1966. Abs., DA, 26, 1966, 6701.

1901   SUNUMA, YOSHITARO. A Study of Paradise Lost. Tokyo Bunrika University English Language and Literature Review, 6, 1939.

1902   SVENDSEN, KESTER. Adam's Soliloquy in Book X of Paradise Lost. CE, 10, 1949, 366-70. Reprinted in Milton: Modern Essays in Criticism. A

Galaxy Book. Ed. by Arthur E. Barker (New York: Oxford Univ. Press, 1965), pp. 328-35.
Discusses the passage as a dramatic monologue and shows its structural relationship to the rest of the poem.

1903 ------. Epic Address and Reference and the Principle of Decorum in Paradise Lost. PQ, 28, 1949, 185-206.
"The first object of this paper is to describe Milton's understanding of the principle of decorum and to examine his exercise of it in the forms of address and reference for the major characters of Paradise Lost. The second object is to suggest the bearing these epithets have on what may be called the structural decorum of the content and strategy of the poem."

1904 ------. "Found out the Massie Ore." N&Q, 177, 1939, 331.
On an emendation of Paradise Lost, 1, 703.

1905 ------. John Martin and the Expulsion Scene of Paradise Lost. SEL, 1, 1961, 63-73.
Examines Martin's twenty-four illustrations (1826-27) of Paradise Lost and compares his Expulsion Scene with those of his predecessors and contemporaries. See also correspondence between Svendsen and Marcia Allentuck, SEL, 2, 1962, 151-5.

1906 ------. Milton and Malleus Maleficarum. MLN, 60, 1945, 118-9.
Adam's remark to Eve concerning the rib (10, 884-8) is clarified by a passage in the Malleus Maleficarum (c. 1484).

1907 ------. Milton's Chariot of Paternal Deity (P. L., VI, 749-759). N&Q, 193, 1948, 339.
Comments of Bartholomew Anglicus in De Proprietatibus Rerum closely parallel Milton's description.

1908 ------. Milton's Paradise Lost, V, 108-111. Expl, 4, 1945, item 2.

1909 ------. Milton's Paradise Lost, IV, 347-350. Expl, 8, 1949, item 11.

1910 ------. Paradise Lost as Alternative. Humanities Association Bulletin, 18, 1967, 35-42.
A lecture originally delivered at Simon Frazer University. Describes the moral alternatives in Paradise Lost and shows "how the structure of the poem asserts them—or . . . how the form into which the poem is cast takes its identity from its moral environment."

1911 ------. The Power to Reason: A Milton Paradox. N&Q, 184, 1943, 368-70.
On Milton and the reasoning ability of animals. See also H. W. Crundell, N&Q, 185, 1943, 113.

1912 ------. Milton and Science. Cambridge: Harvard Univ. Press, 1956. viii, 304pp.
Considers, i.a., Milton's use of natural science in Paradise Lost.

1913 ------. The Prudent Crane: Paradise Lost, VII, 425-431. N&Q, 183, 1942, 66-7.
Testimony of the crane's qualities from popular encyclopedias of science.

1914 ------. Satan and Science. BuR, 9, 1960, 130-42.
Illustrates how the "assumption of Satan's hand in the advance of science

and technology appears in Paradise Lost, and ... in John Martin's nineteenth century mezzotint illustrations for certain of its scenes."

1915 SWARDSON, HAROLD ROLAND, JR. A Study of the Tension Between Christian and Classical Traditions in Seventeenth-Century Poetry. Doctoral diss., Univ. of Minnesota, 1956. Abs., DA, 17, 1957, 1559. Published as Poetry and the Fountain of Light: Observations on the Conflict Between Christian and Classical Traditions in Seventeenth-Century Poetry. London: Allen and Unwin, 1962. 167pp.

> Milton, pp. 104-55. Argues that the conflict between the two traditions creates an unresolved tension in Paradise Lost and that the poem suffers because of this, that it lacks artistic and moral firmness.

1916 SWIDLER, ARLENE A. Milton's Paradise Lost, II, 866-70. Expl, 17, No. 6, 1959, item 41.

> On the parody of the Satan-Sin-Death episode.

1917 SYLVESTER, JOSHUA, trans. Bartas His Devine Weeks (1605) and Works. A Facsimile Reproduction with an Introduction by Francis C. Haber. Gainesville, Florida: Scholars Facsimiles and Reprints, 1965. xii, 597pp.

> A reprint of the work which Charles Dunster, George Coffin Taylor, and others have named as a definite influence on Milton in the composition of Paradise Lost.

1918 TAMAKI, ISHITARO. Satan in Paradise Lost. Kwansai Univ. Eigaku, 1, 1954.

1919 TATE, CHARLES D., JR. Milton's Paradise Lost and Vondel's Adam in Ballingschap. Doctoral diss., Univ. of Colorado, 1966. Abs., DA, 28, 1967, 1060-A.

> "Consequently, we cannot say that Milton was indebted to Vondel's play."

1920 TAYLOR, DICK, JR. The Battle in Heaven in Paradise Lost. TSE, 3, 1952, 69-92.

> Milton fused traditional epic practice and traditional Biblical interpretation, "... integrat[ing] the action of the warfare so richly into his design that it did him highly important service both structurally and thematically...."

1921 ------. Milton and the Paradox of the Fortunate Fall Once More. TSE, 9, 1959, 35-51.

> Insists "that Milton did not believe in a Fortunate Fall and was in no wise proposing the idea in Paradise Lost."

1922 ------. Milton's Treatment of the Judgment and the Expulsion in Paradise Lost. TSE, 10, 1960, 51-82.

> Sets Milton's treatment of the Judgment and Expulsion "against the background of the long developed tradition dealing with this episode." Supports Milton's optimism in later stages of Paradise Lost and the concept of a gentle and kind God.

1923 TAYLOR, GEORGE C. Did Milton Read Robert Crofts' A Paradise within Us or The Happie Mind? PQ, 28, 1949, 207-10.

> Expresses the affirmative view.

1924 ------. Milton on Mining. MLN, 45, 1938, 24-7.
On the background of two passages in Paradise Lost directed against the
mining of metals in the earth.

1925 ------. Milton's Use of Du Bartas. Cambridge: Harvard Univ. Press;
London: Milford, 1934. Reprinted, New York: Octagon Books, 1966.
129pp.
Rev: TLS, Aug. 23, 1934, pp. 578-9; H. F. Fletcher, JEGP, 34, 1935, 119-20;
H. O. Wilde, Ang. Bbl., 46, 1935, 237-8; D. Saurat, RES, 12, 1936, 216-8, and
MLN, 51, 1936, 263-4; B. A. Wright, MLR, 31, 1936, 84-5; J. H. Hanford,
MP, 35, 1937, 200-1.

1926 TAYLOR, JOHN CHESLEY. A Critical History of Miltonic Satanism.
Doctoral diss., Tulane Univ., 1966. Abs., DA, 27, 1966, 1348-A-1349-A.

1927 TAYLOR, MYRON WILFRED. Two Analogies for Poetry in the
Seventeenth Century. Doctoral diss., Washington Univ., 1961. Abs., DA,
21, 1961, 3772.
Chapters 7 and 8 on Paradise Lost.

1928 TCHAKIRIDES, JOHN PETER. Epic Prolepsis and Repetition as Structural Devices in Milton's Paradise Lost. Doctoral diss., Yale Univ.,
1968. Abs., DA, 29, 1968, 881-A-2-A. 227pp.

1929 Tercentenary Conferences and Volumes. MN, 2, 1968, 7.
Comments on conferences at Goucher College, the College of Notre Dame
of Maryland (Baltimore), and the University of York.

1930 [Tercentenary Exhibition]. BJRL, 50, 1967, 1.
Announces a library exhibition to celebrate the tercentenary of Paradise Lost.
Of the six issues of the first edition, the John Rylands Library possesses all
but the second. Accompanied by a facsimile of the title page of the first issue.

1932 TERRY. Paradise Lost, Book I: A Complete Paraphrase. Sixth Edition.
The Normal Milton. Farnham, Surrey: The Normal Press, 1961. 20pp.

1933 THOMPSON, ELBERT N.S. Essays on Milton. New York: Russell and
Russell, 1967. 217pp.
A reprint of Stevens' No. 2416, published in 1914. "An interesting collection
of studies with original contributions. Contains: Milton, The Last of the
Elizabethans; Milton's Temperament and Ideals; The True Bearing of Mil-
ton's Prose; Epic Structure of Paradise Lost; The Sources of Paradise Lost;
The Theme of Paradise Lost; Milton's Art" (Stevens' annotation).

1934 ------. For Paradise Lost, XI-XII. PQ, 22, 1943, 376-82.
In refutation of C. S. Lewis, the author expresses a liking for the books
and argues that they are artistically justified.

1935 THOMPSON, J. A. K. The Epic Tradition in Modern Times: Milton.
Classical Influences on English Poetry (London: Allen and Unwin,
1951), pp. 53-74.
Indicates lines along which the relation of Milton to Homer and Vergil
may be pursued.

1936 THORSLEV, PETER L., JR. The Romantic Mind Is Its Own Place.
CL, 15, 1963, 250-68.

Analyzes Paradise Lost, 1, 251-9, as a locus classicus of romantic Satanism and briefly traces thematic transmutations of the passage in the romantic mind.

1937 TILLYARD, E. M. W. On Annotating Paradise Lost, Books IX and X. JEGP, 60, 1961, 808-16.
Problems encountered in editing a school edition of Books 9 and 10.

1938 ------. The Causeway from Hell to the World in the Tenth Book of Paradise Lost. SP, 38, 1941, 266-70.
Establishes the purpose of the rich references cited in making up Milton's description of the bridge over Chaos.

1939 ------. The Crisis of Paradise Lost. Milton: A Collection of Critical Essays. Ed. by Louis L. Martz (Englewood Cliffs, N.J.: Prentice-Hall, 1966), pp. 156-82.
A reprint of a chapter from Tillyard's Studies in Milton.

1940 ------. The English Epic Tradition. Warton Lecture on English Poetry. Proceedings of the British Academy, 22. London: Humphrey Milford, 1936. 23pp. Reprinted in The Miltonic Setting (Cambridge: Cambridge Univ. Press, 1938), pp. 141-67.
I.a., considers Paradise Lost as an epic which "resumes the essential medieval theme and combines with it Renaissance culture and exuberance and with neo-classic compression of form."
Rev: E. C. Batho, MLR, 33, 1938, 87-8.

1941 ------. Milton. The English Epic and Its Background (New York: Oxford Univ. Press, 1954), pp. 430-7.
Discusses Milton as the nodal figure in the English epic, corresponding to Vergil in Latin.

1942 ------. Milton and Sidney's Arcadia. TLS, Mar. 6, 1953, p. 153.
On the resemblance between Paradise Lost, 11, 836-9, and the passage describing the shipwreck early in the Arcadia.

1943 ------. Milton and Statius. TLS, July 1, 1949, p. 429.
Notices a parallel between Paradise Lost, 9, 886-93, and the Thebiad, 7, 148-50.

1944 ------. Milton and the English Epic Tradition. Seventeenth Century Studies Presented to Sir Herbert Grierson (Oxford: Clarendon Press, 1938), pp. 211-34. Reprinted as The Growth of Milton's Epic Plans in The Miltonic Setting (Cambridge: Cambridge Univ. Press, 1938), pp. 168-204.

1945 ------. Studies in Milton. London: Chatto and Windus, 1951. 176pp. Reprinted, 1955, 1960, 1964.
Contains, i.a., chapters on the crisis of Paradise Lost, on Satan, and on Adam and Eve.
Rev: James H. Hanford, YR, 41, 1951, 634-6; John S. Diekhoff, SRL, Jan. 5, 1952, p. 14; Lionel Stevenson, Pers, 33, 1952, 440; P. Legouis, EA, 5, 1952, 76-7.

1946 TOLA MENDOZA, FERNANDO. Una nota sobre el Paradiso Perdito de Milton. Sphinx (Lima, Peru), 2, No. 3, 1937, 91-4.

1947 TOLIVER, HAROLD E. Complicity of Voice in Paradise Lost. MLQ, 25, 1964, 153-70.
On the rhetoric of the several voices in Paradise Lost.

1948 TREFMAN, SIMON. A Note on the Bridge of Chaos in Paradise Lost and Matthew XVI. 18-19. SCN, 20, 1963, item 204.
Milton's bridge of Chaos echoes the words of Christ in Matthew 16:18-19. The wording in Milton's passage (Paradise Lost, 10, 312-5, 318-24) suggests that the bridge can be equated with the Roman Catholic Church.

1949 TREIP, MINDELE C. Paradise Lost, II, 257-262 and XII, 561-569. N&Q, N.S., 5, 1958, 209-10.
Sardonic parallel in philosophies of Satan, Book 2, and Adam, Book 12.

1950 TSCHUMI, RAYMOND. The Evolution of Myths from Dante to Milton. English Studies Today. Fourth Series. Ed. by Ilva Cellini and Giorgio Melchiori (Roma: Edizioni di Storia e Letteratura, 1966), pp. 237-54. Reprinted as De Dante à Milton. Le Paradis Perdu: 1667-1967. Ed. by Jacques Blondel (Paris: Minard Lettres Modernes, 1967), pp. 141-76.
Cites numerous parallel passages and offers suggestions as to Milton's modifications of his borrowings from Dante.

1951 [TSUJI], HIROKO KUSAKABE. Myth and Language in Milton's Paradise Lost. Annual Reports of Studies (Doshisha Women's College), 15, 1964, 13-33.
Uses the Fall in Book 9 to illustrate the sympathetic relation between the outward and the inward worlds. "... when man laments, so does nature, transforming its features according to man's emotions."

1952 TUNG, MASON. The Abdiel Episode: A Contextual Reading. SP, 62, 1965, 595-609.
Abdiel considered as a foil to Adam and Eve in the total context of Paradise Lost.

1953 TURNER, PAUL. The Dorian Mood (A Note on Paradise Lost, I, 549-61). N&Q, N.S., 4, 1957, 10-11.
Suggests that Milton is alluding to a passage from Plutarch's Lycurgus.

1954 ------. Miltonic Negligence. N&Q, 192, 1947, 358.
On Paradise Lost, 10, 775-9.

1955 ------. Woman and the Fall of Man. ES, 29, 1948, 1-18.
On Adam's attitude toward Eve and the metaphysical love poetry of Milton's age.

1956 TYSON, JOHN PATRICK. The Elements of Aristotelian Tragedy in Paradise Lost. Doctoral diss., Tulane Univ., 1967. Abs., DA, 28, 1968, 3690-A. 170pp.

1957 URGAN, MINA. Satan and His Critics. English Department Studies, Istanbul Univ., 2, 1951, 61-81.
Surveys the Satanist controversy.
Rev: SCN, 13, 1955, 43.

1958 VAN DOREN, MARK. Paradise Lost. The Noble Voice: A Study of Ten Great Poems (New York: Holt, 1946), pp. 122-47. Reprinted, 1962.

"Paradise Lost is as near to greatness as a poem without simple vision can go. Since its vision is not simple, however, or its author's mind made up, as an epic it suffers a serious handicap. It comes last in the great list, walking lame."

Rev: Irwin Edman, NYHTBR, Nov. 24, 1946, p. 3; Carlos Baker, NYTBR, Nov. 24, 1946, p. 3; Delmore Schwartz, SR, 55, 1947, 707-9; M. F. Lindsley, CW, 164, 1947, 476-7.

1959 VARANDYAN, EMMANUEL P. Milton's Paradise Lost and Zoroaster's Zenda Vesta. CL, 13, 1961, 208-20.

A discussion of similarities. "The theme of Milton's Paradise Lost is in essence identical with that of Zoroaster's Zenda Vesta."

1960 VISIAK, E. H. Milton's Magic Shadow. NC, 134, 1943, 135-40.

"Satan is the projection, the shadow-shape of a mind disillusioned by the ideal that had possessed it."

1961 VISWANATHAN, S. Milton and Purchas' Linschoten: An Additional Source for Milton's Indian Figtree. MN, 2, 1968, 43-5.

"The account of the tree given by a Jesuit traveller, John Huighen van Linschoten, in his Voyage to Goa, and Observations of the East India, incorporated in Purchas His Pilgrimes, Vol. X, pp. 222-317, seems to be as immediate a source for Milton as Pliny or Gerard."

1962 WADDINGTON, RAYMOND B. Appearance and Reality in Satan's Disguises. TSLL, 4, 1962, 390-8.

"Milton exploits a consistent level of irony through the idea that Satan thinks he is effectively disguising himself, while the disguises only reveal his nature more effectively to the judicious spectator."

1963 WALDOCK, A. J. A. Masson's Diagram of Milton's Spaces. RES, 22, 1946, 56-7.

On Paradise Lost, 1, 73-4. A reply to B. A. Wright, RES, 21, 1945, 42-3. Rejoinder by Wright, pp. 57-8.

1964 ------. Mr. C. S. Lewis and Paradise Lost. Australian English Assn., Sept., 1943.

A disparagement of the epic.

1965 ------. Paradise Lost and Its Critics. New York and Cambridge: Cambridge Univ. Press, 1947, 1961, 1962, 1964, 1966 (paperback). 147pp.

A controversial study, which has the announced purpose of determining what Milton means in Paradise Lost. Chapters: The Poet and the Theme, The Fall (I), The Fall (II), Satan and the Technique of Degradation, God and the Angels—and Dante, and Unconcious Meanings in Paradise Lost.

Rev: L. C. Martin, YWES, 188-9; TLS, Aug. 2, 1947, p. 395, and Nov. 1, 1947, p. 560; F. R. Leavis and TLS reviewer, TLS, Nov. 22, 1947, p. 603; C. S. Lewis, TLS, Nov. 29, 1947, p. 615; N&Q, 192, 1947, 395; Herman Peschmann, English, 6, 1947, 311-2; W. G., QQ, 54, 1947, 528-30; Joan Bennett, NSN, Aug. 23, 1947, pp. 154-5; Camb. Jour., 1, 1947, 70; H. F. Fletcher, JEGP, 47, 1948, 203; A. N. J., ES, 29, 1948, 94; B. A. Wright, RES, 25, 1949, 75-83; Elizabeth M. Pope, MLN, 64, 1949, 208-9; D. C. Allen, MLQ, 10, 1949, 115-7.

1966 ------. Paradise Lost: The Fall. Milton's Epic Poetry: Essays on Paradise Lost and Paradise Regained. Ed. by C. A. Patrides (Harmondsworth: Penguin Books, 1967), pp. 74-91.

A reprint of portions of Chapter 3 of Waldock's Paradise Lost and Its Critics (1947).

1967 ------. Satan and the Technique of Degradation. Milton: A Collection of Critical Essays. Ed. by Louis L. Martz (Englewood Cliffs, N.J.: Prentice-Hall, 1966), pp. 77-99.
A chapter reprinted from Waldock's Paradise Lost and Its Critics.

1968 WALZL, FLORENCE L. Milton's Paradise Lost, III, 150-166. Expl, 20, 1961, item 11.
Christ's speech is a parallel in miniature to the infernal debate.

1969 WARREN, WILLIAM F. The Universe as Pictured in Milton's Paradise Lost: An Illustrated Study for Personal and Class Use. New York: Gordian Press, 1968. 80pp.
A reprint of Stevens' No. 946, first published in 1915.

1970 WATKINS, WALTER B. C. Creation. Milton: A Collection of Critical Essays. Ed. by Louis L. Martz (Englewood Cliffs, N.J.: Prentice-Hall, 1966), 121-47.
A chapter reprinted from Watkins' An Anatomy of Milton's Verse.

1971 WATSON, J. R. Divine Providence and the Structure of Paradise Lost EIC, 14, 1964, 148-55.
"The aim of this essay is to make some suggestions about the plan of Paradise Lost, and to demonstrate how it emphasises and reinforces Milton's particular justification of the ways of God to men in the poem."

1972 WEATHERS, WINSTON. Paradise Lost as Archetypal Myth. CE, 14, 1952-53, 261-4.

1973 WEBER, BURTON JASPER. The Construction of Paradise Lost. Doctoral diss., Univ. of Minnesota, 1966. Abs., DA, 26, 1966, 6029.

1974 WEIDHORN, MANFRED. The Anxiety Dream in Literature from Homer to Milton. SP, 64, 1967, 65-82.
Classifies and analyzes dreams, including Eve's dream in Paradise Lost.

1975 ------. Dreams and Guilt. HTR, 58, 1965, 69-90.
Concludes that Eve's dream serves "not only as a variation on the theme of temptation but also as an important test probe for Satan," which nevertheless leaves her "guiltless in the eyes of God."

1976 ------. Eve's Dream and the Literary Tradition. TSL, 12, 1967, 39-50.
Interprets Eve's dream in the light of "the use of the dream in ancient civilization: to account for the unknown, the irrational," adding the fact that the essential difference between Eve's dream and earlier examples is that "it evinces greater sophistication in the narrative."

1977 ------. Satan's Persian Expedition. N&Q, N.S., 5, 1958, 389-92.
Some parallels between Satan and Xerxes, as described by Herodotus.

1978 WEINKAUF, MARY STANLEY. The Two Faces of Eve: the Ideal and the Bad Renaissance Wife in Paradise Lost. Doctoral diss., Univ. of Tennessee, 1966. Abs., DA, 27, 1966, 1797-A.
"Thus Eve is an ideal wife before she questions Adam's command of the

household and after she has accepted her guilt and endured his tongue-lashing; she is a bad wife when she goes out to garden alone until she realizes her guilt."

1979 WEISINGER, HERBERT. Tragedy and the Paradox of the Fortunate Fall. London: Routledge and Kegan Paul, 1953. 300pp.
A background study.
Rev: J. A. Bryant, SR, 62, 1954, 319-28.

1980 WEISMILLER, E. R. Materials Dark and Crude: A Partial Genealogy for Milton's Satan. HLQ, 31, 1967, 75-93.
An examination of the influence of Tasso's Jerusalem Delivered (Fairfax translation) upon Paradise Lost, with affirmative conclusions.

1981 ------. The Versification of Paradise Lost and Paradise Regained: A Study of Movement and Structure in Milton's Nondramatic Blank Verse. Doctoral diss., Merton College, Oxford, 1951. xix, 375 pp., and i, 301 pp.

1982 WERBLOWSKY, R. J. ZWI. Lucifer and Prometheus: a Study of Milton's Satan. Introduction by C. G. Jung. London: Routledge, 1952. xix, 120pp.
"The claim made in this study is that Milton's Satan in fact contains Promethean elements, and that these are the reasons for his powerful appeal—an appeal which has proved detrimental to the unity and purpose of the poem."
Rev: NSN, Aug. 9, 1952, 168.

1983 ------. Milton and the Conjectura Cabbalistica. JWCI, 18, 1955, 90-113.
Shows that no direct relation exists between Paradise Lost and the Zohar and argues that kabbalistic influences come from post-Renaissance Kabbalah in its pre-Luranic phase.

1984 WEST, ROBERT H. Milton and the Angels. Athens: Univ. of Georgia Press, 1955. ix, 237pp.
A study of angelology in Europe and in Milton's England and of Milton's handling of the traditions in his own work. Contains a chapter on Milton's heresies on angels.
Rev: R. H. Bowers, SAB, 22, No. 2, 1956, 17-8; Marvin Mudrick, HudR, 9, 1956, 126-33; N&Q, N. S., 3, 1956, 90-1; Charles M. Coffin, QQ, 63, 1956, 138-44; TLS, Jan. 20, 1956, p. 38; Thomas H. English, Georgia Rev., 10, 1956, 19-21; T. S. K. Scott-Craig, Religion in Life, 25, 1956, 477-8; H. F. Fletcher, JEGP, 55, 1956, 323; R. A. Fraser, SAQ, 55, 1956, 388-9; Merritt Y. Hughes, MLN, 71, 1956, 526-9; Kester Svendsen, BA, 30, 1956, 331; Arnold Williams, MP, 54, 1957, 202-3; F. T. Prince, RES, 8, 1957, 348-9; B. A. Wright, MLR, 52, 1957, 101-2.

1985 ------. Milton and Michael Psellus. PQ, 28, 1949, 477-89.
A study of likenesses and differences in demonology and angelology.

1986 ------. Milton's Angelological Heresies. JHI, 14, 1953, 116-23.
Provides the basis for another heresy concerning the goodness of matter.

1987 ------. Milton's Giant Angels. MLN, 67, 1952, 21-3.
On Paradise Lost, 7, 605.

1988 ------. The Names of Milton's Angels. SP, 47, 1950, 211-23.
Only Ithuriel is "not yet certainly found in pre-Miltonic angelological writings."

1989 ------. The Substance of Milton's Angels. SAMLA Studies in Milton. Ed. by J. Max Patrick (Gainesville: Univ. of Florida Press, 1953), pp. 20-53.

1990 ------. The Terms of Angelic Rank in Paradise Lost. Essays in Honor of W. C. Curry (Nashville: Vanderbilt Univ. Press, 1954), pp. 261-8.

1991 WHALER, JAMES. Animal Simile in Paradise Lost. PMLA, 47, 1932, 534-53.
On Milton's iron control over and virtual renunciation of animal similes.

1992 ------. The Compounding and Distribution of Similes in Paradise Lost. MP, 28, 1931, 313-27.
Notes the combinations and frequency of similes in Paradise Lost, examines Dante, Homer and Virgil for precedents, and explains the distribution of similes in Milton's poem.

1993 WHEELER, THOMAS. Milton's Blank Verse Couplets. JEGP, 66, 1967, 359-68.
"What is needed is our recognition that John Milton never read Paradise Lost; he heard it." Advocates a "listening understanding" of the couplets in Paradise Lost, especially those spoken lines, so that a clearer understanding of the characters can be formed.

1994 WHITING, GEORGE W. Abdiel and the Prophet Abdias. SP, 60, 1963, 214-26.
On the relationships between Abdiel and the minor prophet Abdias. "Abdias's prophecy forms a pattern of Abdiel's and there are marked analogies between the character and circumstances of Edom and those of Satan and his host."

1995 ------. And Without Thorn the Rose. RES, N.S., 10, 1959, 60-2.
On Paradise Lost, 4, 256.

1996 ------. Before the Flood: Paradise Lost and the Geneva Bible. N&Q, 194, 1949, 74-5.
Feels that annotations in the Geneva Bible influenced the narrative in Paradise Lost, 11.

1998 ------. Cherubim and Sword. N&Q, 192, 1947, 469-70.
On Paradise Lost, 12, 632-4.

1999 ------. The Golden Compasses in Paradise Lost (Bk. VII, 11. 224-31). N&Q, 172, 1937, 294-5.

2000 ------. Milton and This Pendant World. Austin: Univ. of Texas Press, 1958. xviii, 364pp.
Contains several chapters on Paradise Lost.
Rev: Agnes M. C. Latham, YWES, 181; Wilhelmina Gordon, QQ, 65, 1958, 712-3; SCN, 17, 1959, item 65; Albert H. Carter, RN, 12, 1959, 117-9; Burton O. Kurth, Pers, 41, 1960, 402-3; A. S. P. Woodhouse, MP, 57, 1960, 272-4; Carl S. Meyer, Concordia Theological Monthly, 31, 1960, 392-3; Fitzroy Pyle, RES, 11, 1960, 329-31; Karl Brunner, Eras, 14, 1961, 297-8.

2001 ------. Milton's Crystalline Sphere and Ben Gerson's Heavens. RES, 8, 1932, 450-3.
    Questions Fletcher's interpretation of Paradise Lost, 7, 263-74, in his Milton's Rabbinical Readings (1930).

2002 ------. Tormenting Tophet. N&Q, 192, 1947, 225-30.
    Henry Greenwood's Tormenting Tophet (1624) illustrates the commonplaceness of many elements in Milton's picture of hell.

2003 WHITING, GEORGE W., and ANN GOSSMAN. Siloa's Brook, the Pool of Siloam, and Milton's Muse. SP, 58, 1961, 193-205.
    Holds that the miracle at the pool of Siloam, not the brook of Siloah, is symbolic in Paradise Lost. Siloah's brook inspires the Muse whom Milton invoked.

2004 WICKERT, MARIA. Miltons Entwürfe zu einem Drama vom Sudenfall. Anglia, 73, 1955, 171-206.

2005 WIDMER, KINGSLEY. The Iconography of Renunciation: the Miltonic Simile. ELH, 25, 1958, 258-69. Reprinted in revised form in Milton's Epic Poetry: Essays on Paradise Lost and Paradise Regained. Ed. by C. A. Patrides (Harmondsworth: Penguin Books, 1967), pp. 121-31.
    On Paradise Lost and Paradise Regained. "... a subtle and dialectical reading of the Miltonic texture and tone suggests a fascinating and shocking master simile: the world as evil, and virtue as renunciation."

2006 WILDING, MICHAEL. Paradise Lost and Linguistic Precision. Balcony, No. 5, 1966, 25-31.
    Holds that there are few questionable passages in Paradise Lost, that T. S. Eliot, F. R. Leavis, John Peter, and others "unfortunately came upon the wrong answers by not looking carefully enough."

2007 WILKES, GEORGE A. The Thesis of Paradise Lost. Australian Humanities Research Council Monographs, No. 9. Melbourne: Melbourne Univ. Press, 1961. 42pp.
    Sees Paradise Lost as "a treatment of the operation of Providence, traced through the celestial cycle from the revolt of the angels to the Last Judgment, and its purpose is to justify the workings of Providence to mankind."
    Rev: Agnes M. C. Latham, YWES, 43, 1962, 182; Irène Simon, RLV, 1963, 83-6; Kenneth Muir, CritQ, 5, 1963, 96; TLS, Feb. 15, 1963, pp. 101-2; John M. Steadman, Archiv, 200, 1963, 301-2; F. N. Lees, N&Q, N. S., 11, 1964, 114-6; Edgar Mertner, Anglia, 82, 1964, 247-59.

2008 WILLIAMS, ARNOLD. Commentaries on Genesis as a Basis for Hexaemeral Material in the Literature of the Late Renaissance. SP, 34, 1937, 191-208.
    Suggests that Milton may have followed Ralegh and Sir Thomas Browne in leaning heavily upon Pererius and others.

2009 ------. The Common Expositor: An Account of the Commentaries on Genesis, 1527-1633. Chapel Hill: Univ. of North Carolina Press, 1948. ix, 297pp.
    Renaissance commentaries on Genesis and their influence on Milton and others.
    Rev: L. C. Martin, YWES, 194-5.

2010 ------. Milton and the Book of Enoch—An Alternative Hypothesis. HTR, 33, 1940, 291-9.
Suggests that the fragments themselves are sufficient as a source for Paradise Lost.

2011 ------. Milton and the Renaissance Commentaries on Genesis. MP, 37, 1940, 263-78.
"The thesis of this paper is not that Paradise Lost can be partitioned among a certain group of commentaries, but that, as Milton knew and used a certain group of commentaries, every repeated treatment of a topic by these commentaries is like another blow of the hammer to drive the nail deeper into the wood."

2012 ------. The Motivation of Satan's Rebellion in Paradise Lost. SP, 42, 1945, 253-68. Reprinted in Milton: Modern Judgements, ed. by Alan Rudrum (London: MacMillan, 1968), pp. 136-50.
On the fusion of several motives and the traditions that lie behind them.

2013 ------. Renaissance Commentaries on Genesis and Some Elements of the Theology of Paradise Lost. PMLA, 56, 1941, 151-64.

2014 WILLIAMS, CHARLES. Reason and Beauty in the Poetic Mind. Oxford: Clarendon Press, 1933. xi, 186pp.
Chapter 8, pp. 91-128, suggests that Paradise Lost be read as a psychological poem, the theme of which is obedience and disobedience, and that Milton transcends despair and pathos to a sublimity which consists of the exaltation of power, reason, and beauty.

2015 WILLIAMS, HELEN and PETER. Milton and Music, or The Pandaemonic Organ. Musical Times, 107, 1966, 760-3.
A collection of Milton's references to music, with the suggestion that Paradise Lost, 2, 706-17, is a description of an organ-case that Milton saw in Italy or could have seen illustrated in A. Kircher's Musurgia Universalis (Rome, 1650).

2016 WILLIAMSON, GEORGE. The Education of Adam. MP, 61, 1963, 96-109. Reprinted in Milton: Modern Essays in Criticism, A Galaxy Book, ed. by Arthur E. Barker (New York: Oxford Univ. Press, 1965), pp. 284-307; and in Milton and Others (Chicago: Univ. of Chicago Press; London: Faber and Faber, 1965), pp. 42-65.
On the education of Adam as "a structural element in the epic plot and a didactic element in the meaning of Paradise Lost."

2017 ------. Milton and the Mortalist Heresy. SP, 32, 1935, 553-79. Reprinted in Seventeenth Century Contexts (London: Faber and Faber, 1960), pp. 148-77.
The mortalist controversy and Paradise Lost.

2018 WINKLER, HERTHA. Das biblisch-religiöse Epos des 17. Jahrhunderts bis zu Miltons Paradise Lost. Doctoral diss., Wien, 1949. 249pp.

2019 WINTERICH, JOHN T. Paradise Lost. Twenty-Three Books and the Stories Behind Them (Philadelphia: Lippincott, 1939), pp. 1-12.
General information.

2020 WOLFF, SAMUEL L. Milton's Advocatum Nescio Quem: Milton, Salmasius, and John Cook. MLQ, 2, 1941, 559-600.
  Identifies the advocate as John Cook of Grays Inn and describes the relationship of a speech composed by Cook to Salmasius' tract, and hence to Milton. Offers a series of elucidative annotations on Milton's First Defense.

2021 WOODHOUSE, A. S. P. Pattern in Paradise Lost. UTQ, 22, 1953, 109-27.
  Outlines the connection between theme and pattern and Milton's Christian modification of the traditional epic patterns.

2022 WOODHULL, MARIANNA. The Epic of Paradise Lost. New York: Gordian Press, 1968. 386pp.
  A reprint of Stevens' No. 908, first published in 1907.

2023 WORDEN, W. S. Milton's Approach to the Story of the Fall. ELH, 15, 1948, 295-305.
  Distinguishes three realms in which the Fall occurs: the historical, the psychological, and the allegorical.

2024 WRIGHT, B. A. Counsels Different. N&Q, N.S., 5, 1958, 205.
  On Paradise Lost, 1, 635-7.

2025 ------. Found out the Massie Ore (Paradise Lost, I, 703). TLS, Aug. 9, 1934, p. 553.

2026 ------. Mainly: Paradise Lost, XI, 519. RES, 4, 1953, 143.
  Interprets "mainly" as "considerable, a great deal," not "chiefly."

2027 ------. Masson's Diagram of Milton's Spaces. A Note on Paradise Lost, I, 73-4. RES, 21, 1945, 42-3.
  The "as . . . as" construction indicates a simile, not a comparison of exact measurement.

2028 ------. Milton's Paradise Lost. London: Methuen; New York: Barnes and Noble, 1962. Reprinted, London: University Paperbacks, 1968. 210pp.
  A defense of Paradise Lost against Milton's detractors, beginning with his seventeenth-century critics and continuing to the recent ones. Chapters: The Man and the Poet, The Moral in the Fable, Diction, The Functions of the Epic Simile, Similes from Voyages of Discovery, God and Satan, Angels in Revolt, Satan's Return to Hell, The Creation, Paradise, The Fall, After the Fall, The Last Two Books.
  Rev: Agnes M. C. Latham, YWES, 183; Kenneth Muir, CritQ, 5, 1963, 96; Geoffrey Bullough, English, 14, 1963, 153-4; A. G. Newell, Evangelical Quar., 35, 1963, 174-7; K. M. Lea, RES, 14, 1963, 410-2; TLS, Feb. 15, 1963, pp. 101-2; John M. Steadman, Archiv, 201, 1964, 218-21; Edgar Mertner, Anglia, 82, 1964, 247-59.

2029 ------. Milton's Treason. TLS, June 20, 1929, p. 494.
  On Paradise Lost, 1, 594-9, which, according to Toland, was objected to by the censor.

2030 ------. Milton's Use of the Word Waft. N&Q, N.S., 5, 1958, 341.
  Notes consistent usage in Paradise Lost, 2, 1041-2; 3, 521; 12, 435; Paradise Regained, 1, 103-4; and Lycidas, 164.

2031 ------. Note on Milton's Night-founder'd. N&Q, N.S., 5, 1958, 203-4.
On Paradise Lost, 1, 204.

2032 ------. A Note on Milton's Punctuation. RES, 5, 1954, 170.
On Paradise Lost, 9, 922.

2033 ------. Note on Milton's Use of the Word Danger. RES, 22, 1946, 225-6.
On Paradise Lost, 2, 1004-9. Used in the sense of "power to hurt or harm" or "mischief, harm, and damage."

2034 ------. Note on Milton's Worth Ambition. N&Q, N.S., 5, 1958, 200.
On Paradise Lost, 1, 262.

2035 ------. Note on Paradise Lost, II, 879-83. RES, 22, 1946, 130-1.
"Erebus" used here to designate the dark surrounding void of Chaos out of which hell and the new world of man were created.

2036 ------. Note on Paradise Lost, I, 230. RES, 23, 1947, 146-7.
Suggests that "hue" means not "colour" but "appearance."

2037 ------. Note on Paradise Lost, II, 70-81. N&Q, N.S., 5, 1958, 208-9.
Finds an allusion to Aeneid, 6, 125-9; discusses Milton's use of the word "drench" in Paradise Lost, 2, 70-81, and 11, 367-8, in Comus, 995-1000, and in the first sonnet to Cyriack Skinner.

2038 ------. Note on Paradise Lost, IV, 310, N&Q, N.S., 5, 1958, 341.
"Milton's 'and sweet reluctant amorous delay' is a close translation of Ars Amatoria, II, 718."

2039 ------. Paradise Lost, I, 341. RES, 21, 1945, 238-9.
Suggests the meaning "veering" for "warping."

2040 ------. Paradise Lost, IX, 1079-80. RES, N.S., 10, 1959, 62-3.
Interprets the meaning of "first and last" in the light of The Christian Doctrine, 1, 12, Of the Punishment of Sin.

2041 ------. Stressing of the Preposition Without in the Verse of Paradise Lost. N&Q, N.S., 5, 1958, 202-3.
On Milton's stress variations to achieve artistic rhythm.

2042 WRIGHT, CELESTE T. Something More About Eve. SP, 41, 1944, 156-68.
Collects Renaissance opinions on the nature of women.

2043 YOFFIE, LEAH R. C. Chaucer's White Paternoster, Milton's Angels, and a Hebrew Night Prayer, SFQ, 15, 1951, 203-10.
Suggests that Chaucer and Milton used the prayer.

2044 ------. Creation, the Angels, and the Fall of Man in Milton's Paradise Lost and Paradise Regained, and in the Works of Sir Richard Blackmore. Doctoral diss., Univ. of North Carolina, 1942. Abs., Univ. of North Carolina Record, No. 383, 1942, pp. 77-8.

2045 YOUNG, ANDREW. Milton versus Paradise Lost. Listener, 69, June 13, 1963, 998-9.
On alleged conflicts between Milton's theology and the narrative of Paradise Lost.

2046 ZIEGELMAIER, GREGORY. The Comedy of Paradise Lost. CE, 26, 1965, 516-22.

       Paradise Lost is as much comedy as tragedy because Adam and Eve have the promise of Eternity and within themselves they contain the Infinite.

2047 ZIEGLER, JULIAN. Two Notes on J. T. Williams' Word into Images in Chaucer's Hous of Fame. MLN, 64, 1949, 73-6.

       Feels that there is a connection between Chaucer's poem and Paradise Lost, ll, 14-30, concerning flight from earth to a celestial dwelling place.

PARADISE REGAINED

2048 ADES, JOHN I. The Pattern of Temptation in Comus. PELL, 1, 1965, 265-71.
An examination of the parallels between the temptation in Comus and in Paradise Regained.

2049 ALLEN, DON C. The Harmonious Vision: Studies in Milton's Poetry. Baltimore: Johns Hopkins Univ. Press, 1954.
Contains a chapter on Paradise Regained.

2050 BAKER, STEWART A. The Brief Epic: Studies in the Style and Structure and Genre of Paradise Regained. Doctoral diss., Yale Univ., 1964.

2051 ------. Sannazaro and Milton's Brief Epic. CL, 20, 1968, 116-32.
Believes that Sannazaro, "who had already transformed the genres of the pastoral eclogue and pastoral romance," provides the conceptual basis for the genre of Paradise Regained.

2052 BALDWIN, EDWARD C. Shook the Arsenal: A Note on Paradise Regained. PQ, 18, 1939, 218-22.
On Paradise Regained, 4, 270.

2053 BANKS, THEODORE H. The Banquet Scene in Paradise Regained. PMLA, 55, 1940, 773-6.
Interprets the scene as a connecting device between the first and second temptations.

2054 BARNES, C. L. Error in Paradise Regained. N&Q, 156, 1929, 440.
On Paradise Regained, 1, 383, Cf. N&Q, 157, 1929, 177-8, 251.

2055 BATESON, F. W. Paradise Regained: A Dissentient Appendix. The Living Milton (London: Routledge and K. Paul, 1960), pp. 138-40.
Insists that in Paradise Regained "the words and the word-order exist in a dimension of their own."

2056 BECK, R. J. A Commentary on Paradise Regained. Doctoral diss., St. Andrew's College, 1954.

2057 ------. Urim and Thummin. N&Q, N.S., 4, 1957, 27-9.
On the nature of the gems mentioned by Satan in Paradise Regained, 3, 13-16.

2058 BORINSKI, LUDWIG VON. Milton's Paradise Regained. NS, 6, 1961, 253-74.
On the relationship of Paradise Regained to Milton's artistic development and the cultural development of the seventeenth century.

2059 BOSWELL, JACKSON C. Milton and Prevenient Grace. SEL, 7, 1967, 83-94.
Holds that a reading of Paradise Lost, supported by references to Paradise Regained and the prose works, "demonstrated clearly that Milton did believe in prevenient grace even when he was arguing most strongly for predestination."

2060 BRODRIBB, C. W. A Neglected Correction in Milton (Paradise Regained, IV, 157-158). TLS, May 17, 1941, pp. 239, 241.
Would replace "the" with "thee" as the fourth word in line 157.

2061 CARLISLE, A. I. Milton and Ludwig Lavater. RES, 5, 1954, 249-55.
Believes that Paradise Regained, 1, 365-77, 387-96, 407-53 (Christ's argument with Satan) is taken from Lavater on 2 Chronicles 18.

2062 ------. A Study of the Trinity College MS., Pages 35-41, and Certain Authors Represented in Milton's Commonplace Book, in Their Relationship to Paradise Lost and Paradise Regained. B. Litt. thesis, St. Hugh's, Oxford, 1952.

2063 CHAMBERS, A. B. Absalom and Achitophel: Christ and Satan. MLN, 74, 1959, 592-6.
That Achitophel assumes the role of Satan in the wilderness "is put beyond doubt by the repeated echoing of relevant passages" from Paradise Regained.

2064 CLEVELAND, EDWARD. On the Identity Motive in Paradise Regained. MLQ, 16, 1955, 232-6.
Examines the motive of Satan's attempt to discover Christ's identity against the Old Testament background.

2065 CONDEE, RALPH W. The Formalized Openings of Milton's Epic Poems. JEGP, 50, 1951, 502-8.
Analysis indicative of Milton's attempt to imitate both Homer and Vergil.

2066 COPE, JACKSON I. Satan's Disguises: Paradise Lost and Paradise Regained. MLN, 73, 1958, 9-11.
"The disguises of Satan form a link between the epics."

2067 ------. Time and Space as Miltonic Symbol. ELH, 26, 1959, 497-513.
Considers spatial dimension in Paradise Lost and Paradise Regained "as the aesthetic shape of the myth through which Milton created meaning for the boundless spaces viewed by Galileo...."

2068 COX, LEE SHERIDAN. Food-word Imagery in Paradise Regained. ELH, 28, 1961, 225-43.
Contends "that both imagery and structure reveal that Milton's primary concern throughout the poem is the nature and office of the Word Incarnate and of the Word."

2069 ------. Structural and Thematic Imagery in Samson Agonistes and Paradise Regained. Doctoral diss., Indiana Univ., 1962. Abs., DA, 23, 1963, 4342.

2070 DANIELLS, ROY. Milton, Mannerism and Baroque. Toronto: Univ. of Toronto Press, 1963. 229pp.
A search for analogies between Milton's art and the other arts. Contains a chapter on Paradise Regained.

2071 DAUBE, DAVID. Three Notes on Paradise Regained. RES, 19, 1943, 205-13.
On the second temptation, the order of the temptations, and Schiller's indebtedness in his Fiesko.

2072 DAVIDSON, CLIFFORD. The Dialectic of Temptation. BSUF, 8, Summer, 1967, 11-6.
Holds that Paradise Regained "presents to the reader a dialectic which represents the triumph of wisdom over folly."

2073 DYSON, A. E. The Meaning of Paradise Regained. TSLL, 3, 1961, 197-211.
Suggests that "the force of the poetry, and the realized values" emphasize the similarities between Christ and Satan on the heroic level.

2074 FARNELL, LEWIS R. Milton and Pindar. TLS, Oct. 1, 1931, p. 754.
On Paradise Regained (4, 563-5) and the Ninth Pythian Ode.

2075 FIELDS, ALBERT W. Milton and Self-knowledge. PMLA, 83, 1968, 392-9.
Examines Milton's concept of self-knowledge as seen in Paradise Lost, Paradise Regained, and Samson Agonistes, and compares Milton's view with other Classical and Christian ideas of self-knowledge.

2076 FINK, ZERA S. The Political Implications of Paradise Regained. JEGP, 40, 1941, 482-8.
Summarized in The Classical Republicans (Evanston: Northwestern Univ. Press, 1945), pp. 195-6. On Milton's distrust of seventeenth-century forms of dictatorship.

2077 FIORE, AMADEUS P., O.F.M. The Problem of 17th-Century Soteriology in Reference to Milton. FS, 15, 1955, 48-59, 257-82.
Considers the redemptive element in De Doctrina Christiana, Paradise Lost, and Paradise Regained in relation to the Renaissance milieu.

2078 FIXLER, MICHAEL. The Unclean Meats of the Mosaic Law and the Banquet Scene in Paradise Regained. MLN, 70, 1955, 573-7.
The food is unacceptable because Satan offers food which is proscribed to the Jews, although he says there is no prohibition.

2079 FRISSELL, HARRY L. Milton's Art of Logic and Ramist Logic in the Major Poems. Doctoral diss., Vanderbilt Univ., 1951. Abs., Bulletin of Vanderbilt Univ., 51, 1951, 22-3. Ann Arbor: UM, 1952. 250pp.

2080 FRYE, NORTHROP. The Typology of Paradise Regained. MP, 53, 1956, 227-38. Reprinted in Milton: Modern Essays in Criticism, ed. by Arthur E. Barker (New York: Oxford Univ. Press, 1965), 429-46; and in Milton's Epic Poetry: Essays on Paradise Lost and Paradise Regained, ed. by C. A. Patrides (Harmondsworth: Penguin Books, 1967), pp. 301-21. Revised as Revolt in the Desert. The Return to Eden: Five Essays on Milton's Epics (Toronto: Univ. of Toronto Press, 1965), pp. 118-43.
"In the Book of Job the contest of God and Satan takes the form of a wager on Job's virtue, and the scheme of Paradise Regained is not greatly different, with Christ occupying the place of Job."

2081 GALVIN, ANSELM. Paradise Regained: Milton and the Tradition of the Fathers. Master's thesis, Univ. of Toronto, 1946.

2082 GILLESPIE, EDGAR BRYAN. Paradise Regain'd: A History of the Criticism and an Interpretation. Doctoral diss., Duke Univ., 1966. Abs., DA, 27, 1966, 1820A-1A.
Considers criticism from the seventeenth century to the present.

2083 GORDON, D. J. Two Milton Notes. RES, 18, 1942, 318-9.
      1. Precious Bane: a Recollection of Boethius in Paradise Lost? (1, 692).
      2. The Golden Chersoness. (Paradise Regained, 4, 74).

2084 HOOPER, CHARLOTTE L. The Bible and Paradise Regained. Master's
      thesis, Duke Univ., 1942.

2085 HUGHES, MERRITT Y. The Christ of Paradise Regained and the
      Renaissance Heroic Tradition. SP, 35, 1938, 254-77. Reprinted in Ten
      Perspectives on Milton (New Haven and London: Yale Univ. Press,
      1965), pp. 35-62.
          Tests the "prevailing critical view of Milton's Christ as a self-portrait of an
          aging Puritan taking revenge in Stoicism" by the historical approach and
          recognizes "the contribution of the Middle Ages to Milton's conception of
          his hero."

2086 JONES, CHARLES W. Milton's Brief Epic. SP, 44, 1947, 209-27.
          On the genre of Paradise Regained.

2087 KENDALL, LYLE H., JR. Two Notes on the Text of Paradise Regained.
      N&Q, N.S., 4, 1957, 523.
          On 4, 387, and 2, 485.

2088 KERMODE, FRANK. Milton's Hero. RES, 4, 1953, 317-30.
          "My purpose here is ... to show that Paradise Regained contains within
          itself the reasons why its hero is as he is and not otherwise, and that Milton's
          thought was ... always and heroically consistent."

2089 KLIGER, SAMUEL. The Urbs Aeterna in Paradise Regained. PMLA,
      61, 1946, 474-91.
          On the tradition behind the passage on Rome

2090 LANDY, MARCIA. Tercentenary Celebration of Paradise Lost. SCN, 26,
      1968, 31-3.
          At the Univ. of Pittsburgh. Contains, i.a., a summary of Jackson Cope's Para-
          dise Regained: Inner Ritual.

2091 LANGFORD, THOMAS. The Temptations in Paradise Regained. TSLL,
      9, Spring, 1967, 37-55.
          Suggests that dread and desperation and not uncertainty lie behind Satan's
          behavior.

2092 LASKOWSKY, HENRY J. Miltonic Dialogue and the Principle of
      Antithesis in Book Three of Paradise Regained. Thoth, No. 4, 1963,
      pp. 24-9.
          Examines poetic form of dialogues in Paradise Regained, as exemplified in
          Book 3, in terms of the principle of antithesis.

2093 LAWRY, JON S. The Shadow of Heaven: Matter and Stance in Milton's
      Poetry. Ithaca: Cornell Univ. Press, 1968. xv, 416pp.
          See Chapter 5: Since No Man Comes: God's Ways with His Son in Paradise
          Regained, pp. 289-345.

2094 LEWALSKI, BARBARA KIEFER. Milton's Brief Epic: The Genre,
      Meaning, and Art of Paradise Regained. Providence: Brown Univ.
      Press, 1966; London: Methuen, 1966. xii, 436pp.

"The central argument of this book . . . is that Paradise Regained is conceived as Milton's brief epic, and merits that designation in all its aspects." Contents: Part One, The Genre—Job as Epic, the Brief Biblical Epic (Medieval, Renaissance, and Neoclassical), Job and Paradise Regained. Part Two: Theme and Dramatic Action—Milton's Uses of Typology, Christ in the Several Temptations and/or Scenes. Part Three: The Art of the Poem—Some Aspects of Narrative Method, Structure, and Style. Contains extensive notes.
Rev: TLS, Sept. 1, 1966, p. 779; Stewart Baker, JEGP, 65, 1966, 723-7; James R. McAdams, SCN, 25, 1967, 26-7; William A. Armstrong, English, 16, 1967, 148-9; John Arthos, ELN, 5, 1967, 57-9; John Buxton, RES, 19, 1968, 73-5.

2095 ------. Theme and Structure in Paradise Regained. SP, 57, 1960, 186-220. Revised as Theme and Action in Paradise Regained. Milton's Epic Poetry: Essays on Paradise Lost and Paradise Regained. Ed. by C. A. Patrides (Harmondsworth: Penguin Books, 1967), pp. 322-47.
"In my view, the poem portrays Christ as an essentially dramatic character, seeking fully to understand and realize his nature as God-man, and his mediatorial role."

2096 L[OANE], G[EORGE] G. The Crisis of Paradise Regained. N&Q, 175, 1938, and 187, 1944, 39.

2097 LONG, ANNE BOWERS. The Relations Between Classical and Biblical Allusions in Milton's Later Poems. Doctoral diss., Univ. of Illinois, 1967. Abs., DA, 28, 1968, 5022-A. 382pp.

2098 MACKIN, COOPER R. Aural Imagery as Miltonic Metaphor: The Temptation Scenes of Paradise Lost and Paradise Regained. Explorations of Literature. Ed. by Rima Drell Reck (Baton Rouge: Louisiana State Univ. Press, 1966), pp. 32-42.
Suggests that the aural imagery in Book 9 "is a metaphor for the ultimate meaning of Satan's temptation and that it serves the same function in the temptation scenes in Paradise Regained."

2099 MAJOR, JOHN M. Paradise Regained and Spenser's Legend of Holiness. RenQuar, 20, 1967, 465-70.
Theorizes that Milton, instead of being so greatly influenced by Book 2 of Spenser's Faerie Queene (according to Edwin Greenlaw), was also influenced ("more strongly perhaps") by the first book of the Faerie Queene, Spenser's Legend of Holiness.

2100 MARILLA, ESMOND L. Paradise Regained: Observations on Its Meaning. SN, 27, 1955, 179-91. Reprinted in Milton and Modern Man: Selected Essays (University, Alabama: Univ. of Alabama Press, 1968), pp. 56-67.
Argues that Paradise Regained "is inspired primarily by dynamic interest in the 'practical' problems of the temporal world and that it strives, principally, to set forth the issues which condition the course of human history."

2101 MARTZ, LOUIS L. Paradise Regained: The Interior Teacher. The Paradise Within: Studies in Vaughan, Traherne, and Milton (New Haven and London: Yale Univ. Press, 1964, 1966), pp. 171-201. Reprinted in Milton's Epic Poetry: Essays on Paradise Lost and Paradise Regained. Ed. by C. A. Patrides (Harmondsworth: Penguin Books, 1967), pp. 348-77.

Uses the Augustinian principle of "the indwelling teacher to conclude that Paradise Regained is a rehearsal of the self, where the voice of the inner man discovers what a true Son of God ought to reply to the temptations of Satan."

2102 ------. Paradise Regained: The Meditative Combat. ELH, 27, 1960, 223-47.
    The central contest is "a meditative combat created by Milton's brilliant manipulation of styles, a contest in which the flights of poetic splendor are consistently drawn back by the prevailing net of a frugal, georgic style to the ground of renunciation and temperance."

2103A McADAMS, JAMES R. Milton's Epic Synthesis: A Study of the Association of Paradise Lost and Paradise Regained. Doctoral diss., New York Univ., 1966.

2103B McMANUS, HUGH FRANCIS. Milton's Son of God as Celestial Man. Doctoral diss., Columbia Univ., 1967. Abs., DA, 28, 1968, 5023-A-4-A. 115pp.

2104 MEHL, DIETER VON. Zur Interpretation des Paradise Regained. DVLG, 36, 1962, 340-55.
    Interprets Paradise Regained in terms of the Paradise Lost aim of justifying the ways of God to men.

2105 MENZIES, W. Milton: The Last Poems, E&S, 24, 1938, 80-113.
    Sees Samson Agonistes and Paradise Regained "as the true expression of the poet's inward life at the time, of all he felt and thought during the period."

2106 MOAG, JOSEPH STEWART. Traditional Patterns of Dialogue and Debate in Milton's Poetry. Doctoral diss., Northwestern Univ., 1964. Abs., DA, 25, 1965, 6598-99.

2107 MULDROW, GEORGE McMURRY. An Irony in Paradise Regained. PLL, 3, 1967, 377-80.
    Suggests that Satan "both knows and does not know the identity" of Christ.

2108 ------. The Theme of Man's Restoration in Milton's Later Poetry. Doctoral diss., Stanford Univ., 1960. Abs., DA, 21, 1960, 1193.

2109 NEWELL, SAMUEL WILLIAM, JR. Milton's Paradise Regained: A Historical and Critical Study. Master's thesis, Emory Univ., 1942.

2110 NEWMEYER, EDNA. Beza and Milton: New Light on the Temptation of Learning. BNYPL, 66, 1962, 485-98.
    Concerning the influence of Theodore Beza's Job Expounded (London, 1589?) on Milton's Paradise Regained, 4, 286-364.

2111 NIEMAN, LAWRENCE J. The Nature of the Temptations in Paradise Regained Books I and II. University Review (Kansas City), 34, 1967, 133-9.
    "Underlying the temptations of Satan, then, is the goal of knowledge. For Jesus, at stake is a self-knowledge which will afford him the necessary self-confidence 'to conquer Sin and Death the two grand foes.' And for Satan, at stake is the knowledge of whether this 'Seed of Eve,' this 'Son of God' is that heralded avenger of Adam who is fated to conquer Satan."

2112 NORFORD, DON PARRY. Trial by Contrary: A Study of Milton's Later Poems. Doctoral diss., Columbia Univ., 1966. Abs., DA, 28, 1967, 2218-A.

2113 NOVARR, DAVID. Gray Dissimulation: Ford and Milton. PQ, 41, 1962, 500-4.
On John Ford's The Broken Heart, 4, 2, 99, and Paradise Regained, 1, 497-9. "The peculiarly Miltonic overtones which gray dissimulation has in Paradise Regained make it impossible that Milton had Ford in mind."

2114 ORANGE, LINWOOD E. The Role of the Deadly Sins in Paradise Regained. SoQ, 2, 1964, 190-201.
On Milton's use of the Sins to link "the various temptations of the second day and to provide logical transitions from one day to the next."

2115 ORAS, ANTS. Milton's Blank Verse and the Chronology of His Major Poems. SAMLA Studies in Milton. Ed. by J. Max Patrick (Gainesville: Univ. of Florida Press, 1953), pp. 128-97.
Accepts the traditional chronology.

2116 PARISH, JOHN E. An Unrecognized Pun in Paradise Regained. N&Q, N.S., 11, 1964, 337.
On Paradise Regained, 3, 280.

2117 PATRICK, J. MAX. The Influence of Thomas Ellwood upon Milton's Epics. Essays in History and Literature. Presented by Fellows of the Newberry Library to Stanley Pargellis. Ed. by Heinz Bluhm (Chicago: The Newberry Library, 1965), pp. 119-32.
Holds that Miltonists have underestimated Ellwood in intelligence and judgment and suggests that the didacticism and simplicity of Paradise Regained was a result of the Quaker's reaction to Paradise Lost.

2118 PATRIDES, C. A. The Beast with Many Heads: Renaissance Views on the Multitude. SQ, 16, 1965, 241-6.
Quotes Milton (Paradise Regained, 3, 49-50) and others in reference to the hatred of Shakespeare's Coriolanus for the multitude.

2119 PATRIDES, C. A., ed. Milton's Epic Poetry: Essays on Paradise Lost and Paradise Regained. A Peregrine Book. Harmondsworth, Middlesex, England: Penguin Books, 1967. 428pp.
Contributors on Paradise Regained are N. Frye, B. R. Lewalski, and L. L. Martz. Each essay is listed in this section according to author.

2120 PETIT, HERBERT H. The Second Eve in Paradise Regained. PMASAL, 44, 1959, 365-9.
"The First Eve entices Adam to his Fall and the Fall of Mankind. The Second Eve nurtures the Second Adam in his office."

2121 POPE, ELIZABETH M. Paradise Regained: the Tradition and the Poem. Doctoral diss., Johns Hopkins Univ., 1944. Baltimore: Johns Hopkins Univ. Press, 1947. xvi, 135pp. Reprinted, New York: Russell and Russell, 1961.
Chapters: The Gospel Narrative; The Exalted Man; Motivation: God, Christ, and Satan; The Disguise Assumed by Satan; The Triple Equation; The Banqueting Scene; The Temptation of the Tower; and Minor Traditions.
Rev: L. C. Martin, YWES, 191-2; H. F. Fletcher, JEGP, 47, 1948, 203-4;

E. N. S. Thompson, PQ, 27, 1948, 288; B. A. Wright, RES, 25, 1949, 75-83;
E. Sirluck, MP, 46, 1949, 277-9.

2122 RAJAN, B. Jerusalem and Athens: The Temptation of Learning in
Paradise Regained. Th'Upright Heart and Pure. Ed. by Amadeus P.
Fiore, O.F.M. (Pittsburgh and Louvain: Duquesne Univ. Press, 1967),
pp. 61-74.
Suggests that the Christ of Paradise Regained is perfect man and also the
historic Christ, "exhibiting in his responses an emerging awareness of his
destiny." He reject Satan's offer of classical learning because he realizes "that
he is destined to incarnate that wisdom."

2123 RANSOM, JOHN CROWE. God Without Thunder. New York: Harcourt
Brace, 1930. x, 334pp.
Discusses Paradise Regained, pp. 141-5.

2124 REITER, ROBERT E. In Adam's Room: A Study of the Adamic
Typology of Christ in Paradise Regained. Doctoral diss., Univ. of
Michigan, 1964. Abs., DA, 25, 1964, 3581-2.

2125 RICE, WARNER G. Paradise Regained. PMASAL, 22, 1937, 493-503.
Reprinted in Milton: Modern Essays in Criticism. A Galaxy Book. Ed.
by Arthur E. Barker (New York: Oxford Univ. Press, 1965), pp. 416-28.
Discusses the unorthodox manner in which Milton handles his theme, emphasizing Milton's presentation of the intense inner conflict.

2126 RICHARDS, I. A. Paradise Regained. TLS, Sept. 9, 1960, p. 577.
Replies: A. D. Fitton Brown, TLS, Sept. 16, 1960, p. 593; Philip H. Mankin
and D. H. Woodward, TLS, Oct. 7, 1960, p. 645. Richards raises the question
of substituting "less" for "more" in 1, 383. Finds little support.

2127 RICKS, CHRISTOPHER. Over-Emphasis in Paradise Regained. MLN,
76, 1961, 701-4.
Disagrees with L. Martz (ELH, 27, 1960, 223-47) that all of Paradise Regained
has a "muted, chastened style" and suggests that certain passages of over-
emphatic repetition reflect a style of self-indulgent elaboration.

2128 RIFFE, NANCY LEE. Milton on Paradise Regained. N&Q, N.S., 13,
1966, 25.
On the anecdote of Milton's preference for Paradise Regained over Paradise
Lost.

2129 ROBSON, W. W. The Better Fortitude. The Living Milton (London:
Routledge and Kegan Paul, 1960), pp. 124-37.
Concerned with the question whether "the chosen form of Paradise Regained
corresponds in any intimate way to the chosen matter."

2130 SACKTON, ALEXANDER H. Architectonic Structure in Paradise Re-
gained. UTSE, 33, 1954, 33-45.
Examines the architectural metaphor and the resulting literary values in
Paradise Regained.

2131 SAFER, ELAINE. The Use of Cross Reference to Develop Polarities in
Paradise Lost and Paradise Regained. Doctoral diss., Western Reserve
Univ., 1966. Abs., DA, 28, 1967, 2221-A.

2132 SAMAHA, EDWARD E., JR. The Essential Conflict: Milton's Treatment of Light and Dark as it Culminates in Paradise Regained. Doctoral diss., Tulane Univ., 1967. Abs., DA, 28, 1968, 2695-A-6-A. 220pp.

2133 SAMUEL, IRENE. Milton on Learning and Wisdom. PMLA, 64, 1949, 708-23.
In Paradise Lost and Paradise Regained Milton expands, not retracts, what he has said earlier about studies.

2134 SCHULTZ, HOWARD. Christ and Antichrist in Paradise Regained. PMLA, 67, 1952, 790-808.
Insists that the poem was intended to define the True Church and the True Kingdom and that it is an antiprelatical work.

2135 ------. A Fairer Paradise? Some Recent Studies of Paradise Regained. ELH, 32, 1965, 275-302.
Surveys recent criticism and notes shifts of emphasis regarding some problems of the poem.

2136 SCOTT-CRAIG, T. S. K. Miltonic Tragedy and Christian Vision. The Tragic Vision and the Christian Faith. Ed. by Nathan A. Scott, Jr. (New York: Association Press, 1957), pp. 99-122.
Argues against Johnson and holds that in Paradise Lost and Paradise Regained "we have almost ideal examples of tragic vision illuminated by biblical faith, and of biblical faith transforming the tragic vision of life."

2137 SEAMAN, JOHN E. The Chivalric Cast of Milton's Epic Hero. ES, 49, 1968, 97-107.
In Paradise Lost and Paradise Regained. Discusses Christ in relation to the Homeric hero. "Christ is within the tradition of the young hero of unknown or unproved origin who must fulfill the prophecies about his great promise."

2138 SENSABAUGH, GEORGE F. Milton on Learning. SP, 43, 1946, 258-72.
"Why Milton, in the period of his greatest poetic activity, should renounce intellectual curiosity and belittle his old classic friends calls for an investigation of the forces which helped shape his thought, not only for what such an inquiry might tell of his changed educational views but also for what it might reveal about the state of his mind when he wrote Paradise Lost and Paradise Regained."

2139 SEWELL, ELIZABETH. The Human Metaphor. Notre Dame: Univ. of Notre Dame Press, 1964. 212pp.
Considers, i.a., Paradise Lost, Paradise Regained, and Samson Agonistes in Chapter 4, Individual Life as Myth: The Figure of Suffering and Effort, pp. 114-55.

2140 SHAFER, ROBERT. Milton and Pindar. TLS, Dec. 3, 1931, p. 982.
On Paradise Regained (4, 563-5) and the Ninth Pythian Ode. Cites the existence in the Harvard Library of the Benedictus edition (1620) of Pindar, with marginalia and index in Milton's own hand, as evidence that Milton knew Pindar. See also L. R. Farnell, TLS, Oct. 1, 1931, p. 754.

2141 SHAWCROSS, JOHN T. The Chronology of Milton's Major Poems. PMLA, 76, 1961, 345-58.
Suggests that Paradise Regained "seems to lie near but somewhat later than

Samson Agonistes and, except for late work, before Paradise Lost as it now stands."

2142 SIMS, JAMES H. The Use of the Bible in Milton's Epic Poems. Doctoral diss., Univ. of Florida, 1959. Published as The Bible in Milton's Epics. Gainesville: Univ. of Florida Press, 1962. 283pp.
"Altogether, 1364 individual citations to Scripture have been recorded by Milton's editors from Hume to Hughes. Yet none of the editors, commentators, or scholars have attempted to bring together and systematize Milton's use of the Bible in his major poems; this is the task I have undertaken here, and I have, in the process, added 816 Biblical citations to particular lines of the two epics."

2143 STEADMAN, JOHN M. Felicity and End in Renaissance Epic and Ethics. JHI, 23, 1962, 117-32.
Sees the idea of beatitude as the cornerstone of Milton's argument and fable in Paradise Lost and Paradise Regained.

2144 ------. Like Turbulencies: the Tempest of Paradise Regained as Adversity Symbol. MP, 59, 1961, 81-8. Reprinted in revised form in Milton's Epic Characters: Image and Idol (Chapel Hill: Univ. of North Carolina Press, 1968), pp. 90-101.
Discusses "the most obvious difference between the storm scene and the preceding temptation—the conventional antithesis between trial by prosperity and trial by adversity" as "essential for a proper understanding of Satan's rhetoric, of the symbolism of the tempest episode, and of the relationship of this scene to epic tradition."

2145 ------. Paradise Regained: Moral Dialectic and the Pattern of Rejection. UTQ, 31, 1962, 416-30. Reprinted in revised form in Milton's Epic Characters: Image and Idol (Chapel Hill: Univ. of North Carolina Press, 1968), pp. 123-36.
"...I shall consider two aspects of the knowledge-rejection pattern in this epic: its relation to the tradition of heroic judgment...and the ethical definition of the true and highest good through a method of systematic negation...."

2146 ------. Peripeteia in Milton's Epic Fable. Anglia, 81, 1963, 429-52.
In the major poems Milton makes use of the Aristotelian concept of peripeteia to emphasize the moral process of God's law.

2147 ------. The Suffering Servant and Milton's Heroic Norm. HTR, 54, 1961, 29-43.
In Paradise Lost and Paradise Regained "Milton modelled his exemplary hero not on any ideal extrinsic to the Biblical Messiah, but on the character of the historic Christ as revealed in the Scriptures and interpreted by Protestant theologians."

2148 ------. The Tree of Life Symbolism in Paradise Regain'd. RES, N.S., 11, 1960, 384-91. Reprinted in revised form in Milton's Epic Characters: Image and Idol (Chapel Hill: Univ. of North Carolina Press, 1968), pp. 82-9.
"...the primary significance of Christ's celestial banquet is largely based on conventional Renaissance interpretations of the arbor vitae."

2149 STEIN, ARNOLD. Heroic Knowledge: An Interpretation of Paradise Regained and Samson Agonistes. Minneapolis: Univ. of Minnesota Press; London: Oxford Univ. Press, 1957; Hamden, Conn.: Archon Books, 1965. xi, 237pp.
Paradise Regained, pp. 3-134.
Rev: Agnes M. C. Latham, YWES, 187; T. S. K Scott-Craig, Christian Century, 75, 1957, 669; Louis L. Martz, YR, N.S., 47, 1957, 259; SCN, 16, 1958, 7; William R. Parker, JEGP, 57, 1958, 133-4; Davis P. Harding, CE, 20, 1958, 103; Howard Sargeant, English, 12, 1958, 63-4; Frank Kermode, MLR, 53, 1958, 566-7; Allan Gilbert, SAQ, 57, 1958, 399-400; K. M. Leas, RES, 10, 1959, 415-7; Jackson I. Cope, JA, 17, 1959, 402-3; Bruce Cutler, Poetry, Mar., 1959, pp. 404-8; Edward M. Clark, BA, 33, 1959, 220.

2150 ------. The Kingdoms of the World: Paradise Regained. ELH, 23, 1956, 112-26. Reprinted in Heroic Knowledge (1957), above.

2151 STROUP, THOMAS B. Religious Rite and Ceremony in Milton's Poetry. Lexington: Univ. of Kentucky Press, 1968. ix, 83pp.
Contains a chapter on Paradise Regained, pp. 48-54.

2152 SUNDELL, ROGER HENRY. Internal Commentary in the Major Poems of John Milton. Doctoral diss., Washington Univ., 1966. Abs., DA, 26, 1966, 6701.

2153 SVENDSEN, KESTER. Milton's Aerie Microscope. MLN, 64, 1949, 525-7.
On Paradise Regained, 4, 55-60.

2154 TAMAKI, ISHITARO. A Commentary on Milton's Paradise Regained. Kwansai Univ. Literary Review, 6, 1956.

2155 TAYLOR, DICK, JR. The Storm Scene in Paradise Regained: a Reinterpretation. UTQ, 24, 1955, 359-76.
Sees the scene not as a desperate move by Satan but as a forceful temptation shrewdly devised and carried out.

2156 TENNISSEN, JOHN JAMES. Of Patience and Heroic Martyrdom: The Book of Job and Milton's Conception of Patient Suffering in Paradise Regained and Samson Agonistes. Doctoral diss., The Univ. of Rochester, 1967. Abs., DA, 28, 1967, 1797-A.

2157 THOMAS, CORAMAE. The Classification of Paradise Regained as Epic. Doctoral diss., Texas Christian Univ., 1966.

2158 TILLYARD, E. M. W. The Christ of Paradise Regained and the Renaissance Heroic Tradition. SP, 36, 1939, 247-52. Reprinted in Studies in Milton (London: Chatto and Windus, 1951), pp. 100-6.
Agrees with Hughes with some qualifications.

2159 TUNG, MASON. The Patterns of Temptation in Paradise Regained. SCN, 24, No. 4, 1966, item 2.
There are two interweaving patterns of temptation in Paradise Regained, revealed by Satan's changing motivations in testing Jesus.

2160 WEISMILLER, EDWARD R. The Versification of Paradise Lost and Paradise Regained: A Study of Movement and Structure in Milton's

Nondramatic Blank Verse. Doctoral diss., Merton College, Oxford, 1951.

2161 WENZL, JOSEF. Paradise Regained und seine Stellung innerhalb der geistigen Entwicklung Miltons. Doctoral diss., Wien, 1940. 148pp.

2162 WEST, ROBERT H. Milton's Sons of God. MLN, 65, 1950, 187-91.
      On Paradise Regained, 2, 178-81.

2163 WHITING, GEORGE W. Christ's Miraculous Fast. MLN, 66, 1951, 12-6.
      Emphasizes the divine nature of the Christ of Paradise Regained.

2164 ------. Milton's Taprobane (Paradise Regained IV, 75). RES, 13, 1937, 209-12.
      Identifies Taprobane as Sumatra.

2165 ------. Syene and Meroe. N&Q, N.S., 5, 1958, 200-1.
      On the identity of Syene and Meroe in Paradise Regained, 4, 70-71.

2166 WIDMER, KINGSLEY. The Iconography of Renunciation: the Miltonic Simile. ELH, 25, 1958, 258-69. Reprinted in revised form in Milton's Epic Poetry: Essays on Paradise Lost and Paradise Regained. Ed. by C. A. Patrides (Harmondsworth: Penguin Books, 1967), pp. 121-31.
      On Paradise Lost and Paradise Regained. "...a subtle and dialectical reading of the Miltonic texture and tone suggests a fascinating and shocking master simile: the world as evil, and virtue as renunciation."

2167 WILKENFELD, ROGER B. Act and Emblem: A Study of Narrative and Dramatic Patterns in Three Poems by John Milton. Doctoral diss., Univ. of Rochester, 1964. Abs., DA, 25, 1964, 2969.
      Considers Comus, Samson Agonistes, and Paradise Regained.

2168 ------. Theoretics or Polemics? Milton Criticism and the Dramatic Axiom. PMLA, 82, 1967, 505-15.
      Surveys criticism of Comus, Samson Agonistes, and Paradise Regained and feels that much of it is unhealthy because the vocally and modally dramatic remains confused.

2169 WILKES, G. A. Paradise Regained and the Conventions of the Sacred Epic. ES, 44, 1963, 35-8.
      Examines the conventions and the literary effects of the poem in relation to the minor sacred epic form.

2170 WILLIAMSON, GEORGE. Plot in Paradise Regained. Milton and Others (Chicago: Univ. of Chicago Press; London: Faber and Faber, 1965), pp. 66-84.
      A summary of each book of Paradise Regained, with the conclusion that this poem builds to divine sanction of its protagonist.

2171 WOLFE, DON M. The Role of Milton's Christ. SR, 51, 1943, 467-75.
      Argues that Milton's own principles and prejudices are reflected in the Christ of Paradise Regained.

2172 WOODHOUSE, A. S. P. Theme and Pattern in Paradise Regained. UTQ, 25, 1956, 167-82.
      Pattern in Paradise Regained provides an opportunity for the interweaving

of two themes—the primary theme of Christ the second Adam and the secondary theme of the Spirit who led him into the desert.

2173 WRIGHT, B. A. Milton's Use of the Word Waft. N&Q, N.S., 5, 1958, 341.
Notes consistent usage in Paradise Lost, 2, 1041-2; 3, 521; 12, 435; Paradise Regained 1, 103-4, and Lycidas 164.

2174 ------. Note on Milton's Shook the Arsenal. N&Q, N.S., 5, 1958, 199-200.
On Paradise Regained, 4, 267-71.

2175 ZWICKY, LAURIE B. Kairos in Paradise Regained: The Divine Plan. ELH, 31, 1964, 271-7.
On the theme of divinely appointed time in Paradise Regained.

SAMSON AGONISTES

2176 ALLEN, DON CAMERON. The Harmonious Vision: Studies in Milton's Poetry. Baltimore: Johns Hopkins Univ. Press, 1954.
Contains a chapter on Samson Agonistes.

2177 ARTHOS, JOHN. Milton and the Italian Cities. London: Bowes and Bowes, 1968. xi, 224pp.
Part 2: Milton and Monteverdi, a consideration of music and drama in Italy in relation to Samson Agonistes.

2178 BEERBOHM, SIR MAX. Agonising Samson. Around Theatres (London: British Book Centre, 1953), pp. 527-31.
A reprint of remarks on a performance of Samson Agonistes, a review published on Dec. 19, 1908. See also Beerbohm on Agonizing Samson, MN, 1, 1967, 57.

2179 BEUM, ROBERT. The Rhyme in Samson Agonistes. TSLL, 4, 1962, 177-82.
"Milton wanted a verse whose climaxes would stand out distinctly, and a chorus that could be both actor and serene observer. Rhyme helped solve the problem."

2180 BOUGHNER, DANIEL C. Milton's Harapha and Renaissance Comedy. ELH, 11, 1944, 297-306.
Harapha and his forebears in Italian Renaissance comedy.

2181 BOWRA, SIR CECIL M. Samson Agonistes. Inspiration and Poetry (London: Macmillan, 1955), pp. 112-29.
"In Samson Milton has rediscovered his taste for action and abandoned the quietism of Paradise Regained."

2182 BROADBENT, J. B. Milton: Comus and Samson Agonistes. Studies in English Literature Series, No. 1. Ed. by David Daiches. London: Edward Arnold, 1961. Published also in Barron's Studies in English Literature, Great Neck, New York: Barron's Educational Series, 1961. 63pp.
Introduction and commentary designed for undergraduates.
Rev: R. P. Draper, CritQ, 3, 1961, 275-7; F. N. Lees, DUJ, 24, 1963, 81.

2183 BUCHANAN, EDITH. The Italian Neo-Senecan Background of Samson Agonistes. Doctoral diss., Duke Univ., 1952.

2184 BURKE, KENNETH. The Imagery of Killing. HudR, 1, 1948, 151-67.
In Samson Agonistes Milton unites the images of the suicide and of the warlike death.

2185 CAREY, JOHN. Sea, Snake, Flower, and Flame in Samson Agonistes. MLR, 62, 1967, 395-9.
"In Samson Agonistes ... the imagery does not merely reinforce the drama's triumphant upward arc. On the contrary, it contributes meanings which threaten to invert this arc and bring the weak-minded, vengeful hero to the

level of Dalila and the Philistines. In this way it makes a major contribution to the moral maturity of the work."

2186 CARSON, BARBARA HARRELL. Milton's Samson as Parvas Sol. ELN, 5, 1968, 171-6.
Shows that Milton was aware of Samson's solar associations and suggests he may have used them as the basis for the light and dark imagery in Samson Agonistes.

2187 CHAMBERS, A. B. Wisdom and Fortitude in Samson Agonistes. PMLA, 78, 1963, 315-20.
"Other patterns, as no one would deny, are also at work within the poem, but none, I think, at once so fundamental and so inclusive as sapientia et fortitudo."

2188 CLARE, SISTER MIRIAM. Samson Agonistes: A Study in Contrast. New York: Pageant Press, 1964. 153pp.
Defines antithesis and other figures of contrast, illustrates how they are used in Samson Agonistes, and considers their significance in character and episode.
Rev: Ann Gossman, JEGP, 64, 1965, 584-6.

2189 COX, LEE SHERIDAN. The 'Ev'ning Dragon' in Samson Agonistes: A Reappraisal. MLN, 76, 1961, 577-84.
"Milton uses the term Dragon to symbolize vision which gives birth to power; but he uses the term also to symbolize reborn power.... Later Milton couples Dragon with Eagle and again as reborn power with the phoenix."

2190 ------. Natural Science and Figurative Design in Samson Agonistes. ELH, 35, 1968, 51-74.
"A close study of Milton's imagery reveals a careful craftsman, whose emphasis is on the vision, not the sound, upon the idea, not the word. Beneath the smooth surface rhetoric of his poetry lies a complex structure of metaphor and symbol, a figurative comment which illuminates Samson's struggle and victory, and which, in itself, constitutes a definitive philosophic comment on everyman's conduct and life."

2191 ------. Structural and Thematic Imagery in Samson Agonistes and Paradise Regained. Doctoral diss., Indiana Univ., 1962. Abs., DA, 23, 1963, 4342.

2192 CRUMP, GALBRAITH M., ed. Twentieth Century Interpretations of Samson Agonistes: A Collection of Critical Essays. Englewood Cliffs, N.J.: Prentice-Hall, Inc., 1968. viii, 120pp.
Part One contains reprints of essays by J. H. Hanford, W. R. Parker, F. M. Krouse, D. C. Allen, Arnold Stein, A. E. Barker, and W. G. Madsen. Part Two contains reprints of briefer studies by T. J. B. Spencer, E. M. W. Tillyard, Frank Kermode, Arnold Stein, J. M. Steadman, and Northrop Frye.
Rev: MN, 2, 1968, 31-2.

2193 DANIELLS, ROY. Milton, Mannerism and Baroque. Toronto: Univ. of Toronto Press, 1963. 229pp.
A search for analogies between Milton's art and the other arts. Contains a chapter on Samson Agonistes.

2194 DAVIES, H. NEVILLE. Dryden's All for Love and Thomas May's The
      Tragedie of Cleopatra Queen of Egypt. N&Q, N.S., 12, 1965, 139-44.
          "Samson Agonistes which Dryden apparently had in mind as a dramatic
          model has had a more obvious effect on the plot and language of the play."

2195 DAWSON, S. W., and A. J. SMITH. Two Points of View: Samson
      Agonistes. AWR, 14, 1964-65, 92-101.
          Dawson voices a dislike for the rhetoric and "pathos and bitterness of defeat"
          in Samson Agonistes; Smith calls the poem a consummation of achieved
          artistry.

2196 DURLING, DWIGHT. Coghill's Samson Agonistes at Oxford. SCN, 9,
      1951, 63.
          On a presentation at Oxford in July, 1951.

2197 EBBS, JOHN DALE. Milton's Treatment of Poetic Justice in Samson
      Agonistes. MLQ, 22, 1961, 377-89.
          Surveys recent criticism of Samson and shows that Milton's treatment of
          poetic justice—or Providence—is the primary means by which he teaches the
          lesson in the poem.

2198 ELLIS-FERMOR, UNA. Samson Agonistes and Religious Drama. The
      Frontiers of Drama (London: Methuen, 1945), pp. 17-33.
          Rev: Harley Granville-Barker, RES, 22, 1946, 144-7; Paul Dombey, NSN,
          Jan. 5, 1946, pp. 13-4; Elizabeth Sweeting, MLR, 41, 1946, 324-6; Alwyn
          Andrew, LL, 48, 1946, 130-40.

2199 EMERSON, EVERETT H. Redgrave's Samson. SCN, 24, No. 1, 1966,
      item 3.
          A review of Michael Redgrave's production of Samson Agonistes, during the
          summer of 1965, at Guilford, near London.

2200 EMPSON, WILLIAM. A Defense of Delilah. SR, 68, 1960, 240-55.
          The case for Delilah reveals Milton's love "of adjudicating high and subtle
          points of conscience." "...he has labored to describe her as a high-minded
          great lady, wholly committed to the values of 'the world.'"

2201 ------. Milton's God. London: Chatto and Windus, 1961; Norfolk, Con-
      necticut: New Directions, 1961. 280pp. Revised Edition: London: Chatto
      and Windus, 1965.
          Contains his defense of Dalila, above.

2202 EPSTEIN, E. L., and T. HAWKES. Linguistics and English Prosody.
      Studies in Linguistics: Occasional Papers, 7. Buffalo: Buffalo Univ.
      Press, 1959. 50pp.
          Contains analysis of the prosody of Samson Agonistes, 11. 930-50, pp. 23-9.

2203 FELL, KENNETH. From Myth to Martyrdom: Towards a View of Mil-
      ton's Samson Agonistes. ES, 34, 1953, 145-55.
          On the martyrdom in Samson Agonistes and in Eliot's Murder in the
          Cathedral.

2204 FERRY, ANNE DAVIDSON. Milton and the Miltonic Dryden. Cam-
      bridge: Harvard Univ. Press, 1968. 238pp.
          Part Two: Samson Agonistes and All for Love, pp. 127-218. Shows that al-
          though the two plays present different visions, there are "so many parallel

notions and stylistic devices that the two dramas appear to express very similar attitudes."

2205 FIELDS, ALBERT W. Milton and Self-knowledge. PMLA, 83, 1968, 392-9.
Examines Milton's concept of self-knowledge as seen in Paradise Lost, Paradise Regained, and Samson Agonistes, and compares Milton's view with other Classical and Christian ideas of self-knowledge.

2206 FINNEY, GRETCHEN L. Chorus in Samson Agonistes. PMLA, 58, 1943, 649-64. Reprinted in Musical Backgrounds for English Literature (New Brunswick: Rutgers Univ. Press, 1962), pp. 220-37.
On Samson Agonistes and the Italian dramatic background.

2207 ------. Musical Backgrounds for English Literature, 1580-1650. New Brunswick: Rutgers Univ. Press, 1962. xiii, 292pp.
Relevant chapters: Speculative Musical Imagery in Milton's Poems, pp. 161-74; Comus: Dramma per Musica, pp. 175-94; A Musical Background for Lycidas, pp. 195-219; Chorus in Samson Agonistes, pp. 220-37.

2208 FLATTER, RICHARD. Samson Agonistes and Milton. TLS, Aug. 7, 1948, p. 443.
Replies by F. F. Farnham-Flower and Maurice Kelley, Aug. 21, 1948, p. 471; rejoinder by Flatter, Sept. 4, 1948, p. 499. Flatter believes that the last lines of Samson Agonistes refer to the projected publication of De Doctrina Christiana; Farnham-Flower and Kelley present contradictory evidence.

2209 FOGEL, EPHIM G. Milton and Sir Philip Sidney's Arcadia. N&Q, 196, 1951, 115-7.
The Leonatus episode is the source of the first lines in Samson Agonistes. Milton's use of the passage illustrates his method of composition.

2210 FOGLE, FRENCH. The Action of Samson Agonistes. Essays in American and English Literature Presented to Bruce Robert McElderry, Jr. Ed. by Max F. Schulz (Athens: Ohio Univ. Press, 1967), pp. 177-96.
Calls for recognition of the "divine role in the process of regeneration" rather than the current emphasis on Samson's psychological development toward self-education.

2211 FOX, ROBERT C. Vida and Samson Agonistes. N&Q, N.S., 6, 1959, 370-2.
Suggests Marco Girolamo Vida's the Christiad, 11. 304-334, as a possible source for 11. 710-724 of Samson Agonistes.

2212 FREEDMAN, MORRIS. All for Love and Samson Agonistes. N&Q, N.S., 3, 1956, 514-7.
"I should like to suggest ... that the verbal, thematic, and critical connections between All for Love and Samson are, in sum, so substantial as to indicate that Dryden not only knew Milton well but was modifying Shakespeare through him."

2213 FRISSELL, HARRY L. Milton's Art of Logic and Ramist Logic in the Major Poems. Doctoral diss., Vanderbilt Univ., 1951. Abs., Bulletin of Vanderbilt Univ., 51, 1951, 22-3. Ann Arbor: UM, 1952. 250pp.

2214 GALLAND, RENÉ. Milton et Buchanan. RA-A, 13, 1936, 326-33.
A study of the influence of George Buchanan's Latin tragedy, Baptistes, Sive Calumnia (1577), on Samson Agonistes.

2215 GHOSH, P. C. Samson Agonistes. Bulletin of the Department of English, Univ. of Calcutta, 3, Nos. 3 & 4, 1962.

2216 GILBERT, ALLAN H. Is Samson Agonistes Unfinished? PQ, 28, 1949, 98-106.
Holds that Samson Agonistes is an earlier work which Milton never found time to revise.

2217 GOHN, ERNEST S. The Christian Ethic of Paradise Lost and Samson Agonistes. SN, 34, 1962, 243-68.
"The purpose of this paper is to show that throughout his work, and particularly in Paradise Lost and Samson Agonistes, Milton never lost sight of the didactic aim outlined in his early treatise (Reason of Church Government) .... This paper also purports to demonstrate that the doctrinal ends of Milton's poems become clearer when viewed against a background of Renaissance ethical theory."

2218 GOSSMAN, ANN. Milton's Samson as the Tragic Hero Purified by Trial. JEGP, 61, 1962, 528-41.
Milton uses "the classical model for treating the hero's character ... but has transformed it through the critical ethical evaluation."

2219 ------. Ransom in Samson Agonistes. RN, 13, 1960, 11-5.
Manoa's attempt to ransom Samson has two classical analogues: Crito's attempt to ransom Socrates and King Priam's ransom of the dead Hector.

2220 ------. Samson, Job and the Exercise of Saints. ES, 45, 1964, 212-24.
Discusses "the relation of Samson Agonistes to the Book of Job."

2221 ------. The Synthesis of Hebraism and Hellenism in Milton's Samson Agonistes. Doctoral diss., Rice Univ., 1957.

2222 GREENE, DONALD. The Sin of Pride: A Sketch for a Literary Exploration. NMQ, 34, Spring, 1964, 8-30.
Sees Samson Agonistes as an example of self-psychoanalysis in literature and cites Satan and Eve as examples of neurotic psychology.

2223 GRENANDER, M. E. Samson's Middle: Aristotle and Dr. Johnson. UTQ, 24, 1955, 377-89.
An examination of Aristotelian criteria applicable to Samson Agonistes in light of Johnson's charges against the work.

2224 GRIERSON, H. J. C. A Note upon the Samson Agonistes of John Milton and Sampson of Heilige Wraeck by Joost van den Vondel. Mélanges d'histoire littéraire générale . . . offerts à Fernand Baldensperger (Paris: Champion, 1930), 1, 332-9. Reprinted in Essays and Addresses (London: Chatto and Windus, 1940), pp. 55-64.

2225 GRIFFIN, ERNEST G. The Dramatic Chorus in English Literary Theory and Practice. Doctoral diss., Columbia Univ., 1959. Abs., DA, 20, 1960, 3726-7.
Chapter Two contains a discussion of the chorus in Samson Agonistes.

2226 HAMBURGER, MICHAEL. The Sublime Art: Notes on Milton and Hölderlin. The Living Milton (London: Routledge and Kegan Paul, 1960), pp. 141-61.
A comparison of Holderlin's work and Milton's Samson Agonistes.

2227 HANFORD, JAMES HOLLY. Samson Agonistes and Milton in Old Age. Studies in Shakespeare, Milton, and Donne (New York: Haskell House, 1964), pp. 165-90. Published also in John Milton, Poet and Humanist (Cleveland: Western Reserve Univ. Press, 1966), pp. 264-86.
 Reprints of Stevens' No. 1182, published in 1925. "A significant unifying of materials that shows Milton's intellectual and spiritual changes, particularly the enunciation through Samson of his final acceptances of divine law" (Stevens' annotation).

2228 HARRIS, WILLIAM O. Despair and Patience as the Truest Fortitude in Samson Agonistes. ELH, 30, 1963, 107-20.
 Two choral passages in Samson Agonistes (652-666 and 1268-1296) reflect the doctrinal "concept of Patience as the highest manifestation of Fortitude."

2229 HILL, R. F. Samson Agonistes. TT, April 10, 1963, p. 28.
 "Intellect and character dominate Samson Agonistes, Milton's testament to an erring generation."

2230 HONE, RALPH E. ed. John Milton's Samson Agonistes: The Poem and Materials for Analysis. San Francisco: Chandler Publishing Company, 1966. viii, 284pp.
 A controlled research book. Includes the text of Masson's edition of Samson Agonistes, several sources, and selected criticism of S. Johnson, R. Cumberland, A. W. Verity, J. H. Hanford, U. Ellis-Fermor, W. R. Parker, and E. Sirluck.

2231 HUNTLEY, JOHN. A Revaluation of the Chorus' Role in Milton's Samson Agonistes. MP, 64, 1966, 132-45.
 Argues that "Milton introduces the chorus in a spiritual condition resembling Samson's darkness of mind and paralysis of will" and that the chorus undergoes a change during the play.

2232 HYMAN, LAWRENCE W. Milton's Samson and the Modern Reader. CE, 28, 1966, 39-43.
 Holds that blindness must be interpreted as more than physical, "as a darkness that shrouds God's ways and that this view will broaden the modern reader's view of the poem."

2232A KAUFMANN, R. J. Bruising the Serpent: Milton as a Tragic Poet. Centennial Review, 11, 1967, 371-86.
 Compares Milton's Samson with Oedipus and Job and finds Samson Agonistes lacking as tragedy. Rather, it is "a somber idyl of spiritual self-vindication."

2233 KELLEY, MAURICE. Samson Agonistes and Milton. TLS, Aug. 21, 1948, p. 471.
 On Samson Agonistes, 1423-6.

2234 KERMODE, FRANK. Samson Agonistes and Hebrew Prosody. DUJ, 14, 1953, 59-63.
 On Milton's imitation of Hebrew lyric measures and rhymes.

2235 KIRKCONNELL, WATSON. That Invincible Samson: The Theme of Samson Agonistes in World Literature with Translations of the Major Analogues. Toronto: Univ. of Toronto Press, 1964. viii, 218pp.
 "My purpose...is to go back in every instance to primary sources and to examine all treatments of Milton's theme in all languages for their intrinsic

interest and merit." Contents: Part One: Translations of Analogues by
Hieronymus Zieglerus, Marcus Andreas Wunstius, Theodorus Rhodius, Vin-
cenzo Giattini, and Joost van den Vondel. Part Two: Descriptive Catalogue
(pp. 145-215) containing brief comments on the significance of more than a
hundred analogues.
Rev. James H. Sims, SCN, 23, 1965, 1-2; Ants Oras, MP, 64, 1966, 77-9.

2236 ------. Six Sixteenth-Century Forerunners of Milton's Samson Agonistes.
TRSC, 3rd Series, 43, 1949, 73-85.
Analogues.

2237 KRANIDAS, THOMAS. Dalila's Role in Samson Agonistes. SEL, 6, 1966,
125-37.
An examination of Dalila for her changeableness, virtuosity, and manipula-
tion of fact.

2238 ------. Milton and the Author of Christ Suffering. N&Q, N.S., 15,
1968, 99.
"It is curious that Milton either did not know of the question [of Gregory
Nazianzen's authorship of the play] or chose to ignore it in the Preface to
Samson Agonistes."

2239 KROUSE, F. MICHAEL. Milton's Samson and the Christian Tradition.
Doctoral diss., Johns Hopkins Univ., 1946. Princeton: Princeton Univ.
Press for the Univ. of Cincinnati, 1949. Reprinted, Hamden, Con-
necticut: Shoestring Press, 1963. viii, 159pp.
Chapters: Samson Agonistes and the Critics, The Foundations of the Samson
Tradition, The Samson of the Patristic Period, The Samson of the Scholastic
Period, The Samson Tradition in the Renaissance, and Milton's Samson and
the Tradition.
Rev: L. C. Martin, YWES, 167-8; Moses Hadas, Class. Week., 43, 1949, 28;
H. F. Fletcher, JEGP, 49, 1950, 115-7; E. Sirluck, MP, 48, 1950, 70-2; Arthur
Barker, PQ, 29, 1950, 93-4; A. H. Gilbert, SAQ, 49, 1950, 254-5; A. Williams,
Spect, 25, 1950, 139-41; A. S. P. Woodhouse, MLN, 66, 1951, 116-8; C. T.
Harrison, SR, 59, 1951, 699; E. L. Allen, RES, 2, 1951, 281-2; William R.
Parker, MLQ, 13, 1952, 103-5.

2240 LANDY, MARCIA K. Character Portrayal in Samson Agonistes. TSLL,
7, 1965, 239-53.
On the "artistic reality" of the characters.

2241 ------. Of Highest Wisdom: A Study of John Milton's Samson Agonistes
as a Dramatization of Christian Conversion. Doctoral diss., Univ. of
Rochester, 1962. Abs., DA, 23, 1963, 3354.

2242 ------. Tercentenary Celebration of Paradise Lost. SCN, 26, 1968, 31-3.
At the Univ. of Pittsburgh. Contains, i. a., a summary of Louis L. Martz's
Tragic Transformation in Samson Agonistes.

2243 LAWRY, JON S. The Shadow of Heaven: Matter and Stance in Milton's
Poetry. Ithaca: Cornell Univ. Press, 1968. xv, 416pp.
See Chapter 6: A Person Rais'd: Election and Redemption in Samson
Agonistes, pp. 346-97.

2244 LE COMTE, EDWARD S. Samson Agonistes and Aureng-Zebe. EA, 2,
1958, 18-22.

Holds that Dryden and other late seventeenth-century writers made use of Milton's ideas on marriage in their sentimental comedies.

2245 LEMAY, J. A. LEO. Jonson and Milton: Two Influences in Oakes's Elegie. NEQ, 38, 1965, 90-2.
Insists that diction and imagery in Oakes's poem (1677) were borrowed from Samson Agonistes.

2246 LEWALSKI, BARBARA KIEFER. The Ship-Tempest Imagery in Samson Agonistes. N&Q, N.S., 6, 1959, 372-3.
Suggests a careful integration of the ship simile in Samson Agonistes "into a larger pattern of ship and tempest imagery closely related to the basic themes of the poem."

2247 LITTLE, MARGUERITE. Some Italian Elements in the Choral Practice of Samson Agonistes. Doctoral diss., Univ. of Illinois, 1946. Abs., Urbana: Univ. of Illinois Press, 1946.

2248 LONG, ANNE BOWERS. The Relations Between Classical and Biblical Allusions in Milton's Later Poems. Doctoral diss., Univ. of Illinois, 1967. Abs., DA, 28, 1968, 5022-A. 382pp.

2249 LYNCH, JAMES J. Evil Communications. N&Q, N.S., 3, 1956, 477.
Points out that neither Fielding nor Milton (in his Preface to Samson Agonistes) attributes the phrase to Menander, its original author.

2250 MADSEN, WILLIAM G. From Shadowy Types to Truth. The Lyric and Dramatic Milton. Ed. by Joseph H. Summers (New York and London: Columbia Univ. Press, 1965), pp. 95-114. Reprinted, Milton: Modern Judgements, ed. by Alan Rudrum (London: Macmillan, 1968), pp. 219-32.
Discusses the typology accepted in Milton's day and suggests that Samson Agonistes is both Christian and non-Christian and that it may be regarded as a companion piece to Paradise Regained.

2252 MAHOOD, MOLLY MAUREEN. Milton's Heroes. Poetry and Humanism (New Haven: Yale Univ. Press; London: Jonathan Cape, 1950), pp. 207-51. Reprinted, Port Washington, N.Y.: Kennikat Press, 1967; Milton: Modern Judgements, ed. by Alan Rudrum (London: MacMillan, 1968), pp. 233-69.
On Satan and Samson as contrasting figures.

2253 MARILLA, ESMOND L. Samson Agonistes: An Interpretation. SN, 29, 1957, 67-76. Reprinted in Milton and Modern Man: Selected Essays (University, Alabama: Univ. of Alabama Press, 1968), pp. 68-77.
Shows that the poem embodies a unification of the basic arguments in Paradise Lost and Paradise Regained.

2254 MATHIES GEB. DORNER, MARIA ELIZABETH. Untersuchungen zu Miltons Samson Agonistes. Doctoral diss., Hamburg, 1949. 271pp.

2255 MAXWELL, J. C. Milton's Knowledge of Aeschylus: the Argument from Parallel Passages. RES, N.S., 3, 1952, 366-71.
Conclusions are negative.

2256 ------. Milton's Samson and Sophocles' Heracles. PQ, 33, 1954, 90-1.
Agrees with W. R. Parker on the influence of Sophocles and shows how Milton "transposed the riddling oracle into Christian (or Hebraic) terms by means of the notion of divine inscrutability."

2257 McCALL, LOIS G. Imagery and Symbolism in Samson Agonistes. Master's thesis, Mt. Holyoke College, 1949.

2258 McDAVID, RAVEN I., JR. Samson Agonistes 1096: a Re-examination. PQ, 33, 1954, 86-9.
Favors "wish" instead of "with."

2259 McMANAWAY, JAMES G. Milton and Harrington. TLS, Feb. 20, 1937, p. 131.
Cf. G. M. Young, TLS, Jan. 9, 1937, p. 28. On the ship-woman image.

2260 MITCHELL, CHARLES. Dalila's Return: The Importance of Pardon. CE, 26, 1965, 614-20.
Holds that Dalila seeks Samson's pardon so that she may have fame rather than infamy and that Samson learns through her false seeking of pardon that he deserves genuine pardon from God.

2261 MOAG, JOSEPH STEWART. Traditional Patterns of Dialogue and Debate in Milton's Poetry. Doctoral diss., Northwestern Univ., 1964. Abs., DA, 25, 1965, 6598-9.

2262 MORGAN, CARLA S. Samson, the Tragic Hero. Nota Bene, 3, 1960, 47-52.

2263 MOSS, LEONARD. The Rhetorical Style of Samson Agonistes. MP, 62, 1965, 296-301.
Holds that Milton utilizes Roman and Greek rhetorical patterns to emphasize the dramatic content of Samson Agonistes.

2264 MUELLER, MARTIN. Pathos and Katharsis in Samson Agonistes. ELH, 31, 1964, 156-74.
Applies the critical terms of Aristotle's Poetics to Samson Agonistes and argues that the crucial problem of the play lies "in its pathos, the deed of violence which constitutes the catastrophe."

2265 MULDROW, GEORGE McMURRY. The Theme of Man's Restoration in Milton's Later Poetry. Doctoral diss., Stanford Univ., 1960. Abs., DA, 21, 1960, 1193.

2266 NAKAGIRI, NOBUYA. Samson Agonistes: A Study in Milton. Meiji Gakuin Ronso (Japan), 34, 1954.

2267 NASH, RALPH. Chivalric Themes in Samson Agonistes. Studies in Honor of John Wilcox. Ed. by A. Doyle Wallace and Woodburn O. Ross (Detroit: Wayne State Univ. Press, 1958), pp. 23-38.
Samson has several themes, such as the champion felled by love and the delivered, that are reminiscent of chivalric literature, especially Tasso's Jerusalem Delivered.

2268 NORFORD, DON PARRY. Trial by Contrary: A Study of Milton's Later Poems. Doctoral diss., Columbia Univ., 1966. Abs., DA, 28, 1967, 2218-A.

2269 OCHI, EIJI. Samson's Intellect and the Recognition of its Limitations. Hiroshima Univ. Eigo Eibungaku Kenkyu, 4, 1957.

2270 ORAS, ANTS. Milton's Blank Verse and the Chronology of His Major Poems. SAMLA Studies in Milton. Ed. by J. Max Patrick (Gainesville: Univ. of Florida Press, 1953), pp. 128-97.
Accepts the traditional chronology.

2271 PARKER, WILLIAM RILEY. A Critical Study of Milton's Samson Agonistes. B. Litt. thesis, Oxford Univ., 1934.

2272 ------. The Date of Samson Agonistes. PQ, 28, 1949, 145-66.
"I propose to show, first, that the traditional date is open to very serious doubt; second, that the usual autobiographical inferences are highly questionable; and third, that there are some reasons for dating the inception of Samson Agonistes as early as 1646-1648."

2273 ------. The Date of Samson Agonistes: A Postscript. N&Q, N.S., 5, 1958, 201-2.
Further arguments for a 1646-1648 date of composition.

2274 ------. The Greek Spirit in Milton's Samson Agonistes. E&S, 20, 1934, 21-44.
Concerned with the extent to which Milton's drama is "animated by the spirit, by the dominant idea of the original."

2275 ------. The "Kommos" of Milton's Samson Agonistes. SP, 32, 1935, 240-4.
"The whole passage, from 1. 1660 to the end of the play, is a Kommos."

2276 ------. Milton's Debt to Greek Tragedy in Samson Agonistes. Baltimore: Johns Hopkins Univ. Press; London: Milford, 1937. xvi, 260pp. Reprinted, Hamden, Connecticut and London: Archon Books, 1963; New York: Barnes and Noble, 1968.
"The exact purpose of my study, then, is to establish the major aspects of Milton's debt to Aeschylus, Sophocles, and Euripides in his drama of Samson." "It is Sophocles, however, to whom he is most indebted." Concludes that the Greek element should not be overemphasized.
Rev: L. C. Martin, YWES, 185-6; E. M. W. Tillyard, MLN, 53, 1938, 381-3; D. Grene, MP, 35, 1938, 454-7; E. N. S. Thompson, PQ, 17, 1938, 416; F. Delattre, EA, Oct., 1938, pp. 401-2; A. v. Blumenthal, Ang. Bbl., 49, 1938, 154-5; J. H. Hanford, JEGP, 38, 1939, 456-7; L. R. Lind, CJ, 34, 1939, 178-9.

2277 ------. Misogyny in Milton's Samson Agonistes. PQ, 16, 1937, 139-44.
Mainly a refutation of the view that there is a pervading misogyny in the play.

2278 ------. Notes on the Text of Samson Agonistes. JEGP, 60, 1961, 688-98.
On the problems of editing Samson Agonistes, especially in matters of punctuation, spelling, and capitalization.

2279 ------. Symmetry in Milton's Samson Agonistes. MLN, 50, 1935, 355-60.
Finds that in structural symmetry Milton has followed Greek models.

2280 ------. Tragic Irony in Milton's Samson Agonistes. EA, 1, 1937, 314-20.
Discusses conscious and unconscious irony, the latter effective only because the reader is familiar with the outcome of the story.

2281 ------. The Trinity Manuscript and Milton's Plans for a Tragedy. JEGP, 34, 1935, 225-32.
We can be "certain only that he was interested in writing a tragedy, and had considered Samson, incidentally, as a subject."

2282 PRICE, E. R. The Chorus in Samson Agonistes. B. Litt. thesis, Merton College, Oxford, 1958.

2283 RADZINOWICZ, MARY ANN NEVINS. Eve and Dalila: Renovation and the Hardening of the Heart. Reason and the Imagination: Studies in the History of Ideas, 1600-1800. Ed. by J. A. Mazzeo (New York: Columbia Univ. Press; London: Routledge and Kegan Paul, 1962), pp. 155-81.
Holds that Eve and Dalila are dramatizations of the struggle to achieve true freedom and virtue after a fall. In Eve, Milton depicts renovation; in Dalila, the process of the hardening of the heart.

2284 ------. Samson Agonistes and Milton the Politician in Defeat. PQ, 44, 1965, 454-71.
On Samson Agonistes as an epic of defeat.

2285 Recording of Samson Agonistes. MN, 2, 1968, 7-8.
On a production directed by Peter Wood (Caedmon TC 2028).

2286 SADLER, MARY LYNN VEACH. Samson Agonistes and the Theme of Consolation. Doctoral diss., Univ. of Illinois, 1967. Abs., DA, 28, 1968, 5027-A. 344pp.

2287 SAMS, ALMA F. Samson Agonistes: Its Date and Fallacies in the Autobiographical Interpretation. Master's thesis, Duke Univ., 1942.

2288 SAMUELS, CHARLES THOMAS. Milton's Samson Agonistes and Rational Christianity. DR, 43, 1963. 495-506.
On reason versus faith in Samson Agonistes, Milton's "most unlovely and irrational" work.

2289 SAN JUAN, EPIFAMI, JR. The Natural Context of Spiritual Renewal in Samson Agonistes. BSUF, 6, iii, 1965, 55-60.
Samson represents fallen nature, and we perceive in his regeneration a renewal of man's primeval brightness, symbolized by the image of the phoenix.

2290 SCOTT-CRAIG, T. S. K. Concerning Milton's Samson. RN, 5, 1952, 45-53.
Interprets Samson Agonistes as a lustration, a Protestant equivalent of the Mass.

2291 SELLIN, PAUL R. Milton's Epithet Agonistes. SEL, 4, 1964, 137-62.
On the Greek meanings of agonistes and seventeenth-century connotations.

2292 ------. Sources of Milton's Catharsis: A Reconsideration. JEGP, 60, 1961, 712-30.
A re-examination of the influence of Antonio Minturno and Giambattista Guarini on Milton and a suggestion of another source—Daniel Heinsius' De tragoedise constitutione.

2293 SEWELL, ELIZABETH. The Human Metaphor. Notre Dame: Univ. of Notre Dame Press, 1964. 212pp.

Considers, i.a., Paradise Lost, Paradise Regained, and Samson Agonistes in Chapter 4, Individual Life as Myth: The Figure of Suffering and Effort, pp. 114-55.

2294A SHAWCROSS, JOHN T. The Chronology of Milton's Major Poems. PMLA, 76, 1961, 345-58.
Suggests that Paradise Regained "seems to lie near but somewhat later than Samson Agonistes and, except for late work, before Paradise Lost as it now stands."

2294B ------. The Prosody of Milton's Translation of Horace's Fifth Ode. TSL, 13, 1968, 81-9.
Contains, i.a., suggestions concerning the prosody of Samson Agonistes.

2295 SPENCER, TERENCE [J. B.]. Samson Agonistes in London. SCN, 9, 1951, 35.
On a performance in the Church of St. Martin's-in-the-Fields in May, 1951.

2296 SPENCER, TERENCE [J. B.], and JAMES WILLIS. Milton and Arnobius. N&Q, 196, 1951, 387.
Cites parallels between Samson Agonistes and Arnobius' Libri Septem Adversus Gentes.

2297 STEADMAN, JOHN M. Dalila, the Ulysses Myth, and Renaissance Allegorical Tradition. MLR, 57, 1962, 560-5.
On Samson Agonistes, 1. 934. There is a "close relationship between Renaissance allegorizations of the Ulysses myth and Milton's characterization of Dalila."

2298 ------. Faithful Champion: The Theological Basis of Milton's Hero of Faith. Anglia, 77, 1959, 12-28. Reprinted in Milton: Modern Essays in Criticism. A Galaxy Book. Ed. by Arthur E. Barker (New York: Oxford Univ. Press, 1965), pp. 167-83; and in revised form in Milton's Epic Characters: Image and Idol (Chapel Hill: Univ. of North Carolina Press, 1968), pp. 44-57.
A re-examination of Milton's characterization of Samson as a hero of faith "against the background of his theological beliefs."

2299 ------. Milton's Harapha and Goliath. JEGP, 60, 1961, 786-95.
Harapha derives largely from 1 Samuel 17 and his name from 2 Samuel 21.

2300 ------. The Samson-Nisus Parallel: Some Renaissance Examples. N&Q, N.S., 7, 1960, 450-1.
"Though Milton could legitimately compare Samson with either Atlas or Hercules, a reference to Nisus would probably have seemed an anachronism."

2301 ------. The Tragic Glass: Milton, Minturno and the Condition Humaine. Th'Upright Heart and Pure. Ed. by Amadeus P. Fiore, O.F.M. (Pittsburgh and Louvain: Duquesne Univ. Press, 1967), pp. 101-15.
Concerned with the human condition in Paradise Lost and Samson Agonistes. Notes similarities and differences between Minturno's and Milton's use of the mirror metaphor in tragedy and concludes, "In universalizing Samson's predicament into a 'mirror of our fickle state,' Milton bears eloquent witness to the gravity and universality of the tragic vision."

2302 STEIN, ARNOLD. Heroic Knowledge: An Interpretation of Paradise Regained and Samson Agonistes. Minneapolis: Univ. of Minnesota Press, 1957. xi, 237pp.
   Samson Agonistes, pp. 137-202.

2303 STEPHENSON, ANDREW. Samson Agonistes. Theatre Arts Monthly, 22, 1938, 914-6.
   Reviews Nugent Monck's production of Samson Agonistes at the Maddermarket Theatre.

2304 STRATMAN, CARL J. Milton's Samson Agonistes: A Checklist of Criticism. Restoration and 18th Century Theatre Research, 4, 1965, 2-10.
   Addenda in SCN, 24, No. 3, 1966, item 16, and by Anthony Low, SCN, 25, No. 1, 1967, item 3.

2305 STROUP, THOMAS B. Religious Rite and Ceremony in Milton's Poetry. Lexington: Univ. of Kentucky Press, 1968. ix, 83pp.
   Contains a chapter on Samson Agonistes, pp. 55-62.

2306 SUMMERS, JOSEPH H. The Movements of the Drama. The Lyric and Dramatic Milton. Ed. by Summers (New York and London: Columbia Univ. Press, 1965), pp. 153-75.
   In Samson Agonistes, Milton solved the problem of purgation "by the creation of movements in events, ideas, emotions, perspectives, and language. . . ."

2307 SUNDELL, ROGER HENRY. Internal Commentary in the Major Poems of John Milton. Doctoral diss., Washington Univ., 1966. Abs., DA, 26, 1966, 6701.

2308 TENNISSEN, JOHN JAMES. Of Patience and Heroic Martyrdom: The Book of Job and Milton's Conception of Patient Suffering in Paradise Regained and Samson Agonistes. Doctoral diss., Univ. of Rochester, 1967. Abs., DA, 28, 1967, 1797-A.

2309 THORPE, JAMES. On the Pronunciation of Names in Samson Agonistes. HLQ, 31, 1967, 65-74.
   "I believe that Milton intended his readers to say Dá-li-la, Má-no-ah (or Má-noa), and Há-ra-pha as they read Samson Agonistes, and I should think it might be simpler if we also spoke the names in that way when we referred to the characters of his poem."

2310 TIMBERLAKE, P. W. Milton and Euripides. Parrott Presentation Volume (Princeton: Princeton Univ. Press, 1935), pp. 315-40.
   Cites various examples of Euripides' influence and suggests reasons why Milton found Euripides congenial.

2311 TINKER, CHAUNCEY B. Samson Agonistes. Tragic Themes in Western Literature. Ed. by Cleanth Brooks (New Haven: Yale Univ. Press, 1955, 1960), pp. 59-76.
   Considers the transformation of the Biblical story to drama.

2312 TUNG, MASON. Samson Impatiens: A Reinterpretation of Milton's Samson Agonistes. TSLL, 9, 1968, 475-92.

Examines and reinterprets the major characters in Samson Agonistes, and concludes that "in writing Samson Agonistes, Milton utilized Samson's impatience and formulated his own tragic sense, suitable for a Christian tragedy. This tragic sense is based on the Christian conception of free will and the inevitability of sin—one of Milton's dominant interests in his major poems."

2313 URE, PETER. A Simile in Samson Agonistes. N&Q, 195, 1950, 298.
Cites parallels to the woman-ship figure (710-18) from Jonson's The Devill is an Asse and The Staple of News.

2314 VAN KLUYVE, ROBERT A. Out, Out, Hyaena. AN&Q, 1, 1963, 99-101.
On Samson Agonistes, 748. "The epithet is curious, but singularly appropriate in light of the traditional comments made about the hyena, and an examination of these reveals several levels in Samson's rejection of Dalila."

2315 WAGGONER, GEORGE R. The Challenge to Single Combat in Samson Agonistes. PQ, 39, 1960, 82-92.
On the connotations of single combat for heroic behavior and Milton's use of the concept as "a symbol for Samson's revived will to act."

2316 WEISMILLER, EDWARD. The Dry and Rugged Verse. The Lyric and Dramatic Milton. Ed. by Joseph H. Summers (New York and London: Columbia Univ. Press, 1965), pp. 115-52.
A prosodic analysis of Samson Agonistes, especially the choral odes.

2317 WHITING, GEORGE W. Milton and This Pendant World. Austin: Univ. of Texas Press, 1958. xviii, 364pp.
Contains a chapter on Samson Agonistes.

2318 ------. Samson Agonistes and the Geneva Bible. RIP, 38, 1951, 18-35.
On the Hebraic elements in Milton's drama.

2319 WILKENFELD, ROGER B. Act and Emblem: The Conclusion of Samson Agonistes. ELH, 32, 1965, 160-8.
"In Samson Agonistes Milton actualizes the concept of an eternal recovery of God through the great emblem of the phoenix which technically resolves the poem's structural patterns and makes them most meaningful."

2320 ------. Act and Emblem: A Study of Narrative and Dramatic Patterns in Three Poems by John Milton. Doctoral diss., Univ. of Rochester, 1964. Abs., DA, 25, 1964, 2969.
Considers Comus, Samson Agonistes, and Paradise Regained.

2321 ------. Theoretics or Polemics? Milton Criticism and the Dramatic Axiom. PMLA, 82, 1967, 505-15.
Surveys criticism of Comus, Samson Agonistes, and Paradise Regained and feels that much of it is unhealthy because the vocally and modally dramatic remains confused.

2322 WILKES, G. A. The Interpretation of Samson Agonistes. HLQ, 26, 1963, 363-79.
Regards Samson as an agent of Eternal Providence.

2323 WILLIAMS, ARNOLD. A Note on Samson Agonistes ll. 90-94. MLN, 63, 1948, 537.
Concerning the indivisibility of the soul.

2324 WILLIAMSON, GEORGE. Tension in Samson Agonistes. Milton and Others (Chicago: Univ. of Chicago Press; London: Faber and Faber, 1965), pp. 85-102.
"The conflict in Samson becomes explicit in the lines of action that constitute his drama."

2325 WILSON, J. DOVER. Shakespeare, Milton, and Congreve. TLS, Jan. 16, 1937, p. 44.
"Cleopatra—Dalila—Millamant make a pretty daisy-chain." Reply by G. G. Loane, Jan. 23, 1937, p. 60.

2326 WOODHOUSE, A. S. P. Samson Agonistes and Milton's Experience. TRSC, 3rd Series, 43, Sec. 2, 1949, 157-75.
Argues for the validity of relating Milton's art and his experience; suggests a date of composition in the 1660's.

2327 ------. Tragic Effect in Samson Agonistes. UTQ, 28, 1959, 205-22. Reprinted in Milton: Modern Essays in Criticism. A Galaxy Book. Ed. by Arthur E. Barker (New York: Oxford Univ. Press, 1965), pp. 447-66.
"To say that Samson Agonistes is a classical tragedy with a Christian theme and outlook does not completely define the effect or the means used to attain it; but it puts us, I think, on the right track. It gives us a point of view from which to read and judge the poem."

2328 WRIGHT, E. Samson as the Fallen Champion in Samson Agonistes. N&Q, N.S., 7, 1960, 222-4.
In Samson Agonistes "there seems evidence that Milton still had in mind the romantic conception of the heroic figure, a conception which reveals itself quite steadily in references scattered throughout the drama."

2329 YOUNG, G. M. Milton and Harrington. TLS, Jan. 9, 1937, p. 28.
On the ship-woman image in Milton and Harrington. Reply by J. G. McManaway, Feb. 20, p.131.

MINOR POEMS

2330 ABERCROMBIE, LASCELLES. Milton Sonnet XVII. TLS, April 11, 1936, p. 316.

2331 ABRAMS, M. H. Five Ways of Reading Lycidas. Varieties of Literary Experience. Ed. by Stanley Burnshaw (New York: New York Univ. Press and Peter Owen, 1962), pp. 1-29. Printed also as Five Types of Lycidas in Milton's Lycidas: The Tradition and the Poem. Ed. by C. A. Patrides (New York: Holt, Rinehart, and Winston, 1961), pp. 212-31.
Concerning the interpretations of Hanford, Tillyard, Ransom, Brooks and Hardy, and R. P. Adams, with Abrams' own analysis, that Lycidas is really what it seems.

2332 ADAMS, BERNARD SCHRODER. Milton and Metaphor: The Artis Logicae and the Imagery of the Shorter English Poems. Doctoral diss., Univ. of Pittsburgh, 1964. Abs., DA, 26, 1965, 1629.

2333 ADAMS, HENRY H. The Development of the Flower Passage in Lycidas. MLN, 65, 1950, 468-72.

2334 ADAMS, RICHARD P. The Archetypal Pattern of Death and Rebirth in Milton's Lycidas. PMLA, 64, 1949, 183-8. Reprinted in Myth and Literature: Contemporary Theory and Practice. Ed. by John B. Vickery (Lincoln: Univ. of Nebraska Press, 1966), pp. 187-91; and in condensed form in Milton's Lycidas: The Tradition and the Poem, ed. by C. A. Patrides (New York: Holt, Rinehart, and Winston, 1961), pp. 120-5.
Milton was familiar with the long tradition of death and rebirth imagery, and he draws his own images from a wide variety of sources, with each image having its own immediate purpose and relevancy to the form of the whole.

2335 ADAMS, ROBERT MARTIN. Reading Comus. MP, 51, 1953, 18-32. Reprinted in Ikon: John Milton and the Modern Critics (1955); A Maske at Ludlow: Essays on Milton's Comus. Ed. by John S. Diekhoff (Cleveland: Case Western Reserve Univ. Press, 1968), pp. 78-101.
Believes that modern criticism has been characterized in the "over-reading" of Lycidas, the Nativity Ode, and especially Comus.

2336 ADES, JOHN I. The Pattern of Temptation in Comus. PELL, 1, 1965, 265-71.
An examination of the parallels between the temptation in Comus and in Paradise Regained.

2337 AIMAR, CAROLINE P. The Psalms as Milton Sings Them. Master's thesis, Duke University, 1942.

2338 AINSWORTH, EDWARD G. Reminiscences of the Orlando Furioso in Comus. MLN, 46, 1931, 91-2.

2339 ALLEN, DON CAMERON. Milton as a Latin Poet. Neo-Latin Poetry of the Sixteenth and Seventeenth Centuries (Williams Andrews Clark

Memorial Library, Univ. of California, Los Angeles, 1965), pp. 30-52. Reprinted in Image and Meaning: Metaphoric Traditions in Renaissance Poetry. New Enlarged Edition (Baltimore: Johns Hopkins Press, 1968), pp. 115-37.
>Concerned mainly with the Fifth Elegy, In Adventum Veris, and with Milton's attempting no Latin verse of consequence after 1647.

2340 ------. Milton's Alpheus. MLN, 71, 1956, 172-3.
>In Lycidas.

2341 ------. Milton's Comus as a Failure in Artistic Compromise. ELH, 16, 1949, 104-19. Reprinted with slight change in The Harmonious Vision (1954).
>"The conflict between the dramatic theme and the moral theme is never made quite clear and never artistically compromised."

2342 ------. The Harmonious Vision: Studies in Milton's Poetry. Baltimore: Johns Hopkins Press, 1954.
>Contains chapters on the Nativity Ode, L'Allegro and Il Penseroso, Comus, and Lycidas. One of the chapters, The Higher Compromise: On the Morning of Christ's Nativity and a Mask is reprinted in A Maske at Ludlow: Essays on Milton's Comus. Ed. by John S. Diekhoff (Cleveland: Case Western Reserve Univ. Press, 1968), pp. 58-71.

2343 ------. A Note on Comus. MLN, 64, 1949, 179-80.
>On the Renaissance theory of the generation of diamonds and Comus, 731-5.

2344 ARAI, AKIRA. Milton in Comus. SEL (Japan), 42, 1965, 19-31.
>Feels that in Comus the Grace-motif refines the Nature-motif in presenting the Soul's upward journey from Sense, through Reason, to Faith.

2345 ------. Milton's Heroism in His Sonnet XIX. Research Bulletin, Dept. of General Education, Nagoya Univ. (Japan), 12, 1968, 1-13.
>Feels that Milton's concept of Christian heroism "first came to the fore in Sonnet XIX."

2346 ARNOLD, JAMES A. John Milton's Masque: an Historical and Critical Study of Comus. Doctoral diss., Princeton Univ., 1951. Abs., DA, 13, 1953, 385-6.

2347 ARTHOS, JOHN. Milton, Ficino, and the Charmides. SRen, 6, 1959, 261-74.
>Ficino's commentary on sophrosyne in the Charmides may be the source and explanation of chastity in Comus.

2348 ------. Milton's Haemony and Virgil's Amellus. N&Q, 8, 1961, 172.
>The description in Comus (628-34) is formed after that of the flower amellus in Vergil's Fourth Georgic.

2349 ------. Milton's Sabrina, Virgil, and Porphyry. Anglia, 79, 1962, 204-13.
>Comus is a work of Milton's imagination and "Sabrina owes more to his imagination than to his reason, and more to Virgil than to Porphyry...."

2350 ------. On A Mask Presented at Ludlow-Castle by John Milton. Univ. of Michigan Contributions in Modern Philology, 20. Ann Arbor: Univ. of Michigan Press, 1954. 50pp.
>A critical analysis.

Rev: Arnold Davenport, YWES, 140-1; TLS, June 10 1955, p. 311; J. C. Maxwell, RES, 6, 1955, 202-3; N&Q, N. S., 2, 1955, 275-6; William B. Hunter, Jr., MLN, 70, 1955, 295-6; SCN, 13, 1955, 31; J. B. Broadbent, ES, 39, 1958, 41.

2351 ------. The Realms of Being in the Epilogue of Comus. MLN, 76, 1961, 321-4.

In the Epilogue "the eschatology seems to come from the Phaedo although the correspondences are not as exact as one might wish. In this note I should like to point to elaborations upon this eschatology in Ficino, with particular reference to statements and descriptions that may present something of the context of Milton's thought if they do not in all instances suggest specific sources."

2352 AUSTIN, WARREN B. Milton's Lycidas and Two Latin Elegies by Giles Fletcher, the Elder. SP, 44, 1947, 41-55.

On the influence of Fletcher's elegies on the death of Walter Haddon and that of his son.

2353 AYLWARD, KEVIN JOSEPH. Milton's Latin Versification: The Hexameter. Doctoral diss., Columbia Univ., 1966. Abs., DA, 27, 1966, 1331-A—32-A.

2354 BABB, LAWRENCE. The Background of Il Penseroso. SP, 37, 1940, 257-73.

On the two conceptions of melancholy in the Renaissance, one banished in L'Allegro and the other accepted in Il Penseroso. Presents the same view in The Elizabethan Malady: a Study in English Literature from 1580 to 1642 (East Lansing: Michigan State College Press, 1951), pp. 178-80.

2355 BACHRACH, ALFRED GUSTAVE HERBERT. Het Dichteroog in de Engelse Litterkunde. Amsterdam: N. V. Noord-Hollansche Uitgevers Maatschappij, 1953. 30pp.

A lecture presented at the University of Leiden on October 30, 1953. Comments on "When I consider how my light is spent" and on the twentieth-century criticism of Milton.

2356 BAINES, A. H. J. The Topography of L'Allegro. N&Q, 188, 1945, 68-71.

2357 BALDI, SERGIO. Poesie italiane di Milton. SSe, 7, 1966, 103-50.

Discusses dates of composition, language and meter, the influence of Petrarch, and Milton's Italian style. Includes the texts of six poems and some critical analysis.

2358 BANKS, THEODORE H. A Source for Lycidas, 154-158. MLN, 62, 1947, 39-40.

Pericles, 3, 1, 57-65.

2359 BARBER, C. L. A Mask Presented at Ludlow Castle: The Masque as a Masque. The Lyric and Dramatic Milton. Ed. by Joseph H. Summers (New York and London: Columbia Univ. Press, 1965), pp. 35-63. Reprinted in A Maske at Ludlow: Essays on Milton's Comus. Ed. by John S. Diekhoff (Cleveland: Case Western Reserve Univ. Press, 1968), pp. 188-206.

A study of the form of the masque as noble entertainment and of Milton's strategy in using the masque form to present "Chastity as an obligation of the natural order which could find sublime fulfillment in the order of Grace."

2360 BARKER, ARTHUR E. The Pattern of Milton's Nativity Ode. UTQ, 10, 1941, 167-81. Reprinted in Milton: Modern Judgements, ed. by Alan Rudrum (London: MacMillan, 1968), pp. 44-57.

2361 BARNETT, H. A. A Time of the Year for Milton's Ad Patrem. MLN, 73, 1958, 82-3.
The astronomical reference in 11. 38-40 suggests early spring as the time of composition.

2362 BARRETT, JAMES A. S. A Line in Lycidas (11. 19-22). TLS, Jan. 11, 1934, p. 28.
Reply by G. M. Gathorne-Hardy, Jan. 18, 1934, p. 44.

2363 BARUCH, FRANKLIN ROY. Studies in Milton's Comus. Doctoral diss., Harvard Univ., 1963.

2364 BATESON, F. W. The Money-Lender's Son: L'Allegro and Il Penseroso. English Poetry, a Critical Introduction (London: Longmans, 1950), pp. 149-64.
Also pertinent comment on Lycidas.
Rev: Maynard Mack, YR, 40, 1950, 338-40.

2365 BATTESTIN, MARTIN C. John Crowe Ransom and Lycidas: A Reappraisal. CE, 17, 1955-6, 223-8.
Attacks Ransom's article on Lycidas in Amer. Rev., 1, 1933, 179-203.

2366 BENNETT, J. A. W. Milton's Cato. TLS, April 5, 1963, p. 233.
See also J. C. Maxwell, April 26, p. 314, and May 17, p. 357; and V. Scholderer, May 10, p. 241. A discussion of whether the last line of the sonnet Lawrence of Virtuous Father derives from Disticha Catonis, 3, 7.

2367 BERKELEY, DAVID S. Milton's On the Late Massacre in Piedmont. Expl, 15, 1957, item 58.
Suggests that line 4 is reminiscent of Jeremiah 2:27.

2368 ------. A Possible Biblical Allusion in Lycidas, 1. N&Q, N.S., 8, 1961, 178.
Hebrews 12:26-7, which contains an allusion to Haggai 2:6-7.

2369 ------. The Revision of the Orpheus Passage in Lycidas. N&Q, N.S., 5, 1958, 335-6.
On reasons for Milton's revising 11. 58-61.

2370 BEUM, ROBERT. The Pastoral Realism of Lycidas. WHR, 15, 1961, 325-9.
Defends Milton's choice of the pastoral form and finds that he "transcends the pastoral tradition" by achieving "realism: a slice of life, cut from the inside."

2371 BLENNER-HASSETT, R. Geoffrey of Monmouth and Milton's Comus. MLN, 64, 1949, 315-8.
Concerning the Sabrina episode.

2372 ------. Geoffrey of Monmouth and Milton's Comus: A Problem in Composition. SN, 21, 1949, 216-21.
Insists that the deftness of Milton's transmutation of Sabrina from Geoffrey of Monmouth into the figure in Comus furnishes us with an insight into the processes of artistic re-creation.

2373 BLONDEL, JACQUES. The Function of Mythology in Comus. DUJ, 58, 1966, 63-6.
At this point in his career, Milton is following the Renaissance practice of making mythological figures support Chrisitan doctrine.

2374 ------. Le Thème de la tentation dans le Comus de Milton. Rev. d'hist. et de philosophie religieuses, 28-9, 1948-9, 43-8.

2375 BODDY, MARGARET. Milton's Translation of Psalms 80-88. MP, 64, 1966, 1-9.
Historical events of 1648 and their connection with Milton's translation.

2376 BOLING, EDGAR, JR. The Masque Conventions in Milton's Comus. Master's thesis, Emory Univ., 1955.

2377 BONHAM, M. E. Milton's Comus Lives Again at Ludlow Castle. Scholastic, Sept. 29, 1934, pp. 9-10.
On the tercentenary production.

2378 BOWERS, ROBERT H. The Accent on Youth in Comus. SAMLA Studies in Milton. Ed. by J. Max Patrick (Gainesville: Univ. of Florida Press, 1953), 72-9.
Proposes that the poem be read as concerned with the emotional life of youth, written by a youthful author for an amiable, aristocratic audience.

2379 BOWLING, WILLIAM G. The Travelogue Sections of L'Allegro and Il Penseroso. EJ, 25, 1936, 220-3.

2380 BRADNER, LEICESTER. Musae Anglicanae: A History of Anglo-Latin Poetry, 1500-1925. New York: Modern Language Association; London: Oxford Univ. Press, 1940. xii, 383pp.
Milton's Latin poetry discussed, pp. 111-8.

2381 BRETT, R. L. Milton's Lycidas. Reason and Imagination: A Study of Form and Meaning in Four Poems (London: Oxford Univ. Press, for the Univ. of Hull, 1960), pp. 21-50.
"The poem is concerned then with the battle between the reason and the senses; between humanism and Puritanism; between the Renaissance and the Reformation conceptions of poetry."
Rev: H. A. Smith, MLR, 56, 1961, 237; John A. M. Rillie, RES, 13 1962, 95-6.

2382 BREWER, WILMON. Sonnets and Sestinas. Boston: Cornhill, 1937.
Milton's sonnets discussed in their historical perspective in a chapter called The History of the Sonnet, pp. 91-178.

2383 BRIGGS, KATHARINE MARY. The Anatomy of Puck: An Examination of Fairy Beliefs among Shakespeare's Contemporaries and Successors. London: Routledge and Kegan Paul, 1959; New York: Hillary House, 1959.
Concerned with Comus and L'Allegro.

2384 BROADBENT, J. B. Milton: Comus and Samson Agonistes. Studies in English Literature Series, No. 1. Ed. by David Daiches. London: Edward Arnold, 1961. Published also in Barron's Studies in English

Literature, Great Neck, New York: Barron's Educational Series, 1961. 63pp.
Introduction and commentary designed for undergraduates.

2385 ------. The Nativity Ode. The Living Milton (London: Routledge and Kegan Paul, 1960), pp. 12-31.
Argues against the uniformity of the nativity tradition and feels that Milton subsumes only about half of it in his ode.

2386 BROCKBANK, PHILIP. Comus and the Trials of Our Youth. English Literature, Bulletin of the National Association for the Teaching of English, 3, No. 2, Summer, 1966, 42-54.

2387 BRODRIBB, C. W. Milton and Persius. N&Q, 158, 1930, 39.
Cites several references to Persius in the Latin poems.

2388 ------. Milton's L'Allegro and Il Penseroso. N&Q, 163, 1932, 201.
Believes that the Declaration of Sports, Oct. 10, 1633, prompted Milton to write the poems.

2389 ------. Stoic Fur (Comus, 1. 707). TLS, May 8, 1937, p. 364.

2390 ------. That Two-Handed Engine. TLS, June 12, 1930, p. 496.

2391 ------. That Two-Handed Engine. TLS, June 5, 1943, p. 271.
Replies by Kathleen Tomlinson and by W. R. Dunstan, June 12, 1943, p. 283; by Katharine A. Esdaile, June 19, 1943, p. 295; by H. Beckett, July 3, 1943, p. 319.

2392 BROOKS, CLEANTH. The Light Symbolism in L'Allegro and Il Penseroso. The Well Wrought Urn: Studies in the Structure of Poetry (New York: Reynal and Hitchcock, 1947; London: Dobson, 1949; New York: Harcourt, Brace, 1956), pp. 47-61.
Concerning Johnson's and Tillyard's comments on the poems, with a new analysis.
Rev: D. A. Stauffer, MLN, 62, 1947, 427-9; Dudley Fitts, KR, 9, 1947, 612-6; A. Mizener, SR, 55, 1947, 460-9; William Empson, SR, 55, 1947, 690-7; Theodore Maynard, CW, 165, 1947, 570; R. P. Blackmur, NYTBR, June 8, 1947, p. 6; G. F. Whicher, NYHTBR, April 20, 1947, p. 2; H. W. Wells, SRL, April 12, 1947, p. 50; J. W. R. Purser, MLR, 42, 1947, 541-2; Josephine Miles, JAAC, 6, 1947, 185-6; R. S. Crane, MP, 45, 1948, 226-45; Norman Callan, RES, 24, 1948, 347-9.

2393 BROOKS, CLEANTH, and JOHN E. HARDY. Essays in Analysis: Lycidas. The Poems of Mr. John Milton (New York: Harcourt, Brace, and Co., 1951; London: Dobson, 1957), pp. 169-86. Reprinted in Milton's Lycidas: The Tradition and the Poem. Ed. by C. A. Patrides (New York: Holt, Rinehart, and Winston, 1961), pp. 136-52.

2394 BROOKS, E. L. Lycidas and Bible Pastoral. N&Q, N.S., 3, 1956, 67-8.
On the resemblance between Peter's address in Lycidas and Ezekiel 34.

2395 BRUSER, FREDELLE. Comus and the Rose Song. SP, 44, 1947, 625-44.
On the carpe diem theme and Comus.

2396 BUSH, DOUGLAS. An Allusion in Milton's Elegia tertia. Harvard Library Bulletin, 9, 1955, 392-6.

Lines 9-10 may contain a reference to King James and Maurice, Prince of Orange.

2397 ------. The Date of Milton's Ad Patrem. MP, 61, 1964, 204-8.
Argues for 1631-32.

2398 C., T. C. Milton: Marble for Thinking. N&Q, 184, 1943, 314.
Explanation of the "marble" of the Nativity Ode, On Shakespeare, and Il Penseroso. Comments by Richard Hussey and the editor, p. 381.

2399 CANDY, HUGH C. H. Milton's Early Reading of Browne. N&Q, 158, 1930, 310-2.
Establishes the claim that Browne's influence on Milton was greater, and perhaps earlier, than Sylvester's.

2400 ------. Milton's Early Reading of Sylvester. N&Q, 158, 1930, 93-5.
Suggests Sylvester's influence on Milton's translations of the Psalms and the Ovidian stanzas.

2401 CAREY, JOHN. The Date of Milton's Italian Poems. RES, N.S., 14, 1963, 383-6.
"If Elegy 6, 11. 89-90, refer to the Italian poems, we can date them firmly in or before December 1629."

2402 ------. Milton's Ad Patrem, 35-37. RES, 15, 1964, 180-4.
"In the Ad Patrem, 35-37, Milton claims, then, that his fiery spirit soars even now... to the outermost sphere of the universe and there... joins in the immortal song of the starry choir."

2403 CARPENTER, NAN C. The Place of Music in L'Allegro and Il Penseroso. UTQ, 22, 1953, 354-67.
On the musical passages, which derive from a large body of aural imagery.

2404 ------. Spenser's Epithalamion as Inspiration for Milton's L'Allegro and Il Penseroso. N&Q, N.S., 3, 1956, 289-92.

2405 CARRITHERS, GALE H., JR. Milton's Ludlow Mask: From Chaos to Community. ELH, 33, 1966, 23-42.
"This masque-poem appears to me to be animated by an ideal of community, more particularly a lively established community reinforcing itself by a significantly precarious process of recruitment."

2406 CHANEY, VIRGINIA MILES. The Elegies of George Buchanan in Relation to Those of the Roman Elegists and to the Latin Elegies of John Milton. Doctoral diss., Vanderbilt Univ., 1961. Abs., DA, 22, 1962, 2383.

2407 CHEEK, MACON. Milton's In Quintum Novembris: An Epic Foreshadowing. SP, 54, 1957, 172-84.
Feels that the poem affords an insight into Milton's earliest conception of epic technique and style and into his earliest conception of Satan.

2408 ------. Of Two Sonnets of Milton. Renaissance Papers, 1956 (Columbia: Univ. of South Carolina Press, 1956), pp. 82-91. Reprinted in Milton: Modern Essays in Criticism. A Galaxy Book. Ed. by Arthur E. Barker (New York: Oxford Univ. Press, 1965), pp. 125-35.
A comparison of On Having Arrived at the Age of Twenty-three and On His

Blindness reveals a close sequence of thoughts and images, illustrating the unity in Milton's thinking.

2409 CLARKE, A. H. T. That Two-Handed Engine at the Door. TLS, Apr. 11, 1929, pp. 295-6.
Replies by G. M. Trevelyan, Harold Van Tromp, and George C. Loane, Apr. 25, 1929, p. 338.

2410 CLARKE, C. A Neglected Episode in Comus. The Wind and the Rain, 6, 1949, 103-7.

2411 COFFMAN, GEORGE R. The Parable of the Good Shepherd, De Contemptu Mundi, and Lycidas: Excerpts for a Chapter on Literary History and Culture. ELH, 3, 1936, 101-13.
Emphasizes the "heritage to humanistic culture in Western Europe" of Christ's parable of the good shepherd "as it emerges in two distinct literary productions: De Contemptu Mundi by Bernard of Marlais (or Morval), a Cluniac monk of the twelfth century, and Milton's Lycidas."

2412 COHEN, GERALD. A Comparative Evaluation of the Pastoral Tradition in English and French Literature in the Early Seventeenth Century. Doctoral diss., Univ. of Washington, 1959. Abs., DA, 20, 1959, 1011-2.
Discusses William Browne, John Fletcher, Ben Jonson, John Milton, Molière, d'Urfé, and J. A. deBaïf.

2413 COLLINS, DAN S. The Influence of Formal Rhetoric on the Treatment of Nature in the Early English Poems of John Milton. Master's thesis, Univ. of North Carolina, 1951.

2414 COMBECHER, HANS. Drei Sonette-drei Epochen: Eine Verglecichende Interpretation. NS, 4, 1959, 178-89.
A consideration of Shakespeare's When in disgrace, Milton's On His Blindness, and Wordsworth's Composed upon Westminster Bridge.

2415 Comus Produced in 1953 at Ludlow Castle—Where It Was First Presented in 1634. Illustrated London News, July 11, 1953, p. 75.
Photographs with text.

2416 CONDEE, RALPH W. Mansus and the Panegyric Tradition. SRen, 15, 1968, 174-92.
"By using and at the same time defying the tradition..., Milton creates something which is simultaneously both conventional and unique. It is a poem which praises Manso, but also one which expands beyond an encomium of the old man to a vision of a universe in which such good men live."

2417 ------. Ovid's Exile and Milton's Rustication. PQ, 37, 1958, 498-502.
On the relation of Ovid to Milton's Elegia Prima.

2418 ------. The Structure of Milton's Epitaphium Damonis. SP, 62, 1965, 577-94.
Discusses Milton's use of the pastoral tradition.

2419 COOLIDGE, JOHN S. Boethius and That Last Infirmity of Noble Mind. PQ, 42, 1963, 176-82.
On Boethius' Consolation of Philosophy as a hitherto unnoticed analogue or source for Milton's thought that desire of fame is the "last infirmity of noble mind."

2420 ------. That Two-Handed Engine. PQ, 29, 1950, 444-5.

2421 COPE, JACKSON I. Fortunate Falls as Form in Milton's Fair Infant. JEGP, 63, 1964, 660-74.

Shows that in the poem Milton establishes movement "as symbolic vehicle for the concept of the fortunate fall by embedding its action in a matrix of allusions to a rich syncretic mythology."

2422 COX, LEE SHERIDAN. Milton's I Did but Prompt, 11. 13-14. ELN, 3, 1965, 102-4.

Interprets in the light of the punctuation in the Trinity Manuscript.

2423 CURGENVEN, J. P. Milton and the Lark (L'Allegro, 41-48). TLS, Oct., 18, 1934, p. 715.

Replies by H. J. C. Grierson, Nov. 1, 1934, p. 755; by T. Sturge Moore, Oct. 25, 1934, p. 735; by Moore and B. A. Wright, Nov. 8, 1934, p. 775; by Grierson, E. M. W. Tillyard, and M. Joan Sargeaunt, Nov. 15, 1934, p. 795, by Wright and B. R. Rowbottom, Nov. 22, 1934, p. 840; by Grierson and W. A. Jones, Nov. 29, 1934, p. 856.

2424 CURIOUS. Archie Armstrong and Milton. N&Q, 178, 1940, 353-4.

Milton's Hobson poems and Armstrong's A Banquet of Jests (1630?). Reply by William Jaggard, p. 393. Cf. John T. Shawcross, A Banquet of Jests and Archie Armstrong, LC, 29, 1963, 116-9.

2425 CURRIE, H. MAC L. Silius Italicus Fax Mentis Honestae and Milton. N&Q, N.S., 5, 1958, 106-7.

Two lines from the Punica may have influenced Milton's lines on fame in Lycidas.

2426 DAHLBERG, CHARLES R. Milton's Sonnet 23 on his Late Espoused Saint. N&Q, N.S., 194, July 23, 1949, 321.

Supports the view that the sonnet is addressed to Katherine Woodcock.

2427 DAICHES, DAVID. Some Aspects of Milton's Pastoral Imagery. English Studies Today, Fourth Series (Roma: Edizioni di Storia e Letteratura, 1966), pp. 289-309.

On Milton's problem of counterpointing tradition and personal feelings in the early poems, when he viewed a poem as an art object.

2428 ------. A Study of Literature for Readers and Critics. Ithaca: Cornell Univ. Press, 1948.

Contains a detailed analysis of Lycidas, pp. 170-95, which is reprinted in Milton's Lycidas: The Tradition and the Poem, ed. by C. A. Patrides (New York: Holt, Rinehart, and Winston, 1961), pp. 101-19; also reprinted in revised form in Daiches' Milton (New York: Rinehart, 1957), pp. 73-92.

2429 DANIELS, EDGAR F. Climactic Rhythms in Lycidas. AN&Q, 6, 1968, 100-1.

Believes that parallels in rhythm unite the two climactic moments in Lycidas—the revelation on fame (climaxed in 1. 82) and the revelation on immortality (1.171).

2430 ------. Milton's Lycidas, 29. Expl, 21, 1963, item 43.

Batten means a spar, which is used to block the entrance of a pen.

2431 DAY, MABEL. Hilton and Lydgate. RES, 13, 1947, 144-6.
      Believes that three passages of the Troy Book are reflected in Il Penseroso
      and Comus.

2432 DE BEER, E. S. Milton's Old Damaetas. N&Q, 194, 1949, 336-7.

2433 ------. St. Peter in Lycidas. RES, 13, 1947, 59-63.
      On the two-handed engine.

2434 DE FILIPPIS, MICHELE. Milton and Manso: Cups or Books? PMLA,
      51, 1936, 745-56.
      On Epitaphium Damonis, 181-97.

2435 DEMARAY, JOHN G. Comus as a Masque. Doctoral diss., Columbia
      Univ., 1964. Abs., DA, 28, 1967, 624-A.

2436 ------. Milton and the Masque Tradition: The Early Poems, Arcades, and
      Comus. Cambridge: Harvard Univ. Press, 1968. xii, 188pp.
      "The weight of historical evidence supports the view that Comus was written
      as a masque rather than as a drama, and that it is central to the English
      masque tradition that flowered in the time of Ben Jonson, Inigo Jones, and
      John Milton during the first half of the seventeenth century." Contents: The
      Masque as Dance; The Early Poems and Arcades; Masques at Court, 1631-
      1634; Comus is Invented; Staging Comus at Ludlow; The Literary Masque;
      Appendix: Comus and the Italian Dramma per Musica; Bibliography; Notes;
      Index. Several illustrations.
      Rev: TLS, Sept. 12, 1968, p. 1003; J. A. Wittreich, Genre, 1, 1968, 333-6.

2437 ------. Milton's Comus: The Sequel to a Masque of Circe. HLQ, 29,
      1966, 245-54.
      Offers evidence "that the Comus in Milton's masque is the literary son of the
      Circe in Tempe Restored [1632]."

2438 DENNEY, E. E., and P. LYDDON-ROBERTS. Milton's Comus: A Com-
      plete Paraphrase. Ninth Edition. Farnham, Surrey: Normal Press, 1961.
      22pp.

2439 D'HAEN, CHRISTINE. John Milton: Lycidas. Tirade (Amsterdam), 7,
      1963, 673-83.
      On the pastoral background of Lycidas. Translation of the poem into Dutch,
      pp. 679-83.

2440 DIEKHOFF, JOHN S. Lycidas, Line 10. PQ, 16, 1937, 408-10.

2441 ------, ed. A Maske at Ludlow: Essays on Milton's Comus, with the
      Bridgewater Version of Comus. Cleveland: Case Western Reserve Univ.
      Press, 1968. ix, 280pp.
      Contains one original essay by Diekhoff, A Maske at Ludlow, pp. 1-16, in
      which the author discusses matters concerning the original production. The
      other essays are reprints of studies by A. S. P. Woodhouse, E. M. W. Tillyard,
      Don Cameron Allen, Robert M. Adams, A. E. Dyson, Rosemond Tuve, Sears
      Jayne, C. L. Barber, and Diekhoff. Each is listed in this bibliography accord-
      ing to author. Also included in this volume are The Bridgewater Comus:
      Text of A Maske, pp. 207-40, and The Airs of the Songs by Henry Lawes,
      with His Version of the Words, pp. 241-50. Bibliography, pp. 276-80.
      Rev: MN, 2, 1968, 68.

2442 ------. The Milder Shades of Purgatory. MLN, 52, 1937, 409-10.
Interprets the sonnet to Lawes.

2443 ------. Milton's Craftsmanship as Revealed by the Revisions of the Poems of the Trinity College Manuscript. Doctoral diss., Western Reserve Univ., 1937.

2444 ------. A Note on Comus, Lines 75-77. PQ, 20, 1941, 603-4.

2445 ------. The Punctuation of Comus. PMLA, 51, 1936, 757-68.
Feels that the punctuation of Comus in the Trinity Manuscript should be taken seriously because it serves as a key to Milton's intention.

2446 ------. The Text of Comus, 1634 to 1645. PMLA, 52, 1937, 705-27. Reprinted in A Maske at Ludlow: Essays on Milton's Comus. Ed. by John S. Diekhoff (Cleveland: Case Western Reserve Univ. Press, 1968), pp. 251-75.
Holds that the version of Comus in the Trinity Manuscript is a transcription.

2447 DILLARD, KATHRYN. Milton's Use of the Psalms. Master's thesis, Duke Univ., 1939.

2448 DORFMAN, ARIEL. El Lycidas de Milton, poema barroco. AUC, 123, No. 134, 1965, 194-210.
"En esta nota trataremos de probar que Lycidas no es monierista, sino barroco. La critica a Sypher no tiene por objectivo simplemente des calificar una de sur multiples ejemplificaciones. . . ."

2449 DORIAN, DONALD C. Milton's Epitaphium Damonis, Lines 181-197. PMLA, 54, 1939, 612-3.

2450 ------. Milton's On His Blindness. Expl, 10, 1951, item 16.

2451 ------. Milton's On His Having Arrived at the Age of Twenty-Three. Expl, 8, 1949, item 10.

2452 ------. Milton's Two-Handed Engine. PMLA, 45, 1930, 204-15.

2453 ------. On the New Forcers of Conscience, line 17. MLN, 56, 1941, 62-4.

2454 ------. The Question of Autobiographical Significance in L'Allegro and Il Penseroso. MP, 31, 1933, 175-82.
"I would suggest, then, that L'Allegro and Il Penseroso have, in addition to their artistic excellence and descriptive charm, this significance: they may be regarded as a valuable autobiographical record of an important step in Milton's development—his consideration of the question whether he should suppress either the lighter or the more serious side of his nature, as man and as poet, for the fuller development of the other."

2455 DOYNO, VICTOR. Parallel Structure and Verbal Artifice in Milton's Comus. MN, 2, 1968, 62-3.
An exploration of the antithetical moral roles of the Attendant Spirit and Comus.

2456 DRINKWATER, JOHN. Shropshire. Historical Pageant and Tercentenary Performances of Milton's Masque of Comus at Ludlow Castle, July 2nd-

7th, 1934. Prologue by Sir Owen Seaman. Shrewsbury: Shropshire Historical Pageant Committee, 1934. 96pp.
> Program booklet includes five historical episodes by Drinkwater, as well as
> the text of Comus.

2457 DUNCAN-JONES, E. E. Lycidas and Lucan. N&Q, N.S., 3, 1956, 249.

2458 DYSON, A. E. The Interpretation of Comus. E&S, 8, 1955, 89-114. Reprinted in A Maske at Ludlow: Essays on Milton's Comus. Ed. by John
S. Diekhoff (Cleveland: Case Western Reserve Univ. Press, 1968), pp.
102-25.
> Disagrees with Woodhouse's view and feels that nature and grace are pres-
> ent side by side throughout the poem. The great debate in the poem is
> "between Reason and Passion as controlling factors in human conduct."

2459 ELLEDGE, SCOTT. Milton, Sappho, and Demetrius. MLN, 58, 1943,
551-3.
> On the source of Comus, 631-5, 637.

2460 ------, ed. Milton's Lycidas: Edited to Serve as an Introduction to Criticism. New York and London: Harper and Row, 1966. xxii, 330pp.
> Annotated in this bibliography under Minor Peoms: Editions.

2461 ELTON, WILLIAM. Two Milton Notes. N&Q, 192, 1947, 428-9.
> On the possibility that Thomas Robinson's Life and Death of Mary Magdalene
> (c.1621) is a source for L'Allegro and the Dantean character of "blind
> mouths."

2462 EMERSON, FRANCIS W. Why Milton Uses Cambuscan and Camball.
MLN, 47, 1932, 153-4.
> Suggests that John Lane is the source of the words used in Il Penseroso.

2463 ENKVIS, NILS ERIK. The Functions of Magic in Milton's Comus. NM,
54, 1953, 310-8.
> Milton uses magic to present in concrete form an abstract conflict between
> two wills.

2464 EVANS, G. BLAKEMORE. Milton and the Hobson Poems. MLQ, 4,
1943, 281-90.
> Prints seven poems by various writers on the death of Hobson.

2465 ------. Some More Hobson Verses. MLQ, 9, 1948, 10, 184.
> Prints four additional sets of verses.

2466 ------. Two New Manuscript Versions of Milton's Hobson Poems. MLN,
57, 1942, 192-4.

2467 EVANS, WILLA McCLUNG. Hobson Appears in Comic Song. PQ, 26,
1947, 321-7.

2468 EVANS, WILLA, and WILLIAM SLOANE. Comus Agonistes? SCN,
17, No. 1, 1959, item 28.
> Comments on a New York performance of Comus (October, 1958).

2469 FABIAN, DAVID R. The Blind Mouths Passage in Lycidas. AN&Q, 6,
1968, 136-7.
> Finds the source of the passage in I Samuel 14:27-30. Saul was the blind mouth

that could not see, and the epithet was probably ascribed to the corrupt clergy by a mental process of automatic recollection and reciprocity.

2470 ------. Milton's Sonnet 23 and Leviticus XVII. 19. XUS, 5, 1966, 83-8.
Supports the view that Milton alludes to Mary Powell through re-evaluation in light of Scripture.

2471 FEINSTEIN, BLOSSOM. On the Hymns of John Milton and Gian Francesco Pico. CL, 20, 1968, 245-53.
"By favoring the routing of the pagan gods,... Milton demonstrates in the Nativity hymn-ode that early in his career he is strongly on the side of orthodoxy. Because he returns later to similar antipagan themes, it may be said, not that Milton is the last of the Renaissance poets, but that he is one of the first of the English poets to turn away from certain Renaissance currents."

2472 FINK, ZERA S. Il Penseroso, Line 16. PQ, 19, 1940, 309-13.

2473 ------. Wine, Poetry, and Milton's Elegia Sexta. ES, 21, 1939, 164-5.

2474 FINLEY, JOHN H., JR. Milton and Horace: A Study of Milton's Sonnets. Harvard Studies in Classical Philology, 48, 1937, 29-73.
A detailed study.

2475 FINNEY, GRETCHEN L. Comus, Dramma per Musica. SP, 37, 1940, 482-500. Reprinted in Musical Backgrounds for English Literature, 1580-1650 (1962), below.
Comus and the drama of Italy.

2476 ------. Music, Mirth, and Galenic Tradition in England. Reason and the Imagination. Studies in the History of Ideas, 1600-1800. Ed. by J. A. Mazzeo (New York: Columbus Univ. Press; London: Routledge and Kegan Paul, 1962), pp. 143-54.
On the medical value of music and the place of music in L'Allegro.

2477 ------. Musical Backgrounds for English Literature, 1580-1650. New Brunswick: Rutgers Univ. Press, 1962. xiii, 292pp.
Relevant chapters: Speculative Musical Imagery in Milton's Poems, pp. 161-74; Comus: Dramma per Musica, pp. 175-94; A Musical Background for Lycidas, pp. 195-219; Chorus in Samson Agonistes, pp. 220-37.

2478 ------. A Musical Background for Lycidas. HLQ, 15, 1952, 325-50. Reprinted in Musical Backgrounds for English Literature, 1580-1640 (1962), above.
Lycidas and Italian music.

2479 FLEISCHAUER, WARREN. Johnson, Lycidas, and the Norms of Criticism. Johnsonian Studies. Ed. by Magdi Wahba (Cairo, 1962), pp. 235-6.
Argues that Johnson was right in his criticism of Lycidas, that his remarks are in accord with his norms of criticism.

2480 FLETCHER, G. B. A. Milton's Latin Poems, MP, 37, 1940, 343-50.
Gives many examples of the influence on Milton of Catullus, Lucretius, Vergil, Horace, Tibullus, Ovid, Seneca, and other Latin writers.

2481 FLETCHER, HARRIS F. Grierson's Suggested Date for Milton's Ad

Patrem. Fred Newton Scott Anniversary Papers (Chicago: Univ. of Chicago Press, 1929), pp. 199-205.

Supports Grierson and holds that the poem was written after Milton returned from Italy.

2482 ------. Milton's Apologus and Its Mantuan Model. JEGP, 55, 1956, 230-3.

Milton's lines "derive from a grammar school period exercise, or were begun before 1625, and he kept them for a long time, polishing and repolishing." "It is clear that his model was Mantuan's metrical Latin fable, and that Milton was working in the imitative vein so much used and encouraged by the English schoolmasters of the later sixteenth and earlier seventeenth centuries."

2483 ------. Milton's Demogorgon—Prolusion I and Paradise Lost, II, 960-5. JEGP, 57, 1958, 684-9.

"Milton's two usages . . . almost certainly came directly from a printed edition of Boccaccio's De genealogiis deorum, perhaps that of 1532."

2484 ------. Milton's Old Damoetas. JEGP, 60, 1961, 250-7.

Names three possibilities of identification: William Chappell, Michael Honywood, and Abraham Wheelock. Favors Chappell.

2485 ------. The Seventeenth-Century Separate Printings of Milton's Epitaphium Damonis. JEGP, 61, 1962, 788-96.

"The four-leaf pamphlet discovered by Leicester Bradner in the British Museum in 1932 probably was printed after the Poemata (1645) and was the second printing of Epitaphium Damonis."

2486 FOX, ROBERT C. Milton's Lycidas, 192-193. Expl, 9, 1951, item 54.

2487 ------. A Source for Milton's Comus. N&Q, N.S., 9, 1962, 52-3.

Names Jonson's The Poetaster (1601).

2488 FRANKS, JESSE. Linguistic Awareness in the Teaching of Poetry. BSUF, 9, 1968, 51-6.

Uses On the Late Massacre in Piedmont to show that a knowledge of sentence structure is the first step in understanding the context of a poem.

2489 FRASER, G. S. Approaches to Lycidas. The Living Milton (London: Routledge and Kegan Paul, 1960), pp. 32-54.

Appreciative. Attacks Graves but draws from Tuve.

2490 FRAZIER, HARRIET. Time as Structure in Milton's Nativity Ode. Universitas, 3, 1965, 8-14.

The Boethian time-eternity paradox provides one of the major sources of unity in the poem.

2491 FRENCH, J. MILTON. A Comment on a Book Was Writ of Late. . . . MLN, 70, 1955, 404-5.

Insists that Milton "thought highly of the learning and piety of the age of Sir John Cheke."

2492 ------. The Digressions in Milton's Lycidas. SP, 50, 1953, 485-90.

Holds that the so-called digressions "are actually passages of increasing intensity, and probably the core of the poem."

2493 ------. Light and Work in L'Allegro and Il Penseroso. SAQ, 58, 1959, 123-7.
Comment on Cleanth Brooks' essay in The Well Wrought Urn (1947).

2494 ------. Milton's Two-Handed Engine. MLN, 68, 1953, 229-31.
See also SP, 49, 1953, 548-50.

2495 FRYE, NORTHROP. Literature as Context: Milton's Lycidas. Proceedings of the Second Congress of the International Comparative Literature Association, ed. by W. P. Friederick, Univ. of North Carolina Studies in Comparative Literature, 23, 1959, 44-55. Reprinted in Milton's Lycidas: The Tradition and the Poem. Ed. by C. A. Patrides (New York: Holt, Rinehart, and Winston, 1961), pp. 200-11. Also in Fables of Identity: Studies in Poetic Mythology (New York: Harcourt, Brace, 1963), pp. 119-29.
Discusses Lycidas as a new creation and as a reshaping of familiar conventions of literature.

2496 FRYE, ROLAND MUSHAT. Milton's Sonnet 23 on His Late Espoused Saint. N&Q, 194, 1949, 321.
Insists that the sonnet is addressed to Milton's second wife.

2497 FUSSELL, E. S. Milton's Two-Handed Engine Yet Once More. N&Q, 193, 1948, 338-9.
Reply by Maurice Hussey, p. 503.

2498 GATHORNE-HARDY, G. M. A Line in Lycidas. TLS, Jan. 18, 1934, p. 44.
Believes that lines 20-2 indicate that the poem itself will take the place of an ordinary funeral.

2499 GECKLE, GEORGE L. Miltonic Idealism: L'Allegro and Il Penseroso. TSLL, 9, 1968, 455-73.
Contains a structural analysis of both poems. Feels that they symbolize happiness "in two modes of existence on two levels of perfection" and that Milton's idealism leads him to choose the higher level of Il Penseroso.

2500 GHOSH, P. C. A Note on Comus (95). TLS, Feb. 19, 1931, p. 135.
Reply by A. W. Verity, Feb. 26, 1931, p. 154.

2501 GIAMATTI, A. BARTLETT. Milton and Fairfax's Tasso. RLC, 40, 1966, 613-5.
Suggests, i. a., that Lycidas, 163-4, echoes a passage from Fairfax's translation.

2502 GODOLPHIN, F. R. B. Milton, Lycidas, and Propertius' Elegies, III, 7, MLN, 49, 1934, 162-6.
A source study.

2503 ------. Notes on the Technique of Milton's Latin Elegies. MP, 37, 1940, 351-6.
On Milton's "embellishment of his verse in relation to the devices used by Tibullus, Propertius, and Ovid."

2504 GOLDBERG, S. L. The World, the Flesh, and Comus. MCR, No. 6, 1963, 56-68.
A disparagement of the poem. "Nevertheless, Comus suggests the poetic limit-

ations of treating the ordinary world and 'art' as objects to exploit: a too simplistic consciousness of spirit and flesh lets them drift inertly apart, so that the poetry—no matter what doctrines about them it presents—fails to present them alive to the imagination."

2505 GOODE, JAMES. Milton and Sannazzaro. TLS, Aug. 13, 1931, p. 621.
Borrowings in Milton's Elegy I, 21-2, and Elegy V, 121-2.

2506 GOODMAN, PAUL. Milton's On His Blindness: Stanzas, Motion of Thought. Structure of Literature (Chicago: Univ. of Chicago Press, 1954), pp. 192-215.

2507 GOSSMAN, ANN, and GEORGE W. WHITING. Comus, Once More, 1761. RES, N.S., 11, 1960, 56-60.
"In Samuel Derrick's A Poetical Dictionary; or, The Beauties of the English Poets (1761) a number of passages attributed to Milton's Comus are in fact from Dalton's adaptation."

2508 ------. Milton's First Sonnet on His Blindness. RES, N.S., 12, 1961, 364-70.
Reply to articles by Roger Slakey (ELH, 27, 1960, 122-30) and Fitzroy Pyle (RES, N.S., 9, 1958, 376-87); rejoinder by Pyle, ibid., pp. 370-2. "... with his light spent and his active life definitely at an end, Milton must have thought that his poetic career was also at an end. . . ."

2509 GOTTFRIED, RUDOLF. Milton, Lactantius, Claudia and Tasso. SP, 30, 1933, 497-503.
On the phoenix passage in Epitaphium Damonis, 185-9.

2510 ------. Milton and Poliziano. N&Q, N.S., 5, 1958, 195-6.
The words cruenta and cruentum in Angelo Poliziano's Nutricia may have influenced Milton's using the phrase "his gorie visage" in l. 62 of Lycidas.

2511 GRACE, WILLIAM J. Notes on Robert Burton and John Milton. SP, 52, 1955, 578-91.
On parallels between Burton and Milton in L'Allegro, Il Penseroso, and Lycidas.

2512 GRAVES, ROBERT. Criticizing Poetry. TLS, Feb. 2, 1962, p. 73.
States that eighteen lines of L'Allegro were misplaced.

2513 ------. John Milton Muddles Through. NR, May 27, 1957, pp. 17-9.
Animadversions upon L'Allegro.

2514 GREG, SIR WALTER W. Pastoral Poetry and Pastoral Drama: A Literary Inquiry, with Special Reference to the Pre-Restoration Stage in England. New York: Russell and Russell, 1959.
First published in 1906. Contains two sections on Milton: Milton's Lycidas and Browne's Britannia's Pastorals, pp. 131-40; Milton's Masques: Arcades and Comus, pp. 388-404.

2515 GREWE, EUGENE FRANCIS. A History of the Criticism of John Milton's Comus, 1637-1941. Doctoral diss., Univ. of Michigan, 1963. Abs., DA, 25, 1964, 2512.

2516 GUIDI, AUGUSTO. John Milton. Brescia: Morcelleana, 1940. 195pp.
Contains a section on the minor poems.

2517 H., C. E. The Pansy Freaked with Jet (Lycidas, 1. 144). N&Q, 177, 1939, 98.
    Replies by E. H. V[isiak] and by William Jaggard, p. 139; by V. R., p. 175.

2518 HALE, HILDA HANSON. Conventions and Characteristics in the English Funeral Elegy of the Earlier Seventeenth Century. Doctoral diss., Univ. of Missouri, 1956. Abs., DA, 16, 1956, 2149-50.
    Discusses Milton's elegies.

2519 HALL, BERNARD G. Milton's Shepherd Lad. TLS, Oct. 12, 1933, p. 691.
    In Comus.

2520 HALPERT, V. B. On Coming to the Window in L'Allegro. Anglia, 81, 1963, 198-200.
    Surveys commentary concerning the infinitive in 1. 45 and concludes that the skylark is its subject.

2521 HANFORD, JAMES HOLLY. Haemony (Comus, 616-48). TLS, Nov. 3, 1932, p. 815.

2522 ------. Milton's Poem On the Death of a Fair Infant. RES, 9, 1933, 312-5.
    On the date of composition (1625).

2523 ------. The Pastoral Elegy and Milton's Lycidas. John Milton, Poet and Humanist (Cleveland: Western Reserve Univ. Press, 1966), pp. 126-60.
    A reprint of Stevens' No. 606, first published in 1910. Also reprinted in revised form in Milton's Lycidas: The Tradition and the Poem. Ed. by C. A. Patrides (New York: Holt, Rinehart, and Winston, 1961), pp. 27-55. "Reviews history of pastoral poetry. Concludes that Milton found his material in all great pastorals; that he was more indebted to Vergil than to Theocritus; and that his debt to Spenser is great. A thorough study" (Stevens' annotation).

2524 ------. The Youth of Milton: An Interpretation of His Early Literary Development. Studies in Shakespeare, Milton, and Donne (New York: Haskell House, 1964), pp. 87-164. Published also in John Milton, Poet and Humanist (Cleveland: Western Reserve Univ. Press, 1966), pp. 1-74.
    Reprints of Stevens' No. 2556. "The parts played by reading, imitation, and experience of active life are integrated into a pattern depicting Milton's youthful development. An excellent introductory document for a balanced judgment of the Minor Poems" (Stevens' annotation).

2525 HARDISON, O. B., JR. Milton's On Time and Its Scholastic Background. TSLL, 3, 1961, 107-22.
    The poem is a reminder that Milton's training in Aristotle "greatly deepened the perspective within which he viewed the issues arising in his poetry."

2526 HARDY, JOHN E. The Curious Frame: Seven Poems in Text and Context. South Bend: Univ. of Notre Dame Press, 1962.
    Milton's Lycidas, pp. 22-44. Contains a reprint of the text and analysis of Lycidas in Poems of Mr. John Milton, ed. by Cleanth Brooks and John Hardy (1951).
Cleanth Brooks and Hardy's Poems of Mr. John Milton: the 1645

2527 ------. Reconsiderations; I. Lycidas. KR, 7, 1945, 99-113. Reprinted in

Edition with Essays in Analysis (New York: Harcourt Brace, 1951; London: Dennis Dobson, 1957).

2528 HARRELL, KARL P. The Nature of the Grotesque in Milton's Comus. Master's thesis, Univ. of North Carolina, 1951.

2529 HARRINGTON, DAVID V. Feeling and Form in Milton's Sonnets. WHR, 20, 1966, 317-28.
Analysis of several of Milton's sonnets in order to show that a reader "should be guided by the form of a poem to a comprehension of significant controlled feeling."

2530 HARRISON, T. P., JR. The Latin Pastorals of Milton and Castiglione. PMLA, 50, 1935, 480-93.
Sets forth parallels between Castiglione's Alcon and Milton's Lycidas.

2531 ------. A Note on Lycidas, 91. UTSE, 15, 1935, 22.

2532 ------. The Haemony Passage in Comus Again. PQ, 22, 1943, 251-4.
On Milton's use of Henry Lyte's New Herbal (1578).

2533 ------. The Pastoral Elegy, an Anthology. English Translations by Harry Joshua Leon. Austin: Univ. of Texas Press, 1939. xii, 312pp.
Prints the texts of Lycidas and Lament for Damon: commentary on Milton's pastoral elegies, pp. 289-96.

2534 HARVEY, W. J. Milton and the Late Fantasticks. N&Q, N.S., 4, 1957, 523-4.
Questions Tillyard's view that the Late Fantasticks of At a Vacation Exercise are George Herbert and his group.

2535 HAUG, RALPH A. They also serve. . . . N&Q, 183, 1942, 224-5.
Suggests that I Samuel 30:24 is the origin of the last line of the sonnet On His Blindness.

2536 HAUN, EUGENE. An Inquiry into the Genre of Comus. Essays in Honor of W. C. Curry (Nashville: Vanderbilt Univ. Press, 1954), pp. 221-39.
Holds that Comus is not a proper-masque but a transitional piece in which the music and dance are secondary to the plot.

2537 HAVILAND, THOMAS P. Hugh Henry Brackenridge and Milton's Piedmontese Sonnet. N&Q, 176, 1939, 243-4.

2538 HELLINGS, PETER. A Note on the Sonnets of Milton. LL, 64, 1950, 165-9.
Maintains that speech habits rather than speech rhythms form the basis of the grand manner of the sonnets.

2539 HENRY, NATHANIEL H. Who Meant License When They Cried Liberty? MLN, 66, 1951, 509-13.
On Sonnets 11 and 12. Holds that Milton is referring to the "lunatic fringe" of the Independents.

2540 HERRON, DALE. Poetic Vision in Two Sonnets of Milton. MN, 2, 1968, 23-8.
Compares Sonnets 18 and 19 and finds that "in both, the context of the underlying Biblical allusions dominates much of the tone and the imagery.

The two sonnets are linked through Milton's concern with his own poetic mission; and in both poems Milton considers the issues of true or right seeing and the manifestation of Grace of Light as it is related to inspiration and prophecy."

2541 HEYWORTH, P. L. The Composition of Milton's At a Solemn Musick. BNYPL, 70, 1966, 450-8.
Uses the Trinity manuscript to reconstruct the stages of composition.

2542 HOELTJE, HUBERT H. L'Allegro, Lines 53-55. PMLA, 45, 1930, 201-3.

2543 HOLLANDER, JOHN. Milton's Renewed Song. The Untuning of the Sky: Ideas of Music in English Poetry, 1500-1700 (Princeton: Princeton Univ. Press, 1961), pp. 315-31. Reprinted in Milton: Modern Essays in Criticism. A Galaxy Book. Ed. by Arthur E. Barker (New York: Oxford Univ. Press, 1965), pp. 43-57.
Deals especially with Comus and At a Solemn Musick. Written originally as a section in Hollander's doctoral dissertation (same title as the 1961 book), Indiana Univ., 1959.

2544 HONE, RALPH E. The Pilot of the Galilean Lake. SP, 56, 1959, 55-61.
Insists that the pilot of Lycidas is Christ.

2545 HOOPES, ROBERT. God Guide Thee Guyon: Nature and Grace Reconciled in the Faerie Queene, Book II. RES, N.S., 5, 1954, 14-24.
Analogies with Comus and Paradise Regained, pp. 23-4.

2546 HOWARD, H. WENDELL. Milton's L'Allegro, 136-143. Expl, 24, 1965, item 3.
On various types of music echoed in the passage.

2547 HOWARD, LEON. That Two-handed Engine Once More. HLQ, 15, 1952, 173-84.

2548 HUGHES, R. E. That Two-handed Engine—Again. N&Q, N.S., 2, 1955, 58-9.

2549 HUNTER, WILLIAM B., JR. Milton Translates the Psalms. PQ, 40, 1961, 485-94.
On Milton's translation of Psalms 80-88 in April, 1648. "It is my purpose here to show the tradition of the psalters within which Milton worked and his relationship to it, and to suggest a probable reason why he undertook the work at just this time."

2550 ------. A Note on Lycidas. MLN, 65, 1950, 544.
On the sheep-rot passage.

2551 HUNTLEY, FRANK L. A Background in Folklore for the Blind Mouths Passage in Lycidas (ll. 113-31). MN, 1, 1967, 53-5.
On the long folk tradition of characterizing the clergy as ignorant and covetous wolves, clever but not clever enough to fool anyone for long.

2552 HUNTLEY, JOHN F. The Ecology and Anatomy of Criticism: Milton's Sonnet 19 and the Bee Simile in Paradise Lost, I. 768-76. JAAC, 24, 1966, 383-91.
Discusses "the use of historical fact in the work of literary interpretation,"

with references to Sonnet 19, and "proposes a non-Homeric, non-Virgilian, rather 'Miltonic' interpretation of the bee simile...."

2553   ------. Milton's 23rd Sonnet. ELH, 34, 1967, 368-81.
Reviews the controversy surrounding the identity of "my late espoused Saint" and concludes that "Sonnet 23 recreates the essential features of a universal human experience which can be specified as the genus which encloses many specific instances."

2554   HUTTAR, CHARLES A. English Metrical Paraphrases of the Psalms, 1500-1640. Doctoral diss., Northwestern Univ., 1956. Abs., DA, 17, 1957, 631-2.
Considers Milton's paraphrases in a general way.

2555   HYMAN, LAWRENCE W. Milton's On the Late Massacre in Piedmont. ELN, 3, 1965, 26-9.
Offers thematic interpretation of the poem "as a record ... of the poet's own struggle to overcome his shock at the ways of God to those just men who follow His way."

2556   JACKSON, ELIZABETH. Milton's Sonnet XX. PMLA, 65, 1950, 328-9.
Supports and further substantiates Neiman, PMLA, 64, 1949, 480-3.

2557   JACKSON, JAMES L., and WALTER E. WEESE. . . . Who only Stand and Wait: Milton's Sonnet On His Blindness. MLN, 72, 1957, 91-3.
Interprets "stand" in the light of Ephesians 6:13.

2558   JAY, LEMUEL EUGENE. Background and Justification in Pastoral Poetry for the Attack on Church and Clergy in Lycidas. Master's thesis, Duke Univ., 1942.

2559   JAYNE, SEARS. The Subject of Milton's Ludlow Mask. PMLA, 74, 1959, 533-43. Reprinted in Milton: Modern Essays in Criticism. A Galaxy Book. Ed. by Arthur E. Barker (New York: Oxford Univ. Press, 1965), pp. 88-111; A Maske at Ludlow: Essays on Milton's Comus. Ed. by John S. Diekhoff (Cleveland: Case Western Reserve Univ. Press, 1968), pp. 165-87.
Analyzes Comus from the point of view of the Renaissance Platonists and concludes that Milton "was merely trying his hand at a technique of mythologized Christian Platonism which had been popular ever since the time of Ficino."

2560   JOHNSON, SAMUEL. from The Life of Milton. Milton's Lycidas: The Tradition and the Poem. Ed. by C. A. Patrides (New York: Holt, Rinehart, and Winston, 1961), pp. 56-7.

2561   JONES, KATHERINE. A Note on Milton's Lycidas. AI, 19, 1962, 141-55.
"I have here tried to explain Milton's Lycidas and its inception as the outcome of the ambivalent feeling he had for King."

2562   JONES, WILLIAM M. Immortality in Two of Milton's Elegies. Myth and Symbol: Critical Approaches and Applications. Ed. by Bernice Slote (Lincoln: Univ. of Nebraska Press, 1963), pp. 133-40.
The Fair Infant and Epitaphium Damonis. In both, Milton can never "progress emotionally beyond the initial image of earthly productivity that he found in the Apollo-hyacinth myth...."

2563 JONES-DAVIES, M. T. Note sur la Légende de Sabrina dans le Comus de Milton. EA, 20, 1967, 416-9.
       A study of the influence of the poetry of Thomas Lodge on the thought of Milton. Acomparison is made between Lodge's Scillaes Metamorphosis (1589) and Tragicall Complaint of Elstred (1593) and the legend of Sabrina in Milton's Comus.

2564 KANE, ROBERT J. Blind Mouths in Lycidas. MLN, 68, 1953, 239-40.

2565 KATCHEN, GRETL. Comus Once More. MN, 2, 1968, 46.
       Addenda to Charles C. Mish (MN, 1, 1967, 39-41) on Puteanus' Comus (1608).

2566 KELLEY, MAURICE. Lycidas: the Two-Handed Engine. N&Q, 181, 1941, 273.
       Reply by G. G. Loane, p. 320.

2567 ------. Milton's Later Sonnets and the Cambridge Manuscript. MP, 54, 1956, 20-5.
       On versions of the later sonnets in the Cambridge Manuscript and the date of composition.

2568 KEMP, LYSANDER. On a Sonnet by Milton. HR, 6, 1952, 80-3.
       Feels that "When I consider how my light is spent" refers to the exhaustion of the poet's inspiration.

2569 KENDALL, LYLE H., JR. Melt with Ruth. N&Q, 198, 1953, 145.
       The phrase in Lycidas occurs also in Chaucer and Spenser.

2570 KILLEEN, J. F. Milton, Lycidas, 144: The Pansy Freaked with Jet. N&Q, N.S., 9, 1962, 70, 73.
       Freaked may have been suggested by "the past participle passive of Latin ludere."

2571 KIMMICH, PAUL EDWARD. John Milton's Technical Handling of the Latin Elegy. Doctoral diss., Univ. of Illinois, 1958. Abs., DA, 19, 1958, 1078-9.

2572 KING, BRUCE. Lycidas and Oldham. EA, 19, 1966, 60-3.
       Parallels between Milton's poem and Dryden's To the Memory of Mr. Oldham suggest additional evidence of Milton's influence.

2573 KLEIN, JOAN LARSEN. Some Spenserian Influences on Milton's Comus. AnM, 5, 1964, 27-47.
       A study of similarities and differences with the conclusion that "Comus finally must be seen as an allegorical representation of man's journey through a life filled with peril to its ultimate end with God."

2574 KNAPP, C. A. Milton's Eglantine. N&Q, 176, 1939, 267.
       In L'Allegro.

2575 KOZIOL, HERBERT. Then to Come in Spite of Sorrow. Anglia, 84, 1966, 75.
       On L'Allegro, 1. 45.

2576 KUROTA, KENJIRO. Milton's Juvenilia. Ehime Univ. Reports, 1, 1952.

2577 LAGUARDIA, ERIC HENRY. Nature Redeemed: The Imitation of Order in Three Renaissance Poems. Doctoral diss., State Univ. of Iowa, 1961. Abs., DA, 22, 1962, 2786. The Hague: Mouton; New York: Humanities Press, 1966. 180pp.
> In Comus, as in Books 3 and 4 of the Faerie Queene, there is "a movement from the corruption and disorder of sensual experience to the purity and order of chaste innocence. The resolution of Comus also provides a metaphor for an ordered nature."
> Rev: Joan Grundy, MLR, 63, 1968, 676-7.

2578 LAWRY, JON S. Eager Thought: Dialectic in Lycidas. PMLA, 77, 1962, 27-32. Reprinted in Milton: Modern Essays in Criticism. A Galaxy Book. Ed. by Arthur E. Barker (New York: Oxford Univ. Press, 1965), pp. 112-24.
> "We may . . . take an additional step toward reconciling the supposedly antagonistic modes of statement in Lycidas by considering the poem as in part a dialectical process, in the Hegelian sense. . . ."

2579 ------. The Shadow of Heaven: Matter and Stance in Milton's Poetry. Ithaca: Cornell Univ. Press, 1968. xv, 416pp.
> Deals with several of the minor poems, especially Comus and Lycidas, in the first three chapters.

2580 LEAHY, WILLIAM. Pollution and Comus. EIC, 11, 1961, 111.
> A reply to David Wilkinson, EIC, 10, 1960, 32-43. The Lady's uncompromising resistance stems from the presence of Lady Alice's family in the audience.

2581 LE COMTE, EDWARD S. Lycidas, Petrarch, and the Plague. MLN, 69, 1954, 402-4.

2582 ------. Milton: Two Verbal Parallels. N&Q, 184, 1943, 17-8.
> The reference to "finny drove" in Comus parallels passages in Spenser and Drayton. Reply by Hibernicus, p. 85.

2583 ------. New Lights on the Haemony Passage in Comus. PQ, 21, 1942, 283-98.
> Finds the model for haemony in Gerard's Herball, which "was yet fresh from the press" at the time Milton was writing Comus, and in other sources.

2584 ------. That Two-Handed Engine and Savonarola. SP, 47, 1950, 589-606.

2585 ------. That Two-Handed Engine and Savonarola: Supplement. SP, 49, 1952, 548-50.

2586 ------. The Veiled Face of Milton's Wife. N&Q, N.S., 1, 1954, 245-6.
> Milton's "late espoused saint" is Katherine, not Mary.

2587 LEISHMAN, J. B. L'Allegro and Il Penseroso in Their Relation to Seventeenth-Century Poetry. E&S, N.S., 4, 1951, 1-36. Reprinted in Milton: Modern Judgements, ed. by Alan Rudrum (London: MacMillan, 1968), pp. 58-93.
> Asserts that "many of the most delightful characteristics of seventeenth-century poetry in general are there more perfectly exhibited than elsewhere."

2588 LEWIS, C. S. Above the Smoke and Stir. TLS, July 14, 1945, p. 331.
> Replies by B. A. Wright, TLS, Aug. 4, 1945, p. 367; by Robert Eisler, Sept.

22, 1945, p. 451; by Lewis, Sept. 29, 1945, p. 463; by Wright, Oct. 27, 1945, p. 511. Lewis quotes Henry More as the source of the Spirit in Comus. Wright finds the source in Plato's Phaedo.

2589 ------. From the Latin of Milton's De Idea Platonic Quemadmodum Aristoteles Intellexit. English, 5, 1945, 195.
Reprints De Idea Platonica . . . , "probably intended as a mere academic squib; but genius sometimes laughs at authors' intentions."

2590 ------. A Note on Comus. RES, 8, 1932, 170-6. Reprinted in Studies in Medieval and Renaissance Literature. Ed. by Walter Hooper (Cambridge: Cambridge Univ. Press, 1966), pp. 175-81.
On Milton's changes in the first five versions of the poem.

2591 L[OANE], G[EORGE] G. Milton: Built in th' eclipse (Lycidas, 1. 100). N&Q, 179, 1940, 9.
Reply by T. O. Mabbott, pp. 141-2.

2592 ------. Milton's Eglantine. N&Q, 176, 1939, 225.
Milton's use of "eglantine" in L'Allegro reminiscent of Spenser's in The Faerie Queene, 3, 6, 44.

2593 LITTLE, MARGUERITE. Milton's Ad Patrem and the Younger Gill's In Natalem Mei Parentis. JEGP, 49, 1959, 345-51.
On the possibility that Milton used Gill's poem as a source.

2594 LLOYD, MICHAEL. Comus and Plutarch's Daemons. N&Q, N.S., 7, 1960, 421-3.
On the nature of daemons in Plutarch and Milton.

2595 ------. The Fatal Bark. MLN, 75, 1960, 103-8.
Lycidas, 100-2, "refers to the mortal bark, built in the eclipse man has endured since Adam's fall."

2596 ------. Justa Edouardo King. N&Q, N.S., 5, 1958, 432-4.
A discussion of the various elegies in the volume.

2597 ------. The Two Worlds of Lycidas. EIC, 11, 1961, 390-402.
The poem dramatically contrasts two worlds: the "mortal world self-absorbed" and the supernatural.

2598 LYNSKEY, WINIFRED. A Critic in Action: Mr. Ransom. CE, 5, 1944, 239-49.
Animadversions on Ransom's criticism of Lycidas, pp. 242-3.

2599 MAAS, P. Hid in, Lycidas, 1. 69. RES, 19, 1943, 397-8.
Believes that the editors should restore the "hid in" of the 1638 edition.

2600 MABBOTT, THOMAS O. Lycidas and Lycaeus. N&Q, 172, 1937, 462.
A reply to McColley, N&Q, 172, 1937, 352.

2601 ------. Milton: Built in the eclipse. N&Q, 179, 1940, 141-2.
Reply to Loane, N&Q, 179, 1940, 9. On Lycidas, 100.

2602 ------. Milton's In Effigei Ejus Sculptorem. Expl, 8, 1950, item 58.
On the meaning of the jest in the epigram.

2603 ------. Milton's Latin Poems, TLS, Oct. 27, 1932, p. 790.

2604 ------. Milton's Lycidas, lines 164 and 183-185. Expl, 5, 1947, item 26.

2605 ------. Milton's Sonnet on His Late Espoused Saint. N&Q, 189, 1945, 239.
Disagrees with argument that the sonnet applies to Milton's first wife.

2606 MacLEAN, HUGH N. Milton's Fair Infant. ELH, 24, 1957, 296-305.
Reprinted in Milton: Modern Essays in Criticism. A Galaxy Book. Ed.
by Arthur E. Barker (New York: Oxford Univ. Press, 1965), pp. 21-30.
On the structure and imagery of the poem.

2607 MacCAFFREY, ISABEL G. Lycidas: The Poet in a Landscape. The
Lyric and Dramatic Milton. Ed. by Joseph H. Summers (New York
and London: Columbia Univ. Press, 1965), pp. 65-92.
"Death is the occasion, lost innocence the theme; the poem itself records the
experience provoked by death and loss. The true landscape of Lycidas is the
speaker's consciousness. . . ."

2608 MADDISON, CAROL. Apollo and the Nine: A History of the Ode.
London: Routledge and Kegan Paul, 1960. 427pp.
L'Allegro, Il Penseroso, the Nativity Ode and other early poems discussed,
pp. 318-30. Also passim.

2609 MADSEN, WILLIAM G. The Idea of Nature in Milton's Poetry. Three
Studies in the Renaissance: Sidney, Jonson, Milton. Yale Studies in
English, 138. Ed. by Benjamin C. Nangle (New Haven: Yale Univ.
Press, 1958), pp. 181-283.
Topics: Nature in Comus; Nature in Paradise Lost; Nature, Man and God;
Nature and Grace; The Poetic Vision.

2610 ------. The Voice of Michael in Lycidas. SEL, 3, 1963, 1-7.
"The current confusion about Lycidas, I suggest, has resulted from assuming
that the consolation is spoken by the uncouth swain. We have failed to hear
the voice of Michael."

2611 MAJOR, JOHN M. Comus and The Tempest. SQ, 10, 1959, 177-83.
Holds that The Tempest and Comus share more than a resemblance of
form, theme, dramatic situation, characterization, atmosphere, and language
and that the play served as an actual model for Milton's masque.

2612 MARESCA, THOMAS E. The Latona Myth in Milton's Sonnet XII. MLN,
76, 1961, 491-4.
Concludes that in the sonnet the progeny of Latona and "the mysteries of
the Gospel" are identical.

2613 MARILLA, ESMOND L. That Two-Handed Engine Finally? PMLA, 67,
1952, 1183-4. Reprinted in Milton and Modern Man: Selected Essays
(University, Alabama: Univ. of Alabama Press, 1968), pp. 114-7.
Holds that the passage in Lycidas is "a forecast that, through fulfillment of
divine prophecy, the day of final reckoning for these same 'perverters' of
truth and righteousness [i. e., the Blinde mouthes] is at hand."

2614 MARKS, EMERSON R. Milton's Lycidas. Expl, 8, 1951, item 44.

2615 MARSHALL, GEORGE O., JR. Milton's Lycidas, 15-22. Expl, 17, 1959,
item 66.
Defines the word lucky.

2616   MARTIN, L. C. Thomas Warton and the Early Poems of Milton. Warton
        Lecture on English Poetry. Proceedings of the British Academy, 20.
        Oxford: Oxford Univ. Press, 1934. 21pp.
            Rev. Eric Gillett, Merc, 30, 1934, 374.

2617   MARTZ, LOUIS L. The Poetry of Meditation, a Study in English Re-
        ligious Literature of the Seventeenth Century. YSE, 125. New Haven:
        Yale Univ. Press, 1954. Revised Edition, 1962. x, 375pp.
            The Nativity Ode discussed, pp. 164-7; other poems, passim.

2618   ------. The Rising Poet, 1645. The Lyric and Dramatic Milton. Ed. by
        Joseph H. Summers (New York and London: Columbia Univ. Press,
        1965), pp. 3-33.
            An appreciative essay on the 1645 volume of Milton's poems, with special
            emphasis on the Nativity Ode. Sees the volume as a "tribute to a youthful
            era now past" and as a forecast of more complex poetry to come.

2619   MAXWELL, J. C. Comus, Line 37, N&Q, N.S., 6, 1959, 364.
            The line echoes the Aeneid 9, 391-2.

2620   ------. The Pseudo-Problem of Comus. Camb. Jour., 1, 1948, 376-80.
            The doctrine of virtue.

2621   MAYERSON, CAROLINE W. The Orpheus Image in Lycidas. PMLA,
        64, 1949, 189-207.
            Relates the image to the poet's own conquest of the temptation to fear and
            doubt.

2622   McCOLLEY, GRANT. Lycidas and Lycaeus. N&Q, 172, 1937, 352.
            "Lycidas" may be Milton's poetic transformation of "Lycaeus," a name
            current at the time of composition of Lycidas.

2623   McKENZIE, J. Early Scottish Performances of Comus. N&Q, 198, 1953,
        158-9.
            On Jan. 7 and 14 and Feb. 1, 1751.

2624   ------. Early Scottish Performances of Comus. N&Q, N.S., 1, 1954, 109.
            Additional notices.

2625   McKENZIE, KENNETH. Echoes of Dante in Milton's Lycidas. Italica,
        20, 1943, 121-6.

2626   McQUEEN, WILLIAM. Prevent the Sun: Milton, Donne, and the Book
        of Wisdom. MN, 2, 1968, 63-4.
            Uses Donne's sermon No. 79 in LXXX Sermons as a gloss on the Nativity Ode.

2627   MELLERS, WILFRID. Harmonious Meeting: A Study of the Relation-
        ship Between English Music, Poetry, and Theater, c. 1660-1900. New
        York: Dover Publications, 1965.
            Comus discussed in a chapter called The Genesis of Masque, pp. 153-67. Also
            prints Henry Lawes' Hymns to the Trinity.

2628   MILES, JOSEPHINE. The Primary Language of Lycidas. Milton's
        Lycidas: The Tradition and the Poem. Ed. by C. A. Patrides (New York:
        Holt, Rinehart, and Winston, 1961), pp. 95-100.
            Author's revised version of a section from her The Primary Language of

Poetry in the 1640's (Univ. of California Publications in English, 19, 1948, 86-90).

2629 MITCHELL, CHARLES B. The English Sonnet in the Seventeenth Century, Especially after Milton. Doctoral diss., Harvard Univ., 1939. Abs., Harvard Univ., Summaries of Theses, 1942, pp. 239-43.

2630 MOLONEY, MICHAEL F. The Prosody of Milton's Epitaph, L'Allegro and Il Penseroso. MLN, 72, 1957, 174-8.
Argues that for the Epitaph Milton borrows from the funerary art of Jonson but that the poet used a more traditional heptasyllabic and octosyllabic line in the companion pieces.

2631 MONTEIRO, GEORGE. Milton's On His Blindness (Sonnet XIX). Expl, 24, 1966, item 67.
On Matthew 25:14-30 and Milton's conclusion in the poem.

2632 MONTGOMERY, WALTER A. The Epitaphium Damonis in the Stream of the Classical Lament. Studies for William A. Read (Baton Rouge: Louisiana State Univ. Press, 1940), pp. 207-20.

2633 MORE, PAUL ELMER. How to Read Lycidas. Amer. Rev., 7, 1936, 140-58. Reprinted in On Being Human (Princeton: Princeton Univ. Press, 1936), pp. 184-202; and in Milton's Lycidas: The Tradition and the Poem. Ed. by C. A. Patrides (New York: Holt, Rinehart, and Winston, 1961), pp. 82-95.
Compares the comments of Tillyard and Dr. Johnson on the poem and then attempts to clarify "the relation between the content of a poem and the art of a poem independent of its content."

2634 MORSE, C. J. The Dating of Milton's Sonnet XIX. TLS, Sept. 15, 1961, p. 620.
Immediately following the summer of 1652. Emile Saillens offers further support in TLS, Oct. 6, 1961, p. 672.

2635 MORSE, J. MITCHELL. A Pun in Lycidas. N&Q, N.S., 5, 1958, 211.
Suggests Milton's awareness of the ambiguity of footing.

2636 MOSER, EDWIN. The Order of Fragments of Thoreau's Essay on L'Allegro and Il Penseroso. Thoreau Society Bulletin, 101, 1967, 1-2.
A reconstruction of the text of Thoreau's college essay on the early poems.

2637 MUELLER, MARTIN. The Theme and Imagery of Milton's Last Sonnet. Archiv, 201, 1964, 267-71.
Discusses the interrelation on the images, the significance of the central image of the veil, and the mood of the poem. Offers modification of an interpretation "shared by W. R. Parker and the late Leo Spitzer."

2638 MUTSCHMANN, HEINRICH. That Two-Handed Engine at the Door. TLS, Apr. 25, 1936, p. 356.
Replies by H. L. Savage, TLS, July 25, 1936, p. 616; by Mutschmann, Aug. 8, 1936 p. 645, and Aug. 15, 1936, p. 664; by A. F. Pollard, Aug. 29, 1936, p. 697.

2639 ------. That Two-Handed Engine at the Door. N&Q, N.S., 2, 1955, 515.

2640 MYHR, IVAR L. [Mrs. E. H. Duncan]. Milton's Hymn on the Morning of Christ's Nativity, Stanza 8. Expl, 4, 1945, item 16.

2641 NAKAGIRI, NOBUYA. Lycidas and the Change of Young Milton. Meiji Gakuin Ronso (Japan), 17, 1948.

2642 NEIMAN, FRASER. Milton's Sonnet XX. PMLA, 64, 1949, 480-3.
On the meaning of "spare" (1. 13).

2643 NELSON, LOWRY, JR. Baroque Lyric Poetry. New Haven: Yale Univ. Press, 1961. viii, 244pp.
The Nativity Ode and Lycidas discussed, pp. 41-52 and 67-76, respectively, in Part 2, Time as a Means of Structure; Lycidas discussed again, pp. 138-52, in Part 3, Drama as a Means of Structure.

2644 NEMSER, RUBY. A Reinterpretation of The Unexpressive Nuptial Song. MN, 2, 1968, 1-2.
Believes "that Milton uses 'unexpressive' to indicate that this heavenly song . . . is 'expressionless,' . . . supernatural music of heavenly spirits, ordinarily inaudible on earth."

2645 NEUSE, RICHARD. Metamorphosis and Symbolic Action in Comus. ELH, 34, 1967, 49-64.
A detailed account of various paradigms and "symbolic expressions of man's lower nature" as representations of "nature disjoined from spirit."

2646 NITCHIE, GEORGE W. Lycidas: A Footnote. N&Q, N.S., 13, 1966, 377-8.
Notes that 11. 124-131 "anticipate the rhyme pattern of the ottava rima stanza" which closes the poem.

2647 OMAN, SIR CHARLES. Of Poor Mr. King, John Milton, and Certain Friends. Cornhill, 156, 1937, 577-87.
Reviews the companion pieces of Lycidas in the first memorial volume.

2648 ORAS, ANTS. Metre and Chronology in Milton's Epitaph on the Marchioness of Winchester, L'Allegro, and Il Penseroso. N&Q, 198, 1953, 332-3.

2649 ------. Milton's Early Rhyme Schemes and the Structure of Lycidas. MP, 52, 1954, 14-22.
"The preceding pages have, I hope, provided at least a partial refutation of the views of those critics who regard rhyme in Milton as a kind of unassimilated foreign body of which he gradually rid himself because for him it had no functional meaning."

2650 ------. Milton's Upon the Circumcision and Tasso. N&Q, 197, 1952, 314-5.

2651 PARKER, WILLIAM RILEY. The Dates of Milton's Sonnets on Blindness. PMLA, 73, 1958, 196-200.
Dates When I Consider late 1651, and Cyriack, this three years day 1654, after May.

2652 ------. Milton's Fair Infant. TLS, Dec. 17, 1938, p. 802.

2653 ------. Milton's Hobson Poems: Some Neglected Early Texts. MLR, 31, 1936, 395-402.

2654   ------. Milton's Last Sonnet. RES, 21, 1945, 235-8.
        Favors Mary Powell as the subject. Reply by T. O. Mabbott, N&Q, 189, 1945,
        239.

2655   ------. Milton's Last Sonnet Again. RES, N.S., 2, 1951, 147-52.
        A reply to Pyle, RES, 25, 1949, 57-60, with further comment by Pyle, pp.
        152-4.

2656   ------. Milton's Sonnet: I did but prompt, 6. Expl, 8, 1949, item 3.

2657   ------. Notes on the Chronology of Milton's Latin Poems. A Tribute to
        G. C. Taylor (Chapel Hill: Univ. of North Carolina Press, 1952), pp.
        113-31.

2658   ------. Shakespeare and Milton. MLN, 53, 1938, 556.
        Addendum to Spencer, MLN, 53, 1938, 366-7.

2659   ------. Some Problems in the Chronology of Milton's Early Poems. RES,
        11, 1935, 276-83.
        A detailed discussion of the difficulties involved in dating certain of Milton's
        works.

2660   PATRIDES, C. A. The Cessation of the Oracles: The History of a Legend.
        MLR, 9, 1965, 500-7.
        The legend of the "dumm oracles" in the Nativity Ode goes back to Plutarch,
        and there are many medieval and Renaissance references to the event.

2661   ------, ed. Milton's Lycidas: The Tradition and the Poem. New York:
        Holt, Rinehart, and Winton, 1961. x, 246pp.
        Chapter One contains the texts of Lycidas, with the significant corrections
        made by Milton, and of Epitaphium Damonis, edited by H. W. Garrod and
        translated by Helen Waddell. Chapter Two contains commentaries, all
        previously printed, but with some revisions by James H. Hanford, E. M. W.
        Tillyard, J. C. Ransom, P. E. More, J. Miles, D. Daiches, R. P. Adams, W.
        Shumaker, C. Brooks and J. E. Hardy, F. T. Prince, R. Tuve, N. Frye, and
        M. H. Abrams, all of which are entered individually in this bibliography.
        Appendices: The Text of Lycidas, An Annotated Reading List.
        Rev: B. Rajan, MLR, 60, 1965, 251.

2662   PEPLE, EDWARD C. Notes on Some Productions of Comus. SP, 36,
        1939, 235-42.
        Supplements Thaler, SP, 17, 1920, 269-308.

2663   PEQUIGNEY, JOSEPH. Milton's Sonnet XIX Reconsidered. TSLL, 8,
        1967, 484-98.
        Explicates the sonnet, covering facets of word usage and style, with a lengthy
        discussion of the word "waite."

2664   POST, MARTIN M. Milton's Twin Lyrics at Three Hundred. EJ, 22,
        1933, 567-80.
        Uses L'Allegro and Il Penseroso to refute those who feel that Milton has no
        relation to the modern world.

2665   POTTER, JAMES L. Milton's Talent Sonnet and Barnabe Barnes. N&Q,
        N.S., 4, 1957, 447.
        Barnes' Sonnets 26 and 28 contain puns on the talents of Matt. 24:14-30,
        and Milton uses the puns in the same way.

2666 PRINCE, F. T. The Italian Element in Lycidas. The Italian Element in Milton's Verse (Oxford: Clarendon Press, 1954, 1962), pp. 71-88. Reprinted in Milton's Lycidas: The Tradition and the Poem. Ed. by C. A. Patrides (New York: Holt, Rinehart, and Winston, 1961), pp. 153-66.

2667 ------. Lycidas and the Tradition of the Italian Eclogue. EM, 2, 1951, 95-105.
Lycidas "mirrors the experiments made in Italy to combine the forms of Italian lyric verse with conventions and diction of Greek and Latin eclogues."

2668 PYLE, FITZROY. And Old Damaetas Lov'd to Hear Our Song Hermathena, 71, 1948, 83-92.
Holds that Damaetas is William Chappell.

2669 ------. Milton's First Sonnet on His Blindness. RES, N.S., 9, 1958, 376-87.
Offers objections to Harry F. Robins' interpretation (RES, N.S., 7, 1956, 360-6). Suggests that "Milton has felt passionately indignant and resentful" but "has re-examined himself and . . . finishes in the steady hope that creative power will return."

2670 ------. Milton's Sonnet on His Late Espoused Saint. RES, 25, 1949, 57-60.
Defends the traditional view that Milton has Katherine Woodcock in mind.

2671 R. Quotations from Lycidas. N&Q, 173, 1937, 393.
Finds seventeen quotations listed in Bartlett (10th ed.).

2672 RAJAN, BALACHANDA. Comus: The Inglorious Likeness. UTQ, 37, 1968, 113-35.
A consideration of the best rational approach to reading Comus. Includes references which Milton made to his masque and discusses the problem of defining masque form. Contains rather broad explication, which for the most part consists of material having to do with the logic and language of the work.

2673A ------. Lycidas: The Shattering of the Leaves. SP, 64, 1967, 51-64.
An address delivered to the Milton Society in 1964 and summarized in SCN, 23, 1965, 27-8. "Lycidas is the shattering of the leaves, not simply in the passage from innocence to experience, but in the angry challenge of the poem to the tradition which it inherits and, finally, to its own security and indeed survival."

2673B ------. In Order Serviceable. MLR, 63, 1968, 13-22.
An analysis of the Nativity Ode. Regards it as "initiating the personal tradition of his [Milton's] work.

2674A RAMSAY, PAUL. The Lively and the Just. Univ. of Alabama Studies, 15. University, Alabama: Univ. of Alabama Press, 1962.
Contains a chapter on Lycidas, which Ramsay calls "the best shorter poem in the language."

2674B RANS, GEOFFREY. Mr. Wilkinson on Comus. EIC, 10, 1960, 364-9.
Reply to David Wilkinson, EIC, 10, 1960, 32-43. Insists that "the primary interest must be moral." Defends the Lady's actions through a comparison with Eve.

2675 RANSOM, JOHN CROWE. A Poem Nearly Anonymous. American Review, 1, 1933, 179-203, 444-67. Reprinted in The World's Body (New York: Charles Scribner's Sons, 1938), pp. 1-28; and in Milton's Lycidas:

The Tradition and the Poem, ed. by C. A. Patrides (New York: Holt, Rinehart, and Winston, 1961), pp. 64-81.

> One of the most controversial articles on Lycidas in a generation. A study of the symbolic meaning with the suggestion that "it was written smooth and rewritten rough."

2676 ------. Why Critics Don't Go Mad. KR, 14, 1952, 331-9.

> A review article of Brooks and Hardy's edition of the early poems.

2677 REESING, JOHN. The Decorum of St. Peter's Speech in Lycidas. Milton's Poetic Art: A Mask, Lycidas, and Paradise Lost (Cambridge: Harvard Univ. Press, 1968), pp. 31-49.

> Discusses the two-handed engine. "Decorum, which for Milton is always 'the grand master-piece to observe,' suggests that the two-handed engine must surely be something that we can associate both with shepherds and with bishops, who are Christian shepherds."

2678 ------. Justice for Lycidas. Milton's Poetic Art: A Mask, Lycidas, and Paradise Lost (Cambridge: Harvard Univ. Press, 1968), pp. 19-28.

> Concerned with the justice of the death of Lycidas. "The poem does not answer the question, why? It does develop its own version of that favorite Miltonic theme, the amazing creativity of God, which is always acting redemptively to bring a new and greater good out of discord and evil."

2679 ------. Most Innocent Nature and Milton's Ludlow Mask. Milton's Poetic Art: A Mask, Lycidas, and Paradise Lost (Cambridge: Harvard Univ. Press, 1968), pp. 1-18.

> Holds that Comus "has to do with the relation of mortals to the world of the divine" and that "Its theme is the moral character of the timeless world of permanence and the moral conditions for membership in it." Discusses Milton's revisions of the text and relates the mask to Milton's other early works.

2680 REISS, EDMUND. An Instance of Milton's Use of Time. MLN, 72, 1957, 410-2.

> Shows that in an early poem, Naturam non pati senium, Milton already held that God created time before the world.

2681 RHODES, BYNO R. Milton's Two-Handed Engine. N&Q, N.S., 13, 1966, 24.

> Interprets the passage from Lycidas in light of Revelation 2:16.

2682 RIESE, TEUT ANDREAS. Die Theatralik der Tugend in Miltons Comus. Festschrift für Walter Hübner. Ed. by Dieter Riesner and Helmut Gneuss. (Berlin: Schmidt, 1964), pp. 192-202.

> An exposition on the artistic unity of Comus.

2683 RIGGS, EDITH. Milton's L'Allegro, 41-50. Expl, 23, 1965, item 44.

> Night is in the watch-tower, not the Lark.

2684 RINEHART, KEITH. A Note on the First Fourteen Lines of Milton's Lycidas. N&Q, 198, 1953, 103.

> Believes that Milton consciously approximates the sonnet form to emphasize the two ideas in the first part of the poem.

2685 ROBINS, HARRY F. The Key to a Problem in Milton's Comus. MLQ, 12, 1951, 422-8.
On Comus, 731-5.

2686 ------. Milton's First Sonnet on His Blindness. RES, 7, 1956, 360-6.
Holds that Sonnet 19 is an expression of "Milton's confidence in his ability to triumph over his affliction and to produce the great poetry toward which his ambition had always been directed."

2687 ------. Milton's Two-Handed Engine at the Door and St. Matthew's Gospel. RES, N.S., 5, 1954, 25-36.

2688 ROHR-SAUER, P. V. English Metrical Psalms from 1600 to 1600. A Study in the Religious and Aesthetic Tendencies of that Period. Doctoral diss., Freiburg, 1938. Freiburg: Poppen and Ortmann, 1938. 127pp.
Milton's Psalms discussed, pp. 39-43.

2689 ROONEY, WILLIAM J. J. Discrimination Among Values. JGE, 13, 1961, 40-52.
Relates On His Blindness to his discussion.

2690 ROSS, MALCOLM M. Milton and the Protestant Aesthetic: the Early Poems. UTQ, 17, 1948, 346-60.
Milton recalls traditional Christian symbols as he prepares a new and different tradition.

2691 RØSTVIG, MAREN-SOFIE. The Happy Man: Studies in the Metamorphoses of a Classical Ideal, 1600-1700. Oslo Studies in English, No. 2. Oslo: Akademish forlag; Oxford: Blackwell, 1964. 496pp.
John Milton, pp. 152-60. On the theme of rural retirement in Milton's early poems.

2692 RUDRUM, ALAN. A Critical Commentary on Milton's Comus and Shorter Poems. Macmillan Critical Commentaries. London: Macmillan, 1967. 113pp.
Contains commentary on the Nativity Ode, L'Allegro and Il Penseroso, Comus, Lycidas, and nineteen of the sonnets.

2693 S., W. W. As taint-worm to the weanling flocks (Lycidas, 1. 45). N&Q, 176, 1939, 112-3.
Author's letter of correction, p. 153.

2694 SABOL, ANDREW J. Songs and Dances for the Stuart Masque. Providence: Brown Univ. Press, 1959. 172pp.
Prints the words and music to five of the songs from Comus, pp. 91-9.

2695 SAILLENS, ÉMILE. Une Hypothèse à propos de Comus. EA, 12, 1959, 100-11.
". . . essentiellement, Comus est une confession, dans le sens où l'entendait saint Augustin."

2696 ST. CLAIR, F. Y. The Rhythm of Milton's Nativity Ode. CE, 5, 1944, 448.

2697 SAMUEL, IRENE. The Brood of Folly. N&Q, N.S., 5, 1958, 430-1.
On Erasmus and others as sources of the melancholy of L'Allegro and Il Penseroso.

2698   [Scenes From Comus]. MN, 1, 1967, 45.
         Comments on a production of Hugh Wood's work in London on April 12,
         1967.

2699   SCHAUS, HERMANN. The Relationship of Comus to Hero and Leander
         and Venus and Adonis. UTSE, 25, 1946, 129-41.
         Sees a definite connection between Milton's masque and the two earlier
         poems of Marlowe and Shakespeare.

2700   SCHOECK, R. J. Milton and Neaera's Hair. N&Q, N.S., 3, 1956, 190-1.
         Believes that Neaera in Lycidas is an echo from the Basia of Joannes
         Secundas.

2701   ------. That Two-Handed Engine Yet Once More: Milton, John of Salis-
         bury, and the Sword. N&Q, N.S., 2, 1955, 235-7.

2702   SCHOLDERER, V. Lycidas. TLS, June 28, 1947, p. 323.
         Replies by Richard Bell and by Parry Michael, July 12, 1947, p. 351; rejoinder
         by Scholderer, July 26, 1947, p. 379. Scholderer believes that Lycidas was
         written in a single day; Bell and Michael object.

2703   SCHULTZ, HOWARD. A book was writ of late. MLN, 69, 1954, 495-7.
         On the meaning of the Tetrachordon sonnet.

2704   SEATON, ETHEL. Comus and Shakespeare. E&S, 31, 1945, 68-80.
         Echoes of Shakespeare's plays in Comus.

2705   SEMPLE, W. H. The Latin Poems of John Milton. BJRL, 46, 1963, 217-35.
         Concerned with the autobiographical Latin poems in the 1645 volume. "They
         give me an impression not of haste but of energy, of vigorous intellectual
         power wishing to express, rapidly and flowingly, the thoughts that pour into
         the young poet's mind."

2706   SENSABAUGH, GEORGE F. The Milieu of Comus. SP, 41, 1944, 233-49.
         Argues that the controversy at the court over the cult of Platonic love is
         reflected in the masque.

2707   SHATTUCK, CHARLES H. Macready's Comus: A Prompt-Book Study.
         JEGP, 60, 1961, 731-48.
         On Macready's 1843 production, based on a copy of the prompt-book now in
         the Kean collection of the Folger Shakespeare Library.

2708   SHAWCROSS, JOHN T. Certain Relationships of the Manuscripts of
         Comus. PBSA, 54, 1960, 38-56.
         An examination of the alterations and variations between the Trinity
         Manuscript, the Bridgewater Manuscripts, and the printed versions of Comus,
         showing stages of composition.

2709   ------. The Date of Milton's Ad Patrem. N&Q, N.S., 6, 1959, 358-9.
         Finds that possible exigencies of printing the 1645 edition of the elegies and
         the Sylvae may make William R. Parker's date (before Nov., 1634) ques-
         tionable.

2710   ------. The Date of the Separate Edition of Milton's Epitaphium Damonis.
         SB, 18, 1965, 262-5.
         ". . . the usual date of 1640 (?) seems acceptable . . . , although 1639 (?) has
         . . . much to offer as publication date."

2711 ------. Division of Labor in Justa Edovardo King Naufrago (1638). LC, 27, 1961, 176-9.
On the respective work of Thomas Buck and Roger Daniel in the printing of the 1638 volume of tributes to Edward King.

2712 ------. Epitaphium Damonis: Lines 9-13 and the Date of Composition. MLN, 71, 1956, 322-4.
October or November, 1639.

2713 ------. Establishment of a Text of Milton's Poems Through a Study of Lycidas. PBSA, 56, 1962, 317-31.
Examines the 1638, 1645, and 1673 texts of Lycidas "to point out the kind of analysis needed to establish a text of Milton's poems."

2714 ------. Henry Lawes's Settings of Songs for Milton's Comus. JRUL, 28, Dec., 1964, 22-8.
Variants between the British Museum manuscript and the Lawes manuscript demonstrate both Milton's and Lawes' methods of composition.

2715 ------. The Manuscript of Arcades. N&Q, N.S., 6, 1959, 359-64.
Examines the draft of Arcades in the Trinity Manuscript "to try to determine the form of the mask at the time it was to be set down and the kinds of alterations made."

2716 ------. The Manuscript of Comus: An Addendum. PBSA, 54, 1960, 293-4.
Establishes the existence of an intermediate manuscript of Comus in late 1637, from which the Bridgewater Manuscript would have been derived.

2717 ------. Milton's Fairfax Sonnet. N&Q, N.S., 2, 1955, 195-6.
Cites "two textual errors, both of which create new meaning for a few lines of the poem, and one of which is significant in the analysis of Milton's spelling practices."

2718 ------. Milton's Italian Sonnets: An Interpretation. UWR, 3, 1967, 27-33.
Suggests a religious level of meaning.

2719 ------. Milton's Nectar: Symbol of Immortality. EM, 16, 1965, 131-41.
Considers nectar as a symbol of Christian immortality, a concept of fame, a fusion of Greek and Christian imagery, and a sign of the immanence of God.

2720 ------. Milton's Sonnet 19: Its Date of Authorship and Its Interpretation. N&Q, N.S., 4, 1957, 442-6.
Late 1655. Interpreted in the light of Isaiah 65.

2721 ------. Milton's Sonnet 23. N&Q, N.S., 3, 1956, 202-4.
Agrees with Parker that the deceased wife is Mary Powell.

2722 ------. A Note on Milton's Hobson Poems. RES, 18, 1967, 433-7.
Theorizes that the rash of Hobson poems by Milton and others was due not only to Hobson's popularity, but to the sudden realization of his death after the Christmas recess, with each versifier trying to outdo the others. Cites additional texts and variants.

2723A ------. Of Chronology and the Dates of Milton's Translation from Horace and the New Forcers of Conscience. SEL, 3, 1963, 77-84.
Dates the translation 1646 or later and the New Forcers during the first months of 1647.

2723B ------. The Prosody of Milton's Translation of Horace's Fifth Ode. TSL, 13, 1968, 81-9.
>Quantitative analysis of the Fifth Ode, with suggestions concerning the prosody of some of the other poems.

2724 ------. Speculations on the Dating of the Trinity MS. of Milton's Poems. MLN, 75, 1960, 11-7.
>"...allows the possibility of 1637 as the date of writing of the letter to an unknown friend. On the acceptance of this, all objection to dating the whole Trinity MS. from that date forward is nullified."

2725 ------. Two Milton Notes: Clio and Sonnet 11. N&Q, N.S., 8, 1961, 178-80.
>On the references to Clio in the Fourth Elegy, Ad Patrem and Mansus. "Clio is not only the inspirer of the historiographer and registrar of noble deeds; she is also the personification of man's individual history." Dates "I did but prompt" Sept., 1645.

2726 SHEPPARD, JOHN T. Milton's Cambridge Exercises. Music at Belmont and Other Essays and Addresses (London: Rupert Hart-Davis, 1951), pp. 152-62.

2727 SHUMAKER, WAYNE. Flowerets and Sounding Seas: a Study in the Affective Structure of Lycidas. PMLA, 66, 1951, 485-94. Reprinted in Milton's Lycidas: The Tradition and the Poem, ed. by C. A. Patrides (New York: Holt, Rinehart, and Winston, 1961), pp. 125-35, and in Milton: Modern Judgements, ed. by Alan Rudrum (London: MacMillan, 1968), pp. 94-103.
>Extracts the flower theme and the water theme and shows how the impact of the poem lies in the affective connotations of words, phrases and images in formal combinations.

2728 ------. On Milton's Lycidas. Readings for Liberal Education. Ed. by Louis F. Locke and others. (New York: Rinehart, 1948), pp. 47-55.

2729 SHUSTER, GEORGE N. The English Ode from Milton to Keats. Doctoral diss., Columbia Univ., 1940.
>Publication noted, below.

2730 ------. Milton and the Metaphysical Poets. The English Ode from Milton to Keats. Columbia University Studies in English and Comparative Literature, 150 (New York: Columbia Univ. Press, 1940), pp. 64-92.
>Rev: Douglas Bush, JEGP, 40, 1941, 304-7.

2731 SIGWORTH, OLIVER F. Johnson's Lycidas: The End of Renaissance Criticism. 18th Century Studies, 1, 1967, 159-68.
>"Johnson was a man with a Renaissance education whose experience in life had forced him to doubt most of the literary precepts of that education.... In the long view of literary history, it is we who are idiosyncratic to expect in poetry what Johnson did not find in Lycidas."

2732 SILLS, KENNETH C. M. Milton's Latin Poems. CJ, 32, 1937, 417-23.
>An appreciative essay.

2733 SINGLETON, RALPH H. Milton's Comus and the Comus of Erycius Puteanus. PMLA, 58, 1943, 949-57.
>A source study.

2734 ------. The Sources of Comus. Doctoral diss., Western Reserve Univ., 1939.

2735 SIRLUCK, ERNEST. Some Recent Suggested Changes in the Chronology of Milton's Poems. JEGP, 60, 1961, 773-85.
Printed as an appendix to Sirluck's Milton's Idle Right Hand in the same issue. Questions W. R. Parker's and A. Gilbert's arguments for an early date of composition of Samson Agonistes, accepts Milton's own testimony in the dating of How soon hath time, and agrees with H. J. C. Grierson, E. M. W. Tillyard, and J. Shawcross that Ad Patrem was composed in 1637 or possibly 1638.

2736 SLAKEY, ROGER L. Milton's Sonnet On His Blindness. ELH, 27, 1960, 122-30.
On Milton and the parable of the talents (Matthew 25). "In this sonnet Milton is concerned not with a mere resignation to his fate, but with some kind of spiritual growth."

2737 SMITH, ROLAND M. Spenser and Milton: An Early Analogue. MLN, 60, 1945, 394-8.
Cites parallels between the verse-letter from Spenser to Harvey in 1580 and Milton's sonnet "How soon hath time."

2738 SPENSER, T. J. B., and STANLEY W. WELLS, gen. eds. A Book of Masques in Honour of Allardyce Nicoll. Cambridge: Cambridge Univ. Press, 1967. xv, 448pp.
A collection of 14 masques (composed between 1604 and 1653) edited and modernized by various scholars. Also includes 48 plates, prepared by Sybil Rosenfeld, a general introduction by Gerald E. Bentley, and an essay, These Pretty Devices: A Study of Masques in Plays, by Inga-Stina Ewbank. A valuable background edition for Comus, although an edition of Comus is not included.

2739 SPENCER, THEODORE. Shakespeare and Milton. MLN, 53, 1938, 366-7.
Argues that Milton's Shakespeare was written in imitation of Shakespeare's supposed epitaph on Sir William Stanley.

2740 SPITZER, LEO. Understanding Milton. HR, 4, 1951, 16-27. Reprinted in Essays on English and American Literature. Ed. by Anna Hatcher (Princeton: Princeton Univ. Press, 1962), pp. 116-31.
On Milton's Sonnet 23 and written in reply to F. S. Boas' comments on the poem in The Problem of Meaning in the Arts. Rejoinder by Boas, HR, 4, 1951, 28-30.

2741 STANDLEY, F. L. An Echo of Milton in the Crucible. N&Q, 15, 1968, 303.
Feels that Arthur Miller's play contains a passage similar to one in Milton's Hobson poems.

2742 STAPLETON, LAURENCE. Milton and the New Music. UTQ, 23, 1954, 217-26. Reprinted in Milton: Modern Essays in Criticism. A Galaxy Book. Ed. by Arthur E. Barker (New York: Oxford Univ. Press, 1965), pp. 31-42.
In the Nativity Ode.

2743 STARNES, D. T. The Figure Genius in the Renaissance. SRen, 11, 1964, 234-44.

Briefly mentions Milton's sources and use of the figure Genius in Christ's Nativity, Il Penseroso, Lycidas, and Arcades.

2744 ------. More about the Tower of Fame in Milton. N&Q, 196, 1951, 515-8.
In Quintum Novembris, 170-3.

2745 STAUFFER, DONALD A. Milton's Two-handed Engine. MLR, 31, 1936, 57-60.

2746 STEADMAN, JOHN M. Eyelids of the Morn: A Biblical Convention. HTR, 56, 1963, 159-67.
"Like other elements in Lycidas, Milton's eyelid-metaphor is rooted in a dual tradition; it recalls classical as well as Biblical prototypes."

2747 ------. Haemony and Christian Moly. Hist. Ideas News Letter, 4, 1958, 59-60.
Notes that Budé anticipates Milton in distinguishing between Homeric and Christian moly.

2748 ------. Milton's Haemony: Etymology and Allegory. PMLA, 77, 1962, 200-7.
"We can say with reasonable certitude that haemony means Knowledge; to superimpose additional meanings is to court obscurity again."

2749 ------. Milton's Two-Handed Engine. N&Q, N.S., 7, 1960, 237.
Cites Edward Benlowes' Theophila, or Loves Sacrifice (1652) as "additional support for the view that the 'two-handed engine' of Lycidas, 130, is actually the 'two-edged sword' of the Word of God."

2750 ------. Milton's Two-Handed Engine and Jehan Gerard. N&Q, N.S., 3, 1956, 249-50.

2751 ------. Milton's Walls of Glass (Psalm 136). Archiv, 198, 1961, 34-7.
On Milton's "metrical paraphrase of Psalm 136:15" and Paradise Lost, 7, 293 and 12, 197. ". . . the comparison of the Red Sea to 'Two Wals of Glasse' flanking the route of the Hebrews originated neither with Milton nor with Du Bartas, but with patristic commentators on Exodus 14 and 15 and on Psalm 136."

2752 ------. St. Peter and Ecclesiastical Satire: Milton, Dante, and La Rappresentazione del Di del Giudizio. N&Q, N.S., 5, 1958, 141-2.
On Echoes of Dante and La Rappresentazione del Di del Giudizio in ll. 113-31 of Lycidas.

2753 ------. William Hog and Milton's Two-Handed Engine. N&Q, N.S., 3, 1956, 335.

2754 STEMPEL, DANIEL. John Knox and Milton's Two-Handed Engine. ELN, 3, 1966, 259-63.
Milton's "two-handed engine" may be an oblique reference to John Knox's "two-handed sweard" in his History of the Reformation in Scotland. If so, "it is a call to arms and an accurate prophecy of the course of events in the following years."

2755 STEPHENSON, EDWARD A. Milton's Materials for Comus, 1941. Kentucky Microcards, Series A. Sponsored by South Atlantic MLA, No. 21.
Discusses genre and sources of Comus and considers the Spenser-Milton relationship.

2756 STOEHR, TAYLOR. Syntax and Poetic Form in Milton's Sonnets. ES, 45, 1964, 289-301.
Analyzes structure of several of the sonnets.

2757 STRATHMANN, ERNEST A. Lycidas and the Translation of May. MLN, 52, 1937, 398-400.
On the probability that Milton knew the Latin translation of Spenser's May eclogue, in which the Protestant pastor is called Lycidas.

2758 STROUP, THOMAS B. Aeneas' Vision of Creusa and Milton's Twenty-third Sonnet. PQ, 39, 1960, 125-6.
Notes parallel between Milton's poem and Aeneas' vision of Creusa in the Aeneid, Book 2, a possible source.

2759 ------. Lycidas and the Marinell Story. SAMLA Studies in Milton. Ed. by J. Max Patrick (Gainesville: Univ. of Florida Press, 1953), pp. 100-13.
Suggests that Milton long remembered Spenser's handling of the Marinell-Florimell story and finds many similarities in Lycidas.

2760 ------. Milton's Two-Handed Engine and Fletcher's Two-Edged Sword. N&Q, N.S., 6, 1959, 366-7.
Suggests Phineas Fletcher's The Locusts, or Apollyonists (1627) as a source and explanation of Milton's massy keys and two-handed engine and as confirmation of interpretations by G. W. Whiting and Leon Howard.

2761 ------. Religious Rite and Ceremony in Milton's Poetry. Lexington: Univ. of Kentucky Press, 1968. ix, 83pp.
Contains a chapter on the Minor Poems, pp. 6-14.

2762 STUDLEY, MARIAN H. That Two-Handed Engine. EJ, 26, 1937, 148-51.

2763 SUNDELL, ROGER HENRY. Internal Commentary in the Major Poems of John Milton. Doctoral diss., Washington Univ., 1965. Abs., DA, 26, 1966, 6701.
Contains chapters on On the Morning of Christ's Nativity, Lycidas, and Comus.

2764 SVENDSEN, KESTER. Milton's L'Allegro and Il Penseroso. Expl, 8, 1950, item 49.
Maintains that the unity of the poems derives from the "progressive emphasis in both parts on images of sound and music."

2765 ------. Milton's On His Having Arrived at the Age of Twenty-Three. Expl, 7, 1949, item 53.

2766 ------. Milton's Sonnet on the Massacre in Piedmont. Shakespeare Association Bulletin, 20, 1945, 147-55.
On the rhetoric of the sonnet.

2767 SYKES, P. M. Sweet Poison (Comus, 47). TLS, July 19, 1934, p. 511.

2768 TATE, ELEANOR. Milton's L'Allegro and Il Penseroso—Balance, Progression, or Dichotomy? MLN, 76, 1961, 585-90.
Considers the two poems "as contrasts, depicting two attitudes towards life, rather than . . . as a steady progression from the first through the second."

2769 Tercentenary of the First Performance of Milton's Comus, the Occasion for a Historical Pageant at Ludlow Castle. BJRL, 18, 1934, 268-71.

2770 THALER, ALWIN. Milton in the Theatre. Shakespeare's Silences (Cambridge: Harvard Univ. Press, 1929), pp. 209-56.
On stagings of Comus. A reprint of Stevens' No. 487, first published in 1920.

2771 THOMPSON, CLAUD ADELBERT. That Two-Handed Engine Will Smite: Time Will Have A Stop. SP, 59, 1962, 184-200.
Views 11. 130-1 of Lycidas (and the entire verse paragraph) "in the light of those universal themes which pervade the poem—the themes of death, judgment, and eternity."

2772 THOMPSON, W. LAWRENCE. The Source of the Flower Passage in Lycidas. N&Q, 197, 1952, 97-9.
Insists that the passage derives from Jonson's Pan's Anniversary rather than from Shakespeare's Winter's Tale.

2773 TILLYARD, E. M. W. The Action of Comus. E&S, 28, 1942, 22-37. Reprinted in Studies in Milton (London: Chatto and Windus, 1951), pp. 82-99, with an addendum; A Maske at Ludlow: Essays on Milton's Comus. Ed. by John S. Diekhoff (Cleveland: Case Western Reserve Univ. Press, 1968), pp. 43-57.
Compares the 1634 and 1637 versions and discusses the growth of the plot. Disagrees that Comus is an academic dispute ending in a stalemate.

2774 ------. Milton: L'Allegro and Il Penseroso. English Association Pamphlet No. 82. Oxford Univ. Press, 1932. 19pp. Reprinted in The Miltonic Setting (Cambridge: Cambridge Univ. Press, 1938), pp. 1-28.
Appreciative essay with the suggestion that the poems belong to the Cambridge period.

2775 ------. Remarks on Lycidas. Milton's Lycidas: The Tradition and the Poem. Ed. by C. A. Patrides (New York: Holt, Rinehart, and Winston, 1961), pp. 58-63.
A reprint from Tillyard's 1930 Milton, pp. 79-85.

2776 TILLYARD, PHYLLIS B. What is a Beck? TLS, July 25, 1952, p. 485.
Reply by E. B. C. Jones, TLS, Aug. 8, 1952, p. 517. On L'Allegro, 27-8. To Tillyard, a "beck" is a "nod"; to Jones, "a come hither look."

2777 TREIP, MINDELE C. Lycidas, Lines 130-131. N&Q, N.S., 6, 1959, 364-6.
Endorses M. Kelley's suggestion "that the main reference of Milton's 'two-handed engine' may be to the sword of the Archangel Michael."

2778 TRUESDALE, CALVIN WILLIAM. English Pastoral Verse from Spenser to Marvell: A Critical Revaluation. Doctoral diss., Univ. of Washington, 1956. 342pp. Abs., DA, 17, 1957, 1087.
Special attention to Lycidas.

2779 TURNER, W. ARTHUR. Milton's Two-Handed Engine. JEGP, 49, 1950, 562-5.
Considers various requirements for identifying the engine. Concludes "that the only engine which does meet all the requirements is the lock on St. Peter's door (or the power of the lock), to which he carries the keys."

2780 TUVE, ROSEMOND. Images and Themes in Five Poems by Milton. Cambridge: Harvard Univ. Press, 1957. 161pp.
Chapters: The Structural Figures of L'Allegro and Il Penseroso; The Hymn

on the Morning of Christ's Nativity; Theme, Pattern, and Imagery in Lycidas; Image, Form, and Theme in A Mask. The chapter on Lycidas is reprinted in Milton's Lycidas: The Tradition and the Poem. Ed. by C. A. Patrides (New York: Holt, Rinehart, and Winston, 1961), pp. 167-200. The chapter on L'Allegro and Il Penseroso is reprinted in Milton: Modern Essays in Criticism. Ed. by Arthur E. Barker (New York: Oxford Univ. Press, 1965), pp. 58-76. The chapter on Image, Form, and Theme in a Mask is reprinted in A Maske at Ludlow: Essays on Milton's Comus. Ed. by John S. Diekhoff (Cleveland: Case Western Reserve Univ. Press, 1968), pp. 126-64.

Rev: William F. Irmscher, ArQ, 14, 1958, 79-81; Christopher Hill, Spect, Apr. 4, 1958, p. 436; L. L. Martz, YR, 47, 1958, 259-61; Merritt Y. Hughes, MLN, 73, 1958, 527-32; Millar MacLure, MP, 56, 1958, 64-5; Allan Gilbert, Expl, June, 1958, item 4; Ruth Mohl, SCN, 16, 1958, 6-7; Arnold Stein, JAAC, 17, 1958, 119-21; Howard Sargeant, English, 12, 1958, 63-4; J. B. Broadbent, MLR, 53, 1958, 623-4; Florence Brinkley, SAQ, 57, 1958, 403-4; TLS, Apr. 18, 1958, p. 215; George W. Boyd, Hist. Ideas News Letter, 4, 1958, 87-9; A. J. Smith, RES, 10, 1959, 309-11; R. W. Condee, CE, 20, 1959, 264; E. Saillens, EA, 12, 1959, 352-3.

2781 TUVESON, ERNEST. The Pilot of the Galilean Lake. JHI, 27, 1966, 447-58.

An interpretation of the Petrine passage in Lycidas. "The central fact about the passage, I suggest, is that Peter is introduced in his office as the great Pastor, and only in this character."

2782 ULLRICH, H. Zu Miltons L'Allegro. GRM, 18, 1930, 74.

On the "night-raven" of line 7.

2783 VAN KLUYVE, ROBERT A. Cerberus in L'Allegro. N&Q, N.S., 7, 1960, 220.

Feels that Burton's coat of arms on the title page of Anatomy of Melancholy may have influenced Milton to substitute Cerberus for Erebus in the opening lines of the poem.

2784 VERITY, A. W. A Note on Comus (95). TLS, Feb. 26, 1931, p. 154.

2785 WADDELL, HELEN, trans. Lament for Damon: the Epitaphium Damonis of Milton. UTQ, 16, July, 1947, 341-8. Reprinted in Milton's Lycidas: The Tradition and the Poem. Ed. by C. A. Patrides (New York: Holt, Rinehart, and Winston, 1961), pp. 19-26.

2786 WAGENKNECHT, EDWARD. Milton in Lycidas. CE, 7, 1946, 393-7.

Interprets the poem as a study of the problem of evil.

2787 WALKER, FRED B. Milton's Use of the Bible in His Shorter Poems. Master's thesis, Univ. of Florida, 1947.

2788 WALLACE, JOHN M. Milton's Arcades. JEGP, 58, 1959, 627-36. Reprinted in Milton: Modern Essays in Criticism. A Galaxy Book. Ed. by Arthur E. Barker (New York: Oxford Univ. Press, 1965), pp. 77-87.

Holds that the central symbol of Arcades is the Dowager Countess of Derby, who personifies heavenly wisdom.

2789 WALLERSTEIN, RUTH. Iusta Edouardo King. Studies in Seventeenth Century Poetic (Madison: Univ. of Wisconsin Press, 1950), pp. 96-114.

A discussion of the tributes to Edward King, including Lycidas, and of the funeral elegy in general.

Rev: L. C. Martin, MLR, 46, 1951, 486-7; Roy Daniells, UTQ, 21, 1951, 97-9; L. L. Martz, YR, 40, 1951, 562-5; Allan Gilbert, SAQ, 51, 1952, 177-9; Kathrine Koller, MLN, 67, 1952, 567-9; Pierre Legouis, RES, 3, 1952, 290-2.

2790 ------. Rhetoric in the English Renaissance: Two Elegies. EIE, 1948 (New York: Columbia Univ. Press, 1949), pp. 153-78.
Considers Donne's elegy on Prince Henry and Lycidas.

2791 WATSON, SARA R. An Interpretation of Milton's Haemony. N&Q, 178, 1940, 260-1.
Replies by W. W. S., p. 321; by T. C. C., p. 339.

2792 ------. Milton's Ideal Day: Its Development as a Pastoral Theme. PMLA, 57, 1942, 404-20.
Milton's two days (L'Allegro and Il Penseroso) derive from pastoral tradition rather than from lyrics which immediately preceded his work.

2793 ------. Milton's Use of Phineas Fletcher's Purple Island. N&Q, 180, 1941, 258.
In L'Allegro and Lycidas.

2794 ------. Moly in Drayton and Milton. N&Q, 176, 1939, 243-4.
On the influence of Drayton.

2795 WEST, HERBERT F., JR. Here's a Miltonic Discovery. RenP (for 1958-60), pp. 69-75.
Insists that Graves mistakenly assumes that Milton misplaced 16 lines of L'Allegro because he fails to recognize that it was to be read as a part of Il Penseroso.

2796 WEST, ROBERT H. Historical Scholarship and Critical Judgment. SAB, 32, 1967, 4-6.
On external values in relation to the merits of a work of art. Uses Lycidas to show that some works can be explicated only after what "history can establish about their origins and results."

2797 WHEELER, THOMAS. Magic and Morality in Comus. Studies in Honor of John C. Hodges and Alwin Thaler. Ed. by Richard B. Davis and John L. Lievsay (Knoxville: Univ. of Tennessee Press, 1961), pp. 43-7.
Feels that Milton fails to fuse the moral and magical elements, resulting in a divergence between action and theme.

2798 ------. Milton's Twenty-third Sonnet. SP, 58, 1961, 510-15. Reprinted in Milton: Modern Essays in Criticism. A Galaxy Book. Ed. by Arthur E. Barker (New York: Oxford Univ. Press, 1965), pp. 136-41.
It does not matter whether Milton's sonnet refers to Mary Powell or Katherine Woodcock; rather, it shows his longing for "that apt and cheerful conversation of man with woman that he never found."

2799A WHITING, GEORGE W. Milton and This Pendant World. Austin: Univ. of Texas Press, 1958. xviii, 364pp.
Contains chapters on Comus and Lycidas.

2799B ------. Byblos and the Hymn on the Nativity. N&Q, N.S., 5, 1958, 527-8.
Summarizes Julian Huxley's chapter Byblos: Doorway to Many Posts, in his book From an Antique Land (1954), as an illumination of the passing of paganism in Milton's poem.

2800 ------, and ANN GOSSMAN. Milton and True Love; or Comus, 1741. TLS, Sept. 17, 1954, p. 591.

2801 WILDE, HANS OSKAR. Miltons sonnett On his blindness. Beiträge zur englischen Literaturgeschichte des 17. Jahrhunderts (Breslau: Priebatsch, 1932), pp. 36-49.

2802 WILKENFELD, ROGER B. Act and Emblem: A Study of Narrative and Dramatic Patterns in Three Poems by John Milton. Doctoral diss., Univ. of Rochester, 1964. Abs., DA, 25, 1964, 2969.
Considers Comus, Samson Agonistes, and Paradise Regained.

2803 ------. The Seat at the Center: An Interpretation of Comus. ELH, 33, 1966, 170-97.
"...I believe that the 'hinge' in Comus is neither a 'myth' nor an 'act' but an emblem . . . of the Lady paralyzed in the seat of Comus. As I hope to show, the whole verbal mechanism of Comus is geared to this emblem and from this emblem devolves the 'turn' of Milton's 'device.' "

2804 ------. Theoretics or Polemics? Milton Criticism and the Dramatic Axiom. PMLA, 82, 1967, 505-15.
Surveys criticism of Comus, Samson Agonistes, and Paradise Regained and feels that much of it is unhealthy because the vocally and modally dramatic remains confused.

2805 WILKINSON, DAVID. The Escape from Pollution: A Comment on Comus. EIC, 10, 1960, 32-43.
Complains that the Lady's simple rejection of Comus, though ritualistic, should have been dramatic. Comment by Geoffrey Rons, ibid., pp. 364-9. See also William Leahy, EIC, 11, 1961, 111.

2806 WILLIAMSON, GEORGE. The Context of Comus. Milton and Others (Chicago: Univ. of Chicago Press; London: Faber and Faber, 1965), pp. 26-41.
Uses Milton's elegiac poetry as the background for the ethical ideas in Comus.

2807 ------. The Obsequies for Edward King. Seventeenth Century Contexts (London: Faber and Faber, 1960), pp. 132-47.
Milton's choice of the pastoral elegy as his form in Lycidas enabled him "to organize and unify common topics in a far more effective way than his rival elegists."

2808 WITHIM, PHILIP M. A Prosodic Analysis of Milton's Seventh Sonnet. BuR, 6, No. 4, 1957, 29-34.

2809 WITTREICH, JOSEPH ANTHONY, JR. Milton's Lycidas, 192. Expl, 26, October, 1967, 13, 15.
"One of the many strokes of genius in Lycidas, line 192 reveals Milton's absolute precision of language at the same time that it participates significantly in the circular pattern the poem creates."

2810 WOODHOUSE, A. S. P. The Argument of Milton's Comus. UTQ, 11, 1941, 46-71. Reprinted in A Maske at Ludlow: Essays on Milton's Comus. Ed. by John S. Diekhoff (Cleveland: Case Western Reserve Univ. Press, 1968), pp. 17-42.

Contends that the argument of Comus presupposed an intellectual frame of reference commonly assumed in Milton's day—the assignment of all existence and experience to the level of nature or the level of grace.

2811 ------. Comus Once More. UTQ, 19, 1950, 218-23. Reprinted in A Maske at Ludlow: Essays on Milton's Comus. Ed. by John S. Diekhoff (Cleveland: Case Western Reserve Univ. Press, 1968), pp. 72-7.
Holds that the intervention of Sabrina signalizes the secure achievement of the level of grace.

2812 ------. Milton's Pastoral Monodies. Studies in Honor of Gilbert Norwood (Toronto: Univ. of Toronto Press, 1952), pp. 261-78.
With Lycidas and Epitaphium Damonis the pastoral monody "becomes a powerful outlet for Milton's emotions and an instrument for transcending his problems. . . ."

2813 WRIGHT, B. A. Milton's Use of the Word Waft. N&Q, N.S., 5, 1958, 341.
Notes consistent usage in Paradise Lost, 2, 1041-2; 3, 521; 12, 435; Paradise Regained, 1, 103-4, and Lycidas, 164.

2814 ------. Note on Paradise Lost, II, 70-81. N&Q, N.S., 5, 1958, 208-9.
Finds an allusion to Aeneid, 6, 125-9; discusses Milton's use of the word "drench" in Paradise Lost, 2, 70-81, and 11, 367-8, in Comus, 995-1000, and in the first sonnet to Cyriack Skinner.

PROSE WORKS

2815 ADAMS, BERNARD SCHRODER. Milton and Metaphor: The Artis Logicae and the Imagery of the Shorter English Poems. Doctoral diss., Univ. of Pittsburgh, 1964. Abs., DA, 26, 1965, 1629.

2816 ALEXANDER, PETER. Milton's God. TLS, Feb. 16, 1962, p. 105.
On the Pamela prayer in Eikon Basilike. Replies: W. Empson, TLS, Mar. 2, 1962, p. 137; P. L. Heyworth, TLS, Mar. 9, 1962, p. 161; Peter Alexander, TLS, Mar. 16, 1962, p. 185; W. Empson, TLS, Mar. 23, 1962, p. 201; B. A. Wright, TLS, Mar. 30, 1962, p. 217; Peter Alexander, TLS, Apr. 6, 1962, p. 240; W. Empson, TLS, Apr. 27, 1962, p. 281; Peter Alexander, May 11, 1962, p. 339; W. Empson, May 25, 1962, p. 380; M. Y. Hughes, TLS, July 27, 1962, p. 541. Controversy summarized in SCN, 20, 1963, item 166, and in Yale Prose, 3, 154-5.

2817 ALLEN, JOHN W. Milton's Writings of 1641-1642. English Political Thought, 1603-1644 (London: Methuen, 1938), 1, 323-8.
Emphasizes Milton's importance as a prose writer of the period but censures his abusiveness.

2818 AXELRAD, ARTHUR MARVIN. One Gentle Stroking: Milton on Divorce. Doctoral diss., New York Univ., 1962. Abs., DA, 24, 1963, 280.
Notice in SCN, 20, 1963, item 159.

2819 AYERS, ROBERT W. The Date of the John Phillips—John Milton Joannis Philippi Angli Responsio. PQ, 38, 1959, 95-101.
Final quarter of 1651.

2820 ------. The John Phillips-John Milton Angli Responsio: Editions and Relations. PBSA, 56, 1962, 66-72.
Concerning the order of publication of four 1652 editions.

2821 ------. Milton's Letter to a Friend and the Anarchy of 1659. Journal of Historical Studies, 1, 1968, 229-39.
"The close resemblance of this alternative proposal [a governing council to the abjurement of a single leader] argues Milton's realism and his intimate knowledge of the army's intentions...."

2822 ------. A Suppressed Edition of Milton's Defensio Secunda (1654). PBSA, 55, 1961, 75-87.
The first Vlack edition, suppressed by Alexander More.

2823 BARKER, ARTHUR E. Christian Liberty in Milton's Divorce Pamphlets. MLR, 35, 1940, 153-61.
Milton's doctrine of Christian liberty was arrived at "through his consideration of divorce between 1643 and 1645.... Such steps as he takes after 1645 will not develop his interpretation, for it can be developed no further."

2824 ------. Milton and the Puritan Dilemma, 1641-1660. Toronto: Univ. of Toronto Press; London: Milford, 1942. Reprinted, 1956. xxiv, 440pp.
A study of the prose pamphlets and of principles of liberty in De Doctrina.

The author argues that "Milton's prose is the record of his effort to develop a theory of liberty, religious, private, and political, which should reconcile man's thoughts concerning freedom and those concerning the spirit of Christianity as an other-worldly religion making fresh demands for a rigid orthodoxy."
Rev: L. C. Martin, YWES, 24, 1943, 147-9; J. T. McNeill, AHR, 49, 1943, 96-7; William Haller, SRL, Dec. 18, 1943, p. 18; Edward Wagenknecht, NYTBR, May 23, 1943, p. 10; B. M., DR, 23, 1943-4, 484-5; William Haller, JEGP, 43, 1944, 120-4; Louis B. Wright, PRv, 53, 1944, 312-3; B. A. Wright, RES, 20, 1944, 323-5; H. J. C. Grierson, MLR, 39, 1944, 97-107; G. D., EHR, 61, 1946, 276-7; TLS, Sept. 7, 1956, p. 522; Kester Svendsen, BA, 32, 1958, 80-1.

2825 ------. Milton and the Struggle for Liberty. Master's thesis, Univ. of Toronto, 1934.

2826 ------. Studies in the Background of Milton's Prose. Doctoral diss., Univ. College, Univ. of London, 1937.

2827 BERKELEY, DAVID S. Determinate Sentence in Milton's Of Education. N&Q, N.S., 1, 1954, 25-6.
Interprets "determinate" as "definitive" or "conclusive."

2828 BERGSGÅRD, ARNE. Demokrati og diktatur [Democracy and Dictatorship]. Printed in the series Norske folkeskrifter, No. 81. Olso, 1934.

2829 BERRY, LLOYD E. Giles Fletcher, the Elder, and Milton's A Brief History of Moscovia. RES, N.S., 11, 1960, 150-6.
Shows "the pervasive influence of Giles Fletcher's Russe Common Wealth on Milton's conception of Russia . . . in his Brief History of Moscovia" and "in the light of this pervasive influence" suggests the Horton period (1632-1638) as a new date of composition.

2830 BLAYNEY, GLENN H. Enforcement of Marriage in English Drama (1600-1650). PQ, 38, 1959, 459-72.
Gives some statements from The Doctrine and Discipline of Divorce (1644) and Tetrachordon (1645). "Milton . . . considers the practice of enforcing marriage more cruel than the withholding of the right of divorce from those requiring it."

2831 BOTTKOL, JOSEPH McG. The Holograph of Milton's Letter to Holstenius. PMLA, 68, 1953, 617-27.
Gives a brief account of the letter in the Barberini archives, a transcript of the text, and a collation with the 1674 edition, with comments.

2832 BRIET, S. L'Areopagitica de Milton: Historie d'une traduction par Mirabeau et E. Aignan. RLC, 26, 1952, 446-56.

2833 BROWN, LAURENCE GEORGE. English Historical Thought in the Seventeenth Century: Heylyn, Fuller, and Milton. Doctoral diss., Northwestern Univ., 1952. Abs., Northwestern University Summaries of Doctoral Dissertations, 20, 1952, 348-55.

2834 BRYANT, JOSEPH A., JR. Milton and the Art of History: A Study of Two Influences on A Brief History of Moscovia, PQ, 29, 1950, 15-30.
Polybius and Bacon.

2835 ------. A Reply to Milton's Moscovia Not History. PQ, 31, 1952, 221-3.
Answer to G. B. Parks, PQ, 31, 1952, 218-21.

2836 BULLOUGH, GEOFFREY. Polygamy Among the Reformers. Renaissance and Modern Essays. Presented to Vivian de Sola Pinto in Celebration of His Seventieth Birthday. Ed. by G. R. Hibbard (London: Routledge and Kegan Paul, 1966), pp. 5-23.
Shows that Milton's position is understandable, in the light of the Reformation background.

2837 CAIRNS, E. E. The Theology of Paradise Lost. BS, 105, 1948, 478-91; 106, 1949, 106-18.
Considers De Doctrina Christiana as a gloss on Paradise Lost.

2838 CANDY, HUGH C. H. A Cancel in an Early Milton Tract. Library, 4th Series, 16, 1935, 118.
Addendum to Parker, Library, 15, 1934, 243-6.

2839 ------. Milton, N.LL, and Sir. Tho Urquhart. Library, 4th Series, 14, 1934, 470-6.
Reply by J. W. Pendleton, Library, 15, 1934, 249-50. Concerning signatures on the Letters of State.

2840 CAWLEY, ROBERT R. Milton's Literary Craftsmanship: A Study of A Brief History of Moscovia, with an Edition of the Text. PSE, 24, Princeton: Princeton Univ. Press, 1941. viii, 103pp. Reprinted, Stapleton, New York: Gordian Press, 1965.
Rev: H. F. Fletcher, JEGP, 41, 1941, 547-8; J. H. Hanford, Library Quar., 12, 1942, 326-7; Douglas Bush, MLN, 58, 1943, 220-2.

2841 The Charity of Bitterness. TLS, April 29, 1960, p. 274.
Comments on the public and private bitterness which produced Milton's works edited in Volume 2 of the Yale Prose. Critical of the massiveness of the edition.

2842 CHILDERS, CHARLES L. Milton's Doctrine of God, Studied in the Light of Historical Christianity. Doctoral diss., Vanderbilt Univ., 1959. Abs., DA, 20, 1959, 1781-2.

2843 CHITTICK, ROGER DALE. The Augustinian Tradition in Seventeenth Century English Prose. Doctoral diss., Stanford Univ., 1957. Abs., DA, 17, 1957, 2606.
Considers Milton.

2844 CLYDE, WILLIAM M. The Struggle for the Freedom of the Press from Caxton to Cromwell. London and New York: H. Milford, Oxford Univ. Press for St. Andrew's Univ., 1934.
Milton and the publication of Areopagitica, pp. 77-84.

2845 COOLIDGE, LOWELL W. Milton's Doctrine and Discipline of Divorce (Text of 1643). Doctoral diss., Western Reserve Univ., 1937.

2846 COX, ROBERT. Milton's Areopagitica, an Analytical and Historical Study, with Implications for the College Teacher. Doctoral diss., Univ. of Michigan, 1956. Abs., DA, 17, 1957, 1335-6.

2847 CRAIG, HARDIN. An Ethical Distinction by John Milton. The Written Word and Other Essays (Chapel Hill: Univ. of North Carolina Press, 1953), pp. 78-88.
A discussion of Milton's conception of public and private morality in De Doctrina Christiana.

2848 CURRY, WALTER C. Milton's Dual Concept of God as Related to Creation. SP, 47, 1950, 190-210.
Proposes to "disengage Milton's philosophy of the Divine nature from theological controversy and to show how consistently his dual concept of Diety in relation to the world is developed in the Christian Doctrine and embodied in Paradise Lost."

2849 D[AVENPORT], A[RNOLD]. Milton's Seagull. N&Q, 196, 1951, 339.
Milton's reference to Bishop Hall as a seagull in An Apology for Smectymnuus is a pun on "sea" (bishop).

2850 DANIELS, EDGAR F. Samson in Areopagitica. N&Q, N.S., 11, 1964, 92-3.
Identifies Milton's reference to "a noble and puissant Nation rousing herself" as an allusion to the growth of Samson's hair and Judges 16:15-31.

2851 The Dignity of Kingship Asserted: In Answer to Mr. Milton's Ready and Easie Way to Establish a Free Commonwealth. By. G. S., a Lover of Loyalty. Reproduced in Facsimile from the Edition of 1660, with an Introduction by William R. Parker. New York: Columbia Univ. Press; London: Milford, 1942. xxi, 315pp.
Rev: TLS, Sept. 26, 1942, p. 476; William Haller, MLN, 58, 1943, 401-2; B. A. Wright, RES, 19, 1943, 217-8.

2852 DOWDEN, EDWARD. Puritan and Anglican: Studies in Literature. New York: Books for Libraries Press, Inc., 1967.
A reprint of Stevens' No. 1309, first published in 1900. Discusses Milton on liberty, as reflected in the prose works, pp. 133-97.

2853 DOWNS, ROBERT B. Liberty without License. Moulders of the Modern Mind. College Outline Series (New York: Barnes and Noble, 1961), pp. 71-5.
A summary of Areopagitica.

2854 DREW, HELEN L. The Diction of Milton's Prose. Doctoral diss., Cornell Univ., 1938. Abs., Cornell University Abstracts of Theses . . . 1938, 1939, pp. 29-32.

2855 DUHAMEL, P. ALBERT. Milton's Alleged Ramism. PMLA, 67, 1952, 1035-53.
Holds that recent scholarship "has tended to overstress Milton's adherence to Ramism and to overlook his significant deviations in both theory and practice."

2856 DUNCAN-JONES, ELSIE. Milton's Late Court-Poet. N&Q, N.S., 1, 1954, 473.
Identifies Davenant as the poet mentioned in The Ready and Easy Way.

2857 DUVALL, ROBERT F. Time, Place, Persons: The Background for Milton's Of Reformation. SEL, 7, 1967, 107-18.

Of Reformation "points beyond the immediate context to a visionary conception of history...."

2858 EISENRING, J. TH. Milton's De Doctrina Christiana: An Historical Introduction and Critical Analysis. Fribourg, Switzerland: Society of St. Paul, 1946. x, 162pp.
Discusses the history of the text and analyzes the content in the light of Roman Catholic dogma.

2859 EKFELT, FRED E. The Diction of Milton's Prose. Doctoral diss., Univ. of Iowa, 1942. Abs., (Iowa) Abstracts and References, 3, 1943, 269-76.

2860 ------. The Graphic Diction of Milton's English Prose. PQ, 25, 1946, 46-49.

2861 ------. Latinate Diction in Milton's English Prose. PQ, 28, 1949, 53-71.

2862 EVANS, B. IFOR. The Lessons of the Areopagitica. CR, 166, 1944, 342-6.

2863 ------. Milton and the Modern Press. Freedom of Expression. Ed. by Herman Ould (London: Hutchinson Intellectual Authors, 1945), pp. 26-9.
Argues that the press and the radio should be regulated, that Milton did not foresee present mass propaganda efforts.

2864 EVANS, HELEN WARD. Milton on Liberty of Conscience. Doctoral diss., Stanford Univ., 1966. Abs., DA, 27, 1966, 201A-202A.

2865 EVANS, JOHN X. Imagery as Argument in Milton's Areopagitica. TSLL, 8, 1966, 189-205.
Shows how each sequence of metaphors "contributes in its own way to the development of Milton's arguments."

2866 Felix Culpa. TLS, Apr. 24, 1943, p. 199.
Refers to Yule, RES, 19, 1943, 61-6, 409. "There are errors which may claim squatters' rights; and among them none so securely as Milton's eagle mewing her mighty youth."

2867 FINK, ZERA S. The Classical Republicans: an Essay in the Recovery of a Pattern of Thought in Seventeenth Century England. Northwestern University Studies in Humanities, 9. Evanston: Northwestern Univ. Press, 1945. xii, 225pp. Reprinted, 1962.
The study had its inception in an attempt to investigate the classical element in Milton's thinking. Chapter 5, Immortal Government: the Free Commonwealth, pp. 90-122, is a discussion of Milton's efforts to achieve a mixed state in England. Three appendices are pertinent: B, The Date and Authenticity of Milton's Character of the Long Parliament, pp. 193-4; C, Political Implications in Paradise Regained, pp. 195-6; and D, The Date of Milton's Proposalls for a Firme Government, pp. 197-8.
Rev: L. C. Martin, YWES, 149-50: C. J. Ryan, CQR, 31, 1945, 332-3; A. S. P. Woodhouse, UTQ, 15, 1945, 100-1; D. H. Wilson, SAQ, 45, 1946, 119-20; M. M., QQ, 53, 1946, 106-7; James Hutton, PRv, 56, 1947, 223-5.

2868 ------. The Date of Milton's Proposalls for a Firme Government. MLN, 55, 1940, 407-10. Reprinted as Appendix D in The Classical Republicans (1945), above.
Between Oct. 20 and Dec. 26, 1659.

2869 ------. Venice and English Political Thought in the Seventeenth Century. MP, 38, 1940, 155-72.
> Maintains, pp. 165-72, that the contemporary reputation of Venice is reflected in Milton's Ready and Easy Way.

2870 FIORE, AMADEUS P., O.F.M. The Problem of 17th-Century Soteriology in Reference to Milton. FS, 15, 1955, 48-59, 257-82.
> Considers the redemptive element in De Doctrina Christiana, Paradise Lost, and Paradise Regained in relation to the Renaissance milieu.

2871 FIRTH, SIR C. H. Milton as an Historian. Essays, Historical and Literary (Oxford: Oxford Univ. Press, 1938), pp. 61-102.
> A reprint of Stevens' No. 1311, published in 1907-8.

2872 FISHER, PETER F. Milton's Logic. JHI, 23, 1962, 37-60.
> Attempts a detailed survey of Milton's logic "with some reference to modern terminology and method."

2873 FLETCHER, HARRIS F. Milton's Vicar of Hell. JEGP, 47, 1948, 387-9.
> Identifies Sir Francis Bryan as the courtier alluded to in Areopagitica.

2874 ------. A Note on Two Words in Milton's History of Moscovia. Renaissance Studies in Honor of Hardin Craig (Stanford: Stanford Univ. Press, 1941), pp. 309-19. Printed also in PQ, 20, 1941, 501-11.
> On "cursemay" and "rossomakka."

2875 ------. The Use of the Bible in Milton's Prose. Univ. of Illinois Studies in Language and Literature, 14, No. 3. Urbana: Univ. of Illinois Press, 1929.
> The result of a need for an apparatus with which to study Milton's quotations and citations of the Bible. Discusses various editions and texts used by Milton. Contains a table of Biblical citations.

2876 FLORY, SISTER ANCILLA MARIE. Free Movement and Baroque Perspective in Milton's Areopagitica. XUS, 6, 1967, 93-8.
> Draws parallels between the freedom and boundless space of the Baroque spirit in art and Milton's plan for freedom of the press.

2877 FOGLE, FRENCH R. Milton as Historian. Two Papers on 17th Century English Historiography Presented at a Seminar Held at the Clark Library on December 12, 1964 (Los Angeles: William Andrews Clark Memorial Library, Univ. of California, 1965), pp. 1-20.
> "I should like first to indicate briefly the extent of Milton's historical studies, then to examine some of his statements on the art and purpose of history, and finally to assess some examples of his historical writing."
> Rev: W. A. Speck, N&Q, N.S., 13, 1966, 268-9.

2878 FORSTER, EDWARD M. The Tercentenary of the Areopagitica. Two Cheers for Democracy (New York: Harcourt, 1951, 1962), pp. 51-5.

2879 FRENCH, J. MILTON. The Burning of Milton's Defensio in France. MLN, 56, 1941, 275-7.
> Extracts and summaries of "a detailed account taken directly from the official French records" are given concerning "the inhospitable reception of Milton's Defensio in France."

2880 ------. The Date of Milton's First Defense. Library, 5th Series, 3, 1948, 56-8.
 Feb. 24, 1650/1.

2881 ------. Milton as a Historian. PMLA, 50, 1935, 469-79.
 The writer of the History of Britain is a man "whose interests are primarily prosaic—that is, critical, ratiocinative, scholarly...."

2882 ------. Milton as Satirist. PMLA, 51, 1936, 414-29.
 In the prose works.

2883 ------. Milton, Ramus and Edward Phillips. MP, 47, 1949, 82-7.
 On similarities between Mysteries of Love and Eloquence (1658) and Milton's Art of Logic (1672). Does not feel that Milton plagiarized Phillips.

2884 ------. Some Notes on Milton's Accedence Commenc't Grammar. JEGP, 60, 1961, 641-50.
 An analysis and evaluation.

2885 ------. An Unpublished Reply (1659) to Milton's Defensio. MP, 55, 1958, 164-9.
 Analyzes manuscript by an unknown writer with pseudonyms "Ambiorix Ariovistus" and "Henry Erastius." Presumably the work is still in the Royal Library at Copenhagen.

2886 FRISSELL, HARRY L. Milton's Art of Logic and Ramist Logic in the Major Poems. Doctoral diss., Vanderbilt Univ., 1951. Abs., Bulletin of Vanderbilt Univ., 51, 1951, 22-3. Ann Arbor: UM, 1952. 250pp.

2887 GEHMAN, HENRY SNYDER. Milton's Use of Hebrew in the De Doctrina Christiana. Jewish Quarterly Review, 29, 1938-39, 37-44.
 Demonstrates from errors in accentuation and vocalization that "the copyist did not transcribe directly from a copy of the scriptures in Hebrew" but from dictation or imperfect notes. Feels that "Milton had such a thorough command of Hebrew that he could use it effectively in theological discussions."

2888 GEORGE, J. An Entry in Milton's Commonplace Book. N&Q, N.S., 1, 1954, 383-4.
 Feels that "coitus" is intended for "cujus" in the note (on fol. 116) beginning "cujus sine amore est frigidus."

2889 ------. Milton's The Reason of Church Government. N&Q, N.S., 3, 1956, 157.
 Dates the work after late November, 1641.

2890 GILBERT, ALLAN H. Milton Quotes from Petrarch. MLN, 60, 1945, 496.
 In Of True Religion (Col. Ed., 6, 167).

2891 ------. Ovid's Mulberry in Milton's Pro Se Defensio. MLN, 63, 1948, 190.

2892 GILMAN, W. E. Milton's Rhetoric: Studies in His Defense of Liberty. Doctoral diss., Cornell Univ., 1937. Abs., Cornell Univ. Abstracts of Theses . . . 1937, 1938, pp. 67-70. Published as Univ. of Missouri Studies, 14, No. 3, in condensed and revised form. Columbia: Univ. of Missouri Press, 1939. 193pp.

Rev: Arthur Barker, MLR, 35, 1940, 560-1; E.N.S. T[hompson], PQ, 19, 1940, 414-5; Z. S. Fink, JEGP, 40, 1941, 148-9; J. H. McBurney, QJS, 27, 1941, 323; William Haller, MLN, 56, 1941, 636-7.

2893 GLEASON, JOHN B. The Nature of Milton's Moscovia. SP, 61, 1964, 640-9.
"It is the object of this paper to show that the Moscovia is very far from being a masterpiece of any kind, that it is in fact an abandoned project never intended by Milton for publication."

2894 GORDON, IAN A. The Movement of English Prose. Bloomington: Indiana Univ. Press, 1966; London: Longmans, 1966. 182pp.
References scattered throughout, but see especially Chapter Ten, Latin-base Prose.
Rev: Simeon Potter, MLR, 63, 1968, 451-2.

2895 GRACE, WILLIAM J. Milton, Salmasius, and the Natural Law. JHI, 24, 1963, 323-36.
On Milton's views regarding natural law in his debate with Salmasius.

2896 HALKETT, JOHN GEORGE. Milton and the Idea of Matrimony: A Study of Milton's Divorce Tracts and Paradise Lost. Doctoral diss., Northwestern Univ., 1964. Abs., DA, 25, 1964, 3570.

2897 HALLER, WILLIAM. The Compassionate Samaritane. TLS, Mar. 13, 1930, p. 214.
Wants to examine a copy of the first edition of this anonymous work to determine whether it appeared before or after Areopagitica in 1644.

2898 ------. For the Liberty of Unlicenc'd Printing. ASch, 14, 1945, 326-33.
Explores the historical context of Areopagitica and Milton's attitude toward civil liberties.

2899 ------. John Fox and the Puritan Revolution. The Seventeenth Century (Stanford: Stanford Univ. Press, 1951), pp. 209-24.
Relates Milton's Of Reformation to Fox's ideas.

2900 ------. Liberty and Reformation in the Puritan Revolution. New York: Columbia Univ. Press, 1955. viii, 410pp.
Milton's activities (1640-9) given a prominent place, passim.
Rev: Lewis A. Dralle, TT, Nov. 12, 1955, pp. 1474-5; D. A. Roberts, Nat, Aug. 20, 1955, p. 161; W. S. Hudson, JR, 35, 1955, 260-1; Douglas Bush, MLN, 71, 1956, 306-9; Ernest Sirluck, MP, 53, 1956, 278-82.

2901 ------. The Rise of Puritanism; or, The Way to the New Jerusalem as Set Forth in Pulpit and Press from Thomas Cartwright to John Lilburne and John Milton, 1570-1643. New York: Columbia Univ. Press, 1938. vii, 464pp.
Detailed analyses of Milton's early polemical pamphlets.
Rev: A. S. P. Woodhouse, AHR, 45, 1939, 123-5; M. M. Knappen, JMH, 11, 1939, 209-11; Florence Higham, History, N. S., 24, 1939, 147-8; A. E. Barker, UTQ, 8, 1939, 472-7; T. Wilkinson, LQHR, July, 1939, pp. 399-400; H. J. C. Grierson, MLR, 39, 1944, 97-107.

2902 HALLER, WILLIAM, ed. Tracts on Liberty in the Puritan Revolution. New York: Columbia Univ. Press, 1935. 3 vols. 197, 339, and 405pp.

The first volume contains several commentaries on Milton's prose works. Appendix A is pertinent: Milton's Reputation and Influence, 1643-1647, 1, 128-42.

Rev: L. C. Martin, YWES, 248, 251-2; A. S. P. Woodhouse, UTQ, 4, 1935, 395-404; R. H. Bainton, Church Hist., 4, 1935, 69-70; G. H. Sabine, PRv, 44, 1935, 391-2; W. Kohler, Historische Zeitschrift, 157, 1937, 163-4.

2903 ------. Two Early Allusions to Milton's Areopagitica. HLQ, 12, 1949, 207-12.

In John Hall's An Humble Motion to the Parliament, 1649, and The Panegyrike and the Storm, 1659, probably by Richard Watson.

2904 HALLER, WILLIAM and MALLEVILLE. The Puritan Art of Love. HLQ, 5, 1942, 235-72.

An "account of the teachings of the Puritan pulpit concerning love and marriage... during the three or four generations before the publication of Milton's first divorce tract, in 1643."

2905 HALLER, WILLIAM, and GODFREY DAVIES, eds. The Leveller Tracts, 1647-1653. New York: Columbia Univ. Press; London: Milford, 1944. vi, 481pp.

The emphasis is on John Lilburne. Milton, passim. A valuable background work.

Rev: TLS, Apr. 28, 1945, p. 203; C. J. Ryan, CHR, 31, 1945, 202-3; W. S. Hudson, JMH, 17, 1945, 87; and Church Hist., 14, 1945, 132-3; T. C. Pease, AHR, 50, 1945, 315-6; J. E. C. H., EHR, 55, 1945, 273-4; H. N. Brailsford, NSN, Oct. 20, 1945, p. 270; A. S. P. Woodhouse, UTQ, 15, 1945, 98-9.

2906 HAMILTON, KENNETH G. The Structure of Milton's Prose. Language and Style in Milton: A Symposium in Honor of the Tercentenary of Paradise Lost. Ed. by Ronald David Emma and John T. Shawcross (New York: Frederick Ungar, 1967), pp. 304-32.

Is concerned primarily with Milton's sentence structure. Feels that Milton placed himself "outside the main line of development of seventeenth century prose . . ." and that "the structure of Milton's long sentences is contrary to a style that seems to be part of the natural genius of English prose."

2907 ------. The Two Harmonies: Poetry and Prose in the Seventeenth Century. Oxford: Clarendon Press, 1963. vi, 218pp.

A background study. Milton considered passim, but especially pp. 90-1, on the Art of Logic.

2908 HARMAN, MARIAN. A Greek Proverb in Milton. CP, 38, 1943, 259-60.

"When I dye, let the earth be foul'd in flames" appears in The Reason of Church Government.

2909 HARTMANN, THOMAS RAE. Milton's Prolusions: A Study. Doctoral diss., New York Univ., 1962. Abs., DA, 24, 1963, 727-8.

2910 HAUG, RALPH A. Milton and Bishop Williams. N&Q, 184, 1943, 193.

Explains an allusion in The Reason of Church Government (Col. Ed., 3, 196).

2911 ------. Milton and Sir John Harrington, MLQ, 4, 1943, 291-2.

Notes parallels between The Reason of Church Government and Harrington's The Life of Ariosto.

2912 HENDRICK, A. L. The Political Writings of John Milton, 1608-1674. Master's thesis, London School of Economics, 1953.

2913 HENRY, NATHANIEL H. Milton and Overton. TLS, Oct. 14, 1949, p. 665.
      Believes that Robert, not Richard, Overton was the author of Man's Mortal-itie and concludes that Milton's reference to Robert in The Second Defence becomes more pointed and that Masson's interpretation must be discarded. Reply by Earnest A. Payne, TLS, Oct. 25, 1949, p. 697.

2914 ------. Milton's Last Pamphlet: Theocracy and Intolerance. A Tribute to G. C. Taylor (Chapel Hill: Univ. of North Carolina Press, 1952), pp. 197-210.

2915 HILLWAY, TYRUS. Milton's Theory of Education. CE, 5, 1943-4, 376-9.

2916 HOWELL, WILBUR S. Logic and Rhetoric in England, 1500-1700. Princeton: Princeton Univ. Press, 1956.
      On Milton's interest in Ramistic logic and his Art of Logic, pp. 213-9.

2917 HUGHES, MERRITT Y. The Historical Setting of Milton's Observations on the Articles of Peace, 1649. PMLA, 64, 1949, 1049-73.
      Milton's attitude toward Ormond's terms is resentful because by English standards the Articles of Peace were articles of treasonable surrender.

2918 ------. Milton's Treatment of Reformation History in The Tenure of Kings and Magistrates. The Seventeenth Century (Stanford: Stanford Univ. Press, 1951), pp. 247-63. Reprinted in Ten Perspectives on Milton (New Haven and London: Yale Univ. Press, 1965), pp. 220-39.
      On Milton's "roll call of the Reformers in the Appendix which he added to his second edition in February 1650." The quotations ranging from Luther to Paraeus are "an example of his honesty and skill in handling historical evidence."

2919 ------. New Evidence on the Charge that Milton Forged the Pamela Prayer in the Eikon Basilike. RES, N.S., 3, 1952, 130-40.
      Disavows the charge.

2920 HUGUELET, THEODORE LONG. Milton's Hermeneutics: A Study of Scriptural Interpretation in the Divorce Tracts and in De Doctrina Christiana. Doctoral diss., Univ. of North Carolina, 1959. Abs., DA, 20, 1960, 2803.

2921 HUNTER, G. K. The Structure of Milton's Areopagitica. ES, 39, 1958, 117-9.
      Combines Jebb's sections 3 and 4 (as outlined in his 1918 edition) in order to make a five-division structure.

2922 HUNTER, WILLIAM B., JR. Milton and Richard Cromwell. ELN, 3, 1966, 252-59.
      The "short but scandalous night of interruption" of Milton's Likeliest Means to Remove Hirelings (1659) may refer to "the succession of Richard and his brief reign of nine months. . . ."

2923 ------. Milton on the Incarnation: Some More Heresies. JHI, 21, 1960, 349-69.

"It is my purpose here to explore Milton's conception of the union of God and man which we call the Incarnation, to indicate something of the philosophical and religious background of this conception, and to show how the underlying theories permeate other areas of his thought."

2924 ------. Milton's Arianism Reconsidered. HTR, 52, 1959, 9-35.
"... the various 'Arian' passages in the Christian Doctrine and Paradise Lost fall into place as revelations of a tradition which antedates even the Council of Nicaea. It seems that we may assert positively that Milton was not an Arian."

2925 ------. Milton's Materialistic Life Principle. JEGP, 45, 1946, 68-76.
On the theory of the soul—its origin, propagation, connection with the body, and return after dissolution to the sun—as described in De Doctrina Christiana.

2926 ------. Some Problems in John Milton's Theological Vocabulary. HTR, 57, 1964, 353-65.
On the meaning of substance, subsistence, essence, and hypostasis in The Christian Doctrine.

2927 HUNTLEY, JOHN F. Proairesis, Synteresis, and the Ethical Orientation of Milton's Of Education. PQ, 43, 1964, 40-6.
In choosing to use the word proairesis instead of synteresis in Of Education, Milton is emphasizing a classical, rather than a scholastic, outlook.

2928 ILLO, JOHN. The Misreading of Milton. CUF, 8, ii, 1965, 38-42.
Insists that for three centuries scholars and critics have misinterpreted the Areopagitica. "The restriction of a conditional, not absolute, freedom of expression for the elect is the main proposition" of the work.

2929 IRWIN, HENRY FRANKLIN, JR. Ramistic Logic in Milton's Prose Works. Doctoral diss., Princeton Univ, 1941.

2930 JOCHUMS, MILFORD C. Antiquity Re-Invoked. N&Q, N.S., 11, 1964, 334-6.
Gives attributions and comments on the five citations in the Smectymnuan tract An Answer To a Book Entituled, An Humble Remonstrance, 1641.

2931 ------. As Ancient as Constantine. SEL, 4, 1964, 101-7.
The authority as ancient as Constantine in the 1642 Apology is Sulpicius Severus.

2932 ------. John Rothwell and the Smectymnuan 'An Answer.' N&Q, N.S., 9, 1962, 216-7.
On the Younger Rothwell's printing practices.

2933 ------. The Legend of the Voice from Heaven. N&Q, N.S., 11, 1964, 44-7.
Comments upon and adds to W. W. Skeat's references to the legend in the latter's study of Piers Plowman.

2934 JONES, JOSEPH. Areopagitica: 1644-1944. Library Chronicle of the Univ. of Texas, 1, No. 2, 1944, 25-31.
Praises the timelessness of the work and describes a copy of the first edition in the Univ. of Texas library.

2935 KATO, TAKEO. Milton's Democratic Idea in the English Commonwealth Period. Osaka Univ. Bungakuba Reports, 5, 1957.

2936   KEETON, G. W. The Tercentenary of the Areopagitica. CR, 166, 1944, 280-6.

2937   KELLEY, MAURICE. Additional Texts of Milton's State Papers. MLN, 67, 1952, 14-9.
        Prints four letters of state.

2938   ------. The Composition of Milton's De Doctrina Christiana—The First State. Th'Upright Heart and Pure. Ed. by Amadeus P. Fiore, O.F.M. (Pittsburgh and Louvain: Duquesne Univ. Press, 1967), pp. 35-44.
        Concludes that "Milton's early studies produced two works, now lost, on religion"—the Index Theologicus and A Perfect System of Divinity—and that Milton converted the latter into De Doctrina Christiana.

2939   ------. Milton and 'Arian.' SCN, No. 1, 1965, item 4.
        The term Arian does not distort Milton's views.

2940   ------. Milton and the Nameless Discourse Written at Delft. MLN, 76, 1961, 214-6.
        "The Responsio ad argumenta ... de paraedestinatione (1589) by Arnoldus Cornelisz and Reynier Donteclock is the discourse mentioned in Areopagitica as 'perverting' Arminius."

2941   ------. Milton and the Third Person of the Trinity. SP, 32, 1935, 221-34.
        Examines De Doctrina in order to "determine more precisely Milton's ideas of the origin, the relative rank, the functions, and the importance of the Third Person."

2942   ------. Milton, Ibn Ezra, and Wollebius. MLN, 49, 1934, 506-7.
        Feels that Milton's immediate source of his doctrine of Biblical exegesis was Wollebius' Compendium rather than Ibn Ezra's Commentary.

2943   ------. Milton's Arianism Again Considered HTR, 54, 1961, 195-205.
        Argues against denials of Milton's Arianism by William B. Hunter, Jr. (HTR, 52, 1959, 9-35) and Roland M. Frye (God, Man, and Stan, 1960, pp. 75-6).

2944   ------. Milton's Debt to Wolleb's Compendium Theologiae Christianae. PMLA, 50, 1935, 156-65.
        In De Doctrina Christiana.

2945   ------. The Recovery, Printing, and Reception of Milton's Christian Doctrine. HLQ, 31, 1967, 35-41.
        A factual account of the discovery of the manuscript in 1823, of its translation by Charles Sumner, of its subsequent publication and mixed critical reception, with conclusion that the work received little attention until about 1920.

2946   ------. This Great Argument: a Study of Milton's De Doctrina Christiana as a Gloss upon Paradise Lost. Princeton: Princeton Univ. Press, 1941. Reprinted, Gloucester, Mass.: Peter Smith, 1962. xiv, 269pp.
        Reviews listed under this entry in Paradise Lost: Criticism.

2947   ------. Two Sources for Milton's Hebrew. N&Q, N.S., 13, 1966, 259-60.
        Cites Johann Buxtorf the Elder's Lexicon Hebraicum et Chaldaicum and Johannes Wollebius's Compendium Theologiae Christianae as sources for words in De Doctrina Christiana.

2948 KENDALL, WILLMOORE. How to Read Milton's Areopagitica. Jour. of Politics, 22, 1960, 439-73.
Argues that the Areopagitica is on the pro-freedom lists "only because people have not been reading it carefully. . . ."

2949 KIRK, RUDOLPH. A Seventeenth-Century Controversy: Extremism vs. Moderation. TSLL, 9, 1967, 5-35.
Between Bishop Hall and Henry Burton, before Hall was attacked by Smecty-mnuus and Milton.

2950 KIVETTE, RUTH MONTGOMERY. Milton on the Trinity. Doctoral diss., Columbia Univ., 1960. Abs., DA, 21, 1960, 189-90.

2951 KLIGER, SAMUEL. The Goths in England, a Study in Seventeenth and Eighteenth Century Thought. Cambridge: Harvard Univ. Press, 1952. 304pp.
Milton's views on the ancient Britons and Anglo-Saxons, pp. 146-53.

2952 KNACHEL, PHILIP A., ed. Eikon Basilike. Ithaca: Cornell Univ. Press, 1966.
Supports Madan's position (pp. 183-84) on the alleged insertion of the Pamela prayer.

2953 KOHN, I. John Milton as a Social and Political Thinker. Questions in Philosophy (USSR), No. 1, 1959, 110-20.

2954 ------. John Milton, Ideologist of the English Bourgeoisie of the XVII Century. Leningrad: Leningrad State Pedagogical Institute, 1950. 391pp.
Dissertation for the degree of Candidate of Historical Sciences. Abstract, Leningrad, 1950, 15pp.

2955 ------. The Political Views of John Milton. Academic Notes of the Vologda Pedagogical Institute (USSR), 11, 1951, 89-138.

2956 KRANIDAS, THOMAS. Decorum and the Style of Milton's Antiprelatical Tracts. SP, 62, 1965, 176-87.
On Milton's propriety as "an ideal of unity."

2957 ------. The Fierce Equation: A Study of Milton's Decorum. The Hague: Mouton, 1965. 165pp.
Contains a chapter on decorum in the prose writings.

2958 ------. Milton's Grand Master Peece. AN&Q, 2, 1963, 54-5.
"I would suggest that in Milton's use of the word [in Of Education] master peece comes closer to meaning master trick or plot than master rule."

2959 KRETER, HERBERT. Bildungs- und Erziehungsideale bei Milton. Studien zur englischen Philologie, 93. Halle: Niemeyer, 1938. vi, 64pp.
Rev: E. O. Sisson, MLR, 34, 1939, 637; Paul Meissner, DL, 60, 1939, 918-9; H. Mutschmann, Ang. Bbl., 51, 1940, 146-50; M. Rosler, ESt, 74, 1940, 237-8; W. R. Parker, JEGP, 39, 1940, 599.

2960 KRUMHAAR, HORST. Der Freiheitsbegriff in Miltons Prosaschriften. Doctoral diss., Berlin-Frei, 1962.

2961 KUIĆ, RANKA. Miltonova revolucionarna obrada bibliskog motiva. Savremenik, 9, No. 3, March, 1959, 309-20.

2962 LANDON, MICHAEL. John Milton's History of Britain: Its Place in English Historiography. UMSE, 6, 1965, 59-76.

2963 LASKI, HAROLD J. The Areopagitica after Three Hundred Years. *Freedom of Expression.* Ed. by Herman Ould (London: Hutchinson International Authors, 1945), pp. 168-76.
    Feels that the work was unequalled in the range of freedom it demands until the publication of Mill's *On Liberty.*

2964 LE COMTE, EDWARD S. Milton's Attitude Toward Women in the History of Britain. PMLA, 62, 1947, 977-83.
    Holds that the History of Britain is a major source-book for determining Milton's attitude and that Milton has much in common on this subject with most men of his time.

2965 LEWALSKI, BARBARA KIEFER. Milton on Learning and the Learned-Ministry Controversy. HLQ, 24, 1961, 267-81.
    On Considerations Touching the Likeliest Means to Remove Hirelings out of the Church (1659) and Milton's "distinction between human knowledge and spiritual truth."

2966 ------. Milton: Political Beliefs and Polemical Methods, 1659-60. PMLA, 74, 1959, 191-202.
    Milton's pamphlets of 1659-60 show him to be "an extremely practical, able, and realistic polemicist" who, despite his polemical compromises, adhered constantly to certain fundamental political principles.

2967 ------. Polemic and Principle: A Study of Milton's Tracts on Church and State, 1658-1660. Doctoral diss., Univ. of Chicago, 1957.

2968 LEWIS, CLARISSA OLIVIA. William Dugard, Printer and the Commonwealth, with Particular Reference to the Milton-Salmasian Controversy. Master's thesis, Univ. of Illinois, 1933.

2969 LOOTEN, C. Les Débuts de Milton pamphlétaire. EA, 1, 1937, 297-313.

2970 LØSKE, OLAV. Folkestyretanken i England i Renessansetida. EDDA, 55, 328-37.
    Concerning the idea of democratic government in the English Renaissance. Calls Milton the strongest voice for freedom in Renaissance England. Quotes from the Tenure of Kings and Magistrates.

2971 MADAN, FRANCIS F. Lord Anglesey and the Eikon Basilike. TLS, Aug. 31, 1956, p. 511.

2972 ------. A Revised Bibliography of Salmasius's Defensio Regia and Milton's Pro Populo Anglicano Defensio. Library, 5th Series, 9, 1954, 101-21. Reprinted, London: Bibliographical Society, 1954.
    A revision of an earlier article (Library, N.S., 4, 1923, 119-45), Stevens No. 76.

2973 MADDISON, R. E. The King's Cabinet Opened: A Case Study in Pamphlet History. N&Q, N.S., 13, 1966, 2-9.
    Mentions Milton's reference in Eikonoklastes to the King's letters taken at Naseby.

2974 MAGEALSON, VIOLA. A Study of Syntax in Milton's Areopagitica.

Doctoral diss., Univ. of Pittsburgh, 1934. Abs., Abstracts of Theses, Univ. of Pittsburgh Bulletin, 10, 1934, 552-3.

2975 MAMEMOTO, KAORU. Milton's View of Civil Society and Natural Law. Shiga University Teachers College Reports (Japan), 3, 1954.

2976 MARTIN, L. C. Muing Her Mighty Youth—A Defense. RES, 21, 1945, 44-6.
Questions Yule, RES, 19, 1943, 61-6, 409.

2977 MASON, M. G. Tractate of Education by John Milton. Education, 74, 1953, 213-24.

2978 MAXEY, CHESTER C. Voices of Freedom. Political Philosophies (New York: Macmillan, 1938), pp. 236-64.
Milton discussed, pp. 237-46. An account of his political career and comments on polemical prose.

2979 MAXWELL, J. C. Plato and Milton. MLR, 43, 1948, 409-10.
Milton's statement in Of Education that "The end then of learning is to repair the ruines of our first parents ..." has as its source the Theaetetus.

2980 MAYOUX, JEAN-JACQUES. Un Classique de la Liberté: L'Aréopagitique de John Milton. Critique, 118, 1957, 195-207.

2981 McCARTHY, B. EUGENE. A Seventeenth-Century Borrowing from Milton's A Brief History of Moscovia. N&Q, N. S., 15, 1968, 99-101.
In Jodocus Crull's Antient and Present State of Muscovy (1698).

2982 McDAVID, RAVEN I., JR. Milton as a Political Thinker. Doctoral diss., Duke Univ., 1935.

2983 McNEILL, W. Milton and Salmasius, 1649. EHR, 80, 1965, 107-8.
On Milton's charge that Charles II hired Salmasius to write Defensio Regia pro Carolo I, 1649.

2984 MERRILL, HARRY G. Milton's Secret Adversary: Peter Du Moulin and the Politics of Protestant Humanism. Doctoral diss., Univ. of Tennessee, 1959.
Notice in SCN, 18, 1960, 2-3.

2985 ------. Political Drama of the Salmasian Controversy: An Essay in Perspective. Studies in Honor of John C. Hodges and Alwin Thaler. Ed. by Richard B. Davis and John L. Lievsay (Knoxville: Univ. of Tennessee Press, 1961), 49-56.
A brief account of the Milton-Salmasius-du Moulin-Alexander More controversy.

2986 MILLER, LEO. Milton's Reason of Church Government, Book I, Chapter 5. Expl, 26, September, 1967, 7.
Holds that Milton's "glorious poppy" was not taken from Matthew 13:24-40 but "from what he had actually seen ..., the vivid red poppy which was then as now a most conspicuous weed among the grain fields of England ...."

2987 ------. Peloni Almoni, Cosmopolites. N&Q, N.S., 7, 1960, 424.
As the signature to A Compendious Discourse, which refers to Milton's Of Reformation, the phrase means anonymous.

2988 MILLER, SONIA. Milton's Eikonoklastes: An Annotated Edition. Doctoral diss., Univ. of Illinois, 1958. Abs., DA, 19, 1959, 2602-3.

2989 ------. Two References in Milton's Tenure of Kings. JEGP, 50, 1951, 320-5.
On Milton's references to Gilby de obedientia and England's Complaint against the Canons.

2990 Milton's God. TLS, Aug. 5, 1965, p. 672.
Observation that in the second edition of his Milton's God, W. Empson expands his case for believing Milton forged the Pamela prayer in Eikon Basilike.

2991 MINEKA, FRANCIS E. The Critical Reception of Milton's De Doctrina Christiana. UTSE, 22, 1943, 115-47.
A collection of comments in periodicals, both English and American, following the publication of the work in 1825.

2992 MOODY, LESTER. John Milton's Pamphlets on Divorce. Doctoral diss., Univ. of Washington, 1957.

2993 MURRY, J. MIDDLETON. An Immortal Pamphlet. Part of the Charter of the Fourth Estate, by Murry and V. M. Inamdar. Aryan Path, 15, 1944, 417-24.
Areopagitica.

2994 NASH, RALPH. Milton, Jonson, and Tiberius. CP, 41, 1946, 164.
Believes that Milton may have taken the proverb quoted in The Reason of Church Government from Sejanus.

2995 NEUMANN, JOSHUA H. Milton's Prose Vocabulary. PMLA, 60, 1945, 102-20.
On Milton's contributions to the English language.

2996 NICHOLAS, CONSTANCE. The Editions of the Early Church Historians Used by Milton. JEGP, 51, 1952, 160-2.
He probably used the Historiae Ecclesiasticae Scriptores Graeci, Geneva, 1612.

2997 ------. Introduction and Notes to Milton's History of Britain. Illinois Studies in Language and Literature, 44. Urbana: Univ. of Illinois Press, 1957. 179pp.
Written as a companion to Vol. 10 of the Columbia Edition.
Rev: SCN, 16, 1958, 33-4; Harry Glicksman, JEGP, 57, 1958, 819-23; G. N. Garmonsway, RES, 11, 1960, 203-4.

2998 ------. Milton's Medieval British Readings. Doctoral diss., Univ. of Illinois, 1951. Abs., Urbana: Univ. of Illinois Press, 1951.

2999 NOAH, JAMES E. Oliver Cromwell, Protector, and the English Press. Journalism Quarterly, 39, 1962, 57-62.
On Milton and Cromwell concerning individual liberty.

3000 O'KEEFFE, TIMOTHY J. The Function and Pattern of Imagery in Milton's Prose, 1641-1649. Doctoral diss., New York Univ., 1967. Abs., DA, 28, 1968, 4642-A. 541pp.

"This study explores recurrent patterns of imagery in the early prose and demonstrates how they grow and develop into complex motifs in the pamphlets, supporting the prose arguments. Further, it describes the subtle relationship between the imagery in the prose and in the poetry. The study contains lists of quoted images in chronological order which may be useful for another student of Milton's imagery" (author's annotation).

3001 OLDFATHER, W. A. Pro Ioanne Miltono Poeta Populum Anglicanum Iterum Defendenta. PQ, 19, 1940, 88-9.
Suggests emendations for a poem in the Second Defence.

3002 ONG, WALTER J., S.J. Idea Titles in John Milton's Milieu. Studies in Honor of DeWitt T. Starnes. Ed. by T. P. Harrison and others (Austin: Univ. of Texas Press, 1967), pp. 227-39.
On the background of Milton's use of "voluntary Idea" in Of Education.

3003 OSGOOD, CHARLES G. Areopagitica—1644. PAPS, 89, 1945, 495-8. Reprinted, Creed of a Humanist (Seattle: Univ. of Washington Press, 1963), pp. 105-13.
On Areopagitica in our time.

3004 OULD, HERMAN, ed. Freedom of Expression: A Symposium Based on the Conference Called by the London Centre of the International P.E.N. to Commemorate the Tercentenary of the Publication of Milton's Areopagitica: 22-26th August, 1944. London: Hutchinson International Authors, 1945. 184pp.
Individual articles are listed under their respective authors in this bibliogra-
Rev: A. Closs, Eras, 1, 1947, 157-8.
phy.

3005 OWEN, EIVION. Milton and Selden on Divorce. SP, 43, 1946, 233-57.
On Milton's indebtedness.

3006 PARKER, WILLIAM RILEY. A Cancel in an Early Milton Tract. Library, 4th Series, 15, 1934, 243-6.
In Animadversions. Suggests that in 1641 and 1698 "we narrowly missed receiving nearly two thousand additional words from a master of English prose."

3007 ------. Education: Milton's Ideas and Ours. CE, 24, 1962, 1-14.
Holds that as a writer on educational theory, Milton was a unique and original thinker and deserves to be named with the realistic reformers of Renaissance education.

3008 PARKS, GEORGE B. Milton's Moscovia Not History. PQ, 31, 1952, 218-21.
Questions Bryant's conclusions in PQ, 29, 1950, 15-30.

3009 ------. The Occasion of Milton's Moscovia. SP, 40, 1943, 399-404.
Written "as a guide to diplomatic dealings with Russia."

3010 PARKS, MALCOLM GORDON. Milton and Seventeenth-Century Attitudes on Education. Doctoral diss., Univ. of Toronto, 1963. Abs., DA, 25, 1965, 4128-29.

3011 PATRICK, J. MAX. The Date of Milton's Of Prelatical Episcopacy. HLQ, 13, 1950, 303-11.
June or July, 1641.

3012 ------. Milton and Thomas Ellwood—A Reconsideration. MN, 2, 1968, 2-4.
Questions some of the conclusions of Elizabeth McLaughlin in MN, 1, 1967, 17-28, including those dealing with the state papers and Ellwood's reaction to Paradise Lost. Reply by Mrs. McLaughlin, ibid., pp. 4-5.

3013 ------. Milton's State Papers in the Commonwealth Period. SCN, 18, 1960, 23-6.
An address delivered at the annual dinner meeting of the Milton Society, Chicago, 1959.

3014 ------. Salmasius. SCN, 18, 1960, 50.
Prints a letter, hitherto unnoticed, from the Council of State Letterbook, advising the suppression of Salmasius' book in the Netherlands.

3015 PATRIDES, C. A. As relações, de Milton com Portugal. Revista de Faculdade de Letras de Unversidade de Lisbõa, 6, 1962, 413-9. Translated into Portuguese by Joseph F. de Freitas.
An account of Milton's official correspondence with the Portuguese when he was Latin Secretary.

3016 PETERSEN, VICT. JUUL. Milton—Akademiet. Et Bland af paedagogiske Syners Historie. Edda, 37, 1937, 35-43.
Compares Milton and Comenius.

3017 PORTER, H. C. The Nose of Wax: Scripture and the Spirit from Erasmus to Milton. Transactions of the Royal Historical Society, 5th Series, 14, 1964, 155-74.
On the doctrine of individual interpretation of the Scriptures and the charge of Erasmus and others that some were treating them "as if they were of wax." Uses Milton as the last of several examples of writers who might have fashioned the Bible to suit their own purposes. Cites the divorce pamphlets and De Doctrina Christiana.

3018 PRICE, ALAN F. Incidental Imagery in Areopagitica. MP, 49, 1952, 217-22.
"Although images occur throughout and are plentiful toward the end, Areopagitica is not crammed with imagery. At some stages...Milton makes little use of figurative language. Yet the memorable passages . . . are those charged with imagination."

3019 QUINTANA, RICARDO. Notes on English Educational Opinion During the Seventeenth Century. SP, 27, 1930, 265-92.
Milton's views discussed, pp. 281-3.

3020 R[AMAGE], D[AVID]. Dugard, Milton, and Vane. Durham Philobiblon, 1, 1953, 55-6.
Describes the Cosin copy of the second edition of Pro Populo Anglicano Defensio.

3021 RAMAGE, SARAH THORPE. Milton's Nationalism as Exemplified in His Early Prose. Doctoral diss., Yale Univ., 1942.

3022 READ, HERBERT. The Areopagitica. A Coat of Many Colors (London: Routledge, 1945), pp. 333-46.
Appreciative.

3023 ------. On Milton's Areopagitica. Adelphi, 21, 1944, 9-15. Reprinted in Freedom of Expression (London: Hutchinson International Authors, 1945), pp. 122-9.

3024 REESING, JOHN. The Materiality of God in Milton's De Doctrina Christiana. HTR, 50, 1957, 159-73.

3025 RICE, ELMER. The Supreme Freedom: Three Hundred Years After Milton. Great Expressions of Human Rights. Ed. by R. M. MacIver (New York: Institute for Religious and Social Studies, 1950), pp. 105-25.
Appreciative. Deplores present strictures on media of communication.

3026 RICE, WARNER G. A Note on Areopagitica. JEGP, 40, 1941, 474-81.
Points out that Milton believes in the restraint of bad men and bad books by the virtuous and the learned.

3027 RYAN, CLARENCE J. Theories of Church-State Relationships in Seventeenth Century England. Historical Bulletin, 27, 1949, 29-30, 36-41.
Milton's views discussed, p. 38.

3028 SAILLENS, ÉMILE. Coup d'OE sur les Débuts de Milton en France. EA, 20, 1967, 399-408. Postscript by Pierre Legouis, p. 408.
An examination of the political influence in France of some of Milton's writings during the years 1649-1654. Particular attention is given to the anti-monarchical nature of The Tenure, Eikonoklastes, and Prima Defensio.

3029A SAMARIN, R. The Role of Milton's Prose in the Development of His Creative Method. Reports and Accounts by the Faculty of Philology of the Moscow State Univ., No. 3, 1947, 88-91.

3029B SAMUEL, IRENE. A Theophrastan Character in Milton. N&Q, N.S., 5, 1958, 528-30.
Asserts that Milton's sketch of a religious hypocrite in Areopagitica reflects a Theophrastan pattern "more adequately than any other seventeenth-century writer succeeded in doing."

3030 SASEK, LAWRENCE A. Milton's Patriotic Epic. HLQ, 20, 1956, 1-14.
Milton did plan "definitely to celebrate the heroic deeds of his nation in a patriotic work. Although this aim leads one naturally to think of a Virgilian epic, Milton fulfilled it to his own satisfaction in his prose works."

3031 SAURAT, DENIS. Milton and Du Moulin. TLS, June 14, 1934, p. 424.
Man's Mortality contains a reference to Pierre du Moulin.

3032 SCOTT-CRAIG, T. S. K. The Craftsmanship and Theological Significance of Milton's Art of Logic. HLQ, 17, 1953, 1-15.
Holds that the craftmanship and theological significance of the work have an important bearing on the major poems.

3033 ------. Milton's Use of Wolleb and Ames. MLN, 55, 1940, 403-7.
In De Doctrina Christiana.

3034 SELLIN, PAUL R. Caesar Calandrini, the London Dutch, and Milton's Quarrels in Holland. HLQ, 31, 1968, 239-49.
Milton's reference to "Calandrinus" in his letter to Ezekiel Spanheim (Mar. 24, 1654-55) has long been accepted to mean Jean Louis Calandrini, a wool merchant of Geneva. The more likely link between John Milton and Spanheim was Jean Louis' younger brother Caesar, a resident of London and

minister of the Dutch church at Austin Friars. Feels that Milton probably knew Caesar Calandrini through their mutual friend Diodati and seeks to establish that Milton's relationship with Calandrini and the people of the Austin Friars church allowed him substantial information channels to events and gossip affecting the affairs of Holland in the 1650's.

3035 SENCI, M. Mil'ton o Rossii. Russko-evropejskie literaturnye svjazi: Sbornik statej k 70-letiju so dnja roždenija akademika M. P. Alekseeva (Moscow and Leningrad: Nauka, 1966), pp. 284-92.
      On A Brief History of Moscovia. Feels that Milton's work is a compilation from several sources and that it reflects his patriotic outlook.

3036 SEWELL, ARTHUR. A Study in Milton's Christian Doctrine. London: Oxford Univ. Press and Milford, 1939. Reprinted, Hamden, Conn.: Shoe String Press, 1967. xiii, 214pp.
      Rev: L. C. Martin, YWES, 115-6; TLS, Feb. 18, 1939, p. 100; A. S. P. Wood-house, MLR, 34, 1939, 593-6; D. C. Macgregor, RES, 15, 1939, 479-82; Maurice Kelley, MP, 37, 1939, 102-4; A. H. Gilbert, MLN, 55, 1940, 212-5.

3037 ------. Milton and the Mosaic Law. MLR, 30, 1935, 12-8.
      "We may read the history of the development of Milton's view of Christian Liberty and the change of his attitude to the Mosaic Law in certain passages in his earlier prose works and in alterations and additions made to the manu-script of De Doctrina Christiana."

3038 ------. Milton's De Doctrina Christiana. E&S, 19, 1934, 40-65.
      Concerning the date of composition and significance of the work as a record of Milton's mature thought. Replies by Maurice Kelley, TLS, Sept. 6, 1934, p. 604, and by R. E. C. Houghton, Dec. 6, 1934, p. 875; rejoinder by Sewell, Nov. 29, 1934, p. 856; surrejoinder by Kelley, Feb. 21, 1935, p. 108.
      Rev: L. C. Martin, YWES, 239-40; D. Saurat, MLN, 51, 1936, 263-4.

3039 SHAWCROSS, JOHN T. The Authorship of A Postscript [to the Smectymnuus pamphlet An Answer to . . . An Humble Remonstrance, 1641]. N&Q, N.S., 13, 1966, 378-9.
      Suggests Milton as the author.

3040 ------. Milton's Tenure of Kings and Magistrates: Date of Composition, Editions, and Issues. PBSA, 60, 1966, 1-8.
      Between Jan. 15 and Jan. 29, 1649, while Charles I was standing trial. Uses bibliographic variations in different editions to determine order of publica-tion.

3041 SIEBERT, F. S. The Control of the Press During the Puritan Revolution. Freedom of the Press in England, 1476-1776: The Rise and Decline of Government Controls (Urbana: Univ. of Illinois Press, 1952), pp. 165-236.
      Places Areopagitica in its historical context, pp. 195-7.
      Rev: J. R. Wiggins, AHR, 58, 1953, 349-50.

3042 ------. Regulation of the Press in the Seventeenth Century; Excerpts from the Records of the Court of the Stationers' Company. Journalism Quarterly, 13, 1936, 381-93.

3043 SIRLUCK, ERNEST. Areopagitica and a Forgotten Licensing Contro-versy. RES, 11, 1960, 260-74.
      Discusses the influence (from 1698 to 1707) of Milton's essay on the con-troversy over liberty of the press, specifically on Matthew Tindal's A Letter

To a Member of Parliament, Shewing, that a Restraint On the Press Is inconsistent with the Protestant Religion, and dangerous to the Liberties of the Nation (1698).

3044 ------. The Eikon Basilike: An Unreported Item in the Contemporary Authorship Controversy. MLN, 70, 1955, 331-2.
Adds a seventh to the six items listed by F. F. Madan in his 1954 bibliography of the authorship controversy.

3045 ------. Eikon Basilike, Eikon Alethine, and Eikonoklastes. MLN, 69, 1954, 497-502.
Insists that the Commonwealthsmen were aware of Bishop Gauden's authorship from the beginning.

3046 ------. Milton Revises The Faerie Queene. MP, 48, 1950, 90-6.
On the reference in Areopagitica to Book II of Spenser's epic.

3047 ------. Milton's Critical Use of Historical Sources: An Illustration. MP, 50, 1953, 226-31.
Sarpi, in Areopagitica.

3048 ------. Milton's Criticism of Hall's Grammar. MLN, 73, 1958, 8-9.
Shows that Milton's censure in Animadversions is based on a typographical error found in some copies of Hall's work but not all.

3049 ------. Milton's Political Thought: The First Cycle. MP, 61, 1964, 209-24.
On Milton's theory of natural law. "In the present study we shall examine the pattern, from 1649 to 1654, of formulation, ambivalence, and retreat into an alternative theory."

3050 SMITH, CONSTANCE I. Some Ideas on Education Before Locke. JHI, 23, 1962, 403-6.
Gives some views from Of Education.

3051 SMITH, G. C. MOORE. A Note on Milton's Art of Logic. RES, 13, 1937, 335-40.
Considers the relationship between some passages in the Art of Logic which parallel passages in Paradise Lost.

3052 SPITZ, DAVID. Milton's Areopagitica: Testament for Our Time. Essays in the Liberal Idea of Freedom (Tucson: Univ. of Arizona Press, 1964), pp. 100-10.
". . . Milton's argument for the freedom of unlicensed printing . . . remains a noble and enduring statement of the free spirit. It assures him a permanent place in the history of liberal thought."

3053 ------. Milton's Testament. AR, 13, 1953, 290-302. Reprinted in The First Freedom: Liberty and Justice in the World of Books and Reading. Ed. by Robert B. Downs (Chicago: American Library Assn., 1960), pp. 8-14.
On the timelessness of Areopagitica in view of recent attempts to suppress ideas.

3054 STAPLETON, LAURENCE. Milton's Conception of Time in The Christian Doctrine. HTR, 57, 1964, 9-21.
"...for Milton, the Son, and the 'heaven of heaven,' and the angels, and matter, were all created before the world."

3055 STEADMAN, JOHN M. Areopagitica and the Hieroglyphica of Gropius Becanus. N&Q, N.S., 8, 1961, 181-2.

Milton's fable of the mutilation of Truth by "a wicked race of deceivers" may have been influenced by the Hieroglyphica.

3056 ------. Milton, Valvasone, and the Schoolmen. PQ, 37, 1958, 502-4.
On a possible parallel between Milton's Areopagitica and Valvasone's Angeleida.

3057 STEDMOND, J. M. English Prose of the Seventeenth Century. DR, 30, 1950, 269-78.
Remarks on the poetic qualities of the prose works of Milton, Jeremy Taylor, and Sir Thomas Browne.

3058 STERNE, LAURENCE. A Concordance to the English Prose of John Milton. Doctoral diss., Columbia Univ., 1968. Abs., DA, 1968, 579-A. 4320pp.

3059 STRATHMANN, ERNEST A. Note on the Ralegh Canon. TLS, Apr. 13, 1956, p. 228.
The Cabinet-Council, published by Milton in 1658, not the work of Ralegh but possibly that of Thomas Beddingfield.

3060 SUNUMA, YOSHITARO. Milton's Tractate on Education. English Study and Teaching, 8, 1940.

3061 SVENDSEN, KESTER. Milton and Alexander More: New Documents. JEGP, 60, 1961, 796-807.
Registers of the Council in Geneva confirm Milton's statements about More.

3062 ------. Milton and the Hundred Articles Against Alexander More. Th'Upright Heart and Pure. Ed. by Amadeus P. Fiore, O.F.M. (Pittsburgh and Louvain: Duquesne Univ. Press, 1967), pp. 117-30.
A paper read at the annual meeting of the Milton Society of America, MLA Convention, December, 1966. Concerned with the hundred articles filed in Geneva against More's doctrine and deportment in 1648-49 and with Milton's use of them in 1655 in Pro Se Defensio.

3063 ------. Milton's Pro Se Defensio and Alexander More. TSLL, 1, 1959, 11-29.
"My present object is to recover some of the vocabulary, so to speak, of Pro Se Defensio in order to exemplify the subsurface activity which recommends it as a stylistic analogue to the method of Paradise Lost."

3064 ------. Science and Structure in Milton's Doctrine of Divorce. PMLA, 67, 1952, 435-45.
Illustrates how Milton uses materials from natural science as a deliberate technique of prose argument, in this instance The Doctrine and Discipline of Divorce.

3065 TAFT, FREDERICK L. Milton and the Smectymnuus Controversy, 1641-42. Doctoral diss., Western Reserve Univ., 1942. 372pp.

3066 TAYLOR, GEORGE C. Much Ado about Something. SAB, 18, 1943, 92-5.
Review article of Kelley's This Great Argument (1941).

3067 THOMPSON, E.N.S. Milton's Prose Style. PQ, 14, 1935, 1-15.

3068 TIHANY, LESLIE C. Milton's Brief History of Moscovia. PQ, 13, 1934, 305-6.
"Milton's Brief History of Moscovia furnishes the evidence necessary to prove that Hakluyt's Navigations and Purchas His Pilgrimes influenced the phraseology of Paradise Lost."

3069 TILLYARD, E. M. W. Milton and Longinus. TLS, Aug. 28, 1930, p. 684.
Believes that certain passages quoted from the Prolusions do not necessarily owe anything to De Sublimitate, 35, 2-3, but could as well derive from Plato, or from no source at all.

3070 TREVELYAN, GEORGE MACAULAY. Milton's Areopagitica, 1644. An Autobiography and Other Essays (London: Longmans, 1949), pp. 179-82.
Appreciative.

3071 VISIAK, E. H. Milton's Prose as Represented in the Compendious Milton. NC, 123, 1938, 499-508.
Appreciative essay on the polemical tracts.

3072 WARNER, CHARLES G. Materials for an Edition of Milton's History of Britain. Doctoral diss., Cornell Univ., 1941. Abs., Cornell Univ. Abstracts of Theses, 1941, pp. 57-8.

3073 WEBBER, JOAN. John Milton: The Prose Style of God's English Poet. The Eloquent I: Style and Self in Seventeenth-Century Prose (Madison: Univ. of Wisconsin Press, 1968), pp. 184-218.
On Milton's use of "I" in his prose and on his personal involvement in the early antiprelatical tracts.

3074 WHITING, GEORGE W. Milton and Comets. ELH, 4, 1937, 41-2.
On Digby and the reference to comets in Of Reformation.

3075 ------. Milton and That Learned English Writer. TLS, Jan. 10, 1935, p. 21.
Identifies the writer mentioned in Of Reformation as Sir Francis Bacon.

3076 ------. Milton's Prelatical Pamphlets. TLS, Sept. 5, 1935, p. 552.

3077 ------. Milton's Reply to Lord Digby. RES, 11, 1935, 430-8.
Considers Of Reformation an answer to Digby's Speech.

3078 ------. On the Authorship of Eikon Basilike. N&Q, 162, 1932, 134-5.
Supplements Stevens' and Fletcher's references on the subject.

3079 ------. A Pseudononymous Reply to Milton's Of Prelatical Episcopacy. PMLA, 51, 1936, 430-5.
A Compendious Discourse (1641).

3080 ------. The Satire of Eikonoklastes. N&Q, 170, 1936, 435-8.
Addendum to J. Milton French, PMLA, 51, 1936, 414-29.

3081 ------. The Sources of Eikonoklastes: A Resurvey. SP, 32, 1935, 74-102.
Adds Thomas May's The History of the Parliament of England.

3082 WILEY, MARGARET L. The Subtle Knot: Creative Scepticism in Seventeenth-Century England. London: George Allen, 1952. 303pp.

Uses Areopagitica as a basis for discussion, pp. 257-65, of Milton's relationship to scepticism.
Rev: TLS, Jan. 16, 1953, p. 36; Ernest Sirluck, MP, 51, 1953, 68; F. S. Boas, English, 9, 1953, 142-3.

3083 WILLIAMS, ARNOLD. Areopagitica Revisited. UTQ, 14, 1944, 67-74.
A tercentenary paper. Demonstrates the timelessness of Milton's document.

3084 WOLFE, DON M. Milton in the Puritan Revolution. New York and London: Nelson, 1941. Reprinted, London: Cohen & West; New York: Humanities Press, Inc., 1963. xvi, 496pp.
On Milton's activities during and after the Civil War. Shows that Milton and his fellow rebels spoke for more than their own generation. A thorough study.
Rev: TLS, Oct. 4, 1941, p. 499; J. S. Diekhoff, SR, 49, 1941, 426-8; E. N. S. T[hompson], PQ, 20, 1941, 623-4; Bonamy Dobrée, Spect, Nov. 21, 1941, p. 490; D. A. Roberts, Nat, 153, 1941, 490; A. S. P. Woodhouse, UTQ, 19, 1941, 500, and JEGP, 41 1942, 102-5; J. T. Wiseley, RES, 19, 1943, 85-6; Wallace Notestein, MLN, 59, 1944, 142-3; CR, 167, 1945, 256.

3085 WOODHOUSE, A. S. P. Puritanism and Liberty. UTQ, 4, 1935, 395-404.
Review article of Haller's Tracts on Liberty During the Puritan Revolution (1935).

3086 ------. Puritanism and Liberty: Being the Army Debates (1647-9) from the Clarke Manuscripts, with Supplementary Documents. London: J. M. Dent, 1938. 506pp.
Milton mentioned and quoted often, especially in the Introduction.
Rev: F. Higham, History, 24, 1939, 147-8; F. E. Budd, English, 2, 1939, 313-4; A. E. Barker, UTQ, 8, 1939, 238-41; M. M. Knappen, JMH, 11, 1939, 208-11; J. W. Gough, EHR, 54, 1939, 507-8; William Haller, AHR, 44, 1939, 855-7; R. N. C. Hunt, CQR, 128, 1939, 152-7.

3087 WRIGHT, NATHALIA. Milton's Use of Latin Formularies. SP, 40, 1943, 390-8.
In his letters.

3088 YULE, G. UDNY. The Word "Muing" in Milton's Areopagitica (1644). RES, 19, 1943, 61-6, 409.
Suggests that "muing" is a misprint for "renuing." Reply in TLS, Apr. 24, 1943, p. 199. See also L. C. Martin, RES, 21, 1945, 44-6.

BIOGRAPHY

3089 ADAMS, BROWN, and RICHARD ARMOUR. To These Dark Steps. A Play in Three Acts Suggested by the Life of John Milton. New York: New York Institute for the Education of the Blind, 1943. 72pp.

3090 ADEN, JOHN M. More Georgics Echoes in Cyder. N&Q, N.S., 2, 1955, 484-5.
Presents "some hitherto unremarked parallels in accessible sources" of John Phillips' Cyder.

3091 ALLEN, DON CAMERON. Dr. Gui Patin Looks at England. SAQ, 42, 1943, 179-84.
Views from letters on Englishmen, esp. Milton and Bacon.

3092 ANDERSON, PAUL B. Anonymous Critic of Milton: Richard Leigh? or Samuel Butler? SP, 44, 1947, 504-18.
Assigns three anonymous tracts to Butler.

3093 ANTHONY, H. SYLVIA. Mercurius Politicus under Milton. JHI, 27, 1966, 593-609.
"This Commonwealth-Protectorate journal may show more of Milton's influence than is generally accepted."

3094 ANTHONY, R. M. Onslow Portrait. The Times, Jan. 4, 1962, p. 9d.
Quotes an entry which refers to the portrait from the unpublished diary of Thomas Hollis, dated Sept. 5, 1759.

3095 ARTHOS, JOHN. Milton and the Italian Cities. London: Bowes and Bowes, 1968. xi, 224 pp.
"Accordingly it has seemed to me worth while to attempt to re-create something of the quality of the Italian environment at this time, to look somewhat closely at the particular interests of Milton's friends and at the society and the civilization they were part of and that he was enjoying at first hand." Contents: Part 1: Individual chapters on Florence, Rome, Naples, and Venice. Part 2: Milton and Monteverdi, a consideration of music and drama in Italy in relation to Samson Agonistes.
Rev: MN, 2, 1968, 30-1; TLS, July 25, 1968, p. 795.

3096 ------. Milton in Florence and the Florentine Baroque. Michigan Alumnus Quarterly Review, 64, 1958, 289-97.
Reviews life and the arts in Florence at the time of Milton's visit.

3097 ------. Milton in Venice. Michigan Alumnus Quarterly Review, 65, 1959, 341-9.
A companion to Arthos' article on Florence. Consists mainly of a survey of the Venice that Milton visited.

3098 ASHLEY, MAURICE. John Wildman: Plotter and Postmaster. A Study of the English Republican Movement of the Seventeenth Century. London: Cape, 1947. 319pp.
Passim.

3099 AUBREY, JOHN. Aubrey's Brief Lives. Ed. by Oliver Lawson Dick. London: Secker and Warburg, 1949. cxiv, 408pp.
Milton, pp. 199-203, and passim.

3100 BAINTON, ROLAND H. The Bard of Speech Unbound: John Milton. The Travail of Religious Liberty: Nine Biographical Studies (Philadelphia: Westminster Press, 1951), pp. 179-207.
An account of Milton's political activities.
Rev: L. A. Loetscher, Church Hist., 21, 1952, 82-3; Robert Friedmann, Mennonite Quar. Rev., 26, 1952, 324-5; Theodore Hoyer, Concordia Theological Monthly, 23, 1952, 781-2.

3101 BALDWIN, RUTH M. Alexander Gill, the Elder, High Master of St. Paul's School: An Approach to Milton's Intellectual Development. Doctoral diss., Univ. of Illinois, 1955. Abs., DA, 15, 1955, 1862.

3102 BARKER, ARTHUR. Milton's Schoolmasters. MLN, 32, 1937, 517-36.
What the works of Thomas Young and Alexander Gill "tell us, is ... interesting in respect to Milton, and to some extent, interesting in itself."

3103 BELLER, ELMER A. Milton and Mercurius Politicus. HLQ, 5, 1942, 479-87.
Denies that Milton wrote any of the editorials in this journal.

3104 BELLOC, HILAIRE. Milton. London: Cassell; Philadelphia: Lippincott, 1935. 336pp.
A biased account of Milton the man but penetrating criticism of the works.
Rev: TLS, Apr. 4, 1935, p. 225; Bonamy Dobrée, Merc, May, 1935, pp. 70-1; E. Shanks FR, 143, 1935, 633-4; A. M. Witherspoon, SRL, 11, 1935, 646-7; Blanche Kelly, CW, 141, 1935, 368-70; E. M. W. Tillyard, Spect, 154, 1935, 576; LL, 12, 1935, 105-6; P. Hutchinson, NYTBR, Mar. 24, 1935, pp. 4, 16; E. Wagenknecht, VQR, 11, 1935, 601-6; E. Ryan, CHR, 21, 1936, 458-60; Arnold Wilson, NC, 119, 1936, 495-506.

3105 BENHAM, ALLEN R. The So-Called Anonymous or Earliest Life of Milton. ELH, 6, 1939, 245-55.
Argues against the view that Wood used the anonymous life and favors a date later than Wood's account. Reaffirms this view in reply to Parsons, ELH, 9, 1942, 116-7.

3106 BLOCK, EDWARD A. Milton's Gout. BHM, 28, 1954, 201-11.
Describes symptoms of disease and it effects on the patient. Suggests that Milton probably died from a correlated heart-failure, not from gout itself; hence the tranquility of his death.

3107 BRENNECKE, ERNEST, JR. John Milton the Elder and His Music. Columbia Univ. Studies in Musicology, 2. New York: Columbia Univ. Press, 1938. xiii, 324pp.
"He was a genius in his own right long before he had any children. That, at least, is the thesis of the present essay, a thesis which has emerged from a fresh examination of contemporary documents and from the pleasant labor of scoring and hearing all his music which is known to have survived, in print or in manuscript." Reconstructs the life of the elder Milton and relates his work to that of the poet, especially in Chapter 7, Father and Son (1624-1638).
Rev: W. G. Hill, JEGP, 38, 1939, 618-20; J. A. W., ML, 20, 1939, 197-8; C. S. Smith, MLN, 54, 1939, 628-9; TLS, Apr. 15, 1939, p. 222.

3108 BRODRIBB, C. W. Milton at St. Paul's School. TLS, Oct. 10, 1929, p. 794.

3109 B[RODRIBB], C. W. A Portrait of Milton by Mytens. N&Q, 164, 1933, 389.

3110 BROWN, ARTHUR. John Milton's Cottage: Chalfont St. Giles. The War Cry, June 25, 1966, p. 5.
Contains a brief account of Milton's career, including his years at Chalfont St. Giles.

3111 BROWN, ELEANOR G. Milton's Blindness. Doctoral diss., Columbia Univ., 1934. New York: Columbia Univ. Press; London: Milford, 1934. 167pp.
Considers the probable and improbable causes of Milton's blindness, autobiographical references to his blindness, the problem of Milton autographs, the effects of blindness, and other topics relating to Milton's loss of sight.
Rev: TLS, Aug. 23, 1934, p. 579; A. H. Gilbert, SAQ, 33, 1934, 316-7; E. N. S. Thompson, PQ, 13, 1934, 318; B. A. Wright, MLR, 30, 1935, 231-3; H. O. Wilde, Ang. Bbl., 46, 1935, 241-3; W. H. Wilmer, MLN, 50, 1935, 402-3; G. W. Whiting, MP, 33, 1935, 92-5; Denis Saurat, MLN, 51, 1936, 263-4.

3112 BUSH, DOUGLAS. The Critical Significance of Biographical Evidence: John Milton. EIE, 1946, pp. 5-19. Reprinted in Explication as Criticism: Selected Papers from the English Institute 1941-1952. Ed. by W. K. Wimsatt, Jr. (New York: Columbia Univ. Press, 1963), pp. 131-45.
Biographical evidence is often abused in the case of Milton, but often it is useful in re-creating circumstances of composition and in throwing light on the text.

3113 ------. John Milton: A Sketch of His Life and Writings. Masters of World Literature Series. New York: Macmillan; London: Collier-Macmillan, 1964; London: Weidenfield and Nicolson, 1966; New York: Collier Books (Softcover), 1967. 224pp.
This book is "on its very limited scale, a biographical and critical introduction for those who are reading Milton seriously for the first time or have felt the happy impulse to reread him."
Rev: Joseph Frank, SCN, 23, No. 1-2, 1965, 2; Christopher Ricks, NYTBR, June 9, 1966, p. 27; TLS, Mar. 31, 1966, p. 264; John M. Steadman, Archiv, 204, 1968, 459-60.

3114 CAMERON, KENNETH W. Milton's Library. TLS, Oct. 24, 1936, p. 868.
Concerning the discovery of an unrecorded Milton autograph. See note by Maurice Kelley, TLS, Dec. 19, 1936, p. 1056.

3115 CANDY, HUGH C. H. Milton as Translator. N&Q, 161, 1931, 129-30.
Holds that the English version of May's Breviary of the History of the Parliament of England (1650) was really the work of Milton.

3116 ------. Milton Autographs Established. Library, N.S., 13, 1932, 192-200.
On marginal corrections in Lycidas.

3117 ------. Milton's Prolusio Script. Library, 15, 1934, 330-9.
On Milton's early handwriting.

3118 CARD, WILLIAM M. Milton's Coming of Age. Doctoral Diss., Univ. of

Wisconsin, 1936. Abs., Summaries of Doctoral Diss., Univ. of Wisconsin, 1, 1938, 273-5.
A study of the development of Milton's character and literary interests to his twenty-first year.

3119   Charles Diodati. N&Q, 175, 1938, 145.
A biographical account.

3120   CHESTER, ALLAN G. Milton, Latimer, and the Lord Admiral. MLQ, 14, 1953, 15-20.
Concerning Milton's charge that Latimer was the creature of the politicians.

3121   CHIFOS, EUGENIA. Milton's Letter to Gill, May 20, 1628. MLN, 62, 1947, 37-9.
Dates the letter May 20, 1630.

3122   CLARK, DONALD L. John Milton and William Chappell. HLQ, 18, 1955, 329-50.
On the quarrel between Milton and his first tutor at Christ's College.

3123   ------. John Milton at St. Paul's School, a Study of Ancient Rhetoric in English Renaissance Education. New York: Columbia Univ. Press, 1948. Reprinted, Hamden, Conn: Shoe String Press, 1964. x, 269pp.
Chapters: The Trivium, Milton as a Schoolboy, St. Paul's School, Milton's Schoolmasters, The Course of Study at St. Paul's School, Textbooks, Authors for Imitations, Exercises for Praxis.
Rev: H. F. Fletcher, JEGP, 47, 1948, 308-9; W. A. Turner, JMH, 20, 1948, 367; VQR, 24, 1948, lxxxiii; F. M. Krouse, MLN, 64, 1949 130-2; A. H. Gilbert, SAQ, 48, 1949, 486-7; L. C. Martin, RES, 25, 1949, 362-3; C. T. Harrison, SR, 57, 1949, 709-14; H. W. Wilson, UTQ, 19, 1949, 103-5; I. A. Richards, KR, 11, 1949, 17-30; Lionel Stephenson, Pers, 30, 1949, 207-8.

3124   ------. Milton's Schoolmasters: Alexander Gill and His Son Alexander. HLQ, 9, 1946, 121-47.
Includes a reprint of The Five Senses, now attributed to Alexander Gill.

3125   CLARK, EVERT M. Early Geneva Bibles in the University of Texas Library, TQ, 2, No. 4, 1959, 167-85.
Describes and records the history of the Elizabeth Minshull Bible. "That it was once Elizabeth Milton's Bible, and therefore her husband's there can be no doubt."

3126   ------. The Elizabeth Minshull Milton Bible. N&Q, N.S., 5, 1958, 518-9.
Notes the acquisition of the Bible by the University of Texas.

3127   CLARK, WILLIAM S. Milton and the Villa Diodati. RES, 11, 1935, 51-7.
On the improbability of Milton's having stayed there during his Italian trip.

3128   CLARKE, H. ADAMS. A History of the Parish Church of St. Giles. Pierscourt, Beaconsfield, Burks: H. Adams Clarke, 1961. viii, 97pp.
Sheds some light on the parish during the time of Milton.

3129   CLAVERING, ROSE, and JOHN T. SHAWCROSS. Anne Milton and the Milton Residences. JEGP, 59, 1960, 680-90.
Records pertaining to Anne Milton and her second husband, Thomas Agar, throw light on the Milton residences prior to the Horton period.

3130 ------. Milton's European Itinerary and His Return Home. SEL, 5, 1965, 49-59.
A re-examination of Milton's travel plans with the suggestion that he hurried home for family reasons.

3131 CLYDE, WILLIAM M. Parliament and the Press, 1643-7. Library, 4th Ser., 13, 1933, 399-424; 14, 1933, 39-58.
Milton and the 1643 ordinance, pp. 408-15.

3132 COOLIDGE, LOWELL W. At Any Hour the Italian Tongue. N&Q, 194, 1949, 537.
On Milton's method of learning Italian.

3133 COSTELLO, WILLIAM T., S. J. The Scholastic Curriculum at Early Seventeenth Century Cambridge. Cambridge: Harvard Univ. Press, 1958. 221pp.
Considers the framework of scholasticism, undergraduate arts and sciences, and graduate studies. Milton is mentioned several times, and his attitude toward Cambridge is noted.

3134 CURRIE, H. MAC L. Milton and Dionysius Afer. N&Q, N.S., 5, 1958, 194-5.
Asserts that Milton read with his nephews the works of Dionysius Afer, a rare name for Dionysius Periegetes.

3135 DAICHES, DAVID. Milton. London and New York: Hutchinson's University Library, 1957; New York: Rinehart, 1957. 254pp. Second Edition. London: Hutchinson's University Library, 1959. 254pp. Reprinted also in 1961, 1964, and 1966.
A critical biography. Lengthy chapters on the major works, especially Paradise Lost.
Rev: TLS, Oct. 25, 1957, p. 642; Agnes M. C. Latham, YWES, 181-2; William F. Irmscher, ArQ, 14, 1958, 178-80; Anne Karminster, TT, Jan. 11, 1958, p. 52; Everett H. Emerson, SCN, 16, 1958, 34; S. E. Sprott, DR, 38, 1958, 87-9; Jackson, I. Cope, SAQ, 57, 1958, 512-3.

3136 DARBISHIRE, HELEN. The Chronology of Milton's Handwriting. Library, 4th Ser., 14, 1933, 229-35.
Establishes the date when Milton began using the Italian E instead of the Greek E, just before leaving for Italy in 1637.

3137 ------, ed. The Early Lives of Milton. London: Constable, 1932. lxi, 353pp. Reprinted. London: Constable, 1966.
Contains the accounts of Aubrey, Edward Phillips, Wood, Toland, Richardson, and the anonymous biographer.
Rev: L. C. Martin, YWES, 205-6; TLS, Dec. 1, 1932, p. 918; R. Macaulay, Spect, 149, 1932, 835; B. A. Wright, MLR, 28, 1933, 518-25; L. L. Irvine, Obs, Feb. 12, 1933; Dublin Rev., 193, 1933, 301-4; G. C. M. S., EHR, 48, 1933, 699-700; H. Agar, ER, 56, 1933, 98-100; K. M. L., Oxf. Mag., May 4, 1933, p. 613; Paul Chauvet, RA-A, 10, 1933, 521.

3138 DAVIDSON, AUDREY. Milton on the Music of Henry Lawes. MN, 2, 1968, 19-22.
Discusses Milton's praise of the music of Henry Lawes. "It was Lawes, by his tuneful and well measured song, who stirred the hearts of many, including

that of John Milton. Lawes knew best how to join words, meaning, and rhythmic eloquence with musical pitch, and thereby earned the place granted him by Milton—above Casella's Purgatory in the heavenly choir of Phoebus."

3139   DAVIES, GODFREY. Milton in 1660. HLQ, 18, 1955, 351-63.
"The purpose of this article is to reconstruct as exactly as possible what did happen to Milton [from June to December 1660] and try to furnish an explanation of these happenings."

3140   DAVIS, FRANK. Looking for Mr. Milton. The Illustrated London News, July 22, 1961, p. 138.
On the five recorded portraits of John Milton. Notes the acquisition of an early eighteenth-century copy of the Onslow Portrait by the National Portrait Gallery.

3141   ------. The Lost Milton. The Illustrated London News, Jan. 6, 1962, p. 22.
The Onslow Portrait acquired by the National Portrait Gallery may not be an eighteenth-century copy but "the actual picture which Milton's widow showed to Aubrey" in 1681.

3142   DE BEER, E. S. The Site of Diodati's House. RES, 14, 1938, 78.
On a street in Geneva formerly called the Rue de Boulangerie.

3143   DIEKHOFF, JOHN S., ed. Milton on Himself. Milton's Utterances upon Himself and His Works. With an Introduction and Notes and with a New Preface for this Edition by the Editor. New York: Oxford Univ. Press, 1939. Reprinted, New York: Humanities Press, 1965; London: Cohen and West, 1966. xxvi, 307pp.
"My aim in this book has been to make available in a single volume all of Milton's utterances upon himself and his work and to provide the very slight apparatus necessary to understand and to judge what he has to say."
Rev: M. L. Zisowitz, SRL, June 17, 1939, p. 18; D. Roberts, NYTBR, June 4, 1939, p. 2; TLS, June 10, 1939, p. 346; W. R. Parker, MLN, 55, 1940, 215-8; Z. S. Fink, JEGP, 39, 1940, 286-7; D. C. Macgregor, RES, 16, 1940, 114-5; TLS, Sept. 1, 1966, p. 779.

3144   DORIAN, DONALD C. Charles Diodati at Geneva. PMLA, 59, 1944, 589-91.
Concerning Diodati's departure from England soon after Milton's Sixth Elegy, the dating of all Milton's Italian sonnets, and Milton's own reception in Geneva.

3145   ------. The English Diodatis. A History of Charles Diodati's Family and His Friendship with Milton. Doctoral diss., Columbia Univ. 1950. New Brunswick: Rutgers Univ. Press, 1950. xvii, 365pp.
Rev: Arnold Davenport, YWES, 174-5; N&Q, 195, 1950, 374; Marguerite Little, JEGP, 49, 1950, 585; E. G. Midgley, MLR, 46, 1951, 90-1; A. H. Gilbert, SAQ, 50, 1951, 435-6; D. C. A[llen], MLN, 66, 1951, 570-1; A. E. Barker, UTQ, 20, 1951, 430-2; H. W. Donner, ES, 33, 1952, 35-7.

3146   DOS PASSOS, JOHN R. Liberty to Speak to Print. The Ground We Stand On (New York: Harcourt, 1941), pp. 85-100.
An account of Milton's activities prior to 1640.

3147   DUNCAN-JONES, ELSIE. Milton and Marvell. TLS, July 31, 1953, p. 493.

The "learned man" in Milton's letter to Henry Oldenburg (Aug. 1, 1657) is Andrew Marvell.

3148 ELLWOOD, THOMAS. Davideis. Ed. by Walther Fischer. Heidelberg: Winter, 1936.
The epic written by Milton's friend.

3149 ELTON, WILLIAM. New Light on Milton's Amanuensis. HLQ, 26, 1963, 383-4.
Jeremie Picard, Milton's secretary ca. 1658-1660, may have been a mental patient in Bethlehem Hospital, England, in both 1678 and 1700.

3150 ENGLAND, SYLVIA L. The Site of Diodati's House. RES, 13, 1937, 73-6.
Uses historical and literary pieces to determine the location of the house in the precinct of Geneva.

3151 EVANS, WILLA M. Henry Lawes: Musician and Friend of Poets. MLA Revolving Fund Series, 11. New York: Modern Language Association; London: Oxford Univ. Press, 1941. 250pp. Reprinted, New York: Kraus Reprint Corp., 1967.
A critical biography.
Rev: J. T. Wisely, RES, 19, 1943, 86-8; H. E. Rollins, MLN, 58, 1943, 317-8; John Butt, MLR, 38, 1943, 51-2; E. N. S. Thompson, PQ, 22, 1943, 284-5.

3152 FALCONER, J. P. E. A Portrait-Miniature of John Milton. N&Q, 194, 1949, 142-3.
Falconer owns an oval miniature of Milton executed by Thomas Flatman in 1667, when Milton was totally blind.

3153 FEIL, J. P. The Elder Milton. TLS, Jan. 24, 1958, p. 45.
Concerning a 1612 lawsuit involving the poet's father.

3154 FINK, ZERA S. King and Doge: A Chapter in Anglo-Venetian Political and Literary Relations. English Studies Today, 4th Series (Rome), 1967.
"In the process of repudiating kingship, he [Milton] also lost whatever inclination he may once have had for something like a Duke of Venice."

3155 FLETCHER, HARRIS F. Education of a Literary Genius. Phi Delta Kappan, 35, 1954, 243-6.

3156 ------. The Intellectual Development of John Milton. Urbana: Univ. of Illinois Press, 1956, 1961.
The first two of several projected volumes designed to trace Milton's mental growth to 1654. Vol. 1: The Institution to 1625: From the Beginnings Through Grammar School. iii, 459 pp. Vol. 2: The Cambridge University Period, 1625-32. 693pp. The second volume contains detailed chapters on the Cambridge of Milton's day.
Rev: W. R. Parker, MLN, 72, 1957, 447-51; D. L. Clark, JEGP, 56, 1957, 633-6; TLS, Jan. 25, 1957, p. 50; J. Max Patrick, SCN, 15, 1957, 9; Kester Svendsen, BA, 32, 1958, 80-1; Burton O. Kurth, Pers, 39, 1958, 420; Agnes M. C. Latham, YWES, 42, 1961, 165-6; John Arthos, RN, 15, 1962, 247-8; Alastair Fowler, N&Q, N. S., 10, 1963, 75-6; J. C. Maxwell, EHR, 78, 1963, 782-3; K. M. Lea, RES, 14, 1963, 294-7; TLS, Feb. 15, 1963, pp. 101-2; Nell P. Eurich, SCN, 20, 1963, 56.

3157 ------. Milton's E Nostro Suburbano. JEGP, 51, 1952, 154-9.
Argues against the assumption of Milton's retirement to Horton.

3158 ------. Milton's Private Library—An Additional Title. PQ, 28, 1949, 72-6.
Bernardo Davanzati's Scisma d'Inghilterra con altre Operette (1638).

3159 FRANK, JOSEPH. The Levellers. A History of the Writings of Three
Seventeenth-Century Social Democrats: John Lilburne, Richard Overton, and William Walwyn. Cambridge: Harvard Univ. Press, 1955.
viii, 345pp.
A background study.

3160 FREEDMAN, MORRIS. Dryden's Memorable Visit to Milton. HLQ, 18,
1955, 99-108.
The connection between the visit and the rhymed couplet-blank verse controversy.

3161 ------. Milton's On Shakespeare and Henry Lawes. SQ, 14, 1963, 279-81.
Suggests that Henry Lawes was responsible for the inclusion of Milton's
poem in the second folio.

3162 FRENCH, J. MILTON. An Action Against Milton. TLS, Dec. 21, 1935,
p. 879.
Sir Robert Pye's complaint, Feb. 11, 1646/7.

3163 ------. An Action Against Milton. TLS, Mar. 14, 1936, p. 224.
Milton's reply to Pye's complaint.

3164 ------. The Autographs of John Milton. ELH, 4, 1937, 301-30.
Enumerates extant pieces of Milton's own writing (handwriting) and indicates briefly their location and bibliography. Arrangement of items: "1.
Milton's books (including manuscript drafts, presentation copies, and books
corrected in ink) ; 2. books from Milton's library or otherwise containing his
writing; 3. documents signed by, written to, or closely related to, Milton."

3165 ------. The Baptism of Milton's Daughter Mary. MLN, 63, 1948, 264-5.
Notes the entry of the baptism of Milton's daughter Mary in the parish regis-
ter of the Church of St. Giles in the Fields as it appears in Joseph Hunter's
Chorus Vatum.

3166 ------. The Date of Milton's Blindness. PQ, 15, 1936, 93-4.
About 1651/2.

3167 ------. John Milton, Scrivener, the Temples of Stowe, and Sir John
Lenthall. HLQ, 4, 1941, 303-7.
Three documents concerning the elder Milton.

3168 ------, ed. The Life Records of John Milton, RUSE, 7. New Brunswick:
Rutgers Univ. Press, 1949-58. Five volumes: 1, 1608-1639, 1949, x, 446pp.;
2, 1639-1651, 1950, vi, 395pp.; 3, 1651-1654, 1954, 470pp.; 4, 1956, 1655-
1669, vi, 482pp.; 5, 1670-1674, 1958, 568pp. Reprinted, Stapleton, New
York: Gordian Press, 1966.
Of inestimable value to future biographers. Chronological arrangement.
"Within the limits of present knowledge it attempts to reveal what Milton
and the members of his family were doing each year, month, and even day
during his lifetime." Corrections and addenda in Vol. 5.

Rev: D. C. Dorian, Rutgers Alumni Monthly, Apr., 1950, pp. 18-9; TLS, Apr. 14, 1950, p. 232, and Oct. 5, 1956, p. 583; N&Q, 195, 1950, 198; Dora N. Raymond, AHR, 55, 1950, 970-1; H. F. Fletcher, JEGP, 49, 1950, 416-21; Wilhelmina Gordon, QQ, 57, 1950, 136-7; A. H. Gilbert, SAQ, 49, 1950, 418-9; D. A. Roberts, Nat, Aug. 5, 1950, pp. 132-3, May 12, 1951, p. 448, and Feb. 5, 1955, p. 124; B. A. Wright, RES, 2, 1951, 179-81; Ernest Sirluck, MP, 48, 1951, 273-4; H. W. Donner, ES, 33, 1952, 33-5, and 37, 1956, 18-9; A. S. P. Woodhouse, UTQ, 21, 1952, 193-6; M. M. Mahood, MLR, 47, 1952, 393-4; Ralph W. Condee, CE, 17, 1955, 126; W. B. Hunter, MLN, 70, 1955, 531-2, and 72, 1957, 618-9; N&Q, N.S., 2, 1955, 276; L. C. Martin, MLR, 51, 1956, 102-3; Ruth Mohl, SCN, 14, No. 4, 1956, 3-4; J. B. Broadbent, MLR, 52, 1957, 627; N&Q, N.S., 4, 1957, 90; B. A. Wright, RES, 9, 1958, 207-8; TLS, Dec. 5, 1958, p. 707; H. W. Donner, ES, 40, 1959, 395-7; Wilhelmina Gordon, QQ, 66, 1959, 175; SCN, 17, No. 4-5, 1959, item 24; William B. Hunter, Jr., MLN, 74, 1959, 640-3.

3169 ------. Milton and the Politicians. PQ, 15, 1936, 94-5.
Feels that Milton took his office seriously, but "his respect for his superiors was not blind but open-eyed."

3170 ------. Milton in Chancery; New Chapters in the Lives of the Poet and His Father. MLA Monograph Series, 10. New York: Modern Language Association; London: Milford, Oxford Univ. Press, 1939. x, 428pp.
A collection of recently uncovered details concerning the legal transactions of John Milton the Scrivener and of his son.
Rev: L. C. Martin, YWES, 112-3; TLS, Sept. 14, 1940, p. 475; B. A. Wright, RES, 16, 1940, 467-70; E. N. S. T[hompson], PQ, 19, 1940, 414-5; A. M. Witherspoon, SRL, Jan. 20, 1940, p. 7; N&Q, 178, 1940, 449-50; Dora N. Raymond, AHR, 46, 1940, 703-4; W. R. Parker, MLN, 56, 1941, 393; A. Barker, MLR, 36, 1941, 124-5; H. F. Fletcher, JEGP, 40, 1941, 145-6.

3171 ------. Milton, Needham, and Mercurius Politicus. SP, 33, 1936, 236-52.
On Milton's participation.

3172 ------. The Miltonic Epitaph on Mazarin. N&Q, 168, 1935, 445.
Questions Milton's authorship.

3173 ------. Milton's Family Bible. PMLA, 53, 1938, 363-6.
On the underscoring in the Bible as a clue to Milton's interests.

3174 ------. Milton's Homes and Investments. PQ, 28, 1949, 77-97.
Part One: Gives information concerning the known residences of the poet. Part Two: Supplies material on Milton's investments in real estate (several entries accompanied by exploration).

3175 ------. Milton's Supplicats. HLQ, 5, 1942, 349-59.
Prints the supplicats for the BA and MA degrees.

3176 ------. Mr. Secretary Milton at Work. SAQ, 55, 1956, 313-21.
"The purpose of this paper is to watch Milton in action as seen through the diary and letters of Mylius, from which Milton emerges as a brain among brawn, a scholar among mechanics."

3177 ------. Moseley's Advertisements of Milton's Poems, 1650-1660. HLQ, 25, 1962, 337-45.
Gives examples of Moseley's publicity of Milton's collected Poems and his poems on Henry Lawes and Shakespeare, published as separate pieces.

3178 ------. Mute Inglorious John Miltons. MLQ, 1, 1940, 367-81.
On the John Miltons who were contemporaries of the poet.

3179 ------. A New Letter by John Milton. PMLA, 49, 1934, 1069-70.
Addressed to Sir Bulstrode Whitelocke.

3180 ------. The Powell-Milton Bond. Harvard Studies and Notes, 20, 1938, 61-73.
An analysis of Public Records Office documents and other papers concerning the story of the loan Milton made in 1627 to his future father-in-law, Richard Powell.

3181 ------. The Reliability of Anthony Wood and Milton's Oxford M.A. PMLA, 75, 1960, 22-30.
"The evidence, circumstantial though it is, seems to convince us that Wood had what he considered reasonable ground for naming Milton an Alumnus Oxoniensis."

3182 ------. A Royalist Gibe at Milton's Antagonist Salmasius. PQ, 42, 1963, 109-14.
In an address made by Robert Douglas at the coronation of Charles II in Scotland in 1651.

3183 ------. Some Notes on Milton from Nouvelles Ordinaires de Londres. N&Q, N.S., 9, 1962, 53-60.
Additions to Life Records of John Milton.

3184 ------. Two Notes on Milton and Wither. N&Q, N.S., 1, 1954, 472-3.
Opposes Kendall's views, N&Q, 198, 1953, 473.

3185 FRYE, ROLAND M. Milton's First Marriage. N&Q, N.S., 3, 1956, 200-2.
Contemporary opinion concerning Milton's courtship with Mary Powell.

3186 FULLER, EDMUND. John Milton. Pictures by Robert Ball. New York and London: Harper, 1944. 238pp. Revised Edition. New York: Seabury Press, 1967.
A popular biography.

3187 GAITHER, MARY. Pierre Costar on Milton. N&Q, N.S., 9, 1962, 378.
Quotes a passage from Costar (d. 1660) containing a Miltonic allusion not located by J. M. French (Life Records, 5, 455).

3188 GOLDING, SANFORD. The Sources of the Theatrum Poetarum. PMLA, 76, 1961, 48-53.
Contradicts Harris Fletcher (JEGP, 55, 1956, 36). "A careful study...had convinced me that not only did Milton have no hand in the work but that even his influence, if any, was negligible."

3189 GOODE, JAMES. John Milton, the Making of an Epic Poet. Doctoral diss., Univ. of Birmingham, 1929.

3190 GORDON, GEORGE S. The Youth of Milton. The Lives of Authors (London: Chatto and Windus, 1950), pp. 44-86.
Remarks on Milton delivered at University College, London, Feb., 1926.
Rev: TLS, June 9, 1950, p. 355; R. G. Cox, MGW, May 11, 1950, p. 11.

3191 GOULD, CHARLES. Milton and the Ghouls. SR, 150, 1930, 662-3.
On a pamphlet describing the disinterment of Milton's remains in 1790.

3192 GRABILL, PAUL E. Milton's Residences and Real Estate Holdings. Doctoral diss., Univ. of Illinois, 1954. Abs., DA, 14, 1954, 357-8.

3193 Grant to Preserve Milton's Cottage. The Times, Nov. 5, 1959, p. 16g.
Ministry of Works announces grant for preservation of the cottage at Chalfont St. Giles.

3194 GRAVES, ROBERT. Wife to Mr. Milton: The Story of Marie Powell. London: Cassell, 1943, New York: Creative Age Press, 1944. viii, 372pp.
A biased account as told by Mary herself.
Rev: TLS, Jan. 30, 1943, p. 53; reply by Graves, ibid., Feb. 6, 1943, p. 67.

3195 GUIDI, AUGUSTO. John Milton. Brescia: Morcelleana, 1940. 195pp.
On Milton's Life, pp. 7-42.

3196 HALLER, WILLIAM. Milton and the Levellers. Summarized in The Renaissance Conference at the Huntington Library. HLQ, 1942, 155-201.

3197 HANFORD, JAMES HOLLY. The Chronology of Milton's Private Studies. John Milton, Poet and Humanist (Cleveland: Case Western Reserve Univ. Press, 1966), pp. 75-125.
A reprint of Stevens' No. 2469, published in 1921. "An important study based on Milton's Commonplace Book. Corrects Horwood's datings of some of Milton's studies and shows that Milton followed a systematic plan of historical reading" (Stevens' annotation).

3198 ------. Dr. Paget's Library. BMLA, 33, 1945, 91-9.
The auction sale catalogue of books of Dr. Nathan Paget, dated Oct. 24, 1681, reveals a close affinity of minds between Milton and Dr. Paget.

3199 ------. John Milton, Englishman. New York: Crown Publishers, 1949. Reprinted, London: Victor Gollancz, 1950. 272pp.
An interpretation of Milton the man rather than a straightforward biography. Lengthy comments on the works.
Rev: W. Y. Tindall, NYTBR, Oct. 23, 1949, p. 6; S. C. Chew, NYHTBR, Oct. 30, 1949, p. 5; William Haller, SRL, 32, 1949, 22; Douglas Bush, NR, 121, 1949, 30; E. S. Gohn, MP, 48, 1950, 68-70; A. H. Gilbert, SAQ, 49, 1950, 409-11; TLS, Nov. 24, 1950, p. 739; T. B. Stroup, SCN, 8, No. 1, 1950, 2; H. B. Charlton, MGW, Sept. 14, 1950, p. 12; R. Warner, Spect, Sept. 15, 1950, p. 295; Arnold Davenport, YWES, 31, 1950, 173-4; M. S. Douglas, NYHTBR, Dec. 31, 1950, p. 4; Listener, 45, 1950, 232-3; Edwin Muir, Obs, Aug. 20, 1950, p. 7; H. V. Routh, English, 8, 1951, 202.

3200 ------. John Milton Forswears Physic. BMLA, 32, 1944, 23-34.
Identifies Milton's Paris physician as Maistre François Thevenin and comments on the poet's own attitude toward his affliction.

3201 ------. The Marriage of Edward Phillips and Anne Milton. RES, 9, 1933, 58-60.
On the arrangements made (financial and otherwise) and on Milton's relations with Anne and her sons.

3202 ------. Milton Among the Book Collectors. NLB, 4, 1957, 97-109.
Records data concerning Milton's "acquisition of books by loan or purchase, his familiarity with the book trade, his relations with dealers and librarians, and his acquaintance...with several private owners of distinguished collections."

3203 ------. Milton in Italy. AnM, 5, 1964, 49-63.
      Traces Milton's travel year in Italy and considers its effects on the poet.

3204 ------. Summary of an address on Milton in Italy, delivered at the 1962
      Milton Society Meeting. SCN, 21, 1963, item 19.

3205 ------. Pepys and the Skinner Family. RES, 7, 1931, 257-70.
      Comments on Daniel Skinner, Milton's last amanuensis.

3206 ------. Samson Agonistes and Milton in Old Age. Studies in Shakespeare,
      Milton, and Donne (New York: Haskell House, 1964), pp. 165-90.
      Published also in John Milton, Poet and Humanist (Cleveland: Case
      Western Reserve Univ. Press, 1966), pp. 264-86.
      Reprints of Stevens' No. 1182, published in 1925. "A significant unifying of
      materials that shows Milton's intellectual and spiritual changes, particularly
      the enunciation through Samson of his final acceptances of divine law"
      (Stevens' annotation).

3207 ------. The Youth of Milton: An Interpretation of His Early Literary De-
      velopment. Studies in Shakespeare, Milton, and Donne (New York:
      Haskell House, 1964), pp. 87-164. Published also in John Milton, Poet
      and Humanist (Cleveland: Case Western Reserve Univ. Press, 1966),
      pp. 1-74.
      Reprints of Stevens' No. 2556, published in 1925. "The parts played by
      reading, imitation, and experience of active life are integrated into a pattern
      depicting Milton's youthful development. An excellent introductory docu-
      ment for a balanced judgment of the Minor Poems" (Stevens' annotation).

3208 HAVENS, P. S. A. A Tract Long Attributed to Milton. HLB, 6, 1934,
      109-14.
      On the authorship of A Letter Written to A Gentleman in the Country. See
      Masson, Life, 4, 519-23.

3209 HENDRICKSON, G. L. Milton, Salmasius,—and Synizesis. PQ, 20, 1941,
      597-600.
      Concerning the epigram on Salmasius which is incorporated into Milton's
      Second Defence.

3210 HENRY, NATHANIEL H. Milton's Official Translations. TLS, Aug.
      17, 1933, p. 549.
      Believes that the first Declaration Against the Scots in 1650 was not translated
      by Milton but by Thomas May.

3211 HESSLER, L. B. Attributed to Milton. TLS, June 28, 1934, p. 460.
      Submits a Latin poem, Julii Mazarini, Cardinalis, Epitaphium, found in
      Miscellany Poems Upon Several Occasions . . . (1692), for expression of
      opinion as to its authenticity.

3212 HIRAI, MASAO. John Milton. Tokyo: Kenkyusha, 1958. 261pp.
      A critical biography. Contains a chapter on Milton study in Japan.
      Rev: SCN, 13, No. 1, 1960, item 6.

3213 HOBBS, JOHN L. John Milton's Shrewsbury Connections. Transactions
      of the Shropshire Archaeological Society, 57, 1961, 26-30.
      Describes six documents in the Shrewsbury Borough Library (cf. Ralph E.
      Hone, HLQ, 22, 1958, 63-75) pertaining to the Phillips family. Suggests that

the signature of Gilbert Sheldon on the documents "provides valuable evidence that Milton's two nephews did not share their uncle's strong Republican sympathies" and agrees with Hone that this association "may have been responsible for the special leniency with which the poet was treated after the Restoration."

3214 HONE, RALPH E. Edward and John Phillips: Nephews and Pupils of John Milton. Doctoral diss., New York Univ., 1955. Abs., DA, 18, 1958, 2128.

3215 ------. New Light on the Milton-Phillips Family Relationship. HLQ, 22, 1958, 63-75.
An examination of deeds in the Shrewsbury Public Library and Museum, dated from Jan. 1596-7 to Nov. 1654.

3216 HOWARTH, R. G. Dramatists' Namesakes and Milton's Father. N&Q, N.S., 1, 1954, 83.
Cites a document signed at the home of Milton's father between John Webster, a tallow-chandler, and William Rowley of Clavering.

3217 ------. Edward Phillips' Compendiosa Enumeratio Poetarum. MLR, 54, 1959, 321-8.
On Phillips' Latin catalogue of poets. The work was appended to the seventeenth edition of Johannes Buchler's Sacrarum Profanarumque Phrasium Poeticarum Thesaurus, 1669. Howarth reprints the 1669 texts from the copy in the Folger Shakespeare Library.

3218 HOWE, ENA HAY. Blind Milton, a Dramatic Episode. London: S. French, 1947. 27pp.

3219 HOWELL, A. C. Milton's Mortal Remains and Their Literary Echoes. BSTCF, 4, No. 2, 1963, 17-30.
On the disinterment of Milton's remains in 1790 and the reactions of English men of letters.

3220 HUBBARD, EDITH P. John Milton and Giovanni Battista Doni. N&Q, 8, 1961, 170-1.
The Doni present at the meeting of the Svogliati, in Florence, on March 24, 1639, was Niccolò Doni, not Giovanni Battista Doni.

3221 HUGHES, MERRITT Y. Milton as a Revolutionary. ELH, 10, 1943, 87-116. Reprinted in Ten Perspectives on Milton (New Haven and London: Yale Univ. Press, 1965), pp. 240-75.
Delivered as a lecture before the Tudor and Stuart Club of Johns Hopkins University. Disagrees with the conclusions of G. Wilson Knight in The Chariot of Wrath and feels that Milton was no revolutionary in the modern sense. Rather, "Milton's prime concern was with the perfection of the state and of the individual."

3222 HUNT, HORTON M. Hail Wedded Love. The Natural History of Love (New York: Alfred A. Knopf, 1959; London: Hutchinson, 1960), pp. 210-7.
An account of Milton's marital experiences and of his attitude toward marriage.

3223 HUNTER, WILLIAM B., JR. Some Speculations on the Nature of

Milton's Blindness. The Journal of the History of Medicine, 17, 1962, 333-41.

"In this paper I wish to accept without further argument the hypothesis of glaucoma . . . and apply to it some of the findings of psychology during the past two decades."

3224 HUTCHINSON, FRANCIS E. Milton and the English Mind. Teach Yourself History Series. London: Hodder and Stoughton for the English Universities Press, 1946. vii, 197pp. Reprinted, New York: Collier Books, 1962. 155pp.

A sympathetic biographical account.

Rev: TLS, Mar. 29, 1947, p. 140; Charles Morgan, Sun. Times, Feb. 2, 1947, p. 4; A. N. Jeffares, ES, 28, 1947, 82-4; FR, 161, 1947, 311; H. N. Brailsford, NSN, Feb. 15, 1947, p. 138; Pierre Legouis, Les Langues modernes, 41, 1947, 443-4; B. A. Wright, RES, 24, 1948, 68-9; N. M., QQ, 55, 1948, 366; Lionel Stephenson, Pers, 30, 1949, 207-8.

3225 John Milton. The Great Soviet Encyclopedia. Second Edition, Moscow, 1954, Vol. 27.

3226 JOHNSON, SAMUEL. Milton. Johnson's Lives of the Poets. With an Introduction and Notes by K. Deighton. London: Macmillan; New York: St. Martin's, 1965. xxxvii, 139pp.

This edition first published in 1892. Reprinted 12 times. Contains a Summary of Johnson's Milton, by C. D. Punchard, pp. xxv-xxvii.

3227 KELLEY, MAURICE. Addendum: The Later Career of Daniel Skinner. PMLA, 55, 1940, 116-8.

Follows the career of Skinner for three years after his surrender of the Milton manuscripts.

3228 ------. The Annotations in Milton's Family Bible. MLN, 63, 1948, 539-40.

Addenda to the Columbia notes.

3229 ------. Daniel Skinner, Lord Preston, and Milton's Commonplace Book. MLN, 64, 1949, 522-5.

Prints two letters from Skinner to Lord Preston.

3230 ------. Milton and Machiavelli's Discorsi. SB, 4, 1951, 123-8.

Feels that Milton's notes on Machiavelli were made during 1651-2.

3231 ------. Milton and Mylius. TLS, June 17, 1949, p. 397.

On the discovery of two Milton autographs and a copy of Mylius' diary in the Niedersächsische Staatsarchiv at Oldenburg.

3232 ------. Milton and the Notes on Paul Best. Library, 5th Ser., 5, 1950, 49-51.

Questions Milton's authorship.

3233 ------. Milton's Autographs. TLS, Oct. 2, 1937, p. 715.

Describes "two translations which Milton dictated and corrected; or . . . at least had a hand in revising."

3234 ------. Milton's Commonplace Book, Folio 20. MLN, 62, 1947, 192-4.

Holds that the entry is in the handwriting of Lord Preston.

3235 ------. Milton's Dante-Della Casa-Varchi Volume. BNYPL, 46, 1962, 499-504.
Describes the volume in the New York Public Library (pressmarked KB1529) and makes a case for Milton's ownership of all three parts of the volume.

3236 ------. Milton's Library. TLS, Dec. 19, 1936, p. 1056.
Maintains that the signature discovered by Cameron is not genuine.

3237 ------. Robert Overton (1609-1668?), Friend of Milton. PULC, 4, 1943, 76-8.
Describes a recent acquisition by the Princeton Library, a notebook kept by Overton (370pp.) and compiled after 1665.

3238 KELLEY, MAURICE, AND SAMUEL D. ATKINS. Milton and the Harvard Pindar. SB, 17, 1964, 77-82.
Brings Milton's ownership of the Harvard Pindar into serious question.

3239 ------. Milton's Annotations of Aratus. PMLA, 70, 1955, 1090-1106.
Determines how Milton read Aratus in order to evaluate Milton's Greek scholarship.

3240 ------. Milton's Annotations of Euripides. JEGP, 60, 1961, 680-7.
A discussion of 146 marks, corrections, and notes that do not, according to the authors, belong in the Milton canon; and a report on the time, nature, and competence of what seems to be Milton's own work.

3241 KEMBLE, JAMES. John Milton and His Blindness. Idols and Invalids (London: Methuen, 1933; New York: Doubleday, 1936), pp. 247-92.
Argues that glaucoma was the cause of blindness and attempts to disprove other diagnoses.

3242 KENDALL, LYLE H., JR. A Letter from John Milton to George Wither? N&Q, 198, 1953, 473.
Considers the probability of Milton's composition of a letter included in Wither's Se Defendendo (1643) and signed "J. M."

3243 KENT, WILLIAM. The Milton Window at St. Margaret's Church. N&Q, 193, 1948, 570.
Reply to G. W. Wright, N&Q, 193, 1948, 480. The Story of the Memorial Fountain to Shakespeare at Stratford-upon-Avon contains the sermon preached by Archdeacon Farrar.

3244 KEYNES, GEOFFREY. John Donne's Sermons. TLS, May 28, 1954, p. 351.
Includes a transcription of a Latin letter written by Thomas Egerton to Egerton's father.

3245 KLIGER, SAMUEL. Milton in Italy and the Lost Malatesti Manuscript. SP, 51, 1954, 208-14.
Concerning Malatesti's collection of sonnets, La Tina, and an account of the manuscript which the poet allegedly gave to Milton.

3246 KRAMER, JEROME. The Romantic Biographers of Milton. Doctoral diss., Ohio State Univ., 1966.

3247 LANG, JAMES GILES. Life of Milton . . . written in the year of the Shropshire pageant and the performance of Comus at Ludlow Castle, 1934. 11pp.

3248   LARSEN, ERIK. A Presumed Portrait of John Milton by Anthony Van
Dyck. Pantheon, 24, 1966, 288-93.
On an unsigned portrait probably of Milton in his late twenties.

3249   LAW, D. G. John Milton and Chalfont St. Giles. Chalfont St. Giles:
published by Mrs. Law; printed by A. H. Patridge, Gerrards Cross,
1965. 48pp.
A Tercentenary Publication. Contains a short life of Milton, contemporary
accounts of the Great Plague of London, a discussion of Milton and Thomas
Ellwood, and a list of people who have lived in or visited Chalfont St. Giles.

3250   LAWRENCE, C. E. The Caged Eagle (a drama). Bookman (London),
84, 1933, 277-9.

3251   LE COMTE, EDWARD S. Milton Remembers The Praise of Folly.
PMLA, 71, 1956, 840.
The fourth sentence of the Apology for Smectymnuus echoes a passage from
Moriae Encomium and shows that Milton is "feeling doubts and strains that
will shortly . . . impel him to marriage."

3252   LILJEGREN, S. B. Milton at Florence. Neophil, 43, 1959, 133-7.
Argues that Milton did not visit Galileo and feels that Milton largely
imagined a favorable reception in Italy.

3253   ------. Miltons italienische Reise. Ang. Bbl., 40, 1939, 377-8. Reprinted in
UEIES, 16, 1956, xxvi-xxviii.
On Milton's alleged falsehoods concerning the journey.

3254   Lost Milton Portrait Believed Found. The Times, Dec. 23, 1961, p. 3c.
On the Onslow portrait, now in the National Portrait Gallery.

3255   MABBOTT, THOMAS O. Archie Armstrong and Milton. N&Q, 179,
1940, 14.
The young Milton and humorous verse.

3256   ------. Contemporary Evidence for Royal Favour to Milton. N&Q, 169,
1935, 221.
Cites a passage from Peter Heimbach's message to Milton on June 6, 1666, as
support for the "hypothesis that Charles II did seek to employ Milton in
foreign affairs. . . ."

3257   ------. Milton: Latin Inscription in a Bible. N&Q, 159, 1930, 150.
From a Bible which belonged to Milton's wife.

3258   ------. Milton, Leigh, and Dunkin. TLS, July 19, 1937, p. 512.
Perhaps the unpublished pamphlet mentioned by Edward Phillips refers to a
religious controversy with Robert Dunkin, not Richard Leigh.

3259   ------. Milton: A Marginal Note on Varchi. N&Q, 163, 1932, 189.
Milton's note in a book found in the New York Public Library.

3260   ------. Milton to Mylius: Letter found at Oldenburg. N&Q, 159, 1930, 208.
Reprint of a letter from Milton to Mylius.

3261   ------. The Miltonic Epitaph on Mazarin. N&Q, 167, 1934, 349-50.
Two texts in Miscellany Poems on Several Occasions (1692) may deserve
inclusion in the Milton canon.

3262 ------. The Miltonic Epitaph on Mazarin: Cowper's Opinion. N&Q, 172, 1937, 188.
Cowper considered the epitaph Milton's.

3263 ------. Milton's Manuscript Notes. TLS, Jan. 30, 1937, p. 76.
Seeks information concerning a reported "two pages . . . of manuscript notes, ascribed to John Milton."

3264 ------. Milton's "Overdaled sphears." N&Q, 161, 1931, 459.
Query concerning BM MS 36354.

3265 ------. Notes on Farnaby Ascribed to John Milton. N&Q, 171, 1936, 152-4.
Reproduces the marginalia and an abridgment of the text of the Harvard copy of the Systema Grammaticum (1641) which bears the name "I. Miltoni."

3266 MABBOTT, THOMAS O., and J. MILTON FRENCH. The Grand Case of Conscience Wrongly Attributed to Milton. N&Q, 185, 1943, 302-3.
Explains the decision not to include the work in the Columbia Edition.

3267 ------. Milton: An Apocryphal Story. N&Q, 181, 1941, 204.
A query concerning the origin of the legend that Milton wrote Paradise Lost after marriage and Paradise Regained after Mary's death and that he locked her coffin.

3268 MACAULAY, ROSE. Milton. London: Duckworth, 1933, 1957; New York: Macmillan, 1957. 141pp.
A scholarly and concise biography.
Rev: Clennell Wilkinson, Merc, 29, 1934, 477; Herbert Agar, ER, 58, 1934, 227-31; P. H., NYTBR, Mar. 10, 1934, p. 3; TLS, Jan. 11, 1934, p. 29; B. Dobrée, Spect, 152, 1934, 244; reply by Macaulay, ibid., 275-6; A. M. Witherspoon, SRL, 11, 1935, 646-7; Blanche Kelly, CW, 141, 1935, 368-70; E. Wagenknecht, VQR, 11, 1935, 601-6; R. S. Scholler, Unity, Oct. 7, 1935, pp. 56-7.

3269 MAMEMOTO, KAORU. Milton and the English Revolution. Shiga University Teachers College Reports (Japan), 5, 1956.

3270 MANUEL, M. The Life of Milton in The History of King-Killers, N&Q, N.S., 7, 1960, 426.
Insists that this biography is "a skilful abridgement of Anthony Wood's life of Milton in the Athenae and Fasti Oxonienses (1691)." See also Manuel's Wisconsin dissertation, No. 729.

3271 MARTIN, JOHN RUPERT. The Portrait of John Milton at Princeton and its Place in Milton Iconography. Princeton: Princeton Univ. Press, 1961. 34pp.
Says the portrait is an authentic likeness made from life. Identifies the artist as William Faithorne. Many illustrations.
Rev: Roy C. Strong, MLR, 57, 1962, 417-8; B. A. Wright, RES, 14, 1963, 198-200; Edgar Mertner, Anglia, 82, 1964, 247-59; Donald A. Roberts, SCN, 24, 1966, 22-3.

3272 ------. The Milton Portrait: Some Addenda. PULC, 24, 1963, 168-73.
Supplementary notes to his monograph. Mentions "some additional early likenesses of the poet. . . ."

3273   MASSON, DAVID. The Life of John Milton: Narrated in Connexion with
        the Political, Ecclesiastical, and Literary History of His Time. New
        York: Peter Smith, 1946. 7 vols.
            A reprint of Stevens' No. 2024. Masson's monumental biography was first
            published between 1859 and 1880. The index was published in 1894.

3274   McCOLLEY, GRANT. Milton's Lost Tragedy. PQ, 18, 1939, 73-83.
            Believes that after 1645 Milton designed a tragedy different from the drafts
            found in the Trinity MSS.

3275   McCULLEN, J. T., JR. Milton's Letter to Hartop. N&Q, 3, 1964, 8.
            Seeks to locate a letter to Jonathan Hartop of Aldborough, Yorkshire, who
            reportedly lent Milton fifty pounds.

3276   McLAUGHLIN, ELIZABETH T. Milton and Thomas Ellwood. MN, 1,
        1967, 17-28.
            An appreciative evaluation and analysis of Ellwood's career. Discusses his
            friendship with Milton, and reproduces his epitaph on the poet. Rejoinder by
            J. Max Patrick, MN, 2, 1968, 2-4, with a surrejoinder by Mrs. McLaughlin,
            ibid., pp. 4-5.

3277   McMANAWAY, JAMES G. Parish Registers of St. Giles Without
        Cripplegate. N&Q, N.S., 13, 1966, 14-5.
            Describes registers prior to Milton's time.

3278   MEIKLEJOHN, K. C. Tercentenary at Milton's Cottage. Coming Events
        in Britain, June, 1965, pp. 28-9.
            The curator of the Milton Cottage gives an account of Milton's decision to
            move to Chalfont St. Giles. Also describes the present holdings in the cottage,
            including first editions and memorabilia.

3279   Milton's Cottage. SRL, Apr. 6, 1957, p. 31.
            Pictures and describes briefly the cottage at Chalfont St. Giles.

3280   Milton's God. TLS, Aug. 5, 1965, p. 672.
            Observation that in the second edition of his Milton's God, W. Empson ex-
            pands his case for believing Milton forged the Pamela prayer in Eikon
            Basilike.

3281   MOHL, RUTH. John Milton on Some of the Writing of His Day.
        Studies in Language and Literature in Honour of Margaret Schlauch.
        Ed. by Mieczystaw Brahmer and others (Warsaw: PWN—Polish
        Scientific Publishers, 1966), pp. 261-72.
            Discusses what Milton liked and what he criticized in the writing of his own
            day.

3282   MORAND, PAUL P. The Effects of His Political Life upon John Milton
        (thèse complementaire). Paris: Didier, 1939. 126pp.
            Rev: E. M. W. Tillyard, MLN, 55, 1940, 635-6; E. N. S. T[hompson], PQ, 19,
            1940, 223.

3283   MUIR, KENNETH. John Milton. Men and Books Series. London: Long-
        mans, 1955. Second Edition, 1961, 1962, 1965. 196pp.
            A sympathetic biography containing attacks on the New Critics.
            Rev: B. Evan Owen, CR, 188, 1955, 132-3; Rex Warner, Lon. Mag., 2, No. 8,
            1955, 74-6; NSN, May 14, 1955, p. 694; N&Q, N. S., 2, 1955, 322; TLS, May 6,

1955, p. 238; Owen Chadwick, JEH, 7, 1956, 127; E. H. Emerson, JEGP, 51, 1956, 509-10; F. T. Prince, RES, 8, 1957, 203-4.

3284 NAZARI, EMILIO. Problemi Miltoniani. Palermo: A Priulla, 1951. 250pp.
Two chapters of interest in connection with Milton's biography: Il Viaggio di Milton in Italia e Ondeggiamenti Religiosi, pp. 7-43; Alcune Considerazioni Sulla Vita e Sulla Figura del Milton, pp. 218-47.

3285 NETHERCOT, ARTHUR H. Milton, Jonson, and Young Cowley. MLN, 49, 1934, 158-62.
Possibly the friendship between Jonson and Cowley aroused the envy of Milton.

3286 OCHI, FUMIO. Milton and Diodati. SEL (Japan), 18, 1938, 513-30.
Analyzes the friendship and observes that the severity of Milton's character was softened by Diodati's wit, humor, and laughter.

3287 ------. Milton and Herman Mylius. SEL (Japan), 8, 1957.

3288 ------. Milton and Thomas Young. Zeitschrift for Professor Funahashi. Doshisha Univ., 1939.

3289 ------. Milton in his Early Days. Doshisha Literary Pamphlets, No. 3, 1939. 65pp.

3290 ------. Milton in Florence. SEL (Japan), 20, 1940.

3291 ------. Some Notes on the Milton-Heimbach Correspondence. SEL (Japan), 5, 1955.

3292 [Onslow Portrait]. The Times, July 6, 1961, p. 16e.
Notes purchase of portrait by National Portrait Gallery for £23.

3293 Ormuz and Amurath. TLS, Mar, 30, 1933, pp. 205-6.
Milton's interest in contemporary exploration reflected in his works.

3294 ORUCH, JACK B. Milton as Adjutant-General? SEL, 5, 1965, 61-7.
On Edward Phillips' statement that there was a "design in Agitation" of making Milton "Adjutant-General in Sir William Waller's army."

3295 PARKER, WILLIAM RILEY. Above All Liberties: John Milton's Relations with His Earliest Publishers. PULC, 2, 1941, 41-50.
A discussion of Milton's struggles, quarrels, and friendships with various printers and booksellers in London.

3296 ------. The Anonymous Life of Milton. TLS, Sept. 13, 1957, p. 547.
Cyriack Skinner. Replies by R. W. Hunt, TLS, Oct. 11, 1957, p. 609; and by Maurice Kelley, Dec. 27, 1957, p. 787.

3297 ------. Contributions toward a Milton Bibliography. Library, 4th Ser., 16, 1936, 425-38.
On Milton and his early printers.

3298 ------. John Milton, Scrivener, 1590-1632. MLN, 59, 1944, 532-37.
An account of the elder Milton's career.

3299 ------. Milton and Edward Phillips. TLS, Feb. 28, 1942, p. 108.
Questions Milton's alleged part in the Theatrum Poetarum.

3300   ------. Milton and the Marchioness of Winchester. MLR, 44, 1949, 547-50.
        A manuscript version of the poem (B. M. Sloane MS. 1446, fols 37b-38) "is
        not the work of a careless copyist: either it is a careful bit of meddling by an
        informed person who thought to improve Milton's lines, or it is a copy of an
        earlier version of a poem which Milton later revised slightly."

3301   ------. Milton and the News of Charles Diodati's Death. MLN, 72, 1957,
        486-8.
        On the poet's reaction.

3302   ------. Milton and Thomas Young, 1602-1628. MLN, 53, 1938, 399-407.
        Feels that Young's influence on Milton practically ended when the poet was
        eleven.

3303   ------. Milton as Secretary. N&Q, N.S., 4, 1957, 441-2.
        An attempt to clarify Milton's exact secretarial position at various times
        during the Interregnum.

3304   ------. Milton: A Biography. Oxford: Clarendon Press, 1968. 2 vols. Vol.
        1: xvii, 666pp. Vol. 2: pp. 667-1489.
        A monumental study, forty years in preparation, that will inevitably be
        compared with David Masson's Life of Milton (1859-80), although the author
        in the Preface states that "my own work is no presumptuous attempt to
        supersede so stately a memorial" as Masson's work. This study reflects recent
        scholarship on Milton and changed attitudes toward the man and artist.
        The first volume contains the life, and the second consists of fully docu-
        mented notes, and a full index and finding list. Also, there are two appen-
        dices in the second volume: 1, Milton's Publications, 1628-1700, in the order
        of their appearance, and with the number of surviving copies located in
        public, institutional, or private libraries; 2, Surviving Copies of Seventeenth-
        century Editions of Milton located in public or institutional libraries.
        In Volume Two there are lengthy introductions to the notes for each
        chapter of Volume One. "These introductions, addressed to students and
        scholars (though hopefully of some interest to the general reader also), re-
        view the biographical resources and problems for each period of Milton's
        life, stressing the present limitations of our knowledge and the questions
        still awaiting answers."
        The index and finding list contains much useful information: the names
        mentioned in the text, notes and the subjects discussed. "It includes much
        besides, in an effort to be useful to the curious reader and future investigators
        of Milton's biography. . . . The list also contains many titles of books and can
        serve as a collection of bibliographies."
        Rev: David Daiches, MGW, 99, August 29, 1968, 15; Michael Wilding, NSN,
        76, 1968, 232-3; MN, 2, 1968, 59-62.

3305   ------. Milton, Rothwell, and Simmons. Library, 4th Ser., 18, 1937,
        89-103.
        On Milton and his printers.

3306   ------. Milton's Unknown Friend. TLS, May 16, 1936, p. 420.
        Suggests Thomas Young.

3307   ------. On Milton's Early Literary Program. MP, 33, 1935, 49-53.
        In The Reason Of Church Government: "As it happens, I must record my
        disagreement with both Tillyard and Hanford—indeed with all those writers

who either state or imply that Milton gave us, in this pamphlet, a definite statement of program."

3308 ------. Thomas Myriell. N&Q, 188, 1945, 103.
"Is the rector of St. Stephens, Walbrook, the church where Anne Milton was married, the Thomas Myriell who complied the Tristitiae Remedium, MS collection of music containing ten compositions by Anne's father?"

3309 ------. Three Footnotes to Milton Biography. N&Q, N.S., 5, 1958, 208.
On the date of Deborah Milton's marriage, Cyriack Skinner's marriage, and the baptismal date of the poet's nephew, John Milton.

3310 ------. Wood's Life of Milton: Its Sources and Significance. PBSA, 52, 1958, 1-22.
Reprints Wood's Life of Milton and concludes that Wood's biography is almost "wholly worthless as biographical source material" and is even misleading.

3311 PARKS, GEORGE B. Two Queries About Milton. SCN, 2, No. 1, 1943, 3-4.
On Milton's entry to the Florentine Academy and on the identity of Sir William Hawley.

3312 PARSONS, EDWARD S. The Authorship of the Anonymous Life of Milton. PMLA, 50, 1935, 1057-64.
Questions Darbishire's attribution to John Phillips.

3313 ------. Concerning The Earliest Life of Milton. ELH, 9, 1942, 106-15.
Opposes the view of Benham, ELH, 6, 1939, 245-55.

3314 PATRICK, J. MAX. Milton's Visit to Galileo. SCN, 19, 1961, 62-3.
Milton probably saw Galileo through a grating or window but did not converse with him.

3315 PATTISON, MARK. Milton. English Men of Letters. London: Macmillan, 1932; New York and London: AMS Press, 1968. vi, 227pp.
Reprints of Stevens' No. 1712, published in 1879.

3316 [PHILLIPS, JOHN] A Satyr Against Hypocrites (1655). Introduction by Leon Howard. UCLA Augustan Reprint Soc., 38. Los Angeles: Clark Memorial Library, 1953. iv, 22pp.
A facsimile reproduction. "At best, Milton could have considered this first rhymed flowering of his nephew's satiric humor a pointless piece of scurrility which lacked real wit, coherence, or character."

3317 The Portrait of John Milton at Princeton. PULC, 23, 1961, 24.
Reviews John R. Martin's monograph and reproduces the portrait.

3318 PRAZ, MARIO. John Milton. La letteratura inglese: Dal medioevo all'illuminismo (Firenze: Sansoni, 1967), pp. 253-67.
An account of Milton's career as man and writer.

3319 RACINE, LOUIS. Life of Milton, together with Observations on Paradise Lost. Translated, with an Introduction, by Katherine John. London: Hogarth Press, 1930. v, 158pp.
Rev: Bookman, 79, 1930, 218; TLS, Oct. 23, 1930, p. 869; James Thornton,

Nat. and Ath., 48, 1930, 197; ER, 52, 1931, 118; Oxf. Mag., May 14, 1931, p. 700; D. Saurat, RES, 7, 1931, 472-4; R. F. Russell, Merc, 23, 1931, 507.

3320 RAYMOND, DORA B. Oliver's Secretary: John Milton in an Era of Revolt. New York: Minton, Balch, 1932. 355pp.
A sympathetic biography.
Rev: L. C. Martin, YWES, 206; NR, 74, 1933, 289; A. M. Witherspoon, SRL, 9, 1933, 377; Nat, 134, 1933, 26; G. W. Whiting, MP, 31, 1933, 91-4; W. H. Coates, AHR, 38, 1933, 589-90; E. Hodder, JMH, 5, 1933, 230-1; G. Genzmer, CHR, 20, 1934, 106-7; TLS, Sept. 5, 1935, p. 554; G. D., EHR, 52, 1937, 163.

3321 READ, ALLEN W. The Disinterment of Milton's Remains. PMLA, 45, 1930, 1050-68.
Concludes that the body disinterred in 1790 was that of Milton. Draws information from Philip Neve's account.

3322 REBORA, PIERO. Milton a Firenza. Nuova Antologia, 459, 1953, 147-63. Reprinted in Sei-Settecento (Firenze: Sansoni, 1956), pp. 251-70.
On Milton and various Florentine influences.

3323 RICKWORD, EDGELL. Milton: The Revolutionary Intellectual. The English Revolution 1640 (London: Lawrence and Wishart, 1940), pp. 101-32.
A stimulating account of Milton's political career.

3324 RIFFE, NANCY LEE. Milton and Charles II. N&Q, N.S., 11, 1964, 93-4.
On the origin of Chateaubriand's attributed anecdote involving Milton and Charles II, mentioned in French's Life Records of John Milton.

3325 ROGERS, LAMBERT. John Milton's Blindness: A Suggested Diagnosis. Jour. Hist. Medicine and Allied Sciences, 4, 1949, 468-71.
The author, an M.D., suggests that the blindness was caused by a suprachiasmal cystic tumor.

3326 ROSEN, EDWARD. A Friend of John Milton: Valerio Chimentelli and His Copy of Viviani's De maximus et minimus. BNYPL, 57, 1953, 159-74. Printed also in pamphlet form by the New York Public Library, 1953. 18pp.

3327 ROTH, LEON. Hebraists and Non-Hebraists of the Seventeenth Century. Journal of Semitic Studies, 6, 1961, 204-21.
Holds that Milton had no special knowledge of Hebrew and Hebraic learning.

3328 ROWSE, ALFRED L. The Milton Country. The English Past, Evocations of Persons and Places (New York: Macmillan, 1952), pp. 85-112.
Concerning Milton's ancestors, the countryside around Milton (the town), the Powell house, etc.

3329 RUBINSTEIN, ANNETTE T. John Milton. The Great Tradition in English Literature from Shakespeare to Shaw (New York: Russell and Russell, 1953), pp. 121-63.
An account of Milton's life and works.

3330 RUHE, EDWARD L. Milton and the Duke of York. N&Q, 198, 1953, 524-5.

Quotes the story of Milton and the Duke from Joseph Tower's British Biography (1769).

3331 ------. A Study in the Early Lives of Milton. Doctoral diss., Columbia Univ., 1959. Abs., DA, 20, 1959, 1368.
Considers Aubrey, Wood, Wood's anonymous source, Edward Phillips, and Toland.

3332 SAILLENS, ÉMILE. John Milton, poète combatant. Paris: Gallimard, 1959. 350pp. Published in English as John Milton: Man, Poet and Polemist. New York: Barnes and Noble, 1964; Oxford: Blackwell, 1964. xxii, 371pp.
A sympathetic biography, originally intended to win for Milton "the admiration and respect of my French readers and might induce some of them to read Milton himself." Kathleen Pond assisted in the translation. Bibliography, pp. 355-66, complied by R. W. Gibson.

3333 ------. Milton à l'O.R.T.F. EA, 19, 1966, 201-2.
On Marie Forestier's radio drama Faut-il Pendre John Milton, presented on Jan. 26, 1966. Concerned with possible story of how Milton was saved by Lady Beresford after the Restoration.

3334 SAITO, TAKESHI. John Milton. Tokyo: Kenkyusha, 1933. vi, 150pp.
Written in Japanese. A biographical introduction to Milton and his works.

3335 SAMARIN, R. Tvorčestvo Džona Mil'tona. Moskkva: State Univ. Press, 1964. 485pp.
Chapters (titles translated): Milton's Early Work, The Poet and the Revolution, Apotheosis of the Uprising, In the Name of the Common Cause, Samson Agonistes, Milton's Place in Seventeenth-Century Literature.

3336 SANDS, MAURICE. Milton: Life and Works. Boston: Student Outlines Co., 1956.

3337 SAURAT, DENIS. Milton: 1608-1674. Les Ecrivains Célèbres. Ed. by Raymond Queneau (Paris: Lucien Mazenod, 1952), 2, 130-2.
An appreciative account of Milton's career. Especially admires Milton's portrayal of Satan and of Adam and Eve and the autobiographical passages in Paradise Lost.

3338 ------. Milton: Man and Thinker. Second Edition. London: Dent, 1944, 1946; Hamden, Conn.: Archon Books, 1964; London: Bailey Brothers, 1964. xiv, 291pp.
Originally published in 1925, Stevens' No. 2565. Lengthy annotation in Stevens.

3339 SCHNITTKIND, HENRY T. and DANA A. John Milton. Living Biographies of Great Poets (New York: Garden City Publishing Co., 1941), pp. 47-59.

3340 SCHOLFIELD, A. F. Notes by Milton. TLS, July 17, 1937, p. 528.
The author is trying to locate a certain copy of Harington's translation of Orlando Furioso, said to contain marginal notes in the handwriting of Milton.

3341 SCHRÖDER, A. Milton als Schullektüre. Neuphilologische Mschr., 1, 1930, 177-96.

3342A   SEATON, ETHEL. Literary Relations of England and Scandinavia in the Seventeenth Century. Oxford: Clarendon Press, 1935. 384pp.
Milton, passim.
Rev: L. C. Martin, YWES, 249-50; TLS, Mar. 28, 1936, p. 262; J. Nordström, Lychnos, 1, 1936, 353; J. Kruuse, RLC, July, 1936, 608-12; E. Eckhardt, Ang. Bbl., 47, 1936, 265-7; A. B., Archiv, 169, 1936, 135-6.

3342B   SELLIN, PAUL R. Caesar Calandrini, the London Dutch, and Milton's Quarrels in Holland. HLQ, 31, 1968, 239-49.
This entry is annotated under Prose: Criticism.

3343   SENIOR, H. L. John Milton, the Supreme Englishman. London: W. H. Allen, 1944. 38pp.
Senior, a Communist, emphasizes the "freedom element" in Milton's writings.

3344   SENSABAUGH, GEORGE F. A Milton Ascription. N&Q, 194, 1949, 337.
In a copy of The King's Cabinet opened (1645).

3345   ------. Milton Bejesuited. SP, 47, 1950, 224-42.
On the origin of the idea that Milton died a papist.

3346   SHAWCROSS, JOHN T. The Dating of Certain Poems, Letters, and Prolusions Written by Milton. ELN, 2, 1965, 261-6.
Dates Naturam non pati and De Idea Platonica, 1631; seven Prolusions, 1628-29; redates Letters 3 and 4 of Epistolarum Familiarium.

3347   ------. Division of Labor in Justa Edovardo King Naufrago (1638). LC, 27, 1961, 176-9.
On the respective work of Thomas Buck and Roger Daniel in the printing of the 1638 volume of tributes to Edward King.

3348   ------. Milton's Decision to Become a Poet. MLQ, 24, 1963, 21-30.
Suggests that "during the summer of 1637 Milton decided against a church career and, by the beginning of autumn, in favor of a poetic one."

3349   ------. Notes on Milton's Amanuenses. JEGP, 58, 1959, 29-38.
On John Phillips and others. Questions some of the conclusions of Maurice Kelly (MP, 54, 1956, 20-5) and observes that more information is needed on extant materials in the various amanuenses' hands.

3350   ------. Of Chronology and the Dates of Milton's Translation from Horace and the New Forcers of Conscience. SEL, 3, 1963, 77-84.
Dates the translation 1646 or later and the New Forcers during the first months of 1647.

3351   ------. Speculations on the Dating of the Trinity MS. of Milton's Poems. MLN, 75, 1960, 11-7.
". . . allows the possibility of 1637 as the date of writing of the letter to an unknown friend. On the acceptance of this, all objection to dating the whole Trinity MS. from that date forward is nullified."

3352   SIRLUCK, ERNEST. Milton's Idle Right Hand. JEGP, 60, 1961, 749-85.
Sees Milton's marriage and its failure as the solution to the problem of slight poetic activity between 1641-1660.

3353   SLOANE, WILLIAM. Milton's Rooms at Christ's College. N&Q, N.S., 6, 1959, 357-8.
Suggests Rats' Hall, a temporary structure, as Milton's Cambridge residence.

3354 SORSBY, ARNOLD. On the Nature of Milton's Blindness. British Journal of Ophthalmology, 14, 1930, 339-54.
Suggests myopia.

3355 SPEARS, JEWEL. Milton's Literary Records of His Personal Relationships. Master's thesis, Univ. of Alabama, 1939.

3356 SPENCER, LOIS, and J. MILTON FRENCH. A Supplement to The Life Records of John Milton from the Thomason Manuscript Catalogue. N&Q, N.S., 7, 1960, 424-5.
Presents notes on some of George Thomason's books mentioned in Life Records.

3357 STOYE, J. W. English Travellers Abroad 1604-1667. London: Cape, 1952. 479pp.
Invaluable background study. Milton's Italian journey, passim.
Rev: TLS, July 11, 1952, p. 454.

3358 STROUSSE, FLORA. John Milton, Clarion Voice of Freedom. New York: Vanguard Press, 1962. 283pp.
A book for juveniles.

3359 STUART, DOROTHY MARGARET. Milton and Prynne: Some New Light on the Secret History of the Commonwealth. NSN, N.S., 1, 1931, 15-6.
On Milton's part in Prynne's arrest.

3360 TAAFFE, JAMES G. John Milton's Student, Richard Barry: A Biographical Note. HLQ, 25, 1962, 325-36.
On the "varied and interesting career" of the second Earl of Barrymore. "What he learned or gained from his period with Milton may never be known..."

3361 ------. Milton, the Boyles, and Their Circle. Doctoral diss., Indiana Univ., 1960. Abs., DA, 21, 1960, 905.

3362 ------. Mrs. John Dury: A Sister of Lycidas. N&Q, N.S., 9, 1962, 60-1.
In 1645 Milton had the opportunity to become acquainted with Mrs. John Dury, née Dorothy King.

3363 THOMPSON, KARL F. Milton's Eighteenth Century Biographers. Doctoral diss., Yale Univ. 1950.

3364 TILLYARD, E. M. W. Milton. London: Chatto and Windus; New York: Dial Press, 1930. viii, 396pp. Reprinted, London: Chatto and Windus, 1931; New York: Barnes and Noble, 1963. Revised Edition, with a Preface by Phyllis B. Tillyard. London: Chatto and Windus, 1966; New York: Collier-Macmillan, 1967; Harmondsworth: Penguin Books, 1968. viii, 340pp.
Contains sections on the early poems, the period of the prose, Milton's beliefs, and the later poems. Appendices, i.a., on Thomas Young, the dating of the sonnets, and Spenser's influence on Milton. The revised edition is substantially the same work as the 1930 edition.
Reviews are listed in this bibliography under No. 972.

3365 TURNBULL, GEORGE H. Hartlib, Dury, and Comenius. Gleanings

from Hartlib's Papers. London: Hodder and Stoughton; Liverpool: Univ. Press of Liverpool, 1947. xi, 447pp.
Milton, passim.
Rev: TLS, Apr. 3, 1948, p. 192; J. M. Batten, JR, 28, 1948, 147-8; Dorothy Stimson, Isis, 39, 1948, 181-2.

3366 ------. Notes on John Durie's Reformed Librarie-Keeper. Library, 5th Ser., 1, 1946, 64-7.
Argues that Milton did not instigate the writing of the work.

3367 ------. Samuel Hartlib's Connection with Sir Francis Kynaston's Musaeum Minervae. N&Q, 197, 1952, 33-7.
Describes the private Conservatory from Hartlib's account of it.

3368 TURNER, W. ARTHUR. Cromwell and the Piedmont Massacres. N&Q, 193, 1948, 135-6.
A quote from Jean Leger, representative of the Vaudois, may indicate that "Cromwell's indignation at the outrage was tinged with more diplomacy than we have imagined."

3369 ------. John Winthrop, F. R. S. TLS, Nov. 1, 1947, p. 563.
Letters from Milton to Winthrop may exist.

3370 ------. The Known English Acquaintances of John Milton. Doctoral diss., Ohio State Univ., 1947. Abs., Ohio State Univ., Abstracts of Doctoral Dissertations, No. 53, 1947, pp. 161-7.

3371 ------. Masson's Identification of Milton's Pupil Richard Heath, N&Q, 193, 1948, 383.
Questions Masson's indentification of Heath as the Richard Heath who assisted Brian Walton with the Polyglot Bible.

3372 ------. Milton and Spenser's Grandson. N&Q, 192, 1947, 547.
William Spenser, grandson of the poet, may have been the "Spencer" aided by Milton.

3373 ------. Milton, Marvell, and Dradon at Cromwell's Funeral, PQ, 28, 1949, 320-3.
Calls attention to British Museum MS Lansdowne 95, No. 2, p. 11v, which connects Milton, Marvell, and possibly Dryden with Cromwell's funeral.

3374 ------. Milton's Aid to Davenant. MLN, 63, 1948, 538-9.
"The question is not whether Milton saved Davenant's life, but how he might have helped him."

3375 ------. Milton's Aid to the Polyglot Bible. MLN, 64, 1945, 345.
Two orders of the Council, of July 9 and July 15, 1653, concerning custom-free importation of paper are offered as "more certain evidence of aid to the great project by Milton."

3376 ------. Milton's Friendship with Cromwell's Granddaughter. N&Q, N.S., 1, 1954, 199.
On the possible friendship between Milton and Bridget Bendish.

3377 UNTERMEYER, LOUIS. Blind Visionary: John Milton. Lives of the Poets: The Story of One Thousand Years of English and American Poetry (New York: Simon and Schuster, 1959), pp. 170-92.

An appreciative account of Milton's life. Discusses some of the reasons why Milton is "one of the least read."

3378 VILLANI, FELICE. Milton tra Riforma e Controriforma: L'ideale pedagogico e la Poetica di Milton dopo il viaggio in Italia. Milano: Albrighi, Segati C., 1937. 123pp.
Milton on pedagogy and poetry after his trip to Italy.

3379 VINCE, CHARLES A. Milton in Italy. Lectures and Diversions (London: Elkin Matthews and Marrot, 1931), pp. 49-57.
A reprint of an essay, first published in 1928 in the Central Literary Magazine. Places Milton in the historic tradition of travel to Italy, beginning with Chaucer.

3380 VISIAK, E. H. A Miltonian Puzzle. N&Q, 176, 1939, 200-1.
Holds that the verses sent to Queen Christina with Cromwell's picture are the collaboration of Milton and Marvell.

3381 VISSER, MARTINUS. Het leven van Milton. Amsterdam: H. J. Spruyt's Uitgevers-Mij., 1940. 147pp.

3382 WARNER, OLIVER. English Literature: A Portrait Gallery. London: Chatto and Windus, 1964. 205pp.
Reproduces the Onslow portrait, p. 35.

3383 WHITING, GEORGE W. Milton and the "Postscript." MLR, 30, 1935, 506-8.
Declares that Milton did not write the postscript to An Answer to A Book Entituled An Humble Remonstrance... (1641).

3384 ------. Milton a Jesuit. N&Q, 168, 1935, 150-1.
Concerning the ridiculousness of Pelling's charge (1680).

3385 WILLOUGHBY, EDWIN E. Milton's Taxes (1641-2?). MLR, 26, 1931, 178-9.
Three Aldersgate Ward papers in the Guildhall Library confirm previous deductions that Milton was at this time a prosperous citizen.

3386 WILMER, W. H. The Blindness of Milton. JEGP, 32, 1933, 301-15.
Diagnoses glaucoma.

3387 ------. The Blindness of Milton. BHM, 1, 1933, 85-106.

3388 WITHERSPOON, A. M. Milton as a Statesman. SRL, 9, 1933, 377.
A review article of Dora Raymond's Oliver's Secretary (1932).

3389 ------. Milton is Still Timely. SRL, 11, 1935, 646.
Reviews studies by Rose Macaulay and Belloc and concludes that Roman Catholics and women have been Milton's severest critics.

3390 WOLFE, DON M. Lilburne's Note on Milton. MLN, 56, 1941, 360-3.
Lilburne's favorable appraisal of the last lines of Milton's Defence is an indication of a closer bond with the Levellers than scholars have usually assumed.

3391 ------. Milton and Cromwell: April, 1653. English Studies Today. Fourth Series (Roma: Edizioni di Storia e Letteratura, 1966), pp. 311-24.

Observes that Milton approved of Cromwell's dissolution of the Rump Parliament, but his characterization of Cromwell after its dissolution is ambivalent and contradictory.

3392 ------. Milton in the Puritan Revolution. New York and London: Nelson,
1941. Reprinted, London: Cohen and West; New York: Humanities
Press, Inc., 1963. xvi, 496pp.
On Milton's activities during and after the Civil War.
Reviews listed in this bibliography under No. 3084.

3393 WRIGHT, B. A. The Alleged Falsehoods in Milton's Account of His
Continental Tour. MLR, 28, 1933, 308-14.
"A liar of course he may have been, but not yet a convicted one."

3394 ------. Milton's First Marriage. MLR, 26, 1931, 383-400; 27, 1932, 6-23.
"A coherent story can only be made of Milton's first marriage on the assumption that it occurred in 1642."

3395 WRIGHT, C. J. Milton and Dorset. TLS, 29, 1961, p. 636.
Seeks information on the Dorchester tradition that Milton visited Milton
Abbey and while there planned Il Penseroso.

3396 WRIGHT, G. W. The Milton Window at St. Margaret's. N&Q, N.S., 193,
1948, 480.
Inquires about the window and the printing of a sermon preached by the
Ven. Archdeacon R. W. Farrar, Rector of the church.

3397 YOUNG, R. F. Comenius in England, as Described in Contemporary
Documents. London: Oxford Univ. Press, 1932. 100pp.
Comenius possibly influenced Milton through Hartlib.

3398 ZAGORIN, P. The Authorship of Mans Mortallitie. Library, 5th Ser., 5,
1951, 179-83.
Attributes the tract to Richard Overton the Leveller, not Robert Overton the
friend of Milton.

STYLE AND VERSIFICATION

3399A AYLWARD, KEVIN JOSEPH. Milton's Latin Versification: The Hexameter. Doctoral diss., Columbia Univ., 1966. Abs., DA, 27, 1966, 1331-A—32-A.

3399B BALDI, SERGIO. Poesie italiane di Milton, SSe, 7, 1966, 103-50.
  Discusses dates of composition, language and meter, the influence of Petrarch, and Milton's Italian style. Includes the texts of six poems and some critical analysis.

3399C BANKS, THEODORE H. Milton's Imagery. New York: Columbia Univ. Press, 1950. xiv, 260pp.
  Milton's imagery is discussed under several chapter headings: London Public Life, London Private Life, Travel and War, Nature, Animals, and Books and Learning.
  Rev: A. H. Gilbert, SAQ, 50, 1951, 151-2; Jacques Blondel, LM, 45, 1951, 270; F. Michael Krouse, MLN, 67, 1952, 474-8; A. E. Barker, MLR, 47, 1952, 579-80; B. A. Wright, RES, 3, 1952, 390-2; Kester Svendsen, MLQ, 14, 1953, 312-3.

3400 BEUM, ROBERT. So Much Gravity and Ease. Language and Style in Milton: A Symposium in Honor of the Tercentenary of Paradise Lost. Ed. by Ronald David Emma and John T. Shawcross (New York: Frederick Ungar, 1967), pp. 333-68.
  Surveys previous studies of Milton's versification and counters some of the conclusions of F. T. Prince. Feels that "Milton was an Englishman before he was an eclectic humanist." See also Beum's study of rhyme in Samson Agonistes, No. 2179.

3401 BINYON, LAURENCE. A Note on Milton's Imagery and Rhythm. Seventeenth Century Studies Presented to Sir Herbert Grierson (Oxford: Clarendon Press, 1938), pp. 184-91.
  Concludes that in Milton's poetry image and rhythm affect each other as the instrument affects the kind of picture an artist produces, that "rhythm tends to control the imagery, to give it a certain character."

3402 BORDELON, ROMA BOLOLT. The Use of Verbal Repetition as a Structural Device in the Poetry of Milton. Master's thesis, Louisiana State Univ., 1939.

3403 BOTTRALL, MARGARET. The Baroque Element in Milton. EM, 1, 1950, 31-42.
  "Milton to my mind is the one major poet whose work exemplifies the full grandeur of the baroque style."

3404 BRIDGES, ROBERT. Milton's Prosody. Revised Edition. Oxford: Clarendon Press, 1966, 1967. v, 119pp.
  A reprint of Stevens' No. 2767, published in 1921.

3405 BROADBENT, J. B. Milton's Rhetoric. MP, 56, 1959, 224-42. Reprinted in Milton: Modern Judgements, ed. by Alan Rudrum (London: Macmillan, 1968), pp. 270-95.

Discusses Milton's structural, general, and special poetic uses of "schemes: that is, non-tropal arrangements of words and syntax having a prosodic and therefore often a semantic effect."

3406 ------. The Rhetoric of Paradise Lost. Doctoral diss., St. Catharine's College, Cambridge, 1956.

3407 BROOKE-ROSE, CHRISTINE. A Grammar of Metaphor. London: Secker and Warburg, 1958.
Examples, passim.

3408 ------. Metaphor in Paradise Lost: A Grammatical Analysis. Language and Style in Milton: A Symposium in Honor of the Tercentenary of Paradise Lost. Ed. by Ronald David Emma and John T. Shawcross (New York: Frederick Ungar, 1967), pp. 252-303.
Classifies "Milton's metaphors by form rather than by their content" and "shows their suitability to purposes that have been misunderstood by critics [such as Waldock] working with criteria formulated almost entirely with reference to novels" (editors' Preface).

3409 BROWN, JAMES. Eight Types of Pun. PMLA, 71, 1956, 14-26.
Draws several examples from Milton.

3410 BULLOUGH, GEOFFREY. The Grand Style in English Poetry. CaiSE. Ed. by Magdi Wahba (Cairo: Univ. of Cairo, 1959), pp. 9-25.
A lecture delivered in 1956. Comments on Milton and others, with some observations on the decline of the grand style.

3411 BUSH, DOUGLAS. Calculus Racked Him. SEL, 6, 1966, 1-6. Reprinted in Engaged and Disengaged (Cambridge: Harvard Univ. Press, 1966), pp. 58-66.
Questions Maren-Sofie Røstvig's theory of numerical composition.

3412 CANDY, HUGH C. H. Milton—the Individualist in Metre. N&Q, 159, 1930, 165-7, 189-92. Reprinted, London: Nisbet, 1934, in an expanded version.
Finds Milton's metrical hand in the Ovid stanzas formerly attributed to Milton on other grounds.
Rev: TLS, June 21, 1934, p. 447; B. A. W[right], MLR, 30, 1935, 413.

3413 CHATMAN, SEYMOUR. Milton's Participial Style. PMLA, 83, 1968, 1386-99.
This entry is annotated in this bibliography under Paradise Lost: Criticism.

3414 CLARK, DONALD L. John Milton and 'the fitted stile or lofty, mean, or lowly.' SCN, 11, 1953, suppl., 5-9.
An expanded version of a paper delivered in December, 1952, to the Modern Language Association.

3415 ------. Milton's Rhetorical Exercises. QJS, 46, 1960, 297-301.
Milton's rhetorical exercises were composed to be spoken aloud to an audience; he follows the seventeenth-century rules for oration.

3416 COBB, CARL W. Milton and Blank Verse in Spain. PQ, 42, 1963, 264-7.
An attempt to identify the "Spanish poets of prime note" mentioned by Milton in his defense of blank verse in the Preface to Paradise Lost.

3417 COLLINS, DAN STEAD. Rhetoric and Logic in Milton's English Poems. Doctoral diss., Univ. of North Carolina, 1960. Abs., DA, 21, 1961, 1947.

3418 COOK, ALBERT. Milton's Abstract Music. UTQ, 29, 1960, 370-85. Reprinted in Milton: Modern Essays in Criticism. A Galaxy Book. Ed. by Arthur E. Barker (New York: Oxford Univ. Press, 1965), pp. 398-415.
Discusses Milton's style and versification from the early poems through Samson Agonistes.

3419 DARBISHIRE, HELEN. Milton's Poetic Language. E&S, 10, 1957, 31-52.
Suggests that Milton "holds to the idiom and vocabulary of our common speech as the groundwork of his diction." Discusses Milton's principles of word selection and syntax.

3420 DI CESARE, MARIO A. Advent'rous Song: The Texture of Milton's Epic. Language and Style in Milton: A Symposium in Honor of the Tercentenary of Paradise Lost. Ed. by Ronald David Emma and John T. Shawcross (New York: Frederick Ungar, 1967), pp. 1-29.
"...I will discuss certain motifs of the poem by close examination of some of the words Milton uses, some Latinate elements in his diction and syntax, some images and metaphors, allusions and patterns.... But my major concern is to approach them [the motifs] by way of the stylistic elements that contribute to the texture of Paradise Lost as an epic whole."

3421 DIEKHOFF, JOHN S. Milton's Prosody in the Poems of the Trinity Manuscript. PMLA, 54, 1939, 153-83.
In both the blank verse and the rhymed verse, in terms of the linear unit.

3422 ------. Rhyme in Paradise Lost. PMLA, 49, 1934, 539-43.
Rhymes in Paradise Lost are not mere accident. See also J. M. Purcell, MLN, 59, 1944, 171-2.

3423 ------. Terminal Pause in Milton's Verse. SP, 32, 1935, 135-9.
"Milton considered the line as a more or less isolated unit of verse to be indicated as such by some sort of breath pause or lingering at the end."

3424 ELIOT, T. S. A Note on the Verse of John Milton. E&S, 21, 1936, 32-40. Reprinted in On Poetry and Poets (London: Faber, 1957), pp. 156-64; in The Modern Critical Spectrum, ed. by Gerald J. and Nancy M. Goldberg (Englewood Cliffs, N.J.: Prentice-Hall, 1962), pp. 169-74; and in Milton: A Collection of Critical Essays, ed. by Louis L. Martz (Englewood Cliffs, N.J.: Prentice-Hall, 1966), pp. 12-8.
Milton's rhetoric is "not necessarily bad in itself" but "is likely to be bad in its influence; and it may be considered bad in relation to the historical life of a language as a whole."

3425 ELLEDGE, SCOTT B. Milton's Imagery. Doctoral diss., Cornell Univ., 1941. Abs., Cornell Abstracts of Theses. . . , 1941, pp. 32-5.

3426 ELVIN, LIONEL. Milton and the Artificial Style. Introduction to the Study of Literature (London: Sylvan Press, 1949), 1, 49-90.
Uses Milton's work as an example of "stylized and artificial" in order to teach laymen to read critically.

3427 EMMA, RONALD DAVID. Grammar and Milton's English Style. Language and Style in Milton: A Symposium in Honor of the Tercentenary of Paradise Lost. Ed. by Ronald David Emma and John T. Shawcross (New York: Frederick Ungar, 1967), pp. 233-51.

"...asserts that Milton employed no unique or arbitrary system—certainly not a mere imitation of Virgil's grammar—but that, like most great artists, he worked within the limitations of the grammar of his countrymen acceptable in his day" (editors' Preface).

3428 ------. Milton's Grammar. Doctoral diss., Duke Univ., 1960. Abs., DA, 21, 1961, 2286. London, The Hague, and Paris: Mouton and Co., 1964. 164pp.

"The first seven chapters of this study are devoted to the morphemics of nouns, pronouns, adjectives, adverbs, prepositions, and conjunctions; and an eighth chapter, on clause and sentence pattern, gives some attention to the largest grammatical units." Appendices: (A) List of Pages and Lines in the Columbia Edition Included in the Samples of Milton's Poetry and Prose; (B) Summary of the Numbers and Proportions of the Various Parts of Speech in the Samples of Milton, Shakespeare, and Eliot.
Rev: TLS, Dec. 31, 1964, p. 1182; Raven I. McDavid, Jr., Language, 41, 1965, 674-6; Erwin Mayer, Anglia, 84, 1966, 429-32.

3429 ------, and JOHN T. SHAWCROSS, eds. Language and Style in Milton: A Symposium in Honor of the Tercentenary of Paradise Lost. New York: Frederick Ungar, 1967. xii, 371pp.

A collection of essays by Mario A. Di Cesare, Harold Fisch, Hilda M. Hulme, C. A. Patrides, John T. Shawcross, E. J. Dobson, John M. Steadman, Ronald David Emma, Christine Brooke-Rose, K. G. Hamilton, and Robert Beum, each of which is listed separately under its author in this bibliography. The volume also contains Selected References on Milton's Language and Style, pp. 369-71.
Rev: TLS, July 25, 1968, p. 795.

3430 EPSTEIN, E. L., and T. HAWKES. Linguistics and English Prosody Studies in Linguistics: Occasional Papers, 7. Buffalo: Buffalo Univ Press, 1959. 50pp.

Contains analysis of the prosody of Samson Agonistes, lines 930-50, pp. 23-9

3431 EVANS, ROBERT O. Milton's Elisions. Gainesville: Univ. of Florida Press, 1966. 67pp.

Shows how Milton, while employing the traditional system of metrical elision, exhibited great virtuosity in his treatment of each variety and perfected the entire technique. Appendix lists all the elisions in Paradise Lost and tables contain statistical summaries of elisions in Paradise Lost, Paradise Regained, Samson Agonistes, and Comus.
Rev: R. M. Cummings, N&Q, N. S., 14, 1967, 319-20; Karina Williamson, SN, 39, 1967, 184-6; Purvis E. Boyette, SAB, 32, 1967, 11-2; R. M. Cummings, N&Q, 212, 1967, 319-20. Jack Shadorian, SCN, 26, 1968, 3-4.

3432 ------. The Theory and Practice of Poetic Elision from Chaucer to Milton with Special Emphasis on Milton. Doctoral diss., Univ. of Florida, 1954. Abs., DA, 14, 1954, 2056-7.

3433 FALLON, ROBERT THOMAS. Milton's Military Imagery: Its Growth and Function in His Art. Doctoral diss., Columbia Univ., 1964. Abs., DA, 26, 1966, 4626-7.

3434 FISCH, HAROLD. Hebraic Style and Motifs in Paradise Lost. Language and Style in Milton: A Symposium in Honor of the Tercentenary of Paradise Lost. Ed. by Ronald David Emma and John T. Shawcross (New York: Frederick Ungar, 1967), pp. 30-64.

"Had Milton followed the direction indicated by the style and tone of his Scriptural model and the interpretations provided thereon by the Jewish commentators, he would not, I think, have written an epic poem at all."

3435 FISCHER, WALTHER. Ein wenig bekanntes Autogramm Miltons. Anglia, 57, 1933, 221-4.

Discusses a Milton autograph in the album of Johannes Zollikofer, at St. Gall, and corrects the reading of the Greek text.

3436 FLETCHER, HARRIS F. A Possible Origin of Milton's Counterpoint or Double Rhythm. JEGP, 54, 1955, 521-5. Printed also in Studies by Members of the English Department, Univ. of Illinois, in Memory of John Jay Parry (Urbana: Univ. of Illinois Press, 1955), pp. 61-5.

Latin and Hebrew Prosody.

3437 FRANK, JOSEPH. The Unharmonious Vision: Milton as a Baroque Artist. CLS, 3, 1966, 95-108.

Holds that "Milton's poetry generally becomes more Baroque as his theology becomes less assured, that, in fact, the reciprocal movement is like a teeter-totter: as the see of his aesthetic confidence rises, the saw of his religious conviction sinks."

3438 FREEDMAN, MORRIS. Milton and Dryden on Rhyme. HLQ, 24, 1961, 337-44.

Holds that Milton's remarks on rhyme are an intended settlement of the debate between Sir Robert Howard and Dryden.

3439 FRICKER, ROBERT. Eigenart und Grenzen von Miltons Bildersprache. Ang., 71, 1953, 331-45.

Milton's similes both arabesque and functional.

3440 GRAY, JAMES ARTHUR. The Form and Function of Rhythm in the Versification of Paradise Lost. Doctoral diss., Univ. of Washington, 1967. Abs., DA, 28, 1967, 1785-A.

3441 GROOM, BERNARD. Milton. The Diction of Poetry from Spenser to Bridges (Toronto: Univ. of Toronto Press, 1956), pp. 74-94.

Concerned mainly with the diction of Paradise Lost.

3442 GROSS, CHRISTOPHER WALDO. The Rhetoric of the Miltonic Simile. Doctoral diss., Washington Univ., 1966. Abs., DA, 27, 1966, 1785-A.

"The purpose of this dissertation is first to consider Milton's theory of simile, available in the early Logic, and within Paradise Lost itself, and secondly, to read closely the heroic similes of Milton's first epic with this theory in mind."

3443 HALL, JAMES MARTIN. Milton's Rhetoric in Prose and Poetry. Doctoral diss., Yale Univ., 1967. Abs., DA, 27, 1967, 4220-A.

3444 HALL, VERNON, JR. Milton. A Short History of Literary Criticism (New York: New York Univ. Press, 1963), pp. 52-5.

3445 HAMER, ENID. The Metres of English Poetry. London: Methuen, 1930. 326pp.

Lengthy discussions of Milton's poems, passim.
Rev: TLS, Aug. 21, 1930, p. 671; N. R. Tempest, RES, 7, 1931, 493-4; M. W. Croll, MLN, 46, 1931, 338; A. Brandl, DL, 52, 1931, 357-9; R. Spindler, ESt, 67, 1932, 258-9; B. E. C. D[avis], MLR, 27, 1932, 113; A. Eichler, Ang. Bbl., 44, 1933, 291-4.

3446 HAMILTON, KENNETH G. The Structure of Milton's Prose. Language and Style in Milton: A Symposium in Honor of the Tercentenary of Paradise Lost. Ed. by Ronald David Emma and John T. Shawcross (New York: Frederick Ungar, 1967), pp. 304-32.
Is concerned primarily with Milton's sentence structure. Feels that Milton placed himself "outside the main line of development of seventeenth century prose..." and that "the structure of Milton's long sentences is contrary to a style that seems to be part of the natural genius of English prose."

3447 HAMPSTEN, RICHARD FRANKLIN. Studies in Milton's Blank Verse. Doctoral diss., Univ. of Washington, 1963. Abs., DA, 25, 1964, 1210.

3448 HOBSBAUM, PHILIP. The Criticism of Milton's Epic Similes. SN, 36, 1964, 220-31.
Comments on studies by E. M. W. Tillyard, J. B. Broadbent, D. Daiches, K. Muir, and others.

3449 HOWE, M. L. Anapestic Feet in Paradise Lost. MLN, 45, 1930, 311-2.
Holds that Milton used only iambic feet or at least disyllabic feet in Paradise Lost.

3450 HULME, HILDA M. On the Language of Paradise Lost: Its Elizabethan and Early Seventeenth-Century Background. Language and Style in Milton: A Symposium in Honor of the Tercentenary of Paradise Lost. Ed. by Ronald David Emma and John T. Shawcross (New York: Frederick Ungar, 1967), pp. 65-101.
Considers, i.a., the influence of Shakespeare, Spenser, Giles and Phineas Fletcher, and Du Bartas and tries "to establish what Milton . . . remembered and re-used from those writings of his Elizabethan predecessors which he had read before his blindness or which he was having read to him again while he was at work on his later poems."

3451 HUNTER, WILLIAM B., JR. The Sources of Milton's Prosody. PQ, 28, 1949, 125-44.
Sylvester and metrical psalters.

3452 KATO, SADA. Miltonic Style and Its Criticism. Nanzan Univ. Academia, 18, 1957.

3453A KELLOGG, GEORGE A. Bridges' Milton's Prosody and Renaissance Metrical Theory. PMLA, 68, 1953, 268-85.
Milton's prosody based on Italian and classical precedents.

3453B KERMODE, FRANK. Samson Agonistes and Hebrew Prosody. DUJ, 14, 1953, 59-63.
On Milton's imitation of Hebrew lyric measures and rhymes.

3454 KOEHLER, G. STANLEY. Milton on Numbers, Quantity, and Rime. SP, 55, 1958, 201-17.
"It is our purpose here, first, to suggest what Milton may have meant by

these phrases, 'apt numbers' and 'fit Quantity of syllables'—in so far as it is possible to pin down these elusive phrases at all; second, to consider what may have been the real nature and motive of his objection to rime; and finally, to point to a possible connection between Milton's attitude toward rime and his concept of fit quantity."

3455 KUSAKABE, HIROKO. Syntax and Rhetoric in Milton's Poems. Doctoral diss., Doshisha Women's College, 1966.

3456 LEATHES, SIR STANLEY. Rhythm in English Poetry. London: Heinemann, 1935. vi, 154pp.
Passim.

3457 LERNER, L. D. The Miltonic Simile. EIC, 4, 1954, 297-308.
Similes remind us of the world of humanity of which the poem itself is a part.

3458 MILES, JOSEPHINE. The Continuity of Poetic Language: Studies in English Poetry from the 1540's to the 1940's. Univ. of California Publications in English, 19. Berkeley: Univ. of California Press, 1951. 542pp.
Passim. Concerned with the vocabulary of poetry.
Rev: Siegfried Mandel, SRL, Oct. 13, 1951, p. 46; S. H. Monk, JEGP, 51 1952, 426-8.

3459 ------. Major Adjectives in English Poetry from Wyatt to Auden. Univ. of California Publications in English, 12, 3. Berkeley: Univ. of California Press, 1946.
Finds "heaven" the most frequently recurring word in Milton's poetry. Also passim.
Rev: H. W. Wells, AL, 18, 1946, 267-8.

3460 ------. The Primary Language of Poetry in the 1640's. Part One of The Continuity of Poetic Languages. Berkeley: Univ. of California Press, 1948. 160pp.
Rev: James Sledd, MP, 47, 1949, 140-3; C. T. Harrison, SR, 57, 1949, 709-14.

3461 ------. The Vocabulary of Poetry. Berkeley: Univ. of California Press, 1946.
Passim.
Rev: Ethel Seaton, YWES, 16-7.

3462 MOLONEY, M. F. Donne's Metrical Practice. PMLA, 65, 1950, 232-9.
Considers the possible critical reconciliation of Donne and Milton.

3463 MOSS, LEONARD. The Rhetorical Style of Samson Agonistes. MP, 62, 1965, 296-301.
Holds that Milton utilizes Roman and Greek rhetorical patterns to emphasize the dramatic content of Samson Agonistes.

3464 MOUNG, DAPHNE AYE. Controversy on Miltonic Inversions. N&Q, 180, 1941, 210.
After the 1887 publication of Bridges' Milton's Prosody.

3465 NELSON, LOWRY, JR. Góngora and Milton: Toward a Definition of the Baroque. CL, 6, 1954, 53-63.
Using Góngora's Polifemo and Milton's Nativity Ode, sets forth an analysis of style in terms of the time structure of the lyric.

3466 ORAS, ANTS. Blank Verse and Chronology in Milton. Univ. of Florida
      Monographs, Humanities—No. 20; Gainesville: Univ. of Florida Press,
      1966. 81pp.
           "The following pages present a series of stylistic analyses, in the hope of, in
           some degree, clarifying the much observed issue of the relative chronology of
           Milton's major poems—the internal chronology of Paradise Lost and the
           chronological positions in Milton's poetic output of Paradise Regained and
           Samson Agonistes." Extensive use of tables and graphs.
           Rev: Karina Williamson, SN, 39, 1967, 184-6; J. Max Patrick, SCN, 25,
           1967, 27-8; Purvis E. Boyette, SAB, 32, 1967, 11-2; R. M. Cummings N&Q,
           212, 1967, 319-20.

3467A ------. Echoing Verse Endings in Paradise Lost. South Atlantic Studies
      for Sturgis E. Leavitt (Washington: Scarecrow Press, 1953), pp. 175-90.

3467B ------. Metre and Chronology in Milton's Epitaph on the Marchioness of
      Winchester, L'Allegro, and Il Penseroso. N&Q, 198, 1953, 332-3.

3468A ------. Milton's Blank Verse and the Chronology of His Major Poems.
      SAMLA Studies in Milton (Gainesville: Univ. of Florida Press, 1953),
      pp. 128-97.
           Accepts the traditional chronology.

3468B ------. Milton's Early Rhyme Schemes and the Structure of Lycidas. MP,
      52, 1954, 14-22.
           "The preceding pages have, I hope, provided at least a partial refutation of
           the views of those critics who regard rhyme in Milton as a kind of unassimi-
           lated foreign body of which he gradually rid himself because for him it had
           no functional meaning."

3469 P[ARKER], W[ILLIAM] RILEY. Milton's Meter: A Note. SCN, 2, No. 1,
      1943.

3470 PEARCE, DONALD R. The Style of Milton's Epic. YR, N.S., 52, 1963,
      427-44. Reprinted in Milton: Modern Essays in Criticism. A Galaxy
      Book. Ed. by Arthur E. Barker (New York: Oxford Univ. Press, 1965),
      pp. 368-85.
           Claims "that the 'remote grandeur' of Milton's language in Paradise Lost
           originates in the formalities of classic prose. . . ."

3471 PETIT, HERBERT H. Milton, Aristotle, and the Modern Critics. Class.
      Bull., 25, Nov., 1948, 8-10.
           Feels that the modern critics (e.g., Murry, Eliot, and Tillyard) have not
           solved the problem of Milton's style because they have not sought "to de-
           termine the basis upon which he built his theory of style. . . ." Finds this
           basis in Aristotle and compares Aristotle's requirements and the peculiarities
           of Milton's style as outlined by Havens.

3472 PRAZ, MARIO. Baroque in England. MP, 61, 1964, 169-79.
           Discusses Milton as representing "typical aspects of the Baroque in its various
           phases."

3473 ------. Milton and Poussin. Seventeenth Century Studies Presented to Sir
      Herbert Grierson (Oxford: Clarendon Press, 1938), pp. 192-210. Re-
      printed as Milton e Poussin. Gusto Neoclassico (Florence: Sansoni,
      1940), pp. 9-34. Reprinted in French translation, Le Paradis Perdu:

1667-1967. Ed. by Jacques Blondel (Paris: Minard Lettres Modernes, 1967), pp. 177-201.

On the connection between Milton's stylistic development and the painting of his age.

3474 PRINCE, F. T. Milton's Blank Verse: The Diction. Milton: A Collection of Critical Essays. Ed. by Louis L. Martz (Englewood Cliffs, N.J.: Prentice-Hall, 1966), pp. 61-76.

A reprint of a chapter from Prince's The Italian Element in Milton's Verse (1954).

3475 ------. Reply to Mrs. M. Whiteley. RES, N.S., 9, 1958, 278-9.

Answers Mrs. Whiteley's objections (RES, N.S., 9, 1958, 268-70) to his scansion of the English decasyllabic line and the problem of stress.

3476 PURCELL, J. M. Rime in Paradise Lost. MLN, 59, 1944, 171-2.

Addenda to Diekhoff, PMLA, 49, 1934, 539-43.

3477 RAJAN, BALACHANDRA. The Style of Paradise Lost. Milton's Epic Poetry: Essays on Paradise Lost and Paradise Regained. Ed. by C. A. Patrides (Harmondsworth: Penguin Books, 1967), pp. 276-97.

A reprint, with minor changes, of pp. xix-xxxviii) of Rajan's 1964 edition of Books 1 and 2 of Paradise Lost.

3478 RICKS, CHRISTOPHER. Milton's Grand Style. Oxford: Clarendon Press, 1963, 1968 (paperback). 154pp.

"Milton's Grand Style has been vigorously attacked in the twentieth century, and this book is an attempt to refute Milton's detractors by showing the kind of life which there is in Paradise Lost."

Rev: Helen Gardner, Listener, 70, 1963, 575; Patrick Cruttwell, MGW, Aug. 29, 1963, p. 11; William Empson, NSN, Aug. 23, 1963, p. 230; Kenneth Muir, CritQ, 5, 1963, 275-6; TLS, Sept. 20, 1963, p. 706; Frank Kermode, Encounter, 21, Nov., 1963, 84-5; André Crépine, Les Langues Modernes, 58, 1964, 127-8; Agnes M. C. Latham, YWES, 45, 1964, 241-2; J. M. Couper, AUMLA, 21, 1964, 111-3; Anne Davidson Ferry, JEGP, 63, 1964, 521-4; John M. Steadman, Archiv, 201, 1964, 376-8; Geoffrey Bullough, English, 15, No. 85, 1964, 24-5; Joseph Frank, SCN, 21, No. 4, 1963, 58-9; Jacques Blondel, EA, 18, 1965, 181; J. B. Beer, MLR, 60, 1965, 594-8; Rosemary Freeman, RES, 16, 1965, 313-4; René Rapin, ES, 48, 1967, 553-5.

3479 ------. Milton's Grand Style: Enhancing Suggestions. Milton's Epic Poetry: Essays on Paradise Lost and Paradise Regained. Ed. by C. A. Patrides (Harmondsworth: Penguin Books, 1967), pp. 249-75.

A reprint of pp. 78-102 of Milton's Grand Style (1963), with slight revisions.

3480 ------. Over-Emphasis in Paradise Regained. MLN, 76, 1961, 701-4.

Disagrees with L. Martz (ELH, 27, 1960, 223-47) that all of Paradise Regained has a "muted, chastened style" and suggests that certain passages of over-emphatic repetition reflect a style of self-indulgent elaboration.

3481 RØSTVIG, MAREN-SOFIE. The Hidden Sense: Milton and the Neoplatonic Method of Numerical Composition. The Hidden Sense and Other Essays. NSE, 9 (Oslo: Universitetsforlaget; New York: Humanities Press, 1963), pp. 1-112.

Holds that Spenser, Chapman, Milton, and their contemporaries were in-

fluenced by Ficino, Pico della Mirandola, and others to use symbolic numbers in determining the structure of their poetry.
Rev: Pierre Legouis, EA, 17, 1964, 191-2; Husain Haddawy, SCN, 18, No. 1-2, 1965, 4.

3482 ------. Milton and the Science of Numbers. English Studies Today. Fourth Series (Roma: Edizioni di Storia e Letteratura, 1966), pp. 267-88.
Argues that Milton has a "deeply-rooted concern with numerical symbolism, and a desire to base this symbolism primarily on the great Biblical numbers."

3483 ------. Renaissance Numerology: Acrostics or Criticism? EIC, 16, 1966, 6-21..
Defends the theory of numerical composition in general and of Milton's use of it in the composition of Paradise Lost.

3484 ------, and DOUGLAS BUSH. Correspondence. SEL, 7, 1967, 191-4.
Miss Røstvig defends her theory of numerical composition and Bush offers further objections.

3485 SAINTSBURY, GEORGE. A History of English Prose Rhythm. Bloomington: Indiana Univ. Press, 1965. xiv, 489pp.
A reissue of the 1912 publication as corrected in the second impression (1922) on the qualities of Milton's prose style, pp. 168-76 and passim.

3486 SCHANZER, ERNEST. Verse and Its Feet. RES, N.S., 10, 1959, 292-3.
Letter to the editor. Disagrees with Part 1 of Mrs. Whiteley's article (RES, N.S., 9, 1958, 268-78).

3487 SCHLINGHOFF, MARGOT. Miltons Bildersprache in Paradise Lost. NS, 8, 1959, 263-71.
A study of the imagery in Paradise Lost.

3488A SEIGLER, MILLEDGE BROADUS. Milton's Prosody. Doctoral diss., Duke Univ., 1942.

3488B SHAWCROSS, JOHN T. The Prosody of Milton's Translation of Horace's Fifth Ode. TSL, 13, 1968, 81-9.
Quantitative analysis of the Fifth Ode, with suggestions concerning the prosody of Samson Agonistes.

3489 SHERRY, BEVERLY THELMA CHADWICK. Style and Action in Paradise Lost. Doctoral diss., Bryn Mawr, 1966. Abs., DA, 27, 1967, 3470-A.

3490 SITWELL, EDITH, comp. The Pleasures of Poetry. A Critical Anthology. First Series. Milton and the Augustan Age. London: Duckworth, 1930. 236pp.
Lengthy discussion of Milton's versification in the Introduction, pp. 3-80.
Rev: TLS, Dec. 18, 1930, pp. 918, 1083, and May 28, 1931, p. 422; F. T. Wood, ESt, 66, 1932, 429-32.

3491 SMITH, J. C. Feminine Endings in Milton's Blank Verse. TLS, Dec. 5, 1936, p. 1016.
Especially concerned with the occurrence of such endings in passages expressive of agitation.

3492 SPROTT, S. ERNEST. Milton's Art of Prosody. Oxford: Blackwell, 1953. xi, 147pp.

Contains a special chapter on the prosody of Samson Agonistes.
Rev: TLS, May 15, 1953, p. 318; Ants Oras, SCN, 11, 1953, 30; Wilhelmina Gordon, QQ, 61, 1954, 139-41; Michel Poirier, EA, 7, 1954, 232; F. T. Prince, RES, 5, 1954, 292-4; Edgar Mertner, Anglia, 73, 1955, 229-39.

3493 STEADMAN, JOHN M. Demetrius, Tasso, and Stylistic Variation in Paradise Lost. ES, 47, 1966, 329-41.
Holds that stylistic variation in Paradise Lost is consistent with both the tone of the poem and the quality and action of the characters within the poem and points out that Milton's use of stylistic variation parallels that of his contemporaries.

3494 ------. Verse Without Rime: Sixteenth-Century Italian Defences of Versi Sciolti. Italica, 41, 1964, 384-402.
On the Italian background of Milton's blank verse and similarities between English and Italian theory.

3495 STEIN, ARNOLD. Answerable Style. Milton's Epic Poetry: Essays on Paradise Lost and Paradise Regained. Ed. by C. A. Patrides (Harmondsworth: Penguin Books, 1967), pp. 92-120.
A reprint of pp. 119-62 of Stein's Answerable Style: Essays on Paradise Lost (1953).

3496 ------. A Note on Meter. KR, 18, 1956, 451-60.
Comment by John Crowe Ransom, pp. 473-6. Uses lines from Paradise Lost to illustrate the relation of words and emphasis to context. Deals also with the tension between meter and rhythm.

3497 ------. Structures of Sound in Milton's Verse. KR, 15, 1953, 266-77.
An examination of sound and sense in Milton's poetry.

3498 SYPHER, WYLIE. Four Stages of Renaissance Style. Transformation in Art and Literature 1400-1700. Anchor Books Original. Garden City: Doubleday, 1955. 312pp.
Passim.

3499 THOMPSON, E. N. S. Milton's Prose Style. PQ, 14, 1935, 1-15.
"At any rate, the evidence indicates that his prose compositions, in their essential parts if not in their entirety, were more carefully considered, even when haste was essential, than many have realized."

3500 TILLYARD, E. M. W. A Note on Milton's Style. The Miltonic Setting (Cambridge: Cambridge Univ. Press, 1947), pp. 105-40.
Questions certain objections that have been levelled with some persistence against the style of Milton's mature poems.

3501 TUVE, ROSEMOND. Elizabethan and Metaphysical Imagery. Chicago: Univ. of Chicago Press, 1947. xii, 442pp.
Passim.

3502 VIA, JOHN A. Studies in the Imagery of Milton's Early Poetry and Prose (to 1642). Doctoral diss., Univ. of Illinois, 1967. Abs., DA, 29, 1968, 580-A. 426pp.

3503 WEAVER, RICHARD M. Milton's Heroic Prose. The Ethics of Rhetoric (Chicago: Regnery, 1953), pp. 143-63. Reprinted, 1963.
An exposition of Milton's prose style. Milton's polemical writings "demand a

heroic kind of attention which modern education does not discipline the
majority of our citizens to give."

3504 WEBBER, JOAN. John Milton: The Prose Style of God's English Poet.
The Eloquent I: Style and Self in Seventeenth-Century Prose (Madison:
Univ. of Wisconsin Press, 1968), pp. 184-218.
On Milton's use of "I" in his prose and on his personal involvement in the
early antiprelatical tracts.

3505 WEISMILLER, E. R. The Dry and Rugged Verse. The Lyric and
Dramatic Milton. Ed. by Joseph H. Summers (New York and London:
Columbia Univ. Press, 1965), pp. 115-52.
A prosodic analysis of Samson Agonistes, especially the choral odes.

3506 ------. The Verisification of Paradise Lost and Paradise Regained. A
Study of Movement and Structure in Milton's Nondramatic Blank
Verse. Doctoral diss., Merton College, Oxford, 1951.

3507 WHALER, JAMES. Animal Simile in Paradise Lost. PMLA, 47, 1932,
534-53.
Shows that Milton's choice of imagery, in comparison with Homer's or Vergil's
is distinguished by "an iron control over, a virtual renunciation of, animal
similes."

3508 ------. The Compounding and Distribution of Similes in Paradise Lost.
MP, 28, 1931, 313-27.
Shows the occurrence of Milton's similes and compares them to some of the
similes in the Iliad, the Odyssey and the Aeneid. Uses a graph to illustrate the
frequency of similes in these epics.

3509 ------. Counterpoint and Symbol. An Inquiry into the Rhythm of Milton's
Epic Style. Anglistica, 6. Copenhagen: Rosenkilde and Bagger, 1956.
225pp.
Analyzes "the Miltonic paragraph as a rhythmic analogue to a piece of con-
trapuntal music" and studies the mathematical construction for their symbolic
role.
Rev: Arnold Davenport, YWES, 177-8; E. R. Weismiller, MLN, 72, 1957,
612-8; R. O. Evans, JEGP, 56, 1957, 487-90; V. de S. Pinto, N&Q, N.S., 4,
1957; 273-4; SCN, 15, 1957, 23; Edgar Mertner, Anglia, 76, 1958, 320-2; B. A.
Wright, MLR, 53, 1958, 244-5; F. T. Prince, RES, 9, 1958, 320-2.

3510 ------. Grammatical Nexus of the Miltonic Simile. JEGP, 30, 1931, 327-34.
Predicts "Milton's typical form of grammatical nexus." Says that if the typical
Miltonic simile "be not absolutely undetachable, it always tends to be both
structurally and esthetically organic."

3511 ------. The Miltonic Simile. PMLA, 46, 1931, 1034-74.
A study of what Milton does with the simile and a comparison of his
technique with that of his predecessors.

3512 WHEELER, THOMAS. Milton's Blank Verse Couplets. JEGP, 66, 1967,
359-68.
"What is needed is our recognition that John Milton never read Paradise
Lost; he heard it." Advocates a "listening understanding" of the couplets in
Paradise Lost, especially those spoken lines, so that a clearer understanding
of the characters can be formed.

3513 WIDMER, KINGSLEY. The Iconography of Renunciation: the Miltonic Simile. ELH, 25, 1958, 258-69. Reprinted in revised form in Milton's Epic Poetry: Essays on Paradise Lost and Paradise Regained. Ed. by C. A. Patrides (Harmondsworth: Penguin Books, 1967), pp. 121-31.
On Paradise Lost and Paradise Regained. ". . . a subtle and dialectical reading of the Miltonic texture and tone suggests a fascinating and shocking master simile: the world as evil, and virtue as renunciation."

3514 WILLIAMSON, GEORGE. The Senecan Amble. A Study in Prose from Bacon to Collier. London: Faber, 1951. 377pp.
Milton's ideas concerning style, passim.

3515 WRIGHT, B. A. Stressing of the Preposition Without in the Verse of Paradise Lost. N&Q, N.S., 5, 1958, 202-3.
On Milton's stress variations to achieve artistic rhythm.

3516 WYLD, H. C. Some Aspects of the Diction of English Poetry. Oxford: Basil Blackwell, 1933. 72pp.
Passim.

EDITIONS, TRANSLATIONS,
AND ILLUSTRATIONS

3517 ALLENTUCK, MARCIA, and KESTER SVENDSEN. Correspondence. SEL, 2, 1962, 151-5.
Allentuck questions Svendsen's statements concerning Fuseli as an illustrator of Paradise Lost in SEL, 1, 1961, 63-73. Rejoinder by Svendsen.

3518 ARNOLD, E. J. Edward Hill, M.D. (1741-1830), Editor of Milton. Bulletin of the Friends of the Library of Trinity College, Dublin, 1951, pp. 11-5.

3519 AYERS, ROBERT W. The Date of the John Phillips—John Milton Joannis Philippi Angli Responsio. PQ, 38, 1959, 95-101.
Final quarter of 1651.

3520 ------. The John Phillips-John Milton Angli Responsio: Editions and Relations. PBSA, 56, 1962, 66-72.
Concerning the order of publication of four 1652 editions.

3521 ------. A Suppressed Edition of Milton's Defensio Secunda (1654). PBSA, 55, 1961, 75-87.
The first Vlack edition, suppressed by Alexander More.

3522 BAKER, C. H. COLLINS. William Blake, Painter. HLB, 10, 1936, 135-48.
Reproduces Blake's Satan Comes to the Gates of Hell and Raphael Warns Adam and Eve. Discusses Blake's understanding of the emotions in Paradise Lost.

3523 ------. Some Illustrators of Milton's Paradise Lost (1688-1850). Library, 5th Series, 3, 1948, 1-21, 101-19.
A two-part study of the illustrators of Paradise Lost, including ten plates by Bentley, Tonson, Blake, and others, giving lists of illustrations in individual editions.

3524 BALSTON, THOMAS. Some Illustrators of Milton's Paradise Lost. Library, 5th Series, 4, 1949, 146-7.
Corrects Baker in some instances.

3525 BARNETT, PAMELA R. Theodore Haak, F. R. S. (1605-1690): The First German Translator of Paradise Lost. Anglica Germanica: British Studies in Germanic Languages and Literatures, 3. The Hague: Mouton and Co., 1962. 274pp.

3526 BATESON, F. W. Milton for Everyman. TLS, July 4, 1958, p. 377.
Bateson dislikes both Helen Darbishire's and B. A. Wright's Everyman editions of Paradise Lost because of their dearth of introductory material and the editors' over-concern for Milton's spelling. Reply by Wright, July 18, 1958, p. 409; by Bateson, July 25, 1958, p. 423; by Wright, Aug. 1, 1958, p. 435; by J. C. Maxwell, Aug. 15, 1958; by Peter Alexander, Aug. 22, 1958, p. 471. Wright defends his edition, and Maxwell points out errors in it. Alexander defends Wright.

3527   BATTLE, GUY A. The Box Rule Pattern in the First Edition of Paradise Lost. PBSA, 42, 1948, 315-21.

3528   BECK, RICHARD. Jón Thorláksson—Icelandic Translator of Pope and Milton. JEGP, 32, 1933, 572-85.
An eighteenth-century translator.

3529   ------. Jón Thorláksson, Icelandic Translator of Pope and Milton. Studia Islandica, 16. Reykjavik: H. F. Leiftur, 1957. 60pp.
Based on the author's 1926 Cornell dissertation.

3530   BLAKE, WILLIAM. Milton, A Poem. London: William Blake Trust, 1967.
A color facsimile edition, published in 1967 by The Trianon Press, Château de Boissia, Clairvaux, Jura, France. Described in MN, 1, 1967, 58-9.

3531   BRADNER, LEICESTER. Milton's Epitaphium Damonis. TLS, Aug. 18, 1932, p. 581.
Describes an edition in the British Museum.

3532   BREDSDORFF, ELIAS. John Heath, M.A., Fellow of King's College, Cambridge. Scandinavian Studies: Essays Presented to Henry Goddard Leach on the Occasion of His Eighty-Fifth Birthday. Ed. by Carl F. Bayerschmidt (Seattle: Univ. of Washington Press for the American-Scandinavian Foundation, 1965), pp. 170-201.
Contains an account of Jón Thorláksson and Heath's part in the publication of the first Icelandic translation of Paradise Lost.

3533   BUSH, DOUGLAS. The Complete Prose Works of John Milton. RN, 14, 1961, 207-8.
A statement of the aims and policies of the Yale edition.

3534   The Charity of Bitterness. TLS, April 29, 1960, p. 274.
Comments on the public and private bitterness which produced Milton's works edited in Volume 2 of the Yale Prose. Critical of the massiveness of the edition.

3535   DARBISHIRE, HELEN. The Columbia Edition of Milton. RES, 9, 1933, 61-2, 319.
Criticizes the editors' handling of the text.

3536   ------. The Printing of the First Edition of Paradise Lost. RES, 17, 1941, 415-27.

3537   DI NATALE, LUIGI. Il chirurgo che tradusse Milton. Martinella, 17, 1963, 30-2.
The physician who translated Milton.

3538   DORRIS, GEORGE E. Paolo Rolli and the First Italian Translation of Paradise Lost. Italica, 42, 1965, 213-25.
An appreciative essay on Rolli's translation (1729, 1735) with comments on other translations.

3539   EVANS, G. BLAKEMORE. The State of Milton's Text: The Prose, 1643-48. JEGP, 59, 1960, 497-505.

Review article on the second volume of the Yale edition of Milton's prose, edited by Ernest Sirluck and others.

3540 FLETCHER, HARRIS F. The First Edition of Milton's History of Britain. JEGP, 35, 1936, 405-14.
A description of the various states in which the first edition exists and suggestions for an accurate text.

3541 ------. A Second (?) Title-Page of the Second Edition of Paradise Lost. PBSA, 43, 1949, 173-8.
Describes a title page different from that of other copies of the second edition.

3542 FRENCH, J. MILTON. That Late Villain Milton; History of the Publications of Milton's Letters of State. PMLA, 55, 1940, 102-18.
A supplement to Vol. 13 of the Columbia Edition.

3543 ------. An Unrecorded Edition of Milton's Defensio Secunda (1654). PBSA, 49, 1955, 262-8.
Variants between two editions published by Vlacq at the Hague.

3544 ------. MAURICE KELLEY, and THOMAS O. MABBOTT. The Columbia Milton: Fifth Supplement, N&Q, 197, 1952, 376-8.
Additional information on Milton's Letters of State.

3545 GARDNER, HELEN. Milton's First Illustrator. E&S, 9, 1956, 27-38. Reprinted as appendix B of Gardner's A Reading of Paradise Lost (1965).
John Baptist Medina, illustrator of the 4th edition of Paradise Lost (1688).

3546 GASELEE, S. Milton's Asclepiadean Verses. N&Q, 163, 1932, 249.
Praises the Columbia Edition.

3547 GILLET, JEAN. Remarques sur un Concours Entre Traducteurs de Milton Sous L'Empire. Le Paradis Perdu: 1667-1967. Ed. by Jacques Blondel (Paris: Minard Lettres Modernes, 1967), pp. 203-17.
Discusses rivalry between three French translators of epic poetry. Defends Delille as the translator most faithful to the actual poem.

3548 GOODE, JAMES. The Bohn Edition of Milton's Prose. TLS, Aug. 1, 1929, p. 608.
Corrects three textual errors.

3549 GRANT, ISABELLE FITCH. The Publication of Paradise Lost from 1667 to 1800, with a Handlist of Editions. Master's thesis, Univ. of Illinois, 1937.

3550 GRIERSON, H. J. C. The Columbia Milton. RES, 9, 1933, 316-9.
Feels that Darbishire has been "unduly censorious."

3551 GROSE, CHRISTOPHER. Some Uses of Sensuous Immediacy in Paradise Lost. HLQ, 31, 1968, 211-22.
Demonstrates that Milton actually links sensuous immediacy with rhetoric, that sensuous immediacy in fact is an organic part of Milton's rhetorical argument. Places particular emphasis on Book I.

3552 HANFORD, JAMES HOLLY. Paradise Lost Annotated by Thomas Edwards. PULC, 23, 1962, 123-4.
Recognizes Edwards' extensive notes on Paradise Lost, probably prepared

for publication and now existing "as marginalia in a fine copy of the 'Thirtenth Edition,' published by Jacob Tonson in 1729. . . ."

3553 HARASZTI, ZOLTAN. First Editions of Milton. MB, 7, 1932, 323-35, 375-90.
Comments on the first editions in the Boston Public Library.

3554 HARKNESS, BRUCE. The Precedence of the 1676 Editions of Milton's Literae Pseudo-Senatus Anglicani. SB, 7, 1955, 181-5.

3555 HAVILAND, THOMAS P. Three Early Milton Editions. LC, 9, 1941, 78-82.
Addenda to Howard, below.

3556 HOWARD, LEON. Early American Copies of Milton. HLB, 7, 1935, 169-79.
Gives an account of what is known concerning the existence of copies of Milton's works in America before 1815 and indicates the significance.

3557 HOWELL, A. C. Anibal Galindo's Spanish Translation of Milton's Paradise Lost. RLC, 36, 1962, 438-43.
Prose translation, published in Ghent in 1868. Reviews Galindo's comments on Paradise Lost and notes that the translator, a Colombian, saw in the poem inspiration in the struggle of Latin-American nations to attain liberty.

3558 HUGHES, MERRITT Y. Milton's Poems. TLS, Dec. 31, 1954, p. 853.
Announces the plans for the variorum commentary.

3559 ------. Some Illustrators of Milton: The Expulsion from Paradise. JEGP, 60, 1961, 670-9. Reprinted in Milton: Modern Essays in Criticism. A Galaxy Book. Ed. by Arthur E. Barker (New York: Oxford Univ. Press, 1965) , pp. 357-67.
Shows that an illustrator's interpretation of the closing lines of Paradise Lost reflects his view of felix culpa. Discusses various interpretations of the scene and includes four illustrations.

3560 KAUFMAN, PAUL. A Revolutionary Edition of the Areopagitica. AN&Q, 2, 1964, 116-8.
On James Tosh's edition of 1791.

3561 KELLEY, MAURICE. First Editions of Milton's Literae. TLS, April 29, 1960, p. 273.
Concerning the printers and the order of the first two editions of Milton's Literae Pseudo-Senatus Anglicani (1676) .

3562 ------. A Note on Milton's Pro Populo Anglicano Defensio. Library, 4th Series, 17, 1937, 466-7.
Addenda to editions listed by F. F. Madan (Stevens' No. 76) .

3563 KUETHE, J. LOUIS. Paradise Lost: Fourteenth and Fifteenth Editions. N&Q, 172, 1937, 136.
Argues that the "15th" edition was incorrectly dated 1738.

3564 LEWIS, CLARISSA O. A Further Note on Milton's Pro Populo Anglicano Defensio. Library, 4th Series, 23, 1942, 45-7.
On textual variants in the editions of 1651-2.

3565 LOEWENSON, LEO. E. G. von Berge, Translator of Milton and Russian Interpreter (1649-1722). SEER, 34, 1956, 281-91.

3566 LUTAUD, OLIVIER. Milton le Lutteur: Études et Éditions Récentes de la Prose Miltonienne. EA, 8, 1955, 233-48.
       On the rise of scholarly interest in the prose.

3567 MABBOTT, THOMAS O. The Columbia Milton, Fourth Supplement. N&Q, 195, 1950, 244-6.
       Lists eleven items discovered since the third supplement.

3568 ------. First Supplement to the Columbia Milton. N&Q, 177, 1939, 329-30.
       Supplement of material discovered since "completion of the Eighteenth Volume of the Columbia Edition."

3569 ------. Milton's Asclepiadean Verses. N&Q, 162, 1932, 263-4; 163, 1932, 170.
       Defends the reading of the Columbia Edition.

3570 ------. Milton's Proposalls of Certain Expedients, 1659. N&Q, 173, 1937, 66.
       Asks for information on the Proposalls.

3571 ------. Notes by Milton. TLS, Nov. 17, 1932, p. 859.
       Desires to locate the copy of William Browne's Britannia's Pastorals (1613-16) which contains the marginal notes attributed to Milton.

3572 ------, and MAURICE KELLEY. The Columbia Milton: Second Supplement. N&Q, 178, 1940, 20-1.
       Three additional items.

3573 ------, and J. MILTON FRENCH. The Columbia Milton. Third Supplement. N&Q, 181, 1941, 16-7.
       Addenda.

3574 MACKAIL, J. W. Bentley's Milton. Studies in Humanism (London: Longmans, 1938), pp. 186-209.
       A reprint of Stevens' No. 2691. Analysis of the edition and remarks on the early rise of Milton's reputation.

3575 MADAN, F. F. A Revised Bibliography of Salmasius's Defensio Regia and Milton's Pro populo Anglicano Defensio. Library, 5th Series, 9, 1954, 101-21.
       A revision of an earlier article in The Library, N.S., 4, 1923, 119-45.

3576 MADSEN, WILLIAM G. Editions of Milton for Classroom Use. CE, 27, 1966, 512-4.
       A review of recent editions of the complete poems, Paradise Lost, selected poems, and selected prose.

3577 MAGON, LEOPOLD. Die drei ersten deutschen Versuche einer Übersetzung von Miltons Paradise Lost. Gedenkschrift für Ferdinand Josef Schneider (Weimar, 1956), pp. 39-82.
       On German translations of Paradise Lost.

3578 MANNING, CLARENCE A. A Russian Translation of Paradise Lost. SEER, 13, 1935, 173-6.
       Reproduces and comments on the introduction to a 1780 translation.

3579 MAXWELL, J. C. Correction to Howell (111:85) Milton's Paradise Lost, Book I, Line 506. AN&Q, 4, 1965, 10.
Points out the imitation of longum est dicere in line 507, not 506, has been recorded by Verity.

3580 ------. Milton for Everyman. TLS, Aug. 15, 1958, p. 459.
Reply by Peter Alexander, TLS, Aug. 22, 1958, p. 471. On recent editions.

3581 ------. Milton's Treatise of Civil Power. N&Q, 194, 1949, 60.
Notes mistaken alteration printed in the current editions (Bohn, World's Classics, Columbia).

3582 McC., H. Milton's First Prose Work. MB, 12, 1937, 311.
Describes a copy of the first edition of Of Reformation, recently acquired by the Boston Public Library.

3583 McCAIN, JOHN WALKER, JR. Milton's Artis Logicae. N&Q, 164, 1933, 149-50.
Cites locations of copies of the 1672 edition and seeks information concerning other possible editions.

3584 ------. Further Notes on Milton's Artis Logicae. N&Q, 165, 1933, 56-9.
The apparent identity of the 1672 and 1673 editions.

3585 MILLER, SONIA. The Text of the Second Edition of Milton's Eikonoklastes. JEGP, 52, 1953, 214-20.
Defends Haller's work on the Columbia Edition.

3586 Milton and the Painters. The Times, May 7, 1957, p. 3.
On illustrators during the storm and stress period, e.g., Fuseli and Martin.

3587 MOLIN, SVEN ERIC. John Wesley's Techniques in Revising Literary Masterpieces for His Methodist Audience, with Special Reference to Paradise Lost. Doctoral diss., Univ. of Pennsylvania, 1956. Abs., DA, 16, 1956, 957-8.

3588 ORAS, ANTS. Milton's Editors and Commentators from Patrick Hume to Henry John Todd (1695-1801). A Study in Critical Views and Methods. London: Oxford Univ. Press; Tartu: Univ. of Tartu (Dorpat), 1931. Reprinted, New York: Haskell House, 1964. 381pp.
Rev: TLS, Aug. 6, 1931, p. 611; S. B. Liljegren, Ang. Bbl., 43, 1932, 365-9; R. D. Havens, JEGP, 31, 1932, 299-300; B. A. W[right], MLR, 27, 1932, 364; H. Read, Crit, 11, 1932, 746-7; A. B[randl], Archiv, 161, 1932, 305-6; A. Bosker, MLN, 48, 1933, 204-5; M. Schutt, Literaturblatt, 55, 1933, 27-8.

3589 Paradise Lost in Spanish. SCN, 18, No. 1, 1960, item 8.
Report of a paper by A. C. Howell, in which verse translations are examined in detail.

3590 PARKER, WILLIAM RILEY. Fletcher's Milton: A First Appraisal. PBSA, 41, 1947, 33-52.
An examination of the text and critical apparatus of Fletcher's facsimile edition.

3591 ------. Notes on the Text of Samson Agonistes. JEGP, 60, 1961, 688-98.
On the problems of editing Samson Agonistes, especially in matters of punctuation, spelling, and capitalization.

3592   [PATRICK, J. MAX]. American Scholars and Scotch Reviewers. SCN, 13, 1955, 32-3.
       Objects to a review of Vol. 1 of the Yale prose edition by J. George, Aberdeen Univ. Review, 36, 1955, 55-8.

3593   ------. Milton and the Crystal-Gazer. SCN, 14, No. 3, 1956, 5-6.
       A criticism of the Yale prose edition.

3594   ------. More Errata in the Introduction to [the] Complete Prose Works of John Milton. SCN, 13, 1955, suppl., 5.

3595   ------. Should the Project for a Milton Variorum Be Completely Reconsidered? SCN, 10, 1952, 10.
       Suggests a less expensive edition than the one planned.

3596   PECKHAM, MORSE. Blake, Milton, and Edward Burney. PULC, 11, 1950, 107-26.
       "Burney's designs for Paradise Lost [at the Princeton Univ. Library] had a profound influence on both series of Blake's designs for that poem. . . ."

3597   PERSHING, JAMES H. The Different States of the First Edition of Paradise Lost. Library, 4th Series, 22, 1941, 34-66.

3598   R., V. Milton's Asclepiadean Verses. N&Q, 163, 1932, 209, 371.
       Feels that the editors of the Columbia Edition should not correct the errors in Milton's Latin poems.

3599   R[AMAGE], D[AVID]. Dugard, Milton, and Vane. Durham Philobiblon, 1, 1953, 55-6.
       Describes the Cosin copy of the second edition of Pro Populo Anglicano Defensio.

3600   RIFFE, NANCY LEE. Eighteenth-Century Translations of Milton into Latin. N&Q, N.S., 12, 1965, 144.
       Gives three additional translations, hitherto unnoticed, which appeared in British periodicals between 1740 and 1750.

3601A ROBERTSON, D. S. A Copy of Milton's Eikonoklastes. TLS, June 15 and 22, 1951, pp. 380, 396.
       Textual problems in editing the prose tract.

3601B SCHIFF, GERT. Johann Heinrich Füsslis Milton-Galerie. Zürich and Stuttgart: Fretz & Wasmuth, 1963.
       Discussion of various illustrators of Milton's works, passim. Catalogue of Fusseli's paintings, pp. 141-61.

3602   SHAWCROSS, JOHN T. The Date of the Separate Edition of Milton's Epitaphium Damonis. SB, 18, 1965, 262-5.
       ". . . the usual date of 1640 (?) seems acceptable . . . , although 1639 (?) has . . . much to offer as publication date."

3603   ------. Establishment of a Text of Milton's Poems Through a Study of Lycidas. PBSA, 56, 1962, 317-31.
       Examines the 1638, 1645, and 1673 texts of Lycidas "to point out the kind of analysis needed to establish a text of Milton's poems."

3604 ------. Milton's Tenure of Kings and Magistrates: Date of Composition, Editions, and Issues. PBSA, 60, 1966, 1-8.
> Between January 15 and January 29, 1649, while Charles I was standing trial. Uses bibliographic variations in different editions to determine order of publication.

3605 SHERWIN, OSCAR. Milton for the Masses: John Wesley's Edition of Paradise Lost. MLQ, 12, 1951, 267-85.

3606 SIRLUCK, ERNEST. Certain Editorial Tendencies Exemplified: A New Edition of Milton's An Apology. MP, 50, 1953, 201-5.
> A review article of Jochums' edition.

3607 SVENDSEN, KESTER. John Martin and the Expulsion Scene of Paradise Lost. SEL, 1, 1961, 63-73.
> Examines Martin's twenty-four illustrations (1826-27) of Paradise Lost and compares his Expulsion Scene with those of his predecessors and contemporaries.

3608 THORPE, JAMES. The Presentation Paradise Lost. New Colophon, 1, 1948, 357-65.
> Questions the authenticity of the presentation inscription in the copy in the Princeton library.

3609 TILLYARD, E. M. W. On Annotating Paradise Lost, Books IX and X. JEGP, 60, 1961, 808-16.
> Problems encountered in editing a school edition of Books 9 and 10.

3610 TODD, WILLIAM B. The Issues and States of the Second Folio and Milton's Epitaph on Shakespeare. SB, 5, 1952, 81-108.

3611 TURNER, W. ARTHUR. The Yale Milton. TLS, Sept. 24, 1954, p. 609.
> Replies to adverse reviews of the Yale prose edition.

3612 WHITING, GEORGE W. James Thomson, Editor of Areopagitica. N&Q, 164, 1933, 457.

3613 WITHERSPOON, A. M. Milton Complete. SRL, Aug. 8, 1931, pp. 33-5.
> Reviews the first two volumes of the Columbia Edition and makes appreciative remarks about Milton.

3614 ------. A New Milton Gift. Yale Univ. Library Gazette, 20, 1945, 33-5.
> A first edition of Of Education.

3615 WRIGHT, B. A. Milton for Everyman. TLS, July 18, 1958, p. 409.
> Reply by F. W. Bateson, TLS, July 25, p. 423; rejoinder by Wright, TLS, Aug. 1, p. 435.

3616 ------. A Note on Milton's Diction. Th'Upright Heart and Pure. Ed. by Amadeus P. Fiore, O.F.M. (Pittsburgh and Louvain: Duquesne Univ. Press, 1967), pp. 143-9.
> Lists eighty of Milton's words, all beginning with the letter "a," which are (1) not noted or incorrectly glossed in N.E.D., (2) not noted in N.E.D. and not glossed or incorrectly glossed by editors, or (3) not glossed by editors.

3617 WURTSBAUGH, JEWEL. John Hughes. TLS, Feb. 22, 1934, p. 126.
> Hughes' participation in Tickell's Milton.

FAME AND INFLUENCE

3618 ADLER, JACOB H. A Milton-Bryant Parallel. NEQ, 24, 1951, 377-80.
Notes similarities between On the Late Massacre at Piedmont and The Massacre at Scio.

3619 ALBERT, FRANCIS L. Dryden's Debt to Milton. Master's thesis, Univ. of North Carolina, 1951.

3620 ALBRECHT, MILTON C. Sixty Years of Miltonic Criticism: from Aiken to Masson. Doctoral diss. Univ. of California (Berkeley), 1938.

3621 ALSPACH, RUSSELL K. A Dublin Milton Enthusiast. MLN, 56, 1941, 284-6.
Samuel Whyte (1733-1811).

3622 Anti-Milton Books to Be Burnt. The Times, June 13, 1962, p. 6e.
Reports plans of Cambridge students to burn works of F. R. Leavis and T. S. Eliot.

3623 AUBIN, ROBERT A. Nathanael Salmon on Milton, 1728. MLN, 56, 1941, 214-5.
Comments on Milton from Salmon's History of Hertfordshire.

3624 BACHRACH, ALFRED GUSTAVE HERBERT. Het Dichteroog in de Engelse Litterkunde. Amsterdam: N. V. Noord-Hollansche Uitgevers Maatschappij, 1953. 30pp.
A lecture presented at the University of Leiden on October 30, 1953. Comments on "When I consider how my light is spent" and on the twentieth-century criticism of Milton.

3625 BACKUS, EDYTHE N. The MS. Play, Anna Bullen. PMLA, 47, 1932, 741-52.
Restoration piece containing repeated echoes of Paradise Lost.

3626 BAIRD, J. R. Milton and Edward Ecclestone's Noah's Flood. MLN, 55, 1940, 183-7.
Noah's Flood, an opera (1679), exhibits influence of Paradise Lost.

3627 BAKER, CARLOS. A Note on Shelley and Milton. MLN, 55, 1940, 585-9.
Milton's influence on Shelley more pronounced than admitted by Havens.

3628 BALDENSPERGER, FERNAND, and WERNER P. FRIEDERICH. Bibliography of Comparative Literature. New York: Russell and Russell, 1960.
Contains a bibliography of studies on Milton's influence abroad, pp. 561-2.

3629 BARKER, ARTHUR E. Brotherly Dissimilitudes and Some Onward Things: Reflections on Recent Miltonic Studies. SCN, 19, 1961, 18-21.
Excerpts from his address to the Milton Society, Dec. 27, 1960.

3630 BARUCH, FRANKLIN R. Bellow and Milton: Professor Herzog in His Garden. Crit, 9, 1967, 74-83.

3631 BEER, GILLIAN. Richardson, Milton, and the Status of Evil. RES, 19, 1968, 261-70.
A consideration of Milton's influence in Richardson's Clarissa.

3632 BEER, JOHN. Blake's Humanism. Manchester: Manchester Univ. Press; New York: Barnes and Noble, 1968. xiii, 269pp.
Extensive consideration given to the influence of Milton, passim.

3633 BELL, VEREEN M. Johnson's Milton Criticism in Context. ES, 49, 1968, 127-32.
A consideration of Johnson's criticism in relation to the "growing host of Milton admirers" during the eighteenth century. "It was because of Milton's rising popularity...that Johnson undertook to expose what he considered to be the most conspicuous defects of Milton's creative method."

3634 BERCOVITCH, SACVAN. Cotton Mather Against Rhyme: Milton and the Psalterium Americanum. AL, 39, 1967, 191-3.
Shows Milton's influence on Cotton Mather's defense of unrhymed verse in 1718.

3635 BERGONZI, BERNARD. Criticism and the Milton Controversy. The Living Milton (London: Routledge and Kegan Paul, 1960), pp. 162-80.
A discussion of Milton criticism during the past 30 years, with special attention to that of Lewis, Eliot, and Waldock. Feels that the modern detractors have based their remarks on insufficient criteria.

3636 BLONDEL, JACQUES. Sur dix années de critique miltonienne. EA, 16, 1963, 38-53.
Surveys recent criticism of Paradise Lost and Paradise Regained. Distinguishes two categories: informative and interpretive.

3637 BOGORAD, SAMUEL N. Milton's Paradise Lost and Gay's Trivia: a Borrowing. N&Q, 195, 1950, 98-9.
On Paradise Lost, 4, 814-19 and Gay's Trivia, 3, 382-6.

3638 BOND, HAROLD L. The Literary Art of Edward Gibbon. Oxford: Clarendon Press, 1960. 167pp.
Makes some observations on Gibbon and Milton, passim.

3639 BOND, RICHMOND P. English Burlesque Poetry, 1700-1750. Cambridge: Harvard Univ. Press, 1932. Reprinted, New York: Russell and Russell, 1964.
Discusses many imitations or parodies of Milton.

3640 BOYCE, BENJAMIN. Milton and Thomas Brown's Translation of Gelli. N&Q, 171, 1936, 328-9.
1702

3641 BRINKLEY, R. FLORENCE. Milton in French Literature of the Nineteenth Century. UTQ, 27, 1958, 243-55.
"The presentation of Milton as a character in French literature parallels in the creative field the evidence of Milton's popularity provided by the great number of translations of his poems during the century."

3642 BROADBENT, J. B. Milton and Arnold. EIC, 6, 1956, 404-17.
"Sohrab and Rustum is only an episode but it has the superficies of Paradise Lost—epic simile, catalogue, blank verse, heroic action. I want to show how

differently Milton and Arnold handle these common denominators, so as to suggest something about the nature of Victorian narrative poetry, and the historical significance of Arnold's critical theory and poetry practice."

3643   BROWNE, RAY B. Dryden and Milton in Nineteenth Century Popular Songbooks. BB, 22, 1958, 143-4.
       Milton had six songs, and three falsely assigned; L'Allegro, songs for Comus and Arcades, and Paradise Lost, 4, 641ff.

3644   BRYANT, J. A., JR. Milton in Retreat. SR, 68, 1960, 684-94.
       Comments on the alleged decline of Milton's reputation. Reviews the works of Rosemond Tuve, G. W. Whiting, W. C. Curry, and Arnold Stein.

3645   BURCH, FRANCIS F. Tennyson and Milton: Sources of Reese's Tears. AN&Q, 1, 1963, 115-7.
       Suggests Tennyson's Tears, Idle Tears and Milton's sonnet On His Blindness as dominant sources.

3646   BURKE, CHARLES B. Coleridge and Milton. N&Q, 176, 1939, 42.
       The line "My genial spirits fail" in Coleridge's Dejection: an Ode may echo "my genial spirits droop" in l. 594 of Milton's Samson Agonistes.

3647   BUSH, DOUGLAS. Seventeenth-Century Poets and the Twentieth Century. MHRA Bull., No. 27, 1955, pp. 16-28.
       The Presidential Address. Milton "appears to sit more securely than ever on a throne that has partly new and even more solid foundations."

3648   CANNON, CALVIN. The Miltonic Rhythm of Unamuno's El Cristo de Velazquez. Hisp, 44, 1961, 95-8.
       Points out similarities in technique and finds Miltonic influence.

3649   CHAN, SHAN WING. Nineteenth Century Criticism of Paradise Lost, Paradise Regained, and Samson Agonistes. Doctoral diss., Stanford Univ., 1937. Abs., Abstracts of Diss., Stanford Univ., 12, 1937, 37-9.

3650   CHINOL, ELIO. La questione miltoniana. Cultura e Scuola (Roma), 2, No. 5, 1962, 75-9.
       On T. S. Eliot, F. R. Levis, and others. "L'errore di questi critici è dunque l'errore typico dell'estetismo, un errore di prospettiva storica."

3651   COHEN, B. BERNARD. Paradise Lost and Young Goodman Brown. EIHC, 94, 1958, 282-96.
       On Hawthorne's use of Paradise Lost, 9 and 10. Suggests that "Brown's experience is basically a reversal of the re-birth phase of the Adamic myth."

3652   COLGATE, WILLIAM. Horace Walpole on Milton. A Summary of His Annotations on the Work of Thomas Warton Concerning the Poems of John Milton, from the London Edition of James Dodsley, 1785. Toronto: Printed privately, 1953. 18pp.

3653   CORDASCO, FRANCESCO. Junius and Milton. N&Q, 195, 1950, 250-1.
       On Miltonic borrowings in the letters of Junius.

3654   COUFFIGNAL, ROBERT. Le Paradis Perdu de Victor Hugo à Pierre-Jean Jouve. Le Paradis Perdu: 1667-1967. Ed. by Jacques Blondel (Paris: Minard Lettres Modernes, 1967), pp. 251-74.

Shows Milton's influence on Victor Hugo, Leconte de Lisle, the Symbolists, Verhaeren, Péguy, Spire, Valéry, and Pierre-Jean Jouve.

3655 DAICHES, DAVID. English Literature. The Princeton Studies: Humanistic Scholarship in America. Englewood Cliffs, N.J.: Prentice-Hall, 1964.
    The aim of this book is "to present a critical account of American humanistic scholarship in recent decades." Recent Milton scholarship discussed, pp. 32-48.

3656 DAMON, SAMUEL FOSTER. Blake and Milton. The Divine Vision: Studies in the Poetry and Art of William Blake. Ed. by Vivian de Sola Pinto (London: Gallancy, 1957), pp. 89-96. Reprinted in Damon's A Blake Dictionary (Providence: Brown Univ. Press, 1965), pp. 274-80.
    On the Miltonic influence in Blake's works.

3657 DAVIES, H. NEVILLE. Dryden's All for Love and Thomas May's The Tragedie of Cleopatra Queen of Egypt. N&Q, N.S., 12, 1965, 139-44.
    "Samson Agonistes which Dryden apparently had in mind as a dramatic model has had a more obvious effect on the plot and language of the play."

3658 DAVIES, HUGH SYKES, ed. Milton. The Poets and Their Critics: Chaucer to Collins (Harmondsworth: Penguin Books, 1943), pp. 90-140. Revised edition, London: Hutchinson, 1960, pp. 98-156.
    Contains excerpts from critics ranging from Dryden to T. S. Eliot.

3659 DENNY, MARGARET. The Literary Hero in a Sentimental Age: An Unlisted Reference to Milton. MLN, 63, 1948, 259-61.
    An allusion in a poem by Henry Pickering.

3660 Devil's Advocates. TLS, June 24, 1960, p. 401.
    Remarks on Empson's studies.

3661 DILTHEY, WILHELM. Milton und Klopstock. Die Grosse Phantasiedichtung und andere Studien zur vergleichenden Literaturgeschichte (Gottingen: Vanderhoek und Ruprecht, 1954), pp. 122-8.

3662 DODDS, M. H. Chaucer: Spenser: Milton in Drama and Fiction. N&Q, 176, 1939, 69.
    See letter by T. O. M[abbott], ibid., 89.

3663 DORGAN, RUTH. Milton and Two of His Eighteenth-Century Critics, John Dennis and Joseph Addison. Master's thesis, Louisiana State Univ., 1955.

3664 DRINKWATER, JOHN. Shropshire. Historical Pageant and Tercentenary Performances of Milton's Masque of Comus at Ludlow Castle, July 2nd-7th, 1934. Prologue by Sir Owen Seaman. Shrewsbury: Shropshire Historical Pageant Committee, 1934. 96pp.
    Program booklet includes five historical episodes of Drinkwater, as well as the text of Comus.

3665 DURHAM, FRANK M. A Possible Relationship Between Poe's To Helen and Milton's Paradise Lost, Book IV. AL, 16, 1945, 340-3.
    Suggests that Poe went to Milton for "perfumed sea," "Nicéan barks," and "hyacinth hair," finding them all within the space of less than one hundred and fifty lines of Paradise Lost, Book 4.

3666 ECKMAN, FREDERICK. Karl Shapiro's Adam and Eve. UTSE, 35, 1956, 1-10.
      Points out that Shapiro occasionally follows Paradise Lost.

3667 ELIOT, T. S. Milton. Annual Lecture on a Master Mind. Henriette Hertz Trust of the British Academy. Oxford: Oxford Univ. Press, 1947. 19pp. Reprinted in SR, 56, 1948, 185-209; in On Poetry and Poets (London: Faber, 1957), pp. 165-83; in The Modern Critical Spectrum, ed. by Gerald J. and Nancy M. Goldberg (Englewood Cliffs, N.J.: Prentice-Hall, 1962), pp. 175-86.
      Still does not like Milton the man but retracts somewhat from his 1936 position that Milton's influence has been bad.

3668 ELLEDGE, SCOTT, ed. Eighteenth-Century Critical Essays. Ithaca, New York: Cornell Univ. Press, 1961. 2 vols.
      Contains several essays and excerpts of essays on Milton by writers such as Addison, Dennis, Johnson, and J. Warton.

3669 ERSTLING, JULIUS H. Thomas Wolfe's Knowledge and Use of Milton. Master's thesis, Univ. of Florida, 1941.

3670 EVANS, G. BLAKEMORE. Addison's Early Knowledge of Milton. JEGP, 49, 1950, 204-7.
      "I submit that the change of attitude towards Milton shown in the Spectator papers . . . was in some part the result of a comparatively recently acquired firsthand knowledge of Paradise Lost and the consequent breaking of earlier misconceptions based on fragmentary reading and other people's opinions."

3671 ------. Edward Ecclestone: His Relationship to Dryden and Milton. MLR, 44, 1949, 550-5.
      On Ecclestone's possible borrowings from Paradise Lost and his direct imitation of Dryden's State of Innocence in his Noah's Flood, or the Destruction of the World (1679).

3672 ------. Milton and Lee's The Rival Queens (1677). MLN, 64, 1949, 527-8.
      Milton's Satan reflected in Lee's villain.

3673 An Evening, Dedicated to John Milton. Pravda, Dec. 10, 1958.
      On the three hundred and fiftieth anniversary of Milton's birth.

3674 FAROOQUI, M. A. The Influence of Milton on the Romantic Poets. Thesis, Lucknow Univ., 1946.

3675 FARRELL, ALFRED. Joshua Poole and Milton's Minor Poems. MLN, 58, 1943, 198-200.
      Milton's poems quoted in Poole's The English Parnassus, 1657.

3676 FASEL, IDA. Whitman and Milton. WWR, 8, 1967, 79-87.
      Makes a case for extensive Miltonic influence in Whitman's verse.

3677 FIORE, AMADEUS, O.F.M. A Note on Milton's Critics. FS, 19, 1959, 142-9.
      Surveys adverse criticism. "Despite twentieth century prejudices to the contrary, Milton's poetry can be a valuable experience."

3678 FERRY, ANNE DAVIDSON. Milton and the Miltonic Dryden. Cambridge: Harvard Univ. Press, 1968. 238pp.
> The connections discussed in this study demonstrate "that the two greatest poets of the later seventeenth century ... explored experience in significantly related styles, that Dryden in two of his most successful works [Absalom and Achitophel and All for Love] was able to learn in a variety of ways from his older contemporary." Not, however, a study of developing influence.
> Rev: MN, 2, 1968, 64-5.

3679 FLETCHER, EDWARD G. Defoe on Milton. MLN, 50, 1935, 31-2.
> Finds two previously unnoted Milton references in Vol. 8 of Defoe's Review (1711 and 1712).

3680 FLETCHER, HARRIS F. Nathaniel Lee and Milton. MLN, 44, 1929, 173-5.
> Verses contributed by Lee to Dryden's The State of Innocence.

3681 FOERSTER, DONALD M. The Fortunes of Epic Poetry. A Study in English and American Criticism 1750-1950. Washington: Catholic Univ. of America Press, 1962. xii, 250pp.
> "I have focused attention upon critical estimates of the four greatest epic poets, Homer, Virgil, Dante, and Milton." Contains analyses of evaluations of Paradise Lost.

3682 FOGLE, FRENCH. Milton Lost and Regained. HLQ, 15, 1952, 351-69.
> A discussion of the history of Milton criticism.

3683 FOGLE, RICHARD HARTER. Johnson and Coleridge on Milton. BuR, 14, No. 1, 1966, 26-32.
> To Johnson, Milton's egotism was his besetting sin; to Coleridge, "it is his vital principle, a Platonic idea that Milton both is and expresses."

3684 FOX, ROBERT C. The Barbados Gazette. TLS, June 19, 1959, p. 369.
> Quotes the Barbados Gazette (1738), which contains a passage highly complimentary of Paradise Lost.

3685 FREEDMAN, MORRIS. All for Love and Samson Agonistes. NQ, N.S., 3, 1956, 514-7.
> "I should like to suggest ... that the verbal, thematic, and critical connections between All for Love and Samson are, in sum, so substantial as to indicate that Dryden not only knew Milton well but was modifying Shakespeare through him."

3686 ------. Dryden's Reported Reaction to Paradise Lost. N&Q, N.S., 5, 1958, 14-6.
> Insists that Dryden always preferred rhyme to blank verse, despite some statements to the contrary.

3687 ------. Milton and Dryden. Doctoral diss., Columbia Univ., 1953. Abs., DA, 14, 1954, 109.

3688 ------. Satan and Shaftesbury. PMLA, 74, 1959, 544-7.
> "The close dependence of Absalom and Achitophel on Paradise Lost suggests how aptly Milton's material lent itself to contemporary political commentary and simultaneously, how densely political it was in itself."

3689   FRENCH, DAVID P. Pope, Milton, and the Essay on Man. BuR, 16, 1968, 103-11.
>   Suggests that Pope's poem "is partly both a response and a challenge to Milton's Paradise Lost," that Pope's line "But vindicate the ways of God to man" is an intentional misquote which sums up "both his affinity with Milton's pious intention and his quarrel with Milton's method."

3690   FRENCH, J. MILTON. Blind Milton Ridiculed in Poor Robin, 1664-1674. N&Q, 196, 1951, 470-1.

3691   ------. Lamb and Milton. SP, 31, 1934, 92-103.
>   Shows "that Milton's works were continually fresh in Lamb's mind and his constant joy from his earliest to his latest years."

3692   ------. Milton and the Barbarous Dissonance. TSLL, 4, 1962, 376-89.
>   Selects and comments upon fairly recent adverse criticisms.

3693   FRYE, NORTHROP. Fearful Symmetry: A Study of William Blake. Princeton: Princeton Univ. Press, 1947; Boston: Beacon Press (paperback), 1962. 462pp.
>   Cites numerous references to Blake and Milton.

3694   ------. Notes for a Commentary on Milton. The Divine Vision: Studies in the Poetry and Art of William Blake. Ed. by Vivian de Sola Pinto. London: Gollancz, 1957. 216pp.
>   Contains an analysis of Blake's poem, with stress on the Miltonic influence, pp. 97-137.

3695   GEDDES, GARY. Harnessing the Peruvian Torrents: Johnson and Imagination. QQ, 74, 1967, 523-31.
>   A review of Arieh Sachs' Passionate Intelligence: Imagination and Reason in the Works of Samuel Johnson, 1967. Deals, i.a., with Johnson's criticism of Milton.

3696   GILLESPIE, EDGAR BRYAN. Paradise Regain'd: A History of the Criticism and an Interpretation. Doctoral diss., Duke Univ., 1966. Abs., DA, 27, 1966, 1820A.
>   Considers criticism from the seventeenth century to the present.

3697   GLEASON, MORIECE. Milton, the Man, the Poet, the Philosopher: A Study in Patterns of Milton Criticism from 1640 to 1700. Doctoral diss., Louisiana State Univ., 1966. Abs., DA, 27, 1966, 1336-A.

3698   GORDON, R. K. Keats and Milton. MLR, 42, 1947, 434-6.
>   Keats' "debt to Milton, especially to Paradise Lost, is larger and more pervasive than generally thought."

3699   GOSSMAN, ANN. Harmonius Jones and Milton's Invocations. N&Q, N.S., 1, 1954, 527-9.
>   Sir William Jones' debt to Milton.

3700   ------. Milton Trickt and Frounc't. N&Q, N.S., 2, 1955, 100-2.
>   Paraphrases and adaptations.

3701   ------, and GEORGE W. WHITING. Comus, Once More, 1761. RES, N.S., 11, 1960, 56-60.

"In Samuel Derrick's A Poetical Dictionary; or, The Beauties of the English Poets (1761) a number of passages attributed to Milton's Comus are in fact from Dalton's adaptation."

3702 ------, and ------. Milton, Patron of Marriage. N&Q, N.S., 8, 1961, 180-1.
Quotes The Maid's Soliloquy from The London Magazine, Feb., 1758, in which the author's theme is marriage and in which he invokes Milton as his patron.

3703 GREWE, EUGENE FRANCIS. A History of the Criticism of John Milton's Comus, 1637-1941. Doctoral diss., Univ. of Michigan, 1963. Abs., DA, 25, 1964, 2512.

3704 GROSS, BARRY EDWARD. The Eve of St. Agnes and Lamia: Paradise Won, Paradise Lost. BuR, 13, 1965, 47-57.
Compares the reader's response in both pairs of poems. Sees an affinity between Paradise Lost and Lamia and between Paradise Regained and The Eve of St. Agnes.

3705 GRUSHKIN, A. Pushkin in the Thirties of the Nineteenth Century on the Creative Independence of the Artist (Voltaire, Milton, Chateaubriand). Zwiesda (USSR), 9, 1939, 136-59.

3706 GUIDI, AUGUSTO. Milton e Hopkins. EM, 6, 1955, 31-43.

3707 HABER, TOM BURNS. Is It Miltonic? New York Review of Books, May, 18, 1967, p. 41.
Challenges Richard Wilbur's use of the term Miltonic in a sonnet title (April 6, 1967). Wilbur replies that Milton used sonnets "for a public subject."

3708 HÄGIN, PETER. The Epic Hero and the Decline of Heroic Poetry: A Study of the Neoclassical English Epic with special reference to Milton's Paradise Lost. The Cooper Monographs. Bern: Francke, 1964. 181pp.
Focuses attention on the history of the epic hero. Chapter 5: The Hero of Paradise Lost, pp. 146-69.

3709 HALLER, WILLIAM O. Milton's Reputation and Influence, 1643-1647. Tracts on Liberty in the Puritan Revolution (New York: Columbia Univ. Press, 1935), 1, 128-42.

3710 HARDY, BARBARA. Coleridge and Milton. TLS, Nov. 9, 1951, p. 711.
States that a quotation attributed to S. T. Coleridge was, in fact, copied rather inaccurately from Jonathan Richardson the Elder.

3711 HARDY, J. P. Dr. Johnson as a Critic of the English Poets Including Shakespeare. Doctoral diss., Magdalen College, Oxford, 1965.
Chapter 7: Johnson's Criticism of Paradise Lost.

3712 HAVENS, RAYMOND D. The Influence of Milton on English Poetry. London: Russell and Russell, 1962. xii, 722pp.
A reprint of Stevens' No. 2842, first published in 1922. Part One: The Attitude of the Eighteenth Century Towards Milton; Part Two: The Influence of Paradise Lost; Part Three: The Shorter Poems.
Rev: R. Spindler, ESt, 45, 1931, 283-90.

3713 ------. Milton's Influence on Wordsworth's Early Sonnets. PMLA, 63, 1948, 751-2.
    Disagrees with J. B. McNulty, PMLA, 62, 1947, 745-51.

3714 HAVILAND, THOMAS P. How Well Did Poe Know Milton? PMLA, 69, 1954, 841-60.
    Avoids accusing Poe of plagiarism and concludes that Poe possessed a great familiarity with Milton's works.

3715 ------. A Measure for the Early Freneau's Debt to Milton. PMLA, 55, 1940, 1033-40.
    Traces influence by using Freneau's Power of Fancy.

3716 ------. The Miltonic Quality of Brackenridge's Poem on Divine Revelation. PMLA, 56, 1941, 588-92.

3717 HEALY, SISTER M. AQUINAS, R.S.M. Milton and Hopkins. UTQ, 22, 1952, 18-25.
    Although Hopkins dislikes Milton as man and thinker, he praises Milton the artist and considers him a master, surpassing all other poets.

3718 HELSZTYNSKI, STANISLAS. Milton in Poland. SP, 26, 1929, 145-54.
    An account of Milton's reputation in Poland.

3719 HEWELL, ONYCE OLIVE. The Relation of Carlyle to Milton. Master's thesis, Duke Univ., 1937.

3720 HIBERNICUS. Benlowes and Milton. TLS, Aug. 22, 1929, p. 652.
    On Benlowes' borrowings.

3721 HILL, D. M. Johnson as Moderator. N&Q, N.S., 3, 1956, 517-22.
    Regards Johnson's method in assessing Paradise Lost (Life of Milton) as that of a moderator.

3722 HOLLOWAY, JOHN. Milton and Arnold. EIC, 7, 1957, 226-8.
    A reaction to J. B. Broadbent's article in EIC, 6, 1956, 404-17.

3723 HONAN, PARK. Belial upon Setebos. TSL, 9, 1964, 87-98.
    On parallels between Belial's address (Paradise Lost, 2, 119-225) and Caliban's soliloquy in Browning's Caliban upon Setebos.

3724 HORSFALL, T. E. P. A Study of Milton's Reputation at Home and Abroad Between the Years 1600 and 1718. B. Litt. thesis, St. Hilda's College, Oxford, 1929. cvi, 359pp.

3725 HORTON, KENNETH J. The Influence of John Milton on the Connecticut Wits. Master's thesis, Univ. of Florida, 1940.

3726 HOWARD, LEON. Early American Copies of Milton. HLB, 7, 1935, 169-79.

3727 ------. The Influence of Milton on Colonial American Poetry. HLB, 9, 1936, 63-89.

3728 HOWARTH, HERBERT. Eliot and Milton: The American Aspect. UTQ, 30, 1961, 150-62.
    On T. S. Eliot's attitudes toward Milton.

3729 HUCKABAY, CALVIN. Milton's Literary Reputation During the Victorian Era. Doctoral diss., Louisiana State Univ., 1955.

3730 ------. The Satanist Controversy of the Nineteenth Century. Studies in English Renaissance Literature. Ed. by Waldo F. McNeir (Baton Rouge: Louisiana State Univ. Press, 1962), pp. 197-210.
　　Traces the development of the controversy over Satan's position in Paradise Lost from its inception with William Blake (1790) to its fruition with Sir Walter Raleigh (1900).

3731 HUGHES, MERRITT Y. A Meditation on Literary Blasphemy. JAAC, 14, 1955, 106-15.
　　Attacks on Shakespeare and Milton.

3732 ------. The Seventeenth Century in Contemporary Literary Scholarship: A Critical Review. Ed. by Lewis Leary (New York: Appleton-Century-Crofts, 1958), pp. 67-82.
　　Survey of Milton studies, pp. 74-82.

3733 HUNT, B. C. Wordsworth's Marginalia in Dove Cottage to 1800: A Study of His Relationship to Charlotte Smith and Milton. B. Litt. thesis, Christ Church, Oxford, 1965.

3734 [HUNTER, WILLIAM B., JR.]. The Study of Milton in the Southeastern United States. SCN, 8, No. 4, 1950, 6.
　　During the academic year 1949-50.

3735 JENKINS, HAROLD. Benlowes and Milton. MLR, 43, 1948, 186-95.
　　Benlowes borrowed from Milton.

3736 John Milton: On the 350th Anniversary of His Birth. Trud (USSR), Dec. 10, 1958.

3737 JOHNSON, SAMUEL. from The Life of Milton. Milton's Lycidas: The Tradition and the Poem. Ed. by C. A. Patrides (New York: Holt, Rinehart, and Winston, 1961), pp. 56-7.
　　A reprint of Johnson's famous remarks on Lycidas, first published in 1779.

3738 ------. Milton. Johnson's Lives of the Poets. With an Introduction and Notes by K. Deighton. London: Macmillan; New York: St. Martin's Press, 1965. xxxvii, 139pp.
　　This edition first published in 1892. Reprinted 12 times. Contains a Summary of Johnson's Milton, by C. D. Punchard, pp. xxv-xxvii.

3739 JOHNSON, W. G. Skriften om Paradis and Milton. JEGP, 64, 1945, 263-9.
　　On the relationship of Spegel's poems (1705) to Paradise Lost.

3740 JONES, FREDERICK L. Shelley and Milton. SP, 49, 1952, 488-519.
　　Seeks to "illuminate the relationship between Shelley and Milton."

3741 KATO, R. S. T. Coleridge and His Criticism of Milton. SEL (Japan), 13, 1933, 482-93.

3742 KELLEY, GRACIE LEE. Milton's Reputation in the Eighteenth Century as Reflected in the Gentleman's Magazine and the Monthly Review. Master's thesis, Univ. of Georgia, 1940.

3743 KING, BRUCE. Lycidas and Oldham. EA, 19, 1966, 60-3.
Parallels between Milton's poem and Dryden's To the Memory of Mr. Oldham suggest additional evidence of Milton's influence.

3744 KITTREDGE, PAUL M. Macaulay's Essay on Milton: A Literary, Historical, and Political Evaluation. Master's thesis, Univ. of Florida, 1951.

3745 KNOEPFLMACHER, U. C. The Post-Romantic Imagination: Adam Bede, Wordsworth and Milton. ELH, 34, 1967, 518-40.
Shows that George Eliot is indebted to Milton and to Wordsworth. From Milton she learned "to justify man's lot in the temporal world."

3746 KRAMER, JEROME. The Romantic Biographers of Milton. Doctoral diss., Ohio State Univ., 1966. Abs., DA, 27, 1967, 3012-A.

3747 KUROTA, KENJIRO. The Early Reception of Paradise Lost. Ehime Univ. Helicon (Japan), 3, 1953.

3748 LAVIN, J. A. A Miltonic Echo in Housman. N&Q, N.S., 5, 1958, 486.
Disagrees with George O. Marshall, Jr. (N&Q, N.S., 5, 1958, 258), that Paradise Lost, 11, 485-6, is echoed in A Shropshire Lad, LXII.

3749 Leavis Works Not on Pyre. The Times, June 14, 1962, p. 7f.
Cambridge students defer to F. R. Leavis' retirement but proceed to burn T. S. Eliot's poems.

3750 LE COMTE, EDWARD S. Samson Agonistes and Aureng-Zebe. EA, 2, 1958, 18-22.
Holds that Dryden and other late seventeenth century writers made use of Milton's ideas on marriage in their sentimental comedies.

3751 LEMAY, J. A. LEO. Jonson and Milton: Two Influences in Oakes's Elegie. NEQ, 38, 1965, 90-2.
Insists that diction and imagery in Oakes's poem (1677) were borrowed from Samson Agonistes.

3752 LESLIE, F. ANDREW. An Opera about Milton. SCN, 19, 1961, 49.
Notes the performance of Milton by Gasparo Spontini in 1961 by the Falmouth Opera Singers in England.

3753 LEVIN, GERALD. The Imagery of Ruskin's A Walk in Chamouni. Victorian Poetry, 5, 1967, 283-90.
Deals, i. a., with possible Miltonic influence at the end of the poem.

3754 LILL, JAMES V. Dryden's Adaptations from Milton, Shakespeare, and Chaucer. Doctoral diss., Univ. of Minnesota, 1954.

3755 LOANE, GEORGE G. Shakespeare, Milton, and Pope. TLS, Jan. 23, 1937, p. 60.
Dalila, Millamant, and Pope's treatment of Donne.

3756 MABBOTT, THOMAS O. Chatterton and Milton: a Question of Forgery. N&Q, 177, 1939, 314.
Cf. Columbia Edition, 18, 562, 599.

3757 ------, and J. MILTON FRENCH. A Satyr Against J. M. 1655. N&Q, 173, 1937, 45.
Prints short poem preserved in the notebook of Thomas Stringer,

3758 MALE, R. R., JR. Dual Aspects of Evil in Rappaccini's Daughter. PMLA, 69, 1954, 99-109.
A consideration of Milton's influence, pp. 107-8.

3759 MANNING, C. A. Milton et Njegos. Revue des Études Slaves, 18, 1938, 63-72.
Paradise Lost and Njegos' The Torch of the Microcosm (1845).

3760 MANUEL, M. The Seventeenth-Century Critics and Biographers of Milton. Doctoral diss., Univ. of Wisconsin, 1956. Abs., DA, 16, 1956, 2166-7.
Published in Trivandrum, India, in 1962.

3761 MARSHALL, GEORGE O., JR. A Miltonic Echo in Housman. N&Q, N.S., 5, 1958, 258.
Paradise Lost, 11, 485-6, echoed in A Shropshire Lad, LXII.

3762 MAXWELL, J. C. Melville and Milton. N&Q, N.S., 12, 1965, 60.
On an echo of Paradise Lost, 1, 351-4, in Pierre, Book 9, Chapter 1.

3763 ------. Milton in Wordsworth's Praise of Spenser. N&Q, N.S., 15, 1968, 22-3.
Argues that though Wordsworth places the praise of Milton after the praise of Spenser in Book 3 of The Prelude, the most famous Spenserian lines are "strongly Miltonic."

3764 ------. Pope's Spring and Milton's In Adventum Veris. N&Q, N.S., 13, 1966, 212.
Notes "two details in which Pope is closer to Milton than to Virgil," whom he cited.

3765 McALISTER, FLOYD L. Milton and the Anti-Academics. JEGP, 61, 1962, 779-87.
The reaction against Milton by Ezra Pound, F. R. Leavis, Herbert Read and others is more significant as a revelation of their generation's reaction against authority than as literary criticism.

3766 ------. A Survey of Twentieth-Century Milton Scholarship with Particular Attention to Controversies. Doctoral diss., Univ. of Minnesota, 1958. Abs., DA, 19, 1958, 1365.

3767 McCARTHY, BERNARD EUGENE. Milton Criticism in the First Half of the Eighteenth Century. Doctoral diss., Univ. of Kansas, 1967. Abs., DA, 28, 1968, 3150-A. 276pp.

3768 McFADDEN, GEORGE. Dryden's Most Barren Period—and Milton. HLQ, 24, 1961, 283-96.
"The State of Innocence was an exercise on Dryden's part in developing a technique of internal reinforcement of sound in the manner of Vergil and Milton."

3769 McKILLOP, ALAN D. The Early History of Alfred. PQ, 41, 1962, 311-24.
Mentions Thomson's use of Comus in Alfred: A Masque.

3770 McLAUGHLIN, ELIZABETH T., with the assistance of D. H. ROFFEN-SPERGER. Coleridge and Milton. SP, 61, 1964, 545-72.
Allows Coleridge to defend Milton against charges by Pound, Eliot, and others.

3771   McNULTY, JOHN B. Milton, and Wordsworth's Bucer, Erasmus, and
         Melancthon. N&Q, 197, 1952, 61.
            Wordsworth's reference to the three Renaissance scholars (Prelude, 3, 479-81)
            found in Milton's divorce pamphlets.

3772   ------. Milton's Influence on Wordsworth's Early Sonnets. PMLA, 62,
         1947, 745-51.
            Wordsworth acknowledged a greater debt than he owed.

3773   MEGAFFIN, BLANCHE ISABEL. The Warton Brothers: Their Relation
         to Romanticism and Milton. Master's thesis, Manitoba Univ., 1931.

3774   MILES, JOSEPHINE. The Sublime Poem. The Image of the Work. Ed.
         by Bertrand Evans and others. Univ. of California Publications, English
         Studies, 11 (Berkeley and Los Angeles: Univ. of California Press, 1955),
         pp. 59-85.
            Shows how the sublime poem may be distinguished and regards its continua-
            tion in the eighteenth century in part as extension of the Miltonic style.

3775   MILLER, BRUCE E. The Allusion to Paradise Lost in Keat's Letter on
         Imagination. N&Q, N.S., 11, 1964, 423.
            Suggests a reference to Adam's first dream (Paradise Lost, 8, 283-311), despite
            some contrary opinions.

3776   MILLIGAN, BURTON. An Early American Imitator of Milton. AL, 11,
         1939, 200-6.
            Nathaniel Evans, Poems on Several Occasions (1772).

3777   MILNER, MAX. Le Satan de Milton et L'Épopée Romantique Française.
         Le Paradis Perdu: 1667-1967. Ed. by Jacques Blondel (Paris: Minard
         Lettres Modernes, 1967), pp. 219-40.
            Discusses to what extent Milton's Satan has aided or hampered the develop-
            ment of the epic in France after 1820.

3778   Milton 300. MN, 1, 1967, 29-30.
            A report on a conference held at the Univ. of Rochester, March 17-18, 1967,
            on the tercentenary of Paradise Lost; also, an account of a reading produc-
            tion of Comus.

3779   [Milton Birthday]. The Times, Dec. 10, 1958, p. 8g; Dec. 19, p. 9g.
            Soviet cities celebrate 350th anniversary of Milton's birth with lectures and
            concerts, and the government issues a new stamp.

3780   Milton Regained. TLS, Feb. 15, 1963, pp. 101-2.
            A review of recent studies by B. A. Wright, J. H. Summers, J. I. Cope, D. P.
            Harding, and H. F. Fletcher.

3781   [Milton Stamp]. Linn's Weekly Stamp News, May 15, 1967, p. 39.
            Illustrates a Hungarian stamp issued on May 6, 1967, which reproduces the
            painting by Petrics of Milton dictating to his daughters.

3782   MISH, CHARLES C. Comus and Bryce Blair's Vision of Theodorus
         Verax. MN, 1, 1967, 39-40.
            "There is nothing in Blair's Vision [1671] to lead us to believe that he
            knew Milton's Comus."

3783 MIYANISHI, MITSUO. The Present Day Re-estimate of Milton. Kyoto Univ. Edibungaku Hyoron, 4, 1957.

3784 MONK, S. H. Wordsworth's 'unimaginable touch of time.' MLN, 52, 1937, 503-4.
Borrowed from Of Education.

3785 MOORE, JOHN R. Milton among the Augustans: the Infernal Council. SP, 48, 1951, 15-25.
Examines in part the role of politics in Milton's reputation. The Infernal Council best suited the urgent literary needs of the Augustans, since "It could serve as a pattern for satire against rival Chieftains...."

3786 ------. Milton Improved. SCN, 16, No. 1, 1958, item 55.
Reproduces two passages from Paradise Lost, converted to couplets. Printed first in The Flying Post: or, Weekly Medley, March 8, 1728-9.

3787 MUKHERJI, AMULYADHAN. Miltonic Blank Verse in Bengali. Calcutta Review, 149, 1958, 123-6.
Credits Madhusudan Dutt, the nineteenth-century poet, with the introduction of Miltonic blank verse in Bengali.

3788 MURRAY, PATRICK. Appraisal and Re-appraisal of Milton. Doctoral diss., National Univ. of Ireland, 1964.

3789 ------. Milton: The Modern Phase, A Study of Twentieth Century Criticism. London: Longmans, 1967. ix, 163pp.
"A survey of the work of twentieth-century scholars." Deals exclusively with criticism of Paradise Lost.

3790 ------. Paradise Lost: A Christian Poem in a Post-Christian Age. Studies, 60, No. 219, Autumn, 1966, 277-84.
Suggests that "critics and champions of Milton alike have seriously exaggerated the extent to which his greatest work is out of touch with modern taste."

3791 MUSGROVE, T. J. John Milton's Influence on French Poetry in the Romantic Period (1800-1850). Master's thesis, University College, London, 1957.

3792 MYERS, ROBERT MANSON. Handel and Milton. TSE, 3, 1952, 93-124.
Milton and the eighteenth-century librettists and composers, especially Handel.

3793 ------. Handel, Dryden, and Milton: Being a Series of Observations on the Poems of Dryden and Milton, as alter'd and adapted by Various Hands, and Set to Musick by Mr. Handel, to which are added Authentick Texts of Several of Mr. Handel's Oratorios. Cambridge: Bowes and Bowes, 1956.
Part Two is a study of Handel and Milton. It contains a section on eighteenth-century musical settings of Milton's works.

3794 NANES, LAURA MAY. John Milton's Ideas on Civil and Religious Liberty and Their Acceptance During the Interregnum. Master's thesis, State Univ. of Iowa, 1933.

3795 NELSON, JAMES GRAHAM. The Sublime Puritan: Studies in the Victorian Attitude Toward Milton. Doctoral diss., Columbia Univ., 1961. Abs., DA, 22, 1961, 1160. Published as The Sublime Puritan: Milton and the Victorians. Madison: Univ. of Wisconsin Press, 1963. ix, 209pp.

"Milton, like all powerful figures, was loved by many, hated by some, but ignored by few." Chapters: A Power Amongst Powers; Shakespeare and Milton; The Miltonic Sonnet; The Religious Epic and the Miltonic Sublime; Milton the Puritan: Pro and Con; Milton and Tennyson; Milton the Artist: The Late Victorian View.
Rev: E. Saillens, EA, 16, 1963, 395; Joseph Frank, SCN, 21, 1963, 34; J. Max Patrick, SatR, Sept., 7, 1963, pp. 34-5; Walter J. Ong, S.J., SEL, 4, No. 1, 1964, 180; R. G. Cox, N&Q, N.S., 11, 1964, 352-3; Joseph E. Baker, PQ, 44, 1965, 135-6.

3796 NEWMEYER, EDNA. The Poet's Province: Wordsworth's Manuscript Notes in Paradise Lost. Doctoral diss., The City Univ. of New York, 1966. Abs., DA, 27, 1966, 1343A-4A.

3797 OCHI, FUMIO. Recent Trends in Milton Scholarship in America. The Main Current, 21, 1958.

3798 ORAS, ANTS. Miltonic Elements in Shelley. SCN, 13, 1955, 22.
The Chariot of Paternal Deity appears in Prometheus Bound, 4.

3799 ------. Milton's Editors and Commentators from Patrick Hume to Henry John Todd (1695-1801). A Study in Critical Views and Methods. London: Oxford Univ. Press; Tartu: Univ. of Tartu (Dorpat), 1931. 381pp. Reprinted, New York: Haskell House, 1964.

3800 ------. The Multitudinous Orb: Some Miltonic Elements in Shelley. MLQ, 16, 1955, 247-57.
Considers Prometheus Unbound.

3801 OREL, HAROLD. The Dynasts and Paradise Lost. SAQ, 52, 1953, 355-60.
Discusses the change in meaning of the term epic-drama from Milton to Hardy. "Hardy's recognition of the change manifests itself in a work which radically modifies the Miltonic relationship between man and God. . . ."

3802 PARKER, W. M. Lockhart's Notes on Paradise Lost. English (London), 12, 1958, 48-53.
Lockhart's notes, which first appeared in 1826, provided insight into his scholarship on Milton.

3803 PARKER, WILLIAM RILEY. Milton on King James the Second. MLQ, 3, 1942, 41-4.
The pamphlet Pro Populo Adversus Tyrannos (1689) mostly a reprint of The Tenure of Kings and Magistrates.

3804 ------. Milton's Contemporary Reputation, an Essay, Together with a Tentative List of Printed Allusions to Milton, 1641-1674, and Facsimile Reproductions of Five Contemporary Pamphlets Written in Answer to Milton. Columbus: Ohio State Univ. Press, 1940. xii, 229pp.
Includes a list of printed allusions to Milton between 1641 and 1674, photostatic copies of several tracts, with notes. The title essay establishes a valid

evaluation of Milton's popular stature at the time of his greatest political activity.

Rev: L. C. Martin, YWES, 172-3; Arthur Barker, MLR, 36, 1941, 529-30; William Haller, MLQ, 2, 1941, 322-7; E. N. S. Thompson, PQ, 20, 1941, 191-2; TLS, Mar. 22, 1941, p. 143; J. S. Diekhoff, MLN, 57, 1942, 403-4; J. H. Hanford, JEGP, 41, 1942, 236-8; B. A. Wright, RS, 18, 1942, 232-5.

3805 ------. Milton's Harapha. TLS, Jan. 2, 1937, p. 12.
   Replies by E. N. Allen, Jan. 16, 1937, p. 44; by Jacob Leveen and H. Loewe, Jan. 23, 1937, p. 60. A discussion of the reference to Milton's poetry in Edward Phillips' New World of Words (1671 ed.).

3806 PATRIDES, C. A. John Milton: The Poet Who Gave Us Paradise. Obs., Aug. 13, 1967, pp. 3-9.
   Emphasizes the influence of Milton's picture of Eden on the popular imagination and on the visual arts.

3807 PELLETIER, ROBERT R. The Revolt of Islam and Paradise Lost. KSJ, 14, 1965, 7-13.
   Investigates some of the abundant verbal similarities between Shelley's poem and Paradise Lost.

3808 ------. Satan and Prometheus in Captivity. N&Q, N.S., 7, 1960, 107-8.
   Presents some verbal similarities in descriptions of Satan and Shelley's Prometheus as captives.

3809 ------. Shade and Bower Images in Milton and Shelley. N&Q, 8, 1961, 21-2.
   Cites parallels between Shelley's Alastor and Milton's Comus and Paradise Lost.

3810 ------. Shelley's Ahasuerus and Milton's Satan. N&Q, N.S., 7, 1960, 259-60.
   On some parallels to Paradise Lost and Lycidas in Shelley's The Wandering Jew's Soliloquy.

3811 ------. Shelley's Debt to Milton in The Wandering Jew. N&Q, N.S., 8, 1961, 462-4.
   Notes parallels to Paradise Lost, L'Allegro, and the Nativity Ode. Supports 1809-10 as date of composition.

3812 ------. Unnoticed Parallels Between Ahasuerus and Satan. KSJ, 11, 1962, 12-4.
   Notes verbal similarities in Queen Mab and Paradise Lost. Concludes that the grandeur of Shelley's Ahasuerus (Queen Mab) derives from Milton's Satan.

3813 PETTET, E. C. Milton and the Modern Reader. Orion. Ed. by C. Day Lewis and others (London: Nicholson and Watson, 1945), pp. 3, 68-81.
   Argues that Milton has been dislodged because "his language and rhythm are extravagantly artificial and narrowly restricted."

3814 PETTIGREW, RICHARD C. Emerson and Milton. AL, 3, 1931, 45-59.
   Feels that Emerson was preoccupied with content rather than with style in his criticism of Milton.

3815 ------. Lowell's Criticism of Milton. AL, 3, 1932, 457-64.
   "I have felt that an analysis of the criticism of James Russell Lowell must be

of definite assistance in any final estimate of his critical rank. Such a study also partially examines the nature of Milton's American reputation."

3816 ------. Milton in the Works of Emerson, Lowell, and Holmes. Doctoral diss., Duke Univ., 1930.

3817 PITTS, ARTHUR W., JR. Hopkins' The Wreck of the Deutschland, Stanza 29. Expl, 24, 1965, item 7.
Suggests that Hopkins is alluding to Paradise Regained, 4, 44-50.

3818 PLUNKETT, FRANK W. The Miltonic Tradition in One of Its Phases. The Criticism of Milton as Found in Leading British Magazines of the Pre-Romantic and Romantic Periods (1779-1832). Doctoral diss., Indiana Univ., 1931. Printed in summary form, State College, Arkansas: Arkansas State College Press, 1934. 15pp.

3819 POLLITT, JOE DONALD. Ralph Waldo Emerson's Debt to John Milton. Marshall Review (Huntington, West Virginia), 3, Dec., 1939, 13-21.

3820 POMMER, HENRY F. Milton and Melville. Doctoral diss., Yale University, 1946. Pittsburgh: Univ. of Pittsburgh Press, 1950. 172pp.
Traces the influence of Milton on Melville and explains how the various types of influence help to explain the development of Melville's art.
Rev: R. E. Spiller, AL, 23, 1951, 384-5; Sherman Paul, NEQ, 24, 1951, 550-2; Leon Howard, NCF, 6, 1951, 76.

3821 PORTER, HELEN ELIZABETH. Milton's Influence on Tennyson. Master's thesis, Duke Univ., 1938.

3822 POTTS, ABBIE F. Spenserian and Miltonic Influence in Wordsworth's Ode and Rainbow. SP, 29, 1932, 607-16.
Examines the philosophical and descriptive properties of the two in relation to Wordsworth's thought and impressions.

3823 RABEN, JOSEPH. Milton's Influence on Shelley's Translation of Dante's Matilda Gathering Flowers. RES, N.S., 14, 1963, 142-56.
Discusses "Shelley's distinct reliance for both diction and imagery on the verse of Milton" and his theory of translation.

3824 RACINE, LOUIS. Life of Milton. Trans. with an Introduction by Katherine John. London: Hogarth Press, 1930.
The Introduction, pp. 9-94, contains a history of Milton's reputation in France.

3825 RAINE, KATHLEEN. Blake's Debt to Antiquity. SR, 71, 1963, 352-450.
Contains scattered references to Milton's influence on Blake.

3826 REDMAN, HARRY, JR. Albert Joseph Ulpein Hennet, Early French Miltonist. RomN, 1, 1959, 122-6.
Hennet (1758-1828) often cited Milton in his Poétique Anglaise (1806) and especially praised Paradise Lost.

3827 ------. Villemain on Milton: A Document in Romantic Criticism. CL, 10, 1958, 241-5.
A paper presented at the Kentucky Foreign Language Conference on April 27, 1957. Places Villemain in the tradition of Romantic criticism of Paradise Lost and suggests that he anticipated Hugo in the latter's Cromwell.

3828 RIFFE, NANCY LEE. An Early Miltonic Burlesque. N&Q, N.S., 11, 1964, 296.

"The burlesque poem, originally printed in 1713 and attributed to John Phillips, appears in The Bee, No. 11 (1733, 497-9)."

3829 ------. Eighteenth-Century Translations of Milton into Latin. N&Q, N.S., 12, 1965, 144.

Gives three additional translations, hitherto unnoticed, which appeared in British periodicals between 1740 and 1750.

3830 ------. A Fragment of Milton, from the Italian. PQ, 45, 1966, 447-50.

Suggests that the poem A Fragment is a free translation by Aaron Hill of Milton's Italian canzone.

3831 ------. Milton and Eighteenth-Century Whigs. N&Q, N.S., 11, 1964, 337-8.

"Hitherto unnoted comments in two early Whig periodicals of the eighteenth century showed that Milton continued to be revered by this party."

3832 ------. Milton in the Eighteenth-Century Periodicals: Hail, Wedded Love! N&Q, N.S., 12, 1965, 18-9.

"In a period in which the divorce tracts were virtually forgotten, Milton may have been considered a misogynist by some, but for more he seems to have been a kind of patron saint of marriage."

3833 ------. Milton's Minor Poetry in British Periodicals Before 1740. N&Q, N.S., 12, 1965, 453-4.

Shows that the shorter poems were neither unknown nor neglected before Handel called attention to them.

3834 ------. A Study of Milton's Eighteenth Century Reputation in British Periodicals, 1711-1788. Doctoral diss., Univ. of Kentucky, 1963.

3835 RYLEY, ROBERT M. Isaac D'Israeli and Warburton's Plagiarism from Milton. N&Q, N.S., 13, 1966, 217.

Refers to J. Steadman, N&Q, N.S., 6, 1959, 367. D'Israeli found Milton's prose " 'ridiculous' when he thought it Warburton's."

3836 SAMARIN, R. John Milton. Culture and Life (USSR), 2, 1959, 54-5.

In this entry and the three that follow, Samarin writes on the three hundred fiftieth anniversary of Milton's birth, emphasizing Milton's revolutionary ideas.

3837 ------. John Milton and the Controversy About Him. Questions in Literature (USSR), 1, 1959, 155-72.

3838 ------. John Milton i spori o nem (John Milton: Various Opinions of His Life and Work). Voprosi Literaturi, 1, 1959, 155-72.

3839 ------. A Mighty Talent. Literary Gazette (USSR), Dec. 10, 1958.

3840 ------. The Works of John Milton as Evaluated by Pushkin. Reports and Accounts by the Faculty of Philosophy of the Moscow State Univ., No. 6, 1948, 62-70.

3841 SANDERLIN, GEORGE. The Influence of Milton and Wordsworth on the Early Victorian Sonnet. ELH, 5, 1938, 225-51.

Part of a doctoral dissertation, The Sonnet in English Literature, 1800-1850,

Johns Hopkins Univ., 1938. Printed in pamphlet form by the Johns Hopkins Press, 1938.

3842 SANKEY, BENJAMIN T., JR. Coleridge on Milton's Satan. PQ, 41, 1962, 504-8.
On the philosophical background of Coleridge's interpretation.

3843 SATŌ, KIYOSHI. Eishi-no-Seizui (Essence of English Poetry). Tokyo: Kenkyūsha, 1930.
Contains an account of Blake's Milton.

3844 ------. Samuel Johnson on Milton and Shakespeare. SEL (Japan), 19, 1939, 339-50.

3845 SAURAT, DENIS. Blake and Milton. London: Stanley Nott, 1935. Reprinted, London: Russell and Russell, 1965. 159pp.
Rev: London Merc, 33, 1935, 262; Charles Madge, Crit, 15, 1936, 527-9.

3846 SCHAUPP, ROSCOE F. Blake's Correction of Milton in Poem and Picture. Doctoral diss., Ohio State Univ., 1934.

3847 SCHERPBIER, H. Milton in Holland: A Study of Literary Relations of England and Holland before 1730. Doctoral diss., Amsterdam. Amsterdam: H. J. Paris, 1933. 220pp.
Rev: Thomas Weevers, ES, 16, 1934, 69-72.

3848 SCHICK, GEORGE B. Appreciation of Milton as a Criterion of Eighteenth-Century Taste. N&Q, N.S., 4, 1957, 113-4.
On Joseph Warton's belief that an appreciation of Milton was a criterion of true literary taste.

3849 SCHULTZ, MAX F. Coleridge, Milton, and Lost Paradise. N&Q, N.S., 6, 1959, 143-4.
Notes similarities between Paradise Lost and Coleridge's Reflections.

3850 SCHUMBOHM, DIETRICH. Les Martyrs und die Kritik Chateaubriands an Milton und Tasso, Aufsätze zur Themen- und Motivgeschichte: Festschrift für Hellmuth Petriconi zum siebzigsten Geburtstag am 1. April, 1965, von seinen Hamburger Schülern (Hamburg: Cram, de Gruyter, 1965), pp. 111-34.
On Chateaubriand's criticism of Milton.

3851 SENDRY, JOSEPH. In Memoriam and Lycidas. PMLA, 82, 1967, 437-43.
A study of influence. Tennyson directly echoes Miltonic themes and "follows Milton's precedent of paying homage to the the literary decorum that governs the pastoral elegy."

3852 SENSABAUGH, GEORGE F. Adaptations of Areopagitica. HLQ, 13, 1950, 201-5.
In 1679 and 1681, in connection with attempts to regulate the press.

3853 ------. Areopagitica Adapted. MLN, 61, 1946, 166-9.
In 1681.

3854 ------. Jefferson's Use of Milton in the Ecclesiastical Controversies of 1776. AL, 26, 1955, 552-9.
Jefferson used The Reason of Church Government and Of Reformation.

3855 ------. Milton and the Attempted Whig Revolution. The Seventeenth Century (Stanford: Stanford Univ. Press, 1951), pp. 291-305.
Holds that Lord Russell "may in a very real sense be called one of Milton's disciples" and that "Oxford University officials, in their inquiry into the causes of the Rye House Plot, thus made no mistake in placing Milton on their list of subversive authors."

3856 ------. Milton and the Doctrine of Passive Obedience. HLQ, 13, 1949, 19-54.
A study of Milton's influence on Rev. Samuel Johnson and other Whig writers; argues that Milton played an important role "in shaping events which accompanied the Whig rise to power."

3857 ------. Milton at the Trial of Thomas Paine. N&Q, N.S., 2, 1955, 212-3.
Areopagitica quoted by Thomas Erskine, Paine's defense attorney, at the trial in 1792.

3858 ------. Milton in Early America. Princeton: Princeton Univ. Press, 1964. xii, 320pp.
"To measure American interest in Milton from Colonial days through the first twenty-five years of the Republic is the task of the present inquiry."
Rev: Agnes M. C. Latham, YWES, 242; Gordon S. Wood, NEQ, 37, 1964, 543-6; James G Nelson, JEGP, 63, 1964, 784-7; James H. Sims, SCN, 22 No.1, 1964, 6-7; TLS, Dec. 31, 1964, p. 1182; DR, 45, 1965, 227; Lewis Leary, AL, 37, 1965, 75.

3859 ------. Milton in Early American Schools. HLQ, 19, 1956, 353-83.
From the Revolution through the first quarter of the nineteenth century.

3860 ------. Milton in the Revolution Settlement. HLQ, 9, 1946, 175-208.
The influence of Pro Populo Adversus Tyrannos.

3861 ------. That Grand Whig, Milton. Stanford Univ. Pubs., Univ. Ser., Lang. and Lit., 11. Stanford: Stanford Univ. Press, 1952. ix, 213pp. Reprinted, New York: Benjamin Blom, 1968.
The study "purposes to trace the impact of Milton's arguments in the battle of ideas which led to the acceptance of the Settlement and the Bill of Rights. . . ."
Rev: J. W. Gough, EHR, 68, 1953, 478-9; TLS, June 5, 1953, p. 371; Ernest Sirluck, MP, 52, 1954, 63-7; Allen R. Benham, MLQ, 16, 1955, 171-3.

3862 SEPIANU, F. C. Milton's Reputation in France in the Seventeenth Century. B. Litt thesis, St. Hilda's College, Oxford, 1941.

3863 SHARROCK, ROGER. Godwin on Milton's Satan. N&Q, N.S., 9, 1962, 463-5.
"William Godwin in his Political Justice issued what may well be the first manifesto of the Satanist school."

3864 Shelley Exposed—By Computer. The Times, Sept. 12, 1964, p. 8a.
Computer compares Paradise Lost and Prometheus Bound and concludes that Shelley "borrowed heavily from Milton to refute the latter's philosophy."

3865 SHUDOFSKY, M. MAURICE. An Early Eighteenth-Century Rhymed Paraphrase of Paradise Lost, II, 1-225. MLN, 56, 1941, 133-4.
In Reflections . . . on the Vices and Follies of the Age (1707-9).

3866 SIDDIQUI, M. N. Milton and the Orient. OJES, 2, 1962, 37-47.

3867 SIRE, JAMES WALTER. Miltonic Criticism and the Problem of the Reader's Belief. Doctoral diss., Univ. of Missouri, 1964. Abs., DA, 25, 1965, 4129.

3868 SIRLUCK, ERNEST. Areopagitica and a Forgotten Licensing Controversy. RES, 11, 1960, 260-74.
On the influence of Milton's essay between 1698 and 1707.

3869 SLOANE, WILLIAM. Chaucer, Milton, and the Rev. William Stukeley, M. D. N&Q, N.S., 7, 1960, 220-2.
On the references to Chaucer and Milton in Stukeley's Family Memoirs.

3870 SMITH, J. H. Shelley and Milton's Chariot of Paternal Deity. MLN, 51, 1936, 215-7.
Holds that the chariot of Paradise Lost, 6, 749ff., had a profound impression on Shelley's imagination.

3871 SPERRY, STUART M., JR. Keats, Milton, and The Fall of Hyperion. PMLA, 77, 1962, 77-84.
"The allegory of The Fall reveals a comprehensive and original assimilation of Paradise Lost that goes far beyond the manifest similarities of structure and style that dominate the earlier version."

3872 SPROTT, S. E. Ode on the Three Hundred and Fiftieth Morning of Milton's Nativity. DR, 47, 1967, 380-2.
A reprint of a poem written to commemorate the 350th anniversary of the birth of John Milton, read at a banquet held by the members of the Department of English of Dalhousie University (Dec. 9, 1958, in the Lord Nelson Hotel in Halifax). Printed here to commemorate the 300th anniversary of the publication of Paradise Lost.

3873 STANTON, ROBERT. Typee and Milton: Paradise Well Lost. MLN, 74, 1959, 407-11.
On "deliberate" echoes of Paradise Lost in Melville's novel.

3874 STARR, HERBERT. An Echo of L'Allegro in Gray's Bard. MLN, 57, 1942, 676.

3875 STAVROU, C. N. Milton, Byron, and the Devil. Univ. of Kansas City Review, 21, 1955, 153-9.
Argues that Cain is a refutation of Milton's theological position in Paradise Lost.

3876 STEADMAN, JOHN M. Areopagitica and A Critical and Philosophical Enquiry: A Milton-Warburton Parallel. N&Q, N.S., 6, 1959, 367.
On Milton's vision of an awakening nation as a model for Warburton's prophecies for the University.

3877 ------. Jaques Delille on Milton's Daughters. N&Q, N.S., 5, 1958, 463.
"Though he deplores Milton's politics, Delille respects his genius, and bestows unqualified praise on his daughters in La Pitié, Poème en Quatre Chants (1803)."

3878 STEVENS, ALBERT K. Milton and Chartism. PQ, 12, 1933, 377-88.
Discusses the tenets of the Chartists and shows how they drew heavily from

Milton in writing their propaganda. Also, shows Milton's influence on the Chartist poets, especially Thomas Cooper.

3879 STOJANOVIĆ, DUŠAN. Milton i Njegoš: ogledi o našim kulturnim dodirima sa Englezima. Belgrade: Luča Biblioteka Zedruge Profesorskoga Društva, 1940. 121pp.
Discusses cultural contact between England and the Slavic people and considers Milton's influence on Njegos.

3880 STROUP, THOMAS B. The Cestus: Manuscript of an Anonymous Eighteenth-Century Imitation of Comus. SEL, 2, 1962, 47-55.
Describes the Egerton Manuscript 3507, now in the British Museum. Dates it between 1784-1790; connects it with the Spenser-Milton revival.

3881 ------, ed. The Cestus: A Mask. Ed. with an Introduction and Notes. Univ. of Florida Monographs, No. 7. Gainesville: Univ. of Florida Press, 1961.
Terms the masque "a rather obvious imitation of Milton and Spenser."

3882 ------. Gay's Mohocks and Milton. JEGP, 46, 1947, 165-7.
Echoes of Milton in Gay's play.

3883 SUMMERS, JOSEPH H. Milton and the Cult of Conformity. YR, 46, 1957, 511-27. Reprinted in Milton: Modern Judgements, ed. by Alan Rudrum (London: Macmillan, 1968), pp. 29-43.
Appreciative analysis of Milton's position in the twentieth century.

3884 SUTHERLAND, W. O. S. Addison's Paradise Lost Criticisms in the Spectator. Master's thesis, Univ. of North Carolina, 1947.

3885 SWAMINATHAN, S. R. The Allusion to Paradise Lost in Keats' Letter on the Imagination. N&Q, N.S., 12, 1965, 195-7.
Reply to Bruce Miller, N&Q, N.S., 11, 1964, 423. "In spite of Mr. Miller's argument for the dream in VIII. 283-322, I should like to support the traditional view that Keats is thinking rather of the second dream, VIII. 452-90."

3886 TAYLOR, GEORGE C. Why Read Milton Now? Twentieth Century English (New York: Philosophical Library, 1946), pp. 453-60.
"Amidst the babel of voices . . . his voice . . . would give carrying power to all emotional and intellectual forces which serve to elevate rather than degrade us in the scale of being."

3887 Tercentenary Conferences. MN, 1, 1967, 55-7.
Of Paradise Lost. Records conferences held at the University of Western Ontario, the University of Pittsburgh, Southampton College of Long Island University, Georgia State College, and Goucher College.

3888 The Tercentenary of Paradise Lost. SCN, 25, 1967, 56-7.
Notes a series of lectures on Milton at the University of Pittsburgh (Nov. 1967-April 1968) in celebration of the tercentenary of Paradise Lost.

3889 THOMPSON, E. N. S. The Rebel Angel in Later Poetry. PQ, 27, 1948, 1-16.
Seen against the background of Milton's treatment.

3890 THOMPSON, KARL F. Milton's Eighteenth Century Biographers. Doctoral diss., Yale Univ., 1950.

3891 THORPE, JAMES. The Decline of the Miltonic Tradition. Doctoral diss., Harvard Univ., 1941. Abs., Harvard Univ., Summaries of theses, 1941, pp. 347-50.

3892 ------, ed. Milton Criticism: Selections from Four Centuries. New York: Rinehart, 1950. Reprinted, London: Routledge and Kegan Paul, 1956, 1962, 1965; New York: Octagon Books, 1966. 376pp.
   Part One contains essays and excerpts from critics ranging from Addison to C. S. Lewis and T. S. Eliot; in Part Two Thorpe presents excerpts and brief comments from critics from Marvell to Arnold.

3893 ------. A Note on Coleridge's Gutch Commonplace Book. MLN, 1948, 130-1.
   A passage on Milton copied from Jonathan Richardson.

3894 TILLYARD, E. M. W. Matthew Arnold on Milton. CQR, 148, 1949, 153-60. Reprinted in Studies in Milton (London: Chatto and Windus, 1951), pp. 1-7.
   A lecture given at St. Paul's using as a background the speech which Arnold gave on Milton over sixty years prior to Tillyard's speech. Considers Arnold's observations and their present validity or invalidity.

3895 TOLLEY, MICHAEL J. References to the Bible and Milton in Blake's Europe. Proceedings of the Ninth Congress of the Australasian Universities Languages and Literature Association (Melbourne: Univ. of Melbourne, 1965), pp. 41-2.
   Summary of a paper on Blake's uses of the Bible and Milton in his Europe.

3896 TOYODA, MINORU. Nippon-Eigakushi-no-Kenkyu (A Study of English Studies in Japan). Tokyo, 1939.

3897 ------. Tracing Milton in Japan. English Language and Literature (Hiroshima Bunrika Univ.), 4, May, 1933.

3898 TUVE, ROSEMOND. A Name to Resound for Ages. Listener, 60, 1958, 312-3.
   On nineteenth- and twentieth-century attitudes toward Milton's images and religious themes.

3899 UNGER, LEONARD. Yeats and Milton. SAQ, 61, 1962, 197-212.
   On Miltonic echoes in Yeats' poetry and prose.

3900 VAHID, S. A. Iqbal and Milton. Pakistan Quar., 8, Summer, 1957, 52-5.
   Considers Milton's influence on the Persian poet.

3901 VALLESE, TARQUINIO. Un presunto plagio di Milton. Naples: R. Pironti, 1949. 35pp.

3902 VISIAK, E. H. The Arcturan Shadow (A Complement to Milton's Satan). N&Q, 178, 1940, 225-7.
   Satan and David Lindsay's A Voyage to Arcturus (1920).

3903 V[ISIAK], E. H. A Curious Double Parallel Between Milton and Fielding. N&Q, 176, 1939, 260.

In Milton's of Education and An Apology against a Pamphlet and Fielding's Tom Jones.

3904 ------. The Portent of Milton: Some Aspects of His Genius. London: W. Laurie, 1958.
Contains a chapter on the Victorian veneration of Milton.

3905 WALZ, JOHN. Miltonic Words in the German Poetic Vocabulary: Empyreum, Hyazinthene Locken. Monatschrift für deutschen Unterricht, 37, 1946, 92-200.

3906 WASSERMAN, EARL R. Early Evidence of Milton's Influence. MLN, 58, 1943, 293-5.
Addenda to Havens' list.

3907 ------. The Source of Motherwell's Melancholye. MLN, 55, 1940, 296.
Il Penseroso.

3908 WATSON, TOMMY G. Johnson and Hazlitt on the Imagination in Milton. SoQ, 2, 1964, 123-33.
Examines "the treatment of the importance of the imagination in explaining the genius of Milton as viewed by Samuel Johnson in his life of John Milton and William Hazlitt in his lecture on Shakespeare and Milton."

3909 WEIGEL, JOHN A. The Miltonic Tradition in the First Half of the Nineteenth Century. Doctoral diss., Western Reserve Univ., 1939.

3910 WHITING, GEORGE W. Colley Cibber and Paradise Lost. N&Q, 164, 1933, 171-2.
Quotations from Paradise Lost in Cibber's The Refusal (1721) were intended to ridicule the idealism of Milton's conception of love.

3911 ------. Dalton's Comus Again. N&Q, N.S., 6, 1959, 220-1.
Suggests that Act 2 of Dalton's Comus is quoted in The Lady's Magazine, or Entertaining Companion for the Fair Sex, August, 1775 (VI, 422-3); comments on eighteenth-century poetic taste.

3912 ------. A Late Seventeenth Century Milton Plagiarism. SP, 31, 1934, 37-50.
A Letter from General Ludlow borrows from Eikonklastes.

3913 ------. Milton and Lord Brooke on the Church. MLN, 51, 1936, 161-6.
Borrowings from Of Prelatical Episcopacy.

3914 ------. Mrs. M—and Milton. N&Q, N.S., 2, 1955, 200-1.
An unidentified Mrs. M. gives Milton special praise in a poem, The Progress of Poetry (1759).

3915 ------. Mrs. M—and M. M. N&Q, N.S., 4, 1957, 446-7.
Identifies the author of The Progress of Poetry as Mrs. Madan.

3916 ------. Ode on Milton. TLS, July 26, 1957, p. 457.
A poem by J. Lawes (1793).

3917 ------. The Politics of Milton's Apostate Angels. N&Q, 163, 1932, 384-6.
Considers an episode in the London Chronicle, 1763-4, as an episode in the history of Milton's reputation.

3918 ------. Rowe's Debt to Paradise Lost. MP, 32, 1935, 271-80.
Cites several examples of Miltonic influence in Rowe's Tamerlane, Fair
Penitent, The Royal Convert, Jane Shore, Lady Jane Gray, and other works.

3919 ------. A Whig Reference to Paradise Lost, 1682. TLS, June 7. 1934,
p. 408.
In A Pleasant Conference upon the Observator. . . .

3920 ------. Woodward's Debt to Milton in 1644. SP, 33, 1936, 228-35.
Woodward's A Dialogue contains borrowed passages from the anti-episocpal
pamphlets.

3921 WILCOX, STEWART C., and JOHN M. RAINES. Lycidas and Adonais.
MLN, 67, 1952, 19-21.
Parallels.

3922 WILDING, MICHAEL. Milton's Critics: Another Ten Years. MCR, No.
7, 1964, pp. 126-35.
"The essential case, in fact, against Milton hasn't in any real way been
answered."

3923 WILLIAMSON, GEORGE. Dryden's View of Milton. Milton and Others
(Chicago: Univ. of Chicago Press; London: Faber and Faber, 1965),
pp. 103-21.
On Dryden's various pronouncements regarding heroic verse and his operatic
version of Paradise Lost.

3924 WILSON, EDMUND. T. S. Eliot. NR, 60, 1929, 341-9.
Believes that Milton's poetic reputation has declined with the ascendancy of
Eliot.

3925A WITTREICH, JOSEPH ANTHONY, JR. Blake's Philosophy of Contraries: A New Source. ELN, 4, 1966, 105-10.
Shows that Milton exerted a strong influence on Blake's philosophy of
contraries, an influence more pervasive than Boehme's.

3925B ------. Milton, Man and Thinker: Apotheosis in Romantic Criticism. BuR,
16, 1968, 64-84.

3925C ------. A Note on Blake and Milton. Blake Newsletter, 2, 1968, 17-8.

3926A ------. A Power Amongst Powers: Milton and his Romantic Critics. Doctoral diss., Western Reserve, 1966. Abs., DA, 27, 1967, 3436-A.

3926B ------. The Satanism of Blake and Shelley Reconsidered. SP, 65, 1968,
816-33.

3927 WOLFE, DON M. Milton and Mirabeau. PMLA, 49, 1934, 116-28.
Feels that Mirabeau's tracts show that Milton's voice had become a weapon
during the French Revolution.

3928 WOODHOUSE, A. S. P. The Historical Criticism of Milton. PMLA, 66,
1951, 1033-44. Reprinted in The Modern Critical Spectrum. Ed. by
Gerald J. and Nancy M. Goldberg (Englewood Cliffs, N.J.: Prentice-
Hall, 1962), pp. 233-43.
A paper read before the Milton group of MLA on Dec. 28, 1950.

3929 WORDSWORTH, JOHN and WILLIAM. Milton and Wordsworth. TLS, Oct. 4, 1947, p. 507.
Call attention to a copy of Milton owned by Wordsworth during his Cambridge days.

3930 WYNKOOP, WILLIAM MAGEE. Three Children of the Universe: Emerson's View of Shakespeare, Bacon, and Milton. Doctoral diss., Columbia Univ., 1962. Abs., DA, 23, 1963, 3358-9. The Hague: Mouton, 1966. 199pp.
Chapter 3: Milton as the Sayer, pp. 137-77. Shows that Emerson regarded Milton as representative of the third stage of the English Renaissance. Contains an analysis of Emerson's view of the poet.
Rev: John P. Pritchard, BA, 41, 1967, 219-20; Sherman Paul, AL, 39, 1967, 224-5.

3931 YANIGIDA, IZUMI. Meiji-Shoki-no-Miruton (Milton in the Early Meiji Period). Sekai-Bungaju-Gippō (Monthly Journal of World Literature), December, 1929.
Discusses how Milton was introduced to the Japanese in the early Meiji period.

3932 ZIMMERMAN, LESTER F. Some Aspects of Milton's American Reputation to 1900. Doctoral diss., Univ. of Wisconsin, 1950. Abs., Summaries of Doctoral Diss., Univ. of Wisconsin, 11, 1951, 358-60.

INDEX

Reference figures are to item numbers.

Kermode, Frank, 259, 680, 1066, 1478, 2088, 2192, 2234, 3453B.
Keyes, Clinton W., 77.
Keynes, Geoffrey, 3244.
Kiknadze, Z., 381.
Killeen, J. F., 2570.
Kim, Sun Sook, 1479.
Kimmich, Paul Edward, 2571.
King, Bruce, 2572, 3743.
King, Roy, 681.
Kirk, Rudolf, 296, 2949.
Kirkconnell, Watson, 814, 1480-2, 2235-6.
Kirkland, E. C., 682.
Kittredge, Paul M., 3744.
Kivette, Ruth Montgomery, 1483, 2950.
Klammer, Enno, 1484.
Klein, David, 24.
Klein, Joan Larsen, 2573.
Kliger, Samuel, 2089, 2951, 3245.
Knachel, Philip A., 2952.
Knapp, Charles A., 77, 2574.
Knight, Douglas, 1485.
Knight, G. Wilson, 683-5.
Knightley, William J., 1486.
Knoepflmacher, V. C., 3745.
Knott, John R., Jr., 1487-8.
Koehler, George Stanley, 686, 3454.
Kohn, I., 2953-5.
Koretz, Gene, 1489.
Koziol, Herbert, 2575.
Kramer, Jerome, 3246, 3746.
Kranidas, Thomas, 688-9, 1490-2, 1496, 2237-8, 2956-8.
Krapp, George Philip, 77.
Krebs, A. C., 384.
Kreipe, Christian E., 367.
Kreter, Herbert, 2959.
Kristo, Alqi, 336, 344.
Krouse, F. Michael, 1493, 2192, 2239.
Krumhaar, Horst, 2960.
Kuethe, J. Louis, 3563.
Kuíc, Ranka, 2961.
Kuntz, Joseph M., 2.
Kurota, Kenjiro, 1494, 2576, 3747.
Kurth, Burton O., 690, 1495.
Kusakabe, Hiroko, 3455.
Kvitaišvili, E., 381.

Laguardia, Eric Henry, 2577.
Landon, Michael, 2962.
Landy, Marcia K., 1496, 2090, 2240-2.
Lang, James Giles, 3247.
Langdon, Ida, 691.
Langenfelt, Gösta, 1497.

Langford, Thomas, 2091.
Langton, Edward, 1498.
Laredo, Pablo, 332.
Larsen, Erik, 3248.
Larson, Martin A., 692.
Lascelles, Mary, 1499.
Laski, Harold J., 2963.
Laskowsky, Henry J., 2092.
Lauter, Paul, 1500.
Lavin, J. A., 3748.
Law, Dorothy G., 43, 3249.
Lawes, Henry, 265.
Lawrence, C. E., 3250.
Lawrence, W. B., 693.
Lawry, Jon S., 694, 1501-3, 2093, 2243, 2578-9.
Leahy, William, 2580.
Leary, Louis, 656.
Leathes, Sir Stanley, 3456.
Leavis, F. R., 687, 695-7.
Le Comte, Edward S., 118, 698-700, 1504, 2244, 2581-6, 2964, 3251, 3750.
Lee, Chang-bae, 343.
Lee, Herbert G., 1505.
Legouis, Emile, 701-2.
Legouis, Pierre, 703, 1506.
Leishman, J. B., 2587.
Leitão, Antônio José de Lima, 333, 348.
Lejosne, Roger, 1507.
Lemay, J. A. Leo, 2245, 3751.
Le Plastrier, Constance Mary, 139.
Lerner, L. D., 110, 3457.
Leslie, F. Andrew, 3752.
Lever, J. W., 1508.
Lever, Katherine, 704.
Levin, Gerald, 3753.
Levin, Harry, 1509.
Levinson, Ronald B., 705.
Levy, Babette, 1510.
Levy, F. A., 540.
Lewalski, Barbara Keifer, 312, 1511-2, 2094-5, 2246, 2965-7.
Lewis, Clarissa Olivia, 2968, 3564.
Lewis, C. S., 706-7, 1513-5, 2588-90.
Lewis, Richard B., 1516.
Ley, Charles David, 368.
Lieb, Michael J., 1517.
Lievsay, John Leon, 708.
Liljegren, S. B., 709-11, 3253.
Lill, James V., 3754.
Little, Marguerite, 2247, 2593.
Livingstone, Arthur, 77.
Lloyd, Michael, 2594-7.

Loane, George G., 712, 1518-21, 2409, 2591-2, 2601, 3755.

Lockwood, Laura E., 40.

Lodge, Ann, 1522.

Loewenson, Leo, 3565.

Lombardi, Marco, 362.

Long, Anne Bowers, 1523, 2097, 2248.

Looten, C. C., 713-5, 2969.

Looten, M. C., 1524.

Loredano, Giovanno Francesco, 1525.

Løske, Olav, 2970.

Love, Christopher C., 716.

Lovejoy, Arthur O., 1526-7.

Low, Anthony, 61, 1528.

Lucas, F. L., 1529-30.

Lumiansky, Robert M., 717, 1531.

Lumpkin, Ben W., 1532.

Lunch, Humphrey, 382.

Lutaud, Olivier, 391, 3566.

Lutter, Tibor, 718, 1533.

Lyddon-Roberts, P., 2438.

Lynch, James J., 2249.

Lynskey, Winifred, 2598.

Maas, P., 2599.

Mabbott, Thomas O., 77, 635, 1104, 1534, 2600-5, 3255-67, 3544, 3567-73, 3757.

Macaulay, Rose, 3268.

Macaulay, Thomas B., 75, 140, 211, 478.

MacCaffrey, Isabel E. Gamble, 199, 271, 1535-6, 2607.

MacCallum, Hugh Reid, 719-20, 1179, 1537.

MacDonald, Angus, 44.

MacInnes, W. D., 701.

Mack, Maynard, 86.

Mackail, J. W., 721, 3574.

Mackellar, Walter, 209, 722, 1538.

Mackenzie, Donald, 296.

Mackenzie, Phyllis, 723.

Mackin, Cooper R., 1539, 2098.

Mackinnon, Malcolm H. M., 74, 724, 1540.

Macklem, Michael, 725.

MacLean, Hugh N., 56, 2606.

MacLure, Millar, 74.

Macmillan, Dougald, 7.

Macmillan, M., 154.

Madan, Francis F., 2952, 2971-2, 3562, 3575.

Maddison, Carol, 2608.

Maddison, R. E., 2973.

Madsen, William G., 125, 726-7, 1541-3, 2192, 2250, 2609-10, 3576.

Magealson, Viola, 2974.

Magon, Leopold, 1544, 3577.

Mahood, Molly Maureen, 1545, 2252.

Major, John M., 728, 2099, 2611.

Male, R. R., Jr., 3758.

Malone, Kemp, 1546.

Mamemoto, Kaoru, 2975, 3269.

Manley, Frank [Francis], 1548-50.

Manning, Clarence A., 1551, 3578, 3759.

Manuel, M., 729, 3270, 3760.

Maresca, Thomas E., 2612.

Marilla, Esmond L., 730-1, 1552-7, 2100, 2253, 2613.

Marks, Emerson R., 2614.

Marshall, George O., Jr., 2615, 3761.

Marshall, William H., 1558.

Martin, John Rupert, 3271-2.

Martin, L. C., 2616, 2976, 3088.

Martz, Louis L., 732, 762, 1496, 1559, 1565, 2101-2, 2242, 2617-8, 3480.

Mason, M. G., 2977.

Masson, David, 77, 119, 3273.

Mastrostefano, Amina, 353.

Mateos, Juan, 345.

Mathies Geb. Dorner, Maria Elizabeth, 2254.

Maxey, Chester C., 2978.

Maxwell, I. R., 1560.

Maxwell, J. C., 1561-3, 2255-6, 2619-20, 2979, 3526, 3579-81, 3762-4.

Mayerson, Caroline W., 2621.

Maynard, Robert A., 187.

Mayoux, Jean-Jacques, 733, 2980.

Mazières, Thibaut De., 1564.

Mazzeo, Joseph A., 638, 734, 1287.

McAdams, James R., 1565-6, 2103A.

McAlister, Floyd Laverne, 3765-6.

McC., H., 3582.

McCain, John Walker, Jr., 3583-4.

McCall, Lois G., 2257.

McCarthy, B. Eugene, 2981, 3767.

McCarthy, Thomas J., 1567.

McColley, Grant, 735-7, 1568-79, 2600, 2622, 3274.

McCoy, Patricia, 1445.

McCrea, Nelson Glenn, 77.

McCullen, J. T., Jr., 3275.

McDavid, Raven I., Jr., 738, 2258, 2982.

McDill, Joseph M., 739.

McEuen, Kathryn A., 296.

McFadden, George, 3768.

McHugh, Roger J., 159.

McKenzie, Alison, 236.

McKenzie, J., 2623-4.

McKenzie, Kenneth, 2625.

Riley, Sister Mary Geraldine, R. S. M., 862.
Rinehart, Keith, 2684.
Roberti-Fletcher, Lauro, 363.
Roberts, Donald A., 296.
Roberts, Donald R., 863.
Roberts, E. A., 864.
Robertson, D. S., 1729, 3601A.
Robins, Harry F., 865, 1730-4, 2669, 2685-7.
Robson, W. W., 866, 2129.
Roffensperger, D. H., 3770.
Rogers, Katherine M., 867.
Rogers, Lambert, 3325.
Rohr-Sauer, P. V., 2688.
Rooney, William J. J., 2689.
Roscelli, William John, 868-9.
Rosedale, H. G., 746.
Rosen, Edward, 3326.
Rosenberg, Donald Maurice, 1736.
Rosenfeld, Sybil, 2738.
Ross, Malcolm M., 870-2, 1737, 2690.
Røstvig, Maren-Sofie, 1738, 2691, 3481-4.
Roth, Leon, 3327.
Rouse, W. H. D., 97.
Rowse, Alfred L., 3328.
Rozenberg, Paul, 1739.
Rubinstein, Annette T., 3329.
Rudrum, Alan, 873, 1740, 2692.
Rudwin, Maximilian, 1741-2.
Ruhe, Edward L., 3330-1.
Runtz-Rees, C., 874.
Rupp, Ernest Fordon, 1743.
Rusche, Harry, 1744.
Ruzicka, Rudolph, 218-9.
Ryan, C. J., 3027.
Ryken, Leland, 1745.
Ryley, Robert M., 3835.
Rylands, George H. W., 129.

S., W. W., 1746, 2693.
Sabol, Andrew J., 2694.
Sabine, G. H., 293.
Sackton, Alexander H., 2130.
Sadler, Mary Lynn Veach, 2286.
Sáez, Richard, 875.
Safer, Elaine, 1747, 2131.
Saillens, Émile, 354, 2695, 3028, 3332-3.
Saino, Shigeo, 375.
St. Clair, Foster Y., 876, 2696.
St. George, Priscilla P., 1748.
Saintsbury, E. B., 746.
Saintsbury, Geoge, 877, 3485.
Saito, Takeshi, 878, 3334.
Saltmarshe, C., 879.
Samaha, Edward E., Jr., 2132.

Samarin, R., 880-2, 3029A, 3335, 3836-40.
Sambrook, A. J., 883.
Sampson, George, 884.
Sampson, Martin W., 231.
Sams, Alma F., 2287.
Samuel, Irene, 885-7, 1531, 1565, 1749-57, 2133, 2697, 3029B.
Samuels, Charles Thomas, 1758, 2288.
Sanderlin, George, 3841.
Sands, Maurice, 3336.
Sanjuan, Dionisio, 350.
San Juan, Epifami, Jr., 325, 2289.
Sankey, Benjamin T., Jr., 3842.
Sasek, Lawrence A., 1759-61, 3030.
Sato, Kiyoshi, 3843-4.
Saunders, J. W., 888.
Saurat, Denis, 889-90, 1762, 1784, 3031, 3337-8, 3845.
Sauro, Sister Joan Stanislaus, 1763.
Savage, H. L., 2638.
Sayers, Dorothy, 891.
Schaar, Claes, 1764.
Schanzer, Ernest, 1765-6, 3486.
Schaupp, Roscoe F., 3846.
Schaus, Hermann, 2699.
Scherpbier, H., 3847.
Scheuerle, William, 1767.
Schick, George B., 3848.
Schiff, Gert, 3601B.
Schirmer, Walter F., 892, 1768.
Schlinghoff, Margot, 1769, 3487.
Schneider, R., 364, 894.
Schnittkind, Dana A., 3339.
Schnittkind, Henry T., 3339.
Schoeck, R. J., 2700-1.
Scholderer, V., 2702.
Scholfield, A. F., 3340.
Schork, W., 895.
Schröder, A., 3341.
Schücking, Levin L., 1770.
Schultz, Howard, 896-7, 1771-2, 2134-5, 2703.
Schulz, Max F., 1163, 3849.
Schumbohm, Dietrich, 3850.
Scott, William O., 898.
Scott-Craig, T. S. K., 1773-5, 2136, 2290, 3032-3.
Scudder, Harold H., 1776.
Seaman, John Eugene, 1777-9, 2137.
Sears, Minnie E., 58.
Seaton, Ethel, 2704, 3342A.
Sedelow, Sally Yeates, 1780
Seebacher, Jacques, 899.
Seigler, Milledge Broadus, 3488A.
Seldin, M., 1781.

Sellin, Paul R., 900-1, 2291-2, 3034, 3342B.
Selva, Joseph M. Boix, 329, 331.
Semple, W. H., 2705.
Senci, M., 3035.
Sendry, Joseph, 3851.
Senior, H. L., 3343.
Senior, John, 902.
Sensabaugh, George F., 1782, 2138, 2706, 3344-5, 3852-61.
Sepianu, F. C., 3862.
Sergeant, Howard, 112, 262.
Seronsy, Cecil C., 1783.
Sewell, Arthur, 1784, 3036-8.
Sewell, Elizabeth, 903, 1786, 2139, 2293.
Shaaber, M. A., 303, 428.
Shafer, Robert, 2140.
Sharrock, Roger, 1787, 3863.
Shattuck, Charles H., 2707.
Shaw, Marion, 58.
Shawcross, John T., 43, 122, 312, 904-9, 1788-93, 2141, 2294A-B, 2424, 2708-25, 3039-40, 3129-30, 3346-51, 3429, 3488B, 3602-4.
Sheppard, John T., 2726.
Sherry, Beverly Thelma Chadwick, 1794, 3489.
Sherwin, Oscar, 3605.
Shigeno, Tenrai, 316, 236, 351, 355, 1795.
Shillan, David, 153.
Shudofsky, M. Maurice, 3865.
Shumaker, Wayne, 1796-9, 2727-8.
Shuster, George N., 2729-30.
Siddiqui, M. N., 3866.
Siebert, F. S., 3041-2.
Siebert, Theodor, 910-1, 1800.
Siegel, Ben, 912.
Siegel, Paul N., 913, 1801.
Sigworth, Oliver F., 2731.
Sills, Kenneth C. M., 2732.
Simon, Irène, 1802.
Sims, James H., 1803-4, 2142.
Sinclair, T. A., 1064.
Singleton, Ralph H., 2733-4.
Sire, James Walter, 914, 3867.
Sirluck, Ernest, 56, 296, 915-6, 1387, 1805, 2230, 2735, 3043-9, 3352, 3606, 3868.
Sitwell, Edith, 3490.
Skeat, W. W. ,102-3, 226, 232.
Slakey, Roger L., 2736.
Slaughter, E. E., 1806.
Sloane, William, 2468, 3353, 3869.
Slote, Bernice, 2562.
Smart, J. S., 273.
Smith, A. J., 2195.

Smith, Bromley, 77.
Smith, Calvin C., 295, 1807.
Smith, Constance I., 3050.
Smith, G. C. Moore, 3051.
Smith, Hallett, 1808.
Smith, J. C., 604, 3491.
Smith, J. H., 3870.
Smith, Logan Pearsall, 917.
Smith, Paul R., 1809.
Smith, Rebecca W., 1810.
Smith, Roland M., 2737.
Solt, Leo F., 296.
Sorsby, Arnold, 3354.
Spadala, Enrico, 1811.
Spaeth, J. Duncan, 1812.
Spaeth, Sigmund G., 918.
Spears, Jewel, 3355.
Spencer, Lois, 3356.
Spencer, Theodore, 2658, 2739.
Spencer, T. J. B., 919-21, 2192, 2295-6, 2738.
Sperry, Stuart M., Jr., 3871.
Spevack-Husmann, Helga, 922, 1813.
Spingarn, J. E., 304.
Spitz, David, 3052-3.
Spitzer, Leo, 2740.
Sprott, S. Ernest, 3492, 3872.
Stahl, Herbert M., 292.
Standley, F. L., 2741.
Stanley, E. G., 1815.
Stanton, Robert, 3873.
Stapleton, Laurence, 1816, 2742, 3054.
Starkman, M. K., 923.
Starnes, DeWitt T., 924-7, 1817-8, 2743-4.
Starr, Herbert, 3874.
Stauffer, Donald A., 2745.
Stavrov, C. N., 1819, 3875.
Steadman, John M., 928-32, 1387, 1496, 1820-77, 2143-8, 2192, 2297-2301, 2746-53, 3055-6, 3493-5, 3876-7.
Stedmond, J. M., 3057.
Stein, Arnold, 933, 1496, 1878-82, 2149-50, 2192, 2302, 3496-8.
Stempel, Daniel, 2754.
Stephenson, Andrew, 2303.
Stephenson, Edward A., 2755.
Sterne, Laurence, 3058.
Stevens, Albert K., 3878.
Stevens, David Harrison, 5, 60.
Stewart, Florence M., 1883.
Stillman, Donald G., 934.
Stockley, W. F. P., 1884.
Stockwell, N., 266.
Stoehr, Taylor, 2756.
Stojanovi Dušan, 3879.

Stoll, Elmer E., 935-9, 1885-9.

Stollman, Samuel S., 940.

Stoye, J. W., 3357.

Strachey, Lytton, 941.

Strathmann, Ernest A., 2757, 3059.

Stratman, Carl J., 61, 2304.

Straumann, Heinrich, 1890.

Strittmatter, Eugene J., 77.

Strode, Lena Virginia, 1891.

Stroup, Thomas B., 260, 942-3, 1892-3, 2151, 2305, 2758-61, 3880-2.

Strousse, Flora, 3358.

Stuart, Dorothy Margaret, 3359.

Studley, Marian H., 2762.

Suffolk, J. C., 173.

Summer, Claude, 372.

Summers, Joseph H., 944-5, 1496, 1894-9, 2306, 3883.

Sumner, Charles R., 77.

Sundell, Roger Henry, 1900, 2152, 2307, 2763.

Sunuma, Yoshitaro, 1901, 3060.

Sutherland, W. O. S., 3884.

Svendsen, Kester, 296, 946-9, 1902-14, 2153, 2764-6, 3061-4, 3517, 3607.

Swaminathan, S. R., 3885.

Swardson, Harold Roland, Jr., 1915.

Swedenberg, H. T., Jr., 950.

Swidler, Arlene A., 1916.

Sykes, P. M., 2767.

Sylvester, Joshua, 1917.

Sypher, Wylie, 951.

Taaffe, James G., 3360-2.

Taft, Frederick L., 296, 3065.

Taketomo, Torao, 358.

Talbert, Ernest W., 927.

Tamaki, Ishitaro, 1918, 2154.

Tate, Allen, 952, 1178.

Tate, Charles D., Jr., 1919.

Tate, Eleanor, 2768.

Taylor, C. R. H., 63.

Taylor, Dick, Jr., 953, 1920-2, 2155.

Taylor, George C., 954-6, 1923-5, 3066, 3886.

Taylor, H. S., 90, 172.

Taylor, Ivan E., 957.

Taylor, John Chesley, 1926.

Taylor, Myron Wilfred, 1927.

Tchakirides, John Peter, 1928.

Tennissen, John James, 2156, 2308.

Terry, 1932.

Thaler, Alwin, 959-61, 2770.

Thomas, Coramae, 2157.

Thompson, Claud Adelbert, 2771.

Thompson, Elbert N. S., 64, 692, 962, 1933-4, 3067, 3499, 3889.

Thompson, Harley S., 963.

Thompson, J. A. K., 964, 1935.

Thompson, Karl F., 3363, 3890.

Thompson, L. S., 965.

Thompson, W. Lawrence, 2772.

Thorpe, James, 966, 2309, 3608, 3891-3.

Thorslev, Peter L., Jr., 1936.

Thwaites, Michael, 967.

Tickner, F. J., 82.

Tillyard, E. M. W., 163, 165, 258, 281, 968-76, 1028, 1937-45, 2158, 2192, 2773-5, 3069, 3364, 3500, 3609, 3894.

Tillyard, Phyllis B., 163, 258, 281, 296, 2776.

Timberlake, P. W., 2310.

Tinker, Chauncey B., 264, 2311.

Todd, William B., 3610.

Tola Mendoza, Fernando, 1946.

Toliver, Harold E., 1947.

Tolley, Michael J., 3895.

Tousley, Marion, 977.

Toyoda, Minoru, 3896-7.

Treble, H. A., 140.

Trefman, Simon, 1948.

Treip, Mindele C., 1949, 2777.

Trent, W. P., 77, 264.

Trevelyan, George Macaulay, 2409, 3070.

Trinterud, L. J., 978.

Tromp, Harold Van, 2409.

Trotier, Arnold H., 65.

Truesdale, Calvin William, 2778.

Tschumi, Raymond, 1950.

Tsuji, Hiroko Kusakabe, 979, 1951.

Tung, Mason, 980, 1952, 2159, 2312.

Turnbull, Alexander, 63.

Turnbull, George H., 3365-7.

Turner, Alberta T., 5, 267.

Turner, Amy L., 981.

Turner, Paul, 1953-5.

Turner, W. Arthur, 5, 296, 2779, 3368-76, 3611.

Tuve, Rosemond, 687, 982, 2780, 3501, 3898.

Tuveson, Ernest L., 983, 2781.

Tyson, John Patrick, 1956.

Ueki, Toshüchi, 984-5.

Ueno, Seichi, 388.

Ullanaess, S. P. N., 986.

Ullrich, H., 2782.

Ulrich, Hermann, 364, 374.

Umezkai, Mitsuo, 390.